SECOND EDITION

HISTORICAL AND PHILOSOPHICAL FOUNDATIONS OF EDUCATION
A BIOGRAPHICAL INTRODUCTION

GERALD L. GUTEK
Loyola University, Chicago

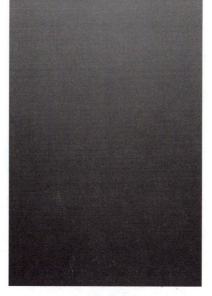

Merrill,
an imprint of Prentice Hall
Upper Saddle River, New Jersey   *Columbus, Ohio*

Library of Congress Cataloging-in-Publication Data

Gutek, Gerald Lee.
    Historical and philosophical foundations of education : a biographical introduction /
Gerald L. Gutek.—2nd ed.
        p.   cm.
    Rev. ed. of: Cultural foundations of education. © 1991.
    Includes bibliographical references and index.
    ISBN 0-13-209743-5
    1. Educators—Biography. 2. Education—History. 3. Education—Philosophy.   I.
Gutek, Gerald Lee. Cultural foundations of education. II. Title.
    LA2301.G88   1997
    370′.92′2—dc20

96-35568
CIP

Editor: Debra A. Stollenwerk
Production Editor: Mary Harlan
Design Coordinator: Karrie M. Converse
Text Designer: Ed Horcharik
Cover Designer: Russ Maselli
Cover art: © Southern Historical Collection, University of North Carolina, Chapel Hill
Production Manager: Deidra M. Schwartz
Director of Marketing: Kevin Flanagan
Advertising/Marketing Coordinator: Julie Shough
Electronic Text Management: Marilyn Wilson Phelps, Matthew Williams, Karen L. Bretz,
    Tracey Ward

This book was set in Life by Prentice Hall and was printed and bound by R.R. Donnelley &
Sons Company. The cover was printed by Phoenix Color Corp.

© 1997 by Prentice-Hall, Inc.
Simon & Schuster/A Viacom Company
Upper Saddle River, New Jersey 07458

Earlier edition, entitled *Cultural Foundations of Education: A Biographical Introduction,* ©
1991 by Macmillan Publishing Company.

Printed in the United States of America

10 9 8 7 6 5 4 3 2 1

ISBN: 0-13-209743-5

Prentice-Hall International (UK) Limited, *London*
Prentice-Hall of Australia Pty. Limited, *Sydney*
Prentice-Hall of Canada, Inc., *Toronto*
Prentice-Hall Hispanoamericana, S. A., *Mexico*
Prentice-Hall of India Private Limited, *New Delhi*
Prentice-Hall of Japan, Inc., *Tokyo*
Simon & Schuster Asia Pte. Ltd., *Singapore*
Editora Prentice-Hall do Brasil, Ltda., *Rio de Janeiro*

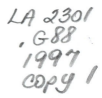

To my students at Loyola University, Chicago

This book is based on my teaching of the history and philosophy of education at Loyola University in Chicago. The identification of the biographies and development of the chapters were stimulated by discussions with my students. My teaching and interaction with students and colleagues have demonstrated that educational biography is a valuable, powerful, but too often neglected medium in preparing teachers, administrators, and other professionals in education. I hope this book will focus more attention on the use of educational biography in professional education programs.

I was also motivated to write this book in response to those who find teacher education programs lacking in historical perspective. My colleagues in the history and philosophy of education have produced many useful and scholarly articles and books on themes that have contributed to the collective memory of our educational past. I hope my colleagues in the discipline will find my work a useful addition to the historical and philosophical foundations of education.

First as a student and then as a teacher of the historical and philosophical foundations of education, I have been intrigued by the interaction of people in historical contexts and the significance and meaning that arise from such interaction. This kind of biographical and historical interest was developed by my graduate education at the University of Illinois in Urbana. Professors J. Leonard Bates, Arthur E. Bestor Jr., and Norman Graebner were masters in developing for their students the importance of people in historical contexts. My study with Professor Harry Broudy emphasized the need for educators to develop a perspective on the development of educational ideas over time. The theme of people interacting within their contexts is a bit Experimentalist and owes much to the introduction to the works of John Dewey that I received from such authorities as William O. Stanley and Joe Burnett. Archibald Anderson, my major professor, provided the insights that helped place the history of education in its broad cultural context. It was Professor Anderson who encouraged me to write my first biography of an educator, my doctoral dissertation on George S. Counts.

New to This Edition

After consultation with professors who used the first edition, I determined to make several changes in the second edition. New chapters examine the biographies and contributions of **Aristotle, Johann Amos Comenius, Mary Wollstonecraft, John Stuart Mill,** and **Mao Tse-tung.** The addition of Aristotle provides readers with a treatment of the origins of Realism in Western philosophy and education that complements the earlier chapter on Plato's Idealism. The new chapter on Comenius illustrates the contributions of an important educational reformer who was transitional between the Reformation and Enlightenment eras. The new chapter on Mary Wollstonecraft presents the biography, ideas, and contributions of a highly gifted crusader for women's rights and education in the late eighteenth century. The added chapter on John Stuart Mill treats a key agent who moved Liberalism from a laissez faire to a reformist direction. A new chapter on Mao Tse-tung continues the theme of providing a global perspective for the study of educational ideas that was found in the first edition. It also provides insights into the ideological struggles that are part of China's educational heritage.

Acknowledgments

I want to thank those who reviewed the prospectus for developing the second edition:

- David W. Dellinger, Bethany College
- Robert V. Farrell, Florida International University
- Albert H. Miller, University of Houston
- Leonard H. Roberts, Troy State University at Dothan

Their comments were very helpful in guiding my organizing and writing of this book.

I appreciate the advice and support of Debbie Stollenwerk, my editor at Prentice Hall, who encouraged me to prepare a second edition. I also want to thank Mary Harlan, who guided the process of developing and editing this project from manuscript to book. Special appreciation is due to Key Metts, who carefully edited the manuscript.

I want to thank my wife, Patricia, for her love and support.

Gerald L. Gutek

CONTENTS

Educational Biography and the Historical and Philosophical Foundations of Education

This book is designed to introduce students to the history and philosophy of education by examining the lives of people who shaped educational theory and practice. It is organized around the theme that key people—by interacting with the forces in the cultural contexts in which they lived—developed ideas about education that continue to affect us today. Some of these people were professional educators, but others were not. By examining the lives, ideas, and contributions of leading personalities on the world scene, this book seeks to illustrate the connection between education and the great transforming events and trends that have shaped our world.

Overview

This book is presented in the form of a historical narrative that describes the context, times and situation, and biography of each world figure examined. Along with this historical narrative, a theoretical analysis of the educational ideas and practices that each person developed and their contemporary meaning is provided. These biographically focused themes in the history and philosophy of education are intended to introduce teachers to the cultural dimensions of teaching.

The narration begins in Chapter 2 with Plato, a founding figure in the establishment of the philosophical traditions of the Western cultural and educational heritage. Chapter 3 continues to develop the Greek contact by examining Aristotle's philosophical and educational contributions. Chapter 4 examines the educational theory and practice of Quintilian, the Roman rhetorician, who furthered the concept of rhetoric education that had originated in ancient Greece with Isocrates. The educational philosophies and ideas of Plato, Aristotle, and Quintilian illustrate the Graeco-Roman contribution to the Western cultural and educational heritage and are used as the point of departure in our study of educational history and philosophy.

Thomas Aquinas' development of theistic realism is discussed in Chapter 5. Using the context of the medieval synthesis, the chapter describes how Christian theology and classical Graeco-Roman philosophy, especially that of Aristotle, were integrated in Western thought and education. Chapter 6 carries the reader from the medieval period to the Renaissance by examining the Christian humanism of Erasmus of Rotterdam. In Chapter 7, the important events emanating from the Protestant Reformation that stimulated universal education and literacy are examined against the background of the life and ideas of the Protestant reformer John Calvin. Chapter 8 deals with the life and educational ideas of Johann Amos Comenius who sought to heal the wounds of religious intolerance through the philosophy of Pansophism.

Educational reform is the underlying theme in Chapter 9, which focuses on Jean-Jacques Rousseau, and Chapter 10 on Johann Heinrich Pestalozzi. Rousseau, a prophet of the Enlightenment, exemplified the themes of naturalism and child permissiveness in educational theory. Pestalozzi, the nineteenth-century Swiss educational reformer, worked desperately to implement the new way of thinking about nature by introducing sensory learning into educational practice.

In Chapter 11, the narrative that has traced the ideas of Western educational thought from ancient Greece through Enlightenment Europe reaches the U.S. social and political context by examining Thomas Jefferson as a proponent of republican civic education. Chapter 12 on Mary Wollstonecraft examines the life of an early feminist who sought to infuse revolutionary thinking into human relationships. Chapter 13, on Horace Mann, describes the work of the man who has been called the "father of the American common school system." Through Jefferson and Mann, the political origins of U.S. public education in the early republican and early national periods are presented. Both Jefferson and Mann are studied in terms of the historical context in which they lived and worked.

In Chapter 14, the life and ideas of Robert Owen, the early nineteenth-century communitarian socialist, points up a new concept in educational theory—the use of education as a means of social change and reconstruction. Owen's work as a social and educational theorist illustrates the ideological underpinnings of many educational theories in the nineteenth and twentieth centuries. Chapter 15 treats the life and times of Friedrich Froebel, the educator who used philosophical idealism as a theoretical foundation for the kindergarten.

Chapter 16 on John Stuart Mill examines the English philosopher's rendition of utilitarian liberalism and defense of the freedom of ideas. Chapter 17, which discusses Herbert Spencer, examines the reformulation of liberalism, a potent ideology in Anglo-American politics and education. Using Darwin's evolutionary theory, Spencer reaffirmed classical liberalism by giving it a scientific rationale based on the survival of the fittest. Spencer's social Darwinism, which had a pervasive influence on U.S. social attitudes and policies, was later attacked by John Dewey in the twentieth century. For students of educational theory, this chapter is intended to help form a perspective that includes liberalism and social Darwinism as formative forces in shaping the modern era.

In Chapter 18, the narrative focuses on Jane Addams, the pioneering social worker and founder of Hull House. Addams' development of the philosophy of "socialized education" and the historical context in which she worked illustrates the significance of urbanization and immigration in transforming the United States from an rural-agrarian to an urban-industrial-technological society.

Chapter 19 examines the life and educational contributions of John Dewey, the United States' leading twentieth-century philosopher of education. By placing Dewey's work in its broad historical and cultural context, it is possible to view his pragmatic philosophy of instrumentalism as the cause of a major reconceptualization of learning and teaching in the United States. His pragmatic philosophy, which endorsed a reconstructed liberalism, challenged Herbert Spencer's social Darwinism.

Chapter 20 examines the work of Maria Montessori. Her theories and practices of early childhood education had an international effect, expanding our views of the child and the processes by which children learn.

The story of Mohandas Gandhi, the subject of Chapter 21, shows how one person challenged the might of a great empire to win freedom and independence for his people. For those who study educational theory, Gandhi's life and ideas represent the turning of the tide against imperialism and colonialism. The examination of Gandhi's educational ideas is particularly instructive for revealing the cultural foundations of education in an Asian cultural context.

Chapter 22 treats the life, ideas, and significance of W. E. B. Du Bois, a sociologist and historian, who was a determined activist for African American civil and educational rights and progress. To comprehend the meaning of Du Bois' struggle, it is necessary to understand the effect of the Reconstruction period in U.S. history and the accommodationist position of Du Bois' chief rival, Booker T. Washington.

Chapter 23, the concluding chapter, examines a figure not usually included in books about the history and philosophy of education: Mao Tse-tung. Mao was not an educator in the sense of being a scholar. However, he and the ideology he developed were instruments of significant change in the People's Republic of China. Marxist-Maoism, which emanated from Mao's ideology, contained powerful implications for education, not only in terms of nonformal education but also for the school as a formal educational agency. By examining Mao's educational ideas, students of educational theory see the effect of ideology in shaping educational policy and practice. Further, they are introduced to Marxism as one of the transforming forces of the twentieth century.

Organization

In treating the effect of these significant figures on the historical and philosophical foundations of education, this book uses four structural devices: (1) historical contexts, (2) educational biographies, (3) the development of educational ideas, and (4) an assessment of significance. Each chapter establishes the historical context in which the particular person lived and worked and then examines how the person's interaction with his or her historical context or environment stimulated that individual to reflect on education and to formulate ideas about education or, in some cases, to develop a complete philosophy of education.

Because ideas occur within a cultural context, the general historical context is used to present the setting and situation in which the educator, theorist, or ideologist such as Plato, Rousseau, or Dewey lived. Each context examined in the book is written to show how educational ideas in the past as well as in our own times were responses to challenges—political, social, economic, religious, and intellectual. For example, Plato was responding to the cultural and political decline of the Greek polis. Jane Addams faced the dilemma of dealing with new Americans, the immigrants, in an urban and industrial society. John Dewey addressed the need for a new social consensus in a society where the old foundations of life were being weakened by social and economic change. W. E. B. Du Bois grappled with the legacy of racism and discrimination that relegated African Americans to the status of second-class citizens.

Using the historical context as an organizing theme illustrates the point that educational ideas originate in particular situations and in a particular time and place. Even though these educational ideas may emerge from a particular context, they often have a larger meaning and value that can be applied in many other contexts. However, we are each our own historian and philosopher of education. The larger meaning that we can gain from studying the lives of educators depends on the challenges we face today. New challenges in different times create the need to revisit and study anew the shaping ideas of our educational heritage.

For students of the historical and philosophical foundations of education, the use of contexts is designed to develop a sense of historical perspective and continuity with our educational past. This past, however, is not to be viewed as completed, or isolated from our educational present. Rather, the varying contexts in which leading educators, philosophers, and ideologists interacted with their environments are viewed as episodes in an ongoing educational experience. It provides us with a historical, philosophical, and ideological map or grid upon which we can locate ourselves as educators today. Such a map of the mind helps us to avoid the rootlessness and presentism that often characterizes too much of the rhetoric about education, teaching, and learning today.

Students of education—prospective teachers, curriculum specialists, administrators, and policy makers—need to develop sensitivity to the theme of contexts. What takes place in the school, as a formal educational setting, does not occur in a cultural vacuum. The world outside of the school's walls determines much of the power—or futility—of the efforts at teaching and learning that go on within. Contemporary educators soon come to recognize that social problems, political issues, and cultural change affect the school's efforts to instruct children. The changing fortunes of the economy obviously determine the extent to which the public will support schools financially.

Although few will argue that the contemporary context of education affects schooling, programs for the preparation of educators have not always examined the development of educational contexts historically. Critics have charged that programs designed to prepare U.S. teachers are intellectually shallow, lacking a sense of historical and cultural perspective. Without a historical memory, U.S. educators are often victims of an all-consuming "presentism." They are "culturally illiterate" in the great ideas and heritage of their own profession. This book seeks to contribute to restoring the collective memory of our educational past.

A second key element, or organizing theme, in this book is the use of educational biography, meaning those events of an educational nature that contributed to forming an individual as a person and shaping his or her intellectual or educational world view. By focusing on important world personalities such as Calvin, Jefferson, and Gandhi, the narrative seeks to illustrate how a significant person, through contextual interaction and challenge, developed insights into educational theory and practice.

The author believes that the study of biography and autobiography, while providing fascinating insights into human behavior, also is useful for educators. If we pause for a moment, we can reflect on and construct our own educational autobiography. The primary sources of our educational autobiography are the formative influence of parents, siblings, friends, adversaries, peers, teachers, politicians, clergy, and others on what we have become and how we view the world. The curriculum, the formal courses we studied in school, and how our teachers taught these courses are also important sources in our educational autobiographies. Our involvement with and participation in informal educational agencies such as churches and the clergy, media and news commentators, libraries and librarians, workplaces, and employers and employees are important in forming us and our attitudes.

In addition to those people and agencies that shape our educational autobiographies, key events in our lives have a special power over our sense of interpretation. How we perceive these events shapes our perspective of reality in its various dimensions—politically, economically, religiously, socially, intellectually, aesthetically, culturally, and educationally. In particular, the key events of a person's childhood and youth take on a special significance, becoming almost like lenses through which he or she establishes a personally meaningful vision of his or her own lifetime. For those who came to maturity during the Great Depression of the 1930s, the stock market crash, the specter of unemployment, reduced family circumstances, and the personality of Franklin D. Roosevelt supply the lenses to interpret what has occurred to them. For the generation of the 1960s, the Civil Rights movement, sit-ins, freedom marches, protests over the Vietnam War, and the power and effect of John Kennedy, Robert Kennedy, and Martin Luther King, Jr., illuminate their vision of subsequent events.

Events in the childhood and youth of the key personalities examined in this book—Pestalozzi, Wollstonecraft, Froebel, Montessori, Jane Addams, and Mao Tsetung—are examined to try to find the lenses through which they glimpsed the sweep of history. Often these key events, those happenings of war and peace, had an effect on the development of their educational theories.

From the interaction of context and biography comes the development of educational ideas. It is the body of educational ideas that forms what we can take from one time and situation to another. Although all educational ideas have contextual origins, some ideas are powerful enough to transcend their time and place. For example, Plato's idealism, Aquinas' Thomism, Erasmus' humanism, Rousseau's naturalism, Jefferson's republicanism, Owen's communitarianism, Spencer's social Darwinism, and Dewey's instrumentalism were powerful bodies of ideas that have shaped our world view and our thinking on human nature and on education. Ideas come to constitute a philosophy of education to answer such questions as, How did the particular theorist conceive of truth, human nature, society, social change, education, schooling, the curriculum, teaching, and learning?

The book's final organizing device deals with the question of historical and educational significance or meaning. The theory's relevance, significance, or meaning depends to a large extent on our own educational context, or situation, and the challenges, issues, and problems that it presents to us as educators. As our educational problems and challenges change, so does the meaning we acquire from studying the lives and contributions of the great thinkers on education. When issues of early childhood education assume a larger importance in today's educational context, then the careers and theories of Pestalozzi, Froebel, and Montessori assume a new significance for us. When contemporary critics allege that our schools have departed from conveying the Western cultural heritage to the young, then a reexamination of the philosophies of Plato, Aristotle, Aquinas, and Quintilian provide a useful perspective on our intellectual and educational origins. As U.S. schools assume the responsibility for educating new immigrants, a reexamination of the work of Jane Addams in helping to assimilate the older stock of immigrants is instructive in understanding the current debates over multiculturalism.

To examine the large organizational themes of historical and cultural contexts, educational biographies, educational theories and philosophies, and historical and educational significance that are used in this book, the following questions may guide the reader:

1. How did the context and the life of a particular theorist shape his or her ideas on education?
2. How did the people presented in this book either reflect or reconstruct the cultural and educational forces and trends that were present in their historical and cultural contexts?
3. Were the people examined in this book agents of educational continuity or change?
4. How did the ideas of key people influence educational policy formulation during their own time and in later history?

Discussion Questions

1. Identify the key personalities of the current cultural context. How do these individuals shape attitudes and values?
2. Assume the proposition that key events during one's childhood and youth provide the lenses through which one sees subsequent events. What are the key events that have shaped your vision? What are the key events that have shaped the collective vision of the students in this course?
3. Discuss the concept of educational autobiography. If you were to write your own educational autobiography, what questions would you ask yourself?
4. Discuss the concept of educational biography and assume that you are planning to prepare an educational biography of another student enrolled in this course. What questions would you ask in an oral history interview?
5. Examine the current cultural context in which we live. What are the major issues, problems, and challenges in the context that face education and educators?
6. Identify one educational event in your life. Why is that event significant?

Research and Essay Topics

1. Go to a bookstore or to your library and do a survey of biographies that have been published in the past year. Prepare an analysis of the general categories of biography, the people treated, and how many of them relate to education formally and informally.
2. Is there a particular person who is a model for you? In an essay, explain why that person is a model.
3. Write your own educational autobiography.
4. Write an educational biography of a student in this course.
5. During the time that you are enrolled in this course, keep a diary or a log of the significant educational events that have occurred. At the end of the course, prepare a summary that indicates which of them remain significant and why.

6. The following journals deal with biography: *Vitae Scholasticae: The Bulletin of Educational Biography* and *Biography: An Interdisciplinary Quarterly*. Read several issues of these journals. Select and review an article on the nature or problems of biography.

Suggestions for Further Reading

Bender, Thomas. *Intellect and Public Life: Essays on the Social History of Academic Intellectuals in the United States.* Baltimore: Johns Hopkins University Press, 1993.

Curti, Merle. *The Social Ideas of American Educators.* Paterson, N.J.: Littlefield, Adams and Co., 1959.

Gutek, Gerald L. *A History of the Western Educational Experience.* Prospect Heights, Ill.: Waveland Press, 1995.

———. *Philosophical and Ideological Perspectives in Education.* Englewood Cliffs, NJ: Prentice Hall, 1996.

Meyers, Jeffrey, ed. *The Craft of Literary Biography.* New York: Schocken Books, 1985.

Middleton, Sue. *Educating Feminists: Life Histories and Pedagogy.* New York: Teachers College Press, Columbia University, 1993.

Smith, Glenn L., ed. *Lives in Education.* New York: St. Martin's Press, 1995.

Stabler, Ernest. *Founders: Innovators in Education, 1830–1980.* Edmonton, Alberta, Canada: University of Alberta Press, 1986.

Van Patten, James J., ed. *Academic Profiles in Higher Education.* Lewiston, N.Y.: Edwin Mellen Press, 1992.

Whittemore, Reed. *Pure Lives: The Early Biographers.* Baltimore: Johns Hopkins University Press, 1988.

West, Elliot, and Petrik, Paula, eds. *Small Worlds: Children and Adolescents in America, 1850–1950.* Lawrence, Kan.: University Press of Kansas, 1992.

Plato: Idealist Philosopher and Educator for the Perfect Society

Engraving of a bust of Plato. Reproduced from the collections of the National Archives.

This chapter examines the life, educational philosophy, and contributions of Plato (427–347 B.C.), one of the major contributors to the development of philosophy in the Western world. Plato was a founding figure in establishing the intellectual foundations of Western civilization, and his philosophical works are still the point of departure for analyzing many educational issues that face us today. For example, Plato speculated on the nature of the universe in which we live, commented on the process by which human learning takes place, and constructed an argument for establishing the good society. Contemporary educators still grapple with questions about the nature of education and the goals and purposes that give it substance and direction.

In this chapter, Plato's influence on Western and U.S. education is analyzed both in terms of the historical context in which it originated and its enduring impact on educational philosophy and policy. First, the social, political, economic, and intellectual contexts of the ancient Greek society in which Plato lived is examined. Second, Plato's biography, education, and career are studied to trace the development of his ideas about education. Third, the continuing effect of Platonic thought on Western philosophy and education is analyzed.

Plato's contributions are most interesting to us as educators because of their multidimensional nature. He sought to answer the basic human question: What is good, true, and beautiful? This enduring question goes to the heart of our concern for educating people who possess a knowledge of reality, are ethical in their behavior, and live lives that are balanced and aesthetically harmonious. As you read this chapter, the following focusing questions are offered to help you organize your thoughts:

- What were the major developments and trends in the historical context of the ancient Athenian society in which Plato lived?
- How did Plato's life shape his philosophy of education?
- How did Plato's educational philosophy shape his educational proposals, policies, and practices?
- What is the enduring impact of Platonic philosophy on Western education?

The Historical Context of Plato's Life

You may be asking why our focus at the beginning of this book is on ancient Athens and on Plato. What fascination do the ancient Greeks hold for us today? What can we learn from them that will illuminate our concerns about society and education?

The ancient Greek world, located on the southern tip of the Balkan Peninsula and the many islands in the Aegean and Ionian seas, was the setting of a remarkable and varied civilization that, although Greek speaking, expressed itself differently in its society and politics.[1] The Greeks lived in separate, autonomous, independent city-states—or poleis—each of which exhibited cultural similarities, but also had some distinctive differences. An examination of the Greek style of life and culture will identify questions that Plato sought to answer in his philosophy of education. We might say that many Greek thinkers, including Plato, were on an intellectual quest to find the meaning of life and of human existence.

Our exploration of Plato's historical and cultural context begins with the theme of the search for meaning. In the history of Western civilization and education, this period of ancient Greece marks a tremendous cultural shift from the earlier despotic Egyptian and Persian empires that still existed at the time.

In the ancient world, the great "oriental empires" that developed in the fertile crescent of the Tigris and Euphrates rivers of Mesopotamia—such as the Assyrian and Persian—and the Egyptian in the Nile River Valley were ruled by powerful emperors who claimed divine origin and godlike powers. Despotically controlling vast empires, these rulers allowed their subjects little or no freedom to make their own choices. According to the belief system in these empires, the emperor or pharaoh was placed on Earth as a semidivine ruler over his subjects, who were to live in abject submission. A priesthood that was part of the ruling structure gave religious sanction to the status quo. This world was to be accepted in a fatalistic way by those who lived in it; they were not to question but to obey. The temple priests said this was the way it had always been and the way it would always be.

In such a closed system of thought, it was an easy task to establish educational goals. The major purpose of education, both formally in schools and informally in society, was to transmit from one generation to the next the ideas and values that supported the status quo. This process of cultural transmission deliberately avoided questions that might challenge the authority of the ruling elite. Much learning consisted of memorizing sacred texts or lists of prescriptions and of imitating the values that reinforced one's station in a hierarchical society.

The ancient Greeks, especially those who lived in the Athenian polis, took a sharply different view of life from that of the despotic empires. Although some Greeks were content with the transmission of traditional religious beliefs, cultural forms, and political institutions, others—especially in Athens—found that tradition did not have all the answers they were seeking. They began a search for the meaning of their existence. This involved developing the kind of education that would assist in that search. Once the Athenians embarked on the search for meaning there were no limits to their inquiry. In the minds of the Greeks, the one answer to life found in the despotic empires was not only inadequate but also undesirable.

As the Greek philosophers probed life's meaning, many possibilities emerged. Plato, one of the philosophers rigorously searching for life's meaning, was both invigorated and disturbed by the intellectual ferment of ancient Athens. He rejected the irrational ordering of society in the despotic empires but he feared that the Greeks, lacking a stable and consistent view, might be falling into intellectual and social anarchy and disorder.

For the ancient Greeks, the place in which life was lived had important consequences for how it was lived. The meaning of place carried with it a sense of social, political, cultural, and educational organization. This organized place called a polis meant a city-state, or a self-governing political unit. Among the Greek poleis were Thebes, Corinth, Delos, and the great rivals Athens and Sparta. Although the concept of the polis included the political meaning of the city-state, it was much more comprehensive. It referred to the total culture of that political place as it found expression in philosophy, religion, art, music, law, and literature. The Greeks commonly embraced this large and integrative view of the polis, although each polis organized its total cultural life differently.

An illustration of how varied the Greek conception of the polis could be is evident in Athens and Sparta, which had extremely different views of life.[2] Sparta was a fascist, military polis in which citizens were regarded as possessions of the state. At a male child's birth, Spartan leaders decided whether he appeared strong and healthy enough to be trained as a soldier. Those babies who were not selected were left to perish. Spartan citizens were expected to be soldiers who would collectively defend their polis against foreign adversaries and keep the majority of "noncitizens," the slave population of helots, under control. The education of Spartan males was directed almost exclusively to military drill, training, and gymnastics. Spartan girls were educated to become mothers of future soldiers. Spartan education, designed to transmit and train citizen-soldiers, was closely censored so that ideas from the outside would not present cultural alternatives. Sparta was like the anthill or the beehive in which the citizens sacrificed their individuality for what had been defined generations earlier as the civic good.

Although Athens went through various stages of historical development, it was a thorough-going democracy at its cultural zenith, the age of Pericles. Citizens were permitted to pursue varying interests and occupations but were also to be involved in the total life of their polis. When Athens was threatened, they were expected to rise to its defense. They were to participate in the assembly that debated and decided policy issues and serve on juries that adjudicated disputes. The art and architecture of Athens' temples and public buildings reflected the aesthetic sense that gave meaning to life. In Athens, a rich life of the mind took place as a succession of philosopher-teachers, including Protagoras, Socrates, Plato, Aristotle, and Isocrates, probed the issue of human meaning with their students.

What emerged from the Greek conception of the polis was the belief that the citizen was to be involved as a participant in the affairs of the city. To be uninterested in or aloof from civic responsibilities diminished human potentiality. However, the larger question then became what kind of sociocultural organization best encouraged the proper development of citizens. Should the polis be organized according to the one-dimensional perspective of Sparta or the multidimensional perspectives found in Pericles' Athens? If one contrasts Spartan singularity of purpose with the varied dimensions of Athenian life, large educational issues emerge. Single-minded training fulfilled the Spartan purpose, whereas the fulfillment of the Athenian purpose encouraged the cultivation of a person who was generally and liberally educated. In this philosophical and educational context, Plato worked his way to a set of answers that were surprisingly conservative for one who lived in democratic Athens.

Closely related to the sociophilosophical issue of the nature of the polis was the question of what constituted the good citizen of this polis. Throughout the Greek city-states, the commonly shared cultural and educational tradition had been derived from Homer's epics, the *Iliad* and the *Odyssey*. In these epic poems, which were transmitted as a oral tradition to Greek youth, an image of the heroic figure emerged. The Greek warrior-knight portrayed in these epics was courageous, cunning, and resourceful in the struggle against Trojan adversaries and eloquent in the councils of his lord, the king Agamemnon. The question at the time of Plato was whether the message and values of Homer's epics were still relevant as educational mediums for Greek society.

Greek philosopher-educators, especially in Athens, debated the nature of the good man and what kind of education was needed to develop him. For Athenian culture, the good man possessed and exhibited *arete,* which was defined as generalized excellence in all those characteristics that made up human nature. For more cerebral theorists, such as Plato and his student Aristotle, the good man was most excellent in rationality, that power that defined the human being.

Not all the theorists and educators of Athens shared Plato's propensity for a model of man that was governed by intellectuality. A group of itinerant teachers, known as the Sophists, who taught for a fee, challenged the intellectual conception of the good man. Responding to the economic prosperity and development that was changing Athenian life, the Sophists claimed that there were many answers, rather than one, to the question of what made a man good.[3] There were also many questions such as: What made a man a good political leader? What made a man a good speaker? What made a man a good soldier? According to the Sophists, the answers to these questions depended on the situation in which one found oneself. Putting forth a theory of cultural relativism, the Sophists claimed they could educate people to be successful in a variety of circumstances. In Athens, where the ability to persuade people in the assembly and in the courts was the key to power, the Sophists concentrated on teaching the skills of persuasion. Their version of rhetorical education supplied the student with a repertoire of information, psychological insights, and public speaking skills that would make them persuasive, successful, and powerful. Much of what Plato would do as a philosopher-orator was designed to counter the appeal of the Sophists.

Plato as an Idealist Philosopher

In examining the life and career of Plato, we will concentrate on those events and experiences in his life that caused him to formulate an idealist philosophy of education and an organic theory of society.[4] Pursuing the Greek search for meaning, Plato established a way of thinking that located a meaningful life in the cosmos as part of the universal order of unchanging reality. The place to experience meaning and to lead the good life was in an idealized and unchanging polis, the republic.

Although he lived in Athens, a polis renowned as the cradle of Western democracy, Plato resisted many of democracy's egalitarian tendencies. His resistance may have been influenced by his aristocratic Athenian family origins or it may have come from his antagonism to the cultural and ethical relativism that he saw as a consequence of popular democracy.

Plato's father, Ariston, claimed to be a descendant of Codrus, the last king of Athens before the establishment of democracy. Perictione, his mother, was a descendant of Solon, the famous lawgiver of ancient Athens. Plato was the youngest of four children. In his *Republic,* he briefly mentioned his brothers Glaucon and Adeimantus. His sister, Potone, was the mother of Speusippus, his successor as the leader of the Academy, the school of philosophy that Plato established in Athens. According to some accounts, Plato's real name was Aristocles, and the name Plato was actually a nickname that referred to his broad shoulders.[5]

During Plato's youth and adulthood, Athens experienced a period of political turmoil and acute social change. After Athens' defeat by Sparta, a conservative pro-Sparta regime was installed. Critias, a cousin of Plato's mother, was the leader of the thirty tyrants who ruled Athens. In the minds of the democratic majority in Athens, the tyrants were merely Spartan puppets.[6] When the democratic faction returned to power, the conservatives who had cooperated with the tyrants were deposed. Their families and associates were purged from state positions. Plato resented his family's fall from political power and resisted the democratization of Athenian life that threatened their favored social and political status. Because of his family connections, a political career was blocked for Plato. Disenchanted with the vicissitudes of everyday politics, Plato turned increasingly to speculation and theory.[7]

Plato's educational conceptions were shaped by his own education as well as by his family background. As a child and youth, Plato received a conventional Athenian education. In primary school he learned to read, write, and compute. He went to the palaestra for gymnastics and physical education. In the school of the citharist, he studied instrumental music, dancing, and singing. It was here that he was exposed to the oral tradition of Greek literature that had been stressed since the time of Homer. When he was 18, Plato spent the year of required military service in the cavalry.

Plato's real education, however, came as a young man when he joined a group of students who were seeking the meaning of their own lives, in particular, and the meaning of life in general. This quest brought Plato, then 22, into the company of Socrates. As is true of many educators, Plato was influenced by his teacher Socrates (470–399 B.C.). Frequenting the agora, the Athenian marketplace, Socrates and his students pursued basic questions about goodness, truth, and beauty. The premise that emerged was the Socratic doctrine that knowledge is the source of the virtuous or reflective life. A good life would be one of wisdom. Socrates challenged the Sophists, who claimed that they could transmit knowledge and virtue to their students from the outside. He did not believe that knowledge could be poured into a student's mind but argued that knowledge lies within each person's mind. The teacher's task, according to Socrates, was to ask stimulating and challenging questions that caused the student to think critically and reflectively. Through the Socratic method, the instructional strategy named for its originator, the ideas that were already in the mind were raised to consciousness. In the Socratic approach, the teacher challenges and prods students to think. Part of the process of critical thinking involves examining beliefs that are held merely because they are traditional and opinions held merely because they are current or popular. Part of the process is to unlearn and cast off false beliefs and opinions.

Through this process of inquiry, Socrates challenged not only the old order of traditional beliefs but also the newer method of the Sophists, who claimed that they could teach students to present a positive public image and manipulate public opinion by the clever combination of fact, myth, crowd psychology, and speech technique. Claiming to be a midwife of ideas, Socrates was an iconoclast who shattered many traditional images of Athenian society.[8]

Charged with impiety to the gods and corruption of the youth of Athens, Socrates was brought to trial, convicted, and sentenced to death by the Athenian court. He was sentenced to take his own life by drinking hemlock, a poison.

Socrates' trial and death made a deep impression on Plato, who wrote about it in his dialogue, *Crito*.[9] Socrates' case was one of the earliest and most famous of a long line of cases involving academic freedom—the right of a teacher to teach and of a learner to learn without interference from either arbitrary political authorities or a countervailing public opinion.

Plato's dramatic account of Socrates' last hours indicates the power of the event on Plato's life. According to Plato's dialogue, Crito and other students urge Socrates to attempt to save his life by running away from Athens or recanting his beliefs. Socrates resists the entreaties of his students, arguing that he must follow the dictates of reason that shape his understanding and his conscience. Socrates claimed that once a person's reason has grasped truth, that person must follow where reason takes him. Socrates explains to Crito that the true end of life is not simply to survive but to live the good life, which means a life guided by truth. A truly wise person, he asserts, both knows and does what is true. If he fled, Socrates claims, he would be escaping one evil by doing another—denying the right to seek the truth for oneself and one's students.

Because of his association with Socrates, Plato, too, was a suspect person. He left Athens on a journey that took him to the cultural centers of the Aegean and Mediterranean worlds. At Megara, a city on the isthmus that links the Peloponnesus with mainland Greece, he studied with Euclid, the famous scholar of geometry. Megara was a prosperous polis with a population estimated at between 25,000 and 40,000 inhabitants. Because of its political stability and economic wealth, Megara had become a cultural center, which explains Plato's attraction to the area.[10]

In Egypt, he encountered the Pythagoreans, a group of scholars who pursued the study of mathematics. As he developed his own philosophy, mathematics, with its power of pure reasoning, continued to intrigue Plato. He later emphasized it in the curriculum that he developed for the training of the philosopher kings, the rulers of the perfect but speculative republic. In Egypt, he may have also encountered oriental philosophy. His theory of reminiscence remarkably resembles the Hindu belief in reincarnation, and the socioeducational structure of the republic resembles the Hindu caste system.

In Sicily, then an outpost of Greek culture, Plato studied the rule of Dionysius I, ruler of Syracuse, who was establishing a strong political state. He questioned the strong personal power that Dionysius wielded in the region. Plato also struck up a friendship with Dion, whose sister was married to Dionysius. Plato incurred the displeasure of Dionysius I, who disapproved of Plato's association with Dion. Dionysius had Plato arrested and sold into slavery. Fortunately for Plato and for the development of Western philosophy, Plato's friend Anniceris purchased his freedom. Plato then returned to Athens.[11]

Influenced by Socrates' search for meaning, Plato immortalized his old teacher by writing about him and by continuing his own quest for truth. Like Socrates, he became a philosopher-educator. Unlike his mentor, who wandered through the agora, Plato taught in an institutional setting. In 387 B.C., Plato founded the Academy, an institution of higher education located in a shady grove near the public gymnasium in Athens. The Academy was granted the status of a legal entity by the government of Athens and had its own constitution.

Although it is not certain that students who applied to study with Plato had to pass an entrance examination, they did have a probationary period during which they had to demonstrate their seriousness of purpose and intellectual ability. Many students were residents at the Academy, where they studied arithmetic, geometry, astronomy, and harmonics, subjects that were designed to prepare them for the study of dialectics.[12] After completing these introductory courses, Plato's students rigorously pursued philosophical questions dealing with metaphysics, the study of ultimate reality; epistemology, the study of the theory of knowledge; and axiology, the examination of values.

Although Plato would argue in *The Republic* that women should have the same education as men because they possessed the same intellectual capacity, students in the Academy were male, as was customary in Athenian education. Women in Athens, with the exception of the heterae, a group of courtesans, were generally secluded from public and educational life. Although Plato was an intellectual, social, and political conservative, his view of women's education was more liberal than other Athenian theorists. Today we can extrapolate the ideas of Plato and the other theorists presented in this book to the education of women. However, during much of the historical period treated in this book, education, especially schooling, was dominated by males and often restricted to them.[13]

While directing the Academy, Plato wrote his leading philosophical works, *The Republic, The Apology,* and *Phaedo.* His philosophical insights were broadened by dialogues with his students and by his organization of lectures. Plato remained at the Academy lecturing, working with students, and writing until his death in 347 B.C.

Plato's Philosophy of Education

In this section, we examine Plato's major philosophical doctrines for their educational implications. The section begins with some situational observations on Plato's background as a possible catalyst for his ideas, and also concentrates on those larger concepts that have shaped Western thinking.

As Plato probed the meaning of life with his students, several trends of thought from his past converged to shape the ideas that formed his philosophical outlook. Plato resented the fact that his family and other families of the old aristocracy had lost their influence to the newly emergent and rising commercial class. Socioeconomic rivalry, which contemporary sociologists of education call conflict theory, was a factor in Plato's theory of education as well as in the theories of later educators. Indeed, it would be a continuing educational issue in Western education. Existing educational institutions and arrangements tend to reflect the belief system and values of the group that benefits from maintaining the status quo. These favored classes seek to maintain control of the institutions and processes, especially the educational ones, by which a person enters positions of power and influence.

In Plato's day, the conflict was induced by the appearance of a new commercial class that wanted the political power and social status they believed their wealth had earned for them. The Sophists developed an educational curriculum that promised the new class access to positions of power and prestige in Athens. Arguing that everything is relative and dependent on circumstances, the Sophists promised to provide their clients with the image that made a person successful. The Sophists claimed they could create a public image for their students by teaching them proper bearing, style of speech, and effective behavior patterns.[14] Thus the Sophists, who claimed their lessons would enable their students to win friends and influence people, were much like modern image makers who create a media image for political candidates. For Plato, these "new people" with their public images not only undermined the old order but were unprincipled opportunists. In the assembly and in the courts, the new people argued a case to win rather than to establish the truth of their case. They were manipulators, who were skillful in using psychology and argumentative techniques and would do anything to gain power.

Plato's aversion to image appeared continually in his philosophical and educational thought. For him, an image was something that had to be penetrated to reach the underlying reality. An Athenian political figure, like a modern-day politician, might appear to be an attractive candidate and deliver speeches that had popular appeal, but it was necessary to penetrate the image or facade to determine if the person possessed knowledge and virtue. Plato's probing of these political issues, which were a kind of civic education, related to the nature of the polis and of those who lived within. They transcended social and political philosophy and became a kind of speculation that was carried to a grand and all-encompassing scale.

At the Academy, Plato and his students sought to go beyond images and appearances to find the underlying truth and meaning of reality. Plato's search led him to develop a philosophical system known as idealism, which asserts that reality is nonmaterial or spiritual. For Plato, what was truly real existed in an eternally stable and unchanging realm of ideas, or pure concepts.

All ideas came from a superior, higher, and all-encompassing idea, called the form of the good.[15] The objects that we sense—see, touch, smell, and hear—are imperfect representations of the perfect ideas of these objects located in the general form of the good. For example, human beings are of different heights, weights, races, ethnic groups, and languages but they are all human beings. To be a human being means that these persons' defining characteristics are found in the idea of the human being, which is part of the all-inclusive concept—the form of the good. This common humanity gives people their "humanness." The same pattern of reality is true of other objects that we sense. We may sense a variety of trees such as pines, oaks, elms, and lindens, but they are what they are—trees—because they reflect the concept of "treeness."

The key to knowing reality is to go beyond the sensory image and reach the true realm of being, the world of ideas. Most important in Plato's version of reality is the human intellectual power to generalize and to abstract. The clearer our knowledge of these concepts, the closer we are intellectually to the form of the good and the more accurate our knowledge of reality.

In our discussion of Plato's metaphysics or conception of reality, we have been discussing knowledge of objects of which we have some sensory experience. It is also possible to use the same general metaphysical strategy for examining questions of virtue, or the values that prescribe ethical and aesthetic behavior. These ethical issues were the important concerns of Socrates, and Plato also explored them. What is it that makes a particular human action an ethical action? Or, what makes a man or a woman a good person?

For the Sophists, answers to these questions were relative and depended on the consequences of a particular situation. The question of what is a good lawyer could be answered by saying: A good lawyer is a person who has the knowledge and skills to win a case. Similarly, a good general is a person who has the military knowledge and strategic skills to win a battle.

For Plato, as for Socrates, such answers were only the beginning points of the learning dialogue rather than the end. Plato would have asked: Is there a moral common ground that applies to both the good lawyer and the good general? Is not the real question what makes a good human being—what makes a good man or good woman? People and their actions are virtuous and ethical as they conform to the universal values found in the form of the good. Plato argued that values are universal regardless of place, time, and circumstances. There are universal standards of moral behavior that have applied across the centuries of human history and they apply equally to people living in different geographical places. What is ultimately good, true, and beautiful does not depend on where you live or when you live. Goodness, truth, and beauty are found in the nature of the universe.

For Plato, then, there is a true intellectual self within and superior to the material human body. There is also a true conceptual world of ideas within and above the material world of time, place, and things that we experience through our physical senses. He explained our search for this true world of ideas through his famous allegory of the cave. Prisoners, confined in the cave, are chained with the sun to their backs so they cannot see the real objects but merely their shadows. In this analogy, objects in the material world such as men, animals, and trees are mere reflections of the idea of the perfect object, like shadows on the wall of a cave. The virtues of human beings are incomplete reflections of the ideal virtues of which the highest is the idea or form of the good. The purpose of life is to strive for knowledge of ultimate and perfect ideas, the form of the good from which all other ideas are derived.

By interpreting the allegory of the cave and Plato's other works, we can analyze his epistemological theory that deals with knowing. How do we know what we know? Epistemological theories are of crucial importance for teachers in that they examine the process by which we come to know. Closely related to theories of knowledge are the issues of how we learn and how we should teach. If our teaching methods follow the way human beings learn, then there is a better chance that they will be effective. In turn, both teaching and learning are parts of the more general question of how human beings know.

For Plato, the process of human knowing is "reminiscence," recalling the knowledge that one knew before the soul was encased in a physical body. Before birth, the soul existed in the world of pure ideas or forms and knew these universal and perfect concepts. At birth, knowledge of these concepts is retained but the shock of being born causes them to be locked away in the unconscious mind. Once the mind is in the body, we are driven by impulses that come into being because of physical needs. The material world and our sensations of it fill us with images. Living in a society that is often based on materialism fills us with opinions, many of which are false. To really know what is real, we must penetrate these sensations and opinions to find the truth.

The search for the truth is an interior search to recall ideas that are latently present in our minds. Through dialogue and the Socratic method, searching questions are asked that cause us to examine our beliefs and values.[16] The interior search for the truth within us may be painful in that it may lead to the abandonment of conventional beliefs or the rejection of popular conventions of public opinion.

The shared dialogue of the symposium is one process used to rediscover the truth, but not the only one. Because the truth is within each of us, it is found deeply within the recesses of the human mind or psyche. The ultimate discovery may require one to distance oneself from sensory and materialistic distractions and in solitary introspection find the interior truth, as Henry David Thoreau at Walden Pond would do many centuries after Plato.

As indicated, Plato's metaphysical and epistemological doctrines directly challenged the Sophists' relativism. Underlying philosophical issues also brought them into conflict about the purpose of education. Was education to cultivate the liberal culture of the person as a generalist or was it to sharpen technical expertise? Here, Plato and his philosophical adversaries were beginning the debate over liberal and technical education that still goes on today.

Plato presents his defense of education for general liberal culture in his dialogue, *Protagoras*. Socrates' adversary in the dialogue, Protagoras, was a famous Sophist and a teacher of rhetoric, or oratory, who insisted that "man is the measure of all things." In the dialogue, Protagoras promises that his method of education will make those who study with the Sophists better people. Socrates pursues the point by demanding to know what there is about the Sophists' education that will make a person more ethical and a better human being. When Protagoras answers that the teaching of political and rhetorical skills will make the student better, Socrates— who is Plato's mouthpiece in the dialogue—leads him into a discussion of whether a particular kind of skill is the same as general knowledge and virtue, which all men should possess. The dialogue concludes with a victory for Socrates, who argues that a genuinely and generally educated person will choose that which is the best. When knowledge is faulty and incomplete, we choose other than the best. What Socrates accomplishes is the integration of knowledge and virtue. If we know the good and the true, we will choose it. Intellectual education and moral preferences are linked in a truly liberal and liberating education.[17]

Plato's *Protagoras* presents the major issues in the debate over liberal versus technical education. For the proponents of technical education, the skill acquired by technical training will make the student a well-paid and valuable contributor to society. Knowledge and skill that come from technical education are not only relevant to social and economic needs but also personally rewarding in a financial sense. Plato's objections in many ways remain the arguments of contemporary proponents of general education. Genuine knowledge is the knowledge that everyone should have because they are human beings. Those who possess such general knowledge will be able to make informed decisions and choices because their actions can be placed in a general context.

Plato's Republic: An Organic Society

In our examination of the historical context in which Plato lived, it was indicated that the polis was the focal and integrative point in Greek culture. Plato, as well as other Greek theorists, sought to develop theories about the kind of polis that would renew and reintegrate Greek life. Plato, who opposed the changes taking place in his native Athens, grappled intellectually with the question: What kind of polis would enable human beings to realize their human potential and live meaningful lives? Plato answered the question by designing an ideal society in *The Republic,* his major work on politics and education.[18]

The Republic presented a plan for the ideal place to live, a utopian design for the good society. Although never implemented, *The Republic* is useful for educators to study because it presents a critique of society and suggests the social, political, and educational structures needed to create the good life on Earth. Those who analyze existing social and educational institutions engage in the kind of social criticism Plato employed in fashioning his idealized design for a polis. The plans for creating new institutions, structures, and processes that are part of policy designs are not unlike what Plato was attempting to do in his classic work.

The Republic is also useful for educators because it clearly points out the intimate connection between education and citizenship. True to the Greek conception that citizens should be totally integrated into the life of their polis, Plato established relationships between the political institutions and responsibilities of citizens and the kind of education that prepared one to fulfill the requirements of citizenship.

Plato's Republic is an organic society in which the socio-political-educational institutions are interrelated and serve the common purpose of maintaining and enhancing the life of the polis.[19] In the same way, the three castes or classes that Plato identified were to function as interrelated and necessary parts of the body politic. Just as the human body is an organism composed of interrelated parts that contribute to its ongoing life, the republic is an organism in which its parts contribute to its survival, well-being, and happiness. Educators who subscribe to an organic theory of society tend to see schools as functioning parts of a total society. Their contribution to the well-being of society gives schools their mission and function.

Metaphysically, Plato saw ultimate reality consisting of perfect ideas or concepts that were derived from the form of the good. Among these perfect metaphysical concepts was the idea of the perfect polis, or political society. It was this perfect city that Plato sought to describe in *The Republic.*

Plato regarded the social, economic, and political changes that were taking place in Athens not as signs of progress but rather as signs of the disintegration of society. He also saw the egalitarianism and social mobility that the Sophists offered as part of their new educational design to be undermining genuine values and debasing learning. Plato took an essentially conservative stance in *The Republic.* Like contemporary conservatives in education, he wanted to reassert the kind of knowledge he considered most valuable and restore what he regarded as genuine values. Once these tasks had been accomplished, it was to endure forever. Plato's position in *The Republic* raises the major issue of what educators should do about social change—ignore it, oppose it, or encourage it?

To escape the discord of social change, Plato proposed an eternal and unchanging city, a perfect polis, that would eliminate the turmoil of the imperfect world. Plato based his perfect city on the principle of justice. Because the state existed to cultivate justice in its citizens, Plato reasoned, the state itself had to be organized according to the principle of justice. In the just society, every citizen was to do what he was suited to do by his nature.

Using the model of the organic society, Plato identified three constituent classes that would perform the necessary functions of the political organism or body. Membership in these three classes—the guardians or philosopher-kings, the defenders or the military, and the workers—was based on the person's capacity to perform the role appropriate to the particular class.

The guardians had the greatest capacity for intellectual activity. They were interested in ideas and pursuing truth. True to Plato's belief that the highest human activity was the power to reason, these people occupied the highest status in *The Republic* and exercised the greatest role. Constituting the republic's "brain trust," they would be the governors, legislators, and policy makers. In the same way the mind thinks for the human being, the philosopher-kings would think for the political body.

In second position in *The Republic* were the defenders, members of the armed forces who possessed the greatest capacity for physical courage and bravery. The defenders were assigned the responsibility of protecting the republic from its enemies. Just as the body's arms protected the human body, the defenders served as the armed forces of the political organism.

In third place were the workers, those who possessed the greatest capacity for economic production. The workers grew the food and provided the goods and services needed to sustain the economic life of the republic. As the human body's digestive system provides nutrients to sustain life, the workers satisfied the economic needs of the society.

Plato believed that selecting individuals for particular assignments based on their natures or capacities was an act of justice. Each would perform the assignments for which their nature had prepared them. The principle of justice was fulfilled by the harmonious relationship of all classes in the republic. The socially integrated society, organized on the basis of intellectuality, is a just society. Justice in the individual consisted of the harmonious integration of the rational, volitional, and appetitive in the human soul, and the social soul of the polis should be likewise integrated.[20] The society that Plato outlined in *The Republic* was hierarchical, based on intellectual capacity. Just as the mind should govern the body and its physical appetites, Plato reasoned, the mind of the polis, the philosopher-kings, should govern those of lesser intellectuality.

The selection of individuals for positions within the hierarchy of society was an important issue for Plato. How people are selected for certain kinds of education and positions following that education remains a crucial policy question today. For Plato, the issue was the relationship of the mass of population to the selected elite, the many to the few. Plato himself came from one of the original elite groups of Athens. In some ways, his philosophy and theory of the organic society is a philosophical rationale for elitism. The elite that would rule the republic was an intrinsically disinterested minority who expected no personal profit from their positions but would use their positions for the good of the polis. From their philosophical orientation in seeking the good, the philosopher-kings were interested only in solving problems, not their own special interests.

Critics of Plato's *Republic* have argued that it is an antidemocratic design for the totalitarian society. The republic was patterned after a version of Sparta but with the important difference that Plato substituted intellect for raw physical stamina and courage. Unlike his rivals the Sophists, who proclaimed the equality of persons and ideas, Plato countered that individuals were not equal in terms of their intellectual ability. The possession of this intellectual ability, or the potential to think abstractly, was not an inherited or ascribed position. Those who were intellectually inferior to the class of their birth were relegated to the class that was appropriate for them. Those who were born into a lower class in the hierarchy but who possessed intellectual acumen would be placed in a higher class. Plato reasoned that those who had the most highly developed minds should be the policy makers of society.

Plato's System of Education

In the broad sense of education as *paideia,* the word the Greeks used for the total cultural formation of the person, Plato's ideas examined in the preceding sections were educational. They were based on his philosophical idealism and his epistemological doctrine of reminiscence. The teacher's task is to effect a kind of intellectual conversion experience in the learner that redirects the person from the sensory world of appearances, images, and opinions to the realm of ideas. Whereas knowing can occur only in the mind of the person, the teacher creates the proper environment and asks the questions that will stimulate the learning process.

Plato believed that early childhood was a crucial stage in the total education of the person. In the child's early years, the attitudes and values—the cultural, social, and intellectual predispositions—of later life were formed. In *The Republic,* Plato specified that state-operated nurseries should be established to rear children from birth to age 6. These nurseries were to be a purified environment free of social evils and the corruptive influences of families who possessed the wrong values. The specific functions of the state nurseries were the following:

- To cultivate a general communal or social disposition that would be supportive of life in the republic.
- To form the proper habits or emotional predispositions to the good life so that when children grew up, they would want the knowledge valued in the republic.
- To provide a curriculum of stories, music, games, and dramas that would be models of the good life that children could imitate.
- To begin the process of identification of those who possessed keen intellectual abilities.

Plato was among the earliest of the educator-philosophers to recognize the importance of childhood in forming predispositions or attitudes that would be conducive to a particular concept of society. Theorists of later eras such as Jean-Jacques Rousseau in *Emile* and Robert Owen in his *New Moral World* would stress the need to shape children in their earliest years in preferred ways.

After spending their first six years in state nurseries, children from 6 to 18 were to attend schools where the curriculum consisted of music, literature, mathematics, and gymnastics.[21] Music, taught according to the broad Greek sense of the term, was designed to create the proper moral spirit. Under the heading of literature, children first learned to read and write and then studied the approved Greek classics. Literature was an important source of character formation in that it provided models that students could imitate. Mathematics, Plato's favorite subject for cultivating abstract reasoning, was an important part of the curriculum. Included in mathematics were geometry and astronomy. Gymnastics promoted character building and physical development, skill, and strength. For Plato, the proper blending of gymnastics and music encouraged a well-balanced and harmonious character. Particular exercises included fencing, archery, javelin throwing, using the sling, and horseback riding.

When they had achieved their level of capacity, students left the school to enter occupations and trades. Those who possessed the capacity to enter the ranks of the military defenders or the philosopher-kings continued for two more years, from ages 18 to 20, to pursue physical and military training. Plato believed the military defenders needed additional training because it related directly to their assigned functions in the republic. The philosopher-kings needed this training because they would be making the overall strategic decisions for the republic.

The education of the future philosopher-kings would continue for ten more years as they studied mathematics, geometry, astronomy, and music. Combining the pursuit of mathematics and philosophy, they would search for underlying principles. Their overarching objective would be to reduce the seemingly vast array of knowledge to the one great unifying principle contained in the form of the good. When they reached age 30, the selection procedure would again be used as those with lesser intellectual powers were assigned to subordinate administrative and educational responsibilities.

For five years after that, the philosopher-kings would concentrate their education on the higher philosophical study of metaphysics, which in Platonic terms is the search to understand the form of the good. In pursuing truth, this select group of students would use the dialectic process, the examination of propositions of truth through critical discussion. At age 35, the philosopher-kings would go into the republic and actually administer and supervise the affairs of state. When they reached age 50, they would become the ruling elite—the most select of the selected ones—and become the policy makers and decision makers of the republic.

Conclusion: An Assessment

Plato remains one of the great and powerful thinkers in the history of Western thought and education. Whether we agree with him—and many of us will not— Plato's basic issues of education still enlist our attention today. Although philosophical idealism is not one of the dominant ways of thinking among contemporary philosophers, Plato's searching questions about the nature of the good, true, and beautiful remain as the continuing human quest. Should not today's teachers seek to cultivate truth, beauty, and goodness in their students?

Although Plato's republic may not appeal to democratic sensibilities today, the issues he raised about the nature of the polis and its citizens still are relevant to education for citizenship in our schools. Public education in the United States is committed to educating citizens who will participate in the political life of their nation. But after this general commitment has been stated, precisely what should be the nature of citizenship education? Is it to be education that nurtures a patriotic love of the country and its traditions and values? Is it to be based on a critical examination of issues even if this process leads students to question inherited values? Although Plato's educational adversaries are no longer with us in the form they took in ancient Greece, what is the educational role of the media? What should teachers in classrooms do about the dynamic and vivid impressionism of television? Although conventional citizenship education is intended to encourage our participation in the political processes of our country, what is the nature of critical thinking when the processes are infused by the dynamic "packaging" of candidates and issues?

In *The Republic,* Plato raised the issue of continuity and change in culture, society, and education. Although few today are likely to endorse Plato's utopian rejection of change, the question remains as to the degree to which schools and teachers should be conservators of the cultural heritage or agents of social change. Is the role of the schools to introduce the young to their cultural heritage by teaching them to read, write, and compute—stressing a stable curriculum of mathematics, history, science, language, and literature as is recommended by the Council on Basic Education? Should the schools incorporate current issues and new technology such as computer literacy into the curriculum? Should teachers boldly seek to help end poverty, pollution, and racism by actively working to build a new social order?

Plato raises the issue of identifying and selecting intellectual individuals in society and in school. What is the role of teachers in the selection process? Should they group students homogeneously? When they do, are they promoting the selective process? Should students be grouped into tracks on the basis of their academic ability as Plato suggested in *The Republic*? Or should educational arrangements promote equality rather than separatism? Should colleges use SAT and ACT tests in their admission processes?

As we pursue questions raised by Plato, we can also think about the hidden factors that modern sociology tells us influence the processes of selection and admission such as gender, race, ethnicity, socioeconomic status, and place of residence. Plato's stress on selection also brings us to the major dilemma facing U.S. education: Is it possible to have excellence and equity in our schools at the same time?

Discussion Questions

1. What issues in the Greek cultural context raised important challenges for education?
2. How did the concept of the polis contribute to the shaping of Greek attitudes about education?
3. How did Plato's family background and early education shape his views on society and education?
4. How did Plato's association with Socrates influence the development of his philosophy of education?
5. Who were the Sophists and why did Plato oppose their social and educational doctrines and methods?
6. Identify and analyze the arguments for liberal and technical education.
7. Examine Plato's republic as an organic society. What are the characteristics of education in such a society?
8. Compare and contrast the process of social and educational selection in Plato's republic with that operating in contemporary U.S. society.
9. Examine the historical context of Athens during Plato's life. Identify and analyze the major socioeducational issues of that time. Are these issues similar to those found in contemporary American society?

Research and Essay Topics

1. In a position paper, use the concept of conflict theory as illustrated in the controversies between Plato and the Sophists to identify and examine a similar conflict in contemporary U.S. education.
2. Write a commentary that analyzes the campaigns of candidates for political office in the United States today according to a Sophist and a Platonic criterion.
3. Examine the contemporary proposals for educational reform in the United States. In an essay, determine if these reflect a liberal or technical approach to education.
4. In an essay, develop a plan for an ideal, or utopian, society and describe the kind of education appropriate for it.
5. In an essay, identify some significant social changes that are taking place in contemporary U.S. society. How would Plato react to these changes? Do you agree with Plato?
6. From the Platonic perspective, prepare a review essay of several books on instructional methods.
7. Design a lesson plan that uses the Platonic approach to teaching.

Notes

1. D. H. F. Kitto, *The Greeks* (Baltimore: Penguin Books, 1962), remains an excellent introduction to Greek civilization.
2. Gerald L. Gutek, *A History of the Western Educational Experience* (Prospect Heights, Ill.: Waveland Press, 1995), 41–48.
3. Harry S. Broudy and John R. Palmer, *Exemplars of Teaching Method* (Chicago: Rand McNally, 1965), 15–30.
4. Biographical and philosophical commentaries on Plato are Alfred E. Taylor, *Plato: The Man and His Work* (London: Methuen, 1966), and Robert W. Hall, *Plato* (London: Allen and Unwin, 1981).
5. Plato's life is discussed in G. C. Field, *Plato and His Contemporaries* (London: Methuen, 1962), 1–39. Also, see Paul Shorey, *What Plato Said* (Chicago: University of Chicago Press, 1968), 1–57.
6. L. Glenn Smith, ed., *Lives in Education* (Ames, Iowa: Educational Studies Press, 1984), 16.
7. Edward J. Power, *Evolution of Educational Doctrines: Major Educational Theorists of the Western World* (New York: Appleton-Century-Crofts, 1969), 55–56.
8. For the life and philosophy of Socrates, see W. K. C. Guthrie, *Socrates* (Cambridge: Cambridge University Press, 1971). Also, see Robert S. Brumbaugh, *The Philosophers of Greece* (Albany: State University of New York Press, 1981).
9. Eric H. Warmington and Philip G. Rouse, eds., *Great Dialogues of Plato,* trans. W. H. D. Rouse (New York: New American Library, 1956), 447–459.
10. Ronald P. Legon, *Megara: The Political History of a Greek City-State to 336 B.C.* (Ithaca, N.Y.: Cornell University Press, 1981), 21–24.
11. G. C. Field, *Plato and His Contemporaries* (London: Methuen, 1962), 16–17.
12. Power, Evolution of Educational Doctrines, pp. 81-83.
13. Commentaries on Plato's views of the education of women are Christine A. Gorside, "Plato on Women," *Feminist Studies 2* (1975), 131–138; Arlene W. Saxonhouse, "The Philosopher and the Female in the Political Thought of Plato," *Political Theory 4* (1978), 195–222.
14. A. E. Taylor, *Plato: The Man and His Works* (New York: Humanities Press, 1952).
15. W. D. Ross, *Plato's Theory of Ideas* (Oxford: Oxford University Press, 1951).
16. Plato, "Meno," in *The Dialogues of Plato,* trans. B. Jowett (Indianapolis: Liberal Arts Press, Bobbs-Merrill, 1949), 37–45.
17. Power, Evolution of Educational Doctrines, pp. 62-68.
18. Among the many editions of Plato's *Republic* are *Plato, The Republic,* trans. Allan Bloom (New York: Basic Books, 1968); *The Republic,* trans. G. M. A. Grube (Indianapolis: Hackett, 1974); *The Republic,* trans. B. Jowett (New York: Random House, 1941).
19. R. M. Hare, *Plato* (Oxford: Oxford University press, 1982), 60–68.
20. S. J. Curtis and M. E. A. Boultwood, *Short History of Educational Ideas* (London: Tutorial Press, 1965), 1–29.
21. Robert S. Brumbaugh and Nathaniel M. Lawrence, *Philosophers on Education: Six Essays on the Foundations of Western Thought* (Boston: Houghton-Mifflin, 1963), 40–43.

Suggestions for Further Reading

Annas, Julia. *An Introduction to Plato's Republic.* Oxford: Oxford University Press, 1981.
Barrow, Robin. *Plato and Education.* London: Routledge and Kegan Paul, 1976.
———. *Plato, Utilitarianism, and Education.* London: Routledge and Kegan Paul, 1975.

Brumbaugh, Robert S. *The Philosophers of Greece.* Albany: State University of New York Press, 1981.

Brumbaugh, Robert S., and Nathaniel M. Lawrence. *Philosophers on Education: Six Essays on the Foundations of Western Thought.* Boston: Houghton-Mifflin, 1963.

Cross, R. C., and A. D. Woozley. *Plato's Republic: A Philosophical Commentary.* New York: St. Martin's Press, 1966.

Field, G. C. *Plato and His Contemporaries.* London: Methuen, 1962.

Grube, G. M. A. *Plato's Thought.* Boston: Beacon Press, 1966.

Gulley, Norman. *Plato's Theory of Knowledge.* London: Methuen, 1962.

Guthrie, W. K. C. *Socrates.* Cambridge: Cambridge University Press, 1971.

Hare, R. M. *Plato.* Oxford: Oxford University Press, 1982.

Lodge, Rupert C. *Plato's Theory of Education.* New York: Russell and Russell, 1970.

Mall, Robert W. *Plato.* London: Allen and Unwin, 1981.

Nettleship, R. L. *The Theory of Education in Plato's Republic.* New York: Teachers College Press, Columbia University, 1968.

Plato. *The Republic.* Trans. Allan Bloom. New York: Basic Books, 1968.

Ross, W. D. *Plato's Theory of Ideas.* Oxford: Oxford University Press, 1951.

Shorey, Paul. *What Plato Said.* Chicago: University of Chicago Press, 1968.

Stalley, R. F. *An Introduction to Plato's Laws.* Oxford: Basil Blackwell Publisher, 1983.

Taylor, Alfred E. *Plato: The Man and His Work.* London: Metheun, 1966.

White, Nicholas P. *A Companion to Plato's Republic.* Indianapolis: Hackett, 1979.

Wilson, John F. *The Politics of Moderation: An Interpretation of Plato 's Republic.* Lanham, Md.: University Press of America, 1984.

Aristotle: Founder of Realism

Aristotle, from an engraved illustration; reproduced from the collections of the Library of Congress.

Chapter 3 examines the life, educational philosophy, and contributions of Aristotle (384–322 B.C.), a philosopher of ancient Greece who developed the theory of Realism. Aristotle, along with Plato, is regarded as a founding father of Western philosophy. In a recent commentary, Barnes wrote that Aristotle "bestrode antiquity like an intellectual colossus. No man before him had contributed so much to learning. No man after him could hope to rival his achievements."[1]

In this chapter, Aristotle's influence on Western thought and education is examined in its historical context and in terms of its enduring impact. First, the general historical context of a Greece undergoing transition from a collection of small city states to the Hellenistic empire is examined. Second, Aristotle's life, his education and career, is analyzed to identify the forces that influenced the development of his philosophical and educational ideas. Third, the key elements in Aristotle's philosophy of Natural Realism are identified and examined. Fourth, we describe his ideas on schooling. Finally, Aristotle's historical and contemporary significance is assessed. By this historical examination, we seek to illuminate those events and factors that contributed to the formulation of one of the Western world's most significant systems of thought.

To help you to organize your thoughts as your read the chapter, you might wish to consider the following focusing questions:

- What were the major trends in the historical context, the time and situation, in which Aristotle lived?
- How did Aristotle's life—his educational biography—shape his philosophical and educational perspective?
- How did Aristotle's philosophy shape his educational ideas and practices?
- What has been the enduring impact of Aristotle's contributions on Western educational theory and practice?

The Historical Context of Aristotle's Life

During Aristotle's time, three major features of Greek culture were of special significance:

1. Basic intellectual concepts.
2. The continuing decline of the polis as a vital cultural focus.
3. The rise of the Hellenistic civilization associated with Alexander the Great.

In addition, many of the characteristics and trends present in Plato's life, discussed in Chapter 2, were still present.

Aristotle's philosophy of education reflects the Greek intellectual tradition that emphasized human reason as that which gives definition, meaning, and purpose to life. While there was also a sense of destiny or fatalism in Greek religion that saw the human being as a toy of the gods, the gods were seen to embody particular human qualities. In contrast to the view that human beings were subject to irrational forces outside of their experience, Aristotle exemplified Greek thinkers who saw human beings' internal rational powers as the proper focus of choice and decision making. He did not rest his theory solely on human responses to the environment, however. The human being, a person of individual character, was part of a universal frame of being. Aristotle moved away from a capricious universe governed by irrational forces to a purposeful world governed by rationality.

Like his mentor Plato, Aristotle's thought embodied the concept that *arete*— human excellence in all things—was an important goal that should direct human purposes. For Aristotle, that excellence ideally exemplified the defining quality of human nature, the pursuit of reason.

Attracted by science and believing that the universe could be explained, Aristotle drew on, refined, and extended the Greek world view. From Thales of Miletus, Aristotle accepted the concept that the physical universe operated rationally and in a way that was knowable to human beings. From Anaximander, Aristotle took the view that a balance of force existed in nature that made things what they were. Aristotle was also knowledgeable about the atomic theory of Parmenides who saw objects as the coming together of material particles. Like Heraclitus who asserted that everything is constantly changing, Aristotle was intrigued by the question of development and of determining what was stable and what was changing. These early Greek scientists contributed to Aristotle's intellectual quest to examine and explain reality.[2]

Aristotle was also heir to the Greek educational tradition, especially as it was practiced in Athens. The Greeks were intellectual system builders who tried to incorporate the parts of their experience—their drama, art, architecture, law, sports, and politics—into a whole. Trying to place bits of experience into an explainable whole was part of their desire to explain the universe in rational terms. The educational content and style they developed reflected the desire for relationship, harmony, and balance.

Greek education, especially for Athens and excluding Sparta, stressed the concept of the liberal arts—studies that were for free men. Except for the militaristic state of Sparta, Greek education was reserved for males. Aristotle shared this gender prejudice, which was common during his time. Important subjects in Greek higher education were grammar (the study of language), rhetoric (persuasive speaking), mathematics, philosophy, and music, which included literature and poetry. Aristotle embraced the Greek version of the liberal arts curriculum. Intrigued by science, his curiosity led him to the natural sciences—to biology, botany, physiology, and zoology—areas that he developed in his own teaching and writing. In his quest to develop a theory that explained reality, Aristotle studied philosophy. He pursued metaphysical issues in his attempt to discover the nature of ultimate reality; he studied epistemological questions in his search to find out how human beings come to know. He developed a system of logic, of deductive reasoning, as the formula for argument. Aristotle was thus the product of the intellectual context that made ancient Greece an important point of origin in the western educational tradition.

During Aristotle's life, from 384 to 322 B.C., the Greek city-states, which embodied the old order of life, were in a process of disintegration. The conviction that the civilized person was an individual who participated in the politics, art, and law of the city-state was yielding to other desires and impulses. Plato had tried to formulate an ideal political-cultural-social state in his *Republic,* which would provide citizens with the needed sense of personal and cultural integration. For Plato, the outline of the perfect republic came from the mind's power to speculate.

Aristotle took a different approach to political organization. He traveled about the world visiting city-states that had different kinds of government and forms of political organization. As the founder of political science, he described actual forms of government—monarchies, oligarchies ruled by elites, and democracies—pointing out their various features and implications for human life.

Aristotle's educational theory was a systemization of the ideas he had developed as he studied various forms of government. *Paideia,* the Greek term for the taking on of culture, had by Aristotle's time changed from meaning the education of children to meaning the cultivation of human character and behavior. In his desire to restore the vitality of the declining polis, Aristotle developed his educational philosophy.

Aristotle's life also coincided with a basic transition in Greek political life from the era of free city-states to the Macedonian empire. In 338 B.C. Philip, king of Macedon from 359 to 336 B.C., defeated the armies of the city-states at the battle of Chaeronea. Two years later, Philip was assassinated and his son, Alexander, came to the throne. Aristotle had tutored Alexander, who in the brief period from 336 to 323 B.C. would conquer the known world. As his armies marched through Asia Minor, they were accompanied by biologists who collected specimens of the plants and animals. Despite his interest in philosophy and literature, Alexander the Great is best known for his military genius and bold use of tactics and strategy.

After putting down a rebellion by some Greek city-states, Alexander extended his empire by conquering the Ionian Greek settlements and the large Persian empire. His conquests extended into the Middle East and reached northern India.

To rule his vast empire, Alexander used Greek governors and settled Greek colonists in key areas. These transplanted Greeks were aided by local non-Greek officials. The end result of the process was to Hellenize, or give a Greek cultural veneer to, the ruling elites in Syria, Egypt, Persia, and other parts of Alexander's empire. Although his reign was brief, the empire that he established continued after his death at age thirty-three in 323 B.C.

By the time Aristotle died, in 322 B.C., the Greek political world of proud, independent city-states had undergone significant change. The polis, which had long been disintegrating as a vital cultural center, had been radically altered by Alexander and his successors. The new world order, while ruled by a Greek-speaking elite, was far different from that of Pericles, Socrates, and Plato.

In the Hellenistic world created by Alexander, his successors were more interested in storing knowledge than in creating it as Socrates, Plato, and Aristotle had done. The great library in Alexandria, Egypt, was such a storehouse of knowledge. On more than a half-million rolls of papyrus, its collection preserved the literature and philosophy of ancient Greece. While there were advances in science, mathematics, and the arts during the Hellenistic period from Alexander's death until the rise of Rome, inquiry followed purely academic paths rather than pursuing the vital issues of truth, justice, and the meaning of life.

Aristotle's Life and Career

Aristotle was born in Stagira, in the northern Greek kingdom of Macedonia, where his father, Nichomachus, was court physician to King Amyntas II. His mother was named Phoestis, but little is known about her background. As was the custom, the court physician not only treated the members of the royal court but also maintained a collection of scientific specimens. As a boy, Aristotle also was attracted to collecting and cataloguing specimens from natural history—minerals, plants, and animals. (Alexander, who studied under Aristotle, is believed to have sent various specimens to his old teacher from lands he had conquered in Asia.) Aristotle's interest in science and medicine continued throughout his life and is reflected in his philosophy of education.[3] Intrigued by natural phenomena, Aristotle sought to catalogue and categorize the objects around him. From his attempts at categorization would come the learned and scientific disciplines that study the various dimensions of reality.

When he was seventeen, Aristotle left Stagira to go to Athens, the center of Greek intellectual life. He studied with Plato, the renowned philosopher who had been a student of Socrates. (For a discussion of the educational ideas of Plato, see Chapter 2.) For the next twenty years, from 367 B.C. to 347 B.C., Aristotle studied with Plato at his philosophical institute, the Academy.

Plato had developed a highly speculative philosophy whose metaphysics asserted that reality was ultimately spiritual or nonmaterial. To understand the real nature of things, Plato argued, one had to transcend the senses and popular opinion and intellectually reach the world of perfect forms or ideas. Plato also emphasized a rigorous intellectual methodology, the Socratic approach of dialogue in which students examined propositions logically and critically. Aristotle held Plato in esteem and learned much from him, particularly the importance of logical and critical thinking. Aristotle would eventually join Plato as a member of that triad of great Greek philosophers who are linked together in western educational history: Socrates, Plato, and Aristotle.

As he developed as a philosopher, Aristotle became more than the lengthened intellectual shadow of Plato. While Aristotle accepted his mentor's concept of form, he disagreed with Plato's metaphysical doctrine that reality was ultimately nonmaterial. Aristotle came to develop a hylemorphic or dualistic position that viewed reality as composed of matter and form. Early in his career, Aristotle combined his scientific curiosity about the natural world around him, learned at his father's side, with the Platonic speculative quest to find a world of truth that existed beyond the senses. While Plato's world view rested on a perfect and unchanging view of reality which could be glimpsed by those who were trained in the method of philosophical speculation, Aristotle began his inquiries with his senses. What would intrigue the young philosopher was a desire to know how things developed and changed. After Plato's death, Aristotle set out to reconcile Plato's theory of perfect forms or ideas with the facts of natural development.[4]

In 347 B.C., Aristotle set out on a educational tour of Asia Minor to study the geography, climate, politics, flora, and fauna of the lands east of Greece. Further, he had at this time no home to which to return. During the conquest of Macedonia, Philip of Macedon had sacked and burned Stagira.

Traveling in Asia Minor, Aristotle lived for several years in the small kingdom of Assos, which was ruled by King Hermias. He joined a small circle of scholars whom Plato had sent earlier to establish a school. The bright young philosopher attracted the attention of Hermias, who engaged him as a tutor and adviser. Aristotle, who was a member of the court, married Hermias' niece Phythias. They had a daughter also named Phythias. While at Assos, Aristotle studied botany and biology. He also traveled to nearby islands where he studied the political institutions, social customs, and plant and animal life.

In 343 B.C., Aristotle was asked by Philip of Macedon to join his court to tutor his son Alexander. He accepted the assignment and was Alexander's tutor for seven years. In 336 B.C., after Philip was assassinated and Alexander became king, Aristotle returned to Athens.

Following in the footsteps of Plato, Aristotle established a school in Athens, the Lyceum. Because Aristotle was a *metic*—a resident alien rather than an Athenian citizen—he could not own land, so the Lyceum happened to be wherever Aristotle was with his students rather than a building in a permanent location. He conducted his school in the public walkways and gathering places. Aristotle taught and wrote in Athens until 323 B.C. He acquired a reputation as a commanding intellectual and philosopher, but he was always regarded as a foreigner and never quite accepted in Athens.

Reflecting the many interests of their teacher, the Lyceum students pursued inquiries in the natural sciences, politics, metaphysics, and ethics. By most accounts, Aristotle is described as a demanding teacher whose lectures were carefully organized and followed a logical progression. He was a good speaker who was capable of including witticisms with his generally profound topics.

It was at the Lyceum that Aristotle developed a theory of natural progression in which natural phenomena were organized in a hierarchy. At the base of the hierarchy were lifeless minerals. Somewhat higher were plants, which while alive, were limited in their potential. Higher in the chain of being, or order of life, were the animals. At the summit of the hierarchy came the human being, who possessed the power of rationality.

Aristotle was a prodigious scholar and writer, and most of his treatises began as lectures to his students. For students of education, important sources include Aristotle's *Metaphysics,* which puts forth his theory of reality; his *Nicomachean Ethics,* which examines the nature of virtue; and his *Politics,* which includes a commentary on schooling. Aristotle wrote on many other subjects, including *On Justice, On the Soul, On the Sciences, The Art of Rhetoric, On Animals,* and *On Plants.* His lectures and writings dealt with a wide range of subjects: logic, the arts and sciences, psychology, physiology, political science, mathematics, zoology, botany, biology, law, metaphysics, epistemology, and astronomy.[5]

As a scholar-philosopher-teacher, Aristotle enjoyed a prestigious reputation but was not immune to the political events taking place in Greece. After Alexander had conquered Athens, Aristotle enjoyed his support and protection. Antipater, Alexan-

der's governor in Athens, saw to Aristotle's personal safety. That protection, however, produced a negative reaction among the Athenian patriots who regarded themselves as captive people. Aristotle, who noted the hostility, advised Alexander to
exercise tact and diplomacy in dealing with his Athenian subjects.[6]

After Alexander's death in 323 B.C., the Athenians revolted against Macedonian
rule. Aristotle was accused of impiety by the faction that had come to power in Athens.
Recalling Socrates' fate on a similar charge, he decided to leave Athens. He retired to
Chalcis in Euboea, where he lived with a slave girl, Herpyllis. (His wife had died many
years earlier.) Herpyllis bore him a son, Nicomachus. Aristotle died in 322 B.C.

Aristotle's Philosophy of Education

For Aristotle, the world in which we live is the world that we experience through our
senses. Unlike those who followed the philosophical Idealism of his mentor Plato,
Aristotle believed that we live in an objective order of reality, a world of objects that
exist external to us and our knowing of them. Through our senses and our reason,
human beings can come to know these objects and develop generalizations about
their structure and function. Theoretical knowledge based on human observation is
the best guide to human behavior, Aristotle said.

Central to Aristotle's metaphysics was his matter-form hypothesis. All the objects
we perceive through our senses are composed of matter. Matter, however, is
arranged according to different designs that Aristotle referred to as form. Without
the element of matter, nothing can exist. However, matter requires a form to
become something. For Aristotle, matter carries with it the principle of potentiality,
which means it has the potential of becoming something but must take a form or
structure. Aristotle referred to taking a form as the principle of actuality.

Aristotle structured reality into two parts: matter and form. Throughout his philosophy, this essential dualism was present. All objects, the specimens of minerals,
plants, and animals that he collected and studied, could be analyzed according to
their matter and their structure. Human beings, too, were made up of matter—tissue, bone, muscles, and sinew—but they possessed the form of the human being.
For Aristotle, the power that raised the human being above the brute world was
rationality. Education, as he conceived of it, was designed to enable human beings
to live socially, politically, and economically in a real world of flesh and blood in
addition to enabling the higher purpose of developing the power of rationality to its
highest possible level.

As a scientist, Aristotle was intrigued by the developmental question of how matter
moved from the state of potentiality to actuality. He explained this process of change
through his theory of the four causes: material, formal, efficient, and final. Every
object that exists has a *material cause,* which is the matter from which it is made. For
example, the chair on which you are sitting may be made of wood, which in Aristotelian terms is the material cause of the chair. The *formal cause* is the form the
object has; it defines the object. Note that the wood of which the chair is composed

could have been made into a desk or a bookcase. It could have been given a different form. The *efficient cause* refers to the agent that brought about the change from the material to the formal. In the case of the chair, it is the woodworker who made the wood into the chair. The *final cause* is that purpose for which the action is done. For the woodworker, the final cause is making the chair so a person can sit on it.

Aristotle's conception of causation, the movement from potentiality to actuality, rested on his view that the universe is purposeful. What goes on in reality, in the patterns of the universe, is meaningful and is tending to an end. Nature is not an accident of atoms coming together by chance. Nature has a symmetry in which every object—every mineral, plant, and animal—has a definite role in the great chain of being.

Aristotle's principle of causation and purpose, like his form-matter hypothesis, has implications for education. It means that human life is meaningful rather than meaningless. It means that human beings, by using rationality, have the power to shape or define themselves by making choices. The meaning of human life in Aristotelian terms is the pursuit of happiness. Happiness is defined as the fulfillment of all human potentiality, especially the power and quality of reason. Aristotle said the purpose of education is to cultivate, to develop, and to exercise each child's potentiality to be fully human.

In analyzing the process of change through the four causes, Aristotle determined that we again have two qualities with which to deal: substance and accident. *Substance,* that which exists by itself, is the stable element while an *accident* is the variable quality. To illustrate Aristotle's distinctions of substance and accidence, you might think of yourself. Your special identity as a person, that which makes you who you are, is your substance. However, you have changed over time in appearance and in human development. While you are essentially the same person you were as an infant, you have grown taller and older. Your appearance has changed, but you are still you.

Aristotle believed education should deal at its highest level with the unchanging elements of human nature. Note that he asserts human beings have an underlying nature that makes them human. Regardless of the historic period or their geographical location, human beings share an essential sameness. For example, all people regardless of race, ethnicity, and culture have the power to reason. While they may speak different languages—English, Chinese, or Polish, for example—all human beings have the power of communication. Thus, it is possible for Aristotelian educators to design curricula according to that which is universal to members of the human race. At the same time, they can also provide subject matter that is pertinent to a given time and place.

Just as he had divided reality into two parts, form and matter, Aristotle's epistemology was dualistic in that it involved two phases, sensation and abstraction. *Sensation* was the process by which the human being acquired sensory data from the material of the object; *abstraction* was the process by which the mind sorted out sensory information and arrived at concepts based on the form of the object.[7]

According to Aristotle, we inhabit a world of objects, and our knowledge of these objects begins with our sensory experience of them. Our eyes, nose, ears, tongue, and fingers are the body's physical organs for coming into contact with objects. Our senses, perceiving the matter of the object, carry information about the object's size, color, hardness or softness, sound, and other data to the mind. Somewhat like a computer, the mind sorts out information into the qualities or conditions that are always present, or necessary to the object, as distinct from those that are occasionally found in the object. The necessary conditions are those that are the basis of a concept. Aristotle defined a concept as based on the formal or essential qualities abstracted from an object. These are the qualities that it shares with other members or individuals of its class but with no other objects.

To illustrate Aristotle's process of abstraction and conceptualization, we can use the human being. People come in a variety of sizes, heights, and colors and speak different languages. Underlying these differences that appear to the senses, the mind is able to abstract a common set of conditions that are necessary to being human. These are common characteristics that people share, regardless of the place and time in which they live. This universal sense of humanness distinguishes human beings from other animate and inanimate objects.

The human powers of sensation and abstraction come to play on all the objects that exist. We see all sorts of trees—pines, palms, firs, apples, and elms—for example, as individual members of a category. These different trees share a commonality—treeness—that makes them part of the general category.

Aristotle's epistemology has important educational implications for both learning and knowledge. If we come to know through our senses and abstraction, then how we learn should follow this pattern of knowing. Instruction—teaching and learning—should provide occasions for students to examine, observe, and deal with objects. It should provide situations in which students create categories of objects that share certain essential characteristics and recognize objects that are similar and different. Later in the early nineteenth century, Pestalozzi's object lesson, which is examined in Chapter 10, followed an essentially Aristotelian epistemological approach.

Aristotle, one of the founding figures of Western science, also pioneered in categorization of objects. From the basic categories of animal, vegetable, and mineral, a highly specialized schema of classification was established. For example, the animal category could be divided into an immense array of subcategories. The information derived from the study of these subcategories could be classified into biology, zoology, anthropology, anatomy, physiology, and so on. In the Aristotelian system, everything that exists can be categorized and classified.

Aristotle's system of classification of objects and of creating bodies of information about them contributed to the organization of knowledge into the arts and sciences. It is these bodies of knowledge that make a person liberally educated or free to make rational choices. Aristotle believed the human being possesses the defining quality of rationality. Through the power of sensing and abstracting, the human mind acquires concepts. Over time, vast arrays of related concepts could be built into a storehouse of knowledge, a kind of intellectual map of reality. To be free and to act rationally, the human being needs to form, weigh, and act on alternatives of action. The human mind is informed by knowledge about the world and how the objects in the world interact and behave according to their structure and function.

The Aristotelian process of liberalization through knowledge can be illustrated by an example. At certain stages in life, people make career choices that shape both their current situation and their future. The list of choices is broad and varied—baker, lawyer, gardener, physician, physicist, computer programmer, teacher, pilot, politician. To rationally make decisions, people need to possess knowledge about these various careers and the preparation needed to enter that particular career. They can go to the library to find information about a particular career, and also investigate institutions and schools that offer programs for particular careers. Using all this information, people can assess their interest and potentiality for the given career.

In Aristotle's view, while human beings have various careers, they all share the most important factor, the exercise of rationality. Reason gives human beings the potential of leading lives that are self-determined. To assist in the process of human self-determination, education should provide the knowledge upon which rational decisions and actions are made.[8]

Congruent with his metaphysical and epistemological perspective, Aristotle developed an ethical orientation. He believed the ultimate good for the human being is happiness, which is defined as the cultivation of rationality, the power that both defines and contains the purpose of human existence. The aim of human life is to live a life governed by reason.

The exercise of virtue is the means of attaining happiness. Aristotle divided virtues—or values—into moral and intellectual virtues. *Moral virtue* is a habit by which the individual exercises a prudent choice, one that a rational person would make. Moral virtues tend to moderation, falling between excess and inhibition. For example, the prudent person would develop a balanced diet based upon the consumption of foods that promote physical health and well-being. Gorging oneself is debilitating to health. At the other extreme, starving oneself into a state of anorexia inhibits what is natural and necessary for the human being's health.

The *intellectual virtues* contribute to the perfection of the human intellect or power of reason. Through science, inquiry, and the search for first principles, the human being develops a theory that arises from observation of the world. This kind of theory has explanatory power in that it tells us about the structure and function of this world. This kind of theory is our surest and best guide to conduct.

While Aristotle's philosophy of education emphasized the development and cultivation of the individual's intellectual potentiality, he also related the cultivation of rational excellence to the well-being of the polis, thus integrating personal and sociopolitical development. Aristotle believed cultivation of both intellectual and ethical virtues takes place in the human community. In the polis, the Greek locus of the human community, shared perceptions of human life arose. The city-state, Aristotle argued, existed so that its inhabitants would have a place to experience happiness, or to live well. The constitution and laws of the city-state should be designed to foster virtue. It is education that creates a commonality among the residents of the city.

Aristotle and Schooling

In addition to the general features of his philosophy of education, Aristotle also held opinions about schooling. While his philosophy has greater meaning for contemporary education, his views of schooling, while positioned in the Greek situation of his day, also have implications for us today.

Aristotle believed the purpose of education is to cultivate human excellence.[9] The human being's psyche, or soul, possesses the rational potentiality that education should develop. The psyche, the locus of the human being's cognitive or reasoning powers, enables people to develop generalizations about the world and its functions. It also enables the mastery of technical skills needed for political, social, and economic survival. Along with developing rationality, education has the function of forming the human being's ethos, or ethical character.

Aristotle believed education is a general process of formation that takes place informally outside of institutions as well as occurring formally in schools. Education in schools is planned deliberately to achieve prescribed outcomes supportive of the human quest for happiness. In structuring the school curriculum, Aristotle would begin the educational process by forming the characters of the young with dispositions favorable to the rational and ethical life. After correct habits are formed, the curriculum turns to pure theory, which explains the universal principles that govern reality. A lower priority would be given to technical skills that relate to the performance of specialized human functions.

Aristotle divided schooling into three stages: primary schooling, which centered on the development of skills that had generative power and the cultivation of moral predispositions conducive to the later life of reason and moderation; secondary schooling, which led from the essential skills and habit formation of the primary years to the intellectual development of higher studies; and higher education, which was almost exclusively intellectual.

Aristotle advocated a system of compulsory schools supervised by state authorities. His belief in compulsory education differed from the general practice in the Greek city-states, where, with the exception of Sparta, schooling was private and voluntary. In Aristotle's plan of school organization, children from the ages of seven to fourteen would attend primary schools. The curriculum would consist of gymnastics to develop coordination, grace of movement, and courage; letters—the study of reading and writing to develop literacy necessary for later learning; music, which also included poetry, literature, and drama; arithmetic; and drawing. Students would have direct experience with elementary skills, especially music and drawing, so that they could practice the appropriate techniques. While these skills required technique, they also were generative in that they led to greater appreciation and enjoyment. Knowing the skills and requirements that went into writing, music, and art would lead to appreciation of literature, music, drama, and other art forms. These various tools or fundamental skills had the power to generate or lead to other areas of learning that were more complex and profound.

Secondary schooling, in Aristotle's plan, was designed for young men from ages fourteen through twenty-one. These youths would continue their studies of music including literature, poetry, drama, choral music, and dancing. These studies were to provide the young with an immersion in the sources of Greek culture and civilization. The last four years of secondary education were to be spent in military drill, tactics, and strategy that would be useful in defending the polis from attack by its enemies.

As a scientist and philosopher who conducted his own school, Aristotle was most concerned with higher education. Higher studies began at age twenty-one and continued as long as a student was interested and capable of pursuing more abstract study. The purpose of higher education was the cultivation of reason and character. More specifically, Aristotle saw higher studies as providing an advanced liberal education for citizens; these good citizens would form an elite who would lead the polis. Higher education, like the other areas of the curriculum, was reserved for male citizens. Women, he believed, were not intellectually capable of abstract studies. Those who were not free citizens were to be trained in performing vocational functions rather than receive a liberal education.

Conclusion: An Assessment

Aristotle, like Plato, is regarded as one of the founding figures of Western philosophy. Courses in Western history and philosophy invariably contain commentaries, sections, readings, and citations related to Aristotle, the founder of Realism. To assess Aristotle's significance, we can look to his influence on later historical development and to the meaning that his work has for contemporary education.

After the collapse of the Roman empire in the West, Aristotle's philosophy suffered a temporary decline. His logic was used in some schools maintained in the early Christian era and found its way into the *compendia,* the small books written to codify the liberal arts. However, the dominant philosophies during Rome's imperial period were Epicureanism and Stoicism rather than Aristotle's. In the early Christian era, study of the Scriptures, theology, and religious studies dominated the curriculum.

In the late twelfth and thirteenth centuries, Aristotle's philosophy was rediscovered by Western scholars and educators. The re-entry of Aristotelian ideas came by way of Arab scholars who had translated Aristotle's works. As Christians came into contact with the Arabic world during the Crusades, they rediscovered the ancient Greek philosophers. Scholastic educators of the Middle Ages, especially those in the medieval universities, began to study Aristotle's philosophy and incorporate it into their teaching and writing. Of particular importance in reincorporating Aristotle's philosophy into Western culture is Thomas Aquinas, the founder of Thomistic philosophy (discussed in Chapter 5). Following some initial debate about the prudence of giving an important role to a non-Christian, or pagan, philosopher, Aristotle's philosophy became an important part of the education of those who attended the medieval universities. Since his rediscovery by the scholastic educators, Aristotle has been regarded as a major influence on Western philosophy and education.

Aristotle is meaningful for contemporary education. His assertion that the human being is endowed with a defining rational nature continues to inspire educators who see the cultivation of the intellect as the primary purpose of education. Educational proposals such as the "Great Books" curriculum and the "Paideia" proposal rest on Aristotelian principles.

Aristotle's argument that human beings should be liberally educated remains a great rationale in support of higher education stressing the liberal arts and sciences.

That people should be educated in the liberal arts so they can frame and choose between rational alternatives is regarded as crucial to the freedom of human choice and self-determination. Much of our world view is the product of Aristotle's quest to find out what things are and how they work. His quest to discover the structure and function of reality has shaped Western thought and education.

Discussion Questions

1. How did the Greek intellectual milieu influence the formation of Aristotle's ideas?
2. Describe the mentor-student relationship that existed between Plato and Aristotle.
3. Compare and contrast Plato's Idealism and Aristotle's Realism.
4. Compare and contrast the nature of research for Plato and Aristotle.
5. What are the educational implications of Aristotle's view of a purposeful universe?
6. Examine the role of knowledge according to the Aristotelian exercise of freedom of choice.
7. Assess the continuing effect of Aristotle on Western thought and eduction.

Research and Essay Topics

1. In an interpretive essay, develop a comparative character sketch of Plato and Aristotle.
2. Design a lesson plan for teaching a particular skill or subject based on Aristotle's philosophy.
3. Based on Aristotle's philosophy, write a defense for liberal arts education.
4. In an essay, examine the relevance of Aristotle's philosophy of education for the contemporary world.
5. In an essay, examine the educational implications of Aristotle's concept of dualism.
6. Examine the liberal arts and science requirements in your degree program. In a position paper, determine Aristotle's reactions.
7. Examine and analyze current proposals for educational reform. In a position paper, indicate if these proposals conform to or differ from Aristotle's philosophy.

Notes

1. Jonathan Barnes, *Aristotle* (New York: Oxford University Press, 1982), 1.
2. H. D. F. Kitto, *The Greeks* (Baltimore: Penguin Books, 1962), 169–94.
3. G. E. R. Lloyd, *Aristotle: The Growth and Structure of His Thought* (Cambridge, Mass.: Cambridge University Press, 1968), 3.
4. E. W. F. Tomlin, *The Western Philosophers* (New York: Harper and Row, 1967), 62.
5. Barnes, 2–3.
6. D. J. Allan, *The Philosophy of Aristotle* (London: Oxford University Press, 1970), 4.
7. John Wild, *Introduction to Realistic Philosophy* (New York: Harper and Brothers, 1948), 441–68.
8. Harry S. Broudy, *Building a Philosophy of Education* (Englewood Cliffs, N.J.: Prentice Hall, 1961), pp. 61–67, 125–26.

9. H. I. Marrou, *The History of Education in Antiquity* (New York: Mentor Books, 1964), 76–136.

Suggestions for Further Reading

Ackrill, J. L. *Aristotle: the Philosopher.* New York: Oxford University Press, 1981.
Aristotle. *Nichomachean Ethics.* Translated by Terence Irwin. Indianapolis: Hackett Publishing Co., 1985.
————. *The Poetics.* Buffalo, N.Y.: Prometheus Books, 1992.
————. *On Rhetoric: A Theory of Civic Discourse.* New York: Oxford University Press, 1991.
Broadie, Sarah. *Ethics with Aristotle.* New York: Oxford University Press, 1991.
Broudy, Harry S. *Building a Philosophy of Education.* Englewood Cliffs, N.J.: Prentice Hall, 1961.
Brumbaugh, Robert S., and Nathaniel M. Lawrence. *Philosophers on Education.* Boston: Houghton Mifflin, 1963.
Burnet, John. *Aristotle on Education.* Cambridge, Mass.: Harvard University Press, 1928.
Chambliss, Joseph J. *The Influence of Plato and Aristotle on John Dewey's Philosophy.* Lewiston, N.Y.: E. Mellen Press, 1990.
Davidson, Thomas. *Aristotle and Ancient Educational Ideals.* New York: Burt Franklin, 1969.
During, Ingemar. *Aristotle in the Ancient Biographical Tradition.* New York: Garland Publishing, 1987.
Edel, Abraham. *Aristotle and His Philosophy.* Chapel Hill, N.C.: University of North Carolina Press, 1982.
Evans, John D. G. *Aristotle.* New York: St. Martin's Press, 1987.
Frankena, William K. *Three Historical Philosophies of Education: Aristotle, Kant, and Dewey.* Chicago: Scott, Foresman, and Co., 1965.
Grene, Marjorie G. *A Portrait of Aristotle.* London: Faber and Faber, 1963.
Irwin, Terence. *Aristotle's First Principles.* Oxford: Clarendon Press, 1988.
Johnson, Curtis N. *Aristotle's Theory of the State.* New York: St. Martin's Press, 1990.
McKirahan, Richard D. *Principles and Proofs: Aristotle's Theory of Demonstrative Science.* Princeton, N.J.: Princeton University Press, 1992.
Randall, John. *Aristotle.* New York: Columbia University Press, 1960.
Rankin, Kenneth. *The Recovery of the Soul: An Aristotelian Essay on Self-Fulfillment.* Montreal: McGill-Queen's University Press, 1991.
Reeve, C. D. C. *Practices of Reason: Aristotle's Nicomachean Ethics.* New York: Oxford University Press, 1992.
Salkever, Stephen G. *Finding the Mean: Theory and Practice in Aristotelian Political Philosophy.* Princeton, N.J.: Princeton University Press, 1990.
Swanson, Judith A. *The Public and the Private in Aristotle's Political Philosophy.* Ithaca, N.Y.: Cornell University Press, 1992.
Verbeke, Gerard. *Moral Education in Aristotle.* Washington, D.C.: Catholic University of America Press, 1990.
White, Stephen A. *Sovereign Virtue: Aristotle on the Relation Between Happiness and Prosperity.* Stanford, Calif.: Stanford University Press, 1992.
Wild, John. *Introduction to Realistic Philosophy.* New York: Harper and Brothers Publishers, 1948.

CHAPTER 4

Quintilian: Rhetorical Educator in Service of the Emperor

Quintilian, from an engraved illustration (detail); photograph from Corbis-Bettmann.

This chapter examines the life, educational philosophy, and contributions of Marcus Fabius Quintilianus, known as Quintilian (A.D. 35–95), a prominent teacher of rhetoric in the Roman Empire. Quintilian's development of rhetorical education is historically significant in that it incorporated important Greek concepts about the education of the orator with a theory of service to the Roman Empire.

In this chapter, Quintilian's educational contributions are discussed in terms of their origins in the historical context of the Roman Empire and in terms of their significance to educational thought. First, the social, political, and cultural context in which Quintilian lived and worked is described. Second, Quintilian's biography, education, and career are examined to trace the evolution of his ideas. Third, Quintilian's significance as a contributor to Western educational thought is assessed. Following the pattern of organization used in the other chapters in this book, we examine the interrelationships of the dynamics of educational history and philosophy. Quintilian lived during a period of social change when the last vestiges of republican Rome had been replaced by imperial rule. Nevertheless, his educational ideas contain elements of continuity, based on transmission of the educational heritage, and of change, based on the altered character of Roman political and social life. Our analysis uses the concepts of continuity and change, which are important for analyzing curriculum, teaching, and education at any time.

To organize your thoughts as you read Chapter 4, you might focus on the following questions:

- What were the major trends in the historical context, the time and situation, in which Quintilian lived?
- How did Quintilian's life, his educational biography, shape his philosophy of education?
- How did Quintilian's educational philosophy determine his educational policies and practices?
- What is the significance of Quintilian's contributions to Western education?

The Historical Context of Quintilian's Life

The history of Rome as a republic and as an empire covers almost 1,000 years of the human record. We shall not attempt to deal with the many political, social, and economic events in this important millennium. Rather, we shall concentrate on certain key concepts and trends that shaped the Roman outlook on life, society, and the world, indicating how this world view shaped the Roman educational vision. We shall then see how Quintilian himself was shaped by that outlook and how he helped to reshape it.

Although Quintilian lived in imperial Rome, certain patterns of Roman life were established during the republican era, from about 450 B.C. to 27 B.C. The Rome of 450 B.C. was a small city-state in central Italy in the vicinity of the present-day Italian capital. The early Romans were primarily an agricultural people who were conservative in their values but assertive in their behavior. Growing restive under the domination of a ruling non-Roman Etruscan elite, they rose up, deposed their rulers, and established their own republic.

During the republic's early years, when contact with non-Romans was minimal, a schema or set of values was developed and prized. These values had weakened and largely eroded by the time of Quintilian, but residues remained. Quintilian and other educators would harken back to the need to restore the cherished traditional values that had made Rome a great empire.

Early Roman society, its knowledge and values, and the education that helped sustain it were originally agricultural. As is true in most agricultural societies, property was emphasized—especially land tenure and ownership. The values of this rural agrarian society were inherited and traditional and sought to maintain the status quo. The tendency in education, which was largely informal and in the hands of parents, called for maintaining tradition and passing it on to the younger generation.

Early Roman republican education, primarily taught by the father as head of the household, was designed to train children, especially sons, to revere their family ancestors and to be aware of their duties to family, the state, and the gods. According to this pattern of values, the good Roman was self-controlled and self-disciplined, respected family ancestors and traditions, maintained property in good order, was thrifty and temperate, and patriotically and courageously performed the military and civil duties needed by the state. Children learned these values by imitating their parents, who were expected to be exemplars of Roman virtues. These basic values were also reinforced by religious rituals and were encoded in the Laws of the Twelve Tables, which every Roman boy was expected to memorize.

During Rome's early years as a republic, these essential values were transmitted in Roman families. When the primary school, the ludus, and the secondary school of the grammaticus were established in the third century B.C., the family's direct role in inculcating these values was shared with these educational agencies. However, the essential values of duty, honor, and patriotism remained dear to the Roman heart and psyche. During the conquests that created its vast empire, Romans encountered greater learning in its captive peoples. The more culturally sophisticated Greeks, for example, caused a weakening of traditional values for some Romans. As we shall see later, the cultural interchange between Greece and Rome affected the continuity of these traditional values in Roman education.

Socioeconomic and status conflicts existed throughout the history of the republic. Rome's two major classes were the patricians, members of the old aristocracy who held title to large landed estates, and the plebeians, who had lower economic and social status. The patricians controlled the Senate, the deliberative and policy making body of Rome. They also elected two consuls who implemented the Senate's military and civil decisions and administered Rome. Much of Rome's political history documents the struggle of the plebeians to gain more of a voice in the affairs of the republic. They gradually gained more rights from the patricians as concessions in return for military service. Over time, some plebeians accumulated fortunes in commerce and bought their way into the ruling circles of the Roman republic.

The Roman Senate was the key institution for wielding influence, debating policies, and making decisions. As in the Congress of the United States or in any deliberative body charged with examining and shaping policies, effective members need to demonstrate several skills:

1. The ability to formulate an agenda to present to the other members of the assembly or body.
2. The ability to win the support of colleagues. Support is won by trade-offs, in which members agree to support each other's programs, or by using influence or exerting pressure.
3. The power of speech and effective argument. Members must be able to debate to persuade others to support their point of view and program.

What emerged in Roman political life in the republic was a recognition of the practical power of oratory or public speaking as a means of influencing people and shaping events. A similar sense of the importance of oratory was found in ancient Greece. In this early stage of the history of Rome, public speaking and its power were appreciated. Cicero, a leading Roman senator, and later Quintilian, among others, would formulate a theory of rhetoric for educating effective public speakers. The important point is that there was a tradition in Rome, from the days of the republic, that prized and valued oratory and Quintilian would embrace it.

Rome was an expansive republic. Roman legions marched out and consolidated Rome's power on the Italian peninsula. After a series of wars with Carthage, Rome became the master of the lands bordering the Mediterranean Sea. Rome even extended its control as far north as modern Germany and present-day England. In its march to power, a significant event occurred that affected Rome's cultural life. In 272 B.C., Rome defeated the Greek armies in the battle of Tarentum. Although Rome conquered Greece militarily, it was heavily influenced by Greek culture. This cultural interchange was significant for Roman education, especially the rhetorical version of it that was Quintilian's life's work.

Not only Greece but much of the eastern Mediterranean region that Rome now ruled had earlier been influenced by Greek culture. The conquests of Alexander the Great had spread Hellenic culture well into Asia Minor. In this region Greek had become the language of the former ruling elites. After the region's conquest by Roman soldiers came Roman governors and officials who were to administer the vast empire. These Roman officials as well as important segments of Rome's aristocracy came to recognize Greek as the language of culture, refinement, and diplomacy in much the same way that French was regarded as the international language in the nineteenth century. Greek slaves were prized as the tutors of the children of well-born Romans, and young Romans of promise made the grand tour of Greece.[1]

As a result of their cultural interchange with Greece, Romans encountered the Greek emphasis on rhetoric originally developed by Plato's educational adversaries, the Sophists (see Chapter 2). The Romans already knew the practical value of oratory in winning Senate debates or in inspiring troops in battle. Now they encountered a people who had refined oratory into an art and developed a well-structured theory of rhetorical education.

Foremost among the Greek rhetoricians who would be studied and cited by the Romans Cicero and Quintilian was Isocrates (436–338 B.C.).[2] A well-regarded teacher of rhetoric in Athens, Isocrates wrote *Against the Sophists,* which described his school and criticized the methods used by his rivals the Sophists; and *Antidosis,* a detailed treatise on rhetorical education. Rejecting the techniques of the Sophists as shallow gimmicks, Isocrates wanted to educate an orator who was both a rational human being and an effective communicator. Such an orator, he reasoned, would be liberally educated in the arts and sciences, would be morally and ethically sensitive, and would be an excellent and effective public speaker. These orator-statesmen, Isocrates believed, would be both visionary and practical leaders who could direct the course of Athenian and, perhaps, Greek life.

Although Isocrates wanted to educate leaders of vision, men who could see events and frame policies in a broad perspective, he rejected Plato's version of the philosopher-king as being too fanciful, speculative, and unrealistic. Neither did Isocrates accept the merely practical approach to oratory in which the Sophists stressed mastery of techniques as being adequate for the statesmanship qualities he saw as necessary to genuine leadership.

When Roman educational theorists such as Quintilian encountered Isocrates' ideas, they found a theory that seemed tailor-made for the preparation of the leaders and officialdom of Rome. Isocrates' stress on the need for liberal education and ethical sensibilities had the potential of raising the level of rhetoric in the Roman Senate. Further, Isocrates' emphasis on the orator as a person who exercised an active function in policy formulation and decision making was well suited to the Roman sense of utility and practicality.

Isocrates' contributions to the history of Western educational ideas have been overshadowed by Socrates, Plato, and Aristotle. However, his ideas on the education of the orator, which significantly contributed to refining the Roman ideal of oratory, also had a long-term effect on the development of rhetorical education in the West.[3] For example, Isocrates redefined philosophy as the practical interpretations that make sense of life and give order to it. A true leader should possess the ability to estimate a situation accurately as it really exists. Such an accurate appraisal would contribute to the formulation of alternatives of action.

The leader who used practical philosophy to guide actions needed, according to Isocrates, a background in the liberal arts.[4] The orator-statesman needed a command of language—of grammar, composition, and literature—which were indispensable in understanding and interpreting the past and assessing the present. He needed a background in geography, mythology, history, archaeology, and politics, because these areas created the contexts of informed discussion. To cultivate ethical sensibilities that would lead to ethical behavior, the orator-statesman needed to study philosophy, jurisprudence, and ethics. With such a background, the student of oratory could then proceed to rhetoric, oratory, debate, and declamation—subjects and skills necessary for the rational and effective communicator that Isocrates hoped to educate.

One of the Romans to make contact with Greek culture, particularly rhetorical education, was the famous Senator Cicero (106–43 B.C.). Cicero's encounter with

Greek culture contributed significantly to the historical and educational context that helped shape Quintilian's ideas. A theme introduced in this section to interpret the Roman context was continuity and change. Cicero, a political conservative from a patrician background, tried to preserve the old Roman values of honor, duty, and service that were part of the legacy of virtue from the early republic. Although some conservative Romans wanted nothing to do with Greek culture, Cicero was impressed by Greek advances in philosophy and rhetoric. He sought to integrate old Roman virtues with those of Greek learning and create a synthesis of educational ideas. In a similar fashion, Thomas Aquinas would attempt a synthesis of Aristotle's philosophy and Christian theology in the Middle Ages. Today's educators who seek to formulate educational philosophy and policy can learn much about the skills of theoretical integration of the past and the present as they deal with the problems as well as the possibilities of continuity and change.

Cicero, a well-born and advantaged Roman youth, spent four years, from 80 to 76 B.C., on a "grand tour" of Greece, where he studied philosophy and rhetoric. On his return to Rome he entered the Senate, where he supported conservative interests and resisted the erosion of republican institutions and values. In 44 B.C., he was implicated in the assassination of Julius Caesar.[5] Cicero believed Caesar was undermining the republic and seeking to create a personal dictatorship. As he sought to flee from Rome, Cicero was killed in retribution for his association with conspirators against Caesar. Although Julius Caesar was assassinated to preserve the republic, the republic gave way to the Roman Empire. Augustus, Julius Caesar's nephew, became the first emperor in 27 B.C.

In 55 B.C., at the height of his political power and influence, Cicero wrote *de Oratorio,* or *About Oratory,* a treatise on the education of the ideal Roman orator. Written to instruct the younger generation of Rome, the book was a skillful blending of old Roman values with the newly encountered Greek philosophy and rhetoric. Cicero admonished parents to make certain their children were adept in using Latin and conversant with its literature. In addition, young Romans should understand and appreciate their cultural heritage, its history, traditions, and values. Like Isocrates, who Cicero called "the master of all rhetoricians," the Roman senator envisioned a liberally educated orator who had studied law, philosophy, ethics, psychology, political science, military strategy, geography, literature, and history. With this background, the student of oratory could turn to rhetoric and declamation. The educated orator, a skilled speaker who possessed a keenly developed ethical sense, should in Cicero's view manifest a variety of skills. He should be subtle in logic, profound in philosophy, clear in diction, poetic in expression, and have the lawyer's command of precedent.[6]

From our foregoing discussion of the historical context that helped shaped Quintilian, certain trends or characteristics emerge. Among them are the following:

1. The Romans, a practical people, recognized the importance of oration as a means of winning and exercising political power.
2. They inherited a well-defined set of values. These values, which were essentially conservative, were challenged and eroded by the forces of change engendered by the transformation of Rome from a small agricultural city-state to a large empire.

3. The Roman encounter with Greek philosophy and rhetoric had a pronounced effect on their views of culture and education, particularly rhetorical education.
4. The republican institutions of Rome were being subverted by what would be imperial Rome.

Quintilian as a Proponent of Rhetorical Education

In this section, we analyze the life, career, and educational ideas of Marcus Fabius Quintilianus. Quintilian was born in A.D. 35 in the provincial town of Callagurris, a Roman city on the Ebro River. Quintilian's birthplace is now the modern Spanish city of Calahorra.

Quintilian's introduction to rhetoric came from his father, who taught the subject. Quintilian's study with his father followed the ancient tradition that had originated in the republic: The father should be the first influence on his son and incline him in the desired direction. Following his father's career, Quintilian decided to become a rhetorician. When he was 16, Quintilian went to Rome, where he worked as an assistant to Domitius Afer, a distinguished rhetorician and lawyer. His legal and rhetorical apprenticeship with Domitius followed the old Roman tradition of the *tricinium fori,* the year a young man spent working with a distinguished person. The goal of this year was to expose the young man to the knowledge and virtues that had contributed to the patron's success. After completing his rhetorical study, he became a lawyer and worked as an assistant to Domitius. When Domitius died in A.D. 58, Quintilian returned to Callagurris, where he was a pleader of cases.

Ten years later, Quintilian returned to Rome, where he established his own rhetorical school. Among his students was Pliny the Younger (A.D. 62–114), who earned a reputation as a poet and author. Quintilian also taught two grandnephews of the emperor Domitian. His skill as a master rhetorician earned Quintilian an outstanding reputation that brought him to the attention of the emperor Vespasian.

Vespasian (A.D. 9–79) was Rome's emperor from A.D. 70 to 79. Known for the simplicity of his court, Vespasian devoted himself to stabilizing the political conditions in Rome. He also embarked on a building program that led to the construction of the Temple of Peace and the Colosseum. He recognized Quintilian's talents and appointed him in A.D. 72 to the imperially endowed chair of Latin rhetoric, a position he held for twenty years.[7]

Quintilian's most important book on the education of an orator was *Institutio Oratoria* or the *Institutes of Oratory,* written between A.D. 93 and 95. In stating his educational purpose and adhering to the philosophical orientation of Isocrates and Cicero, Quintilian announced that the orator he intended to educate would be "a good man" and a "perfect orator." Such an orator would possess "an excellent power of speech" and "all the moral virtues as well."[8]

Quintilian's book, like that of Isocrates, is a thorough exposition not only of rhetorical education but of general education as well. He began with a commentary on human nature and psychology. Human beings possess the power of cognition, which enables them to know and form ideas. They also are emotional and volitional in that they have impulses, needs, and desires. Both thought and action need to be governed by human reason. Thus, at the onset of his work, Quintilian allies himself with rationalism and would have his orator be a reason-governed person.

Because the character needed by the good orator was a product of long-term development, Quintilian reasoned that attention should be paid to early childhood education: From birth to age seven, children are primarily governed by their instincts and impulses. The cognitive powers are present but are unorganized, and reason is not operative. It is most important that children's early years be devoted to creating the positive attitudes that facilitate later learning. Parents were to exercise great care in selecting the child's nurse, tutor, servants, and companions. Quintilian advised that the nurse and the tutor be selected carefully, with particular attention devoted to their speech and behavior. Concerned with the boy's total process of early socialization, Quintilian advised parents to carefully supervise the boy's free time. It was important that his playmates be the "right type" of companions.[9]

Quintilian recognized and accepted the importance of Greek language and culture in rhetorical education. The boy he would prepare to be an orator should be bilingual, learning both Greek and Latin. Greek servants in the household were to use their language correctly so that the boy's acquaintance with their language was correctly formed. That Quintilian was writing for a wealthy audience is clear from his references to servants and tutors. In addition, he clearly is committed to the acceptance of the Greek culture and education.[10]

At age seven, children begin to use their senses to develop ideas of the world about them. They also are highly imitative of adult behavior. Now, the boy goes to the ludus where he learns reading, writing, and calculating.

Quintilian advised upper-class Roman parents to send their sons to school rather than having them tutored at home. Schools, he observed, provided opportunities for socialization and peer group interaction. They also provided the competition needed by orators. In selecting a school, Quintilian advised parents to make sure the teacher was an interesting person of good character who was skilled in instruction. Also, Quintilian was far in advance of his day in his opposition to corporal punishment.

At age thirteen, the boy should go to the school of the grammaticus. At the time Quintilian's book appeared, Roman boys attended two grammar schools that were parallel to each other; one emphasized Greek grammar and literature, whereas the other specialized in Latin grammar and literature. In addition to grammar and literature, Quintilian recommended studying music to develop the voice and geometry to develop mental training.

After completing his studies with the grammaticus, the young man, if he had the aptitude and readiness, could proceed to the rhetorical school. Following the liberal arts approach stressed by Isocrates and Cicero, the curriculum of the rhetorical school included literature, poetry, drama, history, law and jurisprudence, philosophy, and the study of orators and their orations. Of course, the theory and practice of rhetoric, debate, and elocution that were so indispensable to the effective orator also were emphasized. Quintilian identified declamation as the most useful study in the rhetorical school because it provided systematic exercise in public speaking.

Conclusion: An Assessment

Quintilian's conception of the ideal orator was shaped by Roman ethical traditions and by the influence of Isocrates. Quintilian's orator was a moral leader whose ethics reflected the Roman values of honor, responsibility, and duty to the state. Like Isocrates, Quintilian believed that the good orator also needed to be a good human being. His goal was to perfect the human power of speech into eloquence, its highest and noblest expression. Although eloquence had its own value, Quintilian wanted this human excellence to be used for good and noble purposes rather than selfish interests.

Quintilian's theory of rhetorical education can be assessed in three dimensions:

1. As an educational theory using its own internal criteria.
2. In terms of its congruence with the actual realities of Roman political and social life.
3. In terms of its enduring significance for the history of Western educational ideas.

When judged on its own internal criteria, Quintilian's theory of education, particularly as expressed in the *Institutio Oratoria*, was remarkable for its anticipation of later education. His learning theory identified stages of human development, with an appropriate kind of education for each stage. With each stage came a readiness for a certain kind of learning. Quintilian's prescriptions on the importance of early childhood education were prophetic of contemporary research and practice. He recognized, as does the modern early-childhood educator, that the child's earliest years are among the most important. This is the time in which habits and predispositions are formed, and they should be correct ones.

After early childhood comes the stage of growing to cognitive and physical maturity. For Quintilian these years were a time of developing literary skills, learning subjects, and being socialized with the right kind of peers. In the last stage of formal education, in the school of rhetoric, Quintilian stood firmly in the tradition of the liberal arts, which he regarded as essential in forming the properly educated human being.

In developing his educational theory, Quintilian was able to formulate a body of ideas that integrated the continuity of the Roman past with Greek culture. He desired to transmit what he regarded as the value-laden elements in the Roman heritage as a part of moral education. He was well versed in the theory that had been articulated before him, particularly that of Isocrates. As a coherent body of educational doctrines that applied to curriculum and methodology, Quintilian's ideas about education held together and were consistent.

Although Quintilian followed the oratorical model devised by Isocrates, the political changes that had transformed Rome from a republic to an empire also affected rhetorical education. During the republic, oratory could be used as an instrument of power to shape policies. Cicero's death in 43 B.C. marked the end of the republican conception of the orator as a statesman who would dynamically influence public opinion and policy. With the coming of imperial rule, actual power shifted to the person of the emperor. In some situations, real power resided with those who advised, influenced, or actually controlled the emperor. As the Roman Empire began to decline and near its end, power often gravitated to the military and its leading generals, relegating the emperor to more of a figurehead position.

Just how congruent was Quintilian's educational theory with the realities of Roman political life? The question of how well formal education relates to a society's political, economic, and intellectual realities is always serious and difficult for educational policy makers. This question is just as important for our assessment of the adequacy of contemporary U.S. education as it was for Quintilian's Rome. To answer the question for Rome, we can reflect on the consequences of rhetorical education for the determination of policy, for the expression of eloquence, and for administrative service to the state.

In imperial Rome, actual decision making no longer rested with the Senate. Rather, it was lodged in the emperor or the imperial circle or in the army, depending upon the situation. External political institutions remained in the formal sense but had lost their dynamic quality. For instance, the Senate still met, but its functions were changed. Instead of debating and formulating policy, the Senate became a more ceremonial body that met to praise the emperor or commemorate state triumphs and occasions.

Rhetorical education also remained but was growing formalized. For example, Quintilian constantly stated that students of rhetoric should concentrate on real situations and actual life and avoid the fictitious or the imaginative. These continual admonitions show that rhetorical studies were losing their immediate relationship to society and growing more into a classroom or academic study. Rhetoric remained an important preoccupation of the educated Roman elite during the imperial period but the meaning of public service had changed.

Although Quintilian might deny it, his conception of the orator had changed. The use of eloquence as an instrument of persuasion in the public forum had changed to speech that commemorated and ornamented occasions. Like today's commencement and graduation speakers, who rarely shape public policy by their addresses, the Roman orator graced public occasions. As public debate lost its power to influence events, Rome's orators became more stylized, ornamental, and formally eloquent.

The work of Quintilian and Isocrates had an important consequence in that it broadened the concept of the orator from strictly a public speaker to a more generalized public servant. The orator, educated in the rhetorical tradition, was a person prepared for many areas of public service such as teaching, civil administration, and law. In particular, the empire needed civil administrators to represent its interests throughout the Mediterranean world. The kind of education that Quintilian offered was not unlike that of the civil servants who staffed the far-flung British Empire in the nineteenth and early twentieth centuries. Such individuals were educated in the liberal arts to give them a breadth of knowledge. This body of knowledge that originated in the past carried a sense of traditional culture. The logic and organizational skills that made an orator effective at the podium could be recast by the civil servant and effective administrator.

Finally, we come to the enduring significance of Quintilian in the evolution of the history of Western educational ideas. The reconstructed concept of the orator as the civil servant and administrator would slowly turn rhetoric into the art of writing as well as the art of speaking. In the medieval era, the art of writing came to dominate rhetoric and gave it a different educational meaning.

Quintilian was one of those educators who helped shape and transmit the bodies of knowledge known as the liberal arts. These areas of human knowledge survived the fall of the Roman Empire. After much debate, they became part of the educational preparation of the medieval scholastics. Quintilian's ideas on education, along with those of Isocrates, would surface again during the Renaissance when humanist educators such as Vittorino da Feltre and Erasmus looked to the classical traditions of Greece and Rome to guide their efforts at reviving literary humanism. Once they became part of the classical humanism of the Renaissance, they found their way into the preparatory and advanced education of the Reformation and continued onward in the select secondary schools of the post-Reformation era.

Quintilian's efforts to develop a coherent doctrine of rhetorical education remain useful in illustrating several enduring educational issues. In trying to integrate traditional Roman values and the new Greek learning, he had to deal with continuity and change. Educators today face similar problems of integrating cherished values with new ideas and technologies. Quintilian was in many ways the complete educational theorist in that his ideas on education formed a coherent body of doctrines that covered the human life span, from early childhood to maturity. In dealing with Greek culture and education, Quintilian integrated valuable transcultural elements into his conception of education. If Quintilian faced this problem and possibility in the days of limited communication of ideas, just think of how important such integration is today in a world of rapid communication. Finally, in terms of his educational theory, Quintilian was both a victim and victor of changing political and social circumstances. In one way, Rome's political changes made rhetorical education formal and irrelevant, yet in another way gave it a new relevance. Today, the issue of what makes education meaningful and relevant to U.S. society remains a perennial question.

Discussion Questions

1. How appropriate was rhetorical education to the Roman social and political context?
2. Examine rhetorical education as an integration of Greek and Roman educational ideas.
3. Using the educational ideas of Plato and Aristotle as a frame of reference, critique the theory and practice of rhetorical education as developed by Quintilian.
4. Is the theory of rhetorical education applicable to contemporary education?
5. As a theorist of education, what were Quintilian's most useful contributions?
6. Examine the rhetorical or oratorical style of important contemporary speakers. Do you find any similarities between the theory of Quintilian and their styles of oratory?

Research and Essay Topics

1. Prepare a lesson plan for the teaching of speech based on the educational theory of Quintilian.

2. Identify several speeches by leading political or religious leaders. Write a critique of their speeches based on Quintilian's theory of education.
3. In a paper, trace the development of rhetorical education from the ancient Greeks to and including the Romans.
4. In an essay, critique rhetorical education from the Platonic perspective.
5. Review several texts on the teaching of public speaking. Do you find any evidence of rhetorical theory as developed by Isocrates, Cicero, or Quintilian?
6. Prepare a brief that defends the position: Rhetorical education is relevant to the modern media.

Notes

1. H. I. Marrou, *A History of Education in Antiquity* (New York: Mentor Books, 1964), 325–341.
2. For a well-done commentary on Isocrates' contributions to educational theory, see Costas M. Prousis, "The Orator: Isocrates," in Paul Nash, Andreas Kazamias, and Henry Perkinson, eds., *The Educated Man: Studies in the History of Educational Thought* (New York: John Wiley and Sons, 1966), 54–76.
3. For the influence of Isocrates on other educators, see H. M. Hubbell, *The Influence of Isocrates on Cicero, Dionysius and Aristides* (New Haven, Conn.: Yale University Press, 1914).
4. Isocrates' curriculum and methodology are analyzed in Edward J. Power, "Isocrates: A Theory of Literary Humanism," in *Evolution of Educational Doctrine* (New York: Appleton-Century-Crofts, 1969), 25–54. Also see Gerald L. Gutek, *A History of the Western Educational Experience* (Prospect Heights, Ill.: Waveland Press, 1995), 52–54.
5. L. Glenn Smith, ed., *Lives in Education: People and Ideas in the Development of Teaching* (Ames, Iowa: Educational Studies Press, 1984), 30–32.
6. J. J. Chambliss, *Educational Theory as Theory of Conduct: From Aristotle to Dewey* (Albany: State University of New York Press, 1987), 37–38.
7. Power, *Evolution of Educational Doctrine,* 87–90. Also see George Kennedy, *The Arts of Rhetoric in the Roman World: 300 B.C.–A.D. 300* (Princeton, N.J.: Princeton University Press, 1972), 487–514.
8. Aubrey Gwynn, "Quintilian," in *Roman Education from Cicero to Quintilian* (New York: Russell and Russell, 1964), 180–241.
9. Power, *Evolution of Educational Doctrine,* 91–92.
10. Kingsley Price, *Education and Philosophical Thought* (Boston: Allyn and Bacon, 1963), 81–109.

Suggestions for Further Reading

Bonner, Stanley F. *Education in Ancient Rome.* Berkeley, Calif.: University of California Press, 1977.

Chambliss, J. J. *Educational Theory As Theory of Conduct: From Aristotle to Dewey.* Albany: State University of New York Press, 1987.

Cicero, Marcus Tullius. *Cicero's Caesarian Speeches: A Stylistic Commentary.* Chapel Hill, N.C.: University of North Carolina Press, 1993.

———. *On Duties.* New York: Cambridge University Press, 1991.

Fuhrmann, Manfred. *Cicero and the Roman Republic.* Oxford, U.K. and Cambridge, Mass.: Blackwell, 1992.

Gwynn, Aubrey. *Roman Education from Cicero to Quintilian.* New York: Russell and Russell, 1964.

Habicht, Christian. *Cicero: The Politician.* Baltimore, Md.: Johns Hopkins University Press, 1990.

Horne, Herman H. *Quintilian on Education.* New York: New York University Book Store, 1936.

Hubbell, H. M. *The Influence of Isocrates on Cicero, Dionysius and Aristides.* New Haven, Conn.: Yale University Press, 1914.

Kennedy, George A. *The Art of Rhetoric in the Roman World: 300 B.C.–A.D. 300.* Princeton, N.J.: Princeton University Press, 1972.

———. *Classical Rhetoric and Its Christian and Secular Tradition from Ancient to Modern Times.* Chapel Hill: University of North Carolina Press, 1980.

Kerferd, G. B. *The Sophistic Movement.* Cambridge: Cambridge University Press, 1981.

Marrou, H. I. *A History of Education in Antiquity.* New York: Mentor Books, 1964.

Mitchell, Thomas N. *Cicero: Senior Statesman.* New Haven: Yale University Press, 1991.

Nash, Paul, Andreas Kazamias, and Henry Perkinson, eds. *The Educated Man: Studies in the History of Educational Thought.* New York: John Wiley and Sons, 1966.

Power, Edward J. *Evolution of Educational Doctrine.* New York: Appleton-Century-Crofts, 1969.

Price, Kingsley. *Education and Philosophical Thought.* Boston: Allyn and Bacon, 1963.

Quintilian. *The Institutio Oratoria.* Translated by H. E. Butler. London: William Heinemann, 1921.

Smith, L. Glenn. *Lives in Education: People and Ideas in the Development of Teaching.* Ames, Iowa: Educational Studies Press, 1984.

Vasaly, Ann. *Representations: Images of the World in Ciceronian Oratory.* Berkeley, Calif.: University of California Press, 1993.

CHAPTER 5

Thomas Aquinas: Scholastic Theologian and Creator of the Medieval Christian Synthesis

Thomas Aquinas, from a mural painting (detail); photograph from the collections of the National Archives.

This chapter deals with the life, educational philosophy, and contributions of Thomas Aquinas (1225–1274), a prominent theologian and philosopher of the Middle Ages. Aquinas was an educational theorist who developed a theological and philosophical synthesis that incorporated the doctrines of the Christian religion with the inherited tradition of classical philosophy, especially Aristotle's Realism. Aquinas' synthesis of classical Aristotelian philosophy and Christian faith was of great educational importance for medieval times and later decades as well.

Aquinas' contributions to theology and philosophy are examined in the historical context of the Middle Ages and in terms of their enduring effect. First, the cultural, religious, and intellectual context in which Aquinas lived and worked is described. Second, Aquinas' biography, education, and career, are analyzed to determine the evolution of his ideas. Third, the continuing effect of Aquinas' contributions to Western education are assessed. In the case of Aquinas, we shall see the interrelated dynamics of theology, philosophy, and education. With Aquinas, as well as with the educational theorists of the Reformation who will be examined in later chapters, we identify and examine a way of thinking—theology—that was not dealt with earlier in this book. While philosophy can be defined in its broadest terms as speculation about the human being's relationship to the universe or the cosmos, theology can be defined as speculation about the human being's relationship to God. Aquinas grappled with both philosophical and theological issues before coming up with his theistic realism, which blends both dimensions of human thought.

To organize your thoughts as you read Chapter 4, you might focus on the following questions:

- What were the major trends in the medieval historical context in which Aquinas lived?
- How did Aquinas' life, his educational biography, shape his philosophy and theology of education?
- How did Aquinas' theology and philosophy determine his educational policies and practices?
- What is the enduring impact of Aquinas' contributions to Western education?

The Historical Context of Aquinas' Life

In our discussion of the medieval historical context in which Aquinas lived, we shall view the thousand years historians call the Middle Ages as one great historical mosaic. When viewed in this way, the vast temporal landscape is composed of people, events, and situations. It is not our purpose to develop the chronological setting of the Middle Ages in detail but rather to identify the major trends of the period that shaped the world view of Thomas Aquinas. The medieval centuries, which historians say lasted from A.D. 500 to A.D. 1400, are designated the Middle Ages because they lie between the end of the Roman Empire and the beginning of the Renaissance. Historians of the medieval period make many chronological distinctions in this broad sweep of time that we shall not do here.

For educational historians, Rome's collapse as an empire marks the closing of the Graeco-Roman classical period of education as a dynamic time of originating and developing educational ideas. Although it lost its dynamic characteristics, the influence of classical learning has persisted in the Western educational heritage to the present time. With the Renaissance would come a revitalization of classical learning in the West.

To understand the medieval frame of mind and temperament that helped shape Aquinas, it is necessary to identify and examine key elements in the world view. We shall look at the following:

1. The entry of the Christian religion into the West and the medieval formulation of that religion.
2. The destabilization of the political and economic order of the Romans and its replacement with feudalism and manorialism.
3. The hierarchical organization of medieval thought and institutions into a theological-philosophical synthesis.
4. The role of scholastics in the culture of medieval universities.

Christianity, based on the teachings of Jesus of Nazareth, entered the West from Judea as the disciples of the new religion, such as St. Paul, evangelized the Graeco-Roman world. Although early Christians had disagreements about the social and economic arrangements appropriate to the Christian life, they shared a general agreement on such basic doctrines as:

1. Jesus, the Son of God, came to Earth as a man and possessed both a human and divine nature.
2. Jesus' appearance on Earth took place in Judea, at a given historical time and place, in fulfillment of the Hebrew Scriptures, particularly the books of the Old Testament prophets.
3. Jesus was crucified and died to atone for human sin, especially the original sin of Adam and Eve.
4. He rose from the dead, reappeared to his apostles, and then ascended into heaven.
5. By his death and resurrection, Jesus redeemed a fallen humanity and promised those who followed in his way supernatural salvation in heaven.
6. His apostles, disciples, and converts to the new faith were to preach the gospel, the story and message of Jesus as recorded by the Evangelists, to people throughout the world.

The early Christians were proselytizers, or convert seekers, who energetically preached the new religion in Rome and its possessions.

For the early Christians, the true God was a supernatural creator, a supreme and perfect being, not like the Roman emperors, who, although claiming divinity, fell from power and perished like other mortals. There was one God and not the pantheon of many gods that formed the traditional religions of ancient Greece and Rome. The purpose of life on Earth was to merit the eternal reward of the supernatural life that came after the body's death. Service to the emperor and the state was secondary to this higher and otherworldly purpose. Early Christians were viewed by the Roman establishment as dangerous radicals who threatened the status quo and traditional Roman values. They were persecuted by Roman officialdom, with the severity of the persecution dependent on the personality of the emperor and the state of imperial problems and politics. Despite their adversities, Christianity made converts and advanced from being a persecuted sect to a tolerated one to finally being declared the official religion.

Although the early Christian religion was based on a belief in a supernatural order that was eternal, spiritual, and perfect, its original ethical code simply and directly enjoined believers to love God and each other. The teachings of the new religion were found in the Gospels of the New Testament in which Jesus addressed his followers in parables. In addition, there were the sermons and letters that the leaders of the new Church addressed to the congregations of believers throughout the empire. As the Christian church gained respectability and acceptance, church councils were held in which the bishops would meet to formalize or clarify doctrines. The milieu in which Aquinas functioned as a theologian, philosopher, and educator included the doctrines of Christianity.

The Mediterranean and Aegean worlds in which the Christians found themselves already contained a well-developed intellectual and educational heritage that had been articulated by philosophers such as Plato and Aristotle and rhetoricians such as Isocrates, Cicero, and Quintilian. At the core of this intellectual heritage was the body of knowledge known as the liberal arts. For the leaders of the Christian church, the existence of this body of pre-Christian knowledge posed a number of serious questions related to the issue of continuity and change. Classical learning, particularly the philosophical works of Plato, Aristotle, and other thinkers, formed a major part of the continuum of knowledge. The important element of change was the new religious belief system, the doctrines of Christianity. For the Christians, the question was whether this pre-Christian, pagan literature was harmful or beneficial to the believers' faith and morals. Some fathers of the church claimed that its effects were harmful and that it should be destroyed. Others argued that it should be preserved as a legacy from the past but not integrated into Christian education lest it confuse the faithful. Still other church fathers insisted that classical literature, especially the liberal arts, should not only be preserved but also form an integral part of a Christian's higher education.

Although there were many participants in the debate on the relevance of the liberal arts to Christian education, a key role was played by St. Augustine, (354–430), the bishop of Hippo.[1] Augustine's life, education, conversion to Christianity, and rise to prominence as a theologian illustrates in a personal way the intellectual tensions that early Christians experienced. Educated in the liberal arts tradition, Augustine, the son of a Roman official, had studied rhetoric. Before his conversion to Christianity, he was attracted to Manichaeanism, a philosophy that saw the universe locked in a continual struggle between good and evil, and skepticism, which although asserting that thought is a human being's highest pleasure, also denies the possibility of really knowing anything completely. Rejecting these philosophies,

Augustine studied Neoplatonism, a philosophy that stressed Plato's themes of the existence of an intellectual order in the universe, that goodness had a relationship with intelligence, and that the chain of universal being led upward to the supreme and highest good, which is the ultimate object of human knowledge. These Platonic themes related well to Augustine's eventual conversion to Christianity at age 34. He was ordained as a priest and was made a bishop. A learned father of the church, Augustine wrote *The Confessions, On the Trinity, The City of God, On Christian Doctrine,* and *de Magistro,* a treatise on education.

Convinced that the liberal arts were essential components in forming educated Christians, Augustine labored to create a cultural and intellectual kinship between classical and Christian civilization. The liberal arts of classical Greece and Rome— grammar, logic, rhetoric, arithmetic, geometry, music, and astronomy—provided a body of necessary study for higher education. Aided by the spiritual power of grace— the interior light of the mind—the liberal arts led the person onward to seek truth because of the training and discipline they provided. They led to the study of philosophy by which humans speculated about their relationship to the universe. Philosophical pursuits had the power of leading the mind still farther to the Scriptures. The revealed word of God, Augustine believed, leads the inquirer—aided by faith—to theology, the learned discipline by which humans systematically search for divine truth and reflectively examine their relationship to God.[2] Thus, Augustine argued successfully for the incorporation of the liberal arts in the formation of the educated Christian. His educational theory created an intellectual linkage that united elements of Greek and Roman classical culture with elements of Christianity. Aquinas, like Augustine, would continue to build the classical and Christian synthesis.

In addition to this intellectual tension, the Middle Ages represented a time of political and economic destabilization caused by Rome's fall. When Rome ceased to be an empire, the political order and control exerted by the imperial government disintegrated. With the central political authority of the empire gone, political organization and control gravitated to various provinces and localities that had once been under imperial jurisdiction. During the centuries of the medieval millennium, local rulers—kings, dukes, counts—asserted themselves as political authorities. In the feudal system that evolved, these rulers became overlords to vassals who owed them fealty and support. Thus, a politically decentralized system emerged.

Without imperial authority, the broad transportation and trade networks that had linked the Roman world also disintegrated. Economic production and consumption, like political life, devolved on the locality. The large Roman estate, the latifundia, slowly became the manor, a self-contained and largely economically self-sufficient unit of land. In such a localized political and economic situation, ownership of land became the means of survival and the basis of power. The medieval knights, the lords and their vassals who held secular political power, became the great landowners. The serfs, those who worked on the land, although not slaves in the sense of old Rome, were nevertheless bound to labor for their masters.

The medieval social, political, and economic order was a fragile and delicate balance that, although not far from what had been the grandeur and order of imperial Rome, was always in danger of degenerating into barbarism. In this period of political and economic disintegration and reintegration, the Christian church in the West—the Latin or Roman Catholic church—rose to prominence as the most evident and often the most powerful institution. This church provided an institutional framework that extended to ideas and education and within which Thomas Aquinas and other scholastic philosophers and educators worked.

In the West, the church emerged as the sole institution to claim a universal authority that transcended the medieval world's localism and provincialism. The bishop of Rome, located in the old imperial capital, became the pope, the supreme pontiff and visible head of the church on Earth. In many ways, church administration followed that of the old imperial government. The pope became a kind of spiritual emperor and the curia, his administrative and theological advisers, acted as a kind of senate. Although the popes consistently asserted spiritual authority, the degree to which they exercised temporal, or political, authority varied with the style of the particular pope and the degree to which the kings of the various realms sought to challenge him.

The church as it evolved in the Middle Ages came increasingly to stress the concept of hierarchy. (You may recall that Plato, too, used the concept of hierarchy when he structured the social order in *The Republic.*) Coming to dominate medieval thought, the concept of hierarchy was integral to the medieval synthesis in which Aquinas operated. In its broadest sense, a hierarchy means an order or a ranking to reality, to ideas, and to people. The existence of a hierarchy means that not everything and everybody are equal. Depending on the basis for organizing the hierarchy, some ideas, people, and things are higher and, perhaps, even better than other ideas, people, or things.

During the Middle Ages, the church came to be governed by organized bodies of ecclesiastical officials arranged in successive and subordinate ranks. At the summit of the hierarchy was the pope, who held supreme authority over the church. Next were the bishops, who, subject to the pope, held authority in their dioceses, or ecclesiastical districts. At the local or parish level were the priests, who celebrated the liturgy and administered the sacraments to their congregations. The pope, advised by the curia and councils of bishops, determined doctrine and filled appointments when a bishopric fell vacant. The bishops ordained priests, who they assigned to the local parish churches.

In the medieval period, the church exercised control over the majority of schools. At the parish level, there might be a school in which the parish priest or his assistant taught reading, writing, simple arithmetic, and the chants and hymns that were part of the mass, or liturgical service. The bishops maintained cathedral schools that taught the *studium generale,* the general liberal studies and the special studies that prepared a young man for the priesthood. It should be mentioned that only a small minority of the male population attended these schools. The majority of the people—the serfs—were illiterate and unschooled.

In addition to the "secular clergy," so named because they were not members of specific religious communities, were the "regular clergy." The members of the regular clergy included those who lived as monks in monastic communities, such as the Benedictines, who followed the order of St. Benedict (480–543). There were also communities of religious women who followed the monastic way of life and lived in seclusion from the world. By the time of Aquinas, mendicant orders such as the Dominicans, founded by Dominic de Guzman (1170–1221), and the Franciscans, founded by St. Francis of Assisi (1182–1226) had been established. The mendicant orders were not monastic but ministered among the people. Although they differed as to their specific patterns of organized religious life, the orders of priests, brothers, and nuns followed the particular mode of religious life and rules established by their founder. They, too, were subordinate to the authority of the pope. The religious orders performed a variety of educational services. The monasteries became centers for preserving and copying classical and religious texts. They operated monastic schools that taught basic skills along with the pattern of religious life unique to the community. Of importance for Aquinas was the *regula,* or rules of the Dominicans, the order he joined. Known as the "order of preachers," the Dominicans became recognized experts in theology, and Aquinas became the most renowned of these theologians.

Although the principle of hierarchy was most evident in the organization of church government, it also influenced how people thought. The Middle Ages was one of the periods in human history in which basic human concerns were religious in nature. Those ideas, interests, issues, and problems that were spiritual were regarded as most important. Those ideas that pertained to supernatural life ranked higher than those that dealt with the natural order. For the scholastics of the medieval era, the supernatural and the natural orders, although distinct, were complementary. The supernatural was the appropriate sphere for the soul, whereas the natural was the appropriate sphere for the body. Although the two orders were complementary, the spiritual was clearly superior because the life of the soul would be eternal and was destined for heaven.

The world of ideas in which Aquinas worked formed an all-embracing, overarching synthesis in which everything was related and ranked. Presiding over this world view that encompassed the spiritual and physical dimensions of life was the church—the guardian of religious truth and morals. The life of ideas within the synthesis could be vital, exciting, and controversial. Theological issues within the doctrinal synthesis were intensely debated. However, the debate had to take place within the framework and within the context of the first principles that sustained it. To leave the synthesis meant heresy and loss of the church's protection.

The medieval university was the immediate context of Aquinas' scholarly and educational activities. The rise of medieval universities, especially the University of Paris, which was Aquinas' intellectual home, represents the institutionalization of the major intellectual trends of the twelfth and thirteenth centuries. Trends that stimulated the development of higher learning in the medieval world included the entry of knowledge from the Arabic scholars into western Europe between 1100 and 1200. As well as making important original contributions to mathematics and medicine, Arab scholars had preserved works of classical Greek authors that hitherto had been lost to Western scholars. From the intellectual conduit of the Arab scholars, certain texts of Aristotle, Euclid, Ptolemy, and the Greek physicians became known to the West.

In the thirteenth century, the rediscovery of many of Aristotle's works and their entry into the libraries of the scholastics posed a problem of reconciliation analogous to that faced by Augustine. To some Christian scholars, Aristotle's philosophy gave an account of human life that owed nothing to divine creation and revelation. So fearful were some churchmen of the negative effect of Aristotle on the faith of believers that the bishop of Paris condemned a number of the Greek philosopher's works. Like Augustine before him, Aquinas found the task of reconciling the old and the new to be an immense challenge. It was one that he would accomplish in his great synthesis.

Along with establishing contact with the Arabic world of scholarship, the Christian Crusades stimulated the revival of commerce in the medieval world. The revitalization of commercial life led to economic surpluses that helped support institutions of higher learning.

The twelfth and thirteenth centuries also marked the zenith of scholasticism, the method of inquiry associated with this time period. Religious orders such as the Dominicans produced prominent scholars whose lectures attracted large numbers of students. Abelard, the popular author of *Sic et Non,* drew hundreds to Paris to hear his lectures.

This complex of forces—new learning from the Arab scholars, the revival of economic life, and the vitality of the scholastic educators—produced the medieval universities. The existing institutions, such as the cathedral and monastic schools, were inadequate to process and analyze the expanding body of knowledge but were the basis on which to expand. From the cathedral schools, the corpus of fundamental knowledge organized in the liberal arts would remain at the intellectual core of the universities. To this would be added professional schools of theology, law, and medicine and the specialized knowledge that sustained them. The University of Paris developed from the Cathedral school of Notre Dame.[3]

Medieval universities were really corporations or guilds of masters, who were the professors, and students. As a guild, the faculties of the medieval universities were preparing students to become teachers. The professors of the university were organized into faculties of liberal arts, law, medicine, and theology. Each faculty had the power to provide instruction, to conduct examinations, and to grant degrees. The possession of the *licentia docendi,* the forerunner of today's master's and doctoral degrees, meant the recipient had completed the required courses, had written and defended a dissertation, and was competent in the subject. The early universities were cosmopolitan and international in character in that students came from many lands. Because the language of instruction was Latin, these students could communicate with each other and follow their professors' lectures.

The University of Paris received royal recognition from King Philip Augustus of France in 1200 when he gave masters and students the privileged position of being under the jurisdiction of special clerical rather than harsh secular courts. In 1231, the university received recognition from the pope that allowed it to establish its own regulations governing lectures and disputations.

The University of Paris became recognized as the authoritative institution for the study of theology. Not only did it prepare theologians and future doctors of the church, but the faculty of theology was often consulted for its expertise on doctrinal questions. For scholastics such as Aquinas, theology posed the major arena of scholarly inquiry. Characterized by the phrase, "I believe in order that I may know," medieval scholastic thought was framed by the boundaries of Catholic doctrine. Although doctrinal essentials were to be accepted without question, their interpretation made for lively and often controversial debate. As a result of the "new knowledge" from the Arab scholars, the scholastics ventured into the problematic area of reconciling this new element with authoritative theological dogma. The work of the medieval scholastics, especially in theology and philosophy, became so sophisticated and exacting that it produced a body of specialized knowledge. In a world view that located theology at the summit of the hierarchy of knowledge, this area of specialization attracted the best minds of the medieval world, one of whom was Thomas Aquinas.

Thomas Aquinas as a Scholastic Theologian and Philosopher

This section of the chapter examines Aquinas' life, career, and educational contributions. Aquinas was foremost a theologian and a philosopher. To appreciate his ideas on education, it is necessary to see them as a manifestation of his work on theology and philosophy.

Thomas Aquinas, the son of wealthy members of the landowning gentry class, was born in 1225 in the Italian town of Roccasecca. His father's name was Landulf and his mother was Theodora de Aquino. His mother's last name, which referred to the section of the country in which she was raised, also became Thomas's name. Both of his parents were well educated according to the standards of the day. Theodora was Landulf's second wife. The family was large, consisting of nine children plus three sons from Landulf's first marriage.[4] The family home was in the castle at Roccasecca, located in the province of Caserta, near Naples.

When he was five years old, Thomas' parents enrolled him in the monastic school of the famous Benedictine abbey at Montecassino, located in central Italy, east of the Rapido River. The ancient monastery, founded by St. Benedict in 529, was on a hill overlooking the town of Cassino. The abbey was well known for its large library of books on theology and philosophy, especially the writings of the early church fathers. Thomas studied in the monastery school from 1231 to 1239.[5]

In 1239, Aquinas went to the University of Naples, where he enrolled in the *studia generalia,* the liberal arts course. In the medieval universities, the completion of liberal arts studies was preparatory to more professional study. For example, the University of Naples offered the liberal arts program and three professional programs in theology, medicine, and law. It enjoyed a reputation for the scholarship of its legal faculty.

Aquinas began his studies at age 14 and completed them in 1243 when he was 18. His program emphasized the study of texts, or *lectio;* disputations, or *disputationes;* and repetition, or *repetitiones.* Among the texts that Aquinas studied were Aristotle's *Organon;* Boethius' commentaries; Priscian's *Institutiones,* which was a compendium for the study of grammar; Donatus' *Ars Minor* and *Ars Major;* Cicero's *de Inventione* for the study of rhetoric; Euclid's *Elementa,* a geometry text; and

Ptolemy's *Almagest,* a work on astronomy. Thomas thus was educated in the liberal arts tradition that was an intellectual and educational legacy from ancient Greece and Rome. His study at the University of Naples introduced him to Aristotle's logic and philosophy, which were emphasized at this southern Italian university whose location made it accessible to intellectual currents from both Greece and the Arab world. His encounter with the philosophy of Aristotle was of importance later in his career as he developed a grand plan to write a comprehensive book, or *summa,* uniting Aristotelian philosophy with Christian doctrine.[6]

While at Naples, Aquinas encountered the Dominican order and announced his plan in 1244 to join the religious community. The Dominicans were among the most academically oriented religious communities in the Christian church. They tended to specialize in theological studies. His family, especially his mother, opposed his decision to become a Dominican. She did not object to his entry into religious life but preferred that he enter another order. As a Dominican, he could not control the family's wealth. His mother arranged for him to be abducted from Naples and held in the family castle at Roccasecca, where he remained for a year. Steadfast in his determination to become a Dominican, the family relented in its opposition. Thomas was released and returned to the Dominicans in 1245.[7]

Aquinas' superiors in the Dominican order recognized the young man's intellectual powers and decided he should pursue further study. He was sent to the Dominican monastery of the Holy Cross in Cologne, Germany, where he remained until 1252. Here the Dominicans maintained a *studia generalia* used to prepare members of their order intellectually. They also learned the *regula* established by St. Dominic. The general studies, based largely on the liberal arts, and the rule of St. Dominic formed the religious disposition and intellectual perspective of Aquinas and his associates. While at the Monastery of the Holy Cross, Aquinas was ordained a priest. Here he wrote one of his early essays, *On Being and Essence.*

Thus far in the education of Thomas Aquinas, the medieval orientation to learning is clearly visible. His elementary education was under religious auspices of the Benedictines. His secondary education and the beginning of his higher education, too, were heavily influenced by theological concerns and religious practices. His socialization was shaped by religious contact and involvement. Most importantly, for a young man of intellectual promise like Aquinas, the life of the mind was directed to the supernatural concerns that permeated medieval life and set its concerns and priorities.

Aquinas was attracted to the leading academic institution that specialized in theology, the discipline in which he wanted to work, and in 1252, he went to the University of Paris. At this point, Aquinas had already earned his bachelor's degree and had published his essay *On Being and Essence.* Like those who were successful as professors in contemporary colleges and universities, Aquinas possessed promising academic credentials and publications. He was accepted for advanced graduate study leading to the *licentia docendi* and was made an instructor. His academic situation was similar to a graduate teaching assistant in a large modern university who teaches general courses while studying for his or her doctorate, the degree needed to become a professor.

As an instructor at the University of Paris, Aquinas lectured in the area of dogmatic theology, using as a text Peter Lombard's *Libri Quator Sentiiarum,* or *Book of Sen-*

tences. Lombard's book was regarded as an important text because it was a compilation of works by leading fathers of the church. Lombard was among the earliest scholars to develop what came to be called the scholastic method that characterized education in the medieval universities. The course in dogmatic theology that Aquinas taught stressed the truths of revelation. In teaching the course, the lecturer began with a revealed truth and used it as a premise. He then argued rationally to a conclusion based on that truth.

In the scholastic method of teaching, the instructor lectured on the text, reviewed the arguments pro and con, provided explanations, and drew conclusions. The method was essentially book centered and relied on the lecture format, which was organized rhetorically. Aquinas published his interpretations on Lombard's work as *Commentary on the Sentences.* In 1256, he was awarded the licentiate, which qualified him as a fully approved professor.

Devoting himself to scholarship and teaching, Aquinas wrote a treatise, *Summa Contra Gentiles,* the *Summa Against the Gentiles,* in which he defended Christian doctrines against opposing views. *Summa Contra Gentiles,* used as a manual of Christian teaching, was divided into four topics: God, creation, providence, and salvation.[8] In particular, this work was directed to the Arabic world of scholarship. Arab scholars such as Averroes had interpreted Aristotle's philosophy in such a way that its divergence from Christian doctrine was highlighted. In contrast, Aquinas set about to reconcile Aristotle's philosophy with Christianity.[9] Aquinas eventually brought together his arguments in his most comprehensive theological work, the *Summa Theologiae.* Aquinas wrote about education and teaching in *de Magistro.*

From 1259 to 1269, Aquinas left the University of Paris to take up assignments at the request of the Dominicans. He returned to Italy where he traveled about attending provincial chapter meetings of the order. Most of the time, however, he was in residence at Santa Sabina in Rome. Pope Urban IV supported and encouraged Aquinas' scholarship and writing, and Aquinas continued working on *Summa Theologiae.* In 1269, he returned to the University of Paris where he completed this major work and continued teaching and writing until his death in 1274.

Aquinas and Theistic Realism

Thomas Aquinas was one of those rare scholars who was able to effect a great reconciliation of ideas and create an all-embracing synthesis. In building his synthesis in the *Summa Theologiae,* Aquinas sought to integrate into the Christian intellectual heritage two great principles: the importance of Divine revelation as the ultimate source of truth and the validity and efficacy of human reason. Rather than condemn Aristotle's ideas, Aquinas determined to use them in building his synthesis of faith and reason. For him, Aristotle's natural sciences, ethics, and politics expressed an intelligible natural order that could be raised to a higher dimension by faith. Aristotle's natural virtues, when infused by grace, could become supernatural virtues.

Thomism, the philosophy of Aquinas, was a variety of religious or theistic realism. Like Aristotle, who saw reality divided into form and matter, Aquinas conceived of reality in two dimensions: the supernatural and the natural orders. Based on these dualistic conceptions, human nature has a spiritual dimension grounded in the soul and a physical dimension grounded in the body. The human being is an "incarnate spirit," or a "spirit in the world."[10] True to the Christian conception of human nature, Aquinas held that this soul, or spiritual essence, remained after the death and decay of the body. Through the spirit, human beings are related to their Creator.

Aquinas, like Aristotle, recognized that the body positioned human beings in the natural order. They share many characteristics with animals such as instincts, appetites, sexuality, and locomotion. These physical tendencies were raised to a higher dimension by reason and spirituality. All of the earthly tendencies were to be in the service of man but were related to the purpose of existence—the ultimate spiritual goal for which human beings had been created.

Also like Aristotle, Aquinas argued that human ideas originated through the senses, which experienced an external world of objects. The mind, in turn, formed concepts as it extracted the form of the objects conveyed with sensory data. Added to this natural power of cognition or conceptualization was the truth revealed by God through the Scriptures. These scriptural truths and the doctrines of the church added to and completed the knowledge that humans developed through their reason.

The human being was endowed by God with free will—the power to choose between alternatives. It was the power of intellect that enabled human beings to frame alternatives, to weigh them, to choose between them, and to act on them. This power of rationality was essentially as Aristotle had framed it. However, human beings who believed in Christianity had immense assistance in making correct choices from illumination provided by the Scriptures and guidance from church doctrines.

Aquinas was primarily an academic who explored theological and religious themes in his research and writing. He established a conception of human nature possessing complementary spiritual and physical dimensions. Because of their common Creator and their underlying spiritual nature, human beings shared a common human nature. Aquinas' conception of human nature held importance for educational theory. Because human beings shared a common human nature, it was possible to speak about education in general terms. All people possessed a supernatural soul that, if the person cooperated with grace, was destined to experience the beatific vision of God in heaven. For Aquinas, human beings' common nature and destiny were purposeful in that there was meaning to human life within the framework of the universe. A curriculum based on this common nature and destiny should emphasize religious and theological studies that cultivated human spirituality.

Aristotle believed human beings' highest and defining power was reason. He argued that human beings' greatest pleasure was in cultivating rational excellence. Aquinas agreed that reason was one of the distinguishing characteristics of human beings. This power inclined the person to the truth and helped them to know it. Reason, however, needed faith, which endowed human beings with the acceptance of revealed and doctrinal truth. Although Aquinas concurred with Aristotle on the importance of reason, he believed the greatest pleasure human beings could experience came from the supernatural life of the soul in the vision of God after death. The emphasis Aquinas gave to reason encouraged the study of philosophy and the liberal arts that were preparatory to it.

To Aquinas, the human person was a spirit or soul within a body. Although the spiritual side of human nature was of great importance, the physical side was not to be neglected. Each person on Earth inhabited a place at a given time and had a geographical relationship to the Earth and to human history. People were communicators, endowed with powers of speech and hearing. For communication, language studies were important. Because human beings sustained themselves by work and economic activities, these practical endeavors were important.

What emerged in the Thomistic framework of thought was a hierarchical arrangement of human activities with religious studies at the summit, moving gradually downward to those that cultivated rationality, and finally reaching those bounded by space and time that dealt with earning a livelihood and the economic sustenance of society.

Although Thomistic education gave priority to theological and philosophical studies, Aquinas recognized that human beings, endowed with intelligence and free will, could and should act to transform their environment and make it as hospitable as possible. Although religious, the Thomistic view was not fatalistic. Human beings, guided by faith and reason, were to use their powers to formulate plans and actions to improve life on Earth.

Thomas Aquinas can be described as a philosopher who dealt with theological issues or as a theologian who philosophized. He also taught and wrote on educational themes. In *de Magistro,* he developed a theory of education that complemented his broader philosophical and theological work. From his view of human nature, certain themes emerge in Aquinas' philosophy of education:

1. Education, like life itself, is purposeful; it is a means to an end. Human beings' ultimate destiny is the beatific vision of God, and education should contribute to the achievement of that goal.
2. Reality exhibits two dimensions: one that is spiritual and one that is physical. Education relates to both dimensions of human nature: the soul and the body. It should prepare the human being for what needs to be done on Earth and what will contribute to the salvation of the soul.
3. Reality—both supernatural and natural—is hierarchically structured as is society, both secular and religious. Because not all things are equal, education, especially the curriculum, should be structured hierarchically with the most important areas of study receiving the greatest priority.

In true scholastic fashion, Aquinas made some important definitions and distinctions when he dealt with educational matters. Education, broadly construed, was that which contributed to human beings' total formation to the state of excellence or virtue.[11] As the process of total human formation, education encompassed schooling but was much more than formal instruction. Aquinas recognized that many agencies—the family, church, and civil society—had an educative role.

Aquinas referred to formal education, or schooling, as *disciplina,* when a teacher teaches some body of knowledge or skill to a learner.[12] It should be noted that the teaching formula involved three elements: a skill or body of knowledge, a teacher, and a learner.

Aquinas adhered to a basic Aristotelian strategy in structuring instruction. To this he added the scholastic method used in the medieval universities. The subject matter of instruction was *scientia,* an organized body of knowledge in which there were (1) principles, (2) arguments of systematic logical development that supported these principles, (3) analogies and illustrations that served as illustrative examples, and (4) conclusions. This particular format of organizing knowledge was especially suited to theology and philosophy.

Aquinas' model teacher was a person who integrated knowledge and virtue as two interpenetrating elements of professional life. A person was "called" to the life of teaching in a way that was similar to the priest's vocation, which also was a call to service. The teacher's service to humanity was an act of love. Although the sense of loving service was a necessary element in the character of the good teacher, the force of personality was insufficient in itself. Teaching means that the teacher possesses a body of knowledge and the instructional skills to transmit it to students. In the Thomistic conception of instruction, teachers needed to possess rhetorical skills so that they could use language with facility; they also needed logical skills so that instruction was organized according to premises drawn from the body of knowledge.

To Aquinas, a teacher's life was highly integrated in that the various elements of teaching fused harmoniously. First, becoming a teacher meant the person had a commitment to a life of service. Second, through diligent study, the teacher came to possess a body of knowledge. These elements contributed to a life that was both contemplative and active. For the medieval priest, monk, and nun, contemplation was an important aspect of religious life. It meant the person would isolate himself or herself from the concerns of everyday life and, in quietude, reflect on the truly important matters that give purpose and meaning to existence. Contemplation was also important for Plato's preparation of philosopher-kings in *The Republic.* Preparation for teaching also involved contemplation in that the teacher needed to study and reflect on sources and texts so they could be incorporated in lessons. Much of this preparation was done alone in libraries. Although contemplation was a necessary element in teaching, instruction was active in that the teacher was deliberately transmitting a body of knowledge to learners. Knowledge was organized and presented so that students could grasp it.

In the Thomistic world view, all things and all actions are purposeful in that they have an end. Teaching has as its proximate or earthly end the education or formation of students. It is to convey knowledge that will help them attain salvation in heaven and fulfillment on Earth. In the Thomistic view of instruction, teachers can lead students to knowledge but only students have the power to acquire it. Students need to be ready to receive knowledge, to study it, and to appropriate it. The Thomistic educational milieu is a place of activity directed to acquiring bodies of knowledge while recognizing the importance of spiritual grace in inclining students to knowledge.

Based on the Thomistic conception of teaching and learning, it is possible to extrapolate some ideas about a school that reflects the Thomistic orientation. Aquinas was educated in monastic schools and universities. He was shaped by educational environments that were highly religious and highly academic. The

Thomistic school, resting as it does on definite theological and philosophical foundations, would be a learning environment that stressed academic learning of areas of knowledge in a structured and disciplined way. The learning atmosphere would be charged with religious elements that reflected Christian faith and doctrine. Schooling would have a moral purpose in nurturing the habits, dispositions, and outlooks that inclined students to a purposeful life of faith and reason. In such an environment, teachers were to be models of virtue that could be imitated by students.

Conclusion: An Assessment

To assess Aquinas' theory of education, it is necessary to examine certain features of contemporary U.S. society and education that tend to limit its effect. This assessment will also examine certain features of Thomism that have contributed to its viability as an educational theory.

There are undeniable aspects of Thomism—its origin, development, and terminology—that make it medieval. Thomistic theology and philosophy were highly compatible with the hierarchical order of society, which reflected a hierarchical conception of the universe. These medieval origins and structure are out of character with much of the U.S. historical and educational experience. When Europeans colonized the North American continent, the medieval era had already ended. The ideas and institutions the European colonists brought to the New World were more the products of the Renaissance and the Protestant Reformation than the medieval world. Although residues of medievalism, especially in its aristocracy, persisted in Europe, North America was virtually free of medievalism. When the American Revolution ended colonial rule, the United States was a nation conceived in the spirit of the eighteenth-century Enlightenment, not a product of medievalism. The secularism and republicanism of the revolutionary generation of Americans were antagonistic to medieval ideas.

In the history of U.S. public education, medieval ideas and institutions were largely absent. The common school was a product of the twin forces of republicanism and Evangelical Protestantism. Progressive historians, including those who interpreted the history of U.S. schooling, tended to regard the medieval centuries as the "Dark Ages," devoid of those tendencies and inclinations that contributed to a progressive future for humankind.

If Thomism found an intellectual home in the United States, it was in the schools, colleges, and universities established by Roman Catholic immigrants. Separating themselves educationally from what they regarded as Protestant-dominated institutions, Catholics created alternative ones. For a church whose governance was hierarchical and whose liturgy was largely celebrated in ceremonies that were medieval in origin, Thomism, with its blending of theology and philosophy, provided a congenial intellectual perspective. Throughout the centuries, the Catholic church continued to refer to St. Thomas Aquinas as the "philosopher" and the "angelic doctor."

Thomism dominated the philosophical outlook of Roman Catholic institutions of higher education in the United States, and generations of students were intellectualized and socialized in the world view that it provided. Other philosophies were judged in relationship to their conformity or divergence from Thomistic doctrines.

In 1962, Pope John XXIII convened a church council, known as Vatican II, that brought a number of significant changes to the Roman Catholic outlook on the world.[13] Vatican II, with its spirit of ecumenism, inaugurated an opening to the non-Catholic world. It brought about a number of liturgical changes such as the celebration of the mass in the vernacular rather than the traditional Latin. One effect of the church council was to reduce the medievalism that had characterized Roman Catholicism and to reassert what were claimed to be the practices of the early church. Although the philosophy of Thomas Aquinas might retain its esteemed position in the church and in Catholic colleges and universities, its place was no longer exclusive. Philosophical alternatives arose that challenged its supremacy.

Although Thomism can be assessed in terms of its compatibility with the U.S. historical experience and its role in shaping the intellectual outlook of Catholics in the United States, it also can be assessed in terms of its continuing effect on the history of Western educational ideas. Aquinas developed one of the great syntheses in Western educational thought by integrating Aristotle's philosophy of natural realism with the doctrines of the Christian church. This synthesis, which fused the Greek and Roman classical intellectual heritage with the new cultural dynamic of Christianity, provided continuity between the past and the present. For centuries, the Roman church carried both the classical Aristotelian emphasis on reason and the Christian emphasis on faith forward.

Aquinas' dualism, built on the ideas of Aristotle, dichotomized life and learning into two dimensions: the spiritual and the corporal. From this basic categorization came the extension of the spiritual into the intellectual dimension of theory and the corporal into practice. This structuring of education into the theoretical and the practical characterized education long after Aquinas. This Aristotelian-Thomistic dualism would drive John Dewey to attack separations of thought and practice. Despite Dewey's attacks, the theory-practice distinctions has remained an important characteristic of Western education.

Aquinas' emphasis on the rational, the intellectual, and the theoretical did not encourage human beings to be disembodied intellects. He recognized the importance of the corporal or physical element of life as proper to the natural order. Rather than seeing spirit and body locked in perpetual war, he was a reconciler who saw the supernatural and natural orders as compatible and complementary. Perhaps the Thomistic world view that saw the supernatural and the natural as compatible contains possibilities for ongoing synthesis in the modern world, which often sees the spiritual and the material dimensions of human nature at war with each other.

Discussion Questions

1. Examine the educational implications of theology.
2. How did the context of the medieval period contribute to the development of Aquinas' theology and philosophy of education?
3. Compare and contrast the theological views of Augustine and Aquinas.

4. What were the major features of the medieval world view?
5. How was Aquinas' theistic realism a blending of elements of Christian theology and Aristotelian philosophy?
6. Analyze the meaning of the term *hierarchy* and how it might be applied to the governance of educational institutions and to the organization of the curriculum.
7. Compare Plato's use of the concept of the hierarchy in *The Republic* to Aquinas' use of the concept.

Research and Essay Topics

1. In an essay, characterize the medieval outlook and compare and contrast it with that of the contemporary United States.
2. In an essay, develop the character of the teacher as prescribed by Aquinas.
3. Design a lesson plan to teach a subject or skill according to Aquinas' view of education.
4. Analyze several books used in teacher education programs in terms of Aquinas' distinctions between *educatio* and *disciplina*. Are the books as specific in their use of terminology?
5. In a paper, outline a curriculum that is organized according to Thomistic educational principles.
6. In a paper, assess the significance of Aquinas in the history of Western thought and education.
7. In a paper, examine the concept of dualism and describe its educational implications.

Notes

1. Henry Chadwick, *Augustine* (New York: Oxford University Press, 1986).
2. Pearl Kibre, "The Christian: Augustine," in Paul Nash, Andreas Kazamias, and Henry Perkinson, eds. *The Educated Man: Studies in the History of Educational Thought* (New York: John Wiley and Sons, 1965), 96–112.
3. The medieval university is treated in Gordon Leff, *Paris and Oxford Universities in the Thirteenth and Fourteenth Centuries: An Institutional and Intellectual History* (New York: John Wiley and Sons, 1968), and Charles H. Haskins, *The Rise of Universities* (Ithaca: Cornell University Press, 1957).
4. James A. Weisheipl, O. P., *Friar Thomas d'Aquino: His Life, Thought, and Work* (New York: Doubleday, 1974), 3–9.
5. John W. Donohoe, S. J., *St. Thomas Aquinas and Education* (New York: Random House, 1968), 23–57.
6. Ibid., 26–31.
7. Ibid., 27–33.
8. Thomas Aquinas. *On the Truth of the Catholic Faith.* Translated by Anton C. Pegis (Garden City, N.Y.: Image Books, 1955), 17.
9. Ibid., 21–23.
10. Ibid., 62–96.
11. Ibid., 58–96.
12. Ibid.

13. Giancarlo Zizola, *The Utopia of Pope John XXIII* (New York: Orbis Books, 1978), 255–84.

Suggestions for Further Reading

Aquinas, Thomas. *Saint Thomas Aquinas: The Treatise on Law*. Notre Dame: University of Notre Dame Press, 1993.
———. *On the Truth of the Catholic Faith*. Translated by Anton C. Pegis. Garden City, N.Y.: Image Books, 1955.
Blanchette, Oliva. *The Perfection of the Universe According to Aquinas: Teleological Cosmology*. University Park, PA.: Pennsylvania State University Press, 1992.
Chadwick, Henry. *Augustine*. New York: Oxford University Press, 1986.
Davies, Brian. *The Thought of Thomas Aquinas*. New York: Oxford University Press, 1991.
Donohoe, John W., S. J. *St. Thomas Aquinas and Education*. New York: Random House, 1968.
Elders, Leo. *The Metaphysics of Being of St. Thomas Aquinas in a Historical Perspective*. Leiden and New York: E.J. Brill, 1992.
Fatula, Mary Ann. *Thomas Aquinas: Preacher and Friend*. Collegeville, Minn.: Liturgical Press, 1993.
Gilson, Etienne. *The Christian Philosophy of St. Thomas Aquinas*. Notre Dame, Ind.: University of Notre Dame Press, 1994.
———. *History of Christian Philosophy in the Middle Ages*. New York: Random House, 1955.
Hall, Pamela M. *Narrative and the Natural Law: An Interpretation of Thomistic Ethics*. Notre Dame, Ind.: University of Notre Dame Press, 1994.
Haskins, Charles H. *The Rise of Universities*. New York: Cornell University Press, 1957.
Kenny, Anthony J. *Aquinas*. New York: Hill and Wang, 1980.
———. *Aquinas on Mind*. New York: Routledge, 1992.
Klauder, Francis J. *A Philosophy Rooted in Love: The Dominant Themes in the Perennial Philosophy of St. Thomas Aquinas*. Lanham, Md.: University Press of America, 1994.
Leff, Gordon. *Paris and Oxford Universities in the Thirteenth and Fourteenth Centuries: An Institutional and Intellectual History*. New York: John Wiley and Sons, 1968.
McInerny, Ralph M. *Aquinas on Human Action: A Theory of Practice*. Washington, D.C.: Catholic University of America Press, 1992.
———. *A First Glance at St. Thomas Aquinas: A Handbook for Peeping Thomists*. Notre Dame, Ind.: University of Notre Dame Press, 1990.
Murray, Alexander. *Reason and Society in the Middle Ages*. Oxford: Clarendon Press, 1978.
Nelson, Daniel M. *The Priority of Prudence: Virtue and Natural Law in Thomas Aquinas and the Implications for Modern Ethics*. Washington Park, PA..: Pennsylvania State University Press, 1992.
Peters, Edward. *Europe and the Middle Ages*. Englewood Cliffs, N.J.: Prentice-Hall, 1983.
Piltz, Anders. *The World of Medieval Learning*. Totowa, N.J.: Barnes and Noble, 1989.
Selman, Francis J. *Saint Thomas Aquinas: Teacher of Truth*. Edinburgh: T&T Clark, 1994.
Weisheipl, James O. P. *Friar Thomas d'Aquino: His Life, Thought, and Work*. New York: Doubleday, 1974.
Woznicki, Andrew N. *Being and Order: The Metaphysics of Thomas Aquinas in Historical Perspective*. New York: Peter Lang, 1990.

CHAPTER 6

Desiderius Erasmus: Renaissance Humanist and Cosmopolitan Educator

Erasmus, from a 1526 engraving by Albrecht Dürer (detail); reproduction from the collection of the Library of Congress.

This chapter discusses the life, educational philosophy, and contributions of Desiderius Erasmus (1466–1536), one of the leading classical humanist critics and educators of the Renaissance, the period of Western history known for the revival of humanist studies. The Renaissance is important in the history of Western educational ideas because it established patterns that shaped the course of secondary education in both Europe and the United States.

In this chapter, Erasmus' influence on Western education is discussed in its historical context and in terms of its effect on educational philosophy and policy. First, the general intellectual, social, and educational context in which Erasmus lived and worked is described. Second, Erasmus' education and career are analyzed to determine the evolution of his ideas. Third, the continuing effect of Erasmus' contributions to Western education is assessed. By examining the life of this educator, we shall determine how the major historical shift from the late Middle Ages to the Renaissance shaped the educational culture of the times. For example, Erasmus' educational philosophy developed as he confronted the waning of medieval scholasticism (discussed in Chapter 5) and the evolution of the new cultural dynamic of Renaissance classical humanism. As is true of the theorists examined earlier in this book, Erasmus grappled with the problems of educational continuity and change.

To organize your thoughts as you read this chapter, you might focus on the following questions:

- What were the major trends in the historical context of the Renaissance, the time and situation, in which Erasmus lived and worked?
- How did Erasmus' educational biography shape his philosophy of education?
- How did Erasmus' educational philosophy determine his educational policies and practices?
- What is the enduring impact of Erasmus' contributions to Western education?

The Historical Context of Erasmus' Life

Historians call the period from the late fourteenth through the early sixteenth centuries the Renaissance. As is true of most historical periods, there is disagreement about the precise beginning and ending of the period. Erasmus' life, however, squarely locates him in the Renaissance.

The term *renaissance* is used to designate a revival, a rebirth, or a renewal of interest in the humanist dimension of life and culture. The Renaissance period marked the beginning of a "this worldly" view of life in contrast to the "other-worldly" perspective of the Middle Ages. For their sources of inquiry and inspiration, scholars and educators of the Renaissance such as Erasmus looked back to the classics of ancient Greece and Rome. The Renaissance can be seen then as signaling a shift of emphasis from the exclusively spiritual orientation of the Middle Ages to a more humanistic perspective and a renewal of interest in the Greek and Roman classics as commentaries on human life.[1]

Although the generalizations about the Renaissance that introduce the chapter are valid, they need to be examined in view of the complexity of this period, which marks the beginning of the modern era. A brief look at the economic changes of the era and the alterations of the material foundations of life shed some light on the Renaissance. By the late Middle Ages, western Europe was enjoying a period of economic growth and development. City life had been revitalized to the point that a thriving trade existed. Certain principalities such as Venice had built up extensive trade in the eastern Mediterranean area. German merchants, organized in the Hanseatic league, were engaged in brisk trade in northern Europe. With the revival of commercial life came both economic surpluses and new ideas. In the Italian states and principalities, part of the new wealth was directed to creating and supporting new forms of art, architecture, literature, and education. This economically stimulated revival of aesthetic life, centered in Italy, is referred to as the southern Renaissance.

Northern Europe, too, experienced a Renaissance as new art and literary forms were introduced. However, this northern European Renaissance retained a religious emphasis as humanist scholars not only examined classical texts but turned their attention to scriptural and dogmatic works as well. Erasmus devoted his attention to both classical and religious texts.

The critical religious scholarship of northern European humanists such as Erasmus coincided with a weakening of the pope's authority. As the kings of nation-states consolidated and increased their power, they came to resent papal interference in their realms. In fact, disputes between the papacy and the French king grew so intense that King Philip IV invaded Italy, seized Pope Boniface VIII, and imprisoned him. A weakened papacy was moved to Avignon where from 1309 to 1377 it functioned under the scrutiny of the French king. During this period, rival popes claimed to hold authority in Rome. It was not until 1409 that the Council of Pisa ended the dispute.

As a transitional period, important changes in the Western cultural perspective and intellectual orientation occurred, but did not necessarily have a uniform effect throughout Europe. Powerful spiritual and religious interests of the medieval era continued but were diminished in some areas and redirected in others. In certain areas of Europe, especially in the southern Renaissance, creative energies, as well as financial support, shifted from strictly spiritual impulses to more humanistic art and architectural styles. Often, the architectural subjects were still churches and cathedrals but the aesthetic styles of the medieval era yielded to grandiose and palatial edifices. Art forms such as painting and sculpture, too, might still have depicted religious motifs but the figures and themes were earthly rather than ethereal in appearance. Inroads into what once had been dominated by the spiritual continued until a secular or romance literature appeared to carve out its own domain along with the religious. For example, Dante (1265–1321) wrote his *Divine Comedy* in the Italian vernacular rather than in Latin. A writer whose outlook was poised between the medieval and Renaissance worlds, Dante included figures from the classical period but put them in a Christian setting. Petrarch (1304–1374) was a classical scholar who preferred to write his sonnets in Italian.

If religious concerns were diminished among some scholars and educators, they were redirected for others into two areas: active reform and critical scholarship. A number of individuals, primarily clerics who preached against the corruption they observed in the church, urged institutional and personal reformation. John Wycliffe, a professor of theology at Oxford University in England, preached against the growing materialism in the church. He urged a return to the primitive simplicity of the early church and argued that the Bible should be the source of authority for Christians. In Bohemia, Jan Huss challenged papal and civil authority as he preached religious reformation. Huss was seized, tried, and condemned to death. These attempts at religious reformation laid the foundations for the coming Protestant Reformation.

In addition to religious reformers, there were critical humanist scholars like Erasmus who wanted reform but did not want to go outside the institutional and theological framework of a universal Christian church. Especially in the areas touched by the northern Renaissance—the Netherlands and the Low Countries, the German states, and England—religious concerns were still a dominant but redirected set of interests. Aided by their close examination of ancient texts, the classical humanists critically scrutinized medieval works on Scripture, dogma, and doctrine with an eye for detecting errors.[2] As a result of their critical inquiries, the medieval synthesis was weakened but not yet destroyed. The critical scholarship of the northern Renaissance would be a factor that contributed to the Protestant Reformation. (The Protestant Reformation will be treated separately in this book; some historians link it, however, directly with the Renaissance.)

At this point, we can consider the revival of the critical function of the educator. During all periods of history, educators transmit the cultural heritage, the legacy of the past. They also work within the institutional and ideational contexts of the period in which they live. Should educators transmit the heritage or should they attempt to change or reform the culture? Is it possible to do both? Socrates and Plato were dissatisfied with cultural changes that were taking place and tried to reverse them. Socrates criticized the trends of his day and so did Plato. Medieval scholastics were concerned with transmitting the religious and doctrinal heritage. Although they might have been critics, their emphasis was more on integration and synthesis of ideas.

Renaissance humanists transmitted the classical heritage but were also severe critics. Erasmus, in particular, was a caustic critic of people, institutions, and ideas. Renaissance humanists operated as critics in several ways. First, they mastered ancient Greek and Roman texts and became experts in translating and interpreting them. Second, as experts, they made judgments about the authenticity and interpretation of these texts. Not always agreeing with each other, like modern professors, they carried on intense intellectual and academic debates. They also tended to write for each other rather than for a broad audience. They became an intellectual elite, a select group of connoisseurs who regarded themselves as protectors and guardians of knowledge. Most of the time, the cultural criticisms of the humanist scholars stayed within their own academic circles. At other times, particularly when they were involved in institutional criticism, their critiques moved into the larger society, stimulating questions and raising doubts.

Although the economic and intellectual foundations of Western society changed during the Renaissance, a shift in political identities and loyalties also occurred. The political decentralization of the medieval era was replaced by centralizing tendencies in key parts of western Europe. In England, France, Spain, and Portugal, the modern nation-state had emerged. In these countries, monarchies represented the nation in a personal yet symbolic way. The nation was the focus of loyalty, commitment, and identity for those who lived there and were subject to the national monarchies. The rise of nation-states, national monarchies, and nationalism itself set in motion tendencies that eroded the universal authority once held by the Christian church and the pope.

In the Italian peninsula, the German states, and eastern Europe, nationalist impulses also were being felt but were deflected by medieval residues of feudalism. In the myriad German states, nationalist sentiments were present but submerged by the rule of the Holy Roman Empire. Italy was the location of a number of small states, duchies, and principalities, each with their own ruler who was constantly involved in intrigues, alliances, and counteralliances. Niccolo Machiavelli (1469–1527) wrote *The Prince,* a treatise on power politics, to guide his patron in gaining, using, and maintaining power. Machiavelli viewed human beings as weak but greedy individuals who followed what they perceived to be their own self-interests. Such individuals needed to be kept in line by a strong ruler whose primary goal was to preserve, maintain, and extend the power of the state. Using the doctrine that the end justifies the means, Machiavelli's strategy of political manipulation was evidence that new centers of power had developed.[3]

The rise of nation-states and their ruling dynasties had educational consequences. A new educated person came on the scene in the form of the courtier—one who served at the royal court. Baldesar Castiglione described the courtier as an educated and intellectually versatile gentleman equally effective in statecraft, diplomacy, or poetry, depending on the situation.[4] A well-rounded person, the courtier was more versatile than the scholastic. At times, courtiers served as tutors to the children of the king or the lesser nobility. They might be advisers on affairs of state or undertake diplomatic missions for the king.

Once the power of nation-states had been established internally, they began to look outward. Coastal nations such as Spain, France, England, Portugal, and the Netherlands sent navigators on voyages of explorations. The conquest of Constantinople by the Turks had closed trade routes to the east and turned navigators' attention westward. Spurred by dreams of wealth or the conversion of heathen peoples, these nations established trading colonies in Africa, Asia, and North and South America. These colonies represented the beginnings of the diffusion of western European culture across the Earth.

The educational situation of the Renaissance also can be looked at in terms of continuity and change. The various schools associated with the church—the monastic, parish, and cathedral schools and the universities—continued to function as did the scholastic teachers within them. These institutions were joined by a new school, the classical humanist school, and a new kind of educator, the classical humanist. The educational currents of the Renaissance can be examined in terms of particular humanists and educational institutions. Some of the humanists functioned in institutional settings, whereas others operated independently. These humanists were highly individualistic and should be viewed as unique personalities who operated within a shared but loosely structured frame of reference. Among these humanist educators were Thomas Elyot (1490–1546), who, by translating the works of Isocrates, promoted the entry of Greek learning into England. Elyot's *The Boke Named the Governour,* addressing the issue of appropriate education for the statesman, laid out a curriculum of Latin, Greek, the liberal arts, and the ancient classics. Louis Vives (1492–1540), who had been a student of Erasmus, served as a lecturer at Oxford and wrote *de Institutitione Feminae Christianae,* which was a treatise on educating noblewomen in the classical tradition. Roger Ascham (1515–1568), the tutor of Queen Elizabeth I, wrote *The Scholemaster,* which stressed the importance of Cicero and writing according to Ciceronian style.

Some of the humanist educators developed a new kind of educational institution—a school that stressed a curriculum based on the Greek and Latin classics. These classical humanist schools combined both a secondary and a preparatory function. They were secondary schools in that some of the older students had completed the primary branches of instruction, although some younger students entered the humanist school after mastering the basics of their own vernacular and simple arithmetic. The classical humanist schools were preparatory institutions that readied some of their students for admission to colleges and universities. These classical humanist schools—the Latin grammar school in England, the *gymnasium* in Germany, the *lycée* in France, and the *liceo* in Italy—developed into institutions that prepared the children of the upper classes, primarily if not exclusively the males, as the educated elite of Europe. It was this kind of school that was brought to North America in the form of the Latin grammar school in the Massachusetts Bay Colony.

One of the outstanding classical humanist schools was established by the Italian educator, Vittorino da Feltre, who established a court school for his patron, the duke of Mantua.[5] The school was established to educate the children of the duke and his court officials in the classical languages and literatures. In addition, a few children from the lower classes were admitted to the school. Vittorino, following the basic guidelines of humanist education, sought to prepare well-rounded and generally educated persons who could assume leadership positions as civil servants, administrators, and diplomats. The way to accomplish this broad educational objective, he believed, was through the classics, which were the source of ethics, history, morals, and all other kinds of wisdom. Looking back to the Greek and Roman past, Vittorino used the treatises of Quintilian as a guide to curriculum and instruction.

John Collette, an English humanist, visited and was impressed by the classical humanist school in Italy. When he returned to England, he established the classical humanist school of St. Paul's. This school, which originated as a Latin grammar school, became one of the leading preparatory schools in England. On his visit to England, Erasmus visited Collette, and wrote a Latin grammar that was used at St. Paul's.

The Renaissance was a time of intellectual ferment as Western culture moved from the medieval to the modern world. Although there were new political, economic, and aesthetic developments, the greatest effect on education came by way of classical humanism. We now turn our attention to the life of Desiderius Erasmus.

Erasmus: Classical Humanist Educator

The following section examines the life, career, and contributions of Desiderius Erasmus. Although it is well established that Erasmus was born in 1466, many of the events surrounding his birth are shrouded with controversy. The exact situation of his birth and family have been disputed.

According to a recent biographer, Erasmus was born on October 27, 1466, in Rotterdam, in the Netherlands. He is alleged to have been the illegitimate child of Gerard, a priest, and Margaret Rogerius who was employed as Gerard's housekeeper. Erasmus tried to conceal his illegitimate birth and never revealed his father's last name. In 1497, he added the name Desiderius and later adopted the name of the city of his birth, Rotterdam.[6] Erasmus was sensitive about the issue of illegitimacy throughout his life and attempted to create an appearance of legitimacy by altering his birthdate. He later claimed that his father was not ordained until after his mother's death.[7]

When he was six years old, Erasmus was enrolled in the school at Deventer, which was operated by the Brethren of the Common Life, a religious association. The Brethren were founded by the Dutch religious reformer, Gerhard Groote (1340–1384).[8] The Brethren were not a religious order in the strict sense but were rather an association of individuals who gathered to perform charitable and educational good works. The elementary schools that they conducted usually taught the conventional primary subjects of reading, writing, arithmetic, and religion. In addition, the Brethren's schools exemplified a strong moral tone that stressed charity and the imitation of Christ. The religious studies in the schools emphasized the Gospels, the writings of the church fathers, and the lives of the saints.

Although a promising student academically, Erasmus did not enjoy his school days. In his reminiscences he directed a number of criticisms against the Brethren, who he said pressured him into becoming a priest. He claimed that the Brethren were more concerned with empty rituals, their own self-importance, and keeping strict discipline than with genuine learning. Although he found little that was commendable in his teachers, Erasmus held a high opinion of teaching as a vocation. He would write that teaching was the "noblest of occupations" by which dedicated and skilled teachers had the opportunity of embuing the young with "the best literature and the love of Christ."[9] The importance of good literature, which to him was the Greek and Latin classics, and true Christian morality were persistent themes in Erasmus' philosophy of education.

On April 25, 1492, at the age of 23, Erasmus was ordained as a priest and was under the jurisdiction of the Augustinian religious order.[10] He was still associated with the Brethren of the Common Life, who were supervised by the Augustinians. St. Augustine, for whom the order was named, had defended the compatibility of Greek and Roman knowledge with Christianity. For the next two years, he studied at the Augustinian monastery at Steyn, where he wrote *On the Contempt of the World,* a treatise defending the monastic life.

Identified as a promising young man of intellectual talent, Erasmus in 1494 entered the famous University of Paris for further studies in languages and Scripture. While at the university, he became a tutor in Latin grammar and rhetoric, subjects that engaged his interest throughout his life. His work as a tutor also stimulated his interest in teaching. Although published later, it is generally believed that his work as a tutor stimulated Erasmus to write his *Colloquies,* which was subtitled *Formulas of Familiar Conversations by Erasmus of Rotterdam, Useful Not Only for Polishing a Boy's Speech but for Building His Character.*[11]

The *Colloquies* featured conversational dialogues in which participants engaged in intellectual discussions. The characters in these dialogues used correct patterns and styles of speech and also exhibited proper moral values. The *Colloquies* demonstrated Erasmus' conviction that good literature and morality reinforced each other. Another important theme of Erasmus that was manifested by the *Colloquies* was the educational power of conversation. Erasmus believed that the free interchange of ideas between people of knowledge and cultivation was one of the most exciting ways to learn. Such conversations were also a way of learning in the classroom.

While at the University of Paris, Erasmus became a close friend of William Blount, an English aristocrat, who in the Renaissance style became a patron who subsidized a journey to England. In England, Erasmus located at Oxford University. He became acquainted with a circle of humanist scholars such as John Collette, dean of St. Paul's Cathedral and school, and Thomas More, the gifted jurist and diplomat. He wrote a Latin grammar that was used at St. Paul's school. Erasmus developed a lifelong friendship with More, with whom he regularly corresponded. More, called a "man for all seasons," rose to become the chief chancellor of King Henry VIII. When he refused to support the king's divorce from Catherine of Aragon, More fell into disfavor, was tried for treason, convicted, and executed.

After his trip to England, Erasmus traveled frequently. His journeys took him to the intellectual centers of France, Italy, and the Low Countries, where he engaged in learned conversations with Europe's leading humanist scholars. His travels enabled him to sharpen his language as well as his intellectual skills. He continued his study and writing on Scriptures and translated the Greek authors Euripides and Plutarch into Latin. Erasmus saw great educational value in traveling. He was a cosmopolitan scholar who felt at home in the company of other scholars. He especially treasured a Europe that was open to discourse that transcended national boundaries. When he saw religious warfare brewing between Catholics and Protestants, Erasmus feared that the end of cosmopolitan dialogue was approaching.

In 1499, Erasmus published *Adages,* or *Familiar Quotations from the Classics,* a book on his favorite theme of combining literary models with moral instruction. In 1511, his distinguished reputation won him an appointment as a professor of Divinity and Greek at England's Cambridge University. The next several years saw a steady stream of publications come from Erasmus.

In *Encomium Moriae,* or *The Praise of Folly,* Erasmus turned his pen against those whose arrogance and pomposity interfered with true humanist scholarship and teaching. He attacked the teachers of grammar who concentrated on triviality rather than substantial learning. Neither were the philosophers and theologians spared his barbs. Erasmus charged that too many supposedly learned philosophers were building imaginary "castles in the air" rather than developing important ideas that would liberate the human mind from ignorance and superstition. Instead of working to resolve the conflicts in Christianity, Erasmus accused theologians of spinning intricate theological webs in which to trap their unsuspecting victims.[12]

While a professor at Cambridge, Erasmus continued his work in the two areas in which he specialized: the teaching of classical languages and biblical scholarship. In 1512, he published *de Copia,* a compendium of Latin words, phrases, and idioms designed to aid students enlarge their vocabularies. Four years later, Erasmus completed his Greek version of the New Testament.

Erasmus' great work on political philosophy and education, *The Education of the Christian Prince,* appeared in 1516.[13] In this work, Erasmus, like Machiavelli, prescribed the political behavior of those who were born to rule. His advice to future rulers was far different from that of Machiavelli, who urged manipulation and subterfuge if necessary to maintain power. Instead of Machiavellian power politics, Erasmus drew an idealized portrait of a prudent, gentle, and humane ruler. If Machiavelli's treatise put forth one version of policy making, Erasmus' work on the Christian prince offered an alternative version.[14]

Erasmus emphasized that the Christian prince should operate from a base of knowledge grounded in history and geography. He should make every effort to know thoroughly his subjects and his realm, including the location, economy, and demography of the provinces and cities of the kingdom. By studying history, the prince would learn the traditions and customs of each part of his realm. Knowledge of geography and history would give him a sense of time and place and a familiarity with his people.

The Christian prince should be educated in the humanities and the doctrines of religion. Although he would be neither a humanist scholar nor a theologian, the classics would make him an educated person able to deal with other educated people. Knowledge of religion would provide an ethical context for policy formulation and decision making. In addition to informing and guiding his own ethical conduct, a classical humanist education would help him judge the character of others. The prince who governed with a sense of justice could do so only if he was able to appoint advisers, administrators, and diplomats who would conduct the affairs of state fairly and honorably for the good of all the people of the kingdom.

Although the Christian prince would not be a schoolmaster, he had an important educational role to play in his kingdom. As a personification of the good and ethical life, the Christian prince should serve as a model for his subjects. Because the long-term health and prosperity of the realm depended on the proper education of children, he should provide and supervise schools and teachers. Erasmus advised the prince to exercise "greatest care" over teachers and schools so that children were taught by "the best and most trustworthy instructors." They would "learn the teachings of Christ and that good literature which is beneficial to the state."[15] Such an education, Erasmus believed, would incline the population of the realm to right conduct and lessen the need for coercion on the part of state officials.

In *Education of the Christian Prince,* Erasmus was developing a theory of education for peace and international education. He feared that the storm clouds of war, fueled by religious sectarianism and nationalism, were darkening the horizons of Europe. He admonished the Christian prince to study the art of peacekeeping to avoid war. How ironic it was that priests should be blessing contending armies bent on killing fellow Christians in the name of religion. War carried myriad perils for the health and safety of the Christian realm. Even if war appeared to be for just causes, the entry into hostilities had deleterious effects. For Erasmus, even limited wars tended to escalate into larger ones. He admonished that war was like a plague that spreads from place to place. The costs of war were great in human and material resources that could be spent in human betterment rather than in human torment. When disputes among nations threatened to break into violence, Erasmus urged peaceful settlements by international tribunals composed of wise and impartial arbitrators.

Erasmus on Teaching

Although Erasmus saw intrinsic value in studying and commenting on ancient Greek and Roman texts, he also believed these works were of immense educational value in forming educated and moral persons. Along with the classical texts, Erasmus was a Christian humanist who believed that biblical study completed the formation of the educated person. Encompassing both Christianity and the classics, Erasmus' educational ideas were broadly conceived as a total formation, a Christian paideia, of the educated person. Concerned with language education, Erasmus also commented on specific aspects of instruction.

Like his humanist colleagues, Erasmus concentrated on the teaching of the ancient Greek and Latin languages and literature. Classical literature, he believed, was the intellectual wellspring of Western culture where all the knowledge that was of vital importance to humankind could be found.

Erasmus believed classics teachers needed to be well-educated individuals who, although scholars, avoided mindless pedantry. It was crucial that classical humanist teachers possess a commanding knowledge of their subject matter. Not only did they need to be expert in the classical texts, they also needed knowledge of archaeology, astronomy, history, and mythology, which were useful in interpreting and explaining them.

Although some humanist teachers stressed formalism and memorization, Erasmus emphasized the importance of understanding content, theme, and meaning. He outlined a method of presentation structured around six objectives:

1. Discuss the biography of the classical author whose text was being studied.
2. Identify the type of work.
3. Discuss the theme or plot.
4. Comment on the author's writing style.
5. Comment on the moral applications of the literary piece.
6. Extrapolate the cultural and philosophical implications of the work.[16]

Although these objectives were to guide instruction, Erasmus did not want teachers to instruct their students in a rigid, lockstep fashion. He believed intellectual conversation in which students and teacher examined ideas, content, and style of literary works remained the best way to cultivate broadly educated persons.

Conclusion: An Assessment

An assessment of Erasmus as an educator can be approached only in terms of the spirit of Renaissance humanism. Erasmus excelled in the qualities of scholarship and education that marked this era of Western history. He also exhibited its limitations. The criteria of excellence that marked Renaissance humanism called for knowledge of the ancient texts of Greece and Rome. Erasmus' prodigious record of scholarly research, criticism, and publication demonstrates that he was a master of this repository of the Western cultural heritage. It also shows a degree of absorption in scholarship that caused him and other humanists to look backward to a "golden age" rather than forward to a less intellectual but more open universe of thought. What was to guide the human search for truth and meaning was believed to exist in written form in documents of the past.

The sources of the classical past were in the languages of antiquity, Greek and Latin, which meant the humanist needed to master the original languages. Educated people were those who knew the ancient tongues that required years of diligent and careful study. One of the assumptions of the Renaissance was that knowledge was always found in a book, usually written in a classical language rather than the vernacular. Secondary and higher education in the Western world was shaped by the belief that knowledge of Greek and Latin and their literatures was indispensable to the educated person. The entrance requirements and the curricula of secondary schools and colleges reflected this predilection to classical languages until the end of the nineteenth and the beginning of the twentieth centuries. Although Renaissance classical humanism was once a fresh and vital educational force, its long shadow fell over secondary and higher education in the succeeding centuries. Many educational reformers of later years—Rousseau, Pestalozzi, and Owen—would seek to reverse the reverence that educators paid to the authority of the classics.

Like most Renaissance humanists, Erasmus was an elitist who saw himself as an expert guardian and interpreter of the classical heritage. Expertise was not something that could be shared by all, but was a product of serious and careful scholarship. Not every interpretation of the classics was equal; merit depended on the authenticity and genuineness of the text and the degree of interpretive expertise that the scholar brought to understanding it. The humanist scholar and educator was a critic, a commentator, and an interpreter who stood between the body of knowledge and the public. Not everyone was suited by temperament nor prepared educationally to be a humanist. Thus, classical humanist education carried a notion of selectivity and elitism rather than a desire to universalize and diffuse knowledge to the masses. Classical humanists believed in excellence but not in equity.

Erasmus and his humanist colleagues reasserted the conception of the educated man as a generalist, a leader who was versatile, knowledgeable in many subject areas, and comfortable in a variety of situations. The Renaissance man was not a specialist. Not everyone could possess the gift of educated versatility or be a critic of society and its institutions. However, it was possible to have an elite of educated generalists who in the spirit of genuine impartiality could be just, fair, and humane leaders of nations, arbiters of morals, and guardians of knowledge.

Although he could be a biting satirist and critic, Erasmus was not a man of violence. Well read and well traveled, he believed that human beings living in various settings possessed a universality and a commonality. Erasmus had a cosmopolitan attitude acquired in the company of learned books and learned colleagues. Although a purist in scholarship, he was a compromiser in human affairs. He was not the type of man to say, "Here, I stand; I will not and cannot recant," nor the type to die for a moral principle as did his friend, Thomas More. Nor was Erasmus a zealot who would plunge humankind into warfare. For Erasmus, the educated person was urbane and witty, a conversationalist who enjoyed the world of books and found in their pages truth, knowledge, virtue, and pleasure.

Discussion Questions

1. Compare and contrast the cultural and educational ideas of the medieval and Renaissance periods.
2. How did the intellectual context of the Renaissance shape Erasmus' ideas on education?
3. To what extent did Erasmus' educational contributions reflect continuity and change?
4. How was Erasmus a cultural and educational critic?
5. Examine Erasmus' methodology of instruction.
6. Assess Erasmus' significance in the history of educational ideas.

Research and Essay Topics

1. In an essay, examine the Renaissance as a transitional period in the history of Western culture and education.
2. Read and review a biography of a leading Renaissance figure such as Erasmus, Thomas More, Machiavelli, Vittorino da Feltre, Petrarch, Dante, or Boccaccio.
3. In an essay, examine the concept of the educator as critic. What role would such a person perform in the contemporary educational situation?
4. Design a lesson plan that follows Erasmus' methodology.
5. Prepare a character sketch that analyzes Erasmus.
6. Prepare a position paper that either supports or attacks the proposition that Erasmus was primarily a transitional rather than an innovative educational theorist.
7. Reflect on your own educational biography. In a paper, examine the extent to which your education either reflects continuity or change.

Notes

1. A good general history of the Renaissance is De Lamar Jensen, *Renaissance Europe: Age of Recovery and Reconciliation* (Lexington, Mass.: D. C. Heath, 1981).
2. Selected Renaissance theorists such as Petrarch, Thomas More, and Castiglione are treated in Robert Schwobel, ed., *Renaissance Men and Ideas* (New York: St. Martin's Press, 1971).
3. Ibid., 54–65.
4. Baldesar Castiglione, *The Book of the Courtier.* trans. Charles S. Singleton (New York: Doubleday, 1959).
5. William Woodward, *Vittorino da Feltre and other Humanist Educators* (Cambridge, Mass.: Cambridge University Press, 1921).

6. Albert Hyma, *The Youth of Erasmus* (New York: Russell and Russell, 1968), 51–53, 55–56, 59.
7. Christopher Hollis, *Erasmus* (Milwaukee: Bruce Publishing Co., 1933), 4–6.
8. Theodore P. Van Ziji, *Gerhard Groote, Ascetic and Reformer, 1340–1384* (Washington, D.C.: Catholic University of America Press, 1963), 31–39.
9. Hans J. Hillerbrand, ed., *Erasmus and His Age* (New York: Harper and Row, 1970), 92.
10. J. Huizinga, *Erasmus of Rotterdam* (London: Phaido Press, 1952), 9–16.
11. Erasmus, *Colloquies,* trans. Craig R. Thompson (Chicago: University of Chicago Press, 1965).
12. Frank E. Schacht, "The Classical Humanist: Erasmus," in Paul Nash, Andreas Kazamias, and Henry Perkinson, eds., *The Educated Man: Studies in the History of Educational Thought* (New York: John Wiley and Sons, 1965), 140–62.
13. Erasmus, *The Education of the Christian Prince,* trans. Lester K. Born (New York: Columbia University Press, 1936).
14. Gerald L. Gutek, *A History of the Western Educational Experience* (Prospect Heights, Ill.: Waveland Press, 1987), 107–10.
15. Robert Ulich, *Three Thousand Years of Educational Wisdom: Selections from Great Documents* (Cambridge, Mass.: Harvard University Press, 1954), 253.
16. Gutek, 108.

Suggestions for Further Reading

Augustijn, C. *Erasmus: His Life, Works, and Influence.* Toronto: University of Toronto Press, 1991.
Bainton, Roland H. *Erasmus of Christendom.* New York: Charles Scribner's Sons, 1969.
Castiglione, Baldesar. *The Book of the Courtier.* Translated by Charles S. Singleton. New York: Doubleday, 1959.
Demolen, Richard, ed. *Erasmus of Rotterdam: A Quincentennial Symposium.* New York: Twayne Publishers, 1971.
Dorey, T. A., ed. *Erasmus.* London: Routledge and Kegan Paul, 1970.
Erasmus. *Adages.* Translated by Craig R. Thompson. Chicago: University of Chicago Press, 1962.
———. *Colloquies.* Translated by Craig R. Thompson. Chicago: University of Chicago Press, 1965.
———. *Controversies.* Toronto: University of Toronto Press, 1993.
———. *The Education of the Christian Prince.* Translated by Lester K. Born. New York: Columbia University Press, 1936.
———. *The Erasmus Reader.* Toronto: University of Toronto Press, 1990.
———. *The Praise of Folly.* Translated by Hoyt H. Hudson. Princeton, N.J.: Princeton University Press, 1941.
———. *Poems.* Toronto: University of Toronto Press, 1990.
Gordon, Walter E. *Humanist Play and Belief: The Seriocomic Art of Desiderius Erasmus.* Toronto: University of Toronto Press, 1990.
Halkin, Leon E. *Erasmus: A Critical Biography.* Oxford, U.K. and Cambridge, Mass.: Blackwell, 1993.
Hillerbrand, Hans J., ed. *Erasmus and His Age.* New York: Harper and Row, 1970.
Huizinga, J. *Erasmus of Rotterdam.* London: Phaidon Press, 1952.
Hyma, Albert. *The Youth of Erasmus.* New York: Russell and Russell, 1968.
Jardine, Lisa. *Erasmus, Man of Letters: The Construction of Charisma in Print.* Princeton, N.J.: Princeton University Press, 1993.

Jensen, de Lamar. *Renaissance Europe: Age of Recovery and Reconciliation.* Lexington, Mass.: D. C. Heath, 1981.

McConica, James. *Erasmus.* Oxford, U.K. and New York: Oxford University Press, 1991.

Nash, Paul, Andreas Kazamias, and Henry Perkinson, eds. *The Educated Man: Studies in the History of Educational Thought.* New York: John Wiley and Sons, 1965.

Phillips, Margaret M. *Erasmus and the Northern Renaissance.* London: Hodder and Stoughton, 1949.

Rummel, Erika. *Erasmus and His Catholic Critics.* Nieuwkoop, Netherlands: De Graaf, 1989.

Schoeck, Richard J. *Erasmus of Europe: The Making of a Humanist, 1467–1500.* Savage, Md.: Barnes & Noble Books, 1990.

———. *Erasmus Grandescens: The Growth of a Humanist's Mind and Spirituality.* Nieuwkoop, Netherlands: De Graaf, 1988.

Schwobel, Robert, ed. *Renaissance Men and Ideas.* New York: St. Martin's Press, 1971.

Van Ziji, Theodore P. *Gerhard Groote, Ascetic and Reformer, 1340–1384.* Washington, D.C.: Catholic University of America Press, 1963.

Woodward, William. *Vittorino da Feltre and other Humanist Educators.* Cambridge: Cambridge University Press, 1921.

CHAPTER 7

John Calvin: Theologian and Educator of the Protestant Reformation

Portrait of John Calvin; reproduced from the collections of the Library of Congress.

This chapter examines the life, theology, and educational philosophy of John Calvin (1509–1564), a leading figure of the Protestant Reformation. The reformed theology developed by Calvin had momentous significance not only in the history of religious ideas but for society, economics, and education in Europe and North America. Calvin devised a system of religious doctrines known as Evangelical Protestantism. Calvinism, with its sanction of industriousness and economic development, appealed to the rising professional and business middle classes. Relating a righteous earthly life and salvation to knowledge of the Bible, Calvinism also stimulated the tendency to universal literacy and education.

Calvin's influence on Western and U.S. education is examined in the historical context of the Protestant Reformation of sixteenth-century Europe. First, the social, political, economic, and religious context in which Calvin developed his educational ideas is described. Second, Calvin's biography, education, and career are analyzed to determine the evolution of his ideas. Third, the transference of Calvin's theology of Evangelical Protestantism to North America, especially to New England, is examined. Fourth, the continuing significance of Calvinism on education is assessed. By this analysis, we shall determine the relationship of Calvin's reformed theology to educational policy and practices. For example, Calvin's reformed theology, which was articulated in the midst of the Protestant Reformation, had a long-range effect on economic and social policies as well as religious doctrines, beliefs, and practices.

To organize your thoughts as you read Chapter 7, you might focus on the following questions:

- What were the major trends of the Protestant Reformation, the time and situation in which Calvin lived?
- How did Calvin's life—his educational biography—shape his philosophy of education?
- How did Calvin's reformed theology determine his educational policies and practices?
- How did Calvinism influence the development of education in the United States?
- What is the enduring impact of Calvin's contributions to Western and U.S. education?

The Historical Context of Calvin's Life

In the sixteenth and seventeenth centuries, Western life and culture experienced a period of intense religious interest and activity. Historians have designated this period the Protestant Reformation and the Roman Catholic Counterreformation. Although the tendencies of this period were overtly religious, the events of the period were played out against a backdrop of social, political, and economic changes that worked to destroy the medieval synthesis already enfeebled during the Renaissance.[1]

Political centralization had created strong monarchial states in England, France, Spain, and Portugal. Smaller countries such as the Netherlands were also seeking to assert their own political and economic identity. A growing sense of nationalism was surfacing in the divided German states. In England, Henry VIII threw off any commitment to the pope of Rome and established himself as head of the church. In Germany, Martin Luther successfully challenged papal authority. The rise of strong monarchial states and the growing currents of nationalism would unleash new trends that would reshape Western attitudes.

By the sixteenth century, European nationalism had proved to be one of the most potent political and ideological forces in modern Western history. It provided the ideological cement that would unite and hold a people together. In its simplest meaning, nationalism was centered on the nation, a political entity or territory, usually populated by those who were alike in ethnicity, language, and culture. In sixteenth-century Europe, these territorial nations were governed by kings whose people symbolized the nation. The rise of nationalism and national states weakened loyalty and commitment to transnational figures and institutions such as the pope and the Roman Catholic church. Primary loyalty was to the nation as people began to define themselves as English, French, Spanish, and so on.

The religious movements of the Reformation contained a nationalist element. In the German states, there was a seething resentment that an Italian pope should attempt to assert authority over Germans and draw off money to support projects outside of Germany. In England, a similar feeling arose when the pope would not agree to Henry VIII's plans to divorce Catherine of Aragon. Of equal importance to King Henry was the possibility that the expropriation of church property, particularly the extensive monastic holdings, could be used to finance the king's plans to make England into a commanding European power.

Although the rise of nationalism had obvious political importance, it also began to reshape educational institutions. The sense of national identity, loyalty, and commitment was something that had to be acquired or learned. New schools that emerged with the Reformation began to stress nationalism and national identity. In subsequent centuries, the stirrings of nationalism would accelerate and exercise an even greater educational effect.

Another conditioning influence of the Protestant Reformation was economic. In sixteenth-century Europe, new economic structures emerged such as banking, issuance of stock, money exchanges, use of credit, and the charging of interest. Ownership of money and stock brought about a powerful new class of businessmen and bankers. This new class, the bourgeois or middle class, would seek a place of status in the European class structure and would eventually challenge the landed aristocracy for the dominant social, economic, and political positions. Possessing wealth, the middle classes would create and support educational institutions that reflected their views of knowledge and value.

It was against the backdrop of the nation-state, rising currents of nationalism, and economic change that the Protestant Reformation occurred. Although nationalism eroded and destroyed the remains of a European political unity, the Reformation shattered the already debilitated medieval Christian synthesis. The groundwork for the Protestant Reformation has been laid by John Wycliffe (1320–1384), an Oxford theologian. Wycliffe, who condemned the ownership of property by the church, preached against papal interference in English affairs. He translated the Bible into English and urged the formation of a national English church. Although he attracted some support, the time was not ripe for his ideas to flourish.[2] The Reformation's first success would be in Martin Luther's Germany.

Along with John Calvin, Martin Luther was one of the towering figures of the Protestant Reformation.[3] In fact, Luther is often cited as the person who precipitated the Reformation when he posted his *Ninety-five Theses* on the door of the Court Church at Wittenburg. Luther, an Augustinian monk, was assigned as a lecturer to the University of Wittenburg. Growing increasingly restive in his religious order, Luther was becoming disenchanted with Catholic practices such as the earning of indulgences and the veneration of the saints. His study of and lecturing on the Bible brought him to assert the doctrine of "justification by faith alone," which challenged the traditional Catholic teaching that salvation was by faith and the performance of good works. According to Luther, the justice of God was the righteousness by which God's grace and mercy justified human beings through their faith that Jesus Christ was their Savior.[4]

What brought matters to the breaking point for Luther was the sale of indulgences. The issue occurred when Albert of Brandenburg, who was seeking to become the archbishop of Mainz, gave Pope Leo X a contribution to build the new St. Peter's basilica in Rome. The pope, in turn, gave Albert the privilege of dispensing indulgences. (An indulgence is the remission of the temporal punishment, usually in purgatory, due for sins that had been forgiven through the sacrament of penance.) Tetzel, a Dominican monk, was engaged by Albert to urge the faithful to purchase indulgences. Luther, who objected strenuously to the sale of indulgences, nailed his *Ninety-Five Theses* to the door of the church at Wittenberg on October 31, 1517. In his theses, he denied the power of the pope to reduce the penalties of purgatory and rejected the efficacy of indulgences. Luther's theological objection also received a favorable hearing from Germans who opposed the interference of Rome in their internal affairs and opposed sending German money to Rome.

After his initial objections to the sale of indulgences, Luther began to challenge other doctrines of the Catholic church. He contended that the pope's claim to supreme authority was historically rather than Scripturally based and that the pope and the church councils were capable of error. After a series of debates, Luther was condemned as a heretic by the pope. Not accepting the pope's judgment, Luther refused to recant. Instead of exiling him, several German princes protected him. Luther and his supporters circulated his theological writings throughout Germany. Luther became the leader of the Reformation in Germany.

Luther's ideas spread across northern Germany, gaining the support of two influential groups. Members of German nobility, especially Ulrich von Hutten and Franz von Sickingen, who represented the growing sense of German nationalism, gave Luther protection and furthered the diffusion of his theological doctrines. Luther also won the support of some humanist scholars and educators.

An able intellectual and educational ally of Luther was Philipp Melanchthon (1497–1560), whose support demonstrates the relationship between the Protestant Reformation and the northern Renaissance. Melanchthon, a professor of Greek at the University of Wittenberg, encountered Luther teaching Scripture at the university. Luther concurred with Melanchthon's efforts to reform the university curriculum, and Melanchthon agreed with Luther's challenge to the Catholic church.[5]

A brief look at some of Luther's ideas on education provides an overview of the Reformation's effect on education. Luther believed that if the reformed creed was to be sustained after the initial impetus of the Reformation had passed, it needed to be institutionalized in the instruction provided by schools. The young needed to attend school to learn to read so that they could read the Bible. They also needed religious instruction so they could defend their faith against sectarian rivals. In "A Letter to the Mayors and Aldermen of All Cities of Germany in Behalf of Christian Schools," Luther urged these officials to establish schools for religious, political, and economic reasons. Such schools would enable people to read the Bible in their vernacular language and educate citizens who would know and respect the laws of the civil state. Schools would instill habits of industriousness and productivity that would promote the economic prosperity of the state.[6]

Melanchthon helped the rulers of various states of Germany establish primary schools to instill the basics of literacy and the reformed religion in their young subjects. As a humanist, he stressed the need to support classical humanist schools as secondary institutions that would prepare a leadership cadre to be ministers of the Church and officials of the state. Because rival denominations were contending for converts, it was necessary to ensure that teachers instructed their students in the correct religious doctrines. To make sure that teachers taught the tenets of the reformed creed, various German states, with Melanchthon's assistance, prepared school codes that established guidelines for the curriculum and governance of schools.[7]

The care that leaders of the Protestant Reformation such as Luther gave to the supervision of schools brought a new dimension to education. Often supported in their initial efforts by political authorities, leaders of the Protestant Reformation encouraged these authorities to support and control schools. In countries dominated by new Protestant churches, civil authorities came to exercise a large educational role. This tendency was also supported by the rise of nationalism.

In addition to Lutheranism, other Protestant denominations emerged during the Reformation era. A significant number of denominations—the Reformed, Congregational, and Presbyterian churches—followed the theology of John Calvin. In England, Henry VIII established a national church, the Church of England. Pietist denominations such as the Anabaptist, the Moravian, and smaller religious groups emerged to practice religion in their own way.

The period of the Protestant Reformation and Catholic Counterreformation was neither an ecumenical age nor one of religious tolerance. It was a time of intense religious sectarianism and strife. Contentious religious denominations and the rivalries of national states unleashed a period of religious warfare.

Before turning to an examination of John Calvin as a religious and educational reformer, we shall examine the dominant educational ideas and institutions that formed the context for his work. Although education had exhibited a strong religious orientation during the Middle Ages and a somewhat diminished one during the Renaissance, the renewed religious impulses that had an effect on education in the Reformation had a new dimension—the defense of the faith against erring or heretical Christian rivals. Each church, be it Roman Catholic or Protestant, saw other churches as rival bodies following erroneous doctrine. A good part of the education of the young was devoted to instilling religious doctrines certified as correct by the parent church. Young members of the particular denomination also were prepared to defend their faith against rival antagonists.[8] To this end, the catechism became a popular teaching device. Constructed as a series of questions and answers, the catechism's responses contained religious principles. Students were to memorize the catechism, thereby instilling in their minds correct religious positions.

The assertion by Protestant reformers that people should read the Bible in their own language required an extraordinary effort to create a literate populace. The Protestant Reformation was a powerful force in bringing about the extension of primary or elementary schooling to larger sections of the population. Although primary schools had existed in the form of parish and monastic schools, a larger number of such schools were established and a larger attendance occurred as a result of the Reformation. Primary schools were founded by a range of authorities such as the various churches, towns, or districts. Civil authorities either established schools or helped support those established by the churches. The basic curriculum of the primary schools included religion, reading, writing, singing, and arithmetic. Primary schools were designed to educate a literate laity for the reformed churches and a law-abiding citizenry for the civil state. They were the schools of the masses of population and did not lead to secondary or advanced education.

Many of the Protestant reformers such as Luther, Melanchthon, and Calvin had been nurtured intellectually by the currents of the northern Renaissance.[9] They retained a belief that classical humanist education was the best means of preparing a leadership elite for service to church and state. Studying Greek and Latin languages and literatures provided the linguistic tools that ministers needed. The doctrines of the reformed churches were added to the classical languages. These classical humanist schools combined a secondary and preparatory function as young men of promise were prepared for entry to colleges and universities. Mainstream Protestant denominations such as the Lutherans and Calvinists insisted on the need for an educated ministry to lead a literate laity.

John Calvin as a Protestant Reformer and Educator

John Calvin, or Jean Chauvin in French, was born on July 10, 1509, in Noyon in the province of Picardy, France. He was the second son of Geurard and Jeanne Calvin. Of his three siblings, only Charles, his older brother, lived to adulthood.[10] Calvin's mother died when he was six. His father remarried.

Geurard Calvin was the son of a cooper in the city of Pont-l'Eveque, near Noyon. Geurard's education was sufficient to launch him on a career as a civil servant. In 1480, Geurard received an appointment as a government registrar and clerk in Noyon's ecclesiastical Court. Noyon, located on the River Verse fifty-eight miles from Paris, was known for its religious institutions. It was the seat of a bishopric and boasted a cathedral, two abbeys, and four parishes.[11] His father's position in the town placed Calvin socially in the ranks of the bourgeoisie or middle class. The attitudes and values that John Calvin stressed as a religious reformer and leader epitomized middle class mores.

John Calvin's childhood was shaped by his father's position as an official of the ecclesiastical court, a religious institution. His father's work, which was semiadministrative and semilegal, was to influence Calvin in similar directions. Although he was a theologian who would shape the basic doctrines of Evangelical Protestantism, his outlook contained a juridical and legalistic element.

Geurard Calvin's position brought the family into the circle of Charles de Hangest, the bishop of Noyon. The bishop, who recognized young John Calvin's intellectual talent, helped subsidize his education at the College des Capettes. Young Calvin was judged by his teachers to be a promising student, especially in religion and the humanities.

When he was twelve, Calvin was sent to live with the Montmors family, where he received special instruction from the family tutor. He would later claim that he owed a special debt of gratitude to the family for introducing him to the intellectual riches of the arts and humanities.[12]

In 1521, John Calvin went to Paris to attend the College de la Marche. He enrolled in the grammar course, which was preparatory to studying for the arts degree. This grammar course was designed to provide the student with proficiency in Latin so that he could study the arts, which were conducted exclusively in Latin. John Calvin studied under Mathurin Cordier, who was recognized as one of France's preeminent Latin scholars.

At fourteen, John Calvin began the arts course at the College de Montaigu, which was famous for preparing young men to become priests. The college, under the direction of Jean Standonck, was known for its orderliness, academic rigor, and strict discipline. These were important characteristics in the lifestyle the religious followers of Calvin would choose.

Although Calvin showed a keen aptitude for the humanities and theology, he left his studies at the College de Montaigu upon his father's recommendation. He enrolled at the University of Orleans to study civil law, apparently to follow in his father's profession. He applied himself intensively to his studies, displaying the discipline that would characterize his life as a religious reformer. The intensity that he applied to academic work may have caused the stomach disorders that plagued him throughout his life. Once again, he achieved academic distinction. He excelled in debate and even substituted for instructors when they were absent from their classes.

Calvin's education in letters, the humanities, theology, and law took place during the time that Europe was being swept by the intellectual and religious currents of the Reformation. Although France was still securely Roman Catholic, the religious Reformation had reached its academic institutions. The educated people of Europe were discussing Martin Luther's challenge to papal authority and the Roman Catholic church. While a student at the University of Orleans, Calvin came into contact with those who were familiar with Luther's work. An associate, Melchior Wolmar, a German student, introduced Calvin to the reformist theology of Martin Luther.[13]

Calvin completed his study of law and received his licentiate degree. Even before he had completed his legal studies, Calvin's mind kept returning to his earlier and persistent theological interests. His quest for spiritual truth led him to examine the Bible and the writings of the fathers of the early church. He approached his Scriptural study like a lawyer. In his mind, he constructed a legal and theological brief that found the Roman Catholic church to be in conflict with his interpretation of Divine law.

During the midst of his Scriptural investigations, Calvin had an intense religious conversion experience. This personal experience, he said, illuminated his thought "like a flash of light."[15] As a result, he claimed to recognize the irresistible power of God and the need to submit to the Divine Majesty.

Calvin returned to Paris, where he published his commentary on Seneca's *de Clementia.* This publication showed him to be a man with a combination of interests—theology, law, and humanist studies. He encountered a number of religiously inclined intellectuals who supported Luther in his struggle with the Catholic church. He also began to speak at meetings of persons who were moving in the direction of Protestantism. At one of these meetings, on November 1, 1533, Calvin's address to the assembly commented on the importance of the liberal arts and philosophy. Moving from his academic theme, he struck a theological note when he proclaimed salvation by faith alone, putting him squarely in the Protestant camp. Although cautioned to be moderate and not directly challenge the Roman Catholic church, Calvin took a position similar to Luther's refusal to recant his beliefs. Comparing the Catholic church to a decaying structure, Calvin asserted, "The building is too rotten to be patched up. It must be torn down and instead a new one must be built."[16]

In 1536, Calvin's *Institutes of the Christian Religion* was published and recognized as the definitive statement of the Evangelical Protestant doctrinal position.[17] *Institutes* was a forceful and lucid theological exposition framed in legal terms that broke completely with the Roman Catholic hierarchical system of ecclesiastical governance and organization. Claiming that God was too omnipotent and transcendent to be approached sacramentally, Calvin disavowed Catholicism's sacramental system and elaborate ceremonial rituals. Calvin also asserted that people who would be saved were predestined for salvation by God's grace, not through their own actions. This predestined elect would lead disciplined and purified lives according to the laws of the Scriptures.

Calvin claimed that the Evangelical church was the true successor of the early Christian church. In his letter to King Francis I of France, which introduced the *Institutes,* he called upon the French monarch to disband the Catholic church and to make Evangelicalism the official state church. Unlike the German princes who supported Luther, the French king upheld Catholicism as the official church of France and began a persecution of Evangelical and other Protestants.

Faced with persecution by the French government, Calvin fled his native land and sought refuge in Switzerland. He located in Geneva, a city already predisposed to the Protestant Reformation. The famous author of the *Institutes* was given a warm welcome by the Protestant ministers and townspeople of Geneva. They asked him to stay in their city and help build a new and reformed church. Calvin eagerly accepted his assignment in Geneva and set to work to reshape the city into a citadel of Evangelical Protestantism. He wanted to create a theocratic city where the religious and civil authorities worked together to enforce a Scriptural paideia.[18]

Using the theological and legal skills that he had mastered as a student, Calvin prepared a "confession of faith" to proclaim the true beliefs that were to guide the adherents of reformed Christianity.[19] The confession emphasized the authority of the Bible, the importance of a personal experience of guilt for sin, and the need to be reconciled to God through the redemptive act of Jesus Christ. Calvin's proclamation of the Bible as the only infallible rule of faith and life contrasted with the Roman Catholic emphasis on the dual authority of the Scriptures and the tradition of the church. The confession of faith was presented to and accepted by the Council of Two Hundred, Geneva's ruling legislative body. This document would provide the theological basis for the Heidelberg Catechism, which was widely used in the reformed churches.

As a Protestant reformer, Calvin believed that it was not only necessary to purge the corruptions of Catholicism from Christian practice but the young members of the new church had to be instilled with correct doctrine. Like other reformers such as Luther, Calvin turned to the catechistic method to impress the correct version of Christianity on the minds of the young. He condensed the religious principles of the *Institutes* and the confession into an abbreviated version in a catechism that could be studied by children in school.[20]

Reforming religion and life in Geneva did not go smoothly for Calvin, however. There were those in the city who resisted his efforts to remake Geneva into a city governed by the law of the Scriptures. In 1538, Calvin's opponents, dubbed the "libertines" because they opposed the social controls that he imposed on the city, won control of the city council and exiled Calvin from Geneva.

During this exile, Calvin traveled and preached in other Swiss cities until he located in Strasbourg, where he remained until 1541 as the pastor of a church established by Protestant exiles from France. Here, he met and married Idelette de Buren. During the nine years of their marriage, which ended with Idelette's death, the couple had three children, all of whom died shortly after their birth.

Never given to idleness, Calvin used his time in Strasbourg to refine his theological doctrines. He published an expanded edition of the *Institutes* and wrote treatises on the Last Supper and St. Paul's Epistle to the Romans. His growing fame as a theologian of the Protestant Reformation brought him into contact with Philipp Melanchthon, Luther's associate. Calvin and Melanchthon shared a commitment to humanism and religious reformation, and they corresponded with each other. Despite their mutual admiration, they were unable to resolve theological differences between Calvinism and Lutheranism.

During Calvin's absence from Geneva, Pierre de la Baume, the Catholic bishop who had been exiled from the city, returned and attempted to restore Catholicism. A strong reaction occurred against the bishop's efforts. Calvin's supporters regained control of the city council and voted to recall him to Geneva. In 1541, Calvin made a triumphal return to the city and resumed his efforts to make Geneva into a solidly Evangelical Protestant city. He remained in Geneva until his death twenty-three years later on May 27, 1564.

Calvin and Education

In this section, we shall examine the implications of Calvinist theology for education. Calvin's Evangelical Protestantism emphasized the importance of proclaiming the Scriptures through preaching, writing, and reading. Based on the knowledge and authority of the Bible, this religion strongly emphasized the need for the faithful to be literate, to read the Bible, and to govern their lives, their church, and their city according to its laws. The schools of Geneva reflected the Calvinist relationship between education, religious orthodoxy, civil order, and economic prosperity. Geneva's city council required all children to attend school. Parents who failed to comply with the law were fined. Further, the children of the poor were educated at the expense of the city. In Calvin's Geneva, a complete school system was created. Students attended an elementary school called the schola *privata* until age sixteen. The advanced school was called the *schola publica,* which later became the University of Geneva. Its original mission was to prepare clergy for the reformed churches. Its curriculum included theology, Hebrew, Greek, philosophy, mathematics, and rhetoric. The university attracted leading scholars, theologians, and classicists. In Europe and North America, the various churches inspired by Calvinism valued and emphasized education. Schools were necessary instruments in establishing and maintaining the reformed Christian religion.

Because the Bible was the sole religious authority, it was essential that it be translated into the various European vernacular languages and be made accessible to the people. The invention of the printing press made relatively inexpensive editions of the Bible available to more people.[21] Indeed, Protestant reformers urged there be a Bible in every Christian home. The Calvinist theory, as well as the Lutheran educational thrust, was that the members of the church should be literate so they could read their Bibles. Calvinism, in particular, emphasized establishing primary schools to teach basic literacy and religion. This meant that the common people were to learn to read as well as the traditionally educated elites. Thus, a strong beginning was made in the direction of mass systems of primary schools in both Europe and North America.

Although Calvin and other reformers moved in the direction of universal primary schooling, they retained a commitment to the classical humanist view of education developed in the Renaissance. Calvin, like Melanchthon, was a committed humanist. Ministers of the reformed church were to study the Scriptures and preach the Gospel from an informed and educated perspective. A call to ministry was insufficient unless combined with Scriptural and doctrinal studies. For Calvin, the Hebrew, Greek, and Latin languages and literature provided the foundation of knowledge and skills for Scriptural study. For Calvin, it was essential that religious ministers and civil authorities have a classical education. The classical humanist schools were emphasized as a secondary educational track for the educated elites of the Reformation period. It is important to note that Calvin did not envision social mobility through education. The common people would be made literate in primary schools where instruction was conducted in their own vernacular. The religious leaders would be educated in the classics and the Scriptures in humanist schools and in colleges and universities. So although Protestant reformers such as Calvin extended education to the masses of people, it was at an elementary level.

Calvinism in the United States

As a religious creed, Calvinism appealed to the middle classes of western Europe. These loosely defined classes, which had emerged with the economic changes of the

Renaissance era, did not fit neatly into the social structure inherited from the Middle Ages. Although the Middle Ages had a place in the social fabric for the landed aristocracy and the agricultural peasantry, the newly emergent middle classes did not fit. As their name suggests, the people who composed the middle classes were positioned between the aristocracy of birth and the agricultural peasant masses. They included small tradesmen and artisans, businessmen and bankers, and lawyers and other professionals. Although some had earned great wealth, others were merely making a living. What was different about the middle classes was that they had earned their way through their own efforts into the Western scheme of economic and social life rather than benefitting from inherited status.

In the areas of Europe where the middle classes existed, churches based on Calvinism attracted members. In Switzerland, the Calvinist church was the Reformed Church, in the Netherlands it was the Dutch Reformed Church, and in Scotland the Presbyterian church. Of great importance in the settlement of North America were English Calvinists known as Separatists and Puritans. Their settlement in the British colonies in New England especially Massachusetts Bay, would exercise a profound effect on U.S. culture and education.

When the Separatists landed at Plymouth and the Puritans at Massachusetts Bay in 1620, they brought with them strongly held religious beliefs. Just as Calvin had sought to establish a heavenly city in Geneva, so did his English followers in Massachusetts seek to establish a godly commonwealth in the wilderness.[22] The Puritans of Massachusetts Bay Colony enacted some of the earliest ordinances requiring education in North America. The laws of 1642 and 1647 required the towns, the civil authorities, to make sure that children learned to read, write, and know the principles of religion and laws of the commonwealth. In particular, the law of 1647 required larger towns to provide a Latin master who would instruct promising youth in classical languages so that they might attend Harvard College. The significant aspect of these early laws is that they demonstrated the great importance the Puritan settlers in North America gave to education.

The Calvinist religious beliefs that the Puritans had planted in North American soil grew and developed in the late eighteenth and nineteenth centuries into Congregationalism. As a church, Congregationalism grew out of Calvinist theology and the unique pattern of settlement that characterized New England. New towns that grew up on the westward-moving frontier were settled by Congregationalists.

In the Congregational church, each congregation was governed by its own elected trustees. Although Congregational churches had a large degree of autonomy in their governance, they were united by their adherence to Calvin's doctrines. The Congregationalist pattern of local control extended into political organization and education. As political units, New England towns had their own elected boards of trustees. In the governance and control of schools, the pattern was repeated with the residents of districts electing school boards to establish, support, and maintain schools.

Although Calvinism affected how American towns and schools were governed, it also greatly influenced how people viewed each other socially and economically. Resting on the doctrine of predestination, the elect were to exhibit righteous and productive lives. The economic wealth that was the mark of the middle class was not an obstacle to salvation but rather an outward sign of membership in the elect. The possessors of wealth had to use it in the right way, for good purposes and uplifting human beings. Wealthy people were to act as stewards of the economy in much the same way that the good steward in the Bible invested and multiplied the money that his master had given him. Modern stewards were to invest profits to make more profits; in turn, wealth could be used for churches, schools, libraries, and other institutions that ennobled and uplifted life and helped create the Christian common-wealth on Earth. By providing the political and social environment in which Christian men and women could live their lives according to the laws of the Scripture, they would be prepared to enter the heavenly city for eternity.

Although there were a variety of Protestant theologies and churches, Calvinist religious doctrines, with their emphasis on socially and economically productive lives, came to be known as the "Protestant ethic." In the United States, the Protestant ethic had a great formative effect on the institutions of the late eighteenth and nineteenth centuries. The generalized Evangelical Protestantism that was so important to American institution building exemplified Calvinist views of knowledge and values.

The ethic of Evangelical Protestantism in the United States strongly encouraged the establishment of common or public schools that would prepare a literate, law-abiding, Bible-reading, and economically productive citizenry. Common schools were to prepare responsible citizens who could intelligently elect their representatives to office and instill a basic knowledge of and respect for law and order into the young. Skills and values conducive to economic productivity would be stressed along with reading, writing, and arithmetic. Values such as a sense of the importance of time, being diligent in one's work, the need to achieve, the deferring of immediate gratification for long-term success, and other attitudes that made for effective work and management skills in factories, shops, and stores were emphasized in the common schools.

By the late nineteenth and early twentieth centuries, the attitudes and values taught in the common schools came to dominate the public philosophy. Although the religious sectarianism of their Calvinist origins had diminished, they were part of a generalized Protestant ethic. In popular literature, Horatio Alger wrote hundreds of novels in which young men, possessed of the right values, conquered all kinds of adversity. By the merits of their own talents, the heroes of the Alger narratives applied themselves so successfully that they gained the wealth and position they so deserved. A "captain of industry," like Andrew Carnegie, who in Alger-like manner rose from shop boy to industrialist, fulfilled the role of economic stewardship. In his own statement of philosophy, *The Gospel of Wealth,* Carnegie told of an economically prosperous America where modern stewards endowed libraries, universities, and schools.[23]

Conclusion: An Assessment

Calvin's theology, with its stress on literacy and education, cast a lengthened intellectual, as well as religious, shadow over Europe and North America. His connections between religion, civil society, and economic life forged a way of thinking, a religious world view, that became known as the Protestant ethic.

During his own lifetime, Calvin established a strong intellectual basis for reformed Protestant theology. Education became a partner in the effort to design a commonwealth on Earth modeled along the lines of Calvin's reformed doctrines. The "New Jerusalem" was to be a city in which the inhabitants followed a code of civil behavior prescribed by the Bible.

Calvinism also signaled a modernization of Christianity to fit the new economic situation, especially the rise of the middle class. Calvin's doctrines of a righteous people engaged in industrious undertakings that benefitted the commonwealth and the Church suited the modernizing trends of an emergent capitalism. The Calvinist stress on literacy as a tool of salvation fulfilled both religious and economic objectives. As conceived by Calvin and his followers, the school became an institution that emphasized the moral formation of those who attended it.

In the New World, Calvinism would find a setting in which it bore institutional fruit. New England colonies, then states, became the cradle of a transplanted version of Calvinism. The common school movement incorporated the intellectual and moral objectives of a civic culture infused with a sense of religious mission.

Discussion Questions

1. What elements in the historical and cultural context provided the setting for the Protestant Reformation?
2. Examine the elements of continuity and change that existed between the Renaissance and the Protestant Reformation.
3. Compare and contrast the personalities of Martin Luther and John Calvin as leaders of the Protestant Reformation.
4. Examine the relationships between Protestantism and educational change.
5. What were the basic theological elements in Calvin's reformed Protestantism?
6. Why did education become such an important force in Calvin's religious outlook?
7. What is the historical and educational significance of Calvin's reformed theology?

Research and Essay Topics

1. In a comparative essay, analyze the personalities of Luther and Calvin as religious reformers.
2. Write a brief that either supports or challenges the proposition that Calvinism was a religion that expressed the aspirations of the middle classes.
3. Prepare a research paper that examines the Calvinist influence in the New England colonies.
4. Prepare a research paper that examines the influence of Evangelical Protestantism on the common school movement.
5. In a paper, discuss the effect of the Protestant ethic on U.S. life.
6. In a paper, examine the role of the public school as a transmitter of moral values.

Notes

1. A useful general history of the Protestant Reformation is De Lamar Jensen, _Reformation Europe: An Age of Reform and Revolution_ (Lexington, Mass.: D. C. Heath, 1981).

2. Matthew Spinka, ed., _Advocates of Reform: From Wycliffe to Erasmus_ (Philadelphia: Westminster Press, 1953), 22–23.

3. Biographies of Luther are Roland Bainton, _Here I Stand: A Life of Martin Luther_ (Nashville: Abingdon Press, 1959); E. G. Schwiebert, _Luther and His Times: The Reformation from a New Perspective_ (St. Louis: Concordia Press, 1950); Richard Friedenthal, _Luther: His Life and Times_ (New York: Harcourt Brace Jovanovich, 1967); and Bernhard Lohse, _Martin Luther: An Introduction to His Life and Work_ (Philadelphia: Fortress Press, 1986).

4. Bainton, 39–51.

5. Hans Engelland, _Melanchthon on Christian Doctrine: Logi Communes, 1555._ Translated by Clyde L. Manschreck (New York: Oxford University Press, 1965), xxv–xxvii.

6. Robert Ulich, ed., _Three Thousand Years of Educational Wisdom: Selections from Great Documents_ (Cambridge, Mass.: Harvard University Press, 1971), 218–38.

7. Gerald L. Gutek, _A History of the Western Educational Experience_ (Prospect Heights, Ill.: Waveland Press, 1995), 141–143.

8. John H. Leith, ed., _Creeds of the Churches: A Reader in Christian Doctrine from the Bible to the Present_ (New York: Doubleday, 1963).

9. For the interrelationships of the Renaissance and Reformation, see Lewis W. Spitz, _The Renaissance and Reformation Movements_ (Chicago: Rand McNally, 1971); and Lewis W. Spitz, _The Religious Renaissance of the German Humanists_ (Cambridge, Mass.: Harvard University Press, 1963).

10. Williston Walker, _John Calvin: The Organizer of Reformed Protestantism_ (New York: Shocken Books, 1969), 23.

11. Thomas H. Parker, _John Calvin: A Biography_ (Philadelphia: Westminster Press, 1975).

12. Ibid., 4.

13. Walker, 49.

14. Emanuel Stickelberger, _Calvin._ Translated by David G. Gelzer (London: James Clarke and Co., 1959), 16.

15. Ibid., 17.

16. Ibid., 23.

17. John Calvin, _Institutes of the Christian Religion._ Translated by Henry Beveridge (Grand Rapids, Mich.: Eerdmans Publishing Co., 1933).

18. William R. Estep, _Renaissance and Reformation_ (Grand Rapids, Mich.: Eerdmans Publishing Co., 1986), 235–42.

19. John Calvin, _Tracts and Treatises on the Doctrine and Worship of the Church._ Vol. 2. Translated by Henry Beveridge (Grand Rapids, Mich.: Eerdmans Publishing Co., 1958), 137–62.

20. Ibid., 340–57.

21. For the relationships of the printing press and Protestant education, see Carmen Luke, _Pedagogy, Printing and Protestantism: The Discourse on Childhood_ (Albany: State University of New York Press, 1989).

22. Sheldon S. Cohen, _A History of Colonial Education, 1607–1776_ (New York: John Wiley and Sons, 1974), 29–69.

23. Andrew Carnegie, _The Gospel of Wealth and Other Timely Essays_ (Cambridge, Mass.: Harvard University Press, 1962).

Suggestions for Further Reading

Bainton, Roland. *Here I Stand: A Life of Martin Luther.* Nashville: Abingdon Press, 1959.

Calvin, John. *Institutes of the Christian Religion.* Translated by Henry Beveridge. Grand Rapids, Mich.: Eerdmans Publishing Co., 1933.

————. *Calvin's Ecclesiastical Advice.* Louisville, Kentucky: Westminster/John Knox Press, 1991.

————. *Tracts and Treatises on the Doctrine and Worship of the Church.* Translated by Henry Beveridge. Grand Rapids, Mich.: Eerdmans Publishing Co., 1958.

Estep, William R. *Renaissance and Reformation.* Grand Rapids, Mich.: Eerdmans Publishing Co., 1986.

Friedenthal, Richard. *Luther: His Life and Times.* New York: Harcourt Brace Jovanovich, 1967.

Graham, W. Fred. *The Constructive Revolutionary: John Calvin and His Socioeconomic Impact.* Richmond: John Knox Press, 1971.

Jensen, de Lamar. *Reformation Europe: An Age of Reform and Revolution.* Lexington, Mass.: D. C. Heath, 1981.

Leith, John H., ed. *Creeds of the Churches: A Reader in Christian Doctrine from the Bible to the Present.* New York: Doubleday, 1963.

Lohse, Bernhard. *Martin Luther: An Introduction to His Life and Work.* Philadelphia: Fortress Press, 1986.

Luke, Carmen. *Pedagogy, Printing and Protestantism: The Discourse on Childhood.* Albany: State University of New York Press, 1989.

McGrath, Alister, E. *A Life of John Calvin: A Study in the Shaping of Western Culture.* Oxford, U.K., and Cambridge, Mass: Basil Blackwell, 1990.

Parker, Thomas H. *John Calvin: A Biography.* Philadelphia: Westminster Press, 1975.

Schreinter, Susan E. *The Theater of His Glory: Nature and the Natural Order in the Thought of John Calvin.* Durham, N.C.: Labyrinth Press, 1991.

Schwiebert, E. G. *Luther and His Times: The Reformation from a New Perspective.* St. Louis: Concordia Press, 1950.

Spinka, Matthew, ed. *Advocates of Reform: From Wycliffe to Erasmus.* Philadelphia: Westminster Press, 1953.

Spitz, Lewis W. *The Religious Renaissance of the German Humanists.* Cambridge, Mass.: Harvard University Press, 1963.

————. *The Renaissance and Reformation Movements.* Chicago: Rand McNally, 1971.

Towns, Elmer L., ed. *A History of Religious Educators.* Grand Rapids, Mich.: Baker Book House, 1975.

Walker, Williston. *John Calvin: The Organizer of Reformed Protestantism.* New York: Schocken Books, 1969.

Warfield, Benjamin B. *Calvin and Calvinism.* New York: Oxford University Press, 1931.

Johann Amos Comenius: Pansophist Educator and Proponent of International Education

Johann Amos Comenius at age 50, from an engraving; reproduction from the collections of the Library of Congress.

C hapter 8 examines the life, educational philosophy, teaching methods, and contributions of Johann Amos Comenius (1592–1670), an early pioneer in reforming schools. A post-Reformation figure, Comenius lived during a time of intense religious intolerance and persecution. The Moravian Brethren, the small religious denomination that he led, was persecuted by the larger churches. For Comenius, the general enlightenment that resulted from a genuine education was a means of creating a more understanding, tolerant, and humane social order.

In this chapter, the development of Comenius' ideas on education are examined in their historical context and in terms of their continuing significance for teaching and learning. First, the general social, political, and intellectual context of seventeenth-century Europe in which Comenius lived and worked is described. Second, Comenius' life is analyzed to determine its effect on the evolution of his educational ideas. Third, Comenius' contributions to an enlightened concept of childhood, a more humane school environment, and effective methods of teaching are examined. Fourth, the significance of his educational contributions are assessed.

To organize your thoughts as you read this chapter, you might focus on the following questions:

- What were the major trends in the historical context, the time and situation, in which Comenius lived?
- How did Comenius' life, his educational biography, shape his ideas on education?
- How did Comenius' educational philosophy determine his educational policies and practices?
- What has been the enduring effect of Comenius' contributions to education?

The Historical Context of Comenius' Life

Comenius' life coincided with the period of intense religious and nationalistic conflict that swept Europe during the Thirty Years War. Pitting Catholic against Protestant, the sectarian conflict devastated Europe. In addition, the various Protestant denominations were so split on theological issues that they were unable to present a united front against their adversaries.[1]

The war began over religious hostilities, but also was the focus of a power struggle by Europe's great powers to gain supremacy. At various times, the Holy Roman Empire ruled by the Catholic Hapsburg dynasty was pitted against the Protestant kingdoms of Denmark and Sweden. The German states were arrayed on both sides. France, although a Catholic country, fought against the Hapsburgs. The interplay of big power politics and religious hostility took its toll on the smaller states of central Europe, especially Bohemia and Moravia.

Comenius' life and educational contributions need to be considered against the background of European religious, political, and military history, especially the Thirty Years War. A brief examination of the war is helpful in understanding the dilemmas and motivation encountered by educators like Comenius, who sought to develop a theory of international education as a means of bringing about understanding and peace among nations and people. The events of the Thirty Years War, demonstrating the difficulties in keeping conflicts localized, reveal how wars escalate and grow out of control.

The war began in Bohemia, part of the Holy Roman empire, ruled by the Hapsburg Emperor Ferdinand II, a zealous Catholic.[2] An underlying cause of the war was Ferdinand's policy of reversing the effects of the Protestant Reformation and fully restoring Catholicism to his empire. Added to his religious motive was Ferdinand's diplomatic and strategic goal of controlling central Europe.[3]

The specific event that precipitated the war was the "Defenestration of Prague" on May 21, 1618, when Bohemian Protestant rebels seized the palace and threw Ferdinand's governor and representatives from its windows. Although they fell unharmed into a manure pile, the event unleashed a conflict that would devastate central Europe. Like other wars, a conflict that began as a localized incident escalated into a widespread war.

A decisive battle occurred at White Mountain in 1620. Ferdinand II's army supported by his relatives, the Spanish Hapsburgs, were commanded by the master strategists Count Johan Tilly (1559–1632) and Duke Albrecht von Wallenstein (1583–1634). Wallenstein in particular was a skilled commander, who insisted that occupied areas should pay for the support of his army, which had defeated them. In 1620, the armies of the Emperor, the so-called Catholic League, defeated the Protestant army at the Battle of White Mountain. With the Protestant forces routed in Bohemia, the Brethren and other Protestant denominations were subjected to severe repression by the Hapsburg authorities. At this point Denmark, led by King Christian IV, (1577–1648) entered the war on the Protestants' side. Christian, who personally led his armies, enjoyed a great popularity with the middle classes of Norway and Denmark. In 1626, he and his armies were defeated at the battle of Lutter-am-Barenburg by the Catholic armies of Tilly and Wallenstein. After his defeat his fortunes suffered as he lost popular support.

Fearing a total Hapsburg victory, Sweden, a Lutheran bastion, joined the Protestant cause under the leadership of its king, Gustavus Adolphus II (1594–1632), an astute military strategist.[4] Sweden's armies, now the focal point of the Protestant cause, turned the tide in several battles in the German states. It was at this point that Comenius tried to enlist Swedish help in gaining religious recognition and toleration for his church. However, the diplomatic intrigue and territorial objectives of the European great powers became even more complicated and obscured the events that had caused the conflict in the first place.

France, a largely Catholic country whose foreign policy was directed by its wily prime minister, the Roman Catholic Cardinal Richilieu, entered the war against the Catholic Hapsburgs in 1643. France's entry into the war was for strategic rather than religious reasons.

In 1648, the Treaty of Westphalia, a negotiated settlement, ended the war which had begun in 1618. The treaty weakened the position of the Austrian Hapsburg emperor from the exalted position of the Holy Roman Emperor to the status of another European monarch. The provisions of the treaty gave to the various German princes the right to determine the religion of their subjects. The major powers, such as France, gained some territory. The Calvinists were accorded religious recognition and toleration along with the Catholics and Lutherans. However, there was no improvement in the situation of the smaller churches such as Comenius' Brethren.

Along with the military events of the Thirty Years War, the development of Comenius' educational ideas also must be examined in the theological context of his times, especially that of his church. The theology of the Unity of the Brethren, Comenius' small church, was based on the teachings of Jan Hus. The church's membership was located predominantly in Bohemia and Moravia, then part of the Holy Roman Empire and now part of the Czech Republic. Hus (1369—1415) was a Bohemian religious reformer and critic of Catholicism.[5] He was condemned as a heretic by the Council of Constance and burned at the stake on July 6, 1415. After his death, small communities of religious reformers kept his ideas alive. One of these groups was the Unity of the Brethren, the church that Comenius would lead as a bishop. The name of the church, Unity of the Brethren, was based on the strong belief that all Christians should be united in one faith rather than torn apart by denominational tensions, rivalry, and war. While the Brethren believed in Christian unity, they did not believe that the path of salvation came from a single set of theological doctrines and practices. Rather, they took an ecumenical position that the belief in Christ should unite all believers. The age in which Comenius worked and wrote was an intensely religious one. Religion and education went hand-in-hand. Most of the schools that existed were conducted under the auspices of religious denominations.

After the defeat of the Protestant forces at the Battle of White Mountain, the victorious Hapsburgs restored Roman Catholicism as the official religion in Bohemia and Moravia. The Brethren became a people in diaspora. To escape persecution in their native Bohemia and Moravia, the Brethren took refuge in other countries in Europe. Some like Comenius fled to Poland, while others went to Hungary and Germany. To understand Comenius' work on education, he needs to be understood as an exile seeking a home. When he could find no particular country to call his own, his vision grew to encompass a worldwide home.

Although the Thirty Years War ended in the Treaty of Westphalia in 1648, the peace did not end the exile of the Brethren from their native Moravia and Bohemia. The leading powers, exhausted by the protracted conflict, made no provision for the members of the little church. If they returned to Bohemia and Moravia, they had to convert to Catholicism.

The revival of the Brethren stemmed from a group of church members who, fleeing Moravia, were given shelter by a pietistical German nobleman, Count Zinzendorf (1700–1760), on his estate in Silesia. Members of the Brethren on Zinzendorf's estate established a community named Herrnhut. In 1727, a revival revitalized the community and missionaries of the Moravian Brethren came to North America to work among the Indians. Their settlements and schools in North Carolina, Pennsylvania, and Ohio bore the imprint of Comenius' educational work.

Comenius' Life and Career

Comenius was born on March 28, 1592, in Moravia. The Komensky family (Comenius' family name) lived in the Moravian town of Uhersky Brod, where Johann received his elementary education. His parents died in 1604 when he was twelve years old. However, he was able to secure an education and to attend the Universities of Herborn and Heidelberg. After completing his higher education, he returned to his native Moravia and was ordained a minister in the Unity of the Brethren in 1616. In 1618, he was appointed pastor to the congregation of Brethren at Fulnek. In addition to his religious ministry, he also served as principal of the local parish school.[6]

In 1620, the year in which the Protestant army was defeated in the Battle of White Mountain, a series of tragedies began for Comenius, his family, and his church. After the defeat at White Mountain, Protestant leaders were hunted down by the Imperial forces. Comenius' home was burned and he barely escaped with his life. For the next seven years, from 1620 to 1627, Comenius and his family hid in Bohemia. During this time his wife and two small children died, victims of plague. It was at this time that he wrote *The Labyrinth of the World* and *The Paradise of the Heart*. Arising from his experiences as a hunted exile and a victim of war, Comenius' *Labyrinth of the World* described the tortuous path of a pilgrim, an exile like himself, who sought but failed to find peace and security in the world. The pilgrim's quest was satisfied only by union with Christ.[7]

In 1628, Comenius fled across the border into Poland to begin forty-two years of exile from his native Moravia. He located in the city of Leszno, which was forty miles south of the larger city of Poznan, where he ministered to his flock, wrote, and taught. In 1632, he was elected a bishop of the Brethren. In the same year, he also published his *Janua Linguarum Reserata*, which described his method of language instruction. Once again, he and the Brethren were victims of war. During an enemy raid on Leszno, his home was burned along with his manuscripts and books.[8]

In 1641, Comenius visited England as a guest of the educational reformer, Samuel Hartlib (1596–1662), an associate of Oliver Cromwell. While in England, he met with people who were interested in educational and religious reform. Once again war interfered with his educational work. This time the English Civil War between King James' supporters and Cromwell's republicans caused him to leave England in 1642.

Comenius moved to Elbing in Prussia. He continued his efforts to persuade the Swedish government, under Chancellor Oxenstierna (1583–1654), to act as protector of the interests of the Brethren and secure their right to resume their lives in Bohemia and Moravia. By this time, Oxenstierna, weary of central European affairs, was more concerned with reforming Swedish politics and improving its economy. Comenius' efforts to enlist Swedish military and diplomatic assistance were unsuccessful. He returned to the Polish city of Leszno, the site of his first exile.

In 1650, Comenius, once again on the move, located in Saros-Patak in Hungary, which bordered Bohemia and Moravia and brought him close to his native land. Here he organized schools and wrote his religious treatise, *Lux in Tenebris*.

In 1656, Comenius accepted an invitation to locate in Amsterdam in the Netherlands where he attracted the interest and sympathy of Ludovicus de Geer (1587–1652) who became his financial benefactor. Under de Geer's patronage, Comenius was able to complete his major educational work, *Opera Didactica,* published in 1657. Next, in 1658, he published his famous illustrated textbook, *Orbis Pictus*.

In 1668, Comenius published *Via Lucis, The Way of Light,* in which he sought to fashion a plan of international understanding and harmony with which the warring churches and nations of Europe would live in peace. His various works on education were published as *Opera Didactica Omnia* from 1657 to 1668. Throughout his life Comenius was working on a comprehensive publication that encompassed all the world's knowledge. Introductory volumes in this massive work, titled *Panergesia* and *Panaugia,* were published but the work was never completed.[9]

During his life, Comenius was a renowned educator and his advice on educational matters was sought throughout Europe. He continued his research, writing, and educational and religious work until his death in 1670.

Comenius and Pansophist Education

As an educational theorist, Comenius' educational philosophy embraced the broad, overarching goal of Pansophism. Literally meaning all knowledge, Comenius' Pansophism was a synthesis of principles derived from theology, philosophy, and science.[10] Comenius based his theological principles on the tradition of Protestant reformist thought, especially the doctrines preached by Jan Hus. His philosophical underpinnings were in the mode of Realism; there were real objects that could be known by human beings through their senses. Influenced by Francis Bacon, Comenius saw science as an instrument that was complementary to the Bible in providing human beings with knowledge of God's universe. Through the inductive method, human beings could observe their world and find through their observations the principles that governed nature.[11]

Derived from theology, philosophy, and science, Pansophism promised universal knowledge, which was to lead the knower to God, the source of all truth and goodness. Such knowledge was intrinsically valuable to the knower in that it was truth in its purest form. As the funded knowledge of the human race, it was a valuable and indispensable cultural legacy. It was also instrumentally valuable in that the objects of knowledge could be used to secure a better and more peaceful life. Pansophism's claim of providing humankind with universal knowledge was both a way of knowing God and of achieving worldwide peace. While Comenius regarded the Bible as an unerring guide to human conduct, he believed that human knowledge, refined in a structured and orderly way in the various sciences, came from God. As human beings acquired knowledge of the sciences and humanities, they gained greater insights into God. God was all-knowing and hence possessed all knowledge which was revealed to humankind both through scholarly and scientific investigation and by the Holy Scriptures.

Comenius believed that the turmoil, trouble, and conflicts of his age were caused by ignorance. Ignorance, a condition of either not knowing or falsely knowing, contributed to intolerance, discrimination, and prejudice. Both he and the Brethren, the displaced people or refugees of the seventeenth century, were the victims of intolerance. Complete knowledge, Comenius believed, would bring people closer to God and to each other. Thus, Pansophism, an early form of international or peace education, was an argument for universal knowledge and education.

As an international or peace educator, Comenius fully anticipated the creation of a new world order of peace-making and peace-keeping institutions. To create these new institutions, the leaders of the existing institutions—the churches, states, and schools—had to reconstruct or redesign them from rival and contentious institutions into cooperative ones.[12] Further, schools were to be transformed from agencies that indoctrinated children with a sense of their particular church or state's superiority into agencies that cultivated an ecumenical vision of a peaceable kingdom in which all could live in mutual respect.

Through his experiences as an educator, Comenius developed important insights into child nature, psychology, and development. These psychological insights were applied to classroom instruction. Unlike those who regarded childhood as a time of life to be lived through rather than enjoyed, Comenius saw childhood as a crucial part of the whole plan of human growth and development. In drawing his conclusions about child growth and development, Comenius looked to nature. This tendency to relate child development to nature and its processes can also be observed in the work of such educational theorists as Rousseau, Pestalozzi, and Froebel whose ideas are treated in later chapters of the book.

Unlike later naturalistic educators such as Rousseau and Spencer, who emphasized the natural over the supernatural, Comenius viewed the supernatural and natural orders as complementary. Nature, the physical and visible world that human beings observed through their senses, expressed the divine design of its creator. From his reflections and observations of nature, Comenius developed a set of principles for the use of educators. Among them were (1) nature has an appropriate time for growth and development; (2) natural operations are orderly and sequential; (3) nature proceeds gradually and completely; and (4) nature completes whatever it begins.[13]

An important concept, drawn from Comenius' observations, was that in the growth of plants and animals, nature has its own intrinsic time table. Nothing can be hurried to grow unless it is ready to do so. Readiness that cooperates with natural forces and stimuli makes healthy development possible.

Further, based on the concept of readiness, childhood can be broken down into important developmental phases. Each phase has appropriate learning experiences. It was important for teachers to know the stages of development and base their teaching on these stages. The goal of tying instruction to child growth and development was to make both teaching and learning efficient and effective.

Given Comenius' premise that complete knowledge was both possible and desirable, instructional time had to be used efficiently. The lesson needed to be appropriate to the child's readiness and ability to learn as determined by the particular developmental stage. Effectiveness meant the child would succeed in mastering the skill or body of knowledge that was being taught. Comenius' stress on efficiency and effectiveness of instruction did not mean that teaching should be performed in a mechanical and impersonal manner. Rather, he wanted schools to be warm, emotionally secure, and satisfying environments for children. Indeed, schools that were suited to child nature and development would be effective learning centers. For Comenius, schools were made for children rather than children being made for schools.

As a former school principal and educational theorist, Comenius in *The Great Didactic* directed his attention to school reform. Based upon his concept of readiness for learning and natural stages of human growth and development, Comenius designed a sequential system of schools. In *The School of Infancy,* he put forth his ideas on early childhood education, which today would be called parenting education or home learning. From birth until age six, children were to be educated at home by their parents, especially by their mother, the first and best teacher. Anticipating the work of Piaget and Erikson by almost three hundred years, Comenius argued that the first six years were the crucial foundational period for children's later development.[14] The home should be a loving and secure environment where parents embody the values and ethics worthy of imitation by children. Unlike those who saw play as idleness, Comenius advised parents to encourage play activities where children exercised their muscles, renewed themselves, and imitated adult behavior.

The next six years, from six through twelve, was the period of attending primary school. Here, children would become literate and skilled in their native language, the vernacular spoken in their home and community. The primary school curriculum included reading, writing, religious education, mathematics, history, geography, music, art, and crafts.[15]

In his advice on the management of primary schools, Comenius was an early proponent of what is now called "effective schooling." He especially wanted to end the domination of instruction by exclusive reliance on the recitation. According to the recitation method, each child, waiting his or her turn, would come before the teacher's desk and recite a previously memorized lesson.[16] Rather than using children's spontaneous curiosity, the recitation was a cut-and-dried form of monotonous recital. The process of having each child recite individually also was an ineffective use of instructional time. In place of the recitation, Comenius stressed grouping children so they could work on the same lesson simultaneously and interact cooperatively. To facilitate grouping, Comenius developed a design for school organization in which children were clustered in grades or levels.

Comenius also took a radical stand against the corporal punishment and psychological repression commonly practiced in seventeenth-century schools. For him, such schools were "slaughterhouses of the mind." Teachers were to be gentle and persuasive and instruct children without blows, threats, and ridicule. Discipline was to be fair and administered without anger.

After six years of primary school were completed, students would continue for another six years in the Latin grammar school, a secondary institution, which they attended from twelve to eighteen. Here, the curriculum consisted of Greek, Latin, and Hebrew, languages which were then part of a conventional secondary education. Comenius' Latin school curriculum, reflecting his Pansophist ideology, was much enriched over that of conventional grammar schools. It included mathematics, geometry, physical and natural sciences, astronomy, history, ethics, rhetoric, music, and theology.[17] Along with these formal studies, opportunities for recreation were included to refresh the students.

Comenius developed his educational theories at a time when language learning, especially Latin, dominated much of secondary schooling. Like other educators of the period, Comenius continued to stress the importance of learning one's own language as well as the classical languages of Greek and Latin. In his conception of

Pansophist knowledge, language learning was a necessary instrument in acquiring knowledge. Thus Comenius did not attack verbalism to the degree that Rousseau did in the eighteenth century and Pestalozzi did in the nineteenth century. However, he was moving away from teaching that was dominated exclusively by words. He recognized that instruction could be made more realistic and meaningful to children by introducing objects or pictures of objects into the classroom. His book, *Orbis Pictus,* or *The Visible World,* was an innovation in textbooks. The illustrations it provided were a new way of teaching languages.[18]

To complete his system of schools, Comenius developed the idea of the Pansophist university, an institution of higher learning to be attended by the most intellectually gifted students. Here, students would study the entire range of knowledge embraced in the Pansophist philosophy of education. Learned professors would teach classes, lecture, and prepare scholarly books.

Comenius sought to develop strategies for educational effectiveness and efficiency. Concerned with losing valuable instructional time, he urged that the processes of schooling not waste that precious commodity. His work as a textbook writer and pedagogical innovator was directed toward getting the most out of the time allotted for schooling. While he was concerned with using time effectively, Comenius also believed this concern for time should not diminish the humanitarian concern of the teacher for children. During his life he had seen enough of war, torment, and coercion. In the school he envisioned, children were to be liberated to use their senses and not be repressed. Above all, the Comenian ideal in education stressed the mutual respect of teacher and learner.

Conclusion: An Assessment

Perhaps to us who live in a world characterized by the explosion of knowledge, Comenius' vision of Pansophism or the possibility of attaining universal knowledge is naive. The modern world is characterized by ever-increasing new developments in science, medicine, and technology. Modern science and technology is characterized by specialization. Indeed, much of modern education is designed to prepare specialists who have expertise in a limited area of knowledge. Little of modern education is geared to cultivate the generalist who seeks to integrate all knowledge, as Comenius prescribed.

Upon reflection, however, the Comenian vision is not as naive as it appears. While Comenius thought of organizing all knowledge in books, today's information technology might make his vision more a reality in the twenty-first century than was possible in his own time. Computers, with their ability to store and retrieve masses of data and information, may make universal knowledge a reality.

If Comenius were alive today, he would undoubtedly endorse the effectiveness and efficiency of computer-based instruction. The graphics that computerized learning make possible is but a new version of the *Orbis Pictus.* He would endorse the efficient use of time that educational technology makes possible.

At the same time that Comenius would be receptive to educational technology and computer-based instruction, he would remind us that schools were made for children and not vice versa. Regardless of the technology and its efficiency, the child's nature, development, and readiness must always underlie instruction.

Comenius was an ecumenical educator who happened to live and work in a decidedly unecumenical age. Seventeenth-century schools were conducted under church auspices at a time when various denominations were in conflict. Schooling was catechetical and designed to instill the dogmas of the particular religion in an exclusionary way. Children were to learn the doctrines of their particular religion so they could defend their faith against religious adversaries. Comenius, in contrast, believed it was possible to have value-oriented religious education which reflected both denominational uniqueness as well as commonalities. While each could practice religion according to his or her denominational creed, all could feel unity in the commonality of Christian belief. In advance of his age, Comenius argued for a Council of the World's Churches.[19] In the twentieth century, the world's great religions have entered into ecumenical dialogue. Thus, Comenius was a prophet of ecumenism and ecumenical education.

Comenius' world was torn by sectarian contention and nationalistic ambitions. The Thirty Years War devastated Europe. In many parts of the world, war and senseless killing continue today. Just as Comenius and the Brethren were refugees in the seventeenth century, the twenty-first century will still have its victimized men, women, and children. Modern displaced people, the homeless, and refugees remain the people that an education based on the principles of Comenius seeks to restore to wholeness and dignity. Comenius would weep over the acts of terrorism and violence that grow increasingly commonplace today. For him, knowledge and education would still be the road humankind must take to reach the peaceable kingdom.

Discussion Questions

1. How did the context of the European Thirty Years War provide the background for the development of Comenius' educational theory?
2. Was the historical context in which Comenius lived and worked a continuance of the Protestant Reformation and Catholic Counterreformation or was it a new development?
3. How did the key events in Comenius' life shape his outlook on the world and his view of education?
4. Identify and examine the elements of continuity and change in Comenius' educational theory.
5. Debate the relevance of Comenius' Pansophism for contemporary international or peace education.
6. How was Comenius an exponent of children's rights?

Research and Essay Topics

1. In a comparative paper, compare and contrast the theologies of Calvin, discussed in Chapter 7, and Comenius.

2. In a paper, develop a character sketch of Comenius.
3. In an essay, examine the key elements in Comenius' Pansophism.
4. If it is available in your library, review Comenius' *Orbis Pictus.*
5. In a paper, examine the character and competencies of a Comenian teacher.
6. In a paper, examine the themes of continuity and change as exemplified in Comenius' educational philosophy.

Notes

1. Among the histories of the Thirty Years War are David Maland. *Europe at War, 1600–1650* (Totowa, N.J.: Rowman and Littlefield, 1980); and Josef V. Polisensky. *War and Society in Europe, 1618–1644* (Cambridge, Mass.: Cambridge University Press, 1978).
2. Robert Bierley, S. J. *Religion and Politics in the Age of the Counterreformation: Emperor Ferdinand II, William Lamormaini, S.J. and the Formation of Imperial Policy* (Chapel Hill, N.C.: University of North Carolina Press, 1981).
3. Randy Petersen. "The Thirty Years War." *Christian History, VI* (1987), 17.
4. Charles R. L. Fletcher. *Gustavus Adolphus and the Struggle of Protestantism for Existence* (New York: G. P. Putnam's Sons, 1894).
5. Ezra H. Gillett. *The Life and Times of John Huss: The Bohemian Reformation of the Fifteenth Century* (New York: AMS Press, 1978).
6. Eve Chyhova Bock. "Seeking a Better Way." *Christian History, VI* (1987), 7.
7. Ibid., 8.
8. Ibid., 7.
9. Josef Smolik. "Comenius: A Man of Hope in a Time of Turmoil." *Christian History, VI* (1987), 16.
10. Paul Heidebrecht. "Learning from Nature: the Educational Legacy of Jan Amos Comenius." *Christian History, VI* (1987), 23.
11. Ibid.
12. Smolik, 18.
13. Heidebrecht, 23.
14. Jerome K. Clauser. "The Pansophist: Comenius." In Paul Nash, Andreas M. Kazamias, and Henry J. Perkinson, *The Educated Man: Studies in the History of Educational Thought* (New York: John Wiley and Sons, 1965), 165–88.
15. Heidebrecht, 35.
16. Ibid.
17. Lois Le Bar. "What Children Owe to Comenius." *Christian History, VI* (1987), 19.
18. Gerald L. Gutek, *A History of the Western Educational Experience* (Prospect Heights, Ill.: Waveland Press, 1995), 152–56.
19. Smolik, 18.

Suggestions for Further Reading

Busek, Vratislav, ed. *Comenius.* New York: Czechoslovak Society of Arts and Sciences, 1972.
Comenius, John Amos. *The Labyrinth of the World and the Paradise of the Heart.* New York: Arno Press, 1971.
———. *The Orbis Pictus of John Amos Comenius.* Syracuse, N.Y.: C. W. Bardeen Publisher, 1887.

————. *The School of Infancy*. Translated by Ernest M. Eller. Chapel Hill, N.C.: University of North Carolina Press, 1956.

Gillett, Ezra H. *The Life and Times of John Huss: The Bohemian Reformation of the Fifteenth Century*. New York: AMS Press, 1978.

Jakubec, Jan. *Johannes Amos Comenius*. New York: Arno Press, 1971.

Keatinge, M. W. *The Great Didactic of John Amos Comenius*. London: Adam and Charles Black, 1896.

Maland, David. *Europe at War 1600–1650*. Totowa, N.J.: Rowman and Littlefield, 1980.

Monroe, Will S. *Comenius and the Beginnings of Educational Reform*. New York: Arno Press, 1971.

Nash, Paul, Andreas M. Kazamias, and Henry J. Perkinson. *The Educated Man: Studies in the History of Educational Thought*. New York: John Wiley and Sons, 1965.

Polisensky, Josef V. *War and Society in Europe, 1618–1648*. Cambridge, Mass.: Cambridge University Press, 1978.

Spinka, Matthew. *John Amos Comenius, That Incomparable Moravian*. Chicago: University of Chicago Press, 1943.

Young, Robert F. *Comenius in England*. New York: Arno Press and New York Times, 1971.

Jean-Jacques Rousseau: Prophet of Naturalism

Jean-Jacques Rousseau, from an engraved illustration; reproduction from the collections of the Library of Congress.

This chapter discusses the life, educational philosophy, and contributions of Jean-Jacques Rousseau (1712–1778), one of the most intriguing and iconoclastic of the theorists who provoked a revolution in educational thinking and practice. Rousseau's life coincided with what historians have called the Age of Reason, or the Enlightenment, of the eighteenth century. Although Rousseau was a figure of the Enlightenment, he also anticipated the romanticism of the early nineteenth century. In Rousseau's ideas on education, we can feel the tension between reason and romanticism.

In this chapter, Rousseau's influence on Western and U.S. education is discussed in the historical context of the eighteenth-century Enlightenment and in terms of its enduring effect on educational philosophy and policy. First, the general intellectual, social, and political context in which Rousseau lived and worked is described. Second, Rousseau's biography, education, and career are analyzed to determine the evolution of his ideas. Third, the continuing effect of Rousseau's contributions to education is assessed. In this analysis, we shall see how Rousseau's ideas on education, especially as he expressed them in *Emile*, had an effect on the development of educational philosophy and instructional methods in the nineteenth and twentieth centuries. Of special interest is Rousseau's influence on child-centered educational practices.

To organize your thoughts as you read this chapter, you might focus on the following questions:

- What were the major trends of the historical context of the Enlightenment of the eighteenth century, the time and situation, in which Rousseau lived?
- How did Rousseau's life, his educational biography, shape his philosophy of education?
- How did Rousseau's educational philosophy influence educational policies and practices in later centuries?
- What has been the enduring impact of Rousseau's educational ideas?

The Historical Context of Rousseau's Life

Rousseau's life coincided with the century of Western history known as the Enlightenment. Although earlier periods in Western history have had their intellectual revivals, the Enlightenment stands out as the era that unleashed the essential intellectual and cultural trends that created a modern world view.[1] In many respects, Rousseau, who wrote on social, political, and educational philosophy, was a commanding person of the Enlightenment. He helped to break down some of the inherited beliefs and to introduce new ideas that would shape the future.

One of the major trends of the Enlightenment was a new way of thinking about nature and the place of a human being in a natural universe. Since the early Christian era, Western thought and culture had been shaped largely by the supernatural order. The world view of the Middle Ages, the medieval synthesis, rested on a dualistic conception of reality in which the natural order was viewed as inferior to the supernatural order. The age of the Reformation saw a reawakening of human interest in and awe of the supernatural order. The Enlightenment era saw theorists looking to nature to find clues on how life should be lived. Education was important in that, in the minds of the Enlightenment philosophers, it prepared people to live according to the principles of nature.

For many of the thinkers of the Enlightenment, including Rousseau, it was important that human beings stop gazing upward to heaven and begin to look at the natural world about them. They should observe and study natural phenomena and from their observations extract the principles needed to operate in the "real world." The principles of the natural universe could be discovered, the Enlightenment theorists believed, by means of science and use of the scientific method.

The scientific method, as the philosophes conceived of it, was an organized and careful way of observing natural phenomena. Through careful and consistent observation, it was possible to discern the laws or principles that made the universe work, such as the patterns of the revolution of the planets around the sun, the rotation of the Earth, the growth of plants, and the circulation of the blood in the body. There was no end to what humans could discover about their world if they applied themselves to the task correctly. For the Enlightenment generation, science meant actual observation and recording of phenomena and not the study of what the ancient Greek and Roman philosophers had written about nature. In the Enlightenment perspective, nature was "out there" waiting to be discovered.

For these theorists, the scientific method was designed to investigate whatever was observable to the senses, or empirical. The lenses of scientists' telescopes and microscopes were but special extensions of the senses that improved human sight. In the Enlightenment view, the world of objects took on a new meaning and new significance. Truth and meaning were found in the world of things and of people, not by contemplating ideal forms as Plato had insisted or in the spiritual dimension as Aquinas had written. Nor was the Bible the sole authority as Calvin had preached. No, the truth could be found by anyone who used the right approach—the scientific method.

The general intellectual strategy of Enlightenment philosophes including Rousseau, was to demystify. Although earlier thinkers such as Augustine, Aquinas, and Calvin had emphasized the importance and reverence that men and women should accord to their unanswerable questions, to the mysteries of life, the Enlightenment philosophes tried to explain everything. All questions—if they were valid questions—could be answered. With the Enlightenment came two different approaches to viewing reality and organizing education, one based on the assumption that the greatest and most powerful ideas rested on the mystery of life and the other on the assumption that there were no real mysteries. Whereas one version of education exalted mystery, the other sought to demystify life.

In the world view of the Enlightenment, nature was the key to understanding and shaping reality. Nature in the physical sense was all that was out there. This outward world, which human beings experienced through their senses, was orderly in that it manifested and followed certain patterns. Night followed day, the seasons of the year followed each other, the tides rose and fell with a regularity that could be plotted, measured, and predicted. The human body, too, went through stages of observable growth, as did the plants and animals. For the Enlightenment mind, nature was something of which human beings were a part. The natural universe was like a great world machine or clock that was in perpetual, rhythmic movement. Unlike the opinion of modern scientists, the great world mechanism that the Enlightenment philosophes saw as the natural universe was not relative or evolving. It was a beautiful and grandiose but stable world machine.[2]

Since the early Christian era, Western thought—through the Middle Ages, the Renaissance, and the Reformation—had exalted in an idea of a Supreme Being, a divine Creator, a personal God who intervened in world and human affairs. Although most of the Enlightenment theorists continued to believe in a source or origin or creator of some sort, to them this force was impersonal. For many of the Enlightenment thinkers, called deists, this original force was a kind of point of origin that got the universe started and then left it to function on its own perfect mechanism.

With the Enlightenment, the Western intellectual, cultural, and educational heritage experienced the birth of still another set of divergent tensions. The Judeo-Christian tradition with its emphasis on theism, a personal God, and revealed truth represented a strong and continuing part of this heritage. Now, the Enlightenment introduced a new way of thinking—a naturalistic and secular way of thought that insisted on the role of human intelligence to find ways of knowing everything.

It should be pointed out that the philosophes of the Enlightenment, like the humanists of the Renaissance, tended to be an initiated and educated elite. Although the Enlightenment theorists moved in a secular direction, the vast majority of the residents of Europe and the Americas continued to attend their churches and to read and follow their Bibles. Christianity in its Catholic and Protestant creedal formulations continued to be the source of truth and meaning for most people. However, there was an element about the Enlightenment philosophes that was different from the Renaissance classical humanists. Whereas the humanists regarded themselves as the guardians of truth, the philosophes saw themselves as the discoverers and disseminators of truth. Further, the truth of the philosophes was not meant to be merely deposited in libraries, it was intended to remake or reconstruct society along natural principles.

Although preceding eras—the classical Greek and Roman, the medieval, the Renaissance, and the Reformation—looked to the past to find truth, beauty, and wisdom, the Enlightenment theorists looked neither to ancient texts nor sacred books. The Enlightenment philosophes were forward looking and believed that they could shape human destiny. They believed that they could reconstruct or redesign social, political, and economic conditions to get the kind of consequences they desired. In other words, the human future could be made progressively better than the human past. The thinkers of the Enlightenment had a strong belief in the progress of the human race.

The basic strategy that the Enlightenment philosophes designed to make progress a reality was derived from their view of nature and the scientific method. If natural laws could be discovered by observing and identifying the patterns in physical nature, they reasoned, the same was true of society. By observing social, political, and economic interactions, it would be possible to discover the laws that governed human society. However, there was a problem. The intellectual and cultural baggage inherited from the prescientific past created institutional and attitudinal obstacles to social reform. For progress to take place, it would be necessary to purge or remove these obstacles.

Although the social theorists of the Enlightenment agreed that progress was a possibility, they differed on the form of the society of the future and the process that should be used to establish that society. These different views of social forms and processes marked the beginning of the age of ideologies. Initially coined by a group of French theorists called the ideologues, the term *ideology* meant a science of ideas. It was an alternative to the earlier metaphysical concepts that had preoccupied social theorists. What would emerge in the eighteenth, nineteenth, and twentieth centuries would be not one ideology but a number of competing ideologies.[3]

Although the Enlightenment theorists might debate the desired social structure and organization of the future, they generally agreed that established churches and absolute, inherited monarchies blocked the paths to social progress. Further, the educational institutions supported by these inherited residues from the past were agencies of miseducation. For example, the Catholic church in France and Spain and the Orthodox church in Russia were regarded as institutions based on unscientific dogmatic doctrines that suppressed scientific inquiry. Schools that were established and maintained under the auspices of the established churches were agencies of indoctrination rather than of genuine education. For true progress to occur, it would be necessary to disestablish official churches and free schools from their domination. In the political realm, absolute, hereditary monarchies in which kings or queens ruled by the "grace of God" without checks or balances were also regarded as impediments to progress. What was needed were new forms of government. New philosophies of civic education needed to be created that would prepare people to establish and maintain new governments.[4]

In the political realm, the inherited monarchies were in place, buttressed by aristocracies of birth. Some of the monarchs, such as Maria Theresa and Joseph of Austria, Catherine of Russia, and Frederick of Prussia, the "enlightened despots," talked about implementing limited reforms but actually did little. In the British colonies of North America and in France, full-scale revolutions would take place that would replace monarchical rule with republican government.

The currents of the Enlightenment held great importance for the future course of education. The emphasis on nature turned the interests of Enlightened educators to the study of human nature as a means of establishing the content and method of education. Instead of looking to ancient texts for guidance, Enlightenment theorists such as Rousseau urged people to look to the growth and development of the human being. By observing children, it was possible to identify and plot the course of development. Educators merely needed to identify and use the activities that were appropriate to a particular stage of human development.

This emphasis on nature and discovery of natural laws through science also had important implications for learning theory and teaching methods. Enlightened educators such as Rousseau and Pestalozzi and later the American progressive educators would emphasize the role of the senses in learning. Children would learn most effectively and efficiently by using their senses in observing and experiencing the natural objects of their environment.

Although certain key educational reformers such as Rousseau argued for following nature and learning through the senses, the inherited educational institutions were generally resistant to change. The catechism, the classics, and the authority that came from books dominated learning for years to come. Indeed, political, economic, and social changes often preceded the changes in education.

Rousseau as an Educational Theorist of the Enlightenment

The next section examines the life and educational ideas of Jean-Jacques Rousseau, a leading personality, critic, and author of the Enlightenment.[5] Rousseau's autobiographical confessions reveal how his own experiences in early childhood shaped his later view on life and education. The son of Suzanne Bernard and Isaac Rousseau, a watchmaker, Jean-Jacques was born in Geneva, Switzerland, the city where John Calvin once preached the doctrines of the Protestant Reformation. Rousseau's mother died when he was nine days old. Presumably his mother's death contributed to his choice of an orphan boy as the principal character in his educational novel, *Emile.* Jean-Jacques was reared by his father and an aunt. Rousseau claimed that his father favored him over his brother, who ran away from home to escape neglect. He claimed that he was overindulged by his highly emotional, impulsive aunt and his irresponsible, pleasure-loving father.[6]

Rousseau wrote that his father was his first tutor. Together, father and son read widely from an ill-sorted collection of books into the late hours of the night. The reading, ranging from romantic novels to such classic works as Ovid's *Metamorphoses* and Plutarch's *Lives of Famous Men,* stocked his mind with images far removed from reality. In *Emile,* Rousseau warned against introducing books too early in the child's life. It was much better, he advised, that children acquire a stock of direct experiences of their immediate environment before reading about abstract concepts about which they know little or nothing. Although his relationship appears to have been close with his father, it was brief. When Rousseau was ten, his father had an altercation with an army officer and fled Geneva to avoid imprisonment, thus ending the close relationship between father and son. Rousseau was then placed in the care of his uncle, Gabriel Bernard, and received a conventional primary education.

Rousseau went through a series of apprenticeships, first with a notary and then an engraver. Neither worked out satisfactorily. The notary dismissed Rousseau, whom he charged with neglecting his duties. He left the service of the engraver, whom he claimed treated him unfairly and harshly. Early in his life, Rousseau showed that he had difficulty in working as a subordinate and that he would flee from unpleasant situations.[7] Rousseau left Geneva in 1728 and went to Turin, Italy. In Turin, he found short-term employment as a footman for a wealthy family.

The next stage in Rousseau's odyssey took him to Chambery, in Savoy, where he lived with his paramour, a wealthy widow, Madame de Waren. She provided the money that enabled him to acquire a classical education and a knowledge of music. Under her tutelage, he was converted to Catholicism, a religion he would later abandon.

In 1739, when he was 27, Rousseau took a position as tutor to the two sons of M. de Mably. He disliked the actual practice of teaching but was intrigued by the broad issues of education. His experience as tutor in the de Mably household stimulated him to write his first treatise on education, the *Project of the Education of M. de Sainte-Marie.*[8]

In 1741, Rousseau was still searching to establish a place for himself. He went to Paris, where he earned a living by copying music. Paris was then the center of the intellectual ferment of the Enlightenment. Here, Rousseau was attracted to the circle of philosophes of the Enlightenment. Rousseau then received an appointment as secretary to the French ambassador in Venice. Although the appointment could have been the beginning of a diplomatic career, it was not. Rousseau quarreled with his superiors and lost his position.

Rousseau once again returned to Paris. Here, he began a love affair with Therese Levasseur, an illiterate servant. The couple had five children, all of whom were placed in foundling homes shortly after their births. She later became his common law wife. Readers of Rousseau's educational novel, *Emile,* find it ironic that Rousseau, an early proponent of child permissiveness, abandoned his own children.[9]

Established once again in Paris, Rousseau renewed his association with the philosophes and the encyclopedists such as Diderot and d'Alembert. In 1749, Rousseau won a contest for the best essay on "Has the Progress of the Arts and Sciences Contributed More to the Corruption or Purification of Morals?"[10] Unlike the defenders of the arts and sciences over the centuries, Rousseau answered that the arts and sciences tended to corrupt rather than liberate. He wrote articles for Diderot's *Encyclopedia;* his essay, "Discourse on Political Economy," appeared in 1755.[11] Rousseau next returned to Geneva and renounced Catholicism and reconverted to Protestantism. He regained his rights as a citizen of Geneva.

Once again, Rousseau returned to Paris, where he had an affair with the Comtesse d'Handetot. In his novel, *La Nouvelle Heloise,* published in 1761, the countess served as a model of the new woman. Rousseau's influential political commentary, *The Social Contract,* was published in 1762, the same year that he published *Emile.*[12]

Rousseau next went to England, where he was the guest of philosopher David Hume. Here, he started to work on his autobiographical confessions. However, his persistent tendency to quarrel with his friends occurred once again. He imagined that Hume was conspiring against him and quickly left England. In 1767, Rousseau was back in France. He completed the confessions in 1770. At the invitation of Count Wielhorski, Rousseau wrote a constitution for Poland, *The Government of Poland,* in 1772.[13]

On July 2, 1778, Rousseau died of uremia at Ermenonville, some thirty miles from Paris. He was buried on the Girardin estate. On October 11, 1794, his remains were transferred to the Pantheon in Paris.

Rousseau's Educational Writing

Although many of Rousseau's essays and books have educational implications, his didactic novel, *Emile,* is the most significant for education.[14] It exhibits several general features of the Enlightenment, especially the emphasis on nature and naturalism. Those who read Rousseau's *Emile* rarely leave the book in an objective frame of mind. For some readers, it is a challenging argument for education that is almost completely child centered. Others reject it as a wildly utopian book divorced from educational reality.

Like Plato's *Republic,* Rousseau's *Emile* has broad social and political as well as educational implications. Rousseau most likely did not intend that his educational ideas in *Emile* be taken literally. Rather, he wanted the story told in the novel to illustrate certain major principles about education. Foremost among these principles is Rousseau's belief in the original goodness of human nature. The book begins with "Everything is good as it comes from the hands of the Maker of the world but degenerates once it gets into the hands of man." Here, Rousseau is attacking the Calvinist doctrine of human depravity and the Catholic belief in the spiritual deprivation caused by original sin. For Rousseau, human beings are not initially evil or imperfect. Infants, although not moral beings, are intrinsically good. Human beings, Rousseau believed, are corrupted by their socialization in a corrupting society and their education in an artificial culture. For example, children are not born as liars, cheats, thieves, or murderers. They learn these vices in an unnatural and corrupt society. Their intrinsic natural goodness is spoiled by corrupting adults and their institutions. For Rousseau, the challenge is to place Emile in a natural environment in which his intrinsic natural goodness will grow and develop without being tainted by a corrupt society. If this can be accomplished, the child's self-identity can be formed around the natural instinct of *amour de soi,* or self-esteem. Rousseau contrasts amour de soi with *amour propre,* or selfishness, by which a person learns to manipulate others for his or her own purposes. If Emile is educated naturally, perhaps, as the new Adam of the Enlightenment he will be the father of a new, naturally educated race of men and women. In a world inhabited by naturally educated and uncorrupted persons, it might be possible to create social, political, and economic institutions that also function naturally.

The educational challenge for Rousseau is how to educate the new race of human beings. The inherited educational institutions and practices offer no solution. Most of the existing primary or elementary schools were church related. Their educational philosophy, based on theological premises, saw children as inherently corrupt creatures who needed to be disciplined by authoritarian teachers. Secondary schools, too, were agencies of miseducation. They stressed a book-centered, classical curriculum that ignored nature and science.

In his novel, Rousseau tells the story of total upbringing or education of a boy, from infancy to young manhood, by a tutor. The tutor has the sole responsibility of providing for Emile's moral, mental, and physical development. Further, Emile is the only student in that environment. It is in this educational setting that several important themes or elements in Rousseau's theory emerge.

The first element is the location where education takes place. Conventionally, children are educated in schools, institutional settings staffed by teachers and designed specifically to educate. Historically, the school curriculum focused on learning languages, one's own and others. Further, books were regarded as the authoritative sources of knowledge. For Rousseau and other naturalist educators, the conventional school setting was wrong and even miseducative. Child-centered educational reformers sought to replace the conventional school classroom with the "prepared environment." For Rousseau, Emile's prepared environment was a country estate where the growing boy could experience nature directly. Other educational reformers who have followed in Rousseau's theoretical footsteps have tried to redesign schools so that they are more natural settings.

It should be remembered that, although naturalistic reformers such as Rousseau see the conventional school as coercive and argue for greater freedom for the child, the prepared environment can be equally limiting on freedom. When the environment is prepared, it is designed to elicit certain outcomes. The person structuring the environment is creating a design that governs behavior in less direct ways than the conventional school but nonetheless in a controlling manner.

The second element in Rousseau's education of Emile concerns appropriateness in education. In the eighteenth century as well as in later periods, education was closely related to one's socioeconomic class. Although the middle class was a rising new class, the class structure was still based largely on ascription—the status one inherited by birth. In other words, children of an aristocrat were born to rule and enjoy the luxuries of wealth and status. Education was designed to prepare them for specific future roles. The same was true of the children of peasants, who were destined to be agricultural laborers. Although there are many signs that Emile is receiving an education that only a child of the upper classes could afford to receive, Rousseau introduces a new meaning to appropriateness in education—something that nature provides.

As a true son of the Enlightenment, Rousseau's world view saw nature as the sensible reality that human beings inhabited. He saw human nature functioning in parallel terms. In the various dimensions of nature—in plant and animal life—there were stages of development. In human life, too, there were clearly defined stages of development. In the human life span, individuals are born, go through infancy and childhood, come to maturity, reach old age, and eventually die. For each stage of development, there are appropriate kinds of activities and learning that come naturally from the conditions of the developmental stage. Although Rousseau was not the first theorist in the history of education to refer to stages of development, he did so in a dramatic way. Emile was experiencing the natural stages of human development without the intrusion of social and cultural variables.

We now turn to the stages of development that Rousseau identified in *Emile*. What Rousseau calls infancy, the earliest stage of human life, begins with birth and extends until age five. During the first months of infancy, the child is helpless and everything must be done for him. The nurturing process is directed to building a strong, healthy body; the diet consists of simple country food. Although the child is not allowed to harm himself, he is otherwise given freedom of movement so that his muscles are developed. In the early months of life, the infant has only vague feelings of pleasure and pain, rather than ideas. By moving and touching objects, he learns to distinguish himself from objects other than himself. Because ideas are products of data that come from the senses, the child's encounters and experiences with objects are important for learning about the environment. In his earliest years, the child experiences only pleasure and pain that come from the objects encountered in his exploration of the environment. At this stage, memory and imagination are inactive.

In infancy, the young child is like an unspoiled primitive person who is close to the original state of nature. If we want to discover the natural person, the clues to his identity can be found in simple, unaffected, childlike behavior. Education should be based on this behavior. Rousseau's discussion about education for infancy has implications for parenting. He advised parents to love their children, to avoid coercing them physically and emotionally, and to give them as much freedom as possible within a secure environment.

Rousseau emphasizes the mother's role in providing the child's early formative educational experiences.[15] It is through the mother's influence on her child that a general reform of morals will take place. Once women become good and loving mothers, then men will become good husbands and fathers. When the book moves to its conclusion and Emile is about to marry Sophie, her importance in exercising a gentle influence on her husband is stressed.

Like Rousseau, Emile lost his mother in infancy and is a well-to-do orphan. Emile is a strong and healthy boy of average intelligence. To avoid conflict with other adults over how Emile should be raised, the tutor is given complete control over his education.

Rousseau defined the second stage that Emile experiences as boyhood, the period from ages five through twelve. During these years, the boy's physical strength has increased and he is able to do more for himself.[16] It is at this stage that Emile becomes more aware of his personal self-identity and is becoming conscious of happiness and unhappiness. It is at this stage that Rousseau develops two concepts of moral development: *amour de soi* and *amour propre*. *Amour de soi* arises from a person's natural and instinctive self-interests. Natural virtues that arise from *amour de soi* should be cultivated. *Amour propre* is based on social relationships that either make the person a manipulator of other people or an other-directed person. It is important that Emile's educational environment be nonsocial. The tutor should maintain an even temperament in dealing with Emile and should maintain a balance between excessive severity and excessive indulgence.

Rousseau reminds us that children are still amoral and nonreasonable until age twelve. It is a waste of the tutor's time and effort to try to reason with Emile or to give orders and commands. Rousseau's warning against trying to instill morality through preaching essentially attacks the notion that concepts of good and bad and right and wrong can be instilled verbally. What is important is that Emile learn that his actions have consequences. Some actions will bring pleasure and others will bring pain.

Rousseau warns us about the "youthful sage," the boy or girl who is able to memorize and recite dates from history or poetry or literary passages. Those who praise such children have misconstrued words and their recitation with genuine knowledge. Such children adjust their behavior to reflect what adults expect of them. Neither is the child who has memorized the commandments in the catechism necessarily a good person. The youthful sage, although appearing to be intellectually precocious, is not living as a child lives but rather is forcing his behavior to fit patterns of performance designed to please adults.

Rousseau warns against the premature introduction of books. Children should not be pressured into reading. Emile will read when he is ready and needs to read. Rather than verbal learning, Rousseau argues that Emile needs more sensory and physical training. Emile observes the objects in the environment and comes to experience the effects of these objects. Most important at this stage is continued sensory training in which the various senses are used to check each other in estimating the size, shape, and dimensions of objects.

Rousseau defined the third stage in Emile's education as taking place from ages twelve through fifteen.[17] An important object during this stage is to introduce the concept of utility, or purpose. What are the uses of objects? Although nature studies have been an important aspect of Emile's education, they receive special emphasis during this period. Emile observes natural phenomena and asks questions about them. He learns natural science by observing what he sees about him on walks that he takes with his tutor in the forest and by planting vegetables in the garden. Geography, too, is learned firsthand from the study of the immediate environment rather than by studying maps and globes. Emile also learns a manual skill, such as carpentry, to learn the correct combination of mental and physical labor. He gets his first book, *Robinson Crusoe*, which tells how Crusoe, who is shipwrecked on a tropical island, survives in a natural setting. Along with experiencing a tale of the survival, Emile learns about the concept of mutual dependence that arises between Crusoe and Friday.

Emile's next stage of development might be termed adolescence, or the years between age fifteen and eighteen.[18] Emile now develops sexual interests and requires special guidance. When he has a question about sex, the tutor answers him directly, without mystery or coarseness. Emile is also becoming increasingly aware of social relationships and the needs and concerns of others. He is taken on short trips, where he sees people who are in less fortunate circumstances than his. At this point, he develops an awareness of the sufferings of others but is not overexposed to them lest he become insensitive to them.

Emile's next stage of development, from age eighteen to twenty, is referred to as the "age of humanity."[19] It is at this rather advanced stage that Emile enters the moral sphere and becomes involved in moral relationships. Justice and goodness come from the intrinsic primitive affections with which people are endowed at birth. In Rousseau's perspective, these primitive affections are not abstract moral principles created by the intellect but grow and are nurtured throughout the process of development.

It is in the age of humanity that Emile begins to develop a cultural perspective or distance from the immediacy of his environment to broader issues and concerns. He now studies history as a vehicle for examining the human being's basic goodness and the corrupting influence of society. Rousseau warns against the academic historian's narrative of the past that stresses what is bad rather than what is good about human nature. Further, historians often distort history through interpretations that reflect their own prejudices.

Rousseau, who had been a Catholic and a Protestant, commented on the role of religion in Emile's education. In his own thinking about religion, Rousseau eventually reached what could be called a naturalistic deist position. He came to believe that there was a Creator, a God, but this God was approached via nature. Recommending a naturalistic approach to religion, Rousseau warned against the dogmatic catechetical approach in which words, expressed as questions and answers, were regarded as conveying moral principles. He also admonished against the emphasis on mysteries that shrouded the human mind from natural truths. Further, the images formed during childhood about God were carried forward throughout life, often remaining at the level in which they were formed.

At age twenty, Emile reaches the age of manhood and he meets and falls in love with his future wife, Sophie.[20] It is at this point that an interesting inconsistency is revealed in Rousseau's treatment of Sophie. She is the person who, through the natural family, will bring Emile into a natural society. However, much of Rousseau's description of Sophie reflects his male chauvinism. Men, he says, by their nature are active and strong; women are passive and weak. A woman's education is dependent on her relationship to a man. She is to win a man's affection and esteem, to give him companionship, affection, consolation, and counsel. In describing Sophie's character, Rousseau said that she was of a "good disposition" and pleasing appearance. Sophie "loves virtue but has little knowledge of society."

Before marrying Sophie, Emile travels for two years taking the "grand tour," visiting foreign nations and studying their people, languages, forms of government, and customs. When the book ends, Emile informs his tutor that he plans to educate his children as he was educated.

Conclusion: An Assessment

An assessment of the significance of Rousseau's educational contributions can examine only a few selected themes. Rousseau was a far-ranging but undisciplined theorist and writer who was sometimes inconsistent and contradictory in his writing. In the broad sense, however, Rousseau can be seen as a general social, political, and educational theorist who was pointing in his own way to a new but undefined society. Rousseau was tentatively suggesting a society governed by the general will of all citizens in a kind of grand and sweeping consensus. He raised the question of whether it would be possible to replace the artificial social and political orders with a new republic of men and women who functioned in a natural relationship to each other.

The operations of the general will that Rousseau discussed in *The Social Contract* are difficult to pin down. At one point on the political continuum, they might take the form of a primitive and egalitarian society. However, at the other end of the continuum, the concept of the general will could lead to a kind of totalitarian society as it did in the reign of terror under Robespierre after the French Revolution. To be sure, the Rousseauean expression of the general will is very different from John Locke and Thomas Jefferson's political concept in which there was rotation in office and elections decided by majority rule.

When considered as a political and social document as well as an educational document, *Emile* suggests the possibility that a new race of people might be educated that could create a society based on their extended but natural relationships.

The family that Emile and Sophie are establishing in the book might be the first of many families that will create a new society.

It is in terms of education that Rousseau's educational works, particularly *Emile,* have had their greatest effect. Along with other educational theorists such as Comenius, Pestalozzi, and Froebel, Rousseau argued that childhood was a necessary and desirable stage in the human life span. Indeed, childhood experiences often pointed the way to adult behavior, ethics, and values. This sharply contrasted with earlier views that childhood was something to get through as quickly as possible. Rousseau believed that childhood was so important that its stages should take as long as a person needed to fulfill its possibilities. What came from Rousseau's work was a thrust for permissiveness—letting children follow their needs and interests as far as possible. Child-centered educators who followed Rousseau have consistently viewed childhood as a precious and important period of human growth. These educators have designed learning environments that permit the greatest expression of children's freedom.

Although there were educators such as Quintilian and Comenius who outlined learning based on stages of development, Rousseau made a clear statement for the importance of relating appropriate learning activities to the child's development stage. Today educators ask the question, "What learning is the child ready to do?" Readiness for learning is an important theme in modern education. Teachers consider children's readiness as a key element in planning and implementing successful instruction. The importance that Rousseau gave to readiness based on natural stages of development was a warning against rushing or pushing children into forced learning, often of an intellectual nature, for which they were not ready.

Rousseau conceived of a broad and enriched learning environment that went far beyond the four walls of the book-focused conventional classroom. Just as Emile and his tutor explored the hills, valleys, streams, and gardens of a wooded country estate, contemporary teachers and students use field trips to study nature and society.

At the same time that Rousseau is significant for his child-centered perspective, his work is known for its departure from the long Western cultural tradition that stressed the liberal arts. Plato, Aristotle, Quintilian, Aquinas, Erasmus, and Calvin all strongly endorsed the tradition of the liberal arts and sciences. This tradition remains one of the enduring aspects of the Western educational heritage. The concept of a liberal education was brought to the United States, where it has been implemented and maintained in higher education. The subject matter curriculum of secondary education, too, is based on the liberal arts tradition.

Critics of Rousseau, both in his day and today, find an anti-intellectual element in his ideas. His doctrine of child permissiveness suggests that the child should be the guide to his or her own learning. Critics of this notion argue that there are structures of reality and that the liberal arts are the tested and accumulated thinking about this reality. Defenders of liberal education say that it should form the core of an education at the secondary and higher levels and that elementary education with its stress on literacy and mathematical computation should lead to that core. Since the day of Rousseau, this tension between child-centered permissive education and subject matter education remains a point of conflict.

Rousseau was an iconoclast, a breaker of customs, conventions, and traditions. He was a quarrelsome person and an erratic and inconsistent theorist. He advocated child love and permissiveness but placed his own children in orphanages. Nevertheless, Rousseau earned a place among the great theorists and educators of the Western world. His books are still read today and his influence has extended into our times.

Discussion Questions

1. What elements of cultural change during the Enlightenment contributed to Rousseau's educational theory?
2. How did key events in Rousseau's life shape his personality?
3. Compare and contrast the concepts of supernaturalism and naturalism in education.
4. Analyze Rousseau's concept of a stage of human development and indicate its implications for education.
5. What were the important stages in the education of Emile?
6. What was Rousseau's theory of negative education?
7. What kinds of knowledge and attitudes was the tutor seeking to develop in Emile?

Research and Essay Topics

1. Prepare a research paper on the Enlightenment that examines how this period of history differed from preceding eras.
2. In an essay, develop a character analysis of Rousseau.
3. Read *Emile* and develop a paper that outlines his education.
4. In an essay, analyze the educational dynamics that took place between Emile and the tutor.
5. In an essay, examine the concept of permissiveness in education.
6. Do a content analysis on a selected number of books used in teacher education courses, especially those dealing with early childhood education or methods of instruction. Do you find evidence of a Rousseauean point of view?

Notes

1. Robert Anchor. *The Enlightenment Tradition* (New York: Harper and Row, 1967), 34–8.
2. Gerald L. Gutek. *A History of the Western Educational Experience* (Prospect Heights, Ill.: Waveland Press, 1995), 164–67.
3. Gerald L. Gutek. *Philosophical and Ideological Perspectives on Education* (Englewood Cliffs, N.J.: Prentice Hall, 1988), 145–50.
4. Education during the Enlightenment is examined in Harvey Chisick. *The Limits of Reform in the Enlightenment: Attitudes Toward the Education of the Lower Classes in Eighteenth-Century France* (Princeton, N.J.: Princeton University Press, 1981).
5. For his autobiography, see Jean-Jacques Rousseau, *The Confessions.* Translated by J. M. Cohen (Baltimore: Penguin Books, 1954). Biographies of Rousseau are Jakob H. Huizinga, *Rousseau: The Self-Made Saint* (New York: Grossman Publishers, 1976);

George R. Havens, *Jean-Jacques Rousseau* (Boston: Twayne Publishers, 1978); and Gavin R. De Beer, *Jean-Jacques Rousseau and His World* (London: Thames and Hudson, 1972).

6. William Boyd, ed. *The Minor Educational Writings of Jean Jacques Rousseau* (New York: Teachers College, Columbia University, 1962), 7–23.
7. Ibid., 20.
8. Ibid., 24–38.
9. William Kessen. "Rousseau's Children." *Daedalus 107* (Summer 1978), 155–64.
10. Jean-Jacques Rousseau. *The First and Second Discourses.* Edited by Roger D. Masters (New York: St. Martin's Press, 1964).
11. Jean-Jacques Rousseau. *The Political Writings of J. J. Rousseau.* Edited by C. E. Vaughan (Oxford: Basil Blackwell, 1962).
12. Jean-Jacques Rousseau. *The Social Contract.* Translated by Maurice Cranston (Baltimore: Penguin Books, 1969).
13. Jean-Jacques Rousseau. *The Government of Poland.* Translated by Willmoore Kendall (Indianapolis: Bobbs-Merrill, 1972).
14. Jean-Jacques Rousseau. *Emile: or On Education.* Translated by Allan Bloom (New York: Basic Books, 1979).
15. Ibid., 37–74.
16. Ibid., 77–163.
17. Ibid., 165–208.
18. Ibid., 211–355.
19. Ibid., 357–480.
20. Ibid., 357–406.

Suggestions for Further Reading

Becker, Carl L. *The Heavenly City of the Eighteenth Century Philosophers.* New Haven, Conn.: Yale University Press, 1960.

Boyd, William, ed. *The Emile of Jean-Jacques Rousseau.* New York: Teachers College Press, Columbia University, 1966.

———. *The Minor Educational Writings of Jean-Jacques Rousseau.* New York: Teachers College, Columbia University, 1962.

Chisick, Harvey. *The Limits of Reform in the Enlightenment: Attitudes Toward the Education of the Lower Classes in Eighteenth-Century France.* Princeton, N.J.: Princeton University Press, 1981.

Compayre, Gabriel. *Jean-Jacques Rousseau and Education from Nature.* New York: Burt Franklin, 1971.

Cranston, Maurice W. *The Noble Savage: Jean-Jacques Rousseau, 1754–1762* (Chicago: University of Chicago Press, 1991.

———. *Jean-Jacques: The Early Life and Work of Jean-Jacques Rousseau, 1712–1754.* Chicago: University of Chicago Press, 1991.

Cullen, Daniel. *Freedom in Rousseau's Political Philosophy.* DeKalb: Northern Illinois University Press, 1993.

Davidson, Thomas. *Rousseau and Education According to Nature.* New York: AMS Press, 1971.

Ferrara, Alessandro. *Modernity and Authenticity: A Study in the Social and Ethical Thought of Jean-Jacques Rousseau.* Albany: State University of New York Press, 1992.

Grimsley, Ronald. *Jean-Jacques Rousseau.* Sussex, England: Harvester Press, 1983.

Havens, George R. *Jean-Jacques Rousseau.* Boston: Twayne Publishers, 1978.

Huizinga, Jakob H. *Rousseau: The Self-Made Saint.* New York: Grossman Publishers, 1976.

Jackson, Susan K. *Rousseau's Occasional Autobiographies.* Columbus, Ohio: Ohio State University Press, 1992.

Leigh, A., ed. *Rousseau: After Two Hundred Years.* Cambridge: Cambridge University Press, 1982.

Melzer, Arthur M. *The Natural Goodness of Man: On the System of Rousseau's Thoughts.* Chicago: University of Chicago Press, 1990.

Miller, James. *Rousseau: Dreamer of Democracy.* New Haven, Conn.: Yale University Press, 1984.

Misenheimer, Helen E. *Rousseau on the Education of Women.* Washington, D.C.: University Press of America, 1981.

Noble, Richard. *Language, Subjectivity, and Freedom in Rousseau's Moral Philosophy.* New York: Garland Publishers, 1991.

Perkins, Merle L. *Jean-Jacques Rousseau on the Individual and Society.* Lexington, Ky.: University Press of Kentucky, 1974.

Roosevelt, Grace G. *Reading Rousseau in the Nuclear Age.* Philadelphia: Temple University Press, 1990.

Rousseau, Jean-Jacques. *The Confessions of Jean-Jacques Rousseau.* New York: Modern Library, 1945.

———. *Discourses on the Origin of Inequality.* Indianapolis: Hackett Publishing Co., 1992.

———. *Discourses on the Sciences and Arts: First Discourse and Polemics.* Hanover: University Press of New England, 1992.

———. *Emile: or On Education.* Translated by Allan Bloom. New York: Basic Books, 1979.

———. *The First and Second Discourses.* Edited by Roger D. Masters. New York: St. Martin's Press, 1964.

———. *The Government of Poland.* Translated by Willmoore Kendall, Indianapolis: Bobbs-Merrill, 1972.

———. *The Political Writings of J. J. Rousseau.* Edited by C. E. Vaughan, Oxford: Basil Blackwell, 1962.

———. *The Religious Writings of Rousseau.* Edited by Ronald Grimsley. London: Clarendon Press, 1970.

———. *The Social Contract.* Translated by Maurice Cranston. Baltimore: Penguin Books, 1969.

Strong, Tracy B. *Jean-Jacques Rousseau: the Politics of the Ordinary.* Thousand Oaks, Calif.: Sage Publications, 1994.

Trachtenberg, Zev M. *Making Citizens: Rousseau's Political Theory of Culture.* London and New York: Routledge, 1992.

Weiss, Penny A. *Gendered Community: Rousseau, Sex, and Politics.* New York: New York University Press, 1993.

Johann Heinrich Pestalozzi: Proponent of Educating the Heart and Senses

Portrait of Johann Heinrich Pestalozzi; reproduction from the collection of the Library of Congress.

This chapter describes the life, educational philosophy, instructional methodology, and contributions of Johann Heinrich Pestalozzi (1747–1827), a Swiss educational innovator whose development of a natural method of education brought significant changes to teaching and learning. Pestalozzi's educational philosophy and method of education had an effect not only in Europe but in the Americas as well.

In this chapter, Pestalozzi's development of a philosophy of natural education that emphasized both cognitive and affective development is discussed in terms of its historical origins in early nineteenth-century Switzerland, its diffusion to other countries, and its continuing significance for contemporary education. First, the historical context in which Pestalozzi lived and worked is discussed. Second, Pestalozzi's biography as an educator is examined to determine how his educational ideas were developed by certain key events in his life. Third, the crucial phases in the Pestalozzian approach to education—the general method, which required the creation of a learning environment that was emotionally secure for children, and the special method, which included object lessons with form, number, and name units—are analyzed. Fourth, Pestalozzi's significance as an educational innovator is assessed. By this analysis, we shall see how the interaction of Pestalozzi with the important economic, political, and social events and changes of his time contributed to the development of his philosophy and method of education.

To help you organize your thoughts as you read this chapter, the following focusing questions are provided:

- What were the major trends in the historical context—the time and situation—in which Pestalozzi lived?
- How did Pestalozzi's life, his educational biography, shape his philosophy and method of education?
- What were the key elements in Pestalozzi's theory of education?
- What are the continuing contributions of Pestalozzi's educational innovations?

The Historical Context of Pestalozzi's Life

To understand the climate in which Pestalozzi developed his philosophy and methodology of education, an examination of the general historical context of early nineteenth-century Switzerland is useful. In addition, the intellectual and political climate that were part of the larger European scene also illuminates those events that shaped his career and his thought.

In the early nineteenth century, Switzerland was experiencing the social, political, intellectual, and economic currents sweeping the post-Enlightenment Western world. With its French-, German-, and Italian-speaking cantons, Switzerland was divided on religious as well as linguistic lines. It was where the leading Protestant reformers Zwingli and Calvin had developed their theologies. Nevertheless, other Swiss cantons had resisted the Protestant Reformation and remained staunchly Roman Catholic.

Zurich, Pestalozzi's birthplace, was an important cultural and economic center for German-speaking Swiss. Although Zurich's formal political structure appeared to be representative, a small clique of aristocratic families constituted a ruling oligarchy. Supported by the clergy of the reformed Zwinglian church, these leading upper-class families controlled the city's political and economic life. Citizenship, carrying the right to vote, was an inheritance of these favored families that was passed on from father to son.[1]

Pestalozzi's family, although citizens, were not part of Zurich's power structure. As a youth, Pestalozzi came to sympathize with the poor farmers of the countryside surrounding Zurich, who, lacking political power, were exploited by the corrupt bailiff system. Excluded from participation in political decision making, rural communities were administered by bailiffs, officials appointed by the cantonal government in the city. Later in his life, Pestalozzi would write a moving novel, *Leonard and Gertrude,* which portrayed life in a fictional rural community, Bonnal, that is nearly brought to ruin by a dishonest bailiff.

Pestalozzi's career coincided with the French Revolution, beginning in 1789, and leading to the empire created by Napoleon, which ended in 1815. For a time, Pestalozzi believed the French Revolution, with its doctrines of "liberty, equality, and fraternity," would bring positive political, social, and economic changes to Europe. As a middle-class liberal, Pestalozzi was enthusiastic about the revolution's declaration of the "rights of man." He applauded the French revolutionary government's abolition of primogeniture, freeing of serfs, confiscation of church lands, and establishment of free trade.

When the French National Assembly made him an honorary citizen of the republic along with such notables as George Washington, Thomas Paine, and Jeremy Bentham, Pestalozzi was elated and offered his educational services to the republic. Although they expressed interest in his educational theories, the French committee on public instruction was too preoccupied with staying in power to act on Pestalozzi's pedagogy. When the radical Jacobin seizure of power from the more middle-class liberal Girondists began the Reign of Terror, Robespierre's excesses frightened the Swiss educational reformer. Pestalozzi retreated from a semirevolutionary position into a strictly educational one. When Robespierre was overthrown in 1795 and replaced by a middle-class liberal directory, Pestalozzi again looked hopefully to France as the source of reform for Europe. When Napoleon came to power as the first counsel of France in 1799, Pestalozzi believed the general-turned-politician would perform an educational and civilizing mission in Europe. As it turned out, however, Napoleon preferred empire building to pedagogical reform.

Like the rest of Europe, Pestalozzi's Switzerland did not escape the revolutionary climate of opinion sweeping outward across the French frontiers. Spurred by the French invasion of Switzerland in 1790, the country people of Zurich forced concessions from the ruling elite. These concessions, however, did not satisfy the French, who demanded that the Swiss abolish their old government and create a new one pledged to the establishment of liberty, equality, and fraternity on the French model. Facing external threat and internal pressure, the Swiss capitulated to the French demands and established the pro-French revolutionary Helvetian republic in 1798.

Although not an active revolutionary, Pestalozzi, like other liberal Swiss, sympathized with enlightened revolutionary principles and was pleased to see the old power elite displaced. Once the Helvetian republic had been established, Pestalozzi allied with it and volunteered to serve it in an educational capacity. Pestalozzi had a number of friends and supporters in the new republic who gave financial and political support to his educational plans. Supported by the Helvetian minister of education, P. A. Stapfer, Pestalozzi wrote several pamphlets supporting the new regime and was rewarded with positions at Stans and Burgdorf.[2]

The political climate in Switzerland remained unsettled because the Helvetian republic was regarded by many as a puppet of the French. The old elite who had been displaced resented the loss of power and prestige; peasants, especially in the predominantly Roman Catholic cantons, regarded the Helvetian regime as antireligious. The middle-class liberals who dominated the Helvetian government faced internal discontent, French interference, and financial difficulties.

When Napoleon came to power in France, the Helvetian government sent Pestalozzi to Paris as a member of a delegation to win the future emperor's support. Napoleon, however, decreed the Mediation Act of 1803, which restored political decentralization to Switzerland and restored the autonomy of the nineteen Swiss cantons.[3] This change weakened Pestalozzi's political influence.

Napoleon's declining military fortunes after 1812 and his eventual defeat at the battle of Waterloo in 1815 again affected Swiss politics. The coalition armies who opposed Napoleon, especially the Austrians, invaded Switzerland and annulled the Mediation Act. The Swiss factions disagreed on a new political structure, with the conservatives wanting a weak confederation of autonomous cantons and the liberals wanting centralization. Thus, Swiss politics remained an uneasy truce between conservative federalists and liberal centralists during the last decades of Pestalozzi's life.

Intellectually, Pestalozzi's ideas were influenced by the rationalism of the eighteenth-century Enlightenment and by romanticism. Both rationalists and romanticists looked to nature as the source of truth and for the laws that governed human development. The rationalists believed that by applying natural laws to society that they could eradicate social injustice and build a better life on Earth. Through reason, human beings could discover the natural laws of development and, in accordance with these universal laws, could remake society.

John Locke's *An Essay Concerning Human Understanding* and Isaac Newton's *The Mathematical Principles of Natural Philosophy* were important sources of Enlightenment theory. These works, as well as those of Rousseau and the French physiocrats and encyclopedists, contributed to the climate of opinion that shaped Pestalozzi's educational ideas. Denying the existence of innate ideas in the human mind, Locke's *Essay* asserted that ideas originated in the individual's sensory experience of external objects and were formed into concepts by the mind's power of cognition. In his educational theory, Pestalozzi stressed using the senses. Pestalozzi's *anschauung* principle, according to which the mind arrived at concepts, closely corresponded to Locke's epistemology that the mind initially is a *tabula rasa* that gradually forms ideas from data brought to it by the senses.[4]

According to Newton's physics, the universe was a great world machine that functioned according to its own built-in dynamisms. Advocating the scientific method, Newton argued that human beings could discover the natural laws that kept the planet in order and motion. Further, it was possible to give these natural laws mathematical expression. Although Newton wrote as a natural scientist, individuals such as Pestalozzi believed that the same mode of inquiry was applicable to examining social, political, and educational institutions.

The outlook of the Enlightenment contributed to a shift in intellectual circles from a supernatural and theocentric world view to a naturalistic and humanistic orientation. Rejecting the traditional Christian view of man's inherent weakness due to sin, the followers of Enlightenment ideology argued that human beings are naturally good and could perfect themselves through reason. Buttressed by their optimistic belief in human rationality, Pestalozzi and others like him who were inspired by the Enlightenment believed that human institutions, including schools, could be reformed to reflect nature's laws. Although the quest to develop a natural system of education was not Pestalozzi's alone, he embraced a climate of opinion that moved him to devote his life to this cause.

Along with rationalism, Pestalozzi also experienced the evolving force of romanticism. Of the influences on Pestalozzi, the most pervasive was Rousseau, whose writings, especially *Emile,* incorporated both elements of rationalism and romanticism. Like Rousseau, Pestalozzi looked to nature to provide clues to the child's development and distrusted authoritarianism and verbalism in education.[5]

Referring to Rousseau's *Emile,* Pestalozzi said, "My visionary and highly speculative mind was enthusiastically seized by this visionary and highly speculative book."[6] According to Rousseau, the human being was born good but is corrupted by social institutions, traditions, and conventions. In *Emile,* Rousseau sought to develop an education that would permit the child's natural goodness to develop free of the influence of a pernicious society.[7] Rejecting conventional schooling, Rousseau had his fictional pupil educated according to nature. Many of Rousseau's educational principles were included by Pestalozzi in his own novel, *Leonard and Gertrude,* and in his educational experiments at Neuhof, Stans, Burgdorf, and Yverdon. The following Rousseauean principles especially had an effect on Pestalozzi's ideas:

1. Children are naturally good.
2. The source of evil lies in a distorted and corrupt society rather than in human nature.
3. The right kind of education can curb the contagion of a malfunctioning society and stimulate children to develop according to the good impulses of their nature.
4. Human growth proceeds gradually according to well-defined stages.
5. Sensation rather than verbalism is the true source of ideas, and healthy emotional experience rather than moral preachment is the true source of morality.
6. The natural environment is a fruitful scene of educative experiences.

Although Pestalozzi followed Rousseau's injunction against the unnatural and artificial, he did not reject society's role in education nor did he endorse a completely naturalistic religion. Accepting Rousseau's advice to return to nature, Pestalozzi, who was also acquainted with the theories of the French physiocrats, wanted to relate vocational education to agricultural and handicraft production. In

1767, Pestalozzi would study with the physiocratic French agriculturalist Tschiffeli. Once again, the Enlightenment climate of opinion included the doctrines of Francois Quesnay and the physiocratic economists who held land to be the sole source of wealth and agriculture to be the only means of increasing wealth. Opposing mercantilism, Quesnay argued against interfering with natural economic laws. Like Adam Smith, the liberal English economist, Quesnay opposed government interference with the natural law of supply and demand. Thus, Pestalozzi shared much of the intellectual climate of opinion growing out of the Enlightenment.

Although the ideology of the Enlightenment was influencing many of the intellectuals of the Western world, the power and authority of the various churches remained strong. Their influence was particularly pronounced in schools. During Pestalozzi's life, the established state churches in Europe retained their prerogatives, which had been either reaffirmed or won during the Protestant Reformation and the Catholic Counterreformation. In Italy, Spain, France, and the Holy Roman Empire (the Hapsburg empire), the Roman Catholic church maintained its privileged status. In France, Catholicism's fortunes, as the state church, depended on the policies of the faction holding power. With Napoleon, Catholicism was restored as the official religion of the empire. In England, Anglicanism was officially established as the state church. On the European continent, the major Protestant denominations, Lutheranism and Calvinism, were recognized as state churches in non-Catholic countries. For example, the Scandinavian countries and some of the north German states were Lutheran. The Netherlands, Scotland, and some of the Swiss cantons were Calvinist. Religious establishment was a dominant feature of life in eighteenth- and early nineteenth-century Europe.

In Switzerland, the various cantons were either Roman Catholic or reformed Protestant according to the theology of Zwingli and Calvin. Geneva, which had been the home and workplace of John Calvin, had acquired the reputation of being a kind of Protestant Rome. In Zurich, where Pestalozzi was born, the Zwinglian-Calvinist church was supreme.

Although Pestalozzi was familiar with the Calvinist approach to life, he was also influenced by a new theological current that was affecting European religion—pietism. A number of new sects had arisen. Following a "religion of the heart" rather than an intellectualistic theology, these new churches—Janssonist, Rappite, Dunker, Mennonite, Hutterite, and Inspirationist—sought to reaffirm simple and primitive Christian principles.

In Zurich, the officially sanctioned Reformed church emphasized doctrinal conformity and theological purity, whereas the pietists stressed inner religious experience and a life based on the direct message of the Bible. Although the Zwinglian and Calvinist Protestants saw material prosperity as a sign of God's approval, the pietists stressed the simple life and attached no spiritual significance to wealth.[8] Pietism's affirmation of the religion of the heart and the importance of the good-hearted person coincided with Pestalozzi's emphasis on emotional-moral values in human development and education.

It is difficult to identify precisely Pestalozzi's religious persuasion. Educated in the tradition of reformed Protestantism, Pestalozzi did not break completely with his religious heritage. Like Rousseau, he was also influenced by the naturalism of the Enlightenment. Pestalozzi's religious and moral outlook was an amalgamation of the reformed Christianity of his youth, the currents of pietism, the natural religion of Rousseau, and the philosophies of the Enlightenment. As a result, Pestalozzi was a naturalistic Christian humanist who held that, although the powers of human nature were God given, it was each person's responsibility to cooperate with nature and strive for personal and social regeneration.

Pestalozzi's life also coincided with the onset of western Europe's transformation from an essentially agrarian to an industrial economy. In Switzerland, cottage work, or handicraft production, a step in the process of economic change, could be found along with agriculture and new industries. Believing that these new economic conditions required concerted vocational education, Pestalozzi sought to incorporate agricultural and craft activities in his schools. According to Pestalozzi:

> The means to be employed for the salvation of the fatherland seemed clearly discernible and practicable. I believed that I could neutralize the most oppressive consequences of the evils of the feudal system and of the factory system through renewed effort for the education of the people to increased productivity in home and farm work and to a greater degree of self-respect.[9]

Pestalozzi's adherence to Enlightenment naturalism led him to support agriculture as a major human occupation that brought people close to nature. His earliest educational venture at Neuhof was essentially agricultural, and gardening always was a highly rated activity in his schools. In the early nineteenth century, however, agriculture proved to be an inadequate economic base to sustain a growing population. The result was that the rural agricultural classes were becoming impoverished. The physiocratic doctrines of "land wealth" to which Pestalozzi subscribed promised that the application of the principles of scientific agriculture could restore prosperity.

Although agriculture remained an important concern for Pestalozzi, he was well aware of the effect of the Industrial Revolution. The initial phase of that revolution, from 1770 to 1850, increased economic productivity but also brought about exploitation of the working classes. Pestalozzi found the tendency to dehumanize the poor to be deplorable and sought to remedy it through educational means.

Among the major dehumanizing trends of the early factory system was the routine, mechanical, and monotonous nature of work. The factory's specialized routine destroyed the sense of pride in craftsmanship that had characterized handicraft production and the artistry of the older master-apprentice relationship. Although industrialization had some negative consequences for the working classes, it was slowly improving the quantitative conditions of life. Pestalozzi did not believe that the Industrial Revolution could or should be reversed. With more money and more consumer products available, people needed an education that would enable them to benefit fully from these economic changes.

Early industrialization was especially debilitating to family stability. To earn a livelihood, whole families—fathers, mothers, and children—were employed as factory workers. As the factory replaced the home as the workplace, instances of child abandonment and neglect increased. The growing rates of parental neglect and child delinquency reinforced the prejudice that the working class was inherently vicious and depraved. The long-standing doctrine of child depravity that Pestalozzi struggled to overcome now had a dual rationale: the Calvinist concept that children, because of their inheritance of original sin, were born corrupt and the working classes, as the dregs of society, produced offspring who were vicious and mean.

Like Rousseau, Pestalozzi opposed this doctrine and asserted that children were naturally good. Recognizing that children were being physically, mentally, and morally malformed by the factory system, Pestalozzi believed that unwholesome human behavior was caused by environmental factors that greedy and exploitive employers forced upon workers. With natural education, all children could develop into morally respectable, economically productive, and socially useful adults.

The intellectual, political, religious, and economic trends of the early nineteenth century formed the context in which Pestalozzi developed his theory of natural education. One of his goals was to reform the conditions in the schools. During the early nineteenth century, schools were generally unreceptive to the important intellectual currents unleashed by the Enlightenment. Although the ideas of Locke, Rousseau, and Newton stimulated European intellectuals, primary schools were still tied to denominational indoctrination and rote memorization. Although reformers urged pedagogical innovation, schoolmasters persisted in stressing highly verbal and catechetical modes of instruction. Many schools still remained the "slaughterhouses of the mind" that Comenius had condemned in the seventeenth century.

Primary vernacular schools, often conducted under church auspices, stressed basic literacy, writing, singing, arithmetic, and religious conformity and practice. The various Christian denominations were still engaged in doctrinal disputes arising from the Reformation. Children were admonished to defend their particular religion by memorizing catechisms, psalters, primers, and creeds. Schoolmasters were still school keepers rather than teachers and were hired because of their religious orthodoxy and prowess as disciplinarians. Heavy-handed incompetent bigots were often preferred for teaching positions over educated people.

The various secondary schools—the German *gymnasium*, the French *lycée*, and the English grammar and public schools—were slightly more receptive to the Enlightenment than were elementary schools. But here, too, traditionalism generally held the curriculum captive. The secondary school curriculum was designed to prepare an elite group of boys for entry to the universities by instilling in them the language and literatures of the ancient Greek and Latin classics. In higher education, in the universities, a selected few young men studied to become members of the three professions of theology, law, and medicine.

Pestalozzi was touched by the major political, intellectual, religious, economic, and educational currents that formed the context of his life. He was part of that political climate of opinion that experienced the republican revolution with its slogan of "liberty, equality, and fraternity." He knew both the rationalism of the Enlightenment and the emotionalism of romanticism and pietism. Despite the upheavals of his time, he retained an unshakable optimism that human beings were capable of self and social perfection. It was this conviction that inspired Pestalozzi to work among the poor, develop an educational theory, and devote his life to human betterment.

Pestalozzi: The Life of an Educational Reformer

In this section we examine the biography of Johann Heinrich Pestalozzi, the Swiss educational reformer who had an effect on schools and teaching in both Europe and America.[10] Pestalozzi, the son of Johann Baptiste Pestalozzi, a physician, and Susanna Hotz Pestalozzi, was born on January 12, 1747, in Zurich. The Pestalozzis were a middle-class Protestant family of Italian ancestry. Pestalozzi's father died in 1751 at age thirty-three, leaving three surviving children, Johann Baptiste, Anna Barbara, and Johann Heinrich, who was five years old.[11]

According to his reminiscences, Pestalozzi grew up in a household dominated by women. His mother seems to have left the daily management of the household, which often had to struggle to make ends meet, to a trusted servant, Barbara Schmidt, a controlling figure in young Pestalozzi's life. His grandfather, Andreas Pestalozzi, a minister in the village of Hongg in the rural area of the canton of Zurich, was an important influence during young Pestalozzi's formative years. When he reached adulthood, Pestalozzi claimed that it was his grandfather's example and his ministry to the poor that influenced him to devote his life to the education of the economically disadvantaged. In particular, Johann Heinrich recalled driving with his grandfather to visit the poorest members of the parish.

Pestalozzi's memories of his childhood were not particularly happy. Although Babeli, as Barbara Schmidt was called by the family, and his mother were concerned and caring, Pestalozzi believed he was overly protected and isolated from the peer group contacts and associations that were normal for a child of his age. Lacking interaction with other children, he claimed that he knew nothing of children's games and activities. He grew up a socially inept and physically uncoordinated youth. It is interesting to note the similarity in the reflections of Pestalozzi and Friedrich Froebel, the founder of the kindergarten, on their unhappy childhoods. Although Pestalozzi found his own childhood and family to be inadequate, when he developed his educational theory, he based it around a loving mother figure, Gertrude, who presided over a secure and loving household.

Because of the economies practiced in managing their household, Pestalozzi's family was able to finance his education. He attended a local primary school, conducted in the vernacular German that was spoken in Zurich, from 1751 to 1754, where he studied the conventional subjects of reading, writing, arithmetic, and religion. In 1754, he began his Latin and Greek studies at the Schola Abbatissana and then transferred to the Schola Carolina, a more advanced classical preparatory school that resembled the humanist *gymnasium*. He then entered university studies at the Collegium Humanitatis where he studied Latin, Greek, Hebrew language and literature, rhetoric, philosophy, and theology. When he was seventeen, Pestalozzi entered the Collegium Carolinum where he concentrated on languages and philosophy.

Pestalozzi's college years were an exciting release from the introspective shyness of his childhood. He now was part of a circle of young men, who, under the influence of their professor, Jean Jacques Bodmer (1699–1773), dreamed of doing great deeds that would restore their native Switzerland to its past greatness. Bodmer, a historian and literary critic, preached that the revitalization of Swiss life would come from imitating the rugged spirit and simple virtues of the Swiss mountaineers.

Under Bodmer's direction, his followers, organized as the Helvetic Society, intended to lead a rebirth of Swiss life. The young Helvetians, which in addition to Pestalozzi included Johann Caspar Fussli, Caspar Schulthess, Johann Bluntschili, and others who would become lifelong friends, marched off into the mountains to study peasant life and to collect folk stories and songs that represented the virtuous life, uncontaminated by modernity and materialism. Bodmer's emphasis on Swiss folk culture was similar to early nineteenth-century movements elsewhere such as that of the Grimm brothers and Ludwig Jahn in Germany, who combined romanticism and nationalism to find in the purity of the mythical past the key to happiness in the future.

To disseminate their views, the members of the Helvetic Society established and contributed to a weekly publication, *The Monitor*, which in urging reforms along the lines advocated by Bodmer, criticized Zurich's public officials. The officials responded by suppressing publication of *The Monitor* and briefly jailing Pestalozzi and others who had contributed to its pages.

Pestalozzi's foray into political activism and journalism was an exhilarating experience for the young man. He had made some close associates for the first time in his life and had a cause. In reflecting on these days, Pestalozzi wrote:

> Our only wish was to live for freedom, beneficence, sacrifice and patriotism; but the means of developing the practical power to attain these were lacking. We despised all external appearances such as riches, honour, and consideration; and we were taught to believe that by economising and reducing our wants we could dispense with all the advantages of citizen life. We cherished but one aim namely, the possibility of enjoying independence and domestic happiness, without having the strength to acquire and maintain them.[12]

The impressionable Pestalozzi now sought a career that would fulfill his mission of improving life for the less fortunate. His education in the classics, humanities, and religious studies gave him the academic background for the religious ministry. However, he lacked the skill of preaching. His attempt to preach a trial sermon was such an embarrassment that he abandoned religious work. For a while, he toyed with the idea of becoming a lawyer but realized that he was unsuited temperamentally for such a career. In addition, he was regarded as radical because of his association with the Helvetic Society.

In searching for a meaningful career, Pestalozzi decided agriculture would be a suitable vocation. It would enable him to live the simple life of pure Swiss values that Bodmer had emphasized. Further, Pestalozzi had also become an avid disciple of Rousseau. What could be more natural than the life of a farmer? However, because he knew little about farming, he determined to study scientific agriculture with Johann Rudolf Tschiffeli, a well-known agricultural expert who had a model experimental farm near Kirchberg in the canton of Berne. Here, under Tschiffeli's tutelage, Pestalozzi studied to be a scientific farmer.

Pestalozzi married Anna Schulthess, the daughter of an upper middle-class Zurich family and the sister of his close friend Caspar Schulthess. Anna, described as an attractive, patient, and capable young woman, was eight years older than her husband. Her family, who regarded Pestalozzi as an eccentric dreamer, reluctantly consented to the marriage.

With money borrowed from friends and his wife's dowry, Pestalozzi purchased a sixty-acre farm near the village of Birr in the canton of Berne. Here, he built his home, which he called Neuhof, and began his experiment in scientific farming.

Pestalozzi's only child, whom he named Jean Jacques after his literary hero Rousseau, was born in 1770. Jean Jacques was a sickly child who suffered from "violent rheumatic attacks," which may have been another name for epilepsy. Pestalozzi decided that he would use *Emile* as a guide for his son's education. He kept a diary of Jean Jacques' progress. Regarding his son's education, Pestalozzi wrote:

> Whatever you can teach him from the nature of things themselves, do not teach him by words. Leave him to himself to see, hear, find, stumble, rise again, and be mistaken. Give no word when action, or deed is possible. What he can do for himself let him do. Let him be always occupied, ever active, and let the time when you do not worry him be by far the greatest part of his childhood. You will come to learn that nature teaches him better than men.[13]

Pestalozzi followed Rousseau literally in educating his son. When Jean Jacques had difficulty in school and had problems learning to read and write, Pestalozzi decided that although Rousseau was on the right educational track, the method needed to be systematized and based on psychological principles. Jean Jacques eventually married and had a child. He died at the age of thirty.

In 1774, Pestalozzi made education his life's work. Still seeking to uplift the poor economically and morally, he turned his agricultural experiment into an educational experiment as well. His plan was for Neuhof to become a self-supporting farm and handicraft school, where the sale of the children's work would support the educational experiment. This plan bore some resemblance to Gandhi's Wardha plan for basic education in India.

At Neuhof, Pestalozzi accepted orphan children as students and invited poor families in the vicinity of Birr to send their children, both boys and girls, to him for an education. Often, the children came to him in filthy and ragged clothes. He provided them with clean new clothes and put them up in dormitories. In the summer, they did agricultural chores; in the winter they did cotton and wool spinning and weaving and made handicraft items. At its peak, Pestalozzi's school at Neuhof enrolled fifty children. He also instructed them in reading, writing, and counting by using a group method that he called "simultaneous instruction." Aside from his enthusiasm for Rousseau's principles of natural education and his own memories of schooling, Pestalozzi did not yet have any clear ideas of education and instructional methods.

Despite his enjoyment of the experiment at Neuhof and the support of his friends, Pestalozzi's educational venture was proving to be a financial drain. Of the fifty children at the school, ranging in age from six to eighteen, only fourteen were able to work in any concerted fashion. The situation was further complicated by some parents who would withdraw their children after Pestalozzi had provided them with food and clothing. Further, despite his altruism and humanitarian intentions, Pestalozzi was not a good administrator. He was especially inept at balancing accounts and keeping the school operating at a profit. In 1779, for financial reasons, Pestalozzi was forced to close his school. However, he was now convinced that he had found the vocation that would give meaning to his life. He was determined to be an educator.

Pestalozzi turned to writing both to earn a living and to record and disseminate his educational ideas. Deeply impressed with Rousseau's success in diffusing his ideas on natural education through the didactic or teaching novel, Pestalozzi decided that he also would write such a novel. In 1781, Pestalozzi's widely read *Leonard and Gertrude,* was published.[14] In this novel, by using the principles of natural education, Gertrude educates her children. Her success is so great that natural education is used to regenerate the economically depressed village of Bonnal.

In *Leonard and Gertrude,* Pestalozzi developed a cast of characters that personified his views on social and educational change. Gertrude was the devoted mother of a large family who was determined that her children, despite poverty, would grow to be morally, physically, and intellectually well-developed persons. Her husband Leonard, well meaning but weak, was a stonemason by trade. Because of the economic depression in the village, Leonard, like most of the men, was frequently unemployed and idled time away in the village tavern, owned by the corrupt bailiff Hummel, who exploited the village economy for his own gain. Much of the land around the village was owned by Squire Arner, a well-meaning but absent landlord. Squire Arner did not know that the quality of life in the village of Bonnal was deteriorating.

Through a series of simple episodes, Pestalozzi told the story of the good mother-teacher whose actions changed life in the village for the better. Each day, Gertrude would gather her children about the table where they would work together spinning and weaving. As they worked, they recited prayers, said the alphabet, and counted numbers. The children were working and earning to support the family while they were learning. If there were problems of illness in the other households in the village, the kindly, compassionate, and patient Gertrude would be there to help. Gertrude's household and her children became an educational model for the village.

Although Gertrude was managing to raise and educate her children through careful economy and natural education, she realized that her family was part of a larger village community. Mustering her courage, she went to Squire Arner's estate and told him of the deplorable situation in Bonnal. True to the early nineteenth-century pattern, the good squire pleaded innocence. He did not know that his appointee, Bailiff Hummel, was violating his trust and responsibility. Outraged, Squire Arner went with Gertrude to the village where he dismissed Hummel. Together with Gertrude, Squire Arner embarked on an integrated program of educational, social, and economic reform.

An important part of the reform program was to construct a school where Gertrude's method of education could be implemented. Leonard and some of the unemployed village men are employed to build the school. The program of village reconstruction provides work and restores the economy. A teacher is hired who is instructed by Gertrude in the natural method of simultaneous instruction. As a result, Bonnal becomes a shining example of community renewal and humanitarianism. The key message that Pestalozzi was seeking to convey was that education could be the means of more general social reform.

Through the pages of *Leonard and Gertrude,* Pestalozzi made his first attempt to articulate his philosophy of education. His basic educational doctrines were the following:

1. A genuine education will develop each person's intellectual, moral, and physical powers in a harmonious and integrated fashion.
2. To be successful, education needs to unite the home with the school and the school with the whole community.
3. Human beings, despite ignorance, economic depression, and moral deprivation, can be uplifted and regenerated through education.
4. True social reform will be the result of peaceful education rather than violent revolution.
5. Education, conducted humanely, will lead to the development of a humanitarian society.[15]

Pestalozzi's *Leonard and Gertrude* was a best seller. It was republished in numerous editions and brought recognition to its author. The novel won the gold medal awarded by the Economic Society of Berne.

Pestalozzi also produced essays and books on education. He wrote a series of articles, "Essays on the Education of the Children of the Poor," which appeared in *Ephemerides,* a Swiss journal. In 1782, Pestalozzi wrote a sequel to *Leonard and Gertrude,* titled *Christopher and Elizabeth.* The book basically consisted of dialogues in which Christopher led his family in discussions of *Leonard and Gertrude.* The book failed to attract a wide readership.

Between 1782 and 1784, Pestalozzi published his own newspaper, *Ein Schweizer Blatt (The Swiss News),* which carried articles that stressed the importance of the home as an educational force, pointed to the need for a new system of education based on natural principles, and attacked existing schools as being too mechanical and verbal. In 1783, Pestalozzi's *On Legislation and Infanticide* appeared, in which he condemned the practice of killing or abandoning unwanted children. He also examined the broader social and economic causes of crime and indicated how education could be a force in reducing crime. Pestalozzi turned to writing children's books with the publication of *Illustrations for My ABC Book* in 1787 and *Fables for My ABC Book* in 1795.

In 1797, Pestalozzi sought to establish a broad theoretical base for his educational ideas in his *Researches Into the Course of Nature in the Development of the Human Race.* Although harshly criticized as confusing and highly abstract by its reviewers, *Researches* represented an early attempt to create a sociology of education. Writing in the spirit of the Enlightenment, Pestalozzi said human progress would be advanced by education that cultivated inherent human powers. Further, education was not only a matter of schooling and the instruction of children; it was the instrument of advancing human beings to the good society of harmony, morality, and happiness.

In 1799, Pestalozzi, who now enjoyed a reputation as an educational authority because of his publications, was asked to perform an educational service by the new Swiss government, the Helvetian republic. Battles between the French and the Austrian armies had taken place in certain Swiss cantons. French armies had raided the conservative Roman Catholic cantons of Schwyz, Uri, and Unterwalden, which had opposed the pro-French Helvetian republic. Several of Pestalozzi's college friends held posts in the Helvetian government, and they secured his appointment as head of an orphanage in the village of Stans. At age fifty-nine, on January 14, 1799, Pestalozzi resumed active work as an educator. He found himself in charge of eighty children, some of whom had been orphaned as a result of war. His funds were limited, he had the assistance of only a housekeeper and cook, and the residents in the surrounding countryside were hostile. He wrote of his experience at Stans:

> I united in my person the offices of superintendent, paymaster, steward, and sometimes chambermaid, in a half-ruined house. I was surrounded with ignorance, disease, and with every kind of novelty. The number of children rose, by degrees to eighty; all of different ages; some full of pretensions; others inured to open beggary; and all, with a few solitary exceptions, entirely ignorant.[16]

It was at Stans that Pestalozzi made some important educational discoveries. He found that, because of their experiences, the children were suspicious, frightened, and often emotionally withdrawn. To make any progress in their more formal instruction in reading and arithmetic, Pestalozzi realized he first needed to win their affection. He needed to create a home-school atmosphere in which the children's material and emotional needs were satisfied. Only then could he concentrate on their intellectual education. He began to act as a father figure for the children, living with them and providing the security of a caring and loving adult.

In his work at Stans, Pestalozzi came upon an important principle that shaped his educational philosophy. The affective side of human nature, emotional development, was equally important to cognitive development. Neither could proceed in isolation from the other. Further, attention to the attitudinal dimension in the form of creating a learning environment of emotional security had to come before cognitive learning. Hungry, scared, emotionally withdrawn children would have great difficulty in learning skills and mastering more intellectual lessons until their basic needs were satisfied.

Slowly Pestalozzi went about the task of creating in his orphan children at Stans feelings of self-worth and esteem. Gradually, he brought order to disordered lives. Unfortunately, his work at Stans was brought to an abrupt halt July 8, 1799, after only six months of operation. Opposing French and Austrian armies had set up their battle lines in the vicinity, forcing the orphanage to close.

In July 1799, the Helvetian government found a position for Pestalozzi as an assistant to Samuel Dysli, the village schoolmaster of a working-class primary school in Burgdorf. What unfolded next was a conflict between the old, represented by Dysli, and the new in education, represented by Pestalozzi. Dysli, who was a shoemaker, combined his trade with school keeping. The term *school keeping* aptly described Dysli's method of teaching. Dysli would work on shoe repair, while each child came before his bench to recite the lesson that had been assigned the day before. The children memorized the alphabet, which was recited in sing-song fashion. Then they went on to simple phrases. The goal was to have them memorize the catechism, to learn to read, and to count. While one child was standing before Dysli and reciting, the others would wait their turn. A slap across the hand with a rod was used to punish those who had not memorized their lessons or were disobedient.

Almost immediately upon arriving at Burgdorf, Pestalozzi was at odds with Dysli. First, he opposed the use of corporal punishment to instill fear in the children; such an environment, he believed, gave merely the appearance but not the substance of learning. Second, Pestalozzi opposed Dysli's emphasis on memorization of the catechism and passages from the Bible and other books. To Pestalozzi, this approach required the children to mouth words they did not really understand. Rather than parroting words, Pestalozzi believed that children should begin their learning by exploring their immediate environment and the objects that were close at hand.

Thrown together by circumstances in the same classroom, Dysli and Pestalozzi quarreled. Dysli believed that his so-called assistant was really trying to usurp his position. Pestalozzi felt that Dysli was ill prepared as a teacher and was miseducating the children. Soon the quarrel left the school and factions developed around the two men. Dysli spread the word that Pestalozzi was antireligious. The conflict ended with Pestalozzi leaving the position.

Once again, friends in the Helvetian government intervened on Pestalozzi's behalf. They arranged for him to head a new educational institute located in Burgdorf castle. From 1800 to 1804, Pestalozzi directed the Burgdorf Institute, which included a boarding school for students and a teacher education program for educational interns. His years at Burgdorf were of great significance. He developed his educational ideas into a complete philosophy and method of education. By establishing a teacher education program, he ensured that his method of education would be perpetuated and disseminated in Europe and the Americas.

At Neuhof and Stans, Pestalozzi learned that it was of vital importance to create an educational climate of emotional security. Now he developed his theory of sensory learning based on the concept of *anschauung*, a German word that meant the forming of a concept or a clear idea from sense impressions. For Pestalozzi, *anschauung* would bring about an educational revolution. Human beings inhabited, he said, a world that is composed of a multitude of physical objects. People learn in life by having experience with these objects. They see, feel, smell, taste, and hear them. Their eyes, ears, and other senses convey data to the mind. The mind then sorts them out and arranges them into concepts or ideas. Only after the concept is clearly present in the mind is a name, a word that designates it, given to it. If this is the way people learn in life, why should not this method also be used in schools? Instead, schools concentrate on words about which children do not have direct experience. Because they really have no understanding of these words, children are forced to memorize and recite them.

At Burgdorf, Pestalozzi designed his famous object lesson in which children, guided by teachers, examined the form, the shape, and the quantity, the number and weight of objects, and then learned to name the objects only after they had had a direct experience with them. To provide children with direct experience with the many objects present in the environment, Pestalozzi organized nature study field trips into the surrounding countryside. They observed and collected plants and minerals and studied the movement of animals and birds. Geography lessons did not focus on distant oceans and continents but on the immediate vicinity, moving outward from the schoolyard into the neighborhood and then into the countryside.

While at Burgdorf, Pestalozzi finished his most complete and systematic book on educational method, *How Gertrude Teaches Her Children*, in 1801.[17] In this book, he developed his philosophy of the two interrelated phases of education: the general method, which involved the creation of a climate of emotional security, and the special method, which stressed the object lesson of form, number, and sound or name.

At Burgdorf, Pestalozzi trained a number of assistants in his method of education. Among them were Johann Georg Tobler, Johann Christopher Buss, Herman Krusi, and Joseph Neef. Neef introduced the Pestalozzian method to the United States in the early nineteenth century. A number of teachers such as Friedrich Froebel came to Burgdorf from other countries to be prepared in the Pestalozzian method. As his fame spread and his books were translated and published in other languages, Pestalozzi's institute at Burgdorf attracted visitors who observed his method. For example, the U.S. common school leaders Horace Mann and Henry Barnard and the scientist-geologist-philanthropist William Maclure came to observe the Pestalozzian method of education.

In 1804, the Helvetian government was replaced by a more conservative federal government. The canton of Berne repossessed Burgdorf castle and Pestalozzi had to relocate his institute. The municipality of Yverdon invited him to occupy the local castle, which was provided to him without cost. From 1804 until his retirement in 1825, Pestalozzi continued his educational work at Yverdon. Here, he continued to write, prepare teachers, and educate students. In 1827, Pestalozzi died at Neuhof, where he had established his first school.

The Pestalozzian Method of Education

Pestalozzi's method of education was based on his theory of natural education, which was influenced by Rousseau, by the importance that he gave to sensory-based education, and by his experiences as a teacher and teacher-educator. In this section of the chapter, we examine his philosophy and method of education.

Pestalozzi had a conception of human nature in which he saw each person possessing inherent intellectual, moral, and physical powers. In this tripartite view of human nature, the mind was the source of intellectual power, the will the source of moral power, and the body the source of physical power. It was important, he reasoned, that the three powers be cultivated and developed harmoniously and simultaneously. Conventional schooling was oriented to the development of the intellectual powers but neglected the cultivation of the moral and physical powers. Those who succeeded in conventional schools were masters of words and the manipulation of language but not necessarily moral persons. Unfortunately, conventional schooling that ignored true moral education produced individuals who were governed by their appetites. Ignoring physical development, conventional schooling did not provide vocational education, and many individuals, especially children of the poor, left school to join the ranks of the unemployed. It was vitally important that a method of education be used that developed each person's threefold powers—the intellect, the will, and the body—simultaneously and harmoniously.

For Pestalozzi, the education of the individual was closely related to the well-being of society. Crime, injustice, poverty, and the ills of society could be remedied by creating a new kind of society in which the intellectual, moral, and physical needs of people were satisfied by liberating and cultivating the three basic powers common to humanity.

Pestalozzi's theory of instruction can be divided into two phases: the general method and the special method. The general method, which was intended to create schools characterized by a pervasive climate of emotional security, was necessary and preceded the special method. The special method, based on Pestalozzi's *anschauung* principle, stressed sensory learning and conceptualization that came about through the object lesson.[18]

Pestalozzi's concept of the general method was rooted in the basic, simple, and direct needs of early childhood, especially infancy. In the ideal relationship between the mother and the child, the infant had basic needs of food, warmth, and affection. The good and loving mother responded and satisfied these needs. In the first days of life, a bond of love, or a circle of positive emotion, was created between the mother and the child. This bond, arising from natural instincts, was necessary in developing an emotionally secure child.

Emotional security, the positive development of the affective domain, then proceeded through circles of development that extended outward from the initial loving relationship of mother and infant to the larger world. If the relationship between mother and infant had been positive, the child would be responsive to other people and respond to them with love and affection. The next circle involved the other members of the immediate family. The properly functioning family, like Gertrude's family in Bonnal, would be characterized by love and security.

From the family circle, the child's sense of security was extended outward to the people of the neighborhood and the community. Following the premise that marked all of his educational theory, Pestalozzi believed that human development and the education for that development moved from that which was immediate, direct, and close at hand, to that which was more distant, remote, and abstract. Here, Pestalozzi saw the development of psychological-emotional security moving from the ties of blood relationship and closeness that marked the family to the more remote and abstract social relationships of community life with its economic and political implications.

The next stage in emotional development saw the person moving to a still larger and more abstract concept of the nation. If the more immediate village or town community was characterized by conditions of emotional trust, this sense could then be extended to the people of the nation. Moving onward, Pestalozzi saw the nations of the Earth united in an international circle of humanity. People of different languages, nations, and ethnic groups were part of an international human community. If the same essential trust and security that had originated in the mother-child relationship were nurtured and developed, then it could be extended, at a more comprehensive and mature level, to the relationships between peoples and nations.

Slowly, gradually, and surely, the circles of secure human relationships were broadened and extended outward from the person to the society and to the world. These broadening circles of love then took on a religious significance. By loving human beings, the person was led to the love of God, the Father and Creator of all life.

At the vernacular school in Burgdorf, Pestalozzi had argued with Dysli over religious instruction. The conventional teaching of religion in European and U.S. schools in the nineteenth century based instruction on the theology of the religious denomination or the church that controlled the school. Thus, depending on the particular denomination, children learned to be Roman Catholics, Lutherans, Calvinists, and so on. They learned religious principles by memorizing a catechism that structured each religious concept in the form of a question and answer. For Pestalozzi this was a word-centered approach to religion in which children memorized verbal formulas that they really did not understand. Further, the catechetical approach created feelings of religious intolerance. Pestalozzi's approach to religious instruction was based on human relationships that eventually led to God.

Pestalozzi's moral values and moral education were based on his view of how people developed into emotionally secure and psychologically sound individuals. Love originated in the basic human instincts rather than in some abstract principle. Moral and ethical behavior, too, arose from and was associated with the same pattern of development. In a loving relationship, neither person would injure the other.

Pestalozzi, then, took his concept of the genesis of human emotional security and morality and applied it to schools. Conventional schools, he stated, were not places of loving and trusting relationships. Rather, children were treated as ignorant savages who needed to be shaped into "civilized" creatures by psychologically and physically coercive teachers who ruled their classrooms through corporal punishment. These schools needed to be reformed and made into places where the general method, with its emphasis on love and emotional security, could be applied.

In his description of the development of emotional security, Pestalozzi knew he had described the ideal situation. The ideal was not being pursued, however, in many families. As was true of the orphan children that he had ministered to at Neuhof and Stans, the mother-child circle was broken by the mother's death or the breakup of families. Instead of growing up emotionally secure and seeking to extend this security outward to other human relationships, many children, suspicious and mistrustful of others, were either socially withdrawn or socially deviant in their behavior. For these children, the loving and secure climate of the Pestalozzian school would act as a restorative remedy by recreating the conditions that should have been present in the good home.

Pestalozzi was also critical of conventional schooling for its overemphasis on verbalism and the memorization of set passages from books. Memorization of catechism questions and answers and passages from the classics and the Scriptures passed in these schools for intellectual development. Those children who succeeded in conventional schools were little pedants who appeared to be highly intelligent but were "word people" who lacked complete and full development of their emotional and physical powers.

Pestalozzi's stress on creating a school climate characterized by love and emotional security also added a new dimension to teaching. To extend love to children and create a secure environment for their education, teachers needed to be emotionally secure. Conventional teachers in conventional schools were often word-centered and pedantic individuals who preferred books to people and ruled their classrooms like petty tyrants. For Pestalozzi, the true teacher would be a person such as Gertrude who regarded the children in her classroom as a family. Pestalozzi shared meals and recreation with the children in his schools; he accompanied them on their field trips and excursions and expected those he was training to be teachers to follow his example.

Once the children believed they were in an emotionally secure environment with teachers whom they trusted and loved, then the second phase of Pestalozzi's plan of education, the special method, could proceed. At the heart of the special method was Pestalozzi's principle that all knowledge came to human beings through their senses. Pestalozzi's emphasis on the role of senses in bringing information to the mind was similar to Aristotle's Realism. Educators have classified Pestalozzi as a "sense realist." For sense realists, two elements are of utmost importance—the human senses and the objects found in the world. Through the senses—seeing, hearing, tasting, smelling, feeling—information, or sensory data, is conveyed to the mind, which converts it into concepts or ideas that belong to a class of objects.

It was at this point in his epistemology and learning theory that Pestalozzi's important principle of *anschauung* came into play.[19] Here, he was influenced by Rousseau's stress on nature and the natural. Lapsing into romanticism, Pestalozzi claimed that the world appeared at first glance like a forest shrouded in morning mists. *Anschauung* was like the power of the sun, dissipating the mist and bringing each tree that composed the forest into the clear vision of the mind's inner eye.

Because human beings came to know the objects present in their environment through the senses, Pestalozzi reasoned that instruction also should be based on the senses. His special method consisted of a series of object lessons in which children, with the assistance of the teacher, observed, examined, and analyzed objects found in their immediate environment. By using object lessons, children could examine minerals, plants, and animals of the natural order and artifacts made by human beings.

Each object could be studied through a series of "form, number, and name" lessons, which constituted the proper beginning of education rather than reading, writing, arithmetic, and catechism lessons.[20] Every object had a form, a design, or structure that could be studied by observing and touching it. In their drawing exercises, children could trace the outline of small objects or sketch the shape or design of larger objects. By these exercises, they mentally extracted the form of the object and used it to create the concept that referred to that class of objects. For example, by collecting and tracing the leaves of trees and tracing their outline, they came to the mental concept through a concrete physical process.

Along with the form lessons, there were number lessons in which children learned the sense of quantity and number. In conventional schools, children learned to count by reciting numbers; although they could call the numbers off, the numbers they recited often remained mere words. In fact, Pestalozzi admitted that he made this very same mistake in the education of his son. It was important, Pestalozzi stated, that children be able to connect objects in their environment with the quantity of objects present. To develop this skill, Pestalozzi, who always stressed beginning with the immediate and the concrete, had the children collect marbles, stones, or peas and arrange them in groups, beginning with one object, then two objects, three objects, and so forth. Thus, they learned that the number sign referred to a corresponding number of real objects. After they had mastered the skill of counting real objects, they were taught that a dot could be used to represent the object. On paper, they developed a sequence of groups of dots that represented the objects. After they had mastered the ability to represent objects by using dots, a kind of pictograph, then they replaced the dots with number signs so that 1 = one dot, and 2 = two dots, and so on. Just as he had used this system in developing the skill of counting, he used tangible objects to develop the basic computation skills of adding, subtracting, multiplying, and dividing.

Along with the form and number lessons, Pestalozzi developed a series of name or sound exercises. Each object had a name and the children were taught to say that name. Each object also had qualities like color, hardness, and softness and the children were taught to say these qualities. The names were said slowly and often broken down into simple parts that were repeated over and over until mastered. The names of the words and verbs were used to form sentences whose development followed the pattern of going from the simple to the complex.

It was only after the form, number, and name lessons had been thoroughly mastered that Pestalozzi would go on to the lessons in reading, writing, and arithmetic that were conventionally taught in schools. He believed the tracing and drawing exercises that were part of the form lessons naturally led to writing. The name lessons, with their emphasis on breaking down large words and sentences into their smaller parts, led to reading and to clear speaking. The counting exercises led to mathematical computation. After the children had developed clear ideas or concepts in their minds of the objects in their environment, then these concepts were connected with the skills of literacy and computation.

Natural science and geography were taught in a similarly direct fashion and in an integrated way. Led by their teachers, the children would go on excursions, hikes, and field trips through the surrounding countryside. Their first excursions led them out from the school to the village. They were introduced to the local economy and industry by observing the work of the shoemaker, blacksmith, shopkeeper, weaver, and so forth. They then went out into the woods around the village and, following the streams, learned how rivers flow and drain the nearby fields. They collected plants, stones, and other natural objects that were brought back to the school and arranged as a small school museum of natural history. As they walked, they observed the local geography—the location of the streams, hills, roads, and buildings. When they returned to the school, they created a model of the local geography by using clay, sand, paper, and wood. Then they sketched their model on paper, creating a map. It was more realistic for the child to have direct experience with geographical places in this manner than memorizing the names of the oceans, continents, and countries of the world. It was better to see people actually working than to memorize the principal products of various countries.

Throughout the instructional approach developed by Pestalozzi, there was a basic methodological consistency in both the general and the special methods. Both cognitive and affective development began with the child's senses. Development was a result of feeling—both with the senses and the emotions. All learning began with elements directly present in the child's immediate environment. It proceeded slowly and gradually, and did not enter a new stage until the child had mastered the previous stage. Nothing was hurried or forced. Lessons always began with concrete objects in the immediate environment before moving to that which was more abstract and remote in the child's experience. Just as the cognitive form, number, and name lessons moved from the immediate, direct, and concrete to the distant and abstract so did the affective development of values take place in the same way. Children learned to be secure in their social relationships by experiencing security directly.

Not only did Pestalozzi bring about a change in instructional methodology, he also brought about a change in the grouping of children for instructional purposes. The conventional approach to instruction was to have all children in one room and to have one child at a time come before the teacher to recite a previously assigned lesson. Pestalozzi believed this was an inefficient use of time and failed to promote social interaction and development. The group process or simultaneous instruction of children was used to teach object lessons.

Thus, the somewhat odd, eccentric Swiss educator, Johann Heinrich Pestalozzi, who failed at being a farmer, a minister, and a lawyer, succeeded in bringing about a major revolution in education. Much of what he originated is now a regular part of modern education.

Conclusion: An Assessment

Pestalozzianism's effect can be examined in terms of its diffusion from its origin to other places and times. It also can be assessed in terms of its enduring significance for educational theory and practice.

After his death in 1827, Pestalozzi's educational philosophy and method were carried throughout Europe and the United States by those who had studied with him to be teachers. In addition, leading European and American educators who had visited the institutes at Burgdorf and Yverdon brought the Pestalozzian methodology back to their own countries. Although most were inspired by Pestalozzi, the version of Pestalozzianism they diffused was often a pale imitation of the original. Because Pestalozzi's educational philosophy and method was complex and loosely structured, some of his interpreters glimpsed only a part of his total educational edifice.

In assessing Pestalozzi's influence, it should be remembered that the most crucial phase of the general method lies in the creation of an emotionally secure educational environment. Although eccentric, Pestalozzi was a gentle person and a father figure to the children who attended his schools at Neuhof, Stans, Burgdorf, and Yverdon. Unfortunately, not all of those who sought to emulate Pestalozzi were suited temperamentally to be father figures. Because the object lesson was the most visible part of Pestalozzi's method, many followers did not fully comprehend the importance of the less tangible but theoretically pervasive and necessary general method. They did not understand that the full implementation of the method required an emotionally secure environment before proceeding to the object lessons of the special method. As has been true of many educational innovations, the particular innovation loses some of its meaning and vitality when put into practice by those who are distant from the time and place of the innovation's origin.

Despite the difficulty that some of Pestalozzi's disciples had in adequately implementing his method, it was nevertheless widely diffused in Europe and in the Americas. Because Pestalozzi was German speaking and wrote in German, the German states were a natural place for transplanting his method. In the nineteenth century, Prussia, the leader among the German states, introduced the Pestalozzian method. In his *Addresses to the German Nation* in 1808, the Prussian philosopher Johann Gottlieb Fichte urged his nation to adopt the Pestalozzian system. Fichte believed that Pestalozzian education could help revitalize Prussia, which had been defeated by Napoleon's armies. The Prussian government incorporated aspects of Pestalozzianism in its educational reforms of 1809. In England, Pestalozzi's ideas were first introduced with the publication of correspondence between the Swiss educator and the English educator, J. P. Greaves.[21] At their school at Cheam Surrey, Charles and Elizabeth Mayo used the Pestalozzian method but concentrated on the object lesson and tended to neglect the general method. They prepared a number of books for teachers that illustrated the method of teaching the Pestalozzian form, number, and sound lessons.[22] Under their leadership, the Home and Colonial School Society was organized in 1836 to promote Pestalozzianism. The society also established a model school to demonstrate the Pestalozzian method and a training school to prepare teachers in using Pestalozzian pedagogy.

In the United States, Pestalozzi's philosophy and method found a receptive audience. Here, Pestalozzianism experienced three distinct phases:

1. The initial introduction of the method by William Maclure and Joseph Neef.
2. Concerted efforts by Henry Barnard, the common school leader, to publicize the method.
3. Edward A. Sheldon's development of a full-scale program of teacher education at the Normal School at Oswego, New York.[23]

In the early nineteenth century while on one of his many expeditions to Europe, William Maclure, a world traveler and a pioneering student of geology, visited Pestalozzi at Burgdorf. Maclure wanted to diffuse useful scientific knowledge to the U.S. farming and working classes and decided that the Pestalozzian method would be useful in accomplishing his goal. He was so impressed by what he saw at Burgdorf that he recruited Joseph Neef, an assistant of Pestalozzi's, to come to the United

States to introduce the method.[24] Neef, who received a subsidy from Maclure, came to the United States in 1806. He located near Philadelphia, where he established a Pestalozzian school. To introduce Pestalozzian education to a wider U.S. audience, Neef wrote *A Sketch of a Plan and Method of Education* in 1808 and *The Method of Instructing Children Rationally in the Arts of Writing and Reading* in 1813.[25] After he had established Pestalozzian schools in Pennsylvania and Kentucky, Maclure called Neef to New Harmony, Indiana, where in 1824 he had joined Robert Owen's effort to create a communitarian society. Neef was one of several Pestalozzian educators who conducted schools in the Owenite community. Maclure believed that New Harmony could be an important center for scientific research and publication and Pestalozzian education. Even after Owen had abandoned his utopian experiment, the New Harmony school press published scientific and educational works.[26]

A second phase in U.S. Pestalozzianism came with the efforts of Henry Barnard to popularize the method. Barnard, a distinguished educator, was the Connecticut Commissioner of Common schools, editor of the *Connecticut Common School Journal,* the first U.S. commissioner of education, and the editor of the *American Journal of Education.* Barnard was a popular lecturer who conducted numerous teachers' institutes. In pleading the cause of common schools, Barnard also informed his audience about the Pestalozzian method. As a journal editor, he published numerous articles on the Pestalozzian approach. In 1859, Barnard collected his essays on Pestalozzi into a single volume that was published as *Pestalozzi and Pestalozzianism.*[27] Barnard had many associates in the leading educational circles in the United States. He encouraged such individuals as Bronson Alcott, William C. Woodbridge, and William Russell to incorporate Pestalozzian principles in their educational activities.[28]

The work of Edward A. Sheldon (1823–1897) and his associates at the Oswego Normal School in New York State constituted the third major phase of Pestalozzianism in the United States.[29] As superintendent of the Normal School, Sheldon incorporated the Pestalozzian object lesson into the teacher education program. In preparing teachers, the Sheldon faculty stressed the Pestalozzian principle that all knowledge comes from sense impressions and that all instruction should be based on the examination of objects. Sheldon and his associates Margaret Jones, who had been a teacher at the Mayo's Home and Colonial Training School in England, and Herman Krusi, Jr., the son of one of Pestalozzi's teaching assistants, developed an extensive number of object lessons to teach the form, number, and name that constituted the methodological core of the Oswego program. Many of these lessons were published and used at other normal schools throughout the country. The Oswego version of Pestalozzianism attracted attention among teachers. In 1865, a report of the National Teachers' Association endorsed object teaching:

> Whenever this system has been confined to elementary instruction and has been employed by skillful, thorough teachers, in unfolding and disciplining the faculties, in fixing the attention and awakening thought, it has been successful.[30]

Sheldon and the teacher education program at Oswego Normal School improved the methodology of teachers in the common school. The implementation of the object-lesson approach organized instruction so that teachers could exercise greater planning and control in their classrooms. The Oswego approach, however, was less than the full implementation of Pestalozzi's natural method of education. It was rather the implementation of a somewhat formalized version of the object lesson.

The spirit of Pestalozzi also could be found among U.S. progressive educators of the late nineteenth and early twentieth centuries. These progressives, like Pestalozzi, struggled against the formalism and verbalism of traditional schools. Although it was only one of many influences on progressivism, Pestalozzi's general method resembled the U.S. progressive's emphasis on the interests and needs of children. William H. Kilpatrick's project method and Harold Rugg's child-centered school reflected Pestalozzi's focus on the child and on activities as the basis of learning. Unfortunately for Pestalozzi in the nineteenth century and for the progressives in the twentieth century, the traditional school was a mighty fortress. Rather than ushering in a sweeping educational revolution, the work of the reforming Pestalozzi and the later progressives brought about incremental changes that were incorporated slowly into the school's curriculum. The greatest contribution of these educational reformers was to set in motion forces that led to the gradual transformation of the school rather than to its sweeping reformation.

For education today, Pestalozzi's major contribution was developing a philosophy of natural education, which stressed the dignity of children and the importance of a child-centered curriculum. His rejection of child depravity, based on his view of a benevolent human nature, meant that he saw childhood as a uniquely important and special period of human growth. Early childhood education, in particular, was crucial in nurturing attitudes and dispositions that were conducive to later development. Pestalozzi's general method anticipated modern child psychology. The contemporary doctrines of the child-centered school and child permissiveness had their beginnings with Pestalozzi at Neuhof, Stans, Burgdorf, and Yverdon.

The value of Pestalozzi's special method rested on its relationships to children's experience. Pestalozzi anticipated Dewey in insisting on the importance of maintaining a child's continuity of experience. His stress on the need to maintain a continuum of experience caused him to examine and to use the learning possibilities found in children's immediate environment. When used in such an experiential context, Pestalozzi's instructional strategies of "from the simple to the complex" and "from the near to the far" were valuable contributions to educational methodology.

Pestalozzi also was a pioneering theorist in the sociology of education. For him, education had important social implications. Despite his own admission that he had a sentimental and visionary disposition, Pestalozzi was able to understand and interpret the broad educational importance of the political and economic trends of his time.

In terms of the ethical dimension of education, Pestalozzi sought to develop persons whose intellectual, moral, and physical powers were harmoniously developed. Fearing the effects of industrial specialization and dehumanization, he sought to educate persons who were morally sensitive to the conditions of other human beings. His goal of educating the integrated person in a moral society is desirable and defensible for our age as well as his.

Pestalozzi exhibited a basic humanitarianism. As a lover of all humankind, he made love the center of his educational theory and practice. Mother love, the loving family circle, and love of God were persistent themes in his writing. In our age, Pestalozzi's emphasis on the human being's need to be a lover and to be loved may sound simplistic and platitudinous. However, Pestalozzi's philosophy of education was essentially a "love message," in which "Papa Pestalozzi" told children simply to love one another.

Discussion Questions

1. How did the political, social, and economic context of late eighteenth- and early nineteenth-century Switzerland shape Pestalozzi's educational theories?
2. Identify and analyze the major events in Pestalozzi's life that may have shaped his educational ideas.
3. Was Pestalozzi an Enlightenment theorist?
4. Explain and analyze Pestalozzi's general and special methods.
5. To what extent was Pestalozzi a disciple of Rousseau?
6. Trace the diffusion of Pestalozzi's educational ideas.

Research and Essay Topics

1. Write a character sketch of Pestalozzi.
2. In an essay, describe a Pestalozzian school.
3. Develop a lesson plan to teach a subject or skill based on the Pestalozzian method.
4. In an essay, profile a Pestalozzian teacher as you would envision her or him.
5. In a position paper, either support or refute the statement that Pestalozzianism represents the successful transmission of an educational innovation from Europe to the United States.
6. In an essay, assess the influence of Pestalozzi's educational theory on contemporary educational practices.

Notes

1. Kate Silber. *Pestalozzi: The Man and His Work* (London: Routlege and Kegan Paul, 1960), 1–2.
2. Ibid., 108–9.
3. Ibid., 155–56.
4. Ernest E. Bayles and Bruce L. Hood. *Growth of American Educational Thought and Practice* (New York: Harper and Row, 1966), 106.
5. Frederick Mayer. *American Ideas and Education* (Columbus, Ohio: Charles E. Merrill Books, 1964), 156–57.
6. Johann H. Pestalozzi, *How Gertrude Teaches Her Children* (London: Swan Sonneschein and Co., 1907), xvii.
7. Stanley E. Ballinger. "The Natural Man: Rousseau," in Paul Nash, Andreas M. Kazamias, and Henry J. Perkinson, eds., *The Educated Man: Studies in the History of Educational Thought* (New York: John Wiley and Sons, 1965), 225–46.

8. Silber. *Pestalozzi, 2.*

9. Johann H. Pestalozzi. "Views and Experiences," in Lewis F. Anderson, ed., *Pestalozzi* (New York: McGraw Hill Book Co., 1931), 101.

10. Among the biographies of Pestalozzi are Robert B. Downs, *Heinrich Pestalozzi: Father of Modern Pedagogy* (Boston: Twayne Publishers, 1975); Gerald L. Gutek, *Pestalozzi and Education* (New York: Random House, 1968); and Silber, *Pestalozzi.*

11. My treatment of Pestalozzi's biography relies heavily on my earlier *Pestalozzi and Education,* 21–51.

12. Roger de Guimps. *Pestalozzi: His Aim and Work* (Syracuse, N.Y.: Bardeen, 1889), 6–7.

13. Ibid., 20–23.

14. Johann H. Pestalozzi, "Leonard and Gertrude," in Henry Barnard, ed., *Pestalozzi and Pestalozzianism* (New York: F. C. Brownell Publishers, 1862).

15. Gutek, *Pestalozzi and Education,* 35.

16. Pestalozzi, "Pestalozzi's Account of His Own Educational Experience," in Barnard, ed., *Pestalozzi and Pestalozzianism,* 674.

17. Johann H. Pestalozzi, *How Gertrude Teaches Her Children* (Syracuse, N.Y.: Bardeen Publishers, 1900).

18. My account of Pestalozzi's general and special methods relies on my earlier *Pestalozzi and Education,* 101–56.

19. Ibid., 88–89.

20. Ibid., 93–98.

21. Johann H. Pestalozzi. *Letters on Early Education Addressed to J. P. Greaves* (London: Sherwood, Gilbert, and Piper, 1827).

22. Elizabeth Mayo. *Lessons on Objects As Given to Children Between the Ages of Six and Eight in a Pestalozzian School* (London: Seeley and Burnside, 1835), 5–6.

23. Thomas A. Barlow, *Pestalozzi and American Education* (Boulder: Este Es Press, University of Colorado Libraries, 1977).

24. Gerald L. Gutek. *Joseph Neef: The Americanization of Pestalozzianism* (University: University of Alabama Press, 1978).

25. Joseph Neef. *Sketch of a Plan and Method of Education* (Philadelphia: Privately published, 1808), 7.

26. Arthur E. Bestor, Jr. *Backwoods Utopias: The Sectarian and Owenite Phases of Communitarian Socialism in America, 1663–1829* (Philadelphia: University of Pennsylvania Press, 1950).

27. Barnard, ed., *Pestalozzi and Pestalozzianism.*

28. Will S. Monroe. *History of the Pestalozzian Movement in the United States* (Syracuse, N.Y.: C. W. Bardeen Publishers, 1907), 147–55.

29. Ned. H. Dearborn. *The Oswego Movement in American Education* (New York: Teachers College, Columbia University, 1925).

30. Monroe, *History of the Pestalozzian Movement in the United States,* 183–84.

Suggestions for Further Reading

Anderson, Lewis F., ed. *Pestalozzi.* New York: McGraw Hill Book Co., 1931.

Barlow, Thomas A. *Pestalozzi and American Education.* Boulder: Este Es Press, University of Colorado Libraries, 1977.

Barnard, Henry, ed. *Pestalozzi and Pestalozzianism.* New York: F. C. Brownell Publishers, 1862.

Bestor, Arthur E. Jr. *Backwoods Utopias: The Sectarian and Owenite Phases of Communitarian Socialism in America, 1663–1829.* Philadelphia: University of Pennsylvania Press, 1950.

Dearborn, Ned. H. *The Oswego Movement in American Education.* New York: Teachers College, Columbia University, 1925.

DeGuimps, Roger. *Pestalozzi: His Aim and Work.* New York: D. Appleton and Co., 1895.

Downs, Robert B. *Johann Heinrich Pestalozzi: Father of Modern Pedagogy.* Boston: Twayne Publishers, 1975.

Gutek, Gerald L. *Joseph Neef: The Americanization of Pestalozzianism.* University: University of Alabama Press, 1978.

———. *Pestalozzi and Education.* New York: Random House, 1968.

Heafford, Michael R. *Pestalozzi: His Thought and Its Relevance Today.* London: Metheun, 1967.

Jedan, Dieter. *Johann Heinrich Pestalozzi and the Pestalozzian Method of Language Teaching.* Bern: Peter Lang, 1981.

Monroe, Will S. *History of the Pestalozzian Movement in the United States.* Syracuse, N.Y.: C. W. Bardeen Publishers, 1907.

Pestalozzi, Johann Heinrich. *The Education of Man—Aphorisms.* New York: Philosophical Library, 1951.

———. *How Gertrude Teaches Her Children.* London: Swan Sonnenschein and Co., 1907.

———. *Leonard and Gertrude.* Translated by Eva Channing. Boston: D. C. Heath and Co., 1891.

Silber, Kate. *Pestalozzi: The Man and His Work.* London: Routledge and Kegan Paul, 1960.

Walch, Sr. Mary Romana. *Pestalozzi and the Pestalozzian Theory of Education: A Critical Study.* Washington, D.C.: Catholic University Press, 1952.

CHAPTER II

Thomas Jefferson: Advocate of Republican Education

Portrait of Thomas Jefferson; reproduction from the collections of the Library of Congress.

Here we examine the life, political philosophy, and educational ideas of Thomas Jefferson (1743–1826), a statesman and the third president of the United States. Jefferson continues to retain an esteemed position in the "symbolical architecture" of the United States, a "civilized man" with many interests and achievements.[1] Jefferson's general philosophy of education, his plans for establishing a system of elementary and secondary schools in Virginia, and his role in founding the University of Virginia reveal him to be a political leader who developed a broad conception of education's role in republican society. By examining Jefferson's educational philosophy, it is possible to appreciate the necessary role of civic education in the newly created U.S. republic. In the broad expanse of Western educational history and philosophy, Jefferson's contributions are especially illuminating for their relationships between politics and education. In commenting on Jefferson's educational significance, Gordon Lee has noted that "many of the most influential considerations of educational theory . . . have been basically political."[2]

In this chapter, Jefferson's influence on education in the early republic is discussed in its historical context and in its enduring importance for civic education in the United States. First, the general political climate of opinion in which Jefferson lived and worked is examined. Second, Jefferson's biography, his education and career as a political leader and Enlightenment thinker, is analyzed to determine the evolution of his ideas. Third, the continuing impact of Jefferson's contributions on U.S. education, especially on the civic formation of citizens, is examined. This analysis is designed to illustrate the interrelated workings of political and educational philosophy. For example, Jefferson's educational plans were part of his search for political strategies that would make government by the people, through representative institutions, a reality. Although his educational ideas originated in the climate of the American Revolution, Jefferson addressed issues of excellence and equity in education that are still unresolved but are crucial to fulfilling the American dream.

As you read this chapter, the following questions may help you organize your thoughts:

- What were the significant ideas and trends in the historical context, the times and situation, in which Jefferson lived?
- How did Jefferson's life, his educational biography, shape his philosophy of education?
- How did Jefferson's political philosophy shape his educational policies and practices?
- What is the enduring legacy of Jefferson's contributions to U.S. education?

The Historical Context of Jefferson's Life

Jefferson's contributions to the formation and establishment of the United States as an independent and sovereign nation, a republic governed by representative institutions, can best be assessed within the large Euro-American intellectual movement known as the eighteenth-century Enlightenment. Although Jefferson gave an American rendition to the Enlightenment's ideological currents, he was intellectually aware of the more general political and scientific trends in the new pattern of thinking. By adding his own original interpretation to the ideas of the Enlightenment philosophers, he was able to implement and make his ideas a reality.

In his engrossing interpretation of the Enlightenment, the U.S. progressive historian Carl L. Becker used the concept of the "climate of opinion" to examine the Age of Reason's intellectual ferment.[3] The underlying thread that united the various strands of thought of this period was that human beings, by using their reason, possessed the possibility of improving life on Earth. For Becker, the Age of Reason—the age that shaped Jefferson and in turn was shaped by him—was continuous with but also broke with the past. For example, the theologians of the Medieval and Reformation eras construed the universe to be orderly, as did the Enlightenment's philosophers, but their explanations of this cosmic orderliness relied on different sources of authority. For the theologians of the earlier periods, the universe's order was caused by the creative act of God, a supreme supernatural being, who, taking a fatherly concern in the lives of human beings, revealed His word to them in the Bible and intervened in human history at certain crucial periods. For the Enlightenment philosophes and ideologists, the universe and governing natural laws were products of an impersonal deity, a mechanistic first cause or prime mover.

In the earlier times of Thomas Aquinas and John Calvin, the Bible was the principle authority for explaining the universe and educating people about it. For both Catholic and Protestant educators, theology provided the needed explanations. The curriculum of educational institutions under denominational auspices was laden with religiously based knowledge, practices, and values. In contrast, such Enlightenment theorists as Rousseau, Voltaire, Diderot, Condorcet, and Condillac in France and Jefferson and Franklin in the United States chose a decidedly different approach in searching for a principle of authority that explained the universe's workings.[4] For these philosophes, human reason rather than divine revelation was the key to understanding. Human beings, through their powers of reasoning, could come to the necessary truths that explained the laws of nature and to the principles that should govern human society. Human reasoning, however, was not a purely speculative process, disemboweled from political and social realities, but arose from careful and candid observations that science provided.

Jefferson and his Enlightenment colleagues believed that science and the scientific method provided the data upon which human reason should work.[5] According to their conception of science, human beings inhabited an observable natural and social world. They could observe nature and discover its regular operations and patterns. From their careful observations, systematically recorded and analyzed to find patterns, they could find natural laws such as those of gravity, planetary revolutions, the Earth's rotation, the flow of blood in the body's circulatory system, the cycles of plant and animal growth and development, and so on. In their minds, the reasonably lived life was one that followed science. The Enlightenment conception of science was one in which the universe functioned according to an intrinsic and rather mechanical design, almost like a perfect clock that, once it began to tick away seconds, minutes, and hours, would do so perpetually. This universe was stable and patterned, not subject to relativity, variation, and change as later scientists such as Darwin would assert.

Looking to nature and examining it scientifically had immense educational implications. It meant that observation of natural objects and processes was important in the learning process. Those who dealt with epistemological questions, the theory of knowledge and of knowing, such as Etienne Condillac in France and John Locke in England, concluded that the source of ideas is in the human sensory experience of objects that are outside of the mind. From these sensory perceptions—these raw data of experience—humans shaped ideas. Education, so conceived, would be less bookish, verbal, and indirect and more direct and experiential. Ideally, students would learn to think according to the scientific method. In his political theory, Jefferson wrote about principles being based on natural laws. Educators such as Pestalozzi stressed learning by examining and studying the objects found in the students' immediate environment.

In their quest for information about the physical world, the philosophes were vitally interested in collecting scientific data about the world. Their enthusiasm for finding out about nature led to the refinement and scientific development of such natural sciences as geology, chemistry, botany, zoology, and physics. They also had an explorer's curiosity about different places and peoples. For example, it was Thomas Jefferson who as U.S. president, commissioned the expedition of Lewis and Clark to gather information about the regions across the Mississippi River.[6] Further, some of the philosophes turned to anthropology in their search for the unspoiled, natural, primitive human being who lived the simple life according to the laws of nature. Again, the Enlightenment's emphasis on the importance of scientific information as the material for human reasoning had immense educational implications. Wherever they could wield influence, as in Condorcet's plan of education in revolutionary France or in Jefferson's curricular designs for the University of Virginia, they included the natural sciences in the curriculum.

The efforts of Enlightenment thinkers to include the natural sciences in the curricula of schools and colleges was not an easy task. Educational institutions historically have lagged behind in incorporating new knowledge into their curricula. Traditionalists, who staunchly defended Latin, Greek, and the classics, opposed the entry of the natural sciences into the curriculum. Domination by the classics was not the only obstacle, however. When the Enlightenment ideology came upon the intellectual scene, most educational institutions were still being conducted under the auspices and control of religious denominations. The clerics who headed and taught in these institutions believed that the principles that gave them their authority came from the Bible and from their particular church's theology.

Climates of opinion are pervasive in that ideas from one area of inquiry seep into and eventually permeate other areas of thought. The general Enlightenment reliance on scientific inquiry in the natural sciences as the most authoritative kind of reasoning also penetrated into inquiry about social questions. If there were natural laws that governed natural phenomena, was not the same true of human society? Could not political science tell us how to govern ourselves properly? Could not economics provide the principles to bring order to trade, commerce, production, and consumption? Could not anthropology and sociology tell us how human beings lived and should live in mutual association? In their enthusiasm, the philosophes optimistically believed that a new social order, undergirded by natural laws, could be created by enlightened human beings. However, general enlightenment was a necessary condition for the creation of a new society in which people would live unshackled by ignorance, prejudice, and superstition.[7]

The educational implications of the desire to create and live according to the principles of social science were immense. Now, not only would people observe the revolution of the planets, but they would also create a new society on their own planet. Throughout the eighteenth, nineteenth, and twentieth centuries, various social sciences arose and sought entry into the schools' curriculum. For certain philosophes, the social sciences were not merely academic studies, they would provide the designs to create a new social order.

At the point that social science became instrumental in creating a new society, certain Enlightenment theorists, including Jefferson, moved from philosopher to activist and from ideologue to revolutionary. Although the philosophes of the Enlightenment speculated about the possibilities of perfecting human nature, Catholic and Protestant theologians were either pessimistic or suspicious of such claims. Because of original sin, human beings had a fallen and weak human nature that needed the guidance of strong authority figures in church and state. Further, the claims of the new social sciences challenged the authority of theology and philosophy that gave the established educational authorities their legitimacy.

A further obstacle to creating an enlightened commonwealth of reasonable men and women was the political status quo. Europe was governed by hereditary monarchs, many of whom claimed that, because they ruled by the grace of God they were responsible to no one, neither the people nor their representatives. As an impasse developed between the old inherited political order and what promised to be the new, those inspired by the ideological premises and promises of the Enlightenment embarked on a revolutionary course in France and in Britain's thirteen American colonies. One of the significant leaders of this revolution in America was New World philosopher Thomas Jefferson.

From these general patterns of Enlightenment thought, it is possible to become still more specific in establishing the context of Jefferson's thinking. Although he was conversant with the ideas of the French philosophes, Jefferson felt a special intellectual kinship with the political ideology that was developed in England by John Locke, the theorist of the revolution of 1688, which replaced the Stuarts with the more constitutional monarchs, William and Mary. An important figure in the English Enlightenment, Locke's *An Essay Concerning Human Understanding*, expressed the Enlightenment's propensity for science and empiricism.[8] His *Second Treatise on Government* expressed some of the key ideas on representative government that would shape Jefferson's political ideology and hence his educational philosophy.[9]

In *An Essay Concerning Human Understanding*, Locke examined the origin and formation of ideas challenging the Platonic view that ideas were latently present in the mind. Rather, the mind's processes worked, in almost a computerlike fashion, on information that came to it from the senses. By organizing these crude sensory data, the mind formed simple ideas. Several of these simple ideas could be combined into compound ideas and aspects of many of them could be fashioned into complex ideas. The Lockean theory that the data that came to humans through their senses and were refined into ideas was quite egalitarian in that it was available to all. Locke challenged Plato's hierarchical stratification of people based on their ability to recall latent ideas. Although Locke did not assert that all people knew everything equally, his theory did claim that all had an equal possibility of knowing. However, he did not claim that all people would use this possibility. If one extrapolates from Locke's epistemology, a case can be made for providing more people with more educational opportunities.

Although Locke's *An Essay Concerning Human Understanding* held great importance for those who emphasized sensation and empiricism as the foundations of knowledge, his *Second Treatise of Government* was particularly important for Jefferson's political philosophy and as the ideology that would underlie America's Declaration of Independence from Great Britain.[10] Challenging the political authority of hereditary monarchs, Locke asserted that government arises from the consent of the people who are governed. To protect their natural rights of life, liberty, and property, Locke stated that the people joined in a mutual association and elected a government of their representatives. These representatives—divided into a law-making or legislative branch, an adjudicative or legal branch, and a law-enforcing or executive branch—governed the political commonwealth with the consent of the governed. Unlike absolute hereditary monarchs and aristocrats of birth, the members of the government were elected or appointed for a limited term of office. When their term was completed, they returned to the people from which they came. To protect property rights, taxes were to be levied only with the consent of the governed. Jefferson would incorporate these Lockean principles into the Declaration of Independence in 1776 and the framers of the U.S. Constitution would be guided by them in 1788 and 1789.

The Lockean and Jeffersonian emphasis on representative government was based on the principle of election by the people and service by elected officials. Simply stated, the results of elections were determined by counting the votes cast. In such a process, there would be candidates elected by the majority of voters and those who won only the votes of a minority would be defeated. Although the process of counting votes is a simple political procedure, it holds important meaning for republican government and for civic education. It means that those who vote should be educated so that their ballots are cast intelligently. Like the tenure in office of those whom they elect to office, it means that majorities and minorities are temporary coalitions. Today's majority may be tomorrow's minority. Those in the majority are to respect the dissent of the minority. The civic education required to make elective and representative institutions function must have knowledge of the system and a value commitment to it as well. Those who live in a representative republic need a body of knowledge upon which to make decisions, they need to be familiar with the political process, and they need to have the attitudes and demonstrate the behaviors that contribute to its effectiveness.

When Enlightenment theorists such as Locke and Jefferson stated their version of human rights, they generally did so in negative terms. That is, they stated rights that should not be violated by government. For example, Locke asserted that when a government violated the individual rights of life, liberty, and property a revolution against it is justified and the people can rise and overthrow a repressive government. Jefferson's statement of human rights in the Declaration of Independence as life, liberty, and the pursuit of happiness closely paralleled Locke's identification of human rights. The thrust of these statements was that because of their human nature individuals possessed natural and inalienable rights that governments should not violate. The Enlightenment theorists identified government as the most likely violator of human rights because they lived in a time of absolute monarchies, established churches, and hereditary aristocracies. Among such statements of human rights are that government should not interfere with freedom of speech, press, assembly, and religion.[11] Such statements designed to limit the powers of government became closely identified with liberal ideology.

In addition to the requirement that schools should provide knowledge about individual freedoms, the liberal statements regarding freedom also had meaning for education. The right to information meant that teachers should have the academic freedom to teach and that students should have the freedom to learn without censorship of ideas, information, and books. It also implied that teachers and students had the right to raise questions without interference from agents of the church and state. When Jefferson stated that the government that governs best governs least, he was arguing for limited government. When he argued against church control of higher education, he was attempting to remove what he regarded as sectarian limitations on freedom of inquiry.

The context of the age of Jefferson involved, along with the Enlightenment, the momentous events of the American Revolution and the foundational years of the early republic. Because of series of repressive economic and political acts by the British crown, representatives of discontented Americans such as John Adams, Patrick Henry, Richard Lee, and George Washington met as a Continental Congress in 1774 to determine a course of action against British repression. In 1775, actual fighting began between British troops and colonial rebels in the Massachusetts towns of Lexington and Concord.

Thomas Paine's (1737–1809) widely circulated pamphlet, *Common Sense*, expressed the revolutionary ideology's rhetoric. Following the Enlightenment's rationalist reasoning, Paine urged the colonists to free themselves from tyranny and false systems of government. Condemning hereditary monarchy, Paine ripped into George III as a "royal brute" whose arbitrary rule violated Americans' natural right to liberty.[12]

On July 2, 1776, the Continental Congress voted to separate from British rule and commissioned Thomas Jefferson to draft the Declaration of Independence, which was officially proclaimed two days later. For five years, the struggle went on between Great Britain and its former colonies. On October 19, 1781, the surrender of the British General Cornwallis at Yorktown ended hostilities. In 1783, a peace treaty was signed.

Although the military struggle to achieve independence ended in victory for the American cause, founding a new republic remained an unfinished task. Until 1787, the United States was a loose confederation of states governed by the Articles of Confederation. In that year, the Congress authorized the convening of a Constitutional Convention to meet in Philadelphia. Among the fifty-five delegates to the convention were such prominent individuals as George Washington, James Madison, Robert Morris, Benjamin Franklin, and Alexander Hamilton. Jefferson, who was on a diplomatic mission in Europe, was not present.

After long debates, convention members institutionalized the revolutionary process by creating formal structures of government. Following Enlightenment ideology, they devised a threefold division of powers in a federal government, composed of an elected legislative branch, a bicameral Congress, an indirectly elected chief executive, and an appointed judiciary. There was a further division of powers between the federal and state governments. Between 1787 and 1788, the federal Constitution was ratified by eleven of the states and thus became the document that set the processes for governing the new republic.

In 1791, the first ten amendments to the Constitution, a statement of rights in the mode of Enlightenment liberalism, were ratified by the states. The Bill of Rights, as these ten amendments were called, guaranteed the freedoms of assembly, speech, religion, and the press. They preserved the peoples' right to keep and bear arms and prohibited unreasonable search and seizure. The Tenth Amendment, which was especially significant for education, stated that those "powers not delegated to the United States by the Constitution, nor prohibited by it to the States, are reserved to the States respectively, or to the people."

Although the political foundations of the new republic had been laid with the Constitution, it still needed foundations that would educate citizens for the new republic. In place but in disrepair were the inherited schools and colleges of the colonial period. In New England were locally controlled town and district schools and Latin grammar schools that still reflected much control by religious denominations. In Rhode Island and the Middle Atlantic states of New York, New Jersey, Pennsylvania, and Delaware, the schools were generally of the parochial type and tied to religious denominations. School structures were still weaker in the South, where the dominant class of white plantation owners provided tutorial arrangements for their own children but little else for the less economically favored groups. At the summit of the hierarchy of educational institutions were the church-affiliated colleges.

If the schools and colleges in the new republic were weak structurally, they were even less suited to the nation's republican ideology. Although institutions continued to function as they had before the revolution, political and educational theorists argued that a new system of educational institutions, imbued with a republican ideology, had to be created. Leading theorists such as Benjamin Rush, Robert Coram, and Samuel Smith addressed the issue.[13] These theorists, later joined by Jefferson, were engaged in what today might be called strategic planning, or "brainstorming," and developed plans for a new U.S. educational system that embodied Enlightenment theory and a new element—cultural nationalism. Calling for a cultural revolution that would make Americans culturally independent, they wanted an education that stressed the following:

1. The knowledge and virtues that were appropriate and necessary for civic participation in a republic.

2. The inclusion of scientific knowledge, method, and temperament in the curriculum and instruction.
3. The creation of a unique and distinctive United States culture.

It is in terms of this context of the times, the philosophy of the Enlightenment and the rise of a revolutionary American republican ideology, that Jefferson must be studied.

Thomas Jefferson as a Political and Educational Statesman

In this section, we turn to the life and career of Thomas Jefferson. Our goal is to identify those events in his life that made him a political and educational statesman. The third of ten children, Thomas Jefferson, a promising son of prominent parents, was a member of one of Virginia's economically advantaged and socially prestigious families. He was born on April 13, 1743, at Shadwell, Virginia, to Peter Jefferson (1708–1757), owner of a large plantation in Virginia's Albemarle County, and Jane Randolph (1720–1776), a daughter of one of Virginia's most socially prominent families. Shadwell, the Jefferson family's plantation estate, was located near the Rivanna River in Virginia's fertile piedmont region.

Peter Jefferson, a leading figure in Virginia's plantation-owning elite, owned nearly 10,000 acres of land, more than sixty slaves, and large numbers of livestock. Active in politics, Peter Jefferson served at various times as a county sheriff, surveyor, and justice of the peace.[14] Jefferson was also a member of the House of Burgesses, Virginia's elected colonial assembly. Peter Jefferson's interest in politics and service as a government official made him a model that his son Thomas could emulate. Although involvement in public affairs was an expected part of the role that the plantation owner played in society, Jefferson, like his father, made it a lifelong commitment. In the case of the son, the commitment to public service would lead to the presidency of the republic.

Thomas Jefferson's early educational experiences were directed by his father. When his son was five, Peter Jefferson engaged a tutor who taught Thomas the rudiments of reading, writing, and arithmetic. Employing a tutor was typical of the plantation-owning class of Virginia and the other southern states. Unlike the residents of New England's Massachusetts, Connecticut, and New Hampshire who established town schools, the southern gentry regarded education as a private family matter rather than a community responsibility.

When he was nine, Thomas was enrolled in a Latin grammar school conducted by the Reverend William Douglas, minister of St. James parish in Goochland County. Anglican clergymen like Douglas often maintained preparatory schools. Because the school was located some distance from the Jefferson plantation, he boarded at the school. For the next five years, he studied at Douglas' school, where he pursued the typical Latin grammar school curriculum of Latin and Greek. He also studied French.[15] Although he did not regard Douglas as an inspired teacher, Jefferson was introduced to the classical languages, which were still considered indispensable for the educated person. Throughout his life, he would read classical works in their original languages rather than in translations.

When Jefferson was fourteen, his father died and Thomas returned to the family plantation at Shadwell. Despite the loss of his father, Jefferson continued his education and enrolled in a school conducted by the Reverend James Maury, an Anglican minister at Fredericksburg, located twelve miles from Shadwell. From Maury as well as Douglas, Jefferson learned the theology and principles of the Church of England. Although interested in religion, Jefferson as an adult was skeptical that the doctrines of Christianity were divinely inspired. Maury, esteemed as one of Virginia's most learned scholars and teachers, stressed the traditional Latin and Greek classical curriculum, which was a necessary preparation for college admission. In addition to the classics, Jefferson became familiar with English literature and history and benefitted from the opportunity to use Maury's large library.[16] As a complement to his formal schooling, Jefferson also learned to dance, ride, and hunt, skills appropriate to the well-rounded Virginia gentleman.

At seventeen, Jefferson was admitted as a student to the College of William and Mary, located in Williamsburg. Here, in Virginia's capital of 1,500 people, he received a formal education at the college and an informal political education by observing the General Court and the House of Burgesses. At the time of Jefferson's enrollment in 1760, William and Mary enrolled 100 students in its three branches—the grammar school, the Indian school, and the philosophy school. Because Jefferson already had a preparatory education, he was enrolled in the philosophy school. His studies included mathematics, physics, metaphysics, logic, ethics, rhetoric, and literature.[17] Jefferson's educational encounter with the western classical tradition shaped his intellectual development. It encouraged him to build philosophical foundations for what would be political action.

The college's faculty consisted of seven professors, six of whom were Anglican ministers. The seventh professor, Dr. William Small, who specialized in mathematics and natural sciences, was Jefferson's adviser.[18] Opening his mind to science, Jefferson found Small to be a liberalizing influence. He fondly recalled him as "a man profound in most of the useful branches of science, with a happy talent of communication, correct and gentlemanly manners, and an enlarged and liberal mind."[19]

Jefferson completed his studies in the liberal arts and graduated in 1762. He now determined to study law and read in that subject with George Wythe, a learned and influential Williamsburg attorney. Although law was a recognized academic discipline at the large European universities, the general practice for becoming a lawyer in the colonies was to read law. Reading law was a kind of apprenticeship in which the aspiring young man would join the office of an established practicing lawyer and perform an internship. The intern would have access to his mentor's library and experience. Jefferson was fortunate to have Wythe as his legal mentor as he was a member of the House of Burgesses who enjoyed a positive reputation throughout Virginia. Jefferson studied with Wythe for five years. During this time, he read the great legal classics such as Sir Edward Coke's *Institutes of the Laws of England*, Lord Henry Kames' *Historical Law Tracts*, and Bernard Hale's *History of the Common Law*.[20] In 1767, Jefferson was admitted to the practice of law.

Jefferson was fortunate that his college years and years of legal preparation were spent in Williamsburg, the center of Virginia's political and cultural life. His association with Wythe enabled him to meet important and influential political leaders. His political education came from firsthand observation of sessions of the General Court and the House of Burgesses. Here, he followed the great debates over public policy that were slowly but definitely leading the Virginia colonists on the course that would separate them from Great Britain.

When he was 21, Jefferson assumed the role of plantation owner, managing 5,000 acres in Albemarle and adjacent counties. He, like other plantation owners, used enslaved Africans as the agricultural workforce. Although part of the slave system, Jefferson had doubts about it. However, he took no actions against slavery, a gross inconsistency with his espousal of natural rights principles.[21]

Jefferson studied the architectural works of James Gibbs and Robert Morris and implemented his ideas of design in building Monticello, the name he gave to his mountain-top mansion. Throughout his life, he redesigned and added to Monticello—which would be a center of his life, a place of family domesticity, quiet contemplation, and lively sociability. He was interested in horticulture and designed landscape gardens to grace his country estate. On January 1, 1772, Jefferson married Martha Wayles Skelton (1748-1782) who, like Jefferson, was from an influential Virginia family. Jefferson and his wife were the parents of six children. Jefferson was devoted to Martha, and after her death in 1782, Jefferson suffered a deep depression which lifted only very slowly.

By birth, education, and cultural association, Jefferson was prepared to be a member of the gentlemanly southern elite who, along with the New England Yankee, would shape the new republic's course when the revolution brought independence. Versed in law and politics, he continued to read widely, especially in the books that provided the theory of what would become the revolutionary ideology. He read John Locke's *Second Treatise on Government*, Jean Jacques Burlamaqui's *Principles du Droit de la Nature et des gens*, Anthony Elly's *Tracts on the Liberty, Spiritual and Temporal, of Protestants in England*, and Adam Ferguson's *An Essay on the History of Civil Society*.[22] He also poured through the works of Charles Montesquieu, who applied Enlightenment ideology to such questions as inequality, law, and the social compact.[23] A widely read man who valued books, Jefferson spent time and money assembling a large library.[24] Although Jefferson enjoyed the educational opportunities and benefits of wealth and position, he applied himself to a lifelong learning that went beyond his formal schooling. A person of wide-ranging intellectual interests, Jefferson was knowledgeable about philosophy, political theory, archeology, architecture, and horticulture. His presidency was marked by a conception of that office that combined the attributes of the scholar, teacher, and leader. As a political leader, Jefferson was skilled in employing the often-contradictory idioms of the enlightened scholar and popular democrat.[25]

Jefferson's actual political career began with his election to the House of Burgesses in 1769. He arrived in Williamsburg to take his seat at a time when the colonial representatives were protesting the imposition of taxes caused by the Townshend duties. For the next decade, Jefferson supported the colonial cause against

Great Britain. In 1773, he was a member of the Committee of Correspondence that was coordinating colonial strategy against British domination. In 1775, he was elected as one of Virginia's representatives to the Continental Congress in Philadelphia. Jefferson was named to the committee charged with drafting a statement of the colonists' grievances against England and declaring independence. As the Declaration of Independence's principal author, Jefferson envisioned himself as a voice of the people, expressing in words what Americans thought.[26] Succinctly embodying Lockean and Enlightenment political theory, Jefferson's original draft of the Declaration of Independence stated:

> We hold these truths to be sacred & undeniable, that all men are created equal & independent, that from that equal creation they derive rights inherent & inalienable, among which are the preservation of life, & liberty, & the pursuit of happiness; that to secure these ends, governments are instituted among men, deriving their just powers from the consent of the governed; that whenever any form of government shall become destructive of these ends, it is the right of the people to alter or to abolish it, & to institute new government, laying its foundation on such principles & organizing its powers in such form, as to them shall seem most likely to effect their safety & happiness.[27]

In October 1776, Jefferson returned to Virginia to take his place in the state's General Assembly. Here, he turned his attention to a series of proposed reforms that clearly demonstrated his liberal political philosophy and enlightened temperament. By examining his efforts at establishing and reforming political structures in Virginia, it is possible to capture the essence of what in the future would be known as Jeffersonian republicanism. His career in state government is especially illuminating for his concept of civic education.

Influenced by the Enlightenment's general attitude to religion, Jefferson, a "deistic humanist," viewed God abstractly as the "master mind, the supreme artificer, the Creator," rather than according to the Judeo-Christian conception of the Supreme Being as a personal, caring, or law-giving God.[28] Following the principles of Lockean liberalism, Jefferson also opposed state churches, such as the Church of England, which was established as the official church of Virginia. Intellectually, he believed that religious dogmas interfered with the free pursuit of knowledge. A strong believer in separation of church and state, Jefferson introduced a "Bill for Establishing Religious Freedom" in the Virginia Assembly in 1779. In the bill, he stated that "God . . . created the mind free, and manifested his supreme will that free it shall remain by making it altogether insusceptible of restraint." Arguing against religious tests as a basis for citizenship, Jefferson asserted that "civil rights have no dependence on our religious opinions."[29] In a strong statement for separation of church and state, Jefferson's bill, which was enacted in 1786, read:

> We the General Assembly of Virginia do enact that no man shall be compelled to frequent or support any religious worship, place, or ministry whatsoever, nor shall be enforced, restrained, molested, or burthened in his body or goods, nor

shall otherwise suffer, on account of his religious opinions or belief; but that all men shall be free to profess, and by argument to maintain, their opinions in matters of religion, and that the same shall in no wise diminish, enlarge, or affect their civil capacities.[30]

Jefferson's bill for complete religious freedom represented the founding fathers' belief in strict separation of church and state. In the nineteenth and twentieth centuries, the Supreme Court of the United States would uphold the concept of separation between church and state and between the church and public education.[31] Throughout his life, Jefferson opposed the influence of religious denominations over schools and colleges as being inimical to freedom of inquiry. Although Jefferson was effective in disestablishing a state church in Virginia, in other states, especially those of New England, the relationship between religious denominationalism and schooling remained close.

In 1779, Jefferson introduced his bill "for the more general diffusion of knowledge," which was designed to create a state system of schools. Although he was not successful in securing its passage, the bill was an important landmark in U.S. educational history in that it asserted the responsibility of the state and the local community for establishing and maintaining public schools. Because of its importance this bill will be examined in depth in a succeeding section of this chapter.

From 1779 to 1781, Jefferson served as Virginia's governor. He was concerned primarily with coordinating the war effort against the British. In 1783, he was involved with drafting Virginia's new constitution. His next assignment on behalf of the new republic took him to Europe, where he served as ambassador to France. Because of his skill in diplomacy, he was named secretary of state, serving from 1789 to 1793. Along with Benjamin Franklin, Jefferson was one of the early architects of U.S. foreign policy.[32] As a diplomat, he pursued gaining the European powers' recognition of the United States as an independent and sovereign nation.

Jefferson recognized that the United States needed to develop its cultural as well as political identity as an independent nation. Although appreciating the need of Americans to relate to and understand the intellectual, scientific, and cultural achievements of other nations, he believed that the U.S. experience in the New World environment was shaping a new people with their own cultural identity. For him, each generation had its own right to be independent of preceding ones and unfettered by chains of tradition to work out its own destiny.[33] However, the working out of one's own destiny did not take place in cultural isolation. In pursuit of the goal of cultural sovereignty and to satisfy his own intellectual curiosity, Jefferson was in contact with the leading intellectuals of both Europe and the Americas.

In 1780, Jefferson began to work on a manuscript that grew out of inquiries made by Francois Marbois, the secretary of the French minister, about the topography, climate, population, flora, and fauna of Virginia.[34] Marbois was conducting a survey of all of the states and Jefferson was responding for Virginia. Jefferson's manuscript, later published as *Notes on the State of Virginia*, is regarded as one of the most significant scientific and political books on the United States published in the eighteenth century.[35] In it, Jefferson challenged the theory of the French naturalist, Buffon, who had claimed that North American people, plants, and animals were steadily degenerating.[36]

Jefferson's *Notes*, a far-ranging work, encompassed such topics as Virginia's minerals and soils, its river system, the conditions of Indians, the institution of slavery, the servitude of blacks, and the constitution, laws, and politics of the state. The book revealed Jefferson's intellectual flexibility and provided evidence of his preference for political arrangements that rested on freehold, independent farmers and his general reluctance to see a positive influence coming from large urban settings.[37]

In *Notes* he substituted "the pursuit of happiness" for Locke's natural right of "property." He argued that all men, not only property holders, had political rights. *Notes* also included sections on Jefferson's educational views and the condition of Virginia's schools and colleges. He indicated his belief in the possibility of educating a "aristocracy of virtue and talent" that was not defined by property.[38] He also expressed his forebodings about the pernicious effects of slavery on the future of Virginia. Jefferson's scientific contributions were recognized in both Europe and the United States. In 1797, he was elected president of the American Philosophical Society, an organization that sponsored a range of cultural and scientific endeavors and explorations.

As the United States entered the nineteenth century, new political coalitions were at work to form the political party system. Those who favored a strong central government, with limited state power, organized as the Federalist party. Including such individuals as Alexander Hamilton and John Adams, the Federalists saw the federal government as the leading force in developing the new nation. Those who opposed the Federalists gathered in a loose coalition known as the Democratic-Republicans led by Thomas Jefferson. Also known as Jeffersonians, they believed in limited federal power and championed the cause of state rights. Jefferson envisioned a popularly based government with power residing in the hands of freeholders, those who owned small farms. He was suspicious of the concentration of political power in the hands of vested special interests who would pursue their own interests to the sacrifice of the common good.

Although the rival Federalist, or Hamiltonian, and Jeffersonian positions held immense implications for national political policy, they also have important implications for educational philosophy and policy as well. The Hamiltonian position, which resurfaced later as the Whig and then the Republican parties, tended to give the federal government a paramount position in national, especially economic, development. The Whigs and Republicans would follow a policy of "internal improvements" by which the federal government would provide subsidies to certain industries such as canal and railroad building. Within their various states in the nineteenth century, first the Whigs and then the Republicans generally supported common or public schools as a means of national development. (See Chapter 13 on Horace Mann for the Whig role in the common school movement.) Although Jefferson was committed to education and to the provision of schooling, his philosophy rested on a notion of civic education tied to individual and state initiative. He feared concentrations of power.

In 1803, Jefferson's administration successfully negotiated the Louisiana Purchase from France for $15 million. The addition of the vast territory more than doubled the size of the United States and carried the national boundaries far beyond the Mississippi River.[39] In 1804, Jefferson commissioned the transcontinental explorations of Meriwether Lewis and William Clark. The expedition, which took the two explorers from St. Louis, Missouri, to the Pacific Ocean, was intended to assess the economic potential of the new territory and provide scientific and geographical information about the land.[40] It was one of history's ironies that Jefferson, the disciple of limited government, used the presidency and the national government to increase the nation's size.

After leaving the presidency, Jefferson returned to his estate at Monticello, where he pursued his intellectual activities. In 1814, he made another intellectual contribution to his country by offering his library to Congress as a replacement for the holdings of the Library of Congress, which had been destroyed during the British attack on Washington in the War of 1812. Jefferson's vast library of 6,487 volumes was sold to Congress for $23,950. He immediately began a new collection of his own. In the last years of his life, Jefferson energetically devoted himself to founding the University of Virginia. His role in planning and establishing the new university will be discussed in the next section.

Jefferson on Education

Jefferson saw education as the necessary foundation of a free people who governed themselves through representative institutions. His political role in the new republic as well as his own personal intellectual sensitivity produced a deep and sustained interest in educational institutions and processes. Resting upon his political philosophy with its roots in the intellectual climate of the Enlightenment, Jefferson envisioned several broad goals for civic education in the new republic:

1. State-supported and locally controlled schooling should provide the population with a basic literary, mathematical, and historical education.
2. Schools should be agencies of identifying, selecting, and preparing the most talented persons for positions of leadership by providing access to higher education.
3. Popular education should advance the cause of human liberty and freedom by safeguarding the individual's natural rights.

In 1779, as a member of the Virginia legislature, Jefferson introduced a bill for "the more general diffusion of knowledge," which was designed to establish a state system of elementary and secondary schools.[41] Although the bill did not become law then nor in subsequent efforts by Jefferson, it demonstrates Jefferson's early commitment to public schooling as a component of republican citizenship and as a state responsibility. The bill should be considered not only as one of the educational plans of the revolutionary republican generation but as raising important issues about equity and excellence. To state these questions about excellence and equity at the onset of our discussion of Jefferson's bill reveals his thinking on a matter that has been a recurring and debated question in U.S. education.

The question of excellence relates to the idea that educational institutions should identify and cultivate the intellectual abilities of the most gifted students. The assumption is that intellectual ability is unevenly distributed in the general population and that the academically talented are a small minority of the population. The concept of an aristocracy of intellect has been an enduring one in Western civilization, having found expression in such classical statements as Plato's *Republic*. In the European educational tradition, the concept of a gifted minority found institutional expression in the limited access of the general population to secondary and higher education. Although Plato held that the philosopher-kings could be found throughout the population, the history of Western education showed that males from the upper socio-economic classes or the aristocracy dominated secondary and higher education and had the greatest opportunity to occupy leadership positions. Because of circumstances of birth, gender, and class, the majority of people were denied the opportunity to become leaders.

Given the revolutionary ethic of the new republic, the issue of equality of opportunity to educational resources was taking shape. Although it would take two centuries to equalize the educational opportunities of women, racial and other minorities, and the handicapped, Jefferson was beginning to see the dimensions of the equity issue. He also realized that general knowledge, a kind of civic literacy, was indispensable if the representative institutions of the new nation were to function effectively. Jefferson began to deal with the issues of excellence and equity in education in a limited way conditioned by the social and economic realities of the time.

According to Jefferson's plan for the diffusion of knowledge, each of Virginia's counties would be divided into "hundreds," another name for a local district derived from the Anglo-Saxon. In each hundred, an elementary school would be built at a convenient location and maintained at public expense. These hundred schools would enroll all free boys and girls, who would attend for three years. The curriculum would emphasize the basic primary level skills of reading, writing, and arithmetic. The history of Greece, Rome, Great Britain, and North America also would be studied. Although the first three years of elementary schooling would be at public expense, children could continue beyond three years at their parents' expense. By contemporary standards, Jefferson's proposal made an attempt to provide a modest degree of equity to the free children of the state; slave children were excluded. It was an effort to provide the basic literacy needed for representative government.

Jefferson's proposal also provided that twenty grammar, or secondary, schools be established where promising youngsters could continue their education and proceed to college. The grammar school curriculum was to consist of Latin, Greek, English, geography, and advanced mathematics.[42] From clusters of ten elementary schools, the most intellectually promising students whose parents were unable to pay tuition would receive a merit scholarship to attend a grammar school. Students who were able to pay their own tuition were allowed to attend. After one year, one-third of the least promising of the state-supported merit students would be dropped. At the completion of the second year, another selection would be made with only the most promising merit scholars remaining.[43] In each grammar school for each class, the most intellectually able student would continue to study for an additional four years, thus completing the six years of grammar school. In any given year, twenty state-supported merit scholars would complete grammar school. Of these twenty, the top ten would continue their education at the College of William and Mary. The lower ten would become grammar school teachers or enter public service.[44]

Although Jefferson's plan would make elementary education available to all free children, the role he assigned to secondary schooling was highly selective. It did provide an opportunity for a small number of economically deprived children to receive a secondary education, but the thrust of the plan was selectivity. However, this principle was not based on membership in a socially or economically advantaged class. The selection of the intellectually able was free of class bias. Jefferson's compromise between excellence and equity was an uneasy one. The question remains, however, of whether it is possible for education to be equal and academically excellent at the same time. Although not enacted, Jefferson's bill anticipated the promise of public education that would come with the common school movement of the nineteenth century (see Chapter 13).

Throughout his life, Jefferson worked to establish a complete system of educational institutions for Virginia that encompassed elementary, secondary, and higher education. When he found his efforts to establish state-supported elementary and secondary schools frustrated by a reluctant state legislature, Jefferson turned his attention to higher education. Concerned with the educational development of his state, he had at first tried to build an educational system from the lower levels upward. Now he changed his strategy and determined that, if an excellent state university could be established, the momentum that flowed from the top downward would lead to a system of lower schools.

Higher education had long been an interest of the former president who had proposed a reorganization of the College of William and Mary in 1779. When the Virginia legislature failed to act on his proposed reforms, Jefferson, as a member of the board of visitors, worked with William and Mary's president, the Reverend James Madison, on an internal reform of the College. The professorships in the grammar and divinity schools were converted into chairs of medicine, law, and modern languages. However, the conservative board soon reasserted its control and undermined Jefferson's reforms.[45] Jefferson abandoned his plan to make William and Mary the apex of his educational plan.

Jefferson turned his attention to what would become a new state university, the University of Virginia. As was true of his style of leadership throughout his career, Jefferson first did his research. He collected information about the existing colleges and universities of Europe and the United States. Although he appreciated the role that such universities as Oxford and Cambridge had played in preserving and transmitting knowledge, he believed their emphasis on ancient language and literature made them inadequate models for United States' universities. The new republic, an experiment in representative government, needed institutions of higher learning that were open to change and were scientific in outlook. Nor did New England's Harvard and Yale, with their roots in denominational religions, present the model that Jefferson wanted. The university Jefferson envisioned would be state established and publicly supported and controlled. It would be of such an excellent academic character and would boast such superior facilities that it would attract the most able students and the finest faculty. Even before the Virginia legislature authorized a state university, Jefferson was planning the facilities of what would be an "academic village" of attractive classrooms, libraries, and dwellings for professors and students.

In 1816, the Virginia legislature authorized the establishment of what was called the "Central College," which eventually became the new university. The board of visitors, or trustees, of the college included Jefferson; James Madison, another former president; James Monroe, the current president; and three other prominent Virginians. In 1818, Jefferson's plan for the University of Virginia moved forward. Governor James P. Preston appointed a commission to recommend the location of the university. In a meeting on August 1, 1818, at Rockfish Gap in the Blue Ridge Mountains, the commission elected Jefferson as its chairman and voted to locate the new university at Central College.

The Rockfish Gap Report embodied Jefferson's plan for the University of Virginia.[46] It contained his specifications on the architectural design and location of the buildings, the nature of the curriculum, and the appointment of the professors. Wanting the university to provide the useful knowledge that the development of the new republic required, Jefferson saw the overriding educational goal of the institution to be the promotion of scientific inquiry and instruction. The architectural style of the buildings would be classical and reflect the purest style of ancient Greece. By 1819, construction of the buildings was under way and Jefferson had been elected the first rector of the University of Virginia.

A search was conducted to find the finest scholars in Europe and America to serve as the institution's faculty. Appointments were made in the fields of natural history or science, mathematics, ancient languages, modern languages, anatomy and medicine, natural philosophy, and moral philosophy. As rector, Jefferson prepared the bylaws that would govern the university, requirements for examinations and degrees, and even the schedule of classes.[47] On March 7, 1825, the first class of thirty students entered the University of Virginia, which Jefferson dedicated to the pursuit of truth. For Jefferson, the new institution would encourage the "illimitable freedom of the human mind. For here we are not afraid to follow truth wherever it may lead, nor to tolerate any error so long as reason is left free to combat it."[48]

Conclusion: An Assessment

By the standards of his own time as well as those of today, Thomas Jefferson must be judged an exceptional person. A statesman in the most complete sense of the word, he developed many of the political concepts that were embodied in the institutions of the new U.S. republic. His work was larger and more encompassing than political ideology, however. He realized that for a free people to maintain representative institutions of government a system of accessible education was needed. His proposals for the more general diffusion of knowledge and for the establishment of the University of Virginia were attempts to create educational institutions that could enlighten a politically free people.

Jefferson's conception of the role of the political leader, indeed the president, is noteworthy. As a statesman and national leader, Jefferson was a well-read, scholarly person who based his theories on research. His quest for knowledge led him to many areas of scholarship—political theory, philosophy, anthropology, history, literature, horticulture, geography, religion, and architecture. He was the generalist who had a comprehensive understanding of many areas of knowledge. The general breadth of his knowledge enabled him to have a large vision of what the new nation could be. It also enabled him to avoid special interests and to pursue the common good.

Jefferson, who organized a political party and served in a number of appointed and elective offices including the presidency, was a practitioner as well as a theorist. He had the capacity to formulate policy and to seek and often secure its implementation. Although he did not secure passage of his bill for the more general diffusion of knowledge, Jefferson was successful in creating the University of Virginia. His success in founding the new state university provides an excellent example of Jefferson as a policy formulator and implementor. His legacy in this instance is especially significant for what is now known as educational policy studies. Jefferson researched the problem of how to create a new state university by going to the theoretical foundations of higher education and examining relevant aspects of the history, philosophy, and governance of higher education. He then used this theory to devise a policy for a state university that was public, state supported and controlled, and that would advance both general and scientific knowledge. Through a series of political steps—his service on the board of the Central College and as a member of the commission on the state university—Jefferson secured passage of the legislation that established and funded the new university. A study of his life, career, and activities is particularly illuminating as a historical and biographical model that describes the area of educational policy.

Although the United States and its educational system had a number of founding fathers, each of whom brought a special and often different meaning to the philosophy of education for the republic, Jefferson was the father of a particular approach to civic education. For him, education was to be general for all people to provide them with the basic skills needed to participate as citizens of a nation with representative institutions. Although it had the egalitarian component of providing popular enlightenment, Jefferson also saw it as exercising a highly selective role in identifying and educating those who were to be the nation's leaders. He recognized and tried to reconcile the dichotomy that continues to exist in U.S. education between the apparently opposing needs for equity and excellence.

Above all, Jefferson believed in removing the obstacles and impediments to human thought. For him, arbitrary government and state-supported churches that controlled educational institutions were the impediments to freedom of thought, inquiry, teaching, and learning. He was a decided proponent of the principle of separation of church and state, which has come to be a characteristic of U.S. education.

As a representative of the Enlightenment in North America, as a founding father of the republic, and as architect of the University of Virginia, Thomas Jefferson is a commanding figure in U.S. political and educational history. His biography illustrates the relationships between theory and practice.

Discussion Questions

1. What currents of Enlightenment thinking were especially influential in shaping the ideas of the American revolutionary generation?
2. How were the principles of Enlightenment science especially appropriate to the North American situation?
3. Examine the political and educational ideas of Jefferson as a part of an intellectual transaction between Europe and America.
4. How did the key events in Jefferson's life shape his political and educational philosophy?
5. How did Jefferson's educational philosophy include strategies for both selection of an elite and equalitarianism?
6. Describe Jefferson's work in founding the University of Virginia.
7. Analyze Jefferson's concept of civic education.
8. Analyze Jefferson's concept of the president as a mentor of the people.

Research and Essay Topics

1. Read and review Becker's *The Heavenly City of the Eighteenth Century Philosophers* (see Suggestions for Further Reading).
2. Select several books used in courses in U.S. history at the secondary level. In a paper, analyze the treatment that Jefferson receives in these books.
3. Prepare a paper that analyzes Jefferson's style of leadership.
4. Identify Jefferson's major political and educational principles. In a position paper, determine the relevance of these principles for contemporary U.S. society.
5. In a paper, examine Jefferson's use of science as an instrument of national policy.
6. In a paper, apply Jefferson's concepts of selection and equality to contemporary educational institutions.

Notes

1. Peter S. Onuf, "The Scholar's Jefferson," *The William and Mary Quarterly,* 50 (October 1993), 671.
2. Gordon C. Lee, ed., *Crusade Against Ignorance: Thomas Jefferson on Education* (New York: Bureau of Publications, Teachers College Press, Columbia University, 1961), 1.
3. Carl L. Becker, *The Heavenly City of the Eighteenth Century Philosophers* (New Haven, Conn.: Yale University Press, 1932).
4. Douglas L. Wilson, "Thomas Jefferson's Library and the French Connection," *Eighteenth Century Studies,* 26 (Summer 1993), 669–685.
5. John C. Greene, *American Science in the Age of Jefferson* (Ames, Iowa: Iowa State University Press, 1984).
6. Kathleen Tobin-Schlesinger, "Jefferson to Lewis: The Study of Nature in the West," *Journal of the West,* 29 (January 1990), 54–61. Also, see Inguard H. Eide, *American Odyssey: The Journey of Louis and Clark* (Chicago: Rand McNally, 1969).
7. R. R. Palmer, *The Improvement of Humanity: Education and the French Revolution* (Princeton, N.J.: Princeton University Press, 1985).

8. John Locke, *An Essay Concerning Human Understanding*, ed. Raymond Wilburn (New York: Dutton, 1947).

9. John Dunn, *Locke* (Oxford, U.K.: Oxford University Press, 1984), 22–59.

10. Garrett W. Sheldon, *The Political Philosophy of Thomas Jefferson* (Baltimore, Md.: Johns Hopkins Press, 1991), 2–3, 45.

11. Alan L. Golden and James L. Golden, "Thomas Jefferson's Perspectives on the Press as an Instrument of Political Communication," *The American Behavioral Scientist*, 37 (November 1993), 194–99.

12. Thomas Paine, *Common Sense on the Origin and Design of Government in General, with Concise Remarks on the English Constitution; Together with the American Crisis, 1776–1783* (New York: G.P. Putnam's Sons, n.d.).

13. Allen Ol Hansen, *Liberalism and American Education in the Eighteenth Century* (New York: Macmillan Publishing Co., 1926).

14. Robert D. Heslep, *Thomas Jefferson and Education* (New York: Random House, 1969), 31–32.

15. Noble E. Cunningham, Jr., *In Pursuit of Reason: The Life of Thomas Jefferson* (New York: Ballantine Books, 1987), 4.

16. Harold Hellenbrand, *The Unfinished Revolution: Education and Politics in the Thought of Thomas Jefferson* (Newark: University of Delaware Press, 1990), 120.

17. Cunningham, 4.

18. Ludwell H. Johnson III, "Sharper Than a Serpent's Tooth: Thomas Jefferson and His Alma Mater," *The Virginia Magazine of History and Biography*, 99, No. 2 (April 1991), 145.

19. Heslep, 34.

20. Edward Coke, *The Second Part of the Institutes of the Laws of England; Containing the Exposition of Many Ancient and other Statues* (London: E. and R. Brooke, 1799), and Lord Henry Kames, *Historical Law Tracts* (London: 1758).

21. Onuf, 675.

22. Jean Jacques Burlamaqui, *Principes du Droit de la Nature et des gens* (Yverdon, 1768); Anthomy Ellys, *Tracts on the Liberty, Spiritual and Temporal, of Protestants in England* (London: W. Bowyer, 1765); and Adam Ferguson, *An Essay on the History of Civil Society* (London: 1767).

23. Charles de Secondat Montesquieu, *The Spirit of the Laws*, ed., David Wallace (Berkeley: University of California Press, 1977).

24. Arthur E. Bestor, Jr., David C. Mearns, and Jonathan Daniels, *Three Presidents and Their Books* (Urbana: University of Illinois Press, 1955).

25. Onuf, 680.

26. Ibid., 681.

27. "Jefferson's Original Rough Draught of the Declaration of Independence," in eds. Julian P. Boyd, et al., *The Papers of Thomas Jefferson, I* (Princeton, N.J.: Princeton University Press, 1950), as quoted in Heslep, *Thomas Jefferson and Education*, 46.

28. Lee, 10–11.

29. Jefferson, "A Bill for Establishing Religious Freedom," in eds. Julian P. Boyd, et al., *The Papers of Thomas Jefferson, II* (Princeton, N.J.: Princeton University Press, 1950), 545–47, as quoted in Lee, *Crusade Against Ignorance*, 66.

30. Ibid., 68.

31. Roger P. Magnuson, "Thomas Jefferson and the Separation of Church and State," *The Educational Forum* 27 (May 1963), 417–21.

32. Robert W. Tucker and David C. Hendrickson, *Empire of Liberty: The Statecraft of Thomas Jefferson* (New York: Oxford University Press, 1990).

33. Onuf, 681.
34. Cunningham, *In Pursuit of Reason,* 76. Also, see Thomas Jefferson, *Notes on the State of Virginia*, ed. William Peden, (Chapel Hill, N.C.: University of North Carolina Press, 1954).
35. Greene, *American Science in the Age of Jefferson*, 409.
36. Gisela Tauber, "Notes on the State of Virginia: Thomas Jefferson's Unintentional Self-Portrait," *Eighteenth Century Studies* 26 (Summer 1993), 637.
37. Ibid., 635.
38. Ibid., 645.
39. James K. Hosmer, *The History of the Louisiana Purchase* (New York: D. Appleton and Co., 1908), and Lois Houck, *The Boundaries of the Louisiana Purchase* (New York: Arno Press, 1971). Also, see Dan L. Flores, ed., *Jefferson and the Southwestern Exploration: The Freeman and Custis Accounts of the Red River Expedition of 1806* (Norman: University of Oklahoma Press, 1984).
40. Tobin-Schlesinger, "Jefferson to Lewis: The Study of Nature in the West." Also, see Donald Jackson, ed., *Letters of the Lewis and Clark Expeditions, with Related Documents* (Urbana: University of Illinois Press, 1978).
41. Thomas Jefferson, "A Bill for the More General Diffusion of Knowledge," in Boyd et al., eds., *The Papers of Thomas Jefferson II,* 526–33, as quoted in Gerald L. Gutek, *An Historical Introduction to American Education*, 2nd ed. (Prospect Heights, IL: Waveland Press, 1991), 46–52.
42. Ibid.
43. Merle Curti, *The Social Ideas of American Educators* (Paterson, N.J.: Littlefield, Adams & Co., 1959), 34–49.
44. Cunningham, 59.
45. Ludwell H. Johnson III, "Sharper Than a Serpent's Tooth: Thomas Jefferson and His Alma Mater."
46. "Report of the Commissioners Appointed to Fix the Site of the University of Virginia," in Lee, *Crusade Against Ignorance*, 114–33.
47. Cunningham, 337–45.
48. Ibid., 344.

Suggestions for Further Reading

Ambrose, Stephen E. *Meriwether Lewis, Thomas Jefferson, and the Opening of the American West*. New York: Simon and Schuster, 1996.

Becker, Carl L. *The Declaration of Independence: A Study in the History of Political Ideas*. New York: Alfred A. Knopf, 1942.

———. *The Heavenly City of the Eighteenth Century Philosophers*. New Haven, Conn.: Yale University Press, 1932.

Bestor, Arthur E., Jr.; David C. Mearns, and Jonathan Daniels. *Three Presidents and Their Books*. Urbana: University of Illinois Press, 1955.

Boorstin, Daniel J. *The Lost World of Thomas Jefferson*. Boston: Beacon Press, 1960.

Burstein, Meyer L. *Understanding Thomas Jefferson: Studies in Economics, Law and Philosophy*. New York: St. Martin's Press, 1993.

Cunningham, Noble F. Jr. *In Pursuit of Reason: The Life of Thomas Jefferson*. New York: Ballantine Books, 1987.

Dunn, John. *Locke*. Oxford: Oxford University Press, 1984.

Fliegelman, Jay. *Declaring Independence: Jefferson, Natural Language & the Culture of Performance*. Stanford, Calif.: Stanford University Press, 1993.

Greene, John C. *American Science in the Age of Jefferson*. Ames: Iowa State University Press, 1984.

Hansen, Allen O. *Liberalism and American Education in the Eighteenth Century*. New York: Macmillan Publishing Company, 1926.

Hellenbrand, Harold. *The Unfinished Revolution: Education and Politics in the Thought of Thomas Jefferson*. Newark: University of Delaware Press, 1990.

Heslep, Robert D. *Thomas Jefferson and Education*. New York: Random House, 1969.

Honeywell, Roy J. *The Educational Work of Thomas Jefferson*. Cambridge, Mass.: Harvard University Press, 1931.

Jefferson, Thomas. *Notes on the State of Virginia*. Edited by William Peden. Chapel Hill, N.C.: University of North Carolina Press, 1954.

Lee, Gordon C. *Crusade Against Ignorance: Thomas Jefferson on Education*. New York: Bureau of Publications, Teachers College, Columbia University, 1961.

Malone, Dumas. *Jefferson: The Virginian*. Boston: Little, Brown and Co., 1948.

Manent, Pierre. *Tocqueville and the Nature of Democracy*. Translated by John Waggoner. Lanham, Md.: Rowman & Littlefield Publishers, 1996.

Mapp, Alf J., Jr. *Thomas Jefferson: A Strange Case of Mistaken Identity*. Lanham, Md.: Rowman & Little Publishers, 1987.

———. *Thomas Jefferson: Passionate Pilgrim—the Presidency, the Founding of the University, and the Private Battle*. Lanham, Md.: Rowman & Little Publishers, 1991.

Mayer, David N. *The Constitutional Thought of Thomas Jefferson*. Charlottesville, Va.: University Press of Virginia, 1994.

Meltzer, Milton. *Thomas Jefferson, the Revolutionary Aristocrat*. New York: F. Watts, 1991.

Randall, William S. *Thomas Jefferson: A Life*. New York: H. Holt, 1993.

Russell, Phillips. *Jefferson: Champion of the Free Mind*. New York: Dodd, Mead, and Co., 1958.

Sheldon, Garrett W. *The Political Philosophy of Thomas Jefferson*. Baltimore: Johns Hopkins University Press, 1991.

Tucker, Robert W. *Empire of Liberty: The Statecraft of Thomas Jefferson*. New York: Oxford University Press, 1990.

CHAPTER 12

Mary Wollstonecraft: Proponent of Women's Rights and Education

Portrait of Mary Wollstonecraft; reproduced from the collections of the Library of Congress.

This chapter describes the life, writings, and social, political, and educational ideas of Mary Wollstonecraft (1759–1797), a remarkable English woman. Wollstonecraft was a person who was not content to surrender to the patterns that controlled women's lives in the late eighteenth century. Her life was a struggle for her own freedom from the conventions that limited the rights of woman.

To help you organize your thoughts as you read this chapter, you might wish to focus on the following questions:

- How did Mary Wollstonecraft react to the major trends of the historical context in which she lived?
- How did Wollstonecraft's life, her educational biography, shape her philosophy of women's education?
- How did Wollstonecraft's theories about human nature, women, and power shape her educational ideas and practices?
- What is the enduring significance of Wollstonecraft's contributions to women's education?

The Historical Context of Mary Wollstonecraft's Life

Mary Wollstonecraft (1759–1797) was positioned in the second half of the eighteenth century, a momentous period of European and American history. It was a revolutionary era, marked by the American Revolution in 1776 and the French Revolution in 1789.

These initially political revolts against absolutism, aristocracy, and monarchy unleashed significant social and economic movements that sought to construct a new society where people could freely determine their own destinies. While revolutionary change was eroding the old established order, for people like Mary Wollstonecraft, the forces of change were moving too slowly. Largely untouched were the social and economic traditions, conventions, and laws that still relegated much of humanity to a subordinated position. The subordination of women in a male-dominated society was especially onerous to an enlightened woman such as Wollstonecraft.

The late eighteenth and early nineteenth century was a period of conflicting ideologies. Spawned by the revolutions in America and France, contesting ideologists sought to develop the social, political, and economic blueprints for the coming social order. For liberals such as Mary Wollstonecraft, the new social order should be one in which inherited aristocratic ranks and privileges that denied human rights and equality were to be struck down. Conservatives, such as Edmund Burke, presented the counterargument that traditional institutions—monarchy, aristocracy, church, and family—provided that moral foundations that kept a weak human nature in check. These institutions, conservatives asserted, provided cultural continuity between the generations and protected humankind against the ruthlessness of a rootless mob. Wollstonecraft, challenging Burke, perceived these institutions as oppressive agencies of conformity.

Enthusiastic that the French Revolution's "Rights of Man" should be in place everywhere, Wollstonecraft and her intellectual circle interpreted the political document as a bold humanizing text. For her, it was vital that the "rights of man" be generalized into human rights that included women. She battled against the sexist conventions of her day that denied women the right to own property and that gave the first-born male of each family, through primogeniture, the sole privilege to inherit that property. Not only did she battle against the restrictions on women's right to own property, she struggled against the pervasive conventions of the day that ascribed their social role as subordinate in a patriarchal, male-dominated society.

As she dealt with women's rights in a politically revolutionary era, Wollstonecraft began to understand that important socio-economic changes were in progress. Her life coincided with the beginning of the industrial revolution and the rise of the European bourgeois and English middle class. While the social and educational roles of the aristocratic and peasant women had long been established, the emerging positions of middle- and working-class women were still being defined. Women's struggle to create their own self definitions would be long and tortuous. Rousseau, whose ideas Wollstonecraft challenged, had recognized that the bourgeois posed a new and potentially disruptive moral threat. Driven by profit, the restless bourgeois male needed to be tamed, said the author of *Emile,* by the love of a woman who created a natural family for him to lean on and support. Unlike Rousseau, Wollstonecraft did not envision the middle-class woman as a taming influence but rather saw her as an intellectual equal to her male counterpart. For her, educated men and women, as educated persons in their own right, would advance the cause of progress. However, middle-class women had to be educated out of their trivial and subordinate positions. While Rousseau and Wollstonecraft both analyzed the social and moral change heralded by the appearance of the middle class, the question of the education and role of middle-class women remained open. Even in the twentieth century, Jane Addams was a restive seeker for a career that would fulfill her aspirations to do something of significance for humanity.

Educationally, Mary Wollstonecraft was struggling against the long-entrenched doctrine of educational appropriateness. According to the doctrine of appropriateness, a particular kind of education was designed to prepare a person to discharge one's station in life. In a society of rank and privilege, each rung in society has an education appropriate to it. This meant the prince would receive the education appropriate to one who would be king; the aristocrat would receive the education suited to the ruling class; the laborer that of a producer of goods. For women, the doctrine of educational appropriateness was particularly limiting. Because conventional society held that the vast majority of women were to be wives and mothers, the appropriate education was training to be homemakers and mothers. Outside of the conventionally ascribed appropriate roles, a few women might be governesses or teachers of small children. Higher education and alternative careers were closed to them, according to the conventional wisdom.

Unwilling to be confined by the conventions that subordinated women in eighteenth-century Europe, Wollstonecraft mounted an attack on gender-based restrictions. She challenged the traditions that conservatives cherished about the sanctity of established customs, traditions, and institutions. She attacked the stereotypic view of women that portrayed them as "pretty, vain, jealous, fickle creatures." She condemned the traditional female education that reinforced women's intellectual trivialization.[1]

Wollstonecraft: Biographical Sketch

Mary Wollstonecraft was born on April 27, 1759, in London, the second of seven children of Edward and Elizabeth Dickson Wollstonecraft. Her grandfather's financial success as a weaver made it possible for his son, Mary's father, to acquire land and attempt what proved to be an unsuccessful career as a gentleman farmer. Mary's untalented father was unable to maintain his position in the gentry. As his economic fortunes declined, he and his family moved frequently across England and Wales, searching for unrealized better fortunes. Turning more and more to alcohol, he became more abusive and domineering over his wife and family. As an adolescent, Mary attempted to defend her passive mother against her father's abuse. Mary's adult writing reflected her unhappy childhood memories. Her portrayals of marriage and family life in her writings would range from idealized situations to those of abject dysfunctionality.[2]

As child and adult, Mary Wollstonecraft faced the realities of a male-dominated society ruled by grandfathers, fathers, and brothers. According to primogeniture, which was both customary and legal in eighteenth-century England, the first-born male inherited the family property. The Wollstonecraft family fortunes, albeit limited, were invested in Mary's eldest brother, Edward. In addition, Mary presumed that Edward was her mother's favorite child, a preference Mary resented. At this point, Mary was rebelling against a family that gave sons preference over daughters and a society that gave men control over women. She began to feel the alienation against a biased system of gender discrimination.

Although the Wollstonecrafts moved frequently to avoid creditors or to seek their fortune, they did locate for six years in Beverley in Yorkshire. Here, Mary spent her formative years, from nine to fifteen. She attended the local school and made friendships with children and young people outside of her family. Even with her peers, she was trapped emotionally in the behavior patterns that she had experienced in her family. She tended to feel friendships and other social relationships in terms of domination and submission.[3]

When Mary was sixteen, the Wollstonecraft family moved again, locating in 1774 at Hoxton, near London. Here, Mary made a close and lasting friendship with Fanny Blood, a young woman two years older than she. Although Fanny's family was impoverished, Mary saw her new friend as possessing a character worthy of great admiration. In Fanny, Mary found an idealized heroine who would inspire her later writing.

When she was nineteen, Mary left her home to take a position in Bath as a companion to a wealthy widow. Among the few jobs open for young middle-class women were positions as governesses or companions. Never comfortable in situations of subordination, she found her position uneasy and anxiety-provoking. She, herself, resented any situation of subordination and experienced intense feelings against being "in service" to another which meant more domination and control. Further, she disliked the social inferiority her position carried. Her employment, however, broadened her outlook by providing insights outside of her family. From her peripheral social position, she carefully observed the behavior of people of higher social and economic status.

In 1781, Mary was called back to her family to care for her terminally-ill mother. Again, she suffered from mixed emotions—the call to duty expected of a daughter but also resentment against the mother whom she thought had neglected her. After her mother's death, she resided with the Blood family, which she tended to dominate. Again a crisis in the Wollstonecraft family brought her back home. This time, her younger sister, Eliza, who had just borne a child and was suffering severe postpartum depression, had grown to detest her husband. Mary, seemingly prone to impulsivity, which she herself called her "incendiary" behavior, decided that she and her sister would escape the situation by leaving child, husband, and extended family behind. They left and decided to go it alone, a course of action rarely taken by women in the late eighteenth century.

In 1784, Mary, with her sisters Eliza and Everina and Fanny Blood, opened a school at Newington Green, just north of London.[4] Although the school, which closed in 1786, had a brief existence, her time in Newington Green was one of personal and intellectual growth. Here, she joined a group of liberal thinkers who dissented from the Church of England and the traditional institutions and customs of the period. The dissenters were led by Dr. Richard Price, who inspired by the French Revolution, espoused liberal and reformist ideas. The influence of Price's dissenters was important in Wollstonecraft's intellectual development. In late eighteenth-century England, dissenters, though Protestant, faced political and educational discrimination. They were denied the vote and could not attend Oxford or Cambridge Universities. In many respects, the dissenters confronted some of the same restrictions that women suffered. In response, the dissenters, many of whom were England's leading intellectuals, took a proactive stance. They established their own schools and academies.[5] Mary Wollstonecraft, drawing on the dissenters' reactions, also became more assertive intellectually and politically. She began to develop a perspective that enabled her to relate her personal experiences into a larger intellectual framework. She now related her need for personal freedom of choice to the larger issues of social and political change.[6]

Fanny Blood, Mary's closest friend, had married and moved to Portugal, hoping the milder climate would ease her consumption. Unfortunately, Fanny's condition worsened and she died in 1785, with Mary at her deathbed.

In a desperate financial situation, Wollstonecraft turned to writing to earn money. Her book, *Thoughts on the Education of Daughters*, was published in 1787.[7] Her writing was shaped by her own experiences as a woman and her resentment against social and legal conventions that relegated women to subservient status. Wollstonecraft at this stage in her intellectual development, though rebelling against a status quo that victimized women, still accepted their primary roles to be that of wife and mother.

To augment her small royalty from *Thoughts on the Education of Daughters*, Wollstonecraft took a position as governess to the three eldest daughters of Lord and Lady

Kingsborough in Ireland. At that time, the occupation of governess, a live-in tutor for wealthy young women, was one of the few occupations open to unmarried middle-class women. She disliked being a governess, a position which again placed her in a subordinate position in a wealthy household. She especially resented Lady Kingsborough's idle, aristocratic life style. She believed upper-class women, personified by Lady Kingsborough, led undistinguished and trivial lives in which their chief preoccupation was self-amusement. As an outlet for her hostility, she turned to writing, completing her first novel, *Mary, A Fiction*, an idealized autobiographical version of her childhood and youth.[8] By 1787, she and her employers had had enough of each other. She left the Kingsborough household, determined to earn her living as an author.[9]

In 1787, Wollstonecraft located in London to work as an assistant editor of a new journal, the *Analytical Review*, established by Joseph Johnson. Mary found herself in a situation she believed matched her talents as an aspiring writer. Johnson became her literary adviser and introduced her to London's most liberal literary circles. She became acquainted with Tom Paine, the American revolutionist author of *Common Sense*; Heinrich Fuseli, the Swiss painter and friend of Pestalozzi; William Blake, the poet; and William Godwin, the influential political and social theorist.[10]

In 1788, Wollstonecraft's third book appeared, *Original Stories from Real Life, with Conversations, Calculated to Regulate the Affections, and Form the Mind to Truth and Goodness*.[11] In this book, Mary used her life experience and those gleaned from her career as a governess to examine the relationships between mothers and daughters. Mrs. Mason, cast as the model of virtue, teaches two sisters the values of kindness, benevolence, and patience. The book demonstrated Wollstonecraft's growing interest in education and her recognition of the formative importance of early childhood.

The years 1789–1790 found Wollstonecraft an active participant in the ideological debates surrounding the French Revolution that pitted liberals and radicals against conservatives. Wollstonecraft, of course, was squarely on the side of the proponents of the French Revolution. Her friend, Dr. Price, had presented an address which acclaimed the political changes ushered in by the revolution in France. In reply to Price, the conservative ideologue Edmund Burke wrote *Reflections on the Revolution in France*, a work which became the classic statement of the conservative position.[12] Burke assailed the revolutionaries for destroying the cultural connections that tradition gave to the generations past, present, and future. For Burke, traditional institutions safeguarded human freedom against the violence of revolutionary excesses such as those in France. Wollstonecraft was quick to respond to Burke and the conservatives. Her *Vindication of the Rights of Man* expressed her long-seething attitudes against the power of rank, aristocracy, privilege, and wealth in limiting human freedom.[13] She attacked the customs and laws that subordinated one part of humanity to another.[14]

Wollstonecraft's next publication, *A Vindication of the Rights of Woman*, appeared in 1792.[15] In this major work, she argued against Rousseau's portrayal of Sophie in *Emile*, which she considered denigrating to women. Also, contemporary events in revolutionary France motivated her writing on women's rights. The French National Assembly was considering Talleyrand's educational plan which would have provided state-supported schooling for boys but not for girls.[16] While she hoped to influence the French National Assembly to include the education of girls in the projected system, Wollstonecraft addressed the larger and more general topic of women's education. She argued that it was time to effect a revolution in women's educational and social roles.

In December 1792, Wollstonecraft went to France to experience the revolutionary events firsthand. She arrived in Paris as the revolution was growing more radical. The revolutionary impetus had passed to the Paris commune, political prisoners had been massacred, and King Louis XVI had been arrested and tried for treason. Expressing her reactions on paper, Wollstonecraft wrote an essay, "Letter on the Present Character of the French Nation." Saddened by the violent turn of events, she temporarily lost her faith in the power of human rationality to shape events. Her doubts were transitory, however, and she recovered her belief in humanity's inevitable progress. Her *An Historical and Moral View of the Origin and Progress of the French Revolution* emphasized that the momentous revolutionary events should be interpreted dispassionately. While in France, Wollstonecraft witnessed the rise and subsequent dictatorship of Robespierre and the Reign of Terror. Many of her more moderate French friends, especially those associated with the Girondins, fell victim to the terror.

While in France, Wollstonecraft fell in love with Gilbert Imlay, an American financier who hoped to make profits in revolutionary France. A brief affair followed and Mary was left pregnant. In May 1794, her daughter, Fanny Imlay, was born. In 1795, she returned to England, where the unfaithful Imlay was now residing. Abandoned by Imlay, Mary attempted suicide.[17] Imlay, hoping to divert Mary, proposed that she journey to Scandinavia, accompanied by the baby and a nursemaid, to act as his business agent. She accepted his offer and traveled through Sweden, Norway, and Denmark. Following her pattern, she wrote about her experiences, in *Letters Written During a Short Residence in Sweden, Norway, and Denmark*, published in 1796.[18] The letters, part travel account and part introspective, reveal a lonely and rejected, depressed but romantic, wanderer through foreign lands. Returning to England in 1795, she discovered that Imlay had again been unfaithful to her. Again she attempted suicide, by throwing herself in the Thames. It was not until the spring of 1797 that she abandoned her obsessive love and parted with Imlay.[19]

Wollstonecraft encountered William Godwin, a successful author and political theorist. An intellectual leader of Britain's radical reformers and author of *Political Justice*, Godwin, a disciple of the Enlightenment, stressed the power of human reason to improve society. Godwin and Mary became close friends and then fell in love. He wrote of their relationship, " . . . no two persons ever found in each other's society, a satisfaction more pure and refined."[20] When Mary became pregnant, she and Godwin were privately married.

Wollstonecraft continued to work on her novel, *Maria, or The Wrongs of Women* which realistically described the degradation of middle- and lower-class women in a male-dominated society. The novel, like most of Wollstonecraft's writing, was semi-autobiographical. Maria's family was a fictional replica of Wollstonecraft's family, consisting of a tyrannical father, a submissive mother, and four siblings.[21] Further, the heroine, Maria, is victimized by an unfaithful lover.

On August 30, 1797, Wollstonecraft gave birth to a daughter, Mary. The delivery had complications, which led to an infection that claimed her life. She died on September 10, 1797.

Godwin edited and published Wollstonecraft's *Posthumous Works*, in 1798, and wrote *Memoirs of the Author of a Vindication of the Rights of Woman*, which expressed his affection and esteem of his wife.

Mary Wollstonecraft's literary legacy was carried on by her daughter, Mary Wollstonecraft Shelley, a prolific author in her own right. Like her mother, she wrote about her travels through a Europe recovering from the Napoleonic wars in *A Six Weeks Tour*, in 1817. Mary Wollstonecraft Shelley's most famous novel was *Frankenstein*, published in 1818. In this well-known novel, she poses an issue of profound moral values: Will the new age of science and technology improve the human character and values? Or are there weaknesses in human nature that will pervert the new science and technology? In the novel, Dr. Frankenstein, a well-educated physician from a respected family, embarks on a quest to conquer humankind's greatest and most feared enemy, death. By using parts of bodies, he hopes to create a new and deathless man, a new creature for a new age. Using medical science and the new technology, the power of electricity, he creates a new person out of the old. At first the new creature is a childlike giant figure, a noble savage. However, the creature encounters human cruelty that turns him into a monster. Dr. Frankenstein's quest to have power over human nature leads to his own and his creature's destruction.[22]

Wollstonecraft's Major Social and Educational Themes

Mary Wollstonecraft's essays and novels pursue a persistent theme: How can people, both women and men, create a personal state of being and a society based on love, respect for nature, and education rather than on power, control, and domination. In particular, she was concerned with securing women's rights in a male-dominated society in which fathers, husbands, and elder brothers dominated daughters, wives, and sisters. She extended her intellectual compass to include the broader issues of how to reform society, indeed to revolutionize it.

Wollstonecraft's *Thoughts on the Education of Daughters*, in 1787, was one of her early works that dealt with education. Many of its insights, though of a general nature, were remarkable for the period of its publication. Her *Original Stories from Real Life*, in 1791, presented a series of moral episodes designed to illustrate the proper values for young women. Wollstonecraft's *Vindication of the Rights of Woman*, 1792, was her most powerful statement on women's rights. The following sections examine her educational ideas as expressed in these three publications.

Thoughts on the Education of Daughters

In *Thoughts on the Education of Daughters,* Wollstonecraft focuses on women's upbringing and education. However, many of her comments are applicable to both sexes. In commenting on the education of daughters, Wollstonecraft begins with marriage and family. Wollstonecraft's own family life was unsettled and made insecure by frequent moves as her father, an alcoholic and domineering man, unsuccessfully tried to improve his income. She regarded her mother as passive and unsupportive. Further, her sister, Eliza had been pressed into what was an unhappy marriage by her father and eldest brother. Finally, she had suffered an unhappy love affair with Gilbert Imlay.[23] With this unhappy background, she advised her readers that the education of a daughter began with her parents' marriage and family life. Warning about the negative consequences that unhappy marriages have on children's formative development, she advised that the most dysfunctional parent had the power to jeopardize the welfare of the entire household and cause lifelong emotional injury to his or her children.

Based on her reminiscences of her own unhappy childhood and feelings of rejection by her mother, Mary Wollstonecraft called attention to the crucial importance of early childhood experiences in forming a daughter's character. She maintained the need for a close, intimate relationship between mother and daughter during infancy. Giving practical advice, she advised that mothers should nurse their infant daughters rather than employing wet nurses to do so.

Turning to a young woman's intellectual and moral development, Wollstonecraft affirmed her belief that human beings are born with an innate sense of truth, the power of rationality. This innate power can be either stimulated and developed or it can be dulled by miseducation. Like Locke and Pestalozzi, she was a proponent of learning through sensory experience by interaction with the environment. Sensory experience of the natural environment can stimulate a love of nature, build the stock of ideas, and exercise critical thinking. Children can be encouraged to observe natural phenomena. In Lockean fashion, Wollstonecraft examined the process by which ideas are acquired and formed. She said it is important that children learn to build compound and complex ideas by comparing and contrasting the creatures and objects that they observe. Recognizing the basic principles of natural education, she advised that "intellectual improvements, like the growth and formation of the body, must be gradual."[24]

Wollstonecraft believed that children were keen observers of their surrounding. In particular, small animals were likely to capture their attention. She recommended that children be told stories about animals. Then they were to learn to read little stories about animals in which the animals illustrated human virtues and vices.

Disputing the adage that children should be seen but not heard, Wollstonecraft encouraged adults to invite them to enter into conversations and to express their ideas and feelings. It was important for children to develop an ease with the art of conversation. When children ask questions, adults should take their queries seriously and answer them reasonably.

Unlike Rousseau who argued against the premature introduction of books, Wollstonecraft, a prolific author who expressed her ideas and sentiments in writing, emphasized reading. She argued that a "relish for reading, or any of the fine arts, should be cultivated very early in life." While holding the senses to be the primary source of ideas, she theorized that the individual should not be "entirely dependent on the senses for employment and amusement."[25] Her opinion of the value of reading differed, however, from the conventional schoolroom wisdom of the eighteenth century. Reading was for the primary purpose of cultivating human understanding of life, nature, and society. It was for enlightenment. It was not to train the mind to memorize passages which children did not comprehend nor was it to provide a stock of quotations from celebrated authors.

Wollstonecraft was concerned that girls and young women not be indoctrinated by the so-called women's literature of the period, romances and stories that gave a false but conventional portrayal of love and marriage. Many of the books written for women trivialized women's experience. It was especially important that the young woman's judgment and experience be such that she could establish a true perspective on women and not fall victim to novelist's plots that cast them into roles of superficiality and sentimentality.

Although Wollstonecraft was reared in a household without servants and had been in service herself as a governess, her writing was directed to families of some wealth and status. She advised mothers to be closely involved in the upbringing of daughters and not to leave them in the care of servants. If left to servants, they would be prone to acquiring habits of cunning and deceit, which would distort their innate sense of truth. Wollstonecraft believed individuals were born with an innate sense of truth, the power of rational thinking. It was highly important that the sense of truth be stimulated to develop into critical thinking. Despite her later emphasis on human rights, she asserted in her early works on education that daughters should acquire "a proper submission to superiors; and condescension to inferiors."[26]

Wollstonecraft, who had to fight against the expectations of others, advocated that young women be educated to be, and to fulfill, themselves rather than conform to what others wanted them to be. In conventional eighteenth-century society, young women were conditioned to be what others—fathers, then husbands—wanted them to be. The "art" of pleasing others often led to artificiality and insincerity in which the young woman hid or masked her true thoughts and emotions. For example, women were judged to be incapable of abstract thought. Therefore, they were to be uninterested in intellectual and political issues.

In her *Thoughts on the Education of Daughters,* Wollstonecraft was frequently autobiographical, translating her own experiences into her admonitions. In her novels, she was likewise autobiographical, using episodes in her own life to develop her characters. She had been a companion to an older wealthy woman and had worked as a governess for the daughters of a titled family. Both of these employments were unsatisfactory for her. She strongly reacted against being in a subservient situation. In advising on the education of young women, she paid attention to those of the middle class, who while educated, lacked financial means and needed to seek employment. In eighteenth-century England, the few occupations open to educated middle-class women were serving as companions, governesses, or teachers. Commenting on being a companion or governess, she wrote of the humiliation of living with and depending on "intolerably tyrannical" strangers who constantly reminded their employees of their "subordinate state."[27]

Although she sought independence from the conventions of her day, Wollstonecraft was involved in several intense and often stormy love affairs. She was infatuated with and pursued Fuseli, a Swiss painter, who rejected her. She had an obsessive affair with that unfaithful American financier, Imlay. It was with William

Godwin whom she found true love and affection. In *Thoughts on Education,* written before these relationships, she advised on love and marriage, commenting that "people of sense and reflection" are subject to "violent and constant passions."[28] Their strong emotions may cause them to be attracted to a person their reason would reject. Passion, without mutual esteem, she warns, will be temporary or lead to depravity. However, love of a worthy person, rationally considered, was the surest guide to one's own happiness and intellectual and moral improvement.

Cautioning young women against early marriages, Wollstonecraft advised that education, experience, and reflection should be personal guides for deferred but happy marriages. Young women who married before twenty often were wed to men they would reject if they were older and more experienced. Properly educated women, she predicted, were more likely to marry men of principle.

Original Stories

Mary Wollstonecraft wrote *Original Stories, from Real Life, with Conversations, Calculated to Regulate the Affections, and Form the Mind to Truth and Goodness,* published originally in 1788 and reissued by Joseph Johnston in 1791. These stories were designed to be morally instructive for young women. Wollstonecraft assumed that all humans have the God-given power to reason. It is rationality that leads to intelligent behavior. Due to some fault in their early childhood education, a young woman may acquire some character defects. The book, in the genre of eighteenth-century educational "rescue" literature, is intended to provide guidance in freeing a person from moral weakness. The principal characters are Mrs. Mason, the narrator, who is a moral exemplar, and two sisters, Mary and Caroline, who are in her care. The sisters, having been brought up largely by servants, have acquired some undesirable behaviors. Mary, age fourteen, has a "turn for ridicule," and Caroline, age twelve, is "vain of her person."[29]

A typical moral lesson in *Original Stories* is provided by the story of "Jane Fretful," a selfish and continually angry young woman. As a child, Jane's mother was unwilling to set limits on the little girl's demanding behavior. Trying to calm Jane's temper, she let Jane have her own way and tried to satisfy every childish whim. Although Jane had some "tenderness of heart," this virtue was stunted by the constant appeasement of the child. Jane grew to believe that the "world was made only for her." If her friends had a toy that she wanted, she would cry and demand it. Instead of "being a comfort to her tender, though mistaken mother," Jane caused her the anxiety of having to appease an unappeasable child. When she was given a dog that she wanted, Jane, in a fit of rage, gave it such a severe blow that she killed it. As a young woman, Jane continued to rage, demand, cajole and threaten, driving her mother to an early death. When Jane herself died, "no one shed a tear" and she was "soon forgotten."[30]

A Vindication of the Rights of Woman

In *A Vindication of the Rights of Woman,* her most famous work, Wollstonecraft condemned the subordination to which society had relegated women. She attacked the authors of books on education such as Rousseau, arguing that they were written by men who were "more anxious to make" women into "alluring mistresses than affectionate wives and rational mothers."[31] For example, Rousseau, she wrote, regarded that the major goal of female education was to make them pleasing to men.

Convinced that knowledge was power, Wollstonecraft concluded that both parenting and schooling had failed to give women the kind of education that would bring their innate intellectual power to full development. In fact, she argued conventional educational agencies had deliberately dulled their intellectual proclivities by miseducating them. A truly liberating education for all people, including women, would be one that developed rather than retarded rationality. To secure women's rights, it was necessary that they receive the education that would make them into independent rather than subordinate people.

Stating that she recognized that men were stronger physically, Wollstonecraft argued that women should reject the stereotypes that reinforced their subordination. Perpetual subordination had made them into childlike creatures who were educated to amuse and please others rather than realize their own potentialities as independent people. A conventional upper- and middle-class young women's education was often given over to pursuits considered suited for minds that were not to be taxed intellectually. The young women's curriculum of the time consisted of novels, romances, poetry, and music designed to amuse rather than instruct and to make them amusing rather than rational.

Wollstonecraft did not deny that women, if they so chose, were to be wives and mothers. What she quarreled with was the notion that they were to have an education that was so appropriate to their sex that it denied them the knowledge that exercised their rationality. Despite the differences of their sexuality, she argued that both women and men were human beings who through their reason could attain the same truths.

Wollstonecraft rejected the customary view that the most socially appropriate roles for women were to be wives and mothers and that the socially approved occupations were to be midwives, teachers of small children, or governesses. She argued that women should pursue the whole of knowledge and a range of occupations and professions. They might study medicine and be physicians as well as nurses. They might study political science and history and the various lines of business and take their full place in society.

Wollstonecraft had developed into a women of wide interests that included government and politics as well as women's education. She came to recognize that women's issues were interwoven with the general social, political, and economic context and that improvement in the condition of women depended on more general reform.

Influenced by events in revolutionary France, Wollstonecraft developed a plan for a national system of education which was modeled after that proposed by Talleyrand in the French National Assembly. In her plan, she advocated the establishment of government sponsored co-educational day schools. These schools were to be completely free and open to all children regardless of class. Like Owen, she believed that primary schooling, from ages five through nine, should foster a sense of equality. Therefore, children were to wear the same type of clothing and receive the same kind of instruction. The school was to be located in a large area of land in which the children could play, exercise, and engage in gymnastics. The curriculum was to include reading, writing, arithmetic, natural science, and some simple experiments in physical science. Elements of religion, history, and politics were to be taught by way of teacher-student conversations.

Although Wollstonecraft leaned toward political and gender egalitarianism, she nevertheless retained some socio-economic class distinctions in her plan of national education. At age nine, students, both boys and girls, were streamed into different schools according to their intellectual abilities and anticipated vocations. Children intended for domestic employment or mechanical trades were to receive vocational instruction. Boys and girls were to be taught together in the morning. In the afternoons, girls were to attend a separate school where they learned such traditional gender-specific skills as needlework, sewing, and millinery. Again, it is interesting to note that Wollstonecraft, despite her liberal feminism, continued to apply the traditional gender specific curriculum to lower socio-economic class girls. After completing this instruction both boys and girls would enter the work force.

While lower achieving and lower socio-economic class children attended vocational schools, those of superior intellect or economic fortune attended an academic school where they studied classical and modern languages, science, history, politics, and literature. Wollstonecraft made a strong point in stating that their education should be co-educational and that talented young women should have the same opportunities as men. Believing that human progress depended on the education of both men and women, she made a strong case for co-education based on the Enlightenment premise that human progress depended upon knowledge and science.[32]

Conclusion: An Assessment

Mary Wollstonecraft's life was an extraordinary one for a woman of the eighteenth century. She broke the bonds of the limited expectations to which women, especially those of the middle class, were tied. Her own life was a dramatic series of traumas and triumphs.

Wollstonecraft was not afraid to challenge traditional institutions and conventional thinking. She contested the writings of two of the leading theorists of the period: Jean-Jacques Rousseau and Edmund Burke. While Rousseau was a champion of child freedom and political equality, he retained an opinion that saw women's education as designed to make them into people who were to please men. Wollstonecraft challenged Rousseau's view which she believed contributed to women's unequal education and subordination. She also challenged Burke, the champion of British conservatism. Burke's condemnation of the French Revolution and his arguments for preservation of the class-based status quo were repugnant to Wollstonecraft. She believed that women rights and equality were part of a movement of general revolutionary change that would liberate human beings from the tyranny of the past.

Wollstonecraft must be counted among the early leaders for women's rights and feminine equality. Not exclusively a feminist writer, she also was an educational theorist. While she concentrated her attention on the education of women, many of her ideas are applicable to both sexes. Mary Wollstonecraft's works have won a significant place in literature, the history of feminism, and educational thought. Wollstonecraft's work is testimony to what remains an unfinished agenda in women's rights and education.

Discussion Questions

1. Compare and contrast Rousseau and Wollstonecraft's ideas on the education of women.
2. How did Wollstonecraft rebel against the social conventions of her times?
3. Identify and analyze the early childhood experiences that shaped Mary Wollstonecraft's personality and shaped her career.
4. Identify and analyze the knowledge and values that Wollstonecraft regarded as most important in a woman's education.
5. Were inconsistencies present in Wollstonecraft's theory of education?
6. Do you think that Mary Wollstonecraft was a pioneering figure in feminism and women's rights? Why or why not?

Research and Essay Topics

1. Prepare a biographical sketch of Mary Wollstonecraft which discusses the development of her ideas on women's education.
2. Read and review a book by Wollstonecraft.
3. Read and review a biography of Wollstonecraft.
4. In an essay, compare and contrast Wollstonecraft's ideas with those of contemporary feminist education.
5. Consult the syllabi and suggested readings in courses in women's history at your college or university. Determine if Wollstonecraft is included in these courses.
6. Interview a professor on women's history at your college and institution regarding her or his interpretation of Wollstonecraft's contributions and significance.

Notes

1. Moira Ferguson, "Introduction," to Mary Wollstonecraft, *Maria or the Wrongs of Woman* (New York: W. W. Norton & Co., 1975), 10.
2. Ibid., 7.
3. Janet M. Todd, ed., *A Wollstonecraft Anthology* (Bloomington, Ind.: Indiana University Press, 1977), 2.
4. Ibid., 3–4.
5. Mary Wollstonecraft, *Original Stories From Real Life* (Oxford and New York: Woodstock Books, 1990), ii.
6. Todd, 4.
7. Mary Wollstonecraft, *Thoughts on the Education of Daughters* (1787), republished by A. M. Kelley (Clifton, N.J., 1972).

8. Mary Wollstonecraft, *Mary: A Fiction* (1787), republished by Garland Publishing Co. (New York, 1974).
9. Todd, 5–6.
10. Ibid., 6–7.
11. Mary Wollstonecraft, *Original Stories from Real Life* (Oxford and London: Woodstock Books, 1990).
12. Edmund Burke, *Reflections on the Revolution in France* (New York: Liberal Arts Press, 1955).
13. Mary Wollstonecraft, *A Vindication of the Rights of Man* (1790), republished by Scholars' Facsimiles & Reprints (Gainesville, Fla., 1960).
14. Todd, 8–9.
15. Mary Wollstonecraft, *A Vindication of the Rights of Woman* (1792), republished by Norton Co. (New York, 1975).
16. Gerald L. Gutek, *A History of the Western Education Experience*, 2nd ed. (Prospect Heights, IL.: Waveland Press, 1995), 184–87.
17. Todd, 12–13.
18. Mary Wollstonecraft, *Letters Written during a Short Residence in Sweden, Norway, and Denmark* (1796), republished by University of Nebraska Press (Lincoln, 1976).
19. Todd, 14–15.
20. William Godwin, *Memoirs of the Author of A Vindication of the Rights of Woman* (London: Joseph Johnson, 1798), 165, as cited in Todd, 15.
21. Moira Ferguson, "Introduction" to Mary Wollstonecraft, *Maria or the Wrongs of Women* (New York: W. W. Norton & Co., 1975), 13.
22. Betty T. Bennett and Charles E. Robinson, eds., *The Mary Shelley Reader*, (New York and Oxford: Oxford University Press), 3.
23. Moira Ferguson, "Introduction" to Mary Wollstonecraft, *Maria or The Wrongs of Woman* (New York: W. W. Norton & Co., 1975), 13.
24. Mary Wollstonecraft Godwin, *Thoughts on the Education of Daughters* (London: J. Johnson, 1787). Reprinted by Augustus M. Kelley (Clifton, N.J., 1972), 17.
25. Ibid., 48.
26. Wollstonecraft, *Thoughts on the Education of Daughters*, Todd, 29.
27. Ibid., 33.
28. Ibid., 35.
29. Mary Wollstonecraft, *Original Stories from Real Life* (Oxford and New York: Woodstock Books, 1990), iii.
30. Ibid., 31–36.
31. Mary Wollstonecraft, "A Vindication of the Rights of Woman," in Todd, 85.
32. Ibid., 106–11.

Suggestions for Further Reading

Alexander, Meena. *Women in Romanticism: Mary Wollstonecraft, Dorothy Wordsworth, and Mary Shelley*. Savage, Maryland: Barnes and Noble Books, 1989.
Detre, Jean. *A Most Extraordinary Pair: Mary Wollstonecraft and William Godwin*. New York: Doubleday & Co., 1975.
Ferguson, Moira. *Mary Wollstonecraft*. Boston: Twayne Publishers, 1984.
Flexner, Eleanor. *Mary Wollstonecraft: A Biography*. New York: Coward, McCann and Geoghegan, 1972.
George, Margaret. *One Woman's "Situation": A Study of Mary Wollstonecraft*. Urbana: University of Illinois Press, 1970.

Kelly, Gary. *Revolutionary Feminism: The Mind and Career of Mary Wollstonecraft*. New York: St. Martin's Press, 1992.

Lorch, Jennifer. *Mary Wollstonecraft: The Making of a Radical Feminist*. New York: Berg, 1990.

Nixon, Edna. *Mary Wollstonecraft: Her Life and Times*. London: J. M. Dent and Sons, 1971.

Poovey, Mary. *The Proper Lady and the Woman Writer: Ideology as Style in the Works of Mary Wollstonecraft, Mary Shelley, and Jane Austen*. Chicago: University of Chicago Press, 1984.

Sapiro, Virginia. *A Vindication of Political Virtue: The Political Theory of Mary Wollstonecraft*. Chicago: University of Chicago Press, 1992.

Sunstein, Emily. *A Different Face: The Life of Mary Wollstonecraft*. New York: Harper & Row, 1975.

Wardle, Ralph. *Mary Wollstonecraft: A Critical Biography*. Lincoln: University of Nebraska Press, 1967.

Wollstonecraft, Mary. *Collected Letters of Mary Wollstonecraft*. Ithaca, N.Y.: Cornell University Press, 1979.

———. *Mary, A Fiction*. London: Joseph Johnson, 1788. Reprinted by Oxford University Press, New York, 1976.

———. *Original Stories from Real Life*. Oxford, U.K. and New York: Woodstock Books, 1990.

———. *Political Writings*. London: W. Pickering, 1993.

———. *Thoughts on the Education of Daughters with Reflections on Female Conduct, in the More Important Duties Life*. London: Joseph Johnson, 1787. Facsimile by New York: Garland Publishing, Inc., 1974.

———. *A Vindication of the Rights of Man*. Gainesville, Fla.: Scholars' Facsimiles and Reprints, 1960.

———. *A Vindication of the Rights of Woman*. New York: Norton Co., 1975.

———. *The Works of Mary Wollstonecraft*. New York: New York University Press, 1989.

Horace Mann: Leader of the Common School Movement

Portrait of Horace Mann; reproduction from the collection of the Library of Congress.

This chapter examines the life, educational philosophy, and contributions of Horace Mann (1796–1859), a leader in the United States' common school movement, which was the forerunner of today's public school system. Mann's policies as secretary of the Board of Education in Massachusetts in the first half of the nineteenth century have significantly shaped U.S. education.

His influence on U.S. education is discussed in its historical context and in terms of its enduring effect on educational philosophy and policy. First, the social, political, and economic context in which Mann lived and worked is described. Second, Mann's biography, his education and career, is analyzed to determine the evolution of his ideas. Third, the continuing effect of Mann's contributions on U.S. education is examined. By this analysis, we shall see the interrelated dynamics of educational history and philosophy. For example, Mann's educational philosophy emerged as he confronted the issues facing the United States in the early nineteenth century. Although originating in that historical context, his concepts of the nature of common schooling and of the relationship of public education to U.S. society have endured as sustaining elements of the "public school philosophy."

To organize your thoughts as you read this chapter, you might focus on the following questions:

- What were the major trends in the historical context, the time and situation, in which Mann lived?
- How did Mann's life, his educational biography, shape his philosophy of education?
- How did Mann's educational philosophy determine his educational policies and practices?
- What is the enduring impact of Mann's contributions to U.S. education?

The Historical Context of Mann's Life

The first half of the nineteenth century was a time in which the United States, still a young and developing country, was seeking to establish its identity among the nations of the earth. The representative political institutions of life in the United States were still in the early stages of development. The U.S. Constitution had been in effect only eight years in 1796, the year of Mann's birth. As the nineteenth century began, the proper kind of education for a republic such as the United States was still being debated. For such a new nation, it was important that an educational philosophy be developed that would contribute to a sense of national identity. This feeling of group identity or social consensus is also referred to as an ideology. Underlying school systems and their curricula is always a sense of agreement on what knowledge is most worthwhile and what values are most important. As yet the cultural sense of U.S. identity was still lacking. The context into which Mann was born and grew to adulthood coincided with the beginning of the United States as a young and aspiring nation.

The historical context of Mann's life included the ideas of the revolutionary generation who, with the Declaration of Independence in 1776, proclaimed the thirteen colonies' determination to become a free and independent nation and who, with the adoption of the Constitution in 1788, created the institutions to govern the new republic. In 1796 John Adams succeeded George Washington as the second president. Four years later, Thomas Jefferson would take that office. During Mann's childhood, the republic's founders were not historic figures but were still at the helm of the ship of state. Although the revolutionary generation gained political independence for the colonies, many of its educational ideas and institutions were remnants of the era before independence. Educational institutions had to be created that would fulfill the political, social, and economic needs of the new nation. The role education would play in shaping the new U.S. consciousness was still to be determined.

The ideas of the founding statesmen of the republic, especially Benjamin Franklin and Thomas Jefferson, were part of the philosophy of the Age of Reason. According to the ideas of political and scientific enlightenment that shaped the republic's birth, a new kind of education was needed to create a sense of American cultural identity and to apply scientific knowledge to develop the continent's vast natural resources. Benjamin Franklin, proponent of practicality and invention; Thomas Jefferson, proponent of an enlightened and scientific citizenship; and Noah Webster, proponent of American language and cultural identity, each in their own way contributed to ideas that formed Horace Mann's philosophy of education.

The revolutionary impulse, a strong ideological factor in the new republic, posed issues that Mann and those to follow him would face as leaders of public education. What kind of schooling would prepare responsible citizens to participate in elections, serve on juries, and contribute to an enlightened public opinion? What kind of education would cultivate a common cultural identity, a sense of belonging to a people who shared a common language, goals, institutions, and procedures? What kind of education would develop the wilderness beyond the frontier?

If the revolutionary impulses of the Enlightenment were part of the context of Horace Mann's life, still another part of that context came from the revival of Evangelical Protestantism, a religious movement that shaped the moral milieu of the common schools founded from 1830 to 1860.[1]

Many of the clergy who led the Evangelical Protestant revival also supported common, or public, schools. They were active in the common school movement as authors of textbooks, founders of teacher education institutes, and school administrators.[2] Their essential rationale was that U.S. institutions, including schools, should reflect the beliefs and values of the dominant Protestant culture. Schools, in particular, should stress the literacy needed for Bible reading, and the school milieu should reflect Protestant values. Industriousness, frugality, and punctuality were regarded as good Protestant values that promoted economic success as well as social and political order. Along with the Evangelical Protestant emphasis on specific moral values, some Americans, fearful of cultural change, developed a nativism that stereotyped non-Protestants, especially Roman Catholics and Jews, as people to be absorbed into the framework of a general Protestant culture.[3]

The desire to fashion U.S. institutions, especially schools, according to the design of Evangelical Protestantism revealed a continuing tension that has long been part of American life. Although the Enlightenment influence in the U.S. tradition, especially in Jeffersonianism, emphasized separation of church and state and correspondingly separation of public schools and denominational religion, Evangelical Protestantism identified U.S. institutions with a generalized Protestant cultural ethos.

The religious context in which Mann lived was growing still more complicated as immigration accelerated the growth of non-Protestant sectors of the U.S. population, especially Roman Catholics and Jews. Seeds of cultural and religious pluralism had been planted and were quickly germinating in the soil.

During Horace Mann's career, he and other common school leaders faced the issue of religion in the schools. Should the schools be separated completely from sectarian religion, as Jefferson's philosophy prescribed? Or might the emerging common schools reflect the cultural ethos of interdenominational Protestantism? Should the state encourage and support schools established by different religious denominations?

Although political ideology and religious revival were important elements in shaping the common schools that Mann advocated, social and economic realities, then as now, also influenced the development of education. From the older New England states of Connecticut, New Hampshire, Vermont, and Massachusetts—Mann's home state—to the newer states of Ohio, Indiana, and Illinois, which had been part of the Northwest Territory, Americans were pushing the frontier westward. By 1850, the United States had been settled up to the Mississippi River.

The majority of Americans lived in rural areas, on farms and in small towns. Indeed, until 1860, 80 percent of the population of the United States lived in rural areas. The educational needs of this rural and small-town population were basic education for literacy—reading, writing, and simple arithmetic. Although there was general agreement on the need for basic literacy and numeracy, schooling beyond these educational essentials was debated. Common school leaders such as Mann developed the curriculum by adding subjects they believed would meet civic needs.

Although the older habits and values of rural and small-town America set the main pattern of life and educational expectations in the early nineteenth century, industrialization, urbanization, and immigration generated new impulses. These dynamic tendencies would gather momentum and by the century's end transform life in the United States.

Horace Mann witnessed the beginning stages of industrialization that would transform the United States from an agrarian and rural society into an urban, industrial, and modern nation. Cities and factories were growing and creating urban areas. New York City, Philadelphia, and Mann's own Boston, with their large populations, had educational needs and expectations that differed from those of the rural areas.

Along with the industrialization and urbanization processes, different ethnic and language patterns were beginning to change U.S. society from a predominantly English culture to an ethnically, linguistically, and culturally pluralistic one. At the beginning of the nineteenth century, most immigrants were northern Europeans, from Great Britain and the Scandinavian countries. During the 1830s and 1840s, immigration patterns changed as large numbers of immigrants came from Ireland and Germany. In the last two decades of the nineteenth century, another shift would occur as immigrants came from southern and eastern Europe. Of importance was the fact that the United States was becoming culturally pluralistic rather than a nation dominated by English-speaking Protestants. Because many immigrants were Roman Catholics, religious tensions were felt in the schools.

Social and economic changes that began in 1800 and continued throughout the nineteenth century raised a number of questions for Mann and other common school leaders. Among them were the following:

1. What kinds of schools and curriculum should be designed for the children of the growing urban population?
2. What kind of education was needed to prepare workers and managers for the factories, mills, and business enterprises of an industrializing society?
3. How could schools create a civic consensus for a society that was becoming ethnically, linguistically, and culturally diverse?
4. What moral and ethical values should be emphasized as tensions mounted between the Protestant majority and the Roman Catholic minority?

To a degree, all education reflects its political context. The effort to create common schools was part of the political life of the United States. Horace Mann's life, beginning with the last year of George Washington's presidency, spanned the administrations of twelve other U.S. presidents. This half century, characterized as the Age of Jackson, was an era of national expansion and growing sectional controversy between North and South over the slavery issue. This period also saw the United States as a combatant in two wars, that of 1812 against Great Britain, and the Mexican War of 1846–1848.

The Age of Jackson, dominated by Andrew Jackson, who was president from 1829 to 1837, had a great effect on the movement for popular education. Jackson, a Democrat from Tennessee and a hero of the War of 1812, represented the growing power of the recently admitted frontier states. Historians have characterized the Jacksonian era as the period when the common man entered into full political participation through the doctrine of popular sovereignty, which asserted that one man equals one vote. Jackson's political appointees were drawn from those who supported his presidential campaign rather than those of high social status. Leadership was no longer limited to a financial oligarchy as envisioned by the Federalist Alexander Hamilton. Nor were the leaders of the republic to be from an "aristocracy of intellect" as Thomas Jefferson argued. Rather, national leadership, as well as state and local offices, would go to those who won elections and to their supporters. The entry of the common man into politics occurred as many states, especially those on the frontier, reduced or eliminated property requirements for voting. Only 365,000 people had voted in the election of 1824. Four years later, the number of voters had reached 1,155,340.[4]

Jackson's political opponents banded together in an often-fragile coalition known as the Whig party. Just as the opponents to George III in England were called Whigs, Jackson's diverse opponents, who derisively dubbed him "King Andrew," took that name. The leading Whig spokesmen were Senators Henry Clay and Daniel Webster. When he entered politics, Horace Mann identified with the Whigs.

In terms of educational attitudes, Jacksonian democracy implied a broader conception of education in which the common man would be prepared not only to vote in elections but to run for public office as well. Challenging the notion that educational opportunity should be limited to the well-educated upper classes, Jacksonian democracy went hand in hand with universal education. Despite their egalitarian preferences, Jacksonian Democrats generally saw schooling in limited and local terms rather than as a national priority.

The development of educational policy at the state level was more of a concern for the Whigs. For the Whig supporters of common schooling, the development of public elementary schools served two basic purposes: internal improvements and social control. The Whigs believed that both federal and state governments should follow a policy of internal improvements that would contribute to economic development and growth. For example, state-subsidized canals and roads would improve the transportation system that carried agricultural products and raw materials from the western frontier states and territories to the eastern states for manufacturing or export to European markets. If construed as an internal improvement, investments in public schooling would pay the dividends of providing the verbal and mathematical skills needed for national economic development.

Whig politicians often supported common schools because representative political institutions required literate and educated citizens. Beyond this commitment to general literacy, however, Whigs feared that Jacksonian democracy could easily degenerate into "mobocracy," or rule by uneducated, unlettered, ignorant frontiersmen. Whigs also were afraid the growing number of immigrants from Ireland and Germany would become pawns of political bosses or "papist" priests. Common schools, reasoned the Whigs, could instill the "right attitudes and values" into the young and make them orderly, civil, and industrious citizens in a nation modeled on the mores of upper middle-class, English-speaking Protestants. According to this strategy, the dominant socioeconomic classes would use public schooling to mold the outlook and values of the lower classes and control the nation socially.

Still another important impulse running through U.S. thought, especially in New England, was humanitarian reformism. Concurrent with the general reform influence, the movement for common schooling originated in the New England states of Massachusetts, Connecticut, New Hampshire, and Vermont, where Puritanism's gloomy moral prescriptions were being reshaped, especially among intellectuals, into humanistic sentiments seeking to uplift individuals by educating them. Liberating currents of thought stimulated by Ralph Waldo Emerson's philosophical transcendentalism generated ideas for reform that found their way into town meetings and state legislative chambers. Like-minded reformers embraced and argued for a wide range of humanitarian improvements, including the abolition of slavery, recognition of women's rights, public schooling, and prohibition of alcoholic drink. Advocates of common schooling saw the school as an instrument of personal and societal moral regeneration.

Mann's life and work was a drama that was portrayed against the backdrop of a nation seeking to define its national character. The forces that moved across this backdrop represented the ideology of republicanism, the rising tide of frontier democracy, new waves of immigration, and an emerging industrial economy. In the next section of the chapter, we turn to Mann's life and career to see how one of the nation's leading educators shaped the character of life in the United States through the common school system.

Although many people supported public education, Mann is generally acclaimed as the foremost statesman of the common school movement. This lawyer, politician, and educator popularized and established the philosophical and organizational foundations of public schooling through his position as secretary of the Massachusetts Board of Education.[5]

Horace Mann was born on May 4, 1796, at Franklin, Massachusetts, one of five children of Thomas and Rebecca Mann, who were farmers. Franklin was named for Benjamin Franklin, the self-made inventor and statesman and a leading figure of the revolutionary generation, whose practicality appealed to the frugality and industriousness of the New England temperament. Responding to the honor of having the town named for him, Franklin gave it a collection of books that formed the nucleus of a community library. These books would be read by the earnestly studious young Horace Mann.[6]

Later in his life, Mann recalled a childhood dominated by hard work, farm chores, and regular church attendance. At the end of the eighteenth century, society and morality in rural Massachusetts were heavily influenced by the religious creed of orthodox Calvinism, which in Mann's hometown was preached by the imposing and severe "fire and brimstone" clergyman, the Reverend Nathanael Emmons (1773–1827). Mann remembered the town's preacher as:

> [A] man of pure intellect, whose logic was never softened in its severity by the infusion of any kindliness of sentiment. He expounded all the doctrines of total depravity, election, and reprobation and not only the eternity but the extremity of hell torments, unflinchingly and in their most terrible significance, while he rarely if ever descanted upon the joys of heaven, and never, to my recollection, upon the essential and necessary happiness of virtuous life.[7]

Mann, like many other New England children of the time, was expected to attend church services regularly. Preachments about punishment and guilt were part of growing up in the early nineteenth century.[8] As an educator, Mann developed a more generous and sympathetic version of child growth and development. However, the impressions of childhood remain, as Freud would note, to shape a person's psychological outlook and character.

Emmon's stern preaching caused Mann to have psychological fears. At the funeral of Mann's brother, Stephen, Emmons preached about the damnation of those who died unconverted, suggesting that Stephen might be among the damned. This event had a lasting effect on Mann's religious attitudes. As he grew to adulthood, orthodox Calvinism's stern proscriptions lessened their grip on Mann's psyche and he eventually converted to the more liberal Unitarianism. However, the religious perceptions of his childhood remained rooted in him in a cultural sense throughout his life.[9] He continued to believe that a good life must be purposeful and that human purpose must conform to the divine plan. Further, a good life must be strenuously devoted to humanitarian reform that would elevate the human condition by reforming society.

These values guided Mann as a common school leader and found their way into the moral code that became part of the common school philosophy.

Growing up in rural Massachusetts also had a formative effect on Mann. Convinced of the values of hard work, diligence, and seriousness, he exemplified the Protestant work ethic, which saw industriousness and productivity as positive moral values. His educational philosophy would emphasize that children should be educated to respect ethical values and that schools had a duty to "train up" hard-working men and women. The common school philosophy that Mann did so much to form was crystallized in the McGuffey Readers in their portrayal of good little boys and girls who were always truthful, diligent, and obedient. The McGuffey syndrome would be revitalized later in the nineteenth century in Horatio Alger's many novels, which told of the achievement over adversity of industrious youth.

If there is a strong force that shapes a person's educational attitudes, it is one's school experiences. Memories of good teachers and bad ones, no matter how unsophisticated and childlike, always return to the mind to influence a person's educational opinions. Mann was no exception to this tendency. Those school days that he fondly recalled and those that still provoked anxiety affected his educational philosophy.

Mann attended Franklin's local school, which was a remnant of the old district schools that had been inherited from colonial days. The town paid less than $100 annually for the teacher's salary and for heating and maintaining the one-room schoolhouse. Mann remembered a drafty building, a leaking roof, and uncomfortable benches. The school year was brief, limited to about ten weeks. The widely used *New England Primer* was employed to teach the alphabet, reading, and moral instruction. In addition to the *Primer,* students memorized the Westminster Assembly Shorter Catechism.

The education that Mann received at the Franklin town school was typical for the period. Poorly prepared teachers, often young men who were temporarily working at school-keeping on their way to more prestigious careers in law or religion, taught classes. They used corporal punishment to keep their classes in order and heard memorized recitations.

As he recalled his school days in Franklin, Mann assessed the quality of the instruction that he had received. Evaluating teachers was something he would often do in his later career. His teachers, he wrote, were "very good people" but poor instructors. Neglecting children's interests and their sensory experience, his teachers did nothing to develop artistic sensitivity through art and music. He recalled that "the memory for words was the only" faculty the teachers sought to develop in their students. Ignoring the realities of their environment, Mann's teachers emphasized only the information that came from books.[10]

As a common school leader, Mann persistently advocated a broadened curriculum that went beyond the basics of reading, writing, arithmetic, and the catechism. He urged curricular enrichment that included history, geography, health, and music. He also recognized that the school's physical plant was important. He would argue for increased taxation to provide sturdier, more comfortable schools than the one he had attended in Franklin.

In addition to the basic skills learned at the town school, Horace Mann's early education was shaped by two powerful informal educational forces: his family and the town library. Formal schooling is only one part of a person's total education. Informal agencies also are important in that they either supplement and reinforce or they negate what goes on at school.

Mann's parents created a home environment that stimulated his interest in learning and motivated him to seek knowledge. His parents respected learning and learned people and encouraged him to read the books that belonged to the family. Emulating Ben Franklin, Mann frequented the library that Franklin had given to the community and eagerly read works on history and biography.[11]

When his father died in 1809, it appeared that Mann's formal education would end because of his family's reduced income. Mann's desire for further education remained unabated and, with his mother's support, he prepared for entry to Brown University in Providence, Rhode Island. To make up for his educational deficiencies, Mann prepared for the entrance examinations by studying classics and advanced mathematics with private tutors. Passing these subjects, he was admitted to Brown.

Although teachers shape students' attitudes about education, the peer group also has an influence. Mann's fellow students at Brown came primarily from the middle and lower middle socioeconomic classes. They chose Brown for economic reasons, with costs for tuition, room, and board coming to the modest amount of $100 per year. The students lived plainly and generally devoted themselves to their academic programs. Brown at that time lacked the prestige of Harvard and Yale.

Mann's academic program at Brown was typical for students of that era. He studied the classical languages of Latin and Greek, geometry, geography, English, logic, and public speaking. Of particular benefit to Mann was his work in English, which provided effective training in writing and public speaking. His interest in public speaking led him to join the university's literary association and he appeared frequently on its programs. His favorite topics, which anticipated those he would continue to speak on after graduating from college, were politics, philosophy, science, and ethics. Of these, he most enjoyed political issues in which he stressed responsible republicanism, humanitarianism, and social reform. Mann grew to be a master of the spoken and written word, which he used for exhortation, inspiration, and persuasion. His speeches and compositions showed him to be an advocate of gradual reform within the system rather than a proponent of radical change. His annual reports, written when he was secretary of the Massachusetts Board of Education, were cogently and effectively written and remain impressive statements of the public school philosophy. His oratorical abilities made him a popular speaker on public platforms, using his eloquence to further the arguments for publicly supported schooling.

Mann graduated from Brown University in 1819, first in his class. Because of his high academic standing, he was selected as the commencement speaker. The topic of his address, "The Gradual Advancement of the Human Species in Dignity and Happiness," stressed his belief in the possibility of human progress and in the role that science and education were to play in humankind's pursuit of a better future.[12] Mann's address at the commencement revealed what would be a persistent theme in the public school philosophy that he later developed. Harkening back to the Enlightenment belief in progress, Mann looked optimistically forward to a better life. Never a utopian, however, this promise of a better life had to be earned by applying intelligence diligently. Unlike revolution, education—Mann's preferred instrument—would gradually and nonviolently improve the human condition.

After graduating from Brown, Mann read law in the office of J. J. Fiske, an attorney in Wrentham, Massachusetts. Like many other ambitious young men, he saw the legal profession as a means of entering political and public life. He interrupted his legal study to accept a teaching position at his alma mater in 1820. For a salary of $375 a year, he was a Latin and Greek tutor and a librarian. Two years later, he returned to law, studying at Litchfield, Connecticut, with Judge James Gould. Completing his studies in 1823, Mann moved to Dedham, Massachusetts, where he was admitted to the bar. He began to practice law with James Richardson, a prominent attorney.

From 1823 to 1837, Mann successfully practiced law, earned a reputation as an outstanding orator and lawyer, made many prominent friends, and prepared the way for a political career. He married Charlotte Messer, but she died in the early years of their marriage. His second marriage was to Mary Peabody, who was actively interested in social and educational reform.

Mann was elected to the Massachusetts House of Representatives in 1827, serving until 1833, when he was elected to the state Senate for a four-year term. From 1836 to 1837, he had the distinction of serving as president of the Senate.[13] As a legislator, Mann developed a concept of public service that was also to provide the ideological orientation for his civic education. Citizens, like those whom they elected as representatives, should be "principled men who would rise above sectarian and political biases" to determine their political destiny in an enlightened and disinterested fashion.[14] Using this model, Mann acquired a record as an effective advocate of social improvement. His humanitarian efforts led to an investigation by the legislature of conditions in prisons and in asylums for the insane. Mann sponsored legislation to improve the care of the insane and his efforts contributed to the establishment of the Worcester Asylum in 1833, a model institution. Although James G. Carter was the principal originator of the legislation, Mann actively supported the educational bill, "An Act Relating to Common Schools," enacted in 1837. This act established the Massachusetts Board of Education of which Mann later became the first secretary and leading spokesmen.[15]

Mann's career as a legislator is instructive because it tells something of his concept of civic education. He believed it was possible for individuals to put aside their special interests and unite for the common good. The term common school implies that it is possible to generate a shared community of interest that would unite people of different backgrounds in a common cause. In this sense, the common school generated a sense of shared concerns.

Latter day critics of Mann's concept of civic education have argued that he really was not the disinterested and objective legislator and educator that he appeared to be. For these critics, Mann was really advocating a conception of the political and social order based on Whig notions of an orderly society and neo-Evangelical Protestant views of what constituted the good society. For those who did not share these views, the common school ideology was a form of social imposition and control.

Even if one accepts Mann's concept of disinterested civic education as arising from altruism and political objectivity, questions can be asked about its adequacy for our times. Modern U.S. society is characterized by competing interest groups that tend to pursue their own agenda rather than the common good. Is it possible to recreate a sense of commonality and mutuality?

When Horace Mann began his term as secretary of the Massachusetts Board of Education, his specified responsibilities were limited by statutory guidelines that defined the board as an agency to collect educational statistics and dispense educational information. It was also the secretary's responsibility to prepare printed abstracts, based on the data he had collected, for the information of the state legislature to guide it in drafting school laws. The charge to collect information also carried with it the possibility of influencing educational legislation. For example, Mann was to survey the condition of schools throughout the state in order to recommend policies for improving them and the instruction that their teachers provided.[16]

To gather information firsthand, Mann traveled from school to school around the state. His findings, set out in his first annual report of 1838, revealed that many school buildings were poorly constructed and that the district school committees, which were responsible for education in their localities, exercised little supervision and did almost nothing to improve instruction.[17] Further, Mann found that the standards of teaching and methods of instruction were deficient because the teachers were poorly prepared. In his first report, Mann asserted his belief that the state had the responsibility to provide for the education of its children:

> The theory of our laws and institutions undoubtedly is, first, that in every district of every town of the Commonwealth, there should be a free district school, sufficiently safe, and sufficiently good, for all the children within its territory, where they may be well instructed in the rudiments of knowledge, formed to the propriety of demeanor, and imbued with the principles of duty.[18]

Mann's report made clear that he regarded, as did Jefferson, the state as having primary responsibility for supporting and governing public education. He consistently believed that state-supported schools should be available to all and that their quality should exceed that of the private schools. Further, Mann's concept of the common school curriculum was a mixture of basic knowledge and the values that he believed would contribute to an orderly social and political society.

Mann's first annual report was eventually followed by eleven more reports that addressed the educational needs of Massachusetts. Statements in these reports could be taken out of their local context and applied to schools throughout the nation. Among the themes treated by Mann were the policies needed to improve common schools, education's role in preparing a trained and literate work force, and the role common schools played in educating a responsible citizenry. In addition, Mann wrote about the more specific need to improve curriculum, reading, penmanship, and other more immediate problems. For example, Mann concerned himself with the teaching of reading in his second annual report:

> Perhaps the best way of inspiring a young child with a desire of learning to read is, to read to him, with proper intervals, some interesting story, perfectly intelligi-

ble, yet as full of suggestion as of communication; for the pleasure of discovering is always greater than that of perceiving.[19]

Mann's annual reports revealed philosophical depth that related both to the most general national purposes and specific curricular and instructional objectives that were directly related to schooling. In terms of its social significance, Mann wrote, "Education, then, beyond all other devices of human origin, is the great equalizer of the conditions of men—the balance-wheel of the social machinery."[20] Mann set general philosophical goals that were to guide the common schools. He also made sure that the more specific objectives related to curriculum and instruction were derived from and consistent with his general philosophy. For him, educational policies were means by which common school philosophy could be implemented in actual school practice.

To improve the condition of schools in Massachusetts, Mann carefully worked out a strategy that would take the defective district schools and revitalize them into an effective system of common or publicly supported and controlled schools. To do this, he had to define the nature, purpose, and function of common schools. He also had to create a coalition of political support that would endorse the idea of tax-supported schools.

Mann's Concept of the Common School

Mann's career as a lawyer and politician shaped his belief that the common school was directly related to civic competency and to public service. He also subscribed to the Whig ideology that public education was similar to other internal improvements in that it could be an agency for national economic prosperity and civic order. His view of society was not one in which education should be used to preserve the social and economic status quo. Using education as a means of gradual, nonrevolutionary social reform, Mann tied common schooling with the improvement of the human condition. As indicated earlier in the chapter, Mann's ideal of the good society was not an open-ended experimental one; it was shaped by definite views of what made a society and its people good persons and citizens.

Mann's concept of the common school rested on his commitment to the republican conception that the best society was one in which people governed themselves through elected officials and representative institutions. The well-being of society depended, he believed, on literate, diligent, productive, and responsible citizens.[21] Common schools were inextricably related to the political order. They were to educate responsible leaders and citizens who would not respond to political demagogues nor join irresponsible mobs. A proper civic education, Mann argued, should teach basic principles of government, provide insights into representative institutions, and generally form good citizens. The common school would also act as a cultural agency that transmitted the U.S. cultural heritage to young people through literature and history. In this way, the common schools would perpetuate that cultural heritage.

Mann believed the common school could perform its civic, political, and cultural role in a nonpartisan way. He believed the public school, although performing a political role, should not be tied to the platform of any political party. Mann wanted the common schools to do a delicate political balancing act. He wanted them to cultivate a general political consciousness but not instill a set of partisan political objectives. What Mann saw as the desirable civic role of public schools in the nineteenth century still is a challenge for public schools in the late twentieth century.

On closer examination, it can be seen that Mann had definite political ideas and a political ideology that shaped his common school philosophy. Although he was not stridently or overtly partisan, he did have his own opinions about the United States as a nation and the direction that it should take.

Mann's concept of the common school was unlike that of the primary schools in Europe, especially in England and France. European primary schools were used to educate lower socioeconomic class children in reading, writing, and religion. In Europe, upper-class children attended preparatory schools that readied them for entry into selective secondary schools and colleges. Rather than segregating students according to their social and economic class, Mann saw the U.S. common school as an integrative social agency for bringing children of different social and economic classes and religions together in one institution. Mann's common school was also a completely public institution, supported by funds derived from public taxation, governed by publicly elected officials, and responsible to the community that it served.

Mann's concept of the common school embraced two principles that have remained part of the public school philosophy:

1. Common schools should be socially integrative.
2. Common schools are publicly controlled, supported and governed.

Public schools today are seen as agencies that should include rather than exclude different groups of people. Although Mann was primarily concerned about segregation on the basis of socioeconomic class, contemporary policies have made schools inclusive in many other areas. For example, the 1954 Brown v. Board of Education decision by the U.S. Supreme Court struck down laws that justified and supported racially segregated schools. By ending racial segregation, the public schools became instruments to help create a racially integrated society. In similar fashion, legislation pertaining to the education of handicapped persons created the movement for mainstreaming handicapped children in regular classrooms whenever possible. These recent trends reflect the integrationist goal that was part of Mann's concept of the common school.

Along with the integrationist theme is the recurring argument that common schools should be public. By vesting support and control in the hands of the public, Mann believed this would make schooling a matter of public concern. Throughout the history of education in the United States, it has been a public matter. Lay people as well as professional educators have opinions about public education and about the goals, purposes, and curriculum of the public schools.

As indicated, Mann was a philosophically consistent educator in that his immediate objectives were in agreement with his general goals. This consistency was apparent in the manner in which he based the common school curriculum on broad social and political goals. For the common school to create a common civic community that included diverse social and economic as well as religious groups, Mann believed that its curriculum should provide basic knowledge and skills to its students. The common school curriculum should provide the elementary subjects and skills that prepared persons to function successfully as members of the community, as economically productive managers and workers, as ethical persons who shared common values, and as responsible citizens.[22] The common school curriculum, designed to prepare people for everyday life, included reading, writing, spelling, arithmetic, history, geography, health, music, and art—the skills and subjects needed by practical businessmen, skilled workers, and competent citizens. In the first half of the nineteenth century, the United States was in its first stages of industrial transformation. Although the common school curriculum might appear to be incomplete by today's standards, it should be remembered that the nation was still a developing country.

The curriculum Mann endorsed for common schools also should be considered as the forerunner of the contemporary elementary school curriculum. The common school curriculum stressed reading, writing, spelling, and speaking, which today are included in the language arts. Similar to the contemporary curriculum, the nineteenth-century common school stressed mathematics. History and geography, which were introduced into the common school curriculum, remain key elements in the contemporary social studies program. Mann's emphasis on health, music, and art remains with us today. Although much has changed in the history of elementary schooling, particularly in the areas of teaching methods, textbooks, and materials, the line of curriculum development can be traced to the skills and subjects that were part of a common school education.

The values Mann wanted common schools to implant in the young came from the moral codes of his upbringing in rural Massachusetts, from his exposure to Emerson's transcendentalism, and his persistent commitment to republican government. Essentially, he believed common schools should prepare individuals who would and could earn a living, pay taxes, and support their families and their communities. Mann's paramount moral values were those of hard work, effort, honesty, diligence, thrift, literacy, respect for property, and respect for reason. His economic ideas that valued private property and encouraged individual initiative were those of an emerging capitalism and the free-enterprise system. Reflecting the Calvinism of his youth, Mann believed that men of property and position had a special responsibility to be the stewards of society. They were to support schools, improve living and working conditions, and be agents of moral regeneration.

Although his religious values had been liberalized by Unitarianism and transcendentalism, Mann's ethical values remained close to the general orientation of Evangelical Protestantism. To avoid controversy among the Protestant denominations, Mann believed that common schools should cultivate values that were common to Protestants. His compromise that the ethical principles of a common Christianity should be emphasized in the common schools satisfied many but not all of the Protestant denominations. However, Roman Catholics, who were immigrating in larger numbers to the United States, rejected Mann's common Christianity as simply an attempt to indoctrinate their children in the Protestant religion. Of the various compromises Mann developed to promote acceptance of the common school, that of a common Christianity was most fragile. To avoid the "Protestant orientation" of the common schools, Roman Catholics created their own separate parochial school systems that were independent of the public schools. Others who believed that common schooling should be religiously neutral argued and later achieved a public school system that was completely secular and separate from religious denominationalism.

Mann's concept of the common school with its strong emphasis on the cultivation of values was still another element that would shape the institution's development. Americans expect public schools to shape and encourage certain values and behavior. Value formation remains today an important change of public schooling along with its more strictly academic function. Although even in Horace Mann's day the question of what values should be cultivated was intensely debated, the value orientation of today's public schools is even more controversial. The religious value issues that provoked controversy in the nineteenth century still remain. For example, religious differences are part of the context of the debate over the teaching of creationism and evolutionism in the schools. The schools are now involved in many areas of life that used to be dealt with by the church and the family. Questions of the proper kind of sex education, for example, provoke value conflicts in the schools.

Although many issues related to common schooling generated controversy, Mann was a skilled educational leader who was generally able to develop a climate of opinion that was favorable to public education. For Mann, educational administration was a form of political leadership. It was necessary for him to:

1. Define and explain the purposes of common schooling in terms that appealed to wide sectors of the population.
2. Persuade conflicting groups that it was in their interest to support common schools.
3. Mobilize these groups to campaign actively for and support legislation and taxation for public schools.

Among the key groups whose support he needed were the clergy of the major Protestant churches, the businessmen who controlled the economic sector, and the farmers and tradesmen who formed a majority of the population.

The Protestant clergy were often leaders who could shape public opinion in their communities. Initially, some of these clergymen favored schools that were directly affiliated with their churches. Mann and others used the argument that the common schools could emphasize the moral values derived from a generalized interdenominational Protestantism. When the Protestant clergy accepted the compromise of a common Christianity, they generally supported public schooling. Often Protestant clergymen were crucial supporters in molding a climate of public opinion favorable to common schools.[23]

Mann also had to secure the support of the business community—the owners of industries and commercial enterprises. He used the full extent of his persuasive powers to convince them that it was in their best interests to have their property taxed for the purpose of providing common schools for children other than their own. Skillfully using the biblical argument of stewardship, he told them that they were the responsible agents, or the stewards, of the economy. It was their responsibility to make sure that at least a part of their economic profits should be reinvested in society. The best kind of investment was in education, which would pay the dividend of providing a supply of competent managers and skilled workmen. These trained, orderly, and industrious workers would further increase profits that could then stimulate an expansive economy. Mann's argument of stewardship and the relationship of education to national prosperity reflected his Whig political views, which saw common schools as an important internal improvement.

Mann realized that the majority of people were neither religious nor business leaders. They were the common people of the day, the farmers and tradesmen, the people of modest incomes. With this group, he used an argument that is still used to win support for increased taxation for public schools. Public taxation, he told this group, was the best means they had for social and economic mobility. Public schools would make it possible for their sons and daughters to receive an education that would help them to gain better jobs and improve their social status. Mann claimed that the common schools would be the "great leveler," the social agency that would provide an equal opportunity. With an equal educational start, those who succeeded socially, economically, and politically would do so not because they were born into socially prominent families but because of their own merit and achievement.

Using all the rhetorical and oratorical skills that he had acquired at Brown University and had sharpened in the Massachusetts legislature, Mann developed and perfected a consensus style of leadership. Groups that had different interests could be and were united in a common cause. Although their motives for entering into this common cause were different, the result was the same—a climate of public opinion that supported the common schools.

Mann's strategy for creating a system of public education in Massachusetts required that public opinion be favorably inclined and that the necessary legislation was passed. He realized, however, that the success of the common school concept needed more than public and legislative approval. It needed well-prepared teachers who embodied the common school philosophy in their classroom practices. To implement his philosophy of education in public school policy, curriculum, and instruction, Mann developed a proposal to professionalize teachers by improving their qualifications. In this way, Mann was an important figure in the development of teacher education in the United States.

Teachers, Mann believed, should have expert knowledge of the skills and subjects they teach, be competent in the methods of teaching, be skilled in classroom management, and be a role model, an exemplar of moral, civic, and ethical behavior for their students.[24] Mann's concept of the well-prepared teacher differed significantly from the earlier model of the teacher. In the colonial period, elementary school teachers were really just school keepers. Often, they were young men who were preparing for the law or ministry. Their commitment to teaching was secondary and temporary until they could enter careers that had higher status and salaries.

In contrast to the inherited and traditional view of the elementary teacher, Mann believed that those who became teachers should make it their primary career. As a major career commitment, the prospective teacher was to be prepared as a professional educator. To accomplish more professional preparation of teachers, Mann advocated the establishment of normal schools.

The concept of the normal school came originally from France, where it was used to prepare primary school teachers. The "normal ecole," or model school, provided preparation for teaching, which included practice teaching in a demonstration school. Mann, James Carter, and other supporters of common schools believed that normal schools could be used to prepare the teachers who were needed for the public school system. In the United States, the normal school was a two-year institution, specifically designed to prepare prospective teachers.

Convinced by Mann's persuasive arguments for the improvement of teacher qualifications, the Massachusetts legislature authorized the Board of Education to establish a number of normal schools, which were to be located at Lexington, Barre, and Bridgewater. To be admitted to a normal school, applicants had to be sixteen years old, have completed a common school education, be in good health, and sign a declaration of intention to teach. The teacher education curriculum at the normal schools omitted the Latin and Greek classics that had dominated secondary and higher education since the colonial period. Normal school students instead studied English composition and grammar, spelling, geography, arithmetic, health, and history, which were the essential subjects taught in the common schools. The normal school curriculum also emphasized the history and philosophy of education, the principles and methods of teaching, and clinical experience, which involved teaching in a model or demonstration school. The early normal schools, like the common schools, also emphasized the ethics and values of a common Christianity. Daily Bible reading was also required.

The common school and the normal school were related institutions in that the latter prepared the teachers for the former. An important trend was set in motion in these institutions in that elementary school teaching became an occupation that shifted from male to female dominance. The majority of the students who attended the normal schools and went on to become common school teachers were young women. Although they were underpaid and subjected to many restrictions on their personal freedom, the entry of women into teaching was a first stage in the movement of women into other occupations and professions.

The normal schools were also the initial institutional development in the professionalization of teacher education. Although it is too much to claim that teachers enjoyed professional preparation and status in the early nineteenth century, these two-year normal schools were the first step in the process. They were institutions in which educational ideas were developed and innovative methods such as those devised by Johann Heinrich Pestalozzi, Friedrich Froebel, and Johann Herbart were introduced to the United States from Europe. Eventually, many of the normal schools became four-year, degree-granting teachers' colleges. In the mid-twentieth century, many of these teachers' colleges became all-purpose colleges and universities that continued to have as part of their mission the preparation of teachers.

The program used to prepare teachers in the normal schools was the forerunner of the contemporary teacher education program. The preparation of prospective teachers in the skills and subjects they were to teach in the common schools resembles the preparation that contemporary teachers have in the methods and materials related to language arts, social studies, the sciences, and mathematics. The cultural foundations of education—history of education, philosophy of education, and sociology of education—had their origins in the normal schools. Of importance in teacher education is the area of clinical experience and practice teaching, which originated in the early nineteenth-century normal schools.

Conclusion: An Assessment

In this conclusion, we shall assess Horace Mann's influence on U.S. education in four key areas:

1. His role in articulating and explaining the relationship of public education to the U.S. political and social order.
2. His effort in defining the concept of the common school and developing the procedures by which it would be governed, supported, and controlled.
3. His effort to emphasize a particular set of values that common schools were to cultivate.
4. His work in designing a strategy to improve the preparation and status of teachers.

As indicated in this chapter, Mann was inspired by the ideas stemming from the revolutionary republican ideology. He also was a Whig politician who believed in that party's commitment to political stability and to economic development. These factors caused Mann to see a close relationship between public education and the political order. Public education in the institutional form of common schools was to prepare literate citizens who would be capable participants in republican political institutions and processes.

In terms of institutional development and control, Mann's concept of the common school reflected a revitalization of the New England tradition of local control of public institutions, especially educational ones. Important for the future course of public schools was Mann's belief that common schools should be locally controlled and publicly supported institutions. This policy remains a prominent feature of contemporary public education. In addition, as secretary of the Board of Education, Mann was a state official. Common schooling was largely a product of the state's involvement. Common school leaders such as Mann forged a political and educational linkage between the local school district and the state that continues today.

The pattern of public education in the United States that developed out of the common school movement is a combination of local and state control and support. This pattern, which reflects the political ideology of Mann and others, is the pattern that governs public education in the United States today. It should be pointed out that, during Mann's career, it was only one of many alternatives that might have been used. Other possibilities for the development of education in the United States include the following:

1. The schools could have followed a pattern of denominational religious control as was the case in other Western countries.

2. The schools could have been organized on the model of the Lancasterian monitorial schools in which private philanthropists funded mass educational endeavors.

3. The schools might have been linked to definite communitarian efforts designed to transform society radically as attempted by Robert Owen at New Harmony, Indiana.

Instead of these alternatives, the public schools became agencies transmitting a view of society and politics that was stable and orderly rather than socially or culturally reconstructive. Further, public education became a state and local function that fit well with other dominant trends in the United States, such as westward development and capitalism.

In terms of its value orientation, Mann's common schools reflected the dominant Protestant ethos of the time rather than agencies of value change. Public schools were not exclusively academic but were also expected to develop the morals and ethics of the young. The ethical system that Mann embraced merged the values of the Protestant ethic with those of an emergent capitalism. Diligence, hard work, industriousness, punctuality, respect for private property, and an almost habitual tendency to orderly procedures became the creed of public schooling at the time of its origin and continue to dominate public schooling today. Although Mann was successful in imposing this generalized value orientation on the public schools, he was less successful with his compromise position that claimed that the common schools could cultivate a common Christianity. The increasingly pluralistic religious climate in the United States during the mid- and late-nineteenth century was to erode that fragile compromise.

Although Mann was astute in recognizing the common schools' power as an agency of ethical and moral values, the value creed and cultural ethos that he stressed reflected the dominant social, political, and economic group in American society. In his desire to create a consensus climate for the common schools, he also helped to create a view of public education that was culturally monolithic. The school's values reflected a white, English-speaking, Protestant, upper middle-class orientation. With the value presuppositions that Mann helped to create at work throughout the rest of the nineteenth century and the early twentieth century, the public schools were not reflective of the United States' growing ethnic, language, racial, and cultural diversity. Only in the mid- and late-twentieth century was the public school philosophy sufficiently enlarged to reflect the diversity of a culturally pluralistic society.

Finally, Horace Mann contributed the notion that teaching is a field that needs professionalization. The professional preparation Mann inaugurated with the normal schools was a significant point of departure for today's programs of teacher education. It was because of his efforts that teaching was seen as more than a temporary calling a person did on the way to something better. Teaching became a career that required commitment and preparation.

Discussion Questions

1. What was the general social, political, economic, and religious context of Horace Mann's life and career?

2. Analyze Horace Mann's conception of civic education and indicate if it was a form of social continuity or change.
3. What events in Horace Mann's childhood and education shaped his educational philosophy?
4. Identify the values that Mann believed should be cultivated in the common schools. Are these values similar to or different from those emphasized in public education today?
5. Examine the components of your program of teacher education. Are these components similar to or different from those recommended by Mann for the preparation of teachers?
6. Analyze the consensus style of leadership developed by Mann. Is this style of leadership adequate for today's educational leader and administrator?
7. Analyze the common Christianity compromise developed by Mann. Are there any possibilities for such a common ethical creed in today's schools?
8. Examine the public elementary school curriculum. Compare and contrast it with the common school curriculum of Mann's day.

Research and Essay Topics

1. Using Mann's annual reports as a source, prepare a paper that analyzes his conception of civic education.
2. Using Mann's annual reports as a source, prepare a paper that describes his idea of the elementary school curriculum.
3. Using Mann's annual reports as a source, prepare a paper that analyzes his concept of a common Christianity.
4. Read a biography of Horace Mann. Write a paper that identifies the important events that shaped his life and philosophy.
5. Using the *McGuffey Reader* or other books of the period of the 1830s to 1860s, identify and analyze the values conveyed in these reading series or materials.
6. Identify a college that originated as a normal school in your state or region. If a history of that institution is available, write a paper that describes its history as a teacher education institution.

Notes

1. The effect of Evangelical Protestantism is discussed in Perry Miller, *The Life of the Mind in America from the Revolution to the Civil War* (New York: Harcourt Brace Jovanovich, 1965), and Sydney E. Ahlstrom, *A Religious History of The American People* (New Haven: Yale University Press, 1972).
2. Lloyd P. Jorgenson, *The State and the Non-Public School, 1825–1925* (Columbia: University of Missouri Press, 1987), 31–54.
3. Ibid., 69–72.
4. Frederick M. Binder, *The Age of the Common School, 1830–1865* (New York: John Wiley and Sons, 1974), 7–21.

5. The definitive biography of Horace Mann is Jonathan Messerli, *Horace Mann: A Biography* (New York: Alfred A. Knopf, 1972).

6. Robert B. Downs, *Horace Mann: Champion of Public Schools* (New York: Twayne Publishers, 1974), 11.

7. Mary Mann, *Life of Horace Mann* (Boston: Walker Fuller, 1865), 11–12.

8. N. Ray Hiner and Joseph M. Hawes, *Growing Up in America: Children in Historical Perspective* (Urbana: University of Illinois Press, 1986).

9. Lawrence Cremin, ed., *The Republic and the School: Horace Mann on the Education of Free Men* (New York: Bureau of Publications, Teachers College Press, Columbia University, 1957), 4.

10. Mann, 11–12.

11. Downs, 14.

12. Ibid., 17.

13. Ibid., 20.

14. Messerli, 119.

15. Downs, 27–29.

16. Ibid., 29–30.

17. Cremin, 29–33.

18. Ibid., 32.

19. Ibid., 39.

20. Ibid., 87.

21. Merle Curti, *The Social Ideas of American Educators* (Peterson, N.J.: Littlefield, Adams, 1959), 101–138.

22. Lawrence A. Cremin, *The American Common School: An Historic Conception* (New York: Bureau of Publications, Teachers College Press, Columbia University, 1951), 62–63.

23. Jorgenson, 31–54.

24. Downs, 39–41.

Suggestions for Further Reading

Binder, Frederick M. *The Age of the Common School, 1830–1865.* New York: John Wiley and Sons, 1974.

Cremin, Lawrence A. *The American Common School: An Historic Conception.* New York: Bureau of Publications, Teachers College Press, Columbia University, 1951.

———, ed. *The Republic and the School: Horace Mann on the Education of Free Men.* New York: Bureau of Publications, Teachers College Press, Columbia University, 1957.

Downs, Robert B. *Horace Mann: Champion of Public Schools.* New York: Twayne Publishers, 1974.

Hiner, N. Ray, and Joseph M. Hawes. *Growing Up in America: Children in Historical Perspective.* Urbana: University of Illinois Press, 1986.

Jorgenson, Lloyd P. *The State and the Non-public School, 1825–1925.* Columbia: University of Missouri Press, 1987.

Mann, Horace. *Lectures on Education.* New York: Arno Press, 1969.

Messerli, Jonathan. *Horace Mann: A Biography.* New York: Alfred A. Knopf, 1972.

Miller, Perry. *The Life of the Mind in America from the Revolution to the Civil War.* New York: Harcourt Brace Jovanovich, 1965.

Robert Owen: Utopian Socialist and Communitarian Educator

Portrait of Robert Owen; reproduction from the collection of the Library of Congress.

In this chapter we examine the life, educational philosophy, and contributions of Robert Owen (1771–1858), a utopian theorist, proponent of communitarianism, social planner, and an educational innovator. Owen's emphasis on developing planned communities and his stress on the formative effect of the social environment on human beings anticipated contemporary programs of community development and early childhood education. Owen's development of planned communities at New Lanark, Scotland, and New Harmony, Indiana, have intrigued social and educational historians during the years. His many publications on society and education were significant documents about the interconnections of school and society. Owen's influence on Western educational theory and practice is discussed in its historical context and in terms of its effect on educational philosophy and policy. First, the historical context of industrializing, early nineteenth-century England is examined as the situation against which Owen reacted. Second, Owen's biography, his education and career as an industrialist and a theorist, is examined to determine the evolution of his ideas. Third, Owen's theory of human nature and society is analyzed. Fourth, his experiment in schooling at New Lanark is examined. Last, Owen's significance as an educator is assessed.

To help you organize your thoughts as you read this chapter, you might wish to focus on the following questions:

- How did Owen react to the major trends of the historical context in which he lived?
- How did Owen's life, his educational biography, shape his philosophy of education?
- How did Owen's theories about human nature, community, and society shape his educational theories and practices?
- What is the enduring effect of Owen's contributions to education?

The Historical Context of Owen's Life

Robert Owen's work as a social and educational theorist can be viewed in many dimensions. He was a utopian thinker, a social theorist, and an educational practitioner. All these dimensions of his life will be examined but the theme of utopian thinker is especially interesting for educators. By using their imagination, especially their social imagination, utopian thinkers project human nature, culture, and community into the future and try to imagine the contours of a new, better, and different world.[1] Utopian thinkers like Owen use their current context—the social, economic, and educational conditions—as a starting point from which their projections originate. They often reverse the realities of their current situation and in a way turn these realities upside down. Thus, in place of the injustices and ills of the present, they project an improved place on Earth free of the obstacles that retard human happiness. By studying the work of utopian theorists, it is possible to engage in the educational uses of social imagination and project how a perfect system of education could help to create a better world. From such flights of social imagination, future realities may come into being.

As a utopian thinker, Owen's ideas on education were based on the existing social and economic conditions of early nineteenth century Great Britain. As a theorist who wanted to develop a new science of society, Owen believed many of the problems caused by the early Industrial Revolution resulted from a misreading of events.

For Owen, the classical economic theorists such as Adam Smith, David Ricardo, and Thomas Malthus had reached erroneous conclusions about the effect of the Industrial Revolution. Owen came to regard their theories as misleading rationales for the competition, exploitation, and unhappiness that many people, particularly the working classes, were experiencing in the nineteenth century. Classical economists had provided early liberal politicians with a justification for laissez-faire policies that left undone desperately needed reforms, especially of a social and educational nature. As a utopian theorist, Owen wanted to develop a new social theory that would counteract and replace that of laissez-faire.

A prosperous mill owner, Owen was well versed in the factory system's new and efficient modes of industrial production. In no way did he oppose industrialization; rather, he wanted to humanize it by eliminating its negative consequences on the health and welfare of human beings. He believed that machine power was the instrument that could create a new social and economic system. The industrial system made it possible to mass-produce goods, make labor more efficient, and create material abundance. What was wrong, in Owen's opinion, was that wealth created by industrialism benefitted only a few. At the root of the problem was the continuation of an archaic and obsolete system of ownership, private property. In his utopian perspective, a better world would be created if private ownership was ended and an economy and society of cooperative sharing created.

According to Owen's analysis of early nineteenth-century industrialism, private property led to human exploitation and socioeconomic class conflicts. The middle classes of owners, managers, and professionals were becoming locked into an inexorable struggle against the laborers who worked in the factories, mines, and mills. Class antagonisms, based on economic divisions, would lead to social tensions and violence. In the utopia of his dreams, violence would have no place. However, to end the hatred that led to violence, it was necessary to root out its cause—the desire for economic gain at other people's expense.

Although David Ricardo argued that economic prosperity required that profits be reinvested in capital expansion to earn still more profits, Owen claimed that the goods and services of the industrial order should be shared equally by all.[2] Equal sharing would reduce class antagonism, and ownership of property by communities rather than individuals would end class divisions altogether. Completely rejecting the concept of class struggle and antagonism, Owen believed that his projected new community would be classless.

On the issue of class conflict Owen showed himself to be an educator and propagandist rather than the organizer of a political movement as such. He believed that his persuasive abilities would convince the wealthy classes to give up their privileges and property voluntarily for the common good. He also believed he could educate workers to abandon their feelings of antagonism toward their economic oppressors. Peaceful persuasion and education based on his social science would create human harmony and do away with class hatred. By the mid-nineteenth century, scientific socialists—as Karl Marx and Friedrich Engels styled themselves—would praise Owen's assessment of economic conditions as laudable but would condemn the nonviolent social change that he envisioned as unrealistic.

Owen was dismayed by the lack of economic and social planning and coordination that he saw in early nineteenth-century Britain. Nowhere was the absence of coordinated planning more evident than in the mushrooming growth of Britain's cities. The migration of rural agricultural workers to the cities to become factory workers had been unplanned, haphazard, and done without consideration of the social and educational consequences that followed in its wake. Masses of people had crowded into sadly deficient tenements that were ill heated, poorly ventilated, and infested with vermin. The absence of sanitary facilities, supplies of pure water, and adequate sewage disposal made the urban areas—inhabited by the working classes—ripe for the spread of diseases.

Government services such as hospitals, schools, and police were rudimentary at best and unable to cope with the problems created by a burgeoning population. In Owen's reading of events, classical liberal ideology, buttressed by the theories of the Manchester school of economics, further aggravated the situation by endorsing a hands-off, laissez-faire policy. The antidote that Owen developed in his utopian vision of the new social order was one of total involvement by community agencies in human life.

Further, the migration of rural people to the cities produced social changes that affected living conditions and styles of life. The factory system's appetite for cheap labor, especially that of women and children, changed the pattern of family life and early educational practices. The parenting function exercised by both parents, but especially by mothers, changed. Women worked in the factories for long hours, often from early morning to late at night. Children, too, toiled at the monotonous routines of tending the machinery of factory and mill. Education of children, which had been extremely limited for the children of the working poor, was rendered even more inadequate. In the new social order of Owen's dreams, the situation of women and children was to be greatly improved, and education would be the remedy.

Owen was especially concerned about the stereotyped and limited role that women had in the social and economic context of early nineteenth-century England. By law, custom, and social convention, women were held to be unequal and subordinate to men. Women could not legally hold property in their own names. Their property was that of their fathers, husbands, or guardians. Love and marriage in the early nineteenth century were based on property and its control. For the members of a society to be truly free and equal, women had to have equality of educational opportunity and be free to have the kind of social relationships that they chose. In his new world, Owen saw women as equal participants, free from the old gender-defined tasks of cooking, cleaning, and child rearing that had limited them in the past. In the new society, social agencies would perform these functions.

As he surveyed the cultural conditions of the early nineteenth century, Owen believed that unregulated and exploitive industrialism produced a sense of alienation in workers that separated them from involvement with the product they were manufacturing. Unlike the older form of workmanship in which the craftsman had pride in the product he was making with his hands, the worker on the factory assembly line made only one part of the finished item. The worker's alienation from the process and the product was further aggravated, Owen believed, by the fact that the economic profit was expropriated completely by the factory owner. Also, the worker performed his or her labor in social isolation. Thus, in terms of identifying the worker with the product, of providing an economic incentive, and in bringing about societal involvement, the industrial system was lacking.

Although the sense of community was declining, the leading apologists of the classical school of economics and their associates in liberal politics were following the ideological line of Smith, Ricardo, and Malthus that nature should be allowed to take its inexorable course without interference by human planning. Smith argued that government should not interfere with the natural laws of supply and demand; Ricardo argued that profits needed to be maximized even at the expense of workers, and Malthus suggested that plague, famine, or war would check the burgeoning growth of population and that if these natural processes were interfered with, the population would exceed the Earth's potential of feeding it.

Owen believed that conditions of scarcity, unemployment, and economic boom or bust could be altered. To replace the alienation and class antagonism of an exploitive industrial system, it was imperative that a viable sense of community be restored. This could best be developed in villages of mutual cooperation in which the enterprise of the inhabitants was balanced between agriculture and industry. In these villages the inhabitants would come to know each other directly, as in an extended family, although the ties would be based on sociality rather than kinship. The theme of the "machine in the garden" would characterize Owen's utopian plans.

Owen's Life: The Biography of an Utopian

Robert Owen was born in Newtown, a small town in Wales. In his autobiography, Owen, who identified his father, Robert, as an ironmonger and saddler, claimed to be influenced by his parents' habits of hard work, industriousness, and thrift.[3] Owen's autobiography reveals him to be a person with strong self-esteem that his critics claimed bordered on egotism. By all indications, Owen was altruistic but also paternalistic. He took keen delight in hearing his own voice and reading his own words.

Owen's reflections on his childhood are full of self-praise and reveal the confidence of a self-made and mostly self-educated man.[4] He was, he asserts, the fastest runner, the best dancer, the most popular, and the most gifted scholar in Newton. Because of his academic accomplishments, the village schoolmaster relied on Owen to instruct the other children in the school. Imbued with a confidence that he carried throughout his life, Owen's self-generated enthusiasm for his own ideas, words, and plans caused him to operate in a reality of his own making. The eternal optimist, Owen often had difficulty distinguishing between his successes and his failures.

At the age of ten, Owen left Newtown to seek fame and fortune, returning seventy-seven years later, in 1858, to die in the place of his birth. After spending some time in Stamford and London, he took a position as an apprentice in a draper's shop in Manchester, a rapidly growing city in the throes of England's Industrial Revolution.[5] By age 18, Owen, who had worked at various jobs after completing his apprenticeship, had accumulated enough money to invest in a partnership in a firm manufacturing cotton-spinning machinery. He was an ambitious young man intent on making his way up the economic ladder during a time when fortunes could be quickly made and quickly lost. His next venture, in 1792, saw him managing a mechanized cotton mill owned by Peter Drinkwater. Commenting that his business career was an educational experience, Owen noted that he improved the technique of cotton manufacturing, gained expertise in factory management, and was stimulated by association with Manchester's leading entrepreneurs and intellectuals.[6] Owen was quite successful in the profit making that he would later come to see as exploitive.

In 1799, Owen and several associates formed the Chorlton Twist Company, which raised sufficient capital to purchase control of David Dale's New Lanark mills. Cotton manufacturing was then a leading industry in Britain, and Dale's mills, situated in the Clyde Valley near the falls of the River Clyde at New Lanark, Scotland, were among the most prosperous. While negotiating for the properties, Owen met Dale's daughter Caroline and fell in love with her. When he married Caroline Dale, Owen had not only made a business arrangement but had also married into one of nineteenth-century England's leading industrial families.

New Lanark, the scene of Owen's social and educational experimentation from 1799 to 1824, was an industrial village, a mill town. Located halfway between Scotland's large cities of Glasgow and Edinburgh, New Lanark consisted of mill buildings where cotton cloth was manufactured by water-power-driven machinery, many large apartment or row houses for the workers, a company store, and the mansion of the owner.

When he took charge of the mills in 1799, Owen found that he was responsible for managing more than 1,000 workers, including men, women, and children. Surveying the living and working conditions at New Lanark, Owen was disturbed by his findings. The town, he observed, was ridden with delinquency, vice, drunkenness, theft, and vermin. The firsthand encounter with these conditions started the young businessman down the path to utopianism, to communitarianism, and to a life dedicated to social reform. Consistent with the character that he would exhibit throughout his career as a social reformer, Owen acted in the paternalistic fashion that earned him the title of the "benevolent Mr. Owen." His reforms were based on what he claimed to be his great philosophical discovery that "Man's character is made for and not by him."[7] Rejecting the conventional wisdom that poverty and vice were caused by the innate depravity of the human character, Owen argued that human behavior was shaped by the environmental circumstances in which people lived. Better housing, food, clothing, and education would improve the social environment and reform the character of its inhabitants.

Owen had not yet determined that communal ownership of property was a necessary condition for social reform. Still committed to private ownership at New Lanark, he believed that a businessman could earn profits without exploiting his workers. Initially suspicious of Owen's promises to improve their living and working conditions, the New Lanark workers feared that Owen was trying to guile them into working harder and producing more profits for the company. Nevertheless, Owen inaugurated his reform program at New Lanark.

Under Owen's direction, a concerted program of social reform and community renewal were instituted in the Scottish mill town. One set of reforms had to do with the working conditions in the mills. The hours of labor were reduced for all, and children under the age of 10 were not permitted to work in the mills. Owen also ended the practice of wholesale employment of orphan children that had characterized the previous management of the mills. Further, he introduced a system whereby every employee's efficiency was rated daily. Next, he turned to reforming living conditions. The streets were swept, debris was removed, and the mill village generally improved in physical appearance. Inspection teams visited workers' apartments to make sure that they were kept clean. The company store was stocked with fairly priced items.

High on Owen's agenda for the social improvement of New Lanark was education. He established a general school for the education of the town's children, which was characterized by progressive methods. He founded an infant school for the early education of children from the ages of two to six, when they entered the general school. Believing that education was a lifelong undertaking, Owen also established the Institute for the Formation of Character, which featured adult education, after-work lectures, and concerts. Under his direction, New Lanark became a total educational environment.

Word of Owen's reforms at New Lanark traveled widely throughout Europe and the Americas. His fame as a prosperous factory owner and a paternalistic reformer attracted a steady stream of visitors to New Lanark to observe the work in the mills, instruction in the schools, and the general atmosphere of reform. Indeed, new Lanark stood out as a place apart in an era that was content to rely on so-called natural forces of supply and demand rather than on social imagination. Owen spent more time guiding visiting notables around New Lanark than on managing the mills. He began to write tracts describing his reforms and was a frequent speaker to groups throughout England.

Thoroughly enjoying his reputation as a philanthropist and social reformer, Owen decided that his plans for reform should not be limited to New Lanark but should be disseminated throughout the British Isles, through Europe, to the Americas, and even perhaps the rest of the world. He moved from local reform to projects of world renewal. Owen's *Report to the Committee of the Association for the Relief of the Manufacturing and Labouring Poor* in 1817 and his *Report to The County of Lanark* in 1820 reflect his movement to the larger role of social critic and reformer.[8] At this stage in his career, his communitarian ideology began to take shape.

Owen believed that problems of periodic unemployment and inadequate poor relief could not be dealt with in a piecemeal fashion. These issues, he believed, were part of a larger and more pervasive social crisis. Owen believed the Industrial Revolution not only changed economic modes of life, but transformed civilization itself. Industrialization increased productivity and stimulated economic growth, but these benefits were unequally distributed because of an archaic and irrational individualism based on private property. Periodic unemployment, Owen reasoned, was not an inevitable result of industrial modernization as Adam Smith and David Ricardo had argued, but was rather the unnecessary baggage of a competitive and exploitive economy.

In his *Report to the County of Lanark,* Owen, now a full-fledged communitarian socialist, called for the creation of self-supporting "villages of unity and mutual cooperation," not only for the poor but for all classes and all persons. In these villages, where all property would be owned communally, all residential accommodations would be arranged in a parallelogram of connected buildings that would also house schools, apartments, factories, libraries, kitchens, hospitals, dining rooms, and lecture halls. His concept of the "village of unity" quickly developed into a comprehensive communitarian ideology that Owen tried to implement at New Harmony, Indiana, from 1825 to 1828. The Scottish factory town of New Lanark and the frontier village in Indiana became linked by the trans-Atlantic bonds of Owen's communitarian ideology.[9]

Owen's experiences from 1799 to 1824 at New Lanark produced the underlying concepts of his communitarian ideology. He had, largely through his own imaginative efforts, taken a typical factory village and transformed it into a model community. In contrast to the grime, crime, vice, and exploitation that characterized the life of the working class in the early nineteenth century, Owen had brought cleanliness, order, and education to the mill workers of New Lanark, whether they wanted it or not.

In 1824, Owen left New Lanark and came to the United States. For the next four years, Owen sought to establish his new communitarian vision of society and education in New Harmony, which he purchased from the Rappites, a sect of German religious pietists who also had lived a communitarian lifestyle. Attracted to the United States as an open society, Owen believed that the American frontier was the ideal locale for his social experiment. The United States, the New World, was free of the class conscious prejudices and irrational traditions of Europe—the Old World— and would be the place for what he called his "new moral world."

After speaking to sessions of the U.S. Congress attended by the Supreme Court and the president, Owen extended his open invitation to all interested parties to join him at New Harmony. One thousand people came. It was an uneven assortment of humanity that ventured to the Indiana frontier. Some of the United States' leading scholars and scientists, who with William Maclure, the pioneer geologist and philanthropist, came to establish a center for scientific and educational research and dissemination. Among them were Thomas Say, Gerard Troost, both eminent natural scientists, and Joseph Neef, who had been trained by Pestalozzi at Burgdorf. Others were inspired by Owen's vision of a new society in a new land. Some had continually failed and were looking for one last chance to begin again. Still others were opportunists who saw Owen as a naive do-gooder whom they could divest of funds.[10]

Owen planned to create a community of equality at New Harmony in which the town's property would be owned in common by the residents. Education would play a central role in the community, which was to develop a comprehensive set of educational institutions, ranging from nursery schools for children to lectures for adults. Owen predicted that the Indiana community would be so successful and prosperous that other communities would organize to imitate it. With New Harmony at the center of a new communitarian world, Owen envisioned a comprehensive network of satellite cities that would encircle the Earth. Once the parent community had been established, it would serve as the model city. For Owen, communitarian education would create and sustain his envisioned new moral world:

> The world will thus be governed by education alone, since all other governments will then become useless and unnecessary. To train and educate the rising generation will at all times be the first object of society, to which every other will be subordinate.[11]

Owen's educational program at New Harmony was closely related to his communitarian ideology. He believed the small, voluntary, experimental community would quickly reform the behavior and character of its residents. Because social regeneration was to be accomplished peacefully, education was to be the primary instrument of reform. In his insightful commentary on early nineteenth-century education, Arthur Bestor wrote that for the educationists of the era, "the relationship between school and society appeared a reciprocal one." According to Bestor:

> The school should respond to social change, they held, but it should also be an instrument for effecting desirable alterations in society. In their hands educational reform became a branch of social reform.[12]

Conceiving of social reform as a total process, Owen believed the reformed community itself, as an informal educational agency, would be a potent force for societal reform. Schooling would reflect and maintain the values that existed within the community. Although the school alone could not create a new society, it could perpetuate the new social design by transmitting communitarian knowledge, skills, and values to young Harmonists.

Schooling at New Harmony represented a shift in educational theory and practice from the ancient classical languages and literature to utilitarianism. For Owen and his chief associate, William Maclure, the Greek and Latin language curriculum was archaic, a pedagogical residue that was irrelevant to scientific and industrial progress. Based on his experiences at New Lanark, Owen's educational program at New Harmony was designed to serve practical and utilitarian goals as well as contribute to fundamental social reconstruction.

A key provision in Owen's New Harmony plan was the abolition of private property, which he had earlier identified as the primary cause of human and social evils. Common property, supported by common education, would be the "great equalizers" that would end class conflict and violence. On May 1, 1825, the "preliminary society of New Harmony" was organized "to improve the character and conditions of its own members, and to prepare them to become associates in independent communities, having common property."[13]

Ten months later, on February 5, 1826, an overly optimistic Robert Owen proclaimed that New Harmony was now the "community of equality." New Harmony's constitution committed its members to "equality of rights" and "equality of duties" within a society of "cooperative union" and a "community of property. Clearly reflecting Owen's conceptions of character formation, cooperation, and education, the constitution stated that "man's character, mental, moral, and physical, is the result of his formation, his location, and . . . the circumstances within which he exists."[14]

Further, the constitution proclaimed that "all members of the community" were to be "one family." There was to be "similar food, clothing, and education." All were to "live in similar houses" and "be accommodated alike." Restating the importance of education, the document read, "It shall always remain a primary object of the community to give the best physical, moral, and intellectual education to all its members."[15]

Unfortunately for Owen, his ambitious plan for a new social order that was to begin at New Harmony did not succeed. Displaying a chronic tendency to disharmony, the inhabitants of New Harmony endlessly debated with each other over the constitution and its revisions, quarreled over the division of property that Owen continually postponed, and disputed social and educational theories and practices.

With the community in the throes of disintegration, Owen and William Maclure quarreled. After litigation, they divided what was left of the community. In 1828, Owen left New Harmony and returned to England, remaining confident that the new world he envisioned was merely postponed. Convinced of the inevitability of the new social order, Owen continued to write, lecture, and organize societies to promote communitarianism. In the United Kingdom, he organized workers' cooperatives. Some see him as contributing the ideas of what would become one of Britain's major political parties, the Labour party. He continued to work for communitarianism, women's rights, improvement of working conditions, and universal education until his death in 1858.

Owen's Social and Educational Theory

Robert Owen's plan for creating the new moral world was based on his conception of human nature. His often-repeated dictum that "man's character was made for and not by him" expressed his belief that he had made a fundamental and revolutionary discovery that previous generations had ignored. In his "Essays on the Formation of Character," from his *New View of Society,* Owen argued that human character was formed by the interaction of the person's original or germinal nature with environmental circumstances. In Owen's communitarian view of progress, the controlled communitarian environment was the most efficacious setting in which to perfect the human personality. His key beliefs were that character development was completely plastic and that whoever controlled the environment would be able to produce the kind of human character he wanted. Thus, Owen gave himself a great power over human destiny. Although his intentions seem to have been benevolent, the same doctrine of total control could have malevolent effects in the hands of a dictator.

For Owen, individuals were not responsible for their behavior because they had no control over their origins or their early childhood experiences. Human beings, however, were not fated to be hapless victims of accidents of birth and a disordered environment. Given the correct environment, which Owen believed he could establish, the human being could be formed into a good, kindly, sharing person. However, it was crucial that the process of character formation begin as early as possible, even in infancy. Owen's emphasis on early childhood education both at New Lanark and New Harmony have made him one of the pioneering theorists in this field.

Owen saw himself as a behavioral and social engineer and believed that he had discovered the laws of human development. He gave his greatest attention to plans to restructure the environment so that human development followed its proper social course. The communitarian environment was Owen's prescribed setting for character formation and personal socialization. Owen clearly pointed to the importance of the communitarian environment in shaping character when he stated:

> It having been discovered that man at birth is wholly formed by the power which creates him, and that his subsequent character is determined by the circumstances which surround him, acting upon his original or created nature—that does not in any degree form himself, physically or mentally, and therefore cannot be a free or responsible agent: the first practical effects of this knowledge must be, to banish from the mind of man all ideas or merit or demerit in any created object or being—to extirpate from his constitution all the feeling to which such ideas give rise; and thus at once to reconcile him to human nature, to himself, and to all his fellow creatures.[16]

Like Rousseau, Owen rejected views of human nature that asserted that individuals entered life with a depraved character. In contrast, Owen wrote that the human being is "a delightful compound, containing the germs of unalloyed excellence, and which require for their due development, only a kindly soil and a careful cultivation."[17] Evil came not from the human being's nature but from his or her ignorance.

Based on his principle of human character, Owen specified a range or continuum of human behaviors. At one end of the continuum was bad behavior, which was caused by evil surroundings. At the other end was superior character, which resulted from favorable conditions where institutions, laws, and customs conformed to the laws of human nature.

To develop superior character, Owen argued, a favorable environment had to be created and those who resided in it needed the right kind of education. The proper environment was one that had been converted from private to social production, distribution, and consumption of goods and services. It was an environment that had changed from the private to the communitarian system. The right kind of education dispelled the ignorance that came from erroneous education. The vague and mysterious strictures that originated with mythology, found in the classics; and theology, which had dominated education, needed to be displaced. These old thought patterns had to give way to a new world view based on the laws of human nature and social development.

Owen's social theory closely corresponded to his view of human nature. His theory of society and social change, in turn, was heavily influenced by his economic ideas. As a social theorist, Owen began his career as a critic of the capitalist system that had earned him wealth and fame. From the negative role of social critic, he advanced to a proactive role as the prophet of a new social and economic system. Moving beyond its initial economic perspective, Owen's system grew into a comprehensive ideology that rested on the community of equality as the dynamic change agency.

Owen's theory of social change was precipitated by his experiences at New Lanark and by his observations of nineteenth-century English society. Continually reiterating that man's character was formed for and not by him, Owen stressed the environment's role in shaping human behavior. If the environment were properly organized, then those who interacted with it would be shaped by its wholesome stimuli. Owen regarded the cooperative community as the ideal environment for shaping the morality of the inhabitants who would dwell in peace and harmony in the new social order.

Believing that the new moral world would come about by peaceful and nonviolent means, Owen relied on education, both nonformal and formal, as the instrument to create the new society. Through his own polemical tracts, lectures, and books, Owen displayed a missionary zeal and worked to gain converts for his new secular religion. He used nonformal education to disseminate information of his vision of the new society and recruit converts for his cooperative commonwealth. He saw his communities of cooperation as educative environments that would form the new moral order by educating moral citizens. Schools in these egalitarian communities, as formal educational agencies, would train later communitarian generations.

Owen's theory of social change was charged with a secular millennialism that convinced him that the new moral world would, like Marx's classless society, come as a result of historical inevitability. Convinced of the rightness of his ideology, Owen believed that society could be reformed by knowledge, education, and example. His conviction that the new society was inevitable caused him to discount political organization and revolutionary tactics as necessary means of social change. Although he sought to convert heads of state, monarchs, presidents, and politically influential people to his ideology, Owen did not seek to head an organized political movement.

Because of his rejection of revolutionary violence and class warfare, Owen was condemned as a utopian by the Marxists. Holding that social change could be achieved without violence, Owen believed that, when people had been educated to recognize the injustice of the old system, they would replace it with his envisioned humane society. Because Owen held that individuals were not responsible for forming their own character, he regarded class hatred as irrational and irrelevant in achieving the new society.[18]

Owen's rejection of class conflict and revolutionary violence led Marx and Engels to condemn Owenism as utopian socialism—a soft-headed and soft-hearted muddled approach to the class struggle that misled the working classes from their true revolutionary role. Although Engels commended Owen for his analysis of the economic woes of the existing society, he condemned his failure to recognize the revolutionary nature of economic class conflict. Unlike Marx, who believed that the proletariat would be led by an elite vanguard, Owen held that all properly educated people could contribute to establishing the cooperative commonwealth.

In his plans for a new society, Owen's outlook resembled the eighteenth-century philosophers who sought to explain physical and social reality by means of a few fundamental laws of immense power and scope. Like the generation of the Enlightenment, he believed that the orderliness of the natural realm could be extended to society. Convinced that his social science explained the laws governing the universe, Owen believed that he had discovered the natural laws of human and social development. Owen was certain that he had correctly formulated a new social science. For the Owenites, social science, which was synonymous with the ideology of communitarian socialism, was the method of studying society to discover the laws that governed it and formed human character.[19] Following his premise that a controlled environment would produce the desired personality type, Owen was a convinced social engineer. He believed that the social scientist, informed by the laws of social organization and human development, could construct the planned environment—the community of equality—so that its residents would be developed according to a societal blueprint. Because social engineering was a way of creating the new person who would inhabit the world, Owen saw himself in the role of the chief engineer who would create such a reconstructed social order.

Owen's planned reconstruction of the social environment was to lead to a fundamental reshaping of human behavior. By living in an environment based on the laws of social science, the new person would be a moral member of society. Within the context of Owenite social science, education was broadly viewed as a total process of communitarian enculturation, which included but was not limited to schooling. In the past, the old, immoral, and discordant modes of thought of the individualistic society were transmitted to the young both by the culture and by schooling that was dominated by the classics. In the new society, a new form of schooling based on social science would help to create a new form of community. The next section of the chapter describes Owen's actual conduct of schools at New Lanark.

Owen's Schools at New Lanark

Along with socially controlled general reform, Owen emphasized that education, especially for children, was a key element in improving human character. In *An Outline of the System of Education at New Lanark,* Robert Dale Owen, Owen's eldest son, provided a detailed account of schooling in that industrial village.

Robert Dale Owen described the school as a two-story building, constructed of gray stone, as were the other structures at New Lanark. The first story was divided into three large rooms where classes were scheduled on reading, natural science, history, geography, and other subjects. After attempting to teach large classes of 100 pupils, Owen decided instruction would be more effective in smaller classes and limited enrollment in these subjects to 50 pupils.

The school's second story uniquely reflected Owen's educational philosophy. It was divided into two classrooms: The principal schoolroom was ninety feet long, forty feet wide, and twenty feet high, whereas the second classroom was somewhat smaller. Its unique feature was that "the walls are hung round with representations of the most striking zoological and mineralogical specimens, including quadrupeds, birds, fishes, reptiles, insects, shells, minerals, &c."[20] At one end of the room was an upper story gallery for the orchestra; at the other end were hung representations of the hemispheres with the countries and seas indicated by various colors but otherwise unidentified.[21] This room also served as a lecture hall and a ballroom.

The school's physical design and its furnishings reflected Owen's educational theory. Large rooms made it possible for children to move from area to area, depending on the subject being taught. Owen stressed using objects or their representations in the form of drawings and models in instruction. In view of the importance of music and dancing, the orchestra platform was a rare educational feature for a nineteenth-century school.

Frequently called the father of infant education, Owen was a convinced proponent of early childhood education. His emphasis on the importance of early learning experiences rested on his communitarian ideology that reform required children to be educated in a controlled environment away from socially corrupting influences. At New Lanark, the ages of the children attending school ranged from 18 months to 12 years, with some children leaving school at age 10 to work in the mills. Although he wanted to restrict child labor and tried to keep the New Lanark children in school until age 12, Owen yielded to parental demands that they be allowed to work in the mill at age 10. In the early nineteenth century, children's labor and the wages they earned were regarded as a needed contribution to a family's income.

The school day began at 7:30 A.M. and ended at 5 P.M., with long breaks or intervals during the day ranging from one to two hours. Owen believed that instruction was more effective and efficient if interspersed with periods of relaxation. The infant classes, enrolling children from ages two to six, were in session for only half of that time.[22] In addition to the day classes, the school was open at night and instruction was provided for older children and adults.

For infants and older children, instruction was free. For children between the ages of six and ten, a small fee was charged. Owen's rationale for charging this fee was that its payment would prevent parents from negatively regarding the school as a charity institution. In early nineteenth-century England, charity schools were conducted for some children of the dependent poor.

Both boys and girls wore a similar uniform, a white Roman-style cotton tunic. The boy's tunic came to the knee, and the girl's tunic reached the ankle.[23] The uniform dress reflected Owen's belief that schooling should foster a sense of equality.

Within the school, Owen sought to create a permissive but controlled environment in which learning would be a pleasurable experience for the children. Extrinsic rewards and punishments that Owen regarded as contributing to an artificial character were abolished. Owen believed that extrinsic incentives, which substituted false goals for the natural consequences of action, produced people with weak and unstable characters. At New Lanark, no rewards were given for outstanding scholarship or good conduct nor were children punished for idleness or disobedience. The motivation for learning was to come from the child's interests. Good conduct would result from the spirit of amiable cooperation engendered by group membership. Teachers were to treat all children with kindness and use restraint only to protect young children from physical harm.[24]

Owen's emphasis on a child-centered classroom climate was a radical change from the conventional teaching style of the early nineteenth century, which included corporal punishment. Given these guidelines for school management, Owen had difficulty finding properly trained teachers. Because he opposed religious and classical education, he did not want to employ teachers who stressed either catechetical instruction or Latin and Greek. In many British primary schools, conventional teaching practices called for strongly domineering teachers who, with the rod, demanded and obtained strict discipline and rigid conformity. In contrast to teachers trained according to conventional practices, Owen wanted patient teachers who loved children and related to them easily and naturally.

In hiring the first teachers in the New Lanark schools, Owen sought people with the right disposition and attitude toward children rather than pedagogical training or previous teaching experience. Owen identified two individuals who met his requirements: John Buchanan, a local weaver, and Molly Young, a seventeen-year-old mill employee. He regarded these two as unspoiled and sufficiently flexible to teach according to his pedagogical design.[25] As Owen hired other teachers, he selected those with backgrounds and personalities similar to Buchanan and Young. Unfortunately, unlike Pestalozzi and other educational innovators, Owen did not institutionalize his pedagogical style by developing teacher education programs. An exception to his use of untrained teachers were the music and dancing teachers who were skilled in their arts.

Although Owen based instruction on children's interests and emphasized using object lessons, the New Lanark curriculum was more subject-centered than was the case with either Pestalozzi or Froebel. The curriculum for the six- to ten-year-olds consisted of reading, writing, arithmetic, natural science, geography, history, singing, and dancing. In addition, girls were taught sewing and needlework.

In teaching reading, Owen's principle was that "children should never be directed to read what they cannot understand. . . . "[26] The method was to have a child read aloud and then have other pupils in the class question him or her about the content. Understanding was emphasized rather than mimicry of the author's language and style.

Owen anticipated what has come to be called the "broad fields curriculum" in that he stressed that natural science, geography, and history be taught in a correlated manner. The method was for the teacher to present an outline of the topic, which was then slowly filled in with supporting details.[27] According to Robert Dale Owen:

> In . . . Natural History, the division of Nature into the Animal, Vegetable, and Mineral Kingdoms, is first explained to them, and in a very short time they learn at once to distinguish to which of these any object which may be presented to them belongs. The teacher then proceeds to details of the most interesting objects furnished by each of these kingdoms, including descriptions of quadrupeds, birds, fishes, reptiles, and insects—and of the most interesting botanical and mineralogical specimens. The details are illustrated by representations of objects, drawn on a large scale and as correctly as possible.[28]

Owen, who personally enjoyed music and dancing, included art and aesthetic appreciation into the New Lanark school program. Children were instructed in singing by both ear and notes. Dancing, which Owen claimed was a pleasant, natural, and social exercise that improved carriage and deportment and "increased cheerfulness and hilarity," was taught through varied Scotch reels, country dances, and quadrilles.[29] Both boys and girls performed military drill. They were formed into divisions led by young drummers and fifers and moved in unison from place to place in the industrial village.

In addition to the school, Owen designed and constructed a three-storied, multi-functional, educational and cultural center, which formally opened in January 1816 as the Institute for the Formation of Character. It was here that Owen's concept of infant education was more fully implemented. The curriculum and methods in the infant school were child centered, play oriented, and aimed to stimulate children to use their senses to develop skills of careful observation. Teachers placed objects in strategic locations throughout the building to stimulate the children's curiosity and observation. Resistant to book-centered education, Owen wanted children to be taught the nature, qualities, and uses of common objects by direct, exploratory activities and by casual conversation between teacher and child. The teacher was to use natural objects found within the immediate location of the village to excite the children's curiosity. This initial interest was to be reinforced by animated conversation between the youngsters and their teachers, who in turn gained new knowledge about the objects and their pupils.[30] Anticipating the British primary method that reached a height of popularity in the 1970s, Owen developed a method of early childhood education in which children moved about freely and learned by pursuing activities that stimulated their interests.

In his commentary about his father's educational efforts at New Lanark, Robert Dale Owen identified several factors that limited the school's effectiveness. First, the children were in school for only five hours each day. The remaining time was spent with parents and others who lacked the proper disposition to the knowledge and values emphasized in Owen's schools. Later, Owen recommended that children be separated from their parents, raised in communal dormitories and educated in communal boarding schools. Second, it was difficult to locate teachers who possessed the character and temperament that were compatible with Owen's educational philosophy. Although he recognized this problem, Owen did not engage in the kind of teacher education that could institutionalize his educational theories. Third, parents did not support certain features of Owenite education. For example, they wanted their children to read at an age earlier than Owen prescribed. They also wanted them to leave school at age 10 rather than 12 as Owen recommended. Finally, parents wanted religious instruction, which Owen believed was harmful. Throughout his career Owen would meet opposition from religious educators. Owen argued that emphasis on the supernatural and the abstract impeded the formation of concepts based on observation and produced prejudicial attitudes rather than egalitarian sentiments.

When Owen came to New Harmony, Indiana, he already had firm opinions about the conduct of schools that arose from his experience at New Lanark. At New Lanark, Owen had exclusive control of the schools. He established the classroom settings, selected the teachers, and determined the curriculum. At New Harmony, in contrast, educational arrangements were controlled by William Maclure, who was Owen's partner in the communitarian venture.[31] Maclure, who sought to integrate basic scientific research with Pestalozzian pedagogy, had a different educational philosophy from Owen. Differences between Owen and Maclure, and the presence of other educators such as Joseph Neef and Marie Duclos Fretageot, made education at New Harmony a much more complex and often controversial undertaking than it was at New Lanark.

As an educational innovator, Owen should be credited with developing his own theory and practice of education at New Lanark. Important elements in this theory were his stress on the importance of early childhood or infant education and his broad concept of education as a means of bringing about social change. At New Lanark, Owen had mixed motives. For him, education was a philanthropic means of improving the living and working conditions of the residents of the industrial village. It was also a means of social control by which Owen placed himself in the position of chief engineer in shaping the behavior of those who associated with him.

Conclusion: An Assessment

Owen's significance in the history of Western thought needs to be assessed in terms of his contributions to social and educational theory. Too often, historians have viewed him only as a utopian socialist and have not seen him as the creator of a comprehensive social and educational theory. To assess Owen's importance to modern education, he must be viewed as a theorist who recognized that education was inextricably related to society. As a pioneer in the sociology of education, he was not content merely to theorize but rather wanted to use education as an instrument to create a new society.

Owen anticipated in his social theory the very modern proposition that model cities can be designed and that they will, in turn, produce model men and women. His designs to create planned communities anticipated the essential strategies used by contemporary urbanologists and community planners. Corrupt, degenerative, and polluted environments, Owen said, create selfish, sick, and sluggish human beings. Clean, attractive, and wholesome social environments, conversely, would create harmoniously integrated members of society. Although using more sophisticated designs, today's advocates of socially engineered model cities, who regard the social environment as the key to reforming human behavior, still follow many of Owen's premises.

By attacking the traditional schools of the early nineteenth century, Owen rejected and sought to discredit inherited educational practices that he believed retarded children's social development. His concept of early childhood education emphasized, as did the ideas of the later progressive educators, children's interests and experiences. In many respects, Owen was the forerunner of the contemporary British primary school, which stresses the importance of children actively learning by exploring their environment.

Without doubt, Owen's intentions as a social reformer were altruistic and humanitarian. At the same time, he was a benevolent paternalist who invaded the individual's right to privacy and the freedom to develop his or her own subjectivity. A sociological and pedagogical busybody, Owen's planned society interfered with the individual's personal freedom to choose his or her own course of self-development. As a self-annointed prophet and social engineer, Owen sought to shape people according to what he believed was in their best interest. In many respects, Owen was the unwitting predecessor of the molders of public opinion and even of the totalitarians who regard humanity as clay to be molded as they see fit. Although Owen could sincerely claim that benevolence was his guiding principle, his theory also carried with it a deterministic denial of human freedom of choice and of the right to shape one's own destiny.

Perhaps the most useful legacy that Robert Owen left to education was that of the utopian thinker who used social imagination to project a vision of a better world. As a utopian thinker, he provided a useful critique of his times. He also demonstrated how utopian conjectures can lead to social and educational change.

Discussion Questions

1. Analyze the concept of social imagination. How can the theory of social imagination be applied to conjecturing new educational designs and futures?
2. What are the educational uses of studying utopian theories?
3. How was Owen's communitarian socialism a reaction against the existing socioeconomic conditions of early nineteenth-century England?
4. How did the events in Owen's life contribute to shaping his social and educational theories?
5. How was Owenism a transatlantic social and educational theory?
6. How was Owen's school at New Lanark a departure from existing approaches to schooling?
7. Determine Owen's significance as an educational and social theorist.

Research and Essay Topics

1. Using the concept of social imagination, write an essay that describes a community and its schools as you would envision them in the future.
2. Review a book written by a utopian thinker.
3. In an essay, analyze Robert Owen's character.
4. In a position paper, either support or attack the proposition that Robert Owen's plan for creating moral character was designed to liberate people.
5. In an essay, profile the kind of teacher who would be suited to teach in a school conducted by Robert Owen.
6. In an essay, assess the significance of Owen's educational ideas for contemporary education.

Notes

1. Elise Boulding, *Building a Global Civic Culture: Education for an Interdependent World* (New York: Teachers College Press, Teachers College, Columbia University, 1988), 108–17.

2. Michael J. Gootzeit, *David Ricardo* (New York: Columbia University Press, 1975).

3. Robert Owen, *The Life of Robert Owen Written by Himself With Selections from His Writings and Correspondence,* vol. 1 (New York: Augustus Kelley, 1967), 1–2. Published originally in 1857–1858.

4. Gerald L. Gutek, "Education and Reform at Robert Owen's New Lanark," *Journal of the Midwest History of Education Society* 17 (1989), 164–71.

5. Margaret Cole, "Robert Owen Until New Lanark," in *Robert Owen: Industrialist, Reformer, Visionary, 1771–1858* (London: Robert Owen Bicentenary Association, 1971), 4–14.

6. Owen, *The Life of Robert Owen,* 34–38.

7. Harold Silver, "Owen's Reputation As an Educationist," in Sidney Pollard and John Salt, eds., *Robert Owen: Prophet of the Poor* (Lewisburg, Penn.: Bucknell University Press, 1971), 65.

8. Robert Owen, *A Supplementary Appendix to the First Volume of the Life of Robert Owen* (London: Effingham Wilson, 1858), reprinted by Augustus M. Kelley Publishers, 1967. See Appendix I, "Report to the Committee of the Association for the Relief of the Manufacturing and Labouring Poor, 1817," 53–54; also see Appendix S, Report to the County of Lanark, 1820, 263–320.

9. The definitive treatment of Owenism as a trans-Atlantic movement is John F. C. Harrison, *Quest for the New Moral World: Robert Owen and the Owenites in Britain and America* (New York: Charles Scribner's Sons, 1969).

10. Gerald L. Gutek, "New Harmony: An Example of Communitarian Education," *Educational Theory* 22 (Winter 1972), 34–36.

11. Robert Owen, "The New Social System," *The New Harmony Gazette* 2 (January 10, 1827), 113.

12. Arthur E. Bestor, Jr., *Backwoods Utopias: The Sectarian and Owenite Phases of Communitarian Socialism in America, 1663–1829* (Philadelphia: University of Pennsylvania Press, 1950), 134–35.

13. George B. Lockwood, *The New Harmony Movement* (New York: D. Appleton and Co., 1905), 84.

14. Ibid., 105–8.

15. Ibid.

16. Owen, "The New Social System," 113.

17. Ibid.

18. Harrison, 81.

19. Ibid., 79.

20. Robert Dale Owen, *An Outline of the System of Education at New Lanark* (Cincinnati: Deming and Wood, 1825), 11.

21. Ibid., 13.

22. Ibid., 12–13.

23. Ibid., 13.

24. Frank Podmore, *Robert Owen* (London: Hutchinson and Co., 1906), pp. 136–37.

25. Owen, *The Life of Robert Owen,* 140.

26. Robert Dale Owen, 14.

27. Ibid., 16.

28. Ibid., 17.

29. Ibid., 25–26.

30. Owen, *The Life of Robert Owen,* 140–41.

31. Paul K. Bernard, "Irreconcilable Opinions: The Social and Educational Theories of Robert Owen and William Maclure," *Journal of the Early Republic* 8 (Spring 1988), 21–44.

Suggestions for Further Reading

Bestor, Arthur E., Jr. *Backwoods Utopias: The Sectarian and Owenite Phases of Communitarian Socialism in America, 1663-1829.* Philadelphia: University of Pennsylvania Press, 1950.

Boulding, Elise. *Building a Global Civic Culture: Education for an Interdependent World.* New York: Teachers College Press, Teachers College, Columbia University, 1988.

Butt, John, ed. *Robert Owen: Aspects of His Life and Work.* New York: Humanities Press, 1971.

Garnett, Ronald G. *Co-operation and the Owenite Socialist Communities in Britain, 1825-45.* Manchester, England: University Press, 1972.

Harrison, John F. C. *Quest for the New Moral World: Robert Owen and the Owenites in Britain and America.* New York: Charles Scribner's Sons, 1969.

———. *Utopianism and Education: Robert Owen and the Owenites.* New York: Teachers College Press, Columbia University, 1968.

Harvey, Rowland H. *Robert Owen: Social Idealist.* Berkeley: University of California Press, 1949.

Kolmerten, Carol A. *Women in Utopias: The Ideology of Gender in the American Owenite Communities.* Bloomington: Indiana University Press, 1990.

Lockwood, George B. *The New Harmony Movement.* New York: D. Appleton and Co., 1905.

Owen, Robert. *The Life of Robert Owen, Written by Himself with Selections From His Writings & Correspondence.* London: Effingham Wilson, 1857. Reprinted by Augustus M. Kelley, Publishers, New York, 1967.

———. *Selected Works of Robert Owen.* London: W. Pickering, 1993.

Owen, Robert Dale. *An Outline of the System of Education at New Lanark.* Cincinnati: Deming and Wood, 1825.

———. *Threading My Way: Twenty-seven Years of Autobiography.* New York: G. W. Carleton and Co., 1874. Reprinted by Augustus M. Kelley, Publishers, New York, 1967.

Pitzer, Donald E. *Robert Owen's American Legacy.* Indianapolis: Indiana State Historical Society, 1972.

Podmore, Frank. *Robert Owen: A Biography.* London: Hutchinson and Co., 1906. Reprinted by George Allen & Unwin, Ltd. London, 1923. Reprinted by Augustus M. Kelley, Publishers, New York, 1968.

Pollard, Sidney, and John Salt, eds. *Robert Owen: Prophet of the Poor.* Lewisburg, Penn.: Bucknell University Press, 1971.

Silver, Harold, ed. *Robert Owen on Education.* Cambridge: Cambridge University Press, 1969.

CHAPTER 15

Friedrich Froebel:
Founder of the Kindergarten

Portrait of Friedrich Froebel; reproduction from the collection of the Library of Congress.

This chapter discusses the life, educational philosophy, and contributions of Friedrich Froebel (1782–1852), a German educator whose pioneer efforts in early childhood education led to the establishment of the kindergarten. Froebel's innovative experiments in educating young children, conducted originally in Germany, contributed to an enlightened concept of the nature of childhood and had a worldwide influence on early childhood education.

In this chapter, Froebel's role in reshaping early childhood education is discussed in its historical context and in terms of its enduring effect on educational philosophy and policy. First, the general social, political, religious, and intellectual context in which Froebel lived and worked is described. Second, Froebel's biography, his education and career, is analyzed to identify the events that contributed to shaping his ideas. Third, the continuing effect of Froebel's contributions on early childhood education is examined. By this analysis, we shall see how the events of nineteenth-century Germany worked to shape Froebel as a person and his philosophy as an educator. For example, the philosophical idealism that was the dominant philosophy in nineteenth-century Germany had a pronounced influence on how Froebel viewed human growth and development.

To organize your thoughts as you read this chapter, you might focus on the following questions:

- What were the major trends in the historical context of nineteenth-century Germany, in which Froebel lived?
- How did Froebel's life, his own educational biography, shape his philosophy of education?
- How did Froebel's educational philosophy determine his educational policies and practices?
- What is the enduring impact of Froebel's contributions to education?

The Historical Context of Froebel's Life

Friedrich Froebel was in many ways a complex and eccentric personality. He was born in 1782 in the small town of Oberweissbach in the German state of Thuringia. The political weakness and disunity of the various German states had an impact on Froebel as well as on many young people who believed Germans should be united in one nation. The year in which Froebel was born saw Germans living in 300 separate sovereign states or principalities. Although by 1806 the number of German states had been reduced to 100, Germans were still disunited politically. Although Froebel was an educational thinker rather than a political one, part of his philosophy of education contained an element of German unification. For example, he continually stressed the theme of interrelationship and interconnection. Other German politicians and philosophers would echo the theme of Germanic unity and the encompassing role of the nation-state in a more nationalistic manner than Froebel, but nonetheless the spirit of German nationalism is present in his philosophy.

From 1800 to 1815, the forceful emperor of France, Napoleon, dominated the European scene. Until his defeat in Russia in 1812, Napoleon, a consummate military strategist, led the French armies in vanquishing the great powers of Europe on the battlefield. In 1806, Napoleon defeated Prussia and its kindred German allies. Froebel, then age 24, was serving with the German forces that were soundly defeated at the battles of Jena and Auerstadt. Since the days of Frederick the Great, the Prussians had taken pride in their army. Now, defeated by their ancient adversary, the humbled Prussian King Frederick Wilhelm had to watch Napoleon's triumphal entry into Berlin, his capital. Prussians had a feeling of inferiority and a desire for revenge. Throughout Prussia and the German states allied with it, there was a sense of need to rebuild not only the army but the morale of the German people.

After the 1806 defeat, the Prussians set to work rebuilding their forces and recouping their fortunes. The major leader of the effort to regenerate Prussia was Heinrich Friedrich Karl von Stein (1757–1831). Stein embarked on a course of defensive reforms intended to strengthen the basically conservative Prussian state. Stein sought to instill in the Prussian people the will to resist the French by giving them a sense of community spirit and commitment to the nation. He engineered the enactment of legislation designed to streamline the Prussian administrative and military systems.[1] The sense of Prussian community loyalty and service was part of the cultural milieu in which Froebel lived and worked. Under the patriotic Baron von Stein and Chancellor Karl August Hardenberg, the Prussians prepared themselves for another attack on Napoleon. Weakened by his Russian disaster in 1812, Napoleon's army was defeated by the combined forces of England, Austria, Russia, and Prussia in what was called the "Battle of Nations" at Leipzig in the four-day battle from October 16 to October 19, 1813. For the German states allied with Prussia, this was a war of liberation. After the final defeat of Napoleon at Waterloo, Prussia emerged as the most powerful German state.

The years after the defeat of Napoleon saw the restoration of legitimate monarchies in contrast to those established by the usurper Napoleon and the assertion of conservative political ideologies in Europe. The conservative forces, led by the Austrian foreign minister Klemens von Metternich, suppressed liberal intellectual and educational ideas. For example, in the German states, the fraternities that students had organized in the universities to promote German liberalism and nationalism were suppressed. The Carlsbad decrees of 1819 banned liberal-minded professors from teaching in universities as well.

By 1848, the suppression of nationalism and liberalism by European conservative governments was challenged dramatically by a series of popular revolutions in France, Austria, Hungary, Italy, Prussia, and several of the smaller German states. In March 1848, liberals and nationalists in Prussia and other German states took to the streets in demonstrations for reform. The Prussian King Frederick Wilhelm IV responded by abolishing censorship and summoning a constituent assembly. Simultaneously, liberal leaders called an assembly at Frankfurt to prepare a constitution for a united and federated German nation. However, internal disagreements about the form of government for the proposed German confederation deadlocked the Frankfurt assembly. Regaining their strength, the conservative forces in the Prussian government rallied and the liberal Frankfurt assembly was disbanded without accomplishing its goal. It was not until January 18, 1871, that a united German empire would be proclaimed in the Hall of Mirrors at Versailles as a consequence of the victory over France in the Franco-Prussian War.

Froebel's life coincided with a period of rich intellectual development in Germany. Among those who contributed to this flowering of German intellectualism was Johann Gottfried Herder (1744–1803). Herder's *Ideas on the Philosophy of History of Humanity*—a multivolume work—combined biological, ethnographical, and literary insights into his philosophical treatise. His broad view of history and philosophy contributed to philosophical idealism and to the sense of nationalism. Johann Wolfgang von Goethe (1749–1832) was also among the major contributors to early nineteenth-century German intellectual life. Known primarily as the author of Faust and Werther, Goethe was also active in studying and writing on such sciences as anatomy, mineralogy, meteorology, botany, and zoology. Still another intellectual of the period was the scientist and educator Wilhelm von Humboldt (1767–1835). A pioneering scholar of anthropology and linguistics, von Humboldt studied the languages of aboriginal groups such as the American Indians and classical languages such as the Sanskrit of the ancient Indians of Vedic times.[2]

Philosophy in the Western world as well as in Germany was shaped by the great intellectual giant Immanuel Kant (1724–1804), who was a professor at the University of Königsberg. In his famous work, *Critique of Pure Reason,* Kant challenged the strictly empiricist view that all ideas come from sensation. In contrast, Kant argued that the mind possesses categories such as space and time that are *a priori* "modes of perception" or mental structures by which we organize our experience in the real world.[3] In other words, these structures exist in the human mind before sensory experience and are used to catalog or organize that experience. It is impossible to think of objects unless one possesses the prior spatial context in which these objects are positioned. When we experience an object, our consciousness of it has a duration in that it is present in the mind for a given period. Thus, Kant argued that such *a priori* concepts as space and time were necessary mental structures for organizing a coherent and intelligible experience.

Just as space and time exist as organizing structures in the human mind, Kant concluded that universal moral laws also exist.[4] Because they are universal, they are not dependent on changing circumstances. Kant's famous categorical imperative was such a universal ethical principle. All rational beings, he contended, are bound by the moral law that asserts that for an action to be ethical it must be capable of being universally valid.

The effect of idealist philosophy, partially influenced by Kant, produced an intellectual climate of opinion that contributed to the formation of Froebel's ideas. Other philosophers who influenced idealism in Froebel's Germany were Johann Gottlieb Fichte (1762–1814) and Georg Wilhelm Hegel (1770–1831). Like Plato in ancient Greece, these idealists saw reality in nonmaterialist terms. For them, reality was the unfolding of the absolute idea, the perfect all-encompassing form of the good on Earth. Fichte, a university professor and rector of the University of Berlin, delivered a series of lectures to the German people that called for a regeneration of the German spirit. For Fichte, a revitalized form of education would contribute to the regeneration of German culture.[5]

Intellectual life in early nineteenth-century Germany was especially dominated by Hegel, a professor at the University of Berlin and author of many tomes extolling idealism.[6] Like Fichte, Hegel stressed the power of ideas and the mind. The great spiritual force, which is the origin and the culmination of the universe, functions in the individual human mind and is manifested in human cultural and social institutions such as law, education, and art. The highest embodiment of the absolute on Earth was the state, which encompassed all other institutions.

For Hegel, the nature of thought and history occurred through the dialectical process. Thought in the mind of God—or absolute idea—and in the human mind begins with an idea, which is a thesis, and continues with its opposite, an antithesis. The mind then recognizes the positive or related elements in both the thesis and the antithesis and combines them in a synthesis. The synthesis, in turn, is a new idea that contains its antithesis and thus the process is ongoing. Through the dialectical process, ideas are ever-expanding and related to each other in what is an evolving sense of intellectual wholeness or completeness. The result is that all ideas, through this dialectical process, lead to and are derived from the all-encompassing idea.

As described by Hegel, the dialectical process held great appeal for the intellectuals of nineteenth-century Germany. In his own way, Froebel incorporated the dialectic in his theory of human growth. Karl Marx would redefine the process in materialistic terms rather than as the nonmaterial ideas Hegel had originally proposed.

Hegel believed the absolute mind, which is God's mind, functioned according to the dialectical process. The absolute mind contains and encompasses all ideas. Human history is the unfolding of God's mind over time.

In addition to the developments in German literature and philosophy, Froebel's formative years, especially as a university student, coincided with new scientific discoveries and the propounding of new scientific theories. These advances in German sciences occurred in a parallel fashion with the impressive developments being made in philosophy by Kant, Fichte, and Hegel.

Influenced by the idealist frame of reference, the general scientific perspective saw all living things interrelated by a great chain of being rising from lower to higher forms of life. The biologists of the day were laboring to identify the essential structures of plants and animals so they could be classified in such a comprehensive ordering of life. Although scientists were seeking to develop those classifications, they were operating in a pre-Darwinian mode. They believed that every living thing developed according to an archetypal plan common to members of that particular genus or species. However, they did not see the species undergoing evolutionary change. Rather, the creature had been created by God to fill a given assigned rung in what was a complex and hierarchical chain of life.

Just as Froebel was influenced by the dominant trends in idealist philosophy in Germany, so were his ideas shaped by the dominant trends in science. When he developed his educational theory, Froebel continually referred to doctrines of interconnectedness in which all creatures and all ideas were part of a grand, ordered, and systematic universe. Such a universal design had no room for change or accident. Everything had a place and everything was to be in its place.

Froebel's philosophy of early childhood education was filled with religious language, symbolism, and meaning. The son of a Lutheran clergyman, he was born into and came to his maturity in an environment permeated by the Lutheran version of Christianity.

In the late eighteenth and early nineteenth centuries, Lutheranism was experiencing some religious tensions. Most Lutheran synods and congregations followed the creed established by Martin Luther in the Protestant Reformation. This version of Lutheranism adhered to traditional theology and orthodox practices. There were those who felt a need, however, for a more personal and mystical mode of religious experience than the practices of the Lutheran religious establishment. Froebel and other religious people were influenced by the theology of Jacob Böhme (1575–1624) a seventeenth-century Silesian mystic. Although he had little formal education, Böhme, who claimed to have experienced a mystical state, criticized the formalism of the Lutheran church. Among Böhme's writings were *Aurora, or The Dawn* in 1612, *The Three Principles of Divine Being* in 1619, and *The Signature of All Things* in 1622. His stress on the personal quality of religious experience influenced both pietism in religion and romanticism in literature and philosophy. In his kindergarten philosophy, Froebel used a great deal of semireligious symbolism. It is believed that his tendency to express himself through symbolic language and metaphors was influenced by Böhme. The emphasis on a more personalized and pietistical form of religious experience had an effect in Germany where new sects such as the True Inspirationists emerged, and in Sweden where Erik Jansson led a group that departed from the orthodoxy of traditional Lutheranism.

It was this combination of political, philosophical, scientific, and religious events and movements that formed the historical context in which Froebel lived and that influenced his formulation of a philosophy of early childhood education.

Friedrich Froebel: Pioneer Early Childhood Educator

In this section, we turn to the life and career of Friedrich Froebel.[7] Young Froebel, who was formally christened Friedrich Wilhelm August, was born on April 21, 1782. He was the youngest of five sons of Johann Jacob Froebel, a Lutheran minister who was pastor of the church at Oberweissbach.[8] The village of Oberweissbach was located in the Thuringian forests of the small principality of Schwarzburg-Rudolfstadt, one of the many independent states that were part of a fragmented Germany in the early nineteenth century. Today, the village lies about 100 miles southwest of Leipzig.

Froebel's mother died when he was nine months old. When he was four years old, his father remarried. Froebel disliked his stepmother, who he believed neglected him to devote her attention and affection to her own child. This feeling was so intense that as an adult he still complained, "Love was not only withdrawn entirely from me and transferred to her own child, but I was treated with worse than indifference . . . by word and deed, I was made to feel an utter stranger." Froebel felt increasingly alienated from his father, who he recalled considered him to be "stupid, mischievous, and untrustworthy."[9] Whether Froebel's assessment of his childhood was factually accurate is difficult to assess. However, he felt lonely, rejected, and isolated as a child. This feeling of low self-esteem stayed with him throughout his life.

Froebel's memories of an unhappy early childhood had a pronounced effect on the theory of kindergarten education that he developed later in his life. It is interesting to note that Froebel, like Rousseau, lost his mother to death when he was so young that he could not have had a clear memory of her. He also had a stepmother he disliked intensely. When he developed his theory of early childhood education, he created a version of the teacher who was a loving, kindly, and gentle motherlike figure. This concept of the teacher undoubtedly came from his idealized feeling for his own mother.

Further, during his own early childhood, Froebel was often restricted by his father to his home. He was not a particularly attractive child physically and his social relationships with children other than his siblings were rare. This early experience left him shy, introspective, and socially inept. When he created his kindergarten philosophy, he structured learning experiences intended to establish a sense of security and self-esteem in the children.

As a young child, Froebel was fascinated with the woodlands near his home and with plants and animals. He found satisfaction and pleasure in gardening. The mental images of growing and blooming plants that he acquired in his own small garden plot were used in the language that he devised to express his educational philosophy.

Young Friedrich Froebel's first educational experience was in the elementary school for girls at Oberweissbach. His father regarded the village boys as ruffians and determined that Friedrich, whom he apparently regarded as a stupid child, should be sent to the more protected environment of the girls' school. This school followed the conventional curriculum of Bible study, catechism, reading, writing, and arithmetic. With the exception of arithmetic, which was his favorite subject, Friedrich had difficulty with his studies. Attendance at his father's church also affected him; he found comfort in the hymns that were an important feature of the Lutheran religious service.

When Froebel was ten years old, his maternal uncle, Herr Hoffman, decided to intervene in the unhappy situation that his nephew was experiencing. Hoffman invited the youngster to come and stay with him at Stadt-Ilm, where he was a Lutheran archdeacon. Stadt-Ilm was about twenty miles from Froebel's family home at Oberweissbach. Froebel's father agreed and Friedrich spent the next five years at his uncle's home. Froebel described his uncle as a "loving father," a person who was "mild, gentle, and kind-hearted."[10] He attended the town school, where he studied reading, writing, arithmetic, religion, Latin, and geography. He made a good adjustment to school and began to form friendships.

Froebel's next educational experience came as an apprentice to a forester and surveyor in the town of Neuhaus. Froebel's apprenticeship, which began when he was fifteen, lasted two years. The experience was not entirely successful. He believed that the forester, although an experienced person, was unable to convey necessary information and practical skills to him.[11] During this time, the adolescent Froebel read widely in the areas of forestry and botany. His interests became increasingly mystical. Common objects, especially plants, came to have a double meaning for him—one of appearance and another of symbol. While learning the practical skills of forestry, Froebel's fascination with the plant world increased.

When he was seventeen, Froebel was admitted to the University of Jena. As a student, his academic interests ranged widely. He attended lectures in mathematics, mineralogy, physics, chemistry, forestry, architecture, surveying, botany, and other subjects. He was searching for the key to knowledge and wanted to discover how all these subjects related to each other. Either because of his own inability to integrate a variety of subjects or because of the disconnected teaching that he encountered, his goal eluded him. He was a student at Jena for two years, ending his study at age nineteen.[12]

Once again Froebel experienced difficulties with his father. Because of a loan he had made to his brother, Friedrich was unable to pay his own tuition bills. He ended up in the university's debtor's prison. His father agreed to pay his bills and arranged for his release but on the condition that Friedrich officially renounce any future claim to an inheritance from the family estate. Froebel signed the document of agreement. His father died the next year, in 1802, and Friedrich never again set foot in his family home.

After ending his university studies at Jena without completing a degree, Froebel tried to find a suitable career. For a time he worked in the Office of Woods and Forests, then he was a secretary to an estate owner, but these positions proved unsatisfactory to Froebel and his employers.

In 1805, Froebel received an inheritance from his Uncle Hoffman that enabled him to go to Frankfurt to study architecture. Although he pursued architecture for only a brief period, he developed a sense of perspective and proportion that he later transferred to his design of the kindergarten's gifts and occupations. In his educational work, Froebel saw children working, like little architects, with building materials and designing their own structures. He developed the principle that children in their activities should always integrate existing structures into new ones in a synthetic whole.

While in Frankfurt, Froebel met Anton Gruener, the headmaster of the Frankfurt Model School, which was following Pestalozzian principles. Gruener, who believed that Froebel had the correct disposition and inclination for teaching, persuaded him to join the staff of the Model School.

Before assuming his teaching duties, Gruener arranged for Froebel, now twenty-four, to spend two weeks at Yverdon where Johann Henrich Pestalozzi conducted an educational institution. Pestalozzi had developed a method of education that stressed instruction based on object lessons. Instead of beginning children's instructions with reading, writing, arithmetic, and religion, Pestalozzi had devised a series of lessons based on the form, number, and names of objects found in the immediate environment. Challenging the corporal punishment and psychological coercion that were part of traditional teaching, Pestalozzi argued that cognitive learning was most effective in schools where children were made to feel emotionally secure (see Chapter 10).

Froebel was impressed with Pestalozzi. He believed Pestalozzi's respect for the dignity of children and creation of a learning environment of love and emotional security were valuable educational elements that he wanted to incorporate in his own teaching. Although Froebel saw the value of using objects in instruction, he believed the Pestalozzian object lesson lacked a sufficient philosophical base. Unlike the rather direct Pestalozzian object lesson, Froebel designed a more symbolic version in which objects had double meanings. Using his philosophical idealism, Froebel fashioned object lessons in which objects had the meaning of the sensory world and the more symbolic meaning of the mental world.

After his work with Pestalozzi, Froebel returned to Frankfurt and assumed his position as a teacher at the Model School where he taught a class of forty boys, ranging in age from nine to eleven.[13] At last Froebel had found his true vocation. Teaching gave him a sense of personal meaning and fulfillment. He remained a teacher at the Model School for three years. In 1808, he resigned his position and returned to Yverdon for two years of study with Pestalozzi. He learned much from the master Swiss educator but also identified areas that he wanted to improve upon. Froebel was convinced that children's play was an important activity in their development. He planned to devote himself to studying and finding the meaning of play. Play would become the key to his concept of kindergarten education. Froebel believed that children's use of language was also a crucial component in early childhood education. When he left Pestalozzi, Froebel was convinced that he needed further study.

In 1810, Froebel returned to Germany where he spent two years at the University of Gottingen studying Persian, Hebrew, Arabic, and Greek. Like his previous university experience, he was not a consistent nor an in-depth student. However, his study of languages convinced him that the various human languages were somehow related and interconnected. If he could find the structural links in these various languages, he believed he could apply this general structure to the teaching of language. In addition to his language studies, Froebel attended lectures in physics, chemistry, mineralogy, geology, history, and economics. He became interested in geology and mineralogy, which in the early nineteenth century attracted the serious attention of both academic and amateur scientists.

From 1812 to 1816 Froebel was at the University of Berlin, where he studied mineralogy with Professor Christian Samuel Weiss (1780–1856). Weiss, who had studied physics and quantitative mineral analysis, held the chair of mineralogy at the university. Weiss was also immersed in the idealism of Kant and Schelling and developed an abstract theory of crystallography. For him, crystallization reflected the essential process of natural growth.[14] Froebel's work with Weiss made a strong impression on him. He became absorbed in examining the process of crystallization and was convinced that the process of crystal formation followed the same law that governed all creation. The universal process, Froebel now believed, was following a pattern that went from the simple to the complex.[15] Although Pestalozzi, too, had stressed the movement from simple to complex in his instructional methodology, Froebel believed the process of ever-increasing complexity was a divinely ordered cosmic law. Human growth and development, too, were bound by this important philosophical principle.

Froebel's university studies were briefly interrupted in 1812 when he joined the Lutzow Jagers, an infantry division that fought with the German forces against Napoleon's invading French army. Froebel's military service brought him into contact with other young men who shared an interest in education. For example, he became friends with Wilhelm Middendorf and Heinrich Langethal, two soldiers who would later work with him in the kindergarten.[16]

In 1816, ready to strike out on his own as an educator, Froebel established a school at Griesheim, a small town near Darmstadt, which he called the Universal German Educational Institute. The next year he relocated the school in Keilhau. The school had varying success in attracting students. At its peak it enrolled sixty students, and five at its ebb in 1829 when it was forced to close because of low enrollment. Froebel's former military comrades, Middendorf and Langethal, taught at the school. During the thirteen years that the institute functioned, Froebel was able to test some of his educational ideas and develop new insights into child nature and the learning process.

Foremost of the principles that Froebel followed at the institute at Keilhau was that each child should be recognized as an individual and be educated according to his or her own needs and interests. At the same time that children's individual differences were recognized, Froebel believed there were general, universal laws that governed the growth and development of children. Froebel sought to develop a method of instruction that encompassed both a recognition of the universal laws of child development and ways in which each child could express himself or herself creatively according to individual needs. Froebel and his staff maintained an individualized lesson plan for each child that identified needs and indicated achievement.

Froebel's first effort to operate his own school was successful educationally but had serious problems in terms of public relations and administration. Froebel and his teachers had difficulty being accepted into the community. Although Froebel's educational philosophy rested on a religious frame of reference, he was accused of deviating from orthodox Lutheran doctrine. This religious issue generated some hostility in the community. In addition, although Froebel had many ideas about education, he lacked skill in administering a school. He proved inept at organizing and managing a budget. Throughout its thirteen-year history, the institute was frequently on the edge of bankruptcy.

In 1818, Froebel married Henrietta Wilhelmine Hoffmeister (1780–1839), a young lady he had met in Berlin. Henrietta, a well-educated woman, had studied with Fichte. Her father, an official in the Prussian War Ministry, opposed the marriage. Nevertheless, she married Froebel and shared her husband's love of children and of nature. She assisted him in his educational work until her death.[17]

In 1831, Froebel was ready to depart from his faltering institute at Keilhau. He accepted an invitation from the Swiss composer Xavier Schnyder to establish an educational institute at his castle at Wartensee on Lake Sempach in the Lucerne Canton. For a time, Schnyder had taught music at Pestalozzi's institute at Yverdon. With the approval of the Swiss Ministry of Education, Froebel opened his school in Schnyder's castle. Some thirty students enrolled in his school, which offered lessons in arithmetic, languages, history, and gymnastics. The physical environment of the castle proved unsuitable for a school, and Froebel decided to move the school to Willisau. Here, the school prospered, and Froebel gained a reputation as a capable educator.

Froebel accepted an invitation to establish an orphanage at Burgdorf, a town in which Pestalozzi had once operated an educational institute. At Burgdorf, Froebel assumed a number of educational activities. He conducted a school for the town children and a boarding school for those who lived a distance from the town. He also engaged in teacher-training activities. Most importantly for the course of his future educational career, Froebel grew increasingly interested in early childhood education. He established a nursery school for three- and four-year-old children. He turned more attention to preparing materials for the nursery school children. He wrote rhymes and songs and devised physical exercises, activities, and games that could be used in the nursery school. It was at Burgdorf that he began experimenting with the objects and materials that would constitute his kindergarten gifts. True to the emphasis that he gave to play, he stressed the educative role of play in the school.[18] In 1836, Froebel's wife became seriously ill and he returned to Germany.

In 1837, Froebel came back to the Thuringian forest area where he had lived as a child. Perhaps remembering his own unhappy childhood, he decided to create a new kind of school, a child's garden, or kindergarten. Using play, songs, stories, and activities, the kindergarten would be an educational environment in which children could develop in the right direction. The right direction meant that, in their development, children would follow the divinely established laws of human growth through their own activity.

In general, the kindergarten was to be a milieu in which children would develop freely and naturally. Froebel's kindergarten was both a natural and cultural environment. Children's play was a natural activity in which they acted out their interests and satisfied their needs. A specially designed series of gifts, objects to guide and motivate children's activities and occupations, and certain selected activities such as drawing provided the means for stimulating their development. In addition, the songs, stories, and games provided an introduction to the culture. Importantly, children were socialized through group activities. Froebel's fame as a founder of kindergartens spread throughout the German states and a number of these children's gardens were established.

In 1851, a strange controversy developed surrounding the kindergarten in Prussia. Karl von Raumer, the Prussian minister of education, accused kindergartens of undermining traditional Prussian values by spreading atheism and socialism. Although Froebel denied the charges, von Raumer banned the kindergarten in Prussia. In 1852, in the midst of the controversy, Froebel died. Although kindergartens existed in the other German states, they were not permitted to function in Prussia until 1860. By the end of the nineteenth century, kindergartens had been established throughout Europe and North America.

Froebel's Kindergarten Philosophy

In this section, we shall examine Froebel's kindergarten philosophy. This philosophy is most fully expressed in his book, *The Education of Man*, written in 1826.[19] This work reflects the general effect of philosophical idealism as well as Froebel's own study of divergent fields such as linguistics and mineralogy. In *The Education of Man*, Froebel attempted to weave the strands of idealism, Christian mysticism, romanticism, and science into a philosophy of education.

Froebel begins his philosophical commentary by asserting that all existence, including human existence, originates in and with God. His conception of God combined the traditional Lutheran theory of a personal Creator with the Hegelian idealist view of the all-encompassing absolute idea. All creatures, both great and small, have the same spiritual source. Human beings are endowed by their Creator with a divine or spiritual essence and, at the same time, have a body that makes them part of the natural and physical order. Thus, Froebel saw human beings as composed of a spiritual and a physical dimension. It is the spiritual essence, however, that by vitalizing and motivating them leads to human development. In terms of child nature, Froebel asserts that each child at birth has within him or her a spiritual essence, a life force, that seeks to be externalized. Through the child's own activity, the inner spiritual essence is externalized. The kindergarten's gifts, occupations, and activities, especially play, are designed to ensure that this development follows the correct pathway, which is both God's and nature's plan of development.

The human destiny, said Froebel, is to become conscious of the presence of this spiritual essence and to reveal it by externalizing it. In this process of leading the spiritual essence outward, the human being is really growing nearer to God.

Following the idealism that dominated German intellectual thought in the early nineteenth century, Froebel construed ultimate reality to be spiritual rather than physical. All that existed was based on an ideational prototype that existed as a concept in the divine mind, in the absolute. According to this metaphysical view, all ideas were related to and interconnected with each other and culminated in the great all-encompassing idea that was God. All being was united and related in a great chain of being, a universal unity. Although nature appeared to exhibit diversity and individualization, it was in reality one great coherent spiritual unity. In the education of children, the principle of interconnectedness was to be followed. Nothing should be allowed to remain in isolation. In the kindergarten, it was important that children learn that they were members of a great, universal, spiritual community. In Froebel's kindergarten, there was no conflict between the individual and group nor between individual needs and differences and a universal theory of human development. Froebel considered each individual active and autonomous but also associated spiritually with every other person and thing.

For Froebel, child growth and development was essentially based on the doctrine of preformation. Human growth and development was the unfolding of that which was present latently in the mind. All that the child would become as a man or woman was already present at birth. Using an analogy from the plant world, Froebel reasoned that as a seed contains the roots, stalk, leaves, and blossoms of the mature plant, so does the human embryo possess all that the adult person will become. Just as the seed requires a garden with proper soil, moisture, light, and nutrients to grow in the right direction, the child needs a special educative environment for growth—the kindergarten. Just as the plant needs the cultivation of a gardener, children need the care of a loving and kindly teacher.

Like Pestalozzi, Froebel used the concept of an idealized loving mother to develop his view of the kindergarten teacher. The kindergarten teacher was to be an agent who cooperated with God and nature in facilitating the child's growth and development. In a strong sense, the teacher's career was like a religious vocation. To prepare for this vocation, kindergarten teachers were to reflect and reminisce about their own childhood experiences. By this self-analysis, they were to find the hidden clues about childhood that were locked in their memories. Froebel often reflected on his unhappy and melancholy childhood and found in his memories ways to make the early experiences of childhood happier than his own.

Kindergarten teachers were also observers of child life, games, play, and activities. Through such observations, teachers could identify patterns of children's behavior and use these patterns to structure learning activities. It was important, Froebel advised, that teachers have a strong philosophical base for their instruction. True to idealism, the activities of teaching and learning were not separate and disconnected episodes, but were part of a whole that reflected the divine plan.

Once teachers had acquired the philosophy and the attitude conducive to working with children, they could proceed to the distinctive characteristics of the kindergarten. The kindergarten was to be a specially prepared environment in which children could grow and develop. As a special environment, the elements of space and time needed to be considered. Space referred to the actual physical setting of the kindergarten; time referred to the sequencing of activities the children would experience.

In structuring the kindergarten, Froebel was convinced that its primary focus should be directed to play. In terms of the symbolism of Froebel's idealism, he saw play as the means that stimulated children to express their innermost thoughts, needs, and desires in external action. Froebel's exaltation of the role of play was a strikingly different approach from that of many conventional educators up to the nineteenth century. With the exception of Comenius and Pestalozzi, play was regarded as an unworthy element of human life. In the strictly interpreted Calvinist theology, play was a form of idleness that contributed to disorder and laxity. For Froebel, however, play was a natural part of living. Its non-serious mode permitted children to act on their thoughts without the consequences that work entailed. Froebel should be recognized as one of the pioneers in legitimizing the concept of play in Western educational history. When viewed in its most general terms, play became the means by which human beings re-created themselves.[20]

In Froebelian terms, the general concept of play can be analyzed further as a means of cultural recapitulation, imitation of adult vocational activities, and socialization. Froebel believed the human race could be viewed both in its racial, ethnic, and linguistic diversity and as a unity. Froebel believed that the human race, in its collective history, had gone through major periods of cultural development. For example, humans had lived in caves, then in tents or other temporary dwellings as nomadic hunters, then in permanent houses as an agricultural people, and so on. During each of these major epochs, humans added to and refined their culture, moving generally from the simple to the complex. In Froebel's theory of cultural recapitulation, each individual human being repeated the general cultural epoch in his or her own growth and development. Although the human race had taken centuries to go through these cultural epochs, the individual did so in a much more limited time span of a few years.

In the kindergarten, children's play provided the means of living through and experiencing the cultural recapitulation process. For example, children enjoy drawing and often draw pictures on walls. Their drawings are simple and primitive and resemble those of the ancient cave dwellers. Thus, in Froebelian terms, children are living through a particular cultural epoch of the human race. Children like to play hunting and gathering games. In this activity, they are repeating a particular cultural epoch of the human race. The recapitulation process was aided in the kindergarten by the introduction of certain songs and stories that had cultural significance.

In play, children were imitative of the adult society, particularly their social and economic activities. Froebel believed that children should be encouraged to act out in play such activities as cleaning rooms, serving food, and gardening. These and other activities were a means of expressing and acting out their perceptions of adult vocations.

The process of playing at adult vocations took on a highly symbolic religious and philosophical aspect in Froebel's kindergarten. In Lutheran theology and religious practice, the practice of vocations was a form of human industriousness that had been ordained by God. Martin Luther, for example, had admonished parents to make certain that their children learned useful vocations. As an idealist philosopher, Froebel believed that human vocations represented the concrete thoughts of God. Just as God's thoughts had taken on a physical shape and substance in the sensory world, so should human beings give expression to their ideas by transforming thought and raw materials into finished products.

By connecting play with vocations, one can observe the complexity of Froebel's philosophy of early childhood education. If one considers the human vocation of agriculture as an example, it can be recognized as one of humanity's major economic occupations. Children enjoy planting seeds in their gardens and observing the phenomenon of the seeds sprouting, growing, and developing as plants. The raw materials of seeds, soil, water, and fertilizer culminate in products—flowers, vegetables, or fruit. At the same time these obvious physical happenings are occurring in the garden and are perceived by the child's senses, Froebel construed that other events are occurring in the child's spiritual world. The child is recapitulating a major epoch of human culture and is acting out his or her internal impressions of a most significant adult activity. To give gardening a greater cultural significance, songs and stories that relate to planting and harvesting are introduced by the teacher.

Play also was the means for the child's socialization. Through the kindergarten's activities, each individual child was led into the larger world of group life. Froebel regarded his own childhood as a time of isolation, rejection, and loneliness. His kindergarten was designed to encourage children to play and interact with other children under the guidance of a loving teacher. Again, socialization, as a part of play, had a broader symbolic meaning for Froebel. In his idealist view of reality, the world and its beings were part of an all-encompassing spiritual community that came from the mind of God, the Absolute, and sought to return and be reunited with their divine source. Children were born and nurtured in their immediate families. These families were part of a larger village or town community. The town in turn was part of a national community. The next stage in human history would be an international or world community. Although such a worldwide ecumenical vision was broad and grandiose, its beginnings could be found in the kindergarten.

The Kindergarten Curriculum: Gifts and Occupations

A unique feature of Froebel's kindergarten curriculum was the series of gifts and occupations that he developed as teaching and learning materials. The gifts were objects that represented what Froebel defined as fundamental forms. It may be recalled that Pestalozzi had developed an object lesson based on form, number, and sound or name. Like the general tenor of Froebel's philosophy, the gifts had two meanings: that of their actual physical appearance and also a symbolic meaning. Symbolically, they were intended to stimulate the child to bring the fundamental concept that they suggested to mental consciousness. The following is a list of Froebel's gifts:

1. Six soft, colored balls.
2. A wooden sphere, cube, and cylinder.
3. A large cube divided into eight smaller cubes.
4. A large cube divided into eight oblong blocks.
5. A large cube divided into twenty-one whole, six half, and twelve quarter cubes.
6. A large cube divided into eighteen whole oblongs, with three divided lengthwise and three divided breadthwise.
7. Quadrangular and triangular tablets used for arranging figures.
8. Sticks for outlining figures.
9. Whole and half wire rings for outlining figures.
10. A variety of materials that could be used for drawing, perforating, embroidering, paper cutting, weaving or braiding, paper folding, modeling, and interlacing.[21]

The Froebelian kindergarten gifts followed the order of beginning with the simple undifferentiated sphere or circle, which Froebel saw as a fundamental structure, and moving to more complex objects. Froebel believed each gift led the child to the next in the series. He attached great symbolic meaning to the sphere. For example, the Earth, the sun, the moon, and other planets were spheres. In the kindergarten, a large number of activities and games were played with the balls. Many kindergartens featured a large circle that was painted on the floor. Children would join hands around the circle and move in one direction, then the next. The symbolism of this activity was that it represented the unity of all human beings.

Following the idealist predilection for synthesis of opposites, Froebel used cylinders that represented the integration or fusion of the sphere and the cube. The various cubes and their subdivisions were building blocks designed to illustrate the relationships between the whole and the part. Children could use them to create geometrical designs or fashion buildings. Children could use the sticks and rings to trace designs on paper. This activity exercised the small muscles of the hand, developed coordination between hand and eye, and was a first step toward the skill of writing.

Although the gifts were objects given in fixed form to the child, the occupations were items that could be used in making and constructing activities. Among the occupations were paper, pencils, wood, sand, clay, straw, sticks, and other items that could be worked upon to create a picture, an object, or some product.

In addition to the gifts and occupations, the kindergarten repertoire of activities included games, songs, and stories. Froebel would observe children engaged in free play and then from his observation design a game based on what he had observed. His aim was to organize games that would enlist children in social activities, exercise their bodies, and train their powers of observation. A collection of kindergarten songs was published in 1843 under the title of *Mutter-und-Kose-lieder,* or *Mother's Songs, Games, and Stories.*[22] Each song had a motto designed to stress a particular value.

Conclusion: An Assessment

In this section of the chapter, we shall assess the significance of Friedrich Froebel's educational contributions in terms of their diffusion and their significance. Of the various educational innovations of the nineteenth and twentieth centuries, there is little doubt that the kindergarten has been among the most successful, particularly in terms of its diffusion throughout the world. After Froebel's death in 1852, the kindergarten concept was carried throughout Europe and North America by his devoted disciples. In the United Kingdom, Bertha Ronge, a pupil of Froebel's, established several kindergartens.

In the United States, the kindergarten cause attracted a number of advocates. As immigrants came to the United States from Germany following the ill-fated revolution of 1848, they brought with them the concept of the kindergarten. In Watertown, Wisconsin, Margarethe Meyer Schurz, the wife of the future U.S. Senator Karl Schurz, established a kindergarten for German-speaking children in 1856. In New York, Matilda H. Kriege established a kindergarten as part of a German school. She also imported kindergarten materials from Germany to the United States and convinced U.S. manufacturers to produce and market them.

The kindergarten idea gained support among leading proponents such as Henry Barnard, the first U.S. commissioner of education, who popularized Froebel's educational innovation in his *Common School Journal.* In 1860, Elizabeth Palmer Peabody (1804–1894), the sister of Horace Mann's wife, established a kindergarten in Boston. Committed to popularizing the kindergarten, she embarked on an educational tour of Europe to visit kindergartens in 1867. Upon her return, she translated several of Froebel's books into English, formed a kindergarten association called the Froebel Union, and established an institute to train kindergarten teachers. Among her books on the kindergarten are *Moral Culture and Kindergarten Guide,* in 1864; *Kindergarten in Italy,* in 1872; and *Letters to Kindergartners,* in 1886.[23]

The most significant event for making the kindergarten part of the public school system occurred in St. Louis, Missouri, in 1873. Superintendent of Schools William Torrey Harris, (1835–1909), who was a philosophical idealist like Froebel, incorporated the kindergarten into the public school system. Harris believed the years of early childhood were vitally important in directing children's growth in the correct direction. St. Louis, which had a large German population, was also a congenial environment for transplanting Froebel's institution. In his efforts to establish the kindergarten in the public school framework, Harris enlisted Susan Elizabeth Blow (1843–1916), a dedicated proponent of Froebel's work. Blow wrote *Symbolic Education* in 1894, *Letters to a Mother on the Philosophy of Froebel* in 1899, and *Kindergarten Education* in 1900. Together, Blow and Harris succeeded in making St. Louis a center of kindergarten activity. When Harris became the U.S. commissioner of education, he continued to press for the incorporation of kindergartens into the school system. Today, the kindergarten is a part of almost all public school systems in the United States. It also can be found in other countries around the world.

In assessing the significance of Froebel and the kindergarten, it is clear that he succeeded in creating an institution of early childhood that has had an enduring effect. This is shown by the widespread diffusion and permanence of the institution.

Froebel's great contribution was to give us a version of childhood that exalted the dignity of children and their right to be children rather than miniature adults. For him, childhood had a spiritual quality that needed to be recognized and nurtured. Froebel also contributed to legitimizing play at a time when children were often exploited as laborers and play was disdainfully rejected as a form of idleness.

Today, kindergarten teachers continue to emphasize Froebel's ideas of developing the social side of a child's nature and a sense of readiness for learning. The important outcome for the kindergarten child is readiness for the intellectual learning that will come later on in his or her educational career.

The aspect of Froebel's work that has largely disappeared is the mysterious symbolism that clouded much of his philosophy of education. When considered in the context of Froebel's life, when idealism was in vogue in his native Germany, it is not difficult to see why his philosophy contained large allegorical and symbolic elements. For today's teacher, Froebel's message of liberating children and allowing them to develop according to their needs and nature is still of vital significance.

Discussion Questions

1. How did the cultural and intellectual context of early nineteenth-century Germany influence Froebel's educational theory?
2. How was philosophical idealism a factor in Froebel's kindergarten theory?
3. What events in his life and education shaped Froebel's educational theory?
4. Describe Froebel's educational method as a strategy in externalizing the interior or inner qualities of the human being.
5. What is the role of gifts and occupations in Froebel's kindergarten?
6. How was the kindergarten brought to the United States?
7. Assess Friedrich Froebel's significance in the history of educational ideas and practices.

Research and Essay Topics

1. In a paper, develop a character sketch and analysis of Friedrich Froebel.
2. Visit a kindergarten. In a paper, describe what you observed. Are there any elements that reflect Froebel's view of the child?
3. In a paper, comment on those aspects of Froebel's theory that are based on philosophical idealism.
4. In an essay, compare and contrast Froebel's view of the child with that of a theorist examined earlier in this book.

5. Design a lesson plan that follows the Froebelian approach.
6. In an essay, assess the significance of Froebel in the history of Western thought and education.

Notes

1. C. W. Crawley, ed., *War and Peace in an Age of Upheaval, 1793–1830* (Cambridge: Cambridge University Press, 1963), 376–82.
2. Bertrand Russell, *A History of Western Philosophy* (New York: Simon and Schuster, 1967), 701–13.
3. Roland N. Stromberg, *European Intellectual History Since 1789* (Englewood Cliffs, N.J.: Prentice-Hall, 1981), 28–29.
4. Immanuel Kant, *Prolegomena to Any Future Metaphysics* (Indianapolis: Bobbs-Merrill Educational Publishing, 1950).
5. Russell, *A History of Western Philosophy,* 718.
6. J. Loewenberg, *Hegel Selections* (New York: Charles Scribner's Sons, 1959).
7. For his autobiography, see Friedrich Froebel, *Autobiography,* translated by Emilie Michaelis and H. Keatley Moore (Syracuse, N.Y.: C. W. Bardeen Publishers, 1889); a readable and useful biography is Robert B. Downs, *Friedrich Froebel* (Boston: Twayne Publishers, 1978).
8. Froebel, 3–4.
9. Downs, 11–12.
10. Froebel, 17–21.
11. Ibid., 24.
12. Downs, 16–17.
13. Ibid., 19.
14. John C. Greene and John G. Burke, *The Science of Minerals in the Age of Jefferson, Transactions of the American Philosophical Society,* vol. 68 (Philadelphia: American Philosophical Society, 1978). 16–19.
15. Downs, 24.
16. Ibid., 25–26.
17. Froebel, 123.
18. Downs, 34–39.
19. Friedrich Froebel, *The Education of Man,* translated by W. H. Hailman (New York: D. Appleton Sons, 1896).
20. Gerald L. Gutek, *A History of the Western Educational Experience* (Prospect Heights, Ill.: Waveland Press, 1995), 255–69.
21. Downs, 47–50.
22. Friedrich Froebel, *Mother's Songs, Games, and Stories,* translated by Francis and Emily Lord (London: W. Rice, 1910).
23. For the history of the kindergarten in America, see Nina C. Vandewalker, *The Kindergarten in American Education* (New York: Arno Press and New York Times, 1971).

Suggestions for Further Reading

Downs, Robert B. *Friedrich Froebel.* Boston: Twayne Publishers, 1978.
Froebel, Friedrich. *Autobiography.* Translated by Emilie Michaelis and H. Keatley Moore. Syracuse, N.Y.: C. W. Bardeen Publishers, 1889.

————. *The Education of Man.* Translated by W. H. Hailman. New York: D. Appleton Sons, 1896.

————. *Mother's Songs, Games, and Stories.* Translated by Francis and Emily Lord. London: W. Rice, 1910.

Hayward, Frank H. *The Educational Ideas of Pestalozzi and Froebel.* Westport, Conn.: Greenwood Press, 1979.

Headley, Neith. *Education in the Kindergarten.* New York: American Book Co., 1966.

————. *The Kindergarten: Its Place in the Program of Education.* New York: Center for Applied Research in Education, 1965.

Kilpatrick, William H. *Froebel's Kindergarten Principles: Critically Examined.* New York: Macmillan Publishing Company, 1916.

Lawrence, Evelyn ed. *Froebel and English Education.* New York: Schocken Books, 1969.

Lilley, Irene M. *Friedrich Froebel: A Selection from His Writings.* Cambridge: Cambridge University Press, 1967.

Ross, Elizabeth D. *The Kindergarten Crusade: The Establishment of Preschool Education in the United States.* Athens: Ohio University Press, 1976.

Rusk, Robert R. *A History of Infant Education.* London: University of London Press, 1967.

Vandewalker, Nina C. *The Kindergarten in American Education.* New York: Arno Press and New York Times, 1971.

Weber, Evelyn. *The Kindergarten: Its Encounter with Educational Thought in America.* New York: Teachers College Press, Columbia University, 1969.

John Stuart Mill: Proponent of Liberalism

Portrait of John Stuart Mill; reproduction from the collections of the Library of Congress.

Chapter 16 examines the life, educational philosophy and contributions of John Stuart Mill (1806–1873), a proponent of liberalism in philosophy, social policy, and education. Mill's reconceptualization of Liberal ideology, based on a revision of Jeremy Bentham's Utilitarianism, moved Liberalism from a natural rights, laissez-faire position to one of humanitarian social reform. As a writer on education, Mill is best known for his strong defense of human rights and freedom.

This chapter examines the course of Mill's life, as expressed in his *Autobiography,* and his major writings on social and educational philosophy. First, the general social and intellectual context in nineteenth-century England, which influenced and shaped Mill is examined. Particular emphasis is placed on the intellectual context, especially the philosophical ideas of James Mill and Jeremy Bentham. Second, Mill's biography including his education—which was planned and implemented by James Mill and Bentham—and his career as a writer on social and educational themes is examined. Third, key elements in Mill's social and educational philosophy are identified and examined. Fourth, the continuing effect of Mill's concepts of human freedom and disinterested participation in social life and issues is assessed.

Mill's own educational experience is used to illustrate the need in contemporary education for the harmonious integration of the intellectual and emotional dimensions of life. The evolution of Liberalism as a social and political theory is examined for its long-term educational implications.

To organize your thoughts as you read this chapter, you might focus on the following questions:

- What were the major trends, especially those of an intellectual nature, in the historical context in which Mill lived?
- How did Mill's life, particularly his educational biography, shape his philosophy of education?
- How did Mill's social and political philosophy with its emphasis on human freedom and liberty determine his educational policies and practices?
- What has been the enduring impact of Mill's contributions to educational theory and practice?

The Historical Context of John Stuart Mill's Life

In this section, we survey the context, the historical situation and conditions of nineteenth-century England, in which John Stuart Mill lived. When Mill was born in 1806, the United Kingdom had a rapidly growing population that was slightly more than nine million people. This population growth was a by-product of British industrialization. As the nation that gave birth to the Industrial Revolution, Great Britain was well on the way to becoming the factory of the world. Along with its industrial primacy, England had been a leader in the coalition of European nations that had finally vanquished Napoleon who was defeated at Waterloo in 1815 and was in exile on the Island of St. Helena.

Britain's industrialization produced important socioeconomic changes. It brought into being an economic elite of industrial capitalists who garnered great profits and a large and growing industrial working class. Factory workers—men, women, and children—were massed in huge factories to feed and to serve the machines on the assembly lines.[1] For many of these workers, the working day was long, sometimes as long as fourteen to fifteen hours. Workers lived in crowded and dirty tenements.

Such pronounced social change and the pressures of unremitting work caused unrest that sometimes broke into rioting and violence but most often the victims of unregulated industrial change found succor in bottles of cheap gin. Only a very few industrialists such as the utopian socialist, Robert Owen, experimented with communitarian planning and education intended to improve the lot of the working class. (For a discussion of Robert Owen as a communitarian reformer, see Chapter 14). The prevalent educated opinion of the early nineteenth century, especially among theorists of Liberal ideology, was that nature should take its course and that economic prosperity and human progress depended on the government keeping its hands out of the economy and society.

Economic thought in early nineteenth-century Britain was dominated by the theorists of the Manchester school.[2] Adam Smith, the leading authority on the economy, argued that business and the nation prospered when free from regulatory interference from government.[3] For the classical Liberals who followed Smith's dicta, a nonintervention policy without tariffs, trade barriers, and other restrictions was the best to follow. As the Reverend Thomas Malthus asserted in his influential *Essay on the Principle of Population as it Affects the Future Improvement of Society,* published in 1798, population has a constant tendency to increase beyond the supply of food. If war or disease did not check population growth, famine would reduce it to manageable levels that could subsist on the food available. David Ricardo, the proponent of the iron law of wages, provided industrialists with an economic rationale for low wages and long hours of work. If wages rose above the subsistence level, workers would use the increased income to have more children.[4] More children meant a labor surplus in which workers would be forced to work for reduced wages. A far better use of profits was more capital investment in more factories and machinery. The best economic minds of the early nineteenth century were clearly against government intervention and regulation. Nature was to take its course.

At the same time that laissez-faire economic policy was a standard feature of Liberalism, the politics of the ideology continued to stress the Lockean negative freedoms of speech, press, assembly, and religion against a powerful state's interference. The doctrine of the natural rights of human beings, expressed in John Locke's *The Second Treatise of Government,* proclaimed the inviolability of the innate and inherent right to life, liberty, and property. Economically, socially, politically, and educationally, Liberals sought to fashion and bring to power an ideology that asserted the rights of individuals and safeguarded the property rights and interests of the rising middle classes.

Despite Liberalism's ascendancy as the dominant ideology in nineteenth-century Britain, Liberals were dissatisfied with the inherited political, religious, and social structures in their country. For them, too much of the aristocratic past was still present in the control that the Tories, or Conservatives, had over many electoral districts—the so-called rotten boroughs, which with populations much smaller than the growing industrial cities still elected defenders of the old aristocratic status quo to the House of Commons. They were also dissatisfied with the power of the established Church of England over schools and universities. For Liberals, these institutional residues of an archaic and aristocratic past were obstacles to the progressive functioning of society. They felt that institutions would have to be changed to function effectively. How to bring about such change was a major issue that began to divide Liberals.[5]

Liberals were beginning to feel an internal tension about the role that government could and should play in reforming institutions and shaping the future. For the classical Liberals— the followers of Locke, Smith, Malthus, and Ricardo—the future would be better if government stayed out of social and economic affairs. They believed the overripe fruit of the old order was beginning to spoil and would fall from the vine because of its own decay. Other Liberals believed reform was needed to improve both individuals and society. These Liberals, followers of Jeremy Bentham known as Utilitarians, believed that government had a role, albeit a limited one, in bringing about social reform.[6] The Benthamites were an association of like-minded reformers who developed a program of social, economic and political action to reform British life and institutions. Underlying their program was a philosophical methodology that promised to bring about change based on rational calculations that estimated the consequences of action in terms of pleasure and pain. Such a program, they believed, would generate the "greatest good for the greatest number" of people. One of the leading associates of Bentham in the reform movement of Utilitarianism was James Mill, the father of John Stuart Mill. Since Bentham and Mill exerted a strong shaping influence on John Stuart Mill, their lives and ideas were part of the context of his life.

Jeremy Bentham (1748–1832), the son of a wealthy London lawyer, described as a "bookish child" of "dwarfish" appearance, was a precocious youngster who began studying Latin at age four and French at seven. Fond of books, he was nicknamed "the philosopher." In 1755, he was enrolled in Westminster, a venerable "public school." He detested the classical preparatory curriculum and the regimen that required the boys to enthusiastically participate in team sports. In 1760, he was admitted to Queen's College at Oxford University, another prestigious institution that educated England's future leaders. Once again, he found little of interest in his collegiate studies. In 1763, he was awarded his bachelor of arts degree. In 1766, he received a master of arts degree. He then studied law and was admitted to the bar in 1769. However, he never practiced law but used his legal background as a framework for his developing social philosophy, Utilitarianism. Bentham came away from his education with a deep antagonism toward the institutions and the teachers who had educated him. He especially disliked the rigid classical curriculum and the backward-looking mentality of his professors. He viewed the English system of law as a hodgepodge of unrelated and nonrational customs and traditions. Bentham stated that the law was a "jungle of unintelligible distinctions, contradictions, and cumbrous methods through which no man could find his way without the guidance of the initiated, and in which a long purse and unscrupulous trickery gave the advantage over the poor to the rich, and to the knave over the honest man."[7]

Bentham's critique of English law illustrates the Utilitarian temperament and predilection to reform an institution according to rational principles. The legal system was cluttered and the process was riddled with archaic residues that blocked its efficient functioning. To reform the law, Bentham advocated in his *Rationale of Judicial Evidence,* in 1827, a general simplification of the cumbersome system. He advocated a legal code that was easy to apply and that had few rules, could be learned easily, and that used logic rather than custom in deciding cases.

Along with his plan to reform the legal system, Bentham advocated penal reform. He designed a model for a new kind of prison which was intended to reform rather than punish prisoners. In his design for a new prison, called a "panopticon," the warden could observe all inmates from a single vantage point and draw up specific plans for changing their behavior.[8]

Bentham's ideas illustrate the emerging ideology of the Utilitarian Liberals. They were researchers who, like the later progressives in the United States, carefully studied institutions and their functions for the purpose of making them operate more effectively, fairly, and efficiently. They were not activists who took the cause of reform into the streets or organized demonstrations or protests. Rather they wrote proposals that put forth the design of reformed institutions. Although they ventured into politics, their essential methodology for bringing about institutional change was philosophical and educational rather than directly activist. When James Mill enlisted Jeremy Bentham's aid in planning the education of his son, John Stuart, the educational plan for the child resembled that of Bentham's panopticon. The two elder Utilitarians planned to oversee and control completely the child's behavior and turn him into the perfect model of their philosophy.

Bentham put forth his full-blown philosophy in his *Introduction to the Principles of Morals and Legislation.* In this work, he challenged Locke's concept of the existence of inherent human rights that primitive human beings possessed in the state of nature. Likewise, he rejected the idea that government was created as a social contract between the governors and the governed to protect and maintain these natural rights of life, liberty, and property. Bentham insisted that the fundamental principle governing human life, which he called the principle of utility, was the desire to experience pleasure and to avoid pain. The ultimate criterion for human action was the degree to which the action's consequences contributed to pleasure or to pain, and the estimation of pain and pleasure was determined by the individual. For society, the principle was that the policy and its implementation should result in the greatest good for the greatest number of people.

Although Bentham deviated from Lockean and Jeffersonian natural rights Liberalism, his principle of utility was congruent with the Liberal emphasis on the individual. Human beings had, Bentham asserted, self-interests which were goal directed. These goals, based on maximizing pleasure and minimizing pain, were best determined by the individual. However, Bentham's rejection of the inviolability of natural rights also opened the way for regulations that imposed limitations on individual freedoms. Believing that some freedoms might need to be curtailed to expand other freedoms, the Benthamite Utilitarians began, perhaps unwittingly, the movement to social welfare state liberalism.

For Bentham, pleasure and pain could be estimated with almost mathematical precision. Happiness, a pervasive feeling of comfort, was produced by the material consequences of action which were measurable. For example, pleasure and pain could be calculated using questions such as: How intense was the pleasure or pain? How long did it last? How many people would be affected by the pleasure or pain? Thus, Bentham proposed reducing questions of individual decision and social policy-making to adding and subtracting.

Bentham's view of decision-making may sound simplistic and mechanical, but it was a forerunner of the proposition that everything that exists can be measured. It also anticipated the belief popular among some modern educators that all education can be reduced to stated and measurable behavioral objectives. Bentham's view of ethics by estimation was a powerful force in the education of John Stuart Mill.

Bentham's Utilitarian principle of the "greatest happiness or greatest good for the greatest number of people" marked the beginning of the division of Liberals into two factions—the strict individualists who wanted a very limited role for the state in social policy and those who saw the state as the appropriate agency for social reform. (Chapter 17, which examines the life and ideology of Herbert Spencer provides an example of the former type of Liberal. Chapters 18 and 19, which examine the careers and contributions of Jane Addams and John Dewey, deal with progressives in the United States who were Liberal proponents of the welfare state.)

Bentham's Utilitarianism signaled the transition of the social reformist wing of Liberalism from an exclusive concern for the individual to broader social issues. The theoretical challenge that Bentham faced was the question of how to transform individual self-interests into a social good. Again, using mathematical estimation as the basis of ethical policy, Bentham concluded that the public interest was simply the sum of the interests of all individuals who composed society.[9] In terms of calculated happiness, all existing institutions, laws, customs, traditions, and conventions could be examined. If these institutions were not functioning to produce the greatest good for the greatest number, they could be abolished or reformed.

Basic to social reform for Bentham and his followers was parliamentary or political reform. The legislator who followed the principle of utility would be guided by the ever-present question: What use is the institution or law to maximizing the greatest happiness for the greatest number? Using the criteria of pleasure and pain, the new kind of legislature would not be bound by tradition or custom. Through legislation, not revolution, a reformed environment would be created inhabited by rational individuals who calculated their actions. Underlying Bentham's social prescriptions was the Liberal's belief in gradual change that would result in the elimination of aristocratic and feudal privileges but not jeopardize individual freedoms and the sanctity of private property, so dear to the middle class.

As a nonrevolutionary philosophy for gradual and limited social change, the Utilitarians relied heavily on education. Like the later U.S. progressives, they had a journalist's way of educating people. Using the vehicle of informal education, they hoped through their tracts, periodicals, pamphlets and books to mold an informed public opinion. Such an opinion required a literate population, which meant that some system of popular education was needed. Bentham saw popular education as the means by which individuals would know their true self-interests and could participate in the forming of the public interest. Here, the Utilitarians faced an educational dilemma in that they wanted widespread popular education, but not a system of schools controlled by the state.

Like the legal system that he hoped to reform, Bentham, and his associate, James Mill, found the existing educational system to be a hodgepodge of malfunctioning institutions. In the early nineteenth century, the growing population in England was severely undereducated. The elite minority—the children of the landed aristocracy and the new industrialists—attended primary schools that prepared them for college preparatory secondary schools, either grammar schools or the prestigious "public schools" of Eton, Westminster, Rugby, Charterhouse, and Harrow. Despite their misleading name, these schools were private and catered to the rich and well-born. Their stuffy curriculum of Latin and Greek, taught by semireligious clerics, was not the kind of education that would train leaders of Utilitarian reform. The leading universities—Oxford and Cambridge—did not do any better. Bentham was a staunch and unrelenting opponent of these bastions of classical higher education. Under the leadership of Bentham and other Utilitarians, the University of London was established in 1828 to emphasize social philosophy and social science to educate people for the reforms that were needed.

If the education of the upper classes was of the wrong sort, the education of the working classes was either nonexistent or piecemeal and sporadic. The development of English education, especially a system of primary and secondary schools, was retarded by the Church of England's attitude, shared by the Tory Conservatives, that education was largely a private matter. Only in the case of the dependent poor should charity be provided to educate their children. The Liberal stance of little or no government interference did not encourage the development of a school system.

In the early nineteenth century, a limited number of church-supported endowed primary schools enrolled an equally limited number of children, estimated to be about 150,000 students. Another 50,000 children were enrolled in makeshift "dame schools," reading and writing schools conducted for profit by enterprising women. In addition to these primary schools, a small number of factories provided some primary education for their child laborers. At best only a minority of the primary school-age children were attending some sort of school.[10]

With such educational underdevelopment, the Utilitarians faced the dilemma of seeking to bring about educational reform without creating state-controlled schools. They approached the problem cautiously with a variety of gradualistic proposals. Bentham was concerned with the education of both the working classes and the middle classes. Like many middle-class reformers, Bentham was interested in improving the condition of the working classes. In particular, he sought to strengthen their will to resist those vices, especially the drinking of alcohol, to which they were prone. Motivated by both humanitarianism and a desire to minimize the threat that a large and discontented illiterate class constituted to the propertied middle class, Bentham expressed his ideas on the education of the poor in *A Scheme for Improved Pauper Management* in 1797. He endorsed the establishment of "Houses of Industry," which would provide basic education for literacy, moral instruction, and vocational training. In his plan, there was a great deal of latent social control. Like other reformers, Bentham knew what was best for the British underclass. Among the moral values that would be stressed were punctuality, honesty, thrift, self-control especially in terms of sexuality, and respect for private property.[11] Bentham believed that his plan for educating the poor could be paid for primarily by the industries in which the children or their parents worked. Limited government assistance might be provided to those who were unemployed. One important aspect of Bentham's plan was that the parents of poor children would be required to see that their children received the education he prescribed.

Despite some occasional personal and doctrinal disputes of a minor nature, James Mill (1773–1836), the father of John Stuart Mill was one of Bentham's most consistent and devoted disciples. Since James Mill determined that he would educate and guide his son's education according to Bentham's Utilitarian philosophy, a brief commentary on the senior Mill helps illuminate the intellectual context that shaped John Stuart Mill's upbringing and world view.

James Mill was born at Northwater Bridge, in the parish of Logie Port, in Forfarshire in Scotland. His father, James Mill, was the village shoemaker. His mother, Isabel Fenton, who was from a family of higher social status, determined that young James would have the advantages that education could bring. Through his mother's efforts, James attended the local parish school and showed himself to be academically adept. The village minister, a Reverend Peters, took an interest in James and encouraged his attendance at the Montrose Academy, a secondary school. He also came to the attention of Sir John Stuart and Lady Stuart who helped to support him as a student at the University of Edinburgh. At the University, he pursued and completed divinity studies and after graduation in 1798 was licensed as a Presbyterian preacher.[12]

In 1802, James Mill, seeking to improve his economic opportunities, moved to London to pursue a career as a writer and journalist. He continued to enjoy the friendship of Sir John Stuart who introduced him to some of the leading political and public personalities in England's capital. Mill began a successful career as a writer and contributed to such periodicals as the *Literary Journal,* the *British Review,* and the *Philanthropist.* Among Mill's acquaintances were the influential economist, David Ricardo, and the well-known philosopher, Jeremy Bentham. The Bentham-Mill association would have important consequences, not only for the history of philosophy and the development of Liberal ideology, but for the education of John Stuart Mill, whom they planned to make the perfect Utilitarian.

In 1805, James Mill married Harriet Burrow. Nine children were born to the couple, the eldest of whom was John Stuart Mill, the subject of this chapter. In 1818, James Mill secured employment in the London office of the East India Company as Examiner of Correspondence. While there he used records and correspondence to write his multivolume *History of India.* Among his other publications were *Elements of Political Economy* in 1821, *Analysis of the Phenomena of the Human Mind* in 1829, and *A Fragment on Mackintosh* in 1835.

James Mill expressed his educational philosophy in his "Essay on Education."[13] Like Bentham, James Mill saw education directed to securing the greatest happiness for the greatest number of people. According to Mill, an individual can bring happiness to others "either by abstaining from doing harm, or by doing them positive good." Abstention from doing them harm was to Mill the principle of "Justice," and doing them "positive good" was that of "Generosity." The overriding and most general goals of education should then be cultivating the virtues of justice and generosity.[14] These twin virtues required that an individual always balance personal pleasures against the consequences that actions have in the lives of others.

Using a rationale grounded in Utilitarian principles, James Mill saw education as the cultivation of individual and social happiness. In Mill's eyes, human happiness did not mean a hedonistic pursuit of sensual pleasures nor a quick satisfying of the human appetites. Rather, using Bentham's calculus of happiness, actions had to be carefully weighed in terms of their long-run benefits to both individuals and society. The pursuit of genuine happiness involved controlling human appetites and rejecting short-run pleasures for those of long-range human happiness. Mill's properly educated person would be one who would carefully and temperately estimate pleasure and pain.

For Mill, the education of a child required some degree of adult imposition so the youngster would learn to abandon certain immediate desires and direct his or her energy toward others that would improve him or her as an individual and society as well. In tutoring his son, John Stuart, James Mill proved to be a directive teacher who almost completely controlled the child's environment—limiting his peer association and determining the goals that his son would pursue.

John Stuart Mill: Autobiography and Education

In this section of the chapter, we examine the life, education, and career of John Stuart Mill, a determined advocate of human freedom.[15] The life of Mill (1806–1873) coincided with the development of Liberalism, which was both a philosophy and an ideology of political and social reform. The development and changes that occurred in Liberal thought are evident in Mill's education and career. When he was born in 1806, the classical liberal position that held that government should exercise a strictly laissez-faire position of noninterference in social and economic life was challenged by a reform movement within Liberalism known as Utilitarianism which was led by Jeremy Bentham and James Mill, John Stuart Mill's father.

John Stuart Mill was born on May 20, 1806, in Yorkshire, England, the eldest son of James Mill, an essayist and historian and a close associate of Jeremy Bentham, the founder of a new interpretation of Liberalism, known as Utilitarianism. Bentham espoused a philosophy of individual and social reform designed to calculate and obtain the greatest happiness for the greatest number of people. James Mill, influenced by Bentham, determined that his son, John Stuart, would receive a philosophical upbringing, from birth to adulthood, in Bentham's Utilitarianism.

Like Herbert Spencer's father, James Mill dominated his family. Mill's mother appears to be a minor character in his childhood and education. She was a quiet and unassuming woman who devoted her energies to caring for the domestic needs of her husband and children. Mill had little to say about his mother but much to say about his father in later years. He did write that if his mother had been more assertive that she might have brought a more emotional and humane character to the household that was dominated by the icy rationalism and cool logic of James Mill, who even saw family life and child-rearing in terms of Bentham's utilitarian views.[16]

The dominant influences in John Stuart Mill's childhood were his father and Jeremy Bentham. The senior Mill and Bentham wanted John Stuart to become their philosophical heir and eventual leader of the philosophical movement. Bentham looked forward to the opportunity to test his educational theories on young Mill.[17]

When John Stuart was three, James Mill relocated his family into Bentham's home so that Bentham could directly supervise his son's education. Mill and Bentham, who believed that nothing should be left to chance in John Stuart's education, scheduled all the youngster's lessons and activities. Bentham, in particular, believed that human happiness could be mathematically calculated according to the amount of pleasure and pain that a given action had as a consequence. By thorough planning of one life's, the chance element, the unplanned and spontaneous happening, could be reduced. A schedule would use time efficiently and produce effective results, reasoned Mill and Bentham, and so they set about scheduling the childhood of John Stuart Mill.

Mill and Bentham determined John's curriculum, which consisted of the ancient Greek and Latin languages, literature, mathematics, and the physical and natural sciences with an emphasis on chemistry, history, and selected literature. When John Stuart had mastered these bodies of knowledge, they planned to direct his study to logic and the analysis of philosophy. Since the Utilitarian educators saw little utility in art, music and poetry, these subjects were not part of John Stuart's master schedule.

The two philosophers developed a daily routine of study for their young pupil. John Stuart arose at six every morning and studied three hours before taking a half-hour break for breakfast. Then he had a concentrated block of five hours of study with an emphasis on applying his lessons to problems given to him by his father and Bentham. After dinner, he studied for an additional three hours. Thus, a typical day consisted of eleven hours of lessons and study. His only breaks from this routine of concentrated academic effort were discussions with his father on the books that were assigned as readings. John and his father also took a daily walk through nearby woods and gardens during which they pursued an intellectual topic.[18]

John Stuart studied ancient Greek and Latin languages and literature, which were regarded as essential components in the education of upper-class males. However, the method that James Mill used in educating his son differed from the conventional way these languages were taught in nineteenth-century grammar and preparatory schools where students memorized vocabulary from a nomenclature, a book of Latin or Greek words, and studied the principles of grammar. After the rules of grammar and an adequate vocabulary had been acquired, students began translating the classics. Memorization of passages was often the goal rather than comprehension of what was read.

James Mill began his son's study of Greek when John Stuart was three; Latin instruction began when he was eight. Mill devised a set of flash cards with important Greek and Latin words printed on them to acquaint John Stuart with the essential vocabulary. He located the boy in his library and had him read the classical texts, beginning with *Aesop's Fables.* When John Stuart came upon a word or phrase that he did not know, he would interrupt his father, who was working on his multivolume *History of India.* The senior Mill would supply the needed word or phrase and the youngster would continue his lesson. John Stuart later commented that his father, who usually would not tolerate interruptions, did not seem to mind them in such instances.[19]

The relationship between James Mill and his son appeared to be strictly intellectual, without affection at the emotional level. In his *Autobiography,* Mill reflected on his education, which he believed was overly intellectual and without opportunities for association and play with other children, or for enjoying nature, art, or poetry. Although he was an intellectually gifted and precocious child, Mill considered his education uneven and his academic performance to be average. He especially believed that he was lacking in physical dexterity, creativity, and speaking skills. These feelings of inadequacy were reinforced by his father, who, rather than praising his son's achievements, was a critical tutor who consistently heaped on the young boy more academic assignments and challenges. John Stuart Mill later wrote:

> I was constantly meriting reproof by inattention, in observance, and general slackness of mind in matters of daily life. My father was the extreme opposite in these particulars: his senses and mental faculties were always on the alert; he carried decision and energy of character in his whole manner and into every action of life.[20]

John Stuart Mill's approach to his father was one of intellectual awe. His most enjoyable memory of his father revolved around their long daily walks which provided rare opportunities for observing and enjoying nature. However, even on these walks, time was spent with the father asking the son questions about the day's lessons.

As one of the foremost and accomplished disciples of Bentham's Utilitarianism, James Mill wanted to provide his son with a background of knowledge that could be applied to the problems of the day.[21] He wanted his son to develop a critical mind that challenged conventional ways of thinking. However, by concentrating on languages, mathematics, and the sciences to the exclusion of poetry, music, art, and literature, the senior Mill deprived his son of the means for aesthetic appreciation and enjoyment.

John Stuart sought to follow the example of his father, who was a distinguished historian and essayist especially known for his *History of India,* by writing essays at an early age including a history of the Roman republic. In his *Autobiography,* he recalled:

> In my eleventh and twelfth year I occupied myself writing what I flattered myself was something serious. This was no less than a history of the Roman Government. . . . My father encouraged me in this useful amusement, though . . . he never asked to see what I wrote; so that I did not feel that in writing it I was accountable to any one, nor had the chilling sensation of being under a critical eye.[22]

When he was twelve, John Stuart Mill's education took a decided philosophical bent, directed to the analysis of philosophical ideas and principles.[23] His father now concentrated on sharpening his son's powers of logic. He was challenged to analyze philosophical works, to identify their major premises, and to examine the consistency of the case made in the particular philosopher's argument. The daily walks of the father-tutor and pupil-son now became Socratic dialogues in which the young Mill was forced to analyze what he had read and defend his conclusions. John Stuart Mill commented that this rigorous analytical training served him well in his later career as a philosopher and spokesman for the cause of reform. In particular, he believed he learned to avoid fallacious reasoning and vague and ambiguous expression. He claimed that he had learned how to formulate his ideas logically and clearly.

In strongly endorsing the method of philosophical education that his father used, Mill noted that it had the power of forming "exact thinkers, who attach a precise meaning to words and propositions, and are not imposed on by vague, loose or ambiguous terms." Such a philosophical education developed the student's powers of "disentangling the intricacies of confused and self-contradictory thought. . . ."[24]

At age fourteen, Mill's education took another turn. His study regimen grew increasingly independent of his father's supervision. He was permitted to take a long study-and-travel tour of France, during which he encountered the social, political, and educational philosophies that were current on the European continent. During this sojourn in France he began to change from a "little Englander" who viewed life through strictly British lenses to a person with a wider perspective.

However, when Mill returned to England to begin his career his destiny was still largely in the hands of his father. In 1823, James Mill secured a clerical position for his son with the East India Company, a private stock company with some government supervision, which controlled large sectors of the Indian economy. John Stuart Mill worked for the East India Company for the next thirty-five years and eventually was promoted to the rather prestigious position of Examiner of Correspondence with the Native States. As had been true of his father's career, the East India Company provided him with an income while allowing him enough time to pursue his real interest of philosophical writing and editing.

Mill now became actively involved in the Utilitarian cause. He was associated with Bentham and his father in publishing *The Westminster Review,* the official Utilitarian journal. Mill worked on the *Review* as an editor and also contributed his own essays. His articles challenged the views of the philosophical and political opposition, the Conservatives who wanted to retain the old order and the Owenite Socialists who wanted to build a new social order without individual freedom. During his childhood and youth, Mill had been socially isolated but he now was making acquaintances among those who supported Utilitarianism.

To all appearances, John Stuart Mill was the perfectly formed Utilitarian educated in the image and likeness of his father. Inwardly, however, he rebelled against his father's control. Despite his efforts to repress his feelings, his emotions came through. In 1826, at age twenty, John Stuart Mill began to experience what would be a series of episodes of mental depression with symptoms of physical fatigue and exhaustion, loss of interest, and anxiety. Though he continued to work at the East India Company, he found himself unable to engage in the philosophical activities—the writing and editing—that had so intrigued him. He now began to probe his psyche in introspective self-analysis. Plagued by severe self-doubts, he questioned the purpose of his life. In his *Autobiography,* Mill said the cause of reform that had motivated him in the past had lost its meaning. He stated that "the whole foundation on which my life was constructed fell down. . . . I seemed to have nothing left to live for."[25]

Mill's severe mental crisis proved to be the turning point in his life. Although the exact cause of Mill's mental depression has intrigued psycho-biographers, a common interpretation is that he was no longer able to repress his frustration and resentment against an overly controlling father. Still another interpretation is that his overly intellectual education and general lack of social involvement with peers had not prepared him for the emotional side of life, especially as a young adult. In any event, Mill had entered a period of mental and emotional storm and stress. Mill learned that Bentham's philosophy which held that pleasure and pain could be added and subtracted in order to make decisions was totally inadequate for his personal struggle with life.

In struggling to find his way out of his depression, Mill began to feel life as well as to think about it. He found that he needed to develop his emotions and find new creative outlets. Philosophically, Mill began to develop a more flexible and less doctrinaire approach to Liberalism than his previous commitment to Benthamism. He now enjoyed music and art, the aesthetic luxuries that had been denied to him by his Utilitarian tutors.

While Bentham's principles remained a philosophical foundation for him and his father's exacting training in philosophical methodology continued to serve him well, Mill began to shape his own philosophy. He came to the realization that happiness was not a matter of keeping a ledger-like account of credits and debits of pain and pleasure. Mill viewed human happiness as a whole—a blending of the intellectual, emotional, cognitive and affective dimensions of life—not something that could be analyzed and dissected into bits and pieces.

Once, he had overcome his mental depression, Mill began to seek and experience what had been absent in his education—aesthetic appreciation and emotional cultivation. While he continued to prize the intellectual and the logical, Mill broadened and integrated his view of life. At this phase in his life he became personally involved with Harriet Taylor, who became his confidant and companion and later his wife.

When Mill met Taylor, she was in her early twenties, the wife of John Taylor and the mother of two children. She was a member of a Unitarian group to which some friends of Mill belonged. He was strongly attracted to the opinionated young woman who was a firm advocate of women's rights, and she was equally attracted to the young intellectual. In nineteenth-century Victorian England, divorce was out of the question. However, Harriet's husband did not oppose their association which had all the signs of a platonic relationship of kindred spirits. Mill continued to live with his mother and Harriet with her husband. It was not until 1851, two years after John Taylor's death, that John Stuart Mill and Harriet Taylor were married. In 1858, seven years after their marriage, Harriet died and was buried near Avignon in southern France. Mill built a small cottage near the cemetery where she was buried and would retreat there to contemplate and write.[26]

There has been much speculation by historians as to the extent to which Harriet Taylor influenced John Stuart Mill's later philosophical development. That she had a salutory effect on liberating his pent-up emotions there can be little doubt. In many respects, she was a counter-force to the intellectual pressure and control that James Mill had exercised on his son. In any event, Harriet Taylor was a confidant with whom John Stuart Mill shared his ideas. She also was a gentling influence who allowed him to show his feelings and emotions. Harriet, who had strong views about women's rights in society, politics, and education, appeared to influence Mill to take up the cause of women's equality. When Mill was elected to the House of Commons, he introduced a bill for women's suffrage, which was defeated. Harriet Taylor also may have helped push Mill from the laissez-faire Liberal social and economic position in the direction of the social reformist welfare issues of humanitarian Liberalism. However, Benthamite Utilitarianism had already started him in this direction.

John Stuart Mill, in his *Autobiography,* praised Harriet for her intellectual vitality and her compassionate nature. He wrote that her mind was a "perfect instrument, piercing to the very heart and marrow of the matter; always seizing the essential idea or principle." He praised her sensitivity and "her gifts of feeling and imagination."[27]

The rest of Mill's life was spent in philosophical writing. Among his most influential books was *On Liberty,* published in 1859, which expressed Mill's fear of a coming mass society, characterized by a mass morality that would repress individual freedom. His *Utilitarianism,* published in 1863, was a critique of the philosophical position upon which he had been nurtured and educated. In this book, he challenged theories based on a calculus of felicity in which human happiness is regarded to be a measurable, quantitative substance. Human happiness, for Mill, was much more complex and qualitative than Bentham had thought. In terms of suggesting a social policy, Mill argued that while government should provide citizens with equal access to the sources of happiness, it was an individual's right to choose the happiness desired.

In addition to his writing, Mill made a brief foray into active politics and was elected to one term in the House of Commons, serving from 1865 to 1868. Although elected as an independent or unaffiliated member of Commons from the district of Westminster, Mill supported the Liberal Party on most votes. He supported the extension of suffrage to those who were disenfranchised because of property restrictions. He had earlier supported the "great reform" bill of 1832 which reduced property qualifications. As an advocate of universal suffrage, he also supported the reform bill of 1867 which was enacted while he was serving in parliament. He tried to secure legislation that would have enabled women to vote but failed in his efforts.

In 1867, he was made rector of St. Andrews University in Scotland. In his Inaugural Address at St. Andrews, Mill expressed his views on higher education and the proper role of the university. The university, he said, should devote itself to the cultivation of the intellect and not become a training school for the various professions. In his address, Mill also gave education a broad and general meaning. In addition to the recognized formal process of schooling that involves books and lectures, Mill said, education was part of a large informal process that involved the care and ownership of property, one's daily work, and the participation of the person in social and political life.

Mill died in 1873 at Avignon and was buried next to his beloved Harriet.

Mill's Social and Educational Philosophy

John Stuart Mill, the product of an unusual but carefully directed education, was recognized by the end of his life as the foremost theoretician of the new humanitarian

Liberalism. Although he retained his commitment to Bentham's premise that social policy should seek to secure the "Greatest Happiness for the Greatest Number," he rejected the Benthamite methodology that happiness could be calculated with mathematical precision. John Stuart Mill, in his creation of humanitarian Liberalism from his revision of Utilitarianism, came to see human happiness in qualitative rather than quantitative terms which had definite political and educational implications.

Underlying Mill's political and educational philosophy was an emphasis on individual liberty and freedom. Mill stressed the necessity of personal freedom and the free circulation of ideas as necessary conditions for political and social progress. In his much quoted work, *On Liberty,* Mill expresses his belief in the progress of human beings through freedom of thought. According to Mill, "the only purpose for which power can be rightfully exercised over any member of a civilized community, against his will, is to prevent harm to others. His own good, either physical or moral, is not a sufficient warrant."[28] Mill's determination that social reform be accomplished while protecting individual freedom was much different from the position of latter-day humanitarian Liberals, especially the progressives in the United States, who believed that some degree of social control was needed to regulate society and its institutions.

Mill's emphasis on individual liberty was based on his belief that a society benefitted from the presence of critically minded individuals who challenged conventional wisdom and originated new ideas. Liberty and criticism were utilitarian or useful to a society because they cultivated an environment in which new ideas could be expressed and tested in the court of human opinion. Along with political authoritarianism and despotic government, the greatest obstacle to the freedom to originate and circulate ideas was the restraining power of the status quo and the willingness to accept whatever existed as being right and true.

The freedom to hold ideas had a corollary freedom in that individuals should be free to express and communicate their ideas in speech and in print. It was of crucial importance that there be freedom of speech, press, and assembly. It was of equal importance that teachers be free to teach and students be free to learn. This meant that the school should not be an agency to impress conventional wisdom and the status quo on the young but rather an agency to foster individual intellectual initiative, especially the power of critical thinking.

Mill's political philosophy rested on the Liberal ideological commitment to an elected representative government in which legislators were responsible to those who had voted them into office. As a strong defender of civil liberties, Mill believed such freedoms were best secured and maintained under political conditions of self-government. However, representative institutions required that the people, the electorate, have a civic education that made them conscious of the need to maintain their liberties and to elect those to office who would act in the name of liberty. The view that civic education is necessary for the functioning of representative institutions is also found in the ideas of Thomas Jefferson which are examined in Chapter 11 and Horace Mann who is treated in Chapter 13.

Throughout his life and consistently in his writings, Mill opposed any constraint on human liberty, uniqueness, and individuality. As a Liberal, he opposed the obvious tyranny of despotic governments, especially absolute monarchy. He opposed the constraints that established churches sought to impose over freedom of inquiry and institutions. Had he lived in the twentieth century, he could have been expected to oppose the modern political tyrannies of Stalin in the Soviet Union, Mussolini in Italy, and Hitler in Germany. Absolutism in either its ancient or modern form was a political condition that Mill found abhorrent.

To Mill, there was also a variety of tyranny which, while less obvious than dictatorship was just as pernicious to human freedom—the tyranny of the majority, the tendency of the majority to impose prevailing opinions on the minority. His well-founded fears anticipated the dangers of the mass society, mass media, and mass opinion of the twentieth century. In a parliamentary system of government, legislators are elected by the people when receiving a majority of votes. Mill feared that an uneducated mass of voters might be swayed by demagogues who, despite their popular appeal, would act against human rights and freedom if elected. For example, in the 1930s, Adolf Hitler determined that he would gain power in Germany through popular election.

In addition to the danger of the majority of voters electing demagogues and dictators to office, there was the danger that modern society might be a society of the mass mind. The Industrial Revolution had made it possible to mass produce goods that were cheap but uniform. On the assembly line, standardized machines produced standardized products. For example, a shoemaking factory could produce thousands of shoes of the same width, length, and color. If the shoes fit the majority of consumers, the volume of sales would be large. However, the mass-produced shoe might not fit the feet of the minority. Further, the cheapness of the shoes would tend to drive the individual shoemaker with a small shop out of business or force him to restrict his trade to wealthier customers who could afford his services.

The mass production of the industrial factory system had not only economic consequences but threatened to have similar effects on public opinion. Mill feared that mass conformity was a formidable threat to human freedom because it was so socially pervasive. He wrote that it left the individual with "fewer means of escape, penetrating much more deeply into the details of life, and enslaving the soul itself."[29]

A trend in the nineteenth century when Mill lived that has escalated in the twentieth century is gearing information and entertainment to the interests of the majority. In Mill's day, the cheaply produced newspaper made its appearance. The newspaper sold for a few pennies and made its income by circulation. The larger the circulation and sales, the greater the profits. The newspapers that dominated the scene were those that appealed to the largest readership. To attract this readership, the reporting of news and human interest features was geared to the widest possible audience, a mass audience whose taste was based on the average person. Since there is no average person in reality, this fictional character is a composite of individuals. The average implies a sameness that comes from reducing people who do not fit the composite to a common mold. The consequence of such reductionism is that personal uniqueness, individuality, and eccentricity become regarded almost as abnormalities.

While the popular press of the nineteenth century catered to the average person, as a force of informal education it also molded popular opinions, tastes, and values. If Mill were alive today, he would recognize in the mass media—newspapers, magazines, radio, and especially television—new dangers to individuality. To capture the largest possible audience, the media gear their reporting of information and presenting of entertainment to what the majority wants. Once again, the fictional but powerful average person's taste sets the standard. However, in the modern mass society, the average person is computed by sophisticated samplings and public opinion polls. The result is a sameness, a conformity, which while popularly based, restricts ideas, opinions, and tastes that deviate from the average. Unless the proper educational checks were established, Mill feared that the future might be one of the conformism of the mass society and the mass mind—a world view based on the average.

Just as Mill feared the tyranny of the majority might reduce standards to the average, he feared that representative institutions might become places where special interest groups secured legislation to advance their causes rather than those of the greatest number of persons.

At the time that Mill dealt with the question of special interest groups—the contending parties were the industrial employers and the working class employees. Throughout the nineteenth century in the United Kingdom, industrial employers held the advantage. However, in the twentieth century with the rise of large industrial unions and the British Labour Party, the tide would shift. In the Marxist view, the interests of capitalist and worker were irreconcilable and would bring about class conflict, revolution, and the eventual but inevitable triumph of the proletariat.

Mill, raised on Bentham's theory of rational decision-making and committed to Liberal principles of nonviolent social change, took a moderate position. While he was committed to private property, he opposed the exploitation of workers by the capitalist industrialists. While a humanitarian, he feared that undereducated workers could degenerate into a mob that would destroy liberty. Again, Mill looked to education, especially the education of a disinterested group of citizens, who could resolve the dilemma of special interests.

For Mill, a group of well-educated persons, or "disinterested participants," might be able to stem the tide of the tyranny of the majority as well as reconcile the contentions of conflicting special interest groups. A disinterested person was one who was neither biased by personal interests nor motivated by the desire for personal profit. While the disinterested person was unprejudiced, he or she was nonetheless a participant in the social and political processes and not aloof from them. Unlike the member of the special interest group, the disinterested person would not be motivated to seek special privileges or advantages. The quality of disinterestedness implied having an educated perspective that made it possible to evaluate an issue objectively.

In his *Dissertations and Discussion*, written in 1867, Mill argued for the value of disinterested participation in society. Mill, a staunch defender of both individual freedom and representative government, feared that a mass society could, if unchecked, reduce individuals to a state of mass conformity in which personal uniqueness succumbed to the supremacy of the average. Mill also feared that special interests, if unguided by a more general and objective perspective, could destroy the operations of the genuinely representative government.

For Mill, education had the potential of being the great solvent of a free society. Educated people, Mill reasoned, would be concerned with the general good rather than special class interests. Disinterested, critically minded, well-educated people could act as the lever of social policy—a kind of swing vote. As a social voice of criticism, they might exercise the important role of objective decision-making. Mill had a vision of a new kind of scholar—a person disinterested in special gain but a critical thinker—in preparing and advancing legislation that was in the general and public interest.

Mill's argument in *On Liberty* stated that:

- The individual is interested in advancing his or her own welfare
- The individual's welfare is intimately related to promoting the public good.
- New ideas that express human inventiveness and creativity advance both individual and social progress.
- New ideas are generated by individuals or by members of minorities.
- In a social and political climate of freedom of thought and opinion, alternative ideas will be expressed and compete with each other.
- From the competition of ideas, truth will emerge and new policies will be formulated.

Conclusion: An Assessment

John Stuart Mill's life and philosophy are instructive for educators. His *Autobiography* is itself an analysis of educational theory. Like autobiography and biography in general, it is an account of the effects of persons, situations, and ideas in shaping a life. John Stuart Mill's education—at the hands of his Utilitarian tutors, Jeremy Bentham and James Mill—is an account of education that was purposeful but out of balance. It produced a critically minded intellectual who, while skilled in analyzing political and philosophical works, was awkwardly prepared for the totality of life. While Mill's mind was intellectually honed to precision, his education was so one-sided that he was stunted emotionally. What is instructive about studying Mill's life and education for today's teachers is the lesson that it is necessary for a person to have an education that harmoniously blends the intellectual, the cognitive dimension of humanness, and the emotional, or the affective dimension.

In terms of social and educational policy, the educational implications of Mill's stress on individual freedom are clear. In the educative process, the learner is to be appreciated as an individual personality who has his or her own interests, needs, values, and most importantly, ideas. Attention needs to be focused constantly and consistently on the learner who possesses unique potentialities to achieve fulfillment as a human being and to contribute from this unique individuality to the happiness and welfare of others.

In a mass society such as ours, Mill's call to preserve individuality suggests many educational implications. Educational institutions in the United States, like other social institutions, have become large, massive, complex, and bureaucratic places. This massiveness produces a numbing effect on individuality. In corporate education, as well as corporate society, there is the danger that in the desire for efficient programming of instruction, the individual student will have his or her behavior so modified that uniqueness is ground out of the human character. When the individual is lost in the mass and becomes a blur in the faceless crowd of the statistically standardized average, he or she is reduced to an impersonal statistic. In the mass school system as in the mass society, the individual becomes increasingly subject to what Mill called the conformity of the mass. In U.S. schools, the danger to individuality comes also from the pressures to quantify and standardize all modes of education. If large and massive schools bring about a condition of educational conformity and oppressive impersonality, they need to be redesigned according to individual needs rather than reducing the individual to fit institutional requirements.

An educational institution which encourages the development of diverse ideas, in Mill's perspective, is one that is characterized by a pervasive academic freedom. In such schools, teachers are free to teach and students are free to learn. As liberty in the larger society is jeopardized by coercion, bureaucracy, authoritarianism, violence, conformity, and anarchy, these same forces limit academic freedom in schools.

According to Mill, it is possible and desirable to frame social, political, and educational policies that advance the interest of both the individual and society. The kind of society that Mill advocated would recognize the values of individual freedom of thought and expression and encourage disinterested and objective examination and action on social issues. Mill's preferred kind of individualism looks beyond special interests to social progress.

Finally, Mill's modified and revised Utilitarianism was an important stage in the history of Liberalism. While original Liberalism was still alive and while laissez-faire Liberalism would be revived by Herbert Spencer, Mill's emphasis on social policy with a humanitarian conscience was a step in the direction of John Dewey's new liberalism. Mill, who opposed all forms of coercion, unlike Dewey, saw that the group could be an instrument of mass coercion. Mill's Liberal ideology pointed up the importance of the individual and of personal liberty. It raised the Liberal's dilemma that recognizes the need of regulation to protect the interests of the members of society, especially those in disadvantaged situations, but also recognizes in such regulation the beginning of controls on human freedom.

Discussion Questions

1. Describe the Liberal orientation to life, politics, society, and education.
2. What was Jeremy Bentham's methodology for calculating social reform?
3. What was the nature of the division in Liberalism between the classical Liberals and the social reformist Liberals?
4. How did James Mill propose to educate his son, John Stuart Mill?
5. Analyze and evaluate the kind of education that John Stuart Mill received from his father, James Mill, and Jeremy Bentham.
6. What were the basic social and educational ideas of John Stuart Mill?
7. What is the "tyranny of the majority?" Identify some symptoms of the tyranny of the majority in contemporary U.S. life and education?

Research and Essay Topics

1. In an essay review, read and analyze John Stuart Mill's *Autobiography*.
2. In an interpretive essay, analyze the relationship between John Stuart Mill and James Mill.
3. In a paper, examine the proposition that John Stuart Mill was an intellectual genius.
4. In an essay, examine the educational implications of Liberalism.
5. In an essay, analyze John Stuart Mill's concept of the "tyranny of the majority."
6. In an essay, describe an educational situation that exemplifies Mill's concept of the freedom of ideas.

Notes

1. E. P. Thompson, *The Making of the English Working Class* (New York: Random House, 1966).
2. W. D. Grampp, *The Manchester School of Economics* (Stanford: Stanford University Press, 1975).
3. J. Salwyn Schapiro, *Liberalism: Its Meaning and History* (New York: D. Van Nostrand Co., 1958), 112–14.
4. Michael J. Gootzeit, *David Ricardo* (New York: Columbia University Press, 1975).
5. A well done commentary on Liberalism is D. J. Manning, *Liberalism* (New York: St. Martin's Press, 1976).
6. J. Salwyn Schapiro, *Liberalism and the Challenge of Fascism: Social forces in England and France* (New York: McGraw-Hall Book Co., 1949), 43–59.
7. Ibid., 44.
8. Ibid., 44–45.
9. Ibid., 51–53.
10. Elie Halevy, *England in 1815* (New York: Barnes and Noble, 1961), 526–32.
11. Brian W. Taylor, "Useful Education for the Poor: A Benthamite Perspective," paper presented at the annual meeting of the Midwest History of Education Society, 1979, 10.
12. Alexander Bain, *James Mill: A Biography* (London: Longmans, Green and Co., 1892), 23.
13. W. H. Burton, ed., *James Mill on Education* (London: Cambridge University Press, 1969), 41.
14. Ibid., 64–65.
15. For his autobiography, see John Stuart Mill, *The Autobiography of John Stuart Mill* (New York: Columbia University Press, 1944). Among biographies of Mill are: Alan Ryan, *John Stuart Mill* (New York: Pantheon Books, 1970); Peter J. Glassman, *J. S. Mill: The Evolution of a Genius* (Gainesville, Fl.: University of Florida Press, 1985); Richard J. Halliday, *John Stuart Mill* (London: Allan and Unwin, 1976).
16. John Stuart Mill, *Autobiography of John Stuart Mill,* John J. Coss, ed. (New York: Columbia University Press, 1944), 2.
17. John B. Ellery, *John Stuart Mill* (New York: Twayne Publishers, Inc., 1964), 19.
18. Mill, Autobiography, 21.
19. Ibid., 4.
20. Ibid., 25–26.
21. William J. Baker, "Gradgrindery and the Education of John Stuart Mill: A Clarification," *Western Humanities Review,* 24 (Winter, 1970), 51.
22. Mill, *Autobiography,* 9–10.

23. Ibid., 12.
24. Ibid., 14.
25. Ibid., 94.
26. John Stuart Mill and Harriet Taylor Mill, *Essays on Sex Equality,* edited by Alice S. Rossi. (Chicago: University of Chicago Press, 1971), 6.
27. Mill, *Autobiography,* 131.
28. Schapiro, *Liberalism and the Challenge of Fascism,* 281.
29. Ibid., 282.

Suggestions for Further Reading

Atkinson, Charles. *Jeremy Bentham: His Life and Work.* New York: AMS Press, 1971.

Ashton, T. S. *The Industrial Revolution.* London: Oxford University Press, 1948.

Bain, Alexander. *James Mill: A Biography.* London: Longmans, Green, and Co., 1882.

Burston, W. H. *James Mill on Education.* London: Cambridge University Press, 1969.

Carlisle, Janice. *John Stuart Mill and the Writing of Character.* Athens: University of Georgia Press, 1991.

Cavenagh, F. A., ed. *James and John Stuart Mill on Education.* London: Cambridge University Press, 1931.

Cohen, Marshall, ed. *The Philosophy of John Stuart Mill.* New York: The Modern Library, 1961.

Davidson, William. *Political Thought in England: The Utilitarians from Bentham to Mill.* London: Oxford University Press, 1957.

Donner, Wendy. *The Liberal Self: John Stuart Mill's Moral and Political Philosophy.* Ithaca, N.Y.: Cornell University Press, 1991.

Ellery, John B. *John Stuart Mill.* New York: Twayne Publishers Inc., 1964.

Garforth, Francis W. *Educative Democracy: John Stuart Mill on Education in Society.* Oxford: Oxford University Press, 1980.

Garforth, Francis W., ed. *John Stuart Mill on Education.* New York: Teachers College Press, Columbia University, 1971.

Glassman, Peter J. *J. S. Mill: The Evolution of a Genius.* Gainseville, Fla..: University of Florida Press, 1985.

Grote, John. *An Examination of the Utilitarian Philosophy.* Bristol, U.K.: Thoemmes, 1990.

Halevy, Elie. *The Growth of Philosophic Radicalism.* Boston: The Beacon Press, 1966.

Jackson, Julius. *A Guided Tour of John Stuart Mill's Utilitarianism.* Mountain View, Calif.: Mayfield Publishing Co., 1993.

Kahan, Alan S. *Aristocratic Liberalism: The Social and Political Thought of Jacob Burckhardt, John Stuart Mill, and Alexis de Tocqueville.* New York: Oxford University Press, 1992.

Kerner, George C. *Three Philosophical Moralists: Mill, Kant, and Sartre.* New York: Oxford University Press, 1990.

Kinser, Bruce A. *A Moralist In and Out of Parliament: John Stuart Mill at Westminster, 1865–1868.* Toronto: University of Toronto Press, 1992.

Kurer, Oskar. *John Stuart Mill: The Politics of Progress.* New York: Garland Publishing Co., 1991.

Mazlish, Bruce. *James and John Stuart Mill.* New York: Basic Books, 1975.

Mill, John Stuart. *Autobiography.* John J. Coss, ed. New York: Columbia University Press, 1944.

———. *Essays on Equality, Law, and Education.* John M. Robson, ed. Toronto: University of Toronto Press, 1984.

———. *Utilitarianism, Liberty, and Representative Government.* Edited by A. D. Londsay. New York: E.P. Dutton and Co., 1951.

Mill, John Stuart, and Mill, Harriet Taylor. *Essays on Sex Equality.* Edited by Alice S. Rossi. Chicago: University of Chicago Press, 1970.

Plamenatz, John. *The English Utilitarians.* London: Basil Blackwell and Mott, 1966.

Robson, John M. *The Improvement of Mankind: The Social and Political Thoughts of John Stuart Mill.* Toronto: The University of Toronto Press, 1968.

Ryan, Alan. *John Stuart Mill.* New York: Pantheon Books, 1970.

Schapiro, J. Salwyn. *Liberalism and the Challenge of Fascism: Social Forces in England and France.* New York: McGraw-Hill Book Co., 1949.

Smart, Paul. *Mill and Marx: Individual Liberty and the Roads to Freedom.* Manchester, U.K.: Manchester University Press, 1991.

Steintrager, James. *Bentham.* Ithaca, N.Y.: Cornell University Press, 1977.

Stephens, Leslie. *The English Utilitarians.* New York: August M. Kelley, 1978.

Strasser, Mark P. *The Moral Philosophy of John Stuart Mill: Toward Modifications of Contemporary Utilitarianism.* Wakefield, N.H.: Longwood Academic Publishers, 1991.

Thomas, William. *Mill.* Oxford: Oxford University Press, 1985.

Zastoupil, Lynn. *John Stuart Mill and India.* Stanford, Calif. Stanford University Press, 1994.

Zerilli, Linda M. G. *Signifying Woman: Culture and Chaos in Rousseau, Burke, and Mill.* Ithaca, N.Y.: Cornell University Press, 1994.

CHAPTER 17

Herbert Spencer: Advocate of Individualism, Science, and Social Darwinism

Portrait of Herbert Spencer; reproduction from the collections of the Library of Congress.

This chapter analyzes the life, social theory, and educational philosophy of Herbert Spencer (1820–1903), a proponent of science in the curriculum and social Darwinism in society. Spencer, an eminent British intellectual of the Victorian era, developed socioeducational theories that exerted an important trans-Atlantic influence. Spencer, who developed a naturalistic approach to education, also developed the social implications of Charles Darwin's theory of biological evolution.

This chapter looks at Spencer's influence on educational theory in general, and on U.S. society and education, in particular. First, the social, political, and economic context—the historical milieu in which Spencer lived and worked—is described. Second, Spencer's biography, his education and career, is analyzed to determine the evolution of his ideas. Third, the effect of Spencer's educational ideas and of social Darwinism is addressed. By this analysis, it is possible to see the interworkings of ideology and education in society. For example, Spencer's social Darwinism was a potent ideology that provided a rationale for industrialization and modernization in the United States. Although his reputation is inextricably linked to social Darwinism, Spencer also was a major force for educational change, especially in curriculum.

To organize your thoughts as you read this chapter, you might wish to focus on the following questions:

- What were the major trends in the historical context, the time and situation, in which Spencer lived?
- How did Spencer's life, his educational biography, shape his educational theory?
- How did Spencer's "sociology of knowledge" influence his educational philosophy and policies?
- What is the enduring significance of Spencer's educational contributions?

The Historical Context of Spencer's Life

The years of Herbert Spencer's life coincided with the period when Western nations, especially the United Kingdom, the United States, and Germany, were being profoundly changed by the process of industrial modernization.[1] The harnessing of science and engineering to achieve the mass production of the factory system, brought about change not only in the economic system but in society as well. Spencer, an engineer and sociologist, sought to understand the new industrial situation by studying technological change from a variety of perspectives—economic, biological, sociological, political, and educational. From his analysis, he hoped to predict how social change occurs.

Although the processes of industrial and technological change were affecting both the United Kingdom and the United States, they took somewhat different courses in the two nations most influenced by Spencer's ideology. In the United Kingdom, industrialization began in the early nineteenth century with the Industrial Revolution. Water, steam, and then other forces of energy drove the machinery of Britain's mills and factories. Early textile mills were joined by iron and steel foundries to make England the "workshop of the world."

Control of British political life alternated between the Conservative party—largely composed of old aristocracy, landed gentry, small landowners, and supporters of the Church of England—and the Liberal party, composed of industrialists, middle class businessmen, tradesmen, and Nonconformist Protestant dissenters from the established Anglican church. In the Victorian age, named after the long-reigning Queen Victoria, British politics were dominated by Benjamin Disraeli, the Conservative leader, and William Ewart Gladstone, leader of the Liberals.

Conservatives took a largely gentleman's stance to the profound changes sweeping the British Isles, emphasizing the importance of the crown, the church, the aristocracy, and tradition. The Liberals dominated British politics. Early in the nineteenth century, the Liberals, supported by the new money of the rising middle classes, had challenged the traditional Tory, or Conservative, establishment. A party that stressed negative freedoms in the Lockean sense, Liberals sought to advance the interests of the new middle classes by rolling back the privileges of the old aristocracy. The Liberals espoused a number of great reforms that extended the right to vote to more members of the lower classes, restricted child labor, and encouraged greater individual freedom. If the Conservatives were defenders of the great traditions of Britain, the Liberals were the proponents of gradual change and moderate reform.

Industrialization also brought changes in the British class structure. The upper rungs of society were still occupied by the landed aristocracy—the great families of England—and the landed gentry. Their offspring attended the famous "public schools," actually prestigious and exclusive preparatory schools that readied them for entry into the venerable universities of Oxford and Cambridge. By birth, breeding, and education, the privileged classes continued to dominate the upper echelons of the Church of England, the officer corps of the military services, and the imperial civil service.

The British middle classes, ranging from small shopkeepers to large industrialists, challenged the older Tory aristocracy. The "new money" of the middle classes, made in trade and commerce, was earning the power that wealth brought to its possessors in a free enterprise society. Many of the Liberal-sponsored reforms were designed to give the middle classes political power commensurate with their economic power. Wealth brought some power but did not immediately alter the social status quo. Although a number of industrialists' sons entered the great public schools and universities, the middle class established grammar schools and new, practically inclined institutes and universities to educate their children.

Industrialization created a new class, the working class of miners and factory workers. By various reform acts, larger numbers of the working class gained the right to vote. Workers began to organize trade unions to improve working conditions and earn higher wages. For most of the nineteenth century, Conservatives and Liberals vied for the increasing number of working class voters. Neither party, however, truly represented working class interests.

Liberalism, in particular, faced a dilemma that would split it after World War I and severely diminish it as a force in British political life. Originally, the ideology espoused freedom of speech, press, assembly, religion, and trade, opposing any restrictions on these Lockean "negative" freedoms by government. However, if government were to be an agency of reform directed to ameliorating the harsh and exploitive conditions of nineteenth century industrialism such as squalid tenements, unsafe working conditions, and child labor, then it would have to take on regulatory powers that limited the freedom of some to exploit others. Although some Liberal purists, called "classical Liberals," adhered to the socioeconomic doctrines of their founding fathers—John Locke, Adam Smith, David Ricardo, and Thomas Malthus—other Liberals, the "new or modern Liberals," advocated in the utilitarian fashion of Jeremy Bentham and John Stuart Mill gradual reforms to ameliorate exploitive conditions and bring about by legislation the "greatest good for the greatest number."

Within this context of an industrializing British society with its tension between tradition and change, Herbert Spencer, a child of a Nonconformist Protestant middle-class family, lived and worked. By family and class, Spencer was on the side of British liberalism. He resented the privileged position enjoyed by the officially established Church of England. True to liberalism's principles, he wanted the Anglican church's educational role diminished. Largely a self-educated person, Spencer did not value the classically oriented traditional education that characterized the public schools and the older, prestigious universities. Spencer criticized this traditional education as ornamental and of little practical use. England's prestigious secondary and higher educational institutions resisted attempts to add scientific and technological studies to their curricula. For Spencer, securing the entry of new studies that would modernize the economy and production was a determined educational crusade.

Ideologically, Spencer was associated with classical liberalism rather than its more modern socially reformist utilitarian wing. This was not because he was a person of wealth but his ideological convictions led him to oppose any restrictions on individual freedom. Social reformist efforts, regardless of their humanitarian intentions, would inevitably lead to more government regulation. The result would be a super welfare state that intruded into areas of private life. Spencer believed that government involvement in housing, education, and medicine would create inefficient and costly state monopolies. He believed in a government with very limited and specified powers.

In 1859, Charles Darwin (1809–1882) published *The Origin of Species by Means of Natural Selection,* a book that provoked a revolution in biological thinking.[2] Darwin's evolutionary thesis was an important part of the intellectual context of Spencer's world and exerted a powerful influence on his social thinking. Darwin, the official naturalist on an English surveying ship, the *Beagle,* had observed and collected plant and animal specimens that caused him to postulate an evolutionary theory of the origin of species. Hypothesizing that plants and animals had slowly evolved as a result of a process of natural selection, Darwin concluded that all forms of organic life were descended from a small number of primitive prototypes. Existing plants and animals, as well as extinct ones, were descendants of ancestral prototypes that had experienced slow and gradual modifications that, if they enhanced survival, were transmitted to their offspring as inherited characteristics.

In summary, Darwin's thesis held that:

- More individuals of each species were born than could survive.
- There is a struggle, or an intense competition, among these individuals to obtain what they need to survive.

- Those individuals who vary in a profitable way enhance their chances for survival and thus are naturally selected.
- Naturally selected individuals perpetuate themselves by passing on their advantage to their offspring.

Although some scientists disputed Darwin's evolutionary thesis, it received support from such academicians as Joseph Hooker, Charles Lyell, and Thomas Huxley in England, Asa Gray in the United States, and Ernest Haeckel in Germany. Such publications as Lyell's *Antiquity of Man* and Huxley's *Man's Place in Nature* paved the way for a more general application of evolutionary theory to human society.[3]

Charles Darwin's theory of evolution was located in the natural sciences, biology, botany, and zoology, but it also produced dramatic controversies in theology, philosophy, and education. Orthodox theologians, Catholic and Protestant alike, argued that Darwin's theory of changing and evolving species directly contradicted the literal account of creation found in the Bible's book of Genesis, which said that species had been created in their fixed and final form.[4] Later, other theologians would find an accommodation to Darwin's evolutionary theory by reading Genesis in an allegorical way. For religious literalists, there was and continues to be no compromise with evolutionary theory. Spencer, who was not strongly committed to religious doctrine, readily accepted Darwin's theory.

It was neither biology nor religion that attracted Spencer to Darwin's evolutionary theory. He was most intrigued by its social implications. If the natural world of plants and animals followed nature's unyielding evolutionary laws, did not the same laws apply to human society and its institutions? Social Darwinism, the body of social theories emerging from the effect of Darwin's theory of evolution, found a staunch and leading advocate in Herbert Spencer.

Spencer's identification with social Darwinism made him a popular and highly respected theorist in the United States. Like the United Kingdom, the United States after the Civil War was in the throes of industrial and technological change. In the second half of the nineteenth century, the United States was most receptive to social Darwinism and to Spencer's ideas, even more so than his native England.

In the United States after the Civil War, social Darwinism provided an ideological rationale for a public policy that supported the business activities of dominant industrialists such as Andrew Carnegie and John D. Rockefeller, and the trend to industrial modernization. At the same time, social Darwinism could be used to repress the counteractions of discontented agrarian populists and the embryonic trade union movement.[5] After the Civil War, heavy industries—coal, oil, iron, and steel—enjoyed a tremendous expansion with the support of political allies, primarily in the Republican party. Raw materials such as oil, iron ore, and coal were exploited with little concern for environmental protection and human rights. A transcontinental network of railroads was constructed with subsidies from the federal government to link growing cities with the sources of raw materials needed to manufacture products for national and international markets. The leaders of the dominant political party, the Republicans, allied with the "captains of industry" to oppose regulatory legislation. The emergence of social Darwinism as a gospel of economic progress and prosperity provided a useful and apparently coherent "scientific" rationale for these industry leaders and their social, political, and educational allies in the United States.

The attempt of the social Darwinists to use science as a basis for social policy was not new. Since the eighteenth century Enlightenment, theorists had sought to create a science of society that was analogous and parallel to the discoveries and formulations of the physical sciences. Spencer saw physics and chemistry as key subjects in moving humankind along a progressive course. For Spencer and other social theorists such as William Graham Sumner, Darwin's evolutionary view of biology could be adapted to society, politics, and education. The intellectuals of the second half of the nineteenth century seized upon Darwin's theory of evolution as the foundation for an all-encompassing social theory that explained the course of human events.

Ideologically, the United States was a more receptive home for social Darwinism than England. In 1869, Darwin had been honored with membership in the prestigious American Philosophical Society, an organization founded by Benjamin Franklin that numbered Thomas Jefferson as one of its presidents.[6] Herbert Spencer was the favorite philosopher of Carnegie and the capitalist industrialists. The popular acceptance of Darwinism coincided with the high tide of U.S. capitalism and industrial development. In the name of freedom of competition, the advocates of a basically unregulated but growing economy found social Darwinism to be a scientifically based rationale for the following policy assumptions:

- The captains of industry were providing great service to the country by exploiting its resources and establishing an industrial economic base.
- There should be no interference or regulation by either government or misguided social planners and reformers.
- An economy that followed natural principles of supply and demand and encouraged the initiative that came from free enterprise would enjoy progress and economic prosperity.

Herbert Spencer's theories on the evolutionary development of society, private enterprise, and a free and unregulated economy fit well into the cultural milieu of the second half of the nineteenth century. In the following section, we turn to the biography of Herbert Spencer, the nineteenth century's leading apologist for social Darwinism.

Herbert Spencer

Herbert Spencer was born on April 17, 1820, in Derby, England.[7] His father, William George Spencer, an educator and writer, was the author of *Inventional Geometry,* a textbook designed to introduce students to the basic principles of geometry. Spencer's father, the dominant member of the family, had definite opinions about what was wrong and right about English society, politics, economics, and religion. Outspoken, highly opinionated, but coolly rational, William Spencer had a strong influence on his son's education and intellectual outlook. The elder Spencer encouraged his son to think for himself, stand up for his ideas, and be critical of the conventional wisdom of the day. Spencer's mother appears to have been a rather passive person who devoted herself to satisfying the needs of her husband and son. The Spencer household was characterized by the spirit of nonconformity in religion, politics, and social life as well. Spencer's childhood produced an attitude of the strongest kind of individualism and a resistance to infringements on freedom of choice by church or state.[8]

As a child, Herbert Spencer attended school for only a short time. His father regarded the schools as inadequate and ineffective and took charge of his son's education.[9] From his father, Herbert learned the basics of reading, writing, arithmetic, literature, and science, with the greatest stress on mathematics and science. Commenting on his early education, Spencer wrote that he knew virtually nothing of Latin, Greek, ancient history, and literature.[10] It should be noted that these subjects were regarded at the time as forming the necessary education of the English gentleman. Spencer regarded the study of ancient languages and literature to be a waste of time that could be more efficiently spent on a practical education grounded in mathematics and science.

Of equal importance with the subjects that he studied with his father was the style and method of the father-son tutorial relationship. Father and son questioned all existing knowledge, especially assumptions resting on the ancient classics and philosophy. They approached existing beliefs with the skeptic's critical perspective. No philosophical first principles were taken on face value. Nor did they value the Greek and Latin classics. Departing from the Victorian adage that "children should be seen but not heard," William Spencer expected and encouraged his intellectually precocious and highly verbal son to engage adult guests in the Spencer home in discussions of current issues. Spencer's childhood was a prelude to his adult career as a social theorist rather than an opportunity for association with other children and participation in their play, games, and activities. Despite his suffering of periodic episodes of "mental fatigue," Spencer professed gratitude to his father for developing his skills of intellectual analysis and synthesis. Of his father's educational method, Spencer wrote:

> Concerning things . . . and their properties, I knew a good deal more than is known by most boys. My conceptions of physical principles and processes had considerable clearness; and I had a fair acquaintance with sundry special phenomena in physics and chemistry. I had also acquired both in personal observation and by reading, some knowledge of animal life, and especially of insect life. . . . By miscellaneous reading a little mechanical, medical, anatomical, and physiological information had been gained; as also a good deal of information about the various parts of the world and their inhabitants.[11]

In 1832, William Spencer decided that his son would benefit from exposure to the ideas of his brother, the Reverend Spencer. At age 13, Herbert began three years of study with his uncle. He learned small amounts of Latin and Greek but his more formal studies with the Reverend Spencer once again gravitated to mathematics and the natural and physical sciences. Young Spencer particularly enjoyed Euclid's geometry and trigonometry. History, literature, and languages, which the Spencers regarded as ornamental, were purposefully neglected.

After completing his studies, Herbert Spencer pursued a career in civil engineering from age seventeen to twenty-seven. As an engineer, he applied mathematics and science to practical matters. Increasingly, however, his mind went from specific engineering projects to the consideration of larger matters. How had humankind reached its current state of social development? How did social change occur? How should people be educated in a world that was growing steadily more industrial and technological? True to the education that he had received from his father and uncle, Herbert Spencer rejected much of the wisdom of the day and set out on a single-minded intellectual odyssey to find the answers to these questions. He read widely in the sciences, especially the works of Lyell on geology and Lamarck on biology.

In 1842, Spencer began a career as a writer and critic for *The Economist,* a leading periodical. His articles espoused the classical liberal ideology that stressed personal liberty, rugged individualism, and freedom from government interference—themes that concerned him throughout his life.

Spencer's journalistic career was secondary to his primary interest in creating a comprehensive body of knowledge, a sociology of knowledge based on science, that would dethrone theology and metaphysics from their preeminent positions in the intellectual world. He spent his time writing and publishing a large number of essays and books. In 1860, he began work on *The Synthetic Philosophy,* the name he gave to his sociology of knowledge. His work was interrupted by bouts of ill health caused by a regimen of research and writing that left little time for recreation. He regarded many of the recreational outlets that art, literature, drama, and music provided as merely distractions from science. Despite self-diagnosed nervous exhaustion, insomnia, and digestive problems, Spencer continued to labor on his monumental *Synthetic Philosophy,* completing it thirty-six years later.[12]

Spencer's career as an author rather than his personal life stands out in his biography. He was a tireless and ambitious writer. His method of research was more journalistic than scholarly. He claimed that his ideas were his own rather than borrowed from others. His method was to skim articles that appeared in the leading journals and periodicals. Historical and biographical articles received a quick perusal. When he encountered an article on science, engineering, or technology he would study it thoroughly and absorb it.

Spencer's writings would first appear as lectures, articles, and essays. Then, they would be collected, and perhaps be reorganized, into books. His total output was voluminous. Among his most widely read books was his *First Principles of a New System of Philosophy,* which stated his application of evolutionary theory to society. It was a pioneering contribution to sociology. In *First Principles,* Spencer examined the structure and function of social institutions. His book *Social Statics; or the Conditions Essential to Human Happiness Specified, and the First of Them Developed* was a strong statement for individualism, human freedom, and the need to keep state and church from interfering in human affairs. *Essays: Scientific, Political, and Speculative* was a collection of Spencer's ideas on the importance of science and the need to limit government power and regulation. Although his books contained commentaries on education, Spencer addressed education specifically in *Education: Intellectual, Moral, and Physical,* which grew out of his famous and influential essay, "What Knowledge Is of Most Worth?"

Spencer's Social Theory

Spencer's self-determined lifelong task was to create a comprehensive sociology of knowledge capable of explaining the evolution of society and of predicting the course of social change. The study of theories of social change, such as Spencer's, raises the following important questions for educational policy makers:

- Does education, especially schooling, reflect current social conditions and values or can it bring about changes in these conditions and values?
- If one can determine the essential processes that generate social change, is it not possible to formulate educational policies that either accelerate or retard such change?
- Is social change a process that occurs because of natural laws or can it result from deliberate human planning?

These questions about education were intriguing ones for Spencer and remain so for contemporary educational policy makers.

Spencer's opinion about social change was based on a worldview that saw the universe in materialistic terms. Essentially, the matter of the universe was being constantly redistributed by incessant motion. The characteristics of this cosmic redistribution were evolution and dissolution. Evolution, accompanied by the dissipation of motion, resulted in the progressive integration of matter. Dissolution, accompanied by the absorption of motion, brought about the disorganization of matter.[13]

Life itself was inherently an evolutionary process. Organisms, including human beings, were part of an evolutionary chain that went from the very simple, characterized by an incoherent homogeneity, to the complex, characterized by a coherent heterogeneity. That which is homogeneous is unstable because the "persistent force" of motion will cause differences to arise in the course of future development. The simple and homogeneous organisms will eventually become complex and heterogeneous.

Societies, like biological organisms, experience the process of evolution from the simple and primitive to the complex, heterogeneous, and specialized. In the future, advanced societies will reach a state of equilibrium, or perfect balance, that will be stable, harmonious, and capable of providing the greatest happiness to the greatest number.

Although he held a materialistic view of the universe, Spencer believed that true religion dealt with the worship of the "unknowable." In life, decisions had to be made and policies formulated on the basis of the knowable. The guide to the operations of the knowable was science. The surest way of creating a complex and specialized society was by the application of science to the activities that sustained life.

For Spencer, the processes of social change were inextricably tied to natural laws. The dynamic process that affected both natural and social phenomena was that of evolution. According to Spencer, it would be folly to attempt deliberately to change society by either revolution, legislation, or education. The prudent and effective policy was one of efficient adjustment to the environment. The most able individuals would be those who could adjust quickly and intelligently to the circumstances and situations that the natural and social environment posed. The educational policy Spencer endorsed would incorporate and emphasize the scientific method for such efficient adjustment. It would educate scientists, technologists, and specialists who would make their way up the rungs of society by their skill, endurance, and innovation. As society moved to equilibration, the fittest of each generation would survive by skill, scientific intelligence, self-control, discipline, and the ability to adapt.

In such a society, it was crucial that the fittest individuals be not only permitted but also encouraged to excel. For Spencer, ethics meant that the fittest were allowed to compete. The government's role was strictly negative—to make sure that individual freedom was not curtailed. Every person had the right to do as she or he pleased provided that their actions did not violate the natural rights of others to pursue their own self-interests. Government aid, "wars against poverty," and welfare programs were doomed to failure. Not only did they maintain the unfit, they limited the freedom of the fittest. Further, they were not in tune with the natural process of evolution. Driven by the motive of competition and the desire to survive, the fittest by their inventiveness and innovation would bring about a better and more progressive society.

Spencer's Rationale for Curriculum Construction

In addition to being a leading proponent of social Darwinism, Spencer also should be examined as a pioneering educational theorist in his own right. Even before the publication of Darwin's evolutionary theory, Spencer was using naturalistic and scientific principles to urge a more practical and utilitarian curriculum. As a proponent of the principle of naturalism in education, Spencer followed in the tradition of Rousseau and Pestalozzi.

His advocacy of scientific study anticipated the modern school curriculum. Because he was so closely identified with social Darwinism and its highly individualistic and competitive ethic, Spencer has often been cited as representing the kind of social and educational theory that reformers such as Jane Addams (see Chapter 18) and John Dewey (see Chapter 19) opposed. Indeed, many of Addams and Dewey's socioeducational theories need to be seen as an important counterargument against Spencerianism. However, it is equally important to examine Spencer's unique educational contributions.

To see what Spencer was advocating in education, it is useful to examine what he was against. Spencer opposed the "public school" education that he neither experienced nor wanted to experience as a child. In these selective preparatory schools, boys were drilled in Latin and Greek grammar and literature. Advancing to Oxford and Cambridge, they continued to study the classics, literature, philosophy, and history. In the British educational tradition, this kind of study was supplemented by the milieu of living at the preparatory school. Here, one learned to play the game, learn the social graces, and become devoted to the school, a kind of preparatory social club for the larger gentlemen's network that controlled much of British life.

Herbert Spencer, educated by father and self, was not part of the educational milieu that produced cultivated English gentlemen, nor did he want to be part of what he regarded as an obsolete class. The liberally educated gentleman was, in Spencer's opinion, a superfluous person. The modern world, marked by science, technology, and engineering, needed specialists rather than generalists. Just as he opposed the dominant forms of secondary and higher education, Spencer also opposed primary and elementary schooling geared to memorization of textbooks and instilling religious dogmas. The education that he proposed brought together principles of naturalism and of science.

Spencer's best known work on education was his rationale for a new scientific curriculum, titled "What Knowledge Is of Most Worth?" published in 1855.[14] Spencer began by examining the historical conditions that had shaped education. He believed that schooling, from the primary level through higher education, was determined largely by tradition and routine. For example, the dominance of the Latin and Greek classics in the curriculum was largely a matter of tradition. These languages, useful in the theological and philosophical education of the medieval scholastics, no longer served a purpose in a modern industrial society. However, the social and educational establishments, wedded to the past, continued to refer to the ancient classics as the "mark of the educated man" and required them for admission to university study and for entry into governmental positions. Not only were the classical languages obsolete, they also took up time, money, and energy that could be better directed to the study of science, technology, and engineering.

Schooling, controlled by the vested interests of the landed aristocracy and established church, was also a means of social control. In schools, students were taught to conform to, not challenge, traditional expectations and roles. Individual initiative was repressed rather than liberated creatively. Spencer was a determined proponent of liberating individuals from social control, including that fostered by formal education.

Spencer observed that educational attainments such as certificates, diplomas, and degrees had become a kind of "paper chase" used to gain social status and prestige rather than for any instrumental value. The old form of classical education, monopolized by the upper classes, became the educational prize that the new middle class desired.

Rather than relying on tradition, custom, routine, and the desire for social status, Spencer argued there were important questions to be answered in establishing the curriculum:

1. Were not some subjects more important than others in generating added knowledge that was useful?
2. Should not the subjects be taught according to their importance?
3. Might not time be spent more effectively on some subjects than on others?

Using his engineer's mind, Spencer believed curriculum should be determined by estimating the time, money, and energy spent in teaching a subject and the consequences derived from its study: Did the particular subject pay its way?

To answer his overarching question, "What knowledge is of most worth?" Spencer raised a number of related questions to guide construction of the curriculum:

1. How should the human body be treated to maintain its health?
2. How should the human mind, the source of our rational powers, be treated?
3. How should our economic, social, political, and educational affairs be managed?
4. How should our children be reared and educated?
5. How should responsible citizens act?
6. What is the best use of natural resources?

Spencer's focusing questions provided a new rationale for constructing the curriculum that would have a decided influence on U.S. educators, especially those who believed that schooling should be responsive to human needs and produce economically and socially efficient persons.

To answer his own questions, Spencer began to categorize human activities into clusters that could be used as the basis for arranging the curriculum. He found the following clusters of activities, each related to the following areas:

1. Self-preservation—the physical health—of the human body.
2. The self-preservation of human life by providing the necessities of life such as earning a living.
3. Rearing and educating children.
4. Maintaining proper social and political relationships such as civic education.
5. Making time for miscellaneous leisure activities that provide enjoyment and satisfaction such as art, literature, drama, poetry, and music.

Like modern curriculum specialists, Spencer began the task of curriculum construction by identifying important human activities rather than subject matters. Once these activities had been identified, appropriate skills and subjects could be designed to prepare individuals to perform these activities. In examining Spencer's identification of important human activities, it should be noted that he established a priority based on their relationship to each other. The first activity—self-preservation—is necessary for the second—earning a living—and so on. The knowledge that was most useful in performing the first four categories of activities was scientific. The last category—miscellaneous activities—required physical health, economic security, and political order provided by the three preceding categories.

Spencer answered his query on knowledge with a resounding endorsement of the importance of science. Indeed, scientific knowledge could be applied to all the activities that human beings needed to perform. For example, knowledge from anatomy and physiology could be used to enhance physical health. Productivity in an industrial society required knowledge of the properties of raw materials that came from chemistry, botany, and zoology. In a technological society characterized by the application of scientific information to industrial processes, mathematics was indispensable. In a society of mass production and consumption, mathematics was a necessary tool for business—for estimating supply and demand, for conducting trade, and for accounting purposes. Spencer's arguments for a curriculum oriented to mathematics and science may seem commonplace today; however, in the second half of the nineteenth century, it was a bold proposal that challenged traditional education's emphasis on the classics, philosophy, theology, and literature.

In his argument for parenting education, Herbert Spencer was a modernist who anticipated an important contemporary trend. Spencer considered rearing and educating children to be one of the most important but seriously neglected human activities. In this category, Spencer addressed themes related to women's education and to general education.

At the time that Spencer wrote, working-class women in England received little education beyond primary schooling. Middle- and upper-class women enjoyed more educational opportunities but Spencer considered them misguided and misdirected. Women's finishing schools emphasized memorizing "dead languages, reading romantic novels, reciting poetry, and doing needlework," not the practical matters of life, especially child care and education.

In his commentary on the education of children, Spencer shows himself to be in the tradition of such naturalists in education as Rousseau and Pestalozzi. Just as natural laws governed nature and society, they determined patterns of human growth and development. Rather than relying on convention and custom, Spencer advised educators to base instruction on the laws of psychology. Psychology, according to Spencer, tells us that instruction is more effective when it is based on direct experience in the real world rather than on the abstract verbalism of books. Children need a store of experience before they can truly understand what they read.

Spencer recommended that parents and teachers follow a method that emphasized the following:

1. Beginning with children's immediate and direct experience.
2. Using concrete situations before moving to more abstract problems.
3. Letting children learn from the natural consequences of their actions rather than from artificial rewards and punishments.
4. Avoiding the rote memorization of highly verbal lessons.
5. Impressing on children the practical application of what they are learning.

These principles of instruction, Spencer reasoned, constituted the best preparation for dealing with life's real problems and for the later study of advanced mathematics and sciences.

Spencer had specific recommendations related to the proper education for citizens. Civic education, he advised, should be based on the principles of sociology rather than on history. History was too focused on the study of kings and queens, the lives of great men, and battles and military campaigns. Studying history filled the mind with irrelevant and isolated facts that had little value in explaining society and predicting the course of social change. Spencer advised educators to look to social science for the materials of civic education. Sociology, properly organized and taught, could inform us about how human societies had evolved, how institutions functioned, and how individuals related to the social whole. The same laws of change that governed the evolution of species also governed the evolution of society. Social change came about as the fittest individuals made efficient functional adaptations to a changing environment. The proper civic education, like education in general, would encourage the fittest to excel in the race of life. Such a civic education would convince individuals to avoid what Spencer regarded as the false promises of "do-gooders," socialists, and would-be reformers, If nature took its course as it was bound to do, the future would be a progressive and prosperous one for those persons who really mattered in the natural order of things.

Although Spencer must be recognized as a contributor to the natural and scientific education of children and as a pioneering figure in the study and organization of the curriculum, his educational goals were so precise and single-minded that he spent little time discussing the humanities, art, literature, and music. He recognized that arts and letters held potential for aesthetic experience, for recreation, and for leisure but did not see them to be instructive of human behavior. As science, industry, and technology advanced, more time would be available for leisure and recreation, he believed, but the arts and letters were not his major concern.

Conclusion: An Assessment

Herbert Spencer's theories need to be assessed in two dimensions: as social theory and as educational theory. As social theory, Spencer's social Darwinism appeared to be obsolete and irrelevant in the post-Depression and post-World War II eras. In the United Kingdom, the policies of the British Labour party created a welfare state in the decade-and-a-half after World War II. In the United States, Franklin Roosevelt's New Deal policies, designed to alleviate the unemployment of the Great Depression of the 1930s, established a policy of government intervention in the economy that was imitated by subsequent administrations, particularly Truman's Fair Deal, Kennedy's New Frontier, and Johnson's Great Society. In the western European democracies, especially in the Scandinavian nations, the social welfare state was firmly established. The Soviet Union, the socialist states of eastern Europe, and the People's Republic of China were following Marxist policies of total social planning and control. Indeed, Spencerianism and its emphasis on individualism and resistance to state regulation seemed a historical anachronism that was best suited to be an academic counterfoil to the modern state with its regulation, planning, and welfare programs.

In educational philosophy and theory, too, Spencer's social theory appeared to be an anachronism. The socially oriented wing of progressive education led by John Dewey appeared to have won the battle against Spencer's rugged individualism. Dewey's stress on cooperation, echoed by William H. Kilpatrick, rejected individualistic competition as socially unintelligent and economically wasteful. George Counts and other social reconstructionists argued that the school ought to take the lead, or at least join with progressive forces, in creating a new social order. In many respects, progressive social theory, politics, and education was a direct attack against Spencerian social Darwinism.

In the 1980s, however, certain Spencerian themes resurfaced. The neoconservatives in the United States stressed the need for a resurgent individualism and for the deregulation of the economy. Ronald Reagan's presidency called for a return to self-reliant individualism, inventiveness, and innovation. The social welfare programs in the United Kingdom were reduced by Prime Minister Margaret Thatcher. Even in the Soviet Union and its satellite states in eastern Europe, the face of Marxism was being changed by Gorbachev's *perestroika* and *glasnost*. Despite politics' ever-changing circumstances, 1980s and 1990s rhetoric seemed closer to Spencer's ideas than the twentieth century's earlier decades.

Apart from the political relevance that Spencer has today, his ideas exerted an important formative influence on U.S. educational theory. Perhaps it is more accurate to say that his ideas paralleled and theoretically reinforced some important shifts taking place in education in the United States. Spencer's appeal to educators was not unlike his popularity with industrialists and businessmen in the latter half of the nineteenth century.

Spencerianism affected U.S. education in its curricular and value emphasis. Spencer's arguments for a revised curriculum with the physical and natural sciences appealed to educators, particularly those who rebelled against the classically dominated curriculum. Concurrently, Spencer's social Darwinist ideology, with its emphasis on individual initiative, scientific inventiveness, and unregulated competition was congenial to the national mood of industrial expansion. Thus, in terms of its reliance on scientific subject matter and competitive values, Spencer's educational doctrines found a home in U.S. schooling.

Although the United States in the late nineteenth century was still a bastion of Evangelical Protestant religion, the same people who rejected Darwin's theory of evolution supported the competitive ethics of social Darwinism. In many respects, the values of social Darwinism were a modernized version of the older Protestant ethic of hard work, perseverance, diligence, and orderliness that were part of the public school's orientation.

Social Darwinism functioned as a kind of naturalistic Calvinism. The human relationship to nature was similar to the human condition in a predestined theology. Meant to be a time of testing, life was hard and demanding. Life's hardships were a means of developing and encouraging morality and character. In the theological sense, punishment was meted out to the negligent, the shiftless, the wasteful, and the inefficient. In the social Darwinism sense, economic punishment was the deserved consequence of such behavior. Poverty was a sign of personal irresponsibility, not of social conditions beyond the control of the individual.

The United States in the late nineteenth century seemed to many to be a nation enjoying economic prosperity because of individual inventiveness and competitive effort. This economic development occurred because of a government that allowed it to happen rather than trying to regulate it. If individuals were left to compete, then progress would occur. Although there might be immediate hardship for some, in the long run individual and social progress was made inevitable by the course of natural evolution. As Richard Hofstadter suggests, the reigning public policy assumption was that "all attempts to reform social processes were efforts to remedy the irremediable . . . that interfered with the wisdom of nature" and that would "lead only to degeneration."[15]

Spencer's emphasis on slow, gradual, and unhurried evolutionary social development found a parallel in his educational thinking. Spencer argued that learning, too, was a process of gradual and cumulative growth. In this regard, the hard-minded and seemingly hard-hearted evolutionary thinker was in agreement with the romantic Rousseau and the child-centered Pestalozzi and Froebel. Although they might vehemently reject Spencer's rugged individualism and highly competitive ethics, progressive educators in the United States could easily concur with his child-centered view of unhurried, gradual, and direct learning.

The Spencerian concept of unhurried evolutionary development carried immense educational implications. First, it argued for change in the curriculum and methods and challenged the verbalism of schools dominated by rote, routine, and custom. Second, in terms of broad educational policy and social goals, Spencer's evolutionary concept placed the school on the side of the socioeconomic status quo. Because deliberate efforts to bring about social change were not only ill advised but pernicious, the school should be a reflective agency rather than an agency of social change. The school functioned most efficiently when it identified the fittest and provided the educational challenges that caused them to rise to the upper socioeconomic echelons.

In another respect, the vogue of Spencerianism also affected how schools were run. Because the captain of industry was the dominant role model, industrial efficiency became a style for educational administrators. The phrase "run schools like a business" summed up the administrative style. Efficiency and effectiveness were prized by those who would try to create a science of education. Because science had the power to explain nature's fundamental law of evolution and social science explained how society functioned, the same kind of science could be applied to education.

Discussion Questions

1. How was social Darwinism a return to the theories of classical liberalism?
2. How was social Darwinism a radical departure from the earlier view of human development?
3. How were Spencer's ideas on society and education a reaction against the prevalent conditions in nineteenth century England?
4. How were Spencer's ideas on society and education an affirmation of certain of the new trends in nineteenth century England?
5. Why was the United States an especially receptive country for Spencer's ideas?
6. To what degree is there continuity in the ideas of Herbert Spencer with the earlier theories of Rousseau and Pestalozzi?
7. Analyze Spencer's strategy for curriculum construction.

Research and Essay Topics

1. In an essay, compare and contrast Herbert Spencer and John Dewey on their views of society and education.
2. Write a review essay of Herbert Spencer's "What Knowledge Is of Most Worth?"
3. In an essay, assess Spencer's influence on the curriculum.

4. In an outline form, sketch out a curriculum for secondary education that corresponds to Spencer's theory.

5. Prepare a lesson plan for use in an elementary class that reflects Spencer's educational ideas.

6. In a position paper, either defend or attack the statement: Spencer's views on society and education are irrelevant for contemporary U.S. education.

7. In an essay, consider the statement: Spencer's theory was socially conservative and educationally innovative.

Notes

1. C. E. Black, *The Dynamics of Modernization: A Study in Comparative History* (New York: Harper and Row, 1966).

2. Jonathan Howard, *Darwin* (New York: Oxford University Press, 1982). Also, see Michael Ruse, *The Darwinian Revolution* (Chicago: University of Chicago Press, 1979).

3. Carlton J. H. Hayes, *A Generation of Materialism: 1871–1900* (New York: Harper and Row, 1941), 9–13.

4. Neil C. Gillespie, *Charles Darwin and the Problem of Creation* (Chicago: University of Chicago Press, 1979).

5. Richard Hofstadter, *Social Darwinism in American Thought* (Boston: Beacon Press, 1958), 3–12.

6. George Daniels, ed., *Darwinism Comes to America* (Waltham, Mass.: Blaisdell Publishing Co., 1968).

7. For biographical information on Spencer, see *Herbert Spencer, An Autobiography,* 2 vols. (New York: D. Appleton and Co., 1904); David Duncan, *Life and Letters of Herbert Spencer,* 2 vols. (New York: D. Appleton and Co., 1908): Josiah Royce, *Herbert Spencer: An Estimate and Review,* (New York: Fox, Duffield and Co., 1904); and John D. Y. Peel, *Herbert Spencer: The Evolution of a Sociologist,* (New York: Basic Books, 1971).

8. Andreas M. Kazamias, ed., *Herbert Spencer on Education* (New York: Teachers College Press, Columbia University, 1966), 3.

9. William H. Hudson, *Herbert Spencer* (London: Archibald and Constable, 1908), 3–12.

10. Spencer, *An Autobiography,* vol. 1, 100.

11. Ibid.

12. Spencer, *An Autobiography,* vol. 2, 203.

13. Hofstadter, *Social Darwinism in American Thought,* 36–38.

14. There are many editions of Spencer's "What Knowledge Is of Most Worth?" This section of the chapter relies heavily on Kazamias, ed., *Herbert Spencer on Education,* 121–159.

15. Hofstadter, 6–7.

Suggestions for Further Reading

Beale, Truxtun, ed. *The Man Versus the State: A Collection of Essays by Herbert Spencer.* New York: Mitchell Kennerley, 1916.

Bibby, Cyril. *T. H. Huxley: Scientist, Humanist and Educator.* London: C. A. Watts and Co., 1959.

Bowne, Borden P. *Kant and Spencer: A Critical Exposition.* Port Washington, N.Y.: Kennikat Press, 1967.

Carnegie, Andrew. *Autobiography.* New York: Houghton Mifflin Co., 1920.

————. *The Gospel of Wealth and other Timely Essays.* Cambridge, Mass.: Harvard University Press, 1962.

Cashman, Sean D. *America in the Gilded Age.* New York: New York University Press, 1988.

Daniels, George, ed. *Darwinism Comes to America.* Waltham, Mass.: Blaisdell Publishing Co., 1968.

Elliot, Hugh. *Herbert Spencer.* New York: Henry Holt and Co., 1917.

Hacker, Louis. *The World of Andrew Carnegie, 1865-1901.* New York: J. B. Lippincott Co., 1968.

Hofstadter, Richard. *Social Darwinism in American Thought.* Boston: Beacon Press, 1958.

Huxley, Thomas H. *Man's Place in Nature.* Ann Arbor: University of Michigan Press, 1959.

Josephson, Matthew. *The Robber Barons.* New York: Harcourt Brace Jovanovich, 1934.

Kazamias, Andreas M., ed. *Herbert Spencer on Education.* New York: Teachers College Press, Teachers College, Columbia University, 1966.

Kennedy, James G. *Herbert Spencer.* Boston: G. K. Hall and Co., 1978.

Nakamura, Amy. *The Philosophy of Darwin and Spencer.* New York: Thor Publications, 1965.

Paxton, Nancy L. *George Eliot and Herbert Spencer: Feminism, Evolutionism, and the Reconstruction of Gender.* Princeton, N.J.: Princeton University Press, 1991.

Peel, John D. Y. *Herbert Spencer: The Evolution of a Sociologist.* New York: Basic Books, 1971.

————, ed. *On Social Evolution: Selected Writings.* Chicago: University of Chicago Press, 1972.

Persons, Stow. *Evolutionary Thought in America.* New Haven, Conn.: Yale University Press, 1950.

Rumney, Jay. *Herbert Spencer's Sociology: A Study in the History of Social Theory.* New York: Atherton Press, 1966.

Spencer, Herbert. *An Autobiography,* 2 vols. New York: D. Appleton and Co., 1904.

————. *Education: Intellectual, Moral and Physical.* New York: Appleton-Century-Crofts, 1889.

————. *Essays on Education and Kindred Subjects.* New York: AMS Press, 1977.

————. *Essays: Scientific, Political, and Speculative.* New York: D. Appleton Co., 1910.

————. *Facts and Comments.* New York: D. Appleton and Co., 1902.

————. *First Principles.* New York: D. Appleton and Co., 1880. New York: The Principles of Sociology. New York: D. Appleton and Co., 1897.

————. *Political Writings.* Cambridge, U.K.: Cambridge University Press, 1993.

————. *Social Statics.* New York: D. Appleton and Co., 1886.

Taylor, Michael W. *Men Versus the State: Herbert Spencer and Late Victorian Individualism.* New York: Oxford University Press, 1992.

CHAPTER 18

Jane Addams: Advocate of Socialized Education

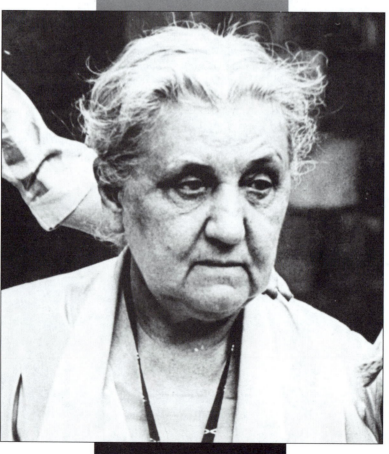

Photograph of Jane Addams (detail); reproduction from the collections of the Library of Congress.

In this chapter, we examine the life, educational philosophy, and contributions of Jane Addams (1860–1935), a founding figure in settlement-house work, social work, and the women's rights movement. Addams was also a pioneering personality in immigrant and urban education. She developed a philosophy of education, "socialized education," which bore some resemblance to the experimentalism and progressivism of John Dewey, who is featured in Chapter 19.

In this chapter, Addams' influence on U.S. education in the broad sense is discussed in its historical context and in terms of its continuing effect on educational philosophy and policy. First, the general social, political, and economic context in which Addams lived and worked is described. Second, Addams' biography, her education and career in settlement-house and social work, is analyzed to determine the evolution of her ideas. Third, the continuing effect of Addams' contributions to social and educational ideas in the United States is assessed. Through this analysis of context, biography, and situation, we shall see how the interrelated dynamics of educational history and philosophy worked to shape Addams' actions in the big city, urban melting pot that was late nineteenth- and early twentieth-century America.

To organize your thoughts as you read Chapter 18, you might focus on the following questions:

- What was the historical context in which Jane Addams worked?
- How did she interpret the major forces of immigration and urbanization that were transforming U.S. life?
- How did Addams's life, her educational biography, shape her social and educational philosophy?
- How did Addams' social and educational philosophy determine her social and educational policies and practices?
- What is the continuing impact of Addams' contributions to U.S. social and educational ideas?

The Historical Context of Addams' Life

Jane Addams was born in 1860, the year of Abraham Lincoln's election as president, and she died in 1935 during the middle year of the Great Depression when Franklin D. Roosevelt was in the White House. During the seventy-five years of her life, the United States was transformed from a predominantly rural and agricultural society to one that was urban and industrial. Addams' work as the founder of Hull House, a settlement house in Chicago, was centered in the vortex of this transformation of U.S. life. Her work can be best interpreted in light of the forces of urbanization and immigration. For the U.S. economy, society, and schools, the shift to an urban and industrial socioeconomic order posed serious policy issues.

After the Civil War ended in 1865, the process of urbanization accelerated and the metropolitan areas of New York, Chicago, Philadelphia, Boston, Detroit, Cleveland, and Los Angeles emerged as major population centers. The population growth of New York City vividly demonstrates the phenomenon of urbanization. In 1860,

New York's population was 1,174,000. By 1910, its population had reached 4,766,000. As of 1910, the population of Chicago, the nation's second largest city and the scene of Jane Addams' work, had reached 2,185,000. Chicago was followed by Philadelphia with a population of 1,549,000. By 1930, more than 25 percent of the population of the United States was living in the seven urban areas of New York, Chicago, Philadelphia, Boston, Detroit, Los Angeles, and Cleveland.[1]

The city of Chicago experienced a phenomenal growth. In 1870, five years after the end of the Civil War and one year after the great fire, Chicago's population was 298,977. In 1880, its population was 503,185. By 1900, the population had tripled—to 1,698,575. In 1910, it had reached 2,185,283. Twenty years later, Chicago had grown to 3,376,438.[2] The city in which Jane Addams was to gain fame as a social settlement worker, like the rest of the United States, was experiencing a continuing upward cycle of population growth.

A primary cause of the growth of urban America was the process of industrialization, which began in the mid-nineteenth century. Stimulated by the Civil War, industrialization accelerated throughout the rest of the century, reaching its peak in the early twentieth century. The factories and mills that produced iron, steel, textiles, and other products were located throughout the United States, but especially in the large urban areas.

Large cities attracted new residents who came looking for a better economic position and style of life. The new urbanites came from several locales. From 1860 to 1935, the number of Americans engaged in agriculture slowly declined while the industrial work force grew. There was a general migration of Americans from farm to city, especially among the young. Jane Addams was particularly concerned not only with the economic placement of these young people but with their moral and social adjustment as well. There was also a movement of African Americans from the rural South to the urban North. No longer did young blacks heed Booker T. Washington's admonition to "cast down your buckets where you are" but instead they migrated to the large northern cities in search of better jobs and improved educational opportunities. In addition there were the hundreds of thousands of immigrants, primarily from southern and eastern Europe, who abandoned their native lands for the United States.

In the urban centers, a large proportion of the population was composed of recent immigrants from Europe. Between 1870 and 1920, some 26,277,000 immigrants entered the United States. As of 1910, it was estimated that one-third of the population of America's eight largest cities were immigrants.[3]

A noticeable shift in the pattern of immigration occurred after 1890. Until that date, 85 percent of the European immigrants came from northern and western Europe, especially from Germany, the United Kingdom, Ireland, and Scandinavia. After 1890, the great majority of immigrants came from southern and eastern Europe, Italy, Russia, Austria-Hungary, and Greece. From the Hapsburg Empire of Austria-Hungary came a variety of ethnic and linguistic groups—Czechs, Slovaks, Slovenes, Croats, and Hungarians. Poles came from their native land, which was then subdivided and ruled by Austria-Hungary, Germany, and Russia. In addition to Russians, Ukranians, and Byelo-Russians, there was a large immigration of Jews from Russia who sought to escape from the tsarist government's anti-Semitic policies. To this great variety of ethnic groups were added Armenians, Assyrians, Syrians, and others from the Ottoman Empire. Serbians, Romanians, and Bulgarians came from the small independent Balkan monarchies. In the 1890s, the number of immigrants from southern and eastern Europe was 1,914,000. The next decade saw a virtual tidal wave of such immigrants as the total number reached 6,224,000. During the next ten years, marked by World War I, the number of immigrants from southern and eastern Europe declined to 2,370,000. After Congress enacted legislation to restrict immigration, the number declined severely.

In 1910, Chicago had a total population of 2,185,000, of whom 1,693,918 were either "foreign born" or classified as "white Foreign stock."[4] The massive influx of new immigrants to cities such as Chicago produced social and educational change and tension. First, there was the effect of demographic changes produced by the entry and location of large numbers of new residents in the cities. As is true of most social change of this magnitude, there was virtually little or no planning to accommodate the increasing population. Municipal governments faced added demands for more public health, sanitation, police and fire protection, public transportation, and educational services.

Public school systems in large urban areas, in particular, responded to the demands of an increased population of school-age children by becoming larger, more standardized, and often more bureaucratic. Using the model of efficient centralization developed by William Torrey Harris in St. Louis, large city systems turned to standardization to solve problems of organization, staffing, attendance, and instruction.[5] The corporate model of organization, which was used in business, was imitated in schools where the general superintendent became the chief organizational officer of the whole system and the building principal became the middle manager for the system. To move large numbers of children through the system with some measure of efficiency, students were organized in what was largely an age-specific graded pattern. Textbooks were standardized into series that corresponded to the prevailing graded pattern.

Trained school administrators attempted to impose the corporate model in the large cities but experienced difficulties that made the results of their labors uneven. Entrenched political machines, often supported by immigrant voting blocks, manipulated or controlled school boards. Machine politicians continued to use the schools for political patronage appointees. Often, schools were the scenes where corporate professionalism was locked in combat with political patronage over appointments and appropriations. Not only did professional administrators have to deal with machine politicians but they had to deal with the distrust of many immigrants who found the public schools to be hostile environments for their children. When Jane Addams served as a member of the Board of Education of the Chicago public schools, she encountered the tensions between professional educators and machine politicians.

Although the weight of sheer numbers had its effect, there were also myriad social and psychological tensions caused by the immigrants' relocation to a new environment and the reaction of the older stock of Americans to the newcomers. The population of the large cities lived in residential areas that tended to segregate on the basis of income, language, ethnicity, race, and often religion. Usually following a grid pattern, neighborhoods might be upper socioeconomic class, middle class, working class, or strictly ethnic. The first generation of immigrants tended to locate in neighborhoods where the residents were members of their own ethnic group. Such ethnic enclaves or urban ghettos were known as "Little Italy," "Greek town," "Polonia," or "Chinatown." There was little assimilation in these neighborhoods, with the exception of the workplace and the public school, because the residents spoke the same language, attended the same church, read the same foreign-language newspaper, and were members of the same fraternal societies and recreational organizations.

By settling in ethnic enclaves, new immigrants gained a sense of security in a strange land. The ethnic areas, which were often located in crowded areas of the city with housing in overcrowded tenements, were also a means by which the older stock of white, English-speaking Protestants isolated themselves from the immigrants. In part, the settlement in ethnic ghettos was self-imposed as the newly arriving immigrants clustered together to find a sense of psychological security with their own. Also in part, the social isolation of the new immigrants was imposed by the dominant social and economic groups in the society. Unlike the South where the racial segregation of blacks had the force of law, the social segregation of immigrants in the North was a de facto condition that resulted from economic forces and controls.

Progressives such as Jane Addams feared the division of society into ethnic and class enclaves was weakening the sense of community that sustained a shared commitment to a democratic society.[6] Although these progressives opposed the domination of the U.S. economy by big business monopolies and trusts, they also were concerned that the representative political processes and shared social concerns had been placed in jeopardy by the changes taking place in the United States at the turn of the century. They feared that the new immigrant masses, inexperienced in exercising the vote and unfamiliar with the processes of representative government, would become pawns of the big city political bosses. Immigrants could form voting blocs that could give the political machines pluralities over reform-minded progressives. They also feared that the division of society into ethnic and language blocs would reduce the commitment to the common good of the great society. In her work at Hull House and in her public speaking and writing, Addams attempted to find solutions to the problem of ethnic, class, and language divisiveness. Her problem was how to maintain the best that each unique heritage had to offer to America while uniting all Americans in a shared vision of the nation's meaning, purpose, and mission.

What would the pattern of life be in the United States in the twentieth century? Would it be one of a solid, uniform version of "Americanism" based on the values of white, Anglo-Saxon, English-speaking Protestants? Or was it possible to devise culturally pluralistic alternatives to such a version of the American heritage?

Ellwood P. Cubberley, one of the country's most respected educators, believed that the pattern of national life already had been established along the lines of an English-speaking and English-behaving society. The task that Cubberley gave to the country's educators was one of assimilating the immigrants into a monolithic version of American life. In his widely used book, *Changing Conceptions of Education,*

Cubberley contrasted the old with the new immigrants. The older immigrants, from western and northern Europe, were easy to assimilate, Cubberley wrote, "All except the Irish came from countries where general education prevailed and where progressive methods of agriculture, trade, and manufacturing had begun to supersede primitive methods." Continuing his favorable assessment of the older immigrants, Cubberley engaged in ethnic stereotyping when he said, "All were from race stock not very different from our own" and possessed a large degree of "courage, initiative, intelligence, adaptability and self-reliance." He praised as good additions to the national life the "good nature of the Irish, the intellectual thoroughness of the German, the respect for law and order of the English, and the thrift of the Scandinavian."[7] In contrast, Cubberley saw the newer immigrants from southern and eastern Europe as "illiterate, docile, lacking in self-reliance and initiative, and not possessing the Anglo-Teutonic conceptions of law, order, and government." Their coming to the United States, he wrote, has diluted "tremendously our national stock" and corrupted "our civic life." Coming down squarely for an Americanization program of assimilation, Cubberley advised educators:

> The great bulk of these people have settled in the cities of the North Atlantic and North Central states, and the problems of proper housing and living, moral and sanitary conditions, honest and decent government, and proper education have everywhere been made more difficult by their presence. Everywhere these people tend to settle in groups or settlements, and to set up here their national manners, customs, and observances. Our task is to break up these groups of people as a part of our American race, and to implant in their children, so far as it can be done, the Anglo-Saxon conception of righteousness, law and order, and popular government, and to awaken in them a reverence for our democratic institutions and for those things in our national life which we as a people hold to be of abiding worth.[8]

The process of assimilating immigrants that educators such as Cubberley prescribed began generally with the immigrants' children rather than the immigrants themselves. Although the children of many Roman Catholic immigrants attended bilingual and bicultural parochial schools that often operated along ethnic lines, the children of immigrants who went to public schools were indoctrinated according to the Americanist ideology. Although there were exceptions, instruction in the public schools was generally in English in most school districts. The immigrant children either learned English or failed.

Equally important to the formal curriculum, the milieu of the school, or the "hidden curriculum," reinforced the ethos and values of the dominant culture that Cubberley praised. Success in school and in the larger society, immigrant children were told, depended on their conformity to the patterns of the dominant group. These children learned that using a foreign language, speaking with an accent, observing different customs and holidays—those things that kept an ethnic heritage alive— were deviations that marked one as a member of an inferior group. Leonardo Covello, in recalling his school days in the New York public schools, reminisced that, "throughout my whole elementary school career, I do not recall one mention of Italy or the Italian language or what famous Italians had done in the world, with the possible exception of Columbus. . . . " Covello, who attended a public school in a predominantly Italian neighborhood, recalled childhood's bitter memories:

> We soon got the idea that "Italian" meant something inferior, and a barrier was erected between children of Italian origin and their parents. This was the accepted process of Americanization. We were becoming Americans by learning how to be ashamed of our parents.[9]

Although spokesmen of the dominant group such as Cubberley put forth the ideology of Americanization that controlled the public schools' policy on the education of immigrants, there were other voices who proposed alternative patterns. An articulate spokesman of cultural pluralism was Horace Kallen, who called for "a democracy of nationalities, co-operating voluntarily and autonomously in the enterprise of self-realization through the perfection of men according to their own kind." Although the common language of the United States was English, each nationality should be free to express "its emotional and voluntary life in its own language, in its own inevitable aesthetic and intellectual forms."[10]

The United States in which Jane Addams lived and worked was a nation gripped by this process of fundamental transformation. It was a country experiencing deep tensions between rural and urban patterns of life and between social configurations that reflected a version of one America or a range of cultural options. It was in this context that Addams sought to formulate a strategy to restore a sense of shared community that embraced diversity.

Jane Addams: Educator of Immigrants

Jane Addams, who would found Hull House and become a leading figure in social settlement work, was born on September 6, 1860, in Cedarville, a small Illinois town near the larger cities of Freeport and Rockford. She was the daughter of John Huy Addams, a prominent local businessman and Republican party leader, and Sarah Weber Addams. In addition to Jane, the Addamses had three older daughters and a son. Sarah Addams died when Jane was two years old. Her formative years were strongly influenced by her father, especially his dedication to public service.

When Jane was eight, John Addams married Anna Haldeman, a well-educated and cultivated widow, whose two sons joined the Addams household. Although she had little formal education, Anna Haldeman Addams considered herself an intellectual. She was a talented musician and an avid reader. Unlike Jane, who would challenge the traditional role of women as household managers, Anna assumed and relished the traditional role assigned to the Victorian woman.[11]

In 1877, seventeen-year-old Jane Addams entered Rockford Seminary, a women's college founded by Presbyterian and Congregational conventions in 1847. She enrolled in a wide range of courses such as Greek, Latin, German, geology,

astronomy, botany, medieval history, civil government, music, literature, Bible studies, and moral philosophy. As a student, she demonstrated an intellectual bent and
was interested in defining a career for herself that went beyond the traditional roles
of wife and mother. Although she completed the course work at Rockford Seminary, she did not receive the bachelor of arts degree until 1882, the year that Rockford Seminary began awarding degrees.[12]

In 1881, when Jane was twenty-one, her father died. He had been a dominant
influence on her and she deeply missed his guidance. She began to experience psychological depression and symptoms of ill health that plagued her periodically for the
next eight years. Feeling trapped by the conventional definition of the role of wife and
mother appropriate for a middle-class young woman at the turn of the century, she
sought to develop a self-definition that would give purpose to her life. Wandering
both physically and intellectually, she took two extended tours of Europe, where she
studied art, architecture, and German. While in England, she became acquainted
with Oxford students who for a time lived and worked among the poor.[13]

In particular, Jane Addams was impressed with the social settlement work of
Canon Samuel A. Barnett, a Church of England clergyman. In 1872, Barnett was
appointed vicar of St. Jude's, in London's Whitechapel district. St. Jude's was one
of the poorest parishes in London's West End. Enlisting the aid of Oxford University students, Barnett embarked on a program to improve the conditions of his
parishioners and other poverty-stricken residents. He established an evening school,
a fund to support children's excursions in the country, and an art gallery. After a
visit by Arnold Toynbee to St. Jude's in 1875, a settlement building was named
Toynbee Hall in his honor. Jane Addams was a frequent visitor at Toynbee Hall and
used Barnett's work as a prototype for Hull House.

While in Europe, Jane Addams determined the course of her life. She would work
among the disadvantaged in the United States in the same way that the young men of
Oxford were working among the poor and indigent of London. She and Ellen Gates
Starr, her longtime friend, established Hull House on Halsted and Polk Streets in
Chicago's near west side. Initially, she approached the polyglot ethnic groups of
Chicago's west side—the Italians, Bohemians, Poles, and Russian Jews—with the
attitude of a middle class reforming progressive who had benefitted from being a
child of the dominant group. She would share the middle-class behaviors and values
of a well-educated and traveled young lady with the less fortunate immigrants who
came to Hull House. By her knowledge and example, she would uplift them intellectually, morally, and spiritually. She and her associates designed a rather formal curriculum of lectures designed to inform those who came to the new settlement house.

Just as Addams planned to educate the immigrants, she in turn was educated by
them. Although moral uplift might be the ideal, the immigrants had practical needs.
They needed to find jobs, pay rent, obtain basic municipal services such as garbage
removal, find health care, and learn to educate their children. Could the genteel and
idealistic young lady from Rockford Seminary help them do things that were basic
to survival as strangers in a new land? Addams was a fast learner who quickly
redesigned her approach to settlement house work and the urban education of
immigrants. She learned from those whom she would teach. She planned the

instruction at Hull House to meet the needs of the immigrants who came there for help. Lectures became less formal and developed into a mutual sharing of information and skills.

Under Addams' leadership, Hull House became a multipurpose settlement house directly related to the lives of the people it served. Although some of its functions such as its adult education courses resembled schooling, much of Hull House's educational work was done informally as groups came together voluntarily to learn particular subjects or skills—the applied knowledge—they needed to survive in the new world. Because many of the neighborhood women needed child-care services, Hull House had a nursery school. Because many had no experience with U.S. finance, Addams established a savings bank. Hull House had a medical dispensary to fill the need for health care. The house was home to the Nineteenth Ward Improvement Club because the immigrants needed to become familiar with the U.S. political process. Because the neighborhood was a working class area, Hull House was used as a meeting place for trade unions. In addition to the activities and organizations that had an informal educational significance, Hull House offered adult education and college extension courses to those who sought to improve their lot through continuing education.

Hull House was also a place in which women could create a new identity and sense of meaning by pursuing careers. Jane Addams and Ellen Gates Starr were joined by other young women, such as Julia Lathrop, who would become the first chief of the Federal Children's Bureau, and Florence Kelley, who would become the chief factory inspector for the Illinois Bureau of Labor Statistics. These educated young women were feminist pioneers in the 1890s.[14]

An important feature of Hull House that went beyond the desire to help the less fortunate was that those who worked there added a knowledge base to their enthusiasm for personal and social reform. Addams and her associates were aided by some of the leading academicians of the progressive era. Richard T. Ely, professor of economics at the University of Wisconsin, visited and advised Addams on how to make the new settlement house an effective agency for reform. John Dewey, then a professor of philosophy, psychology, and pedagogy at the University of Chicago, became a trustee of Hull House and an adviser to Addams. Sociologists and educators from the University of Chicago were frequent visitors to Hull House, where they conducted research and lectured. Thus, Jane Addams moved her work at Hull House from that of the well-intentioned philanthropist to the social worker who used social science as a foundation for her work.[15]

Jane Addams as an Educational Theorist

In addition to founding Hull House and being a pioneering figure in U.S. social work, Jane Addams also developed what might be called a philosophy of education. Her philosophy of "socialized education" was based on her experiences at Hull House as an urban educator and an educator of immigrants. Although rooted in these experiences, her ideas had a broader relevance for the greater society. In this section of the chapter, we shall identify and examine some of Addams's ideas on education.

Jane Addams' socialized education was a multidimensional concept that related to the broad needs of U.S. society. It was designed to help restore a sense of community to a society gripped by a profound transformation from a rural to an urban economy. In particular, the sense of shared common experience was disintegrating as the older set of beliefs and values that had originated in rural America no longer held meaning for the growing urban population, especially the newer immigrants from southern and eastern Europe. Although the settlement house, a society in microcosm, might bring together working-class immigrants with educated reformers, there was a need to foster such social integration on a national scale.

For Addams, the settlement house, like the progressive school, was an experimental setting for solving the social, economic, psychological, and political problems of modern urban life. It was a place in which knowledge, based on the research of social scientists, could be applied to practical problems. As an educational agency, the role of the settlement house was to help people solve their problems by giving them the knowledge they needed. Importantly, it also introduced them to the method they needed to apply that knowledge to life.

Although Addams regarded the settlement house as a social and educational institution, she saw it in relationship to schools and universities rather than a rival or alternative to them. For her, the public school that provided basic skills and subjects was age specific to children and adolescents. It was also time specific to the instructional day and place specific to its location and attendance area. Although Addams recognized the important educative role of the public schools, she saw the education provided by the settlement house as not specific to age, time, or place. The settlement house's educational program reached out from its location into the community—into its housing, entertainment, work, and recreation. It dealt with adults as well as with children. Its hours of operation were flexible and arranged to meet the needs of its people rather than organized around a management prescription to be time and cost efficient.

Although she was a supporter of public schooling, Addams—like Dewey and other progressives—believed that many schools of the time had become removed from the realities and issues of a changing society. The schools' formalism and cultural remoteness often made them and their teachers alien intruders into the ethnic and immigrant community rather than full participants in the total educational process.[16]

Although professors such as Dewey, the philosopher and educator; Albion Small, the sociologist; and Richard Ely, the economist, advised Addams and participated in Hull House's educational program, they saw the university in a special and supportive but distinctive relationship to the settlement house. The settlement house and its population were not to be used for solely academic research. However, it did furnish a place and a population that yielded data that provided evidence for reform legislation to improve health care, working conditions, safety, and housing. True to the progressive model, the results of sociological and demographic research gave reform-minded legislators information on the need and the strategy for legislative reforms.

Jane Addams' concept of socialized education also related to conditions of work in an urban and industrialized society. Industrialization had radically altered the nature of work and the relationships of work to education. Industrialization relied heavily on the machine and the assembly line as the means of mass-producing products. Quickly and cheaply made in comparison with handicraft production, modern industrial manufacturing made a mass supply of goods available to a mass market of consumers. Work on the factory's assembly line was standardized and routine in that each person repeated the same task throughout the day. The industrial employee worked in isolation on only a part, rather than on the whole product as did the craftsman.

Industrialization also altered the concept and process of education for vocations. Until the Industrial Revolution, vocational education—geared to handicraft production—was based on apprenticeship. Apprenticeship was a form of vocational education in which the apprentice, the young person seeking to learn the trade, studied with a craftsman who had mastered the skills of the trade. With the exception of youngsters growing up on farms, industrialization also changed the way children perceived work. Often, handicraft production was done in the home and the children might be involved in the process. In any event, they saw their parents working and earning. In this way, they had direct experience with work and incomes. In an industrial society, work took place away from the home and usually out of the child's neighborhood environment. Work became a remote concept for many children.

For Jane Addams, the occupations of the modern industrial society needed to be infused with social purpose. She recognized the danger that modern industrial work could isolate and alienate workers socially. To avoid this, industrial workers needed the kind of education that would explore social relationships and connections and forge the interconnections that were needed to recreate a sense of community. Addams argued that industrial education, as a part of the larger concept of socialized education, should:

1. Examine the history of the development of industry and the relationship of the individual to it.
2. Develop a perspective in which industrial machines and processes were viewed as products in a long line of evolutionary development.
3. Constantly work at identifying the interrelationships between workers and their common enterprise.
4. Develop the interconnections that led to wholeness within the framework of specialization.[17]

Although she believed children should be introduced to a wide range of vocations as part of their education, Addams opposed child labor and premature vocational education. She believed child labor in factories, mills, and mines was a national disgrace and she worked for the enactment of compulsory school attendance laws and laws restricting child labor. Addams was part of a national network of like-minded progressives who worked for a wide range of reforms. In her fight against child labor, she organized the National Child Labor Committee.

Addams' opposition to child labor rested on her view of the importance of childhood as a crucial stage of human growth and development. Like Rousseau,

Pestalozzi, and Froebel, she believed that play was an important agency of child development. Further, elementary education, with its emphasis on basic skills, was a necessary precondition for subsequent education. Children who were deprived of the opportunities for play and schooling and put to work in the factory, were deprived of childhood and the experiences that contributed to growth and development. Further, it was unfair to children generally to divide them into upper- and middle-class children, who were to have the benefits of childhood, and working-class children, who were to go to work. For Addams, all children should enjoy the benefits of childhood.

It was also important that all children develop an understanding of what it meant to live in an industrialized and urban society. Schools needed to overcome their tendency toward formalism and isolation from social issues and realities. The school curriculum should be redesigned to provide youngsters with a broadened experience that explored children's immediate environment in a way that highlighted connections with an industrial society. For example, the curriculum might include work with the manual arts and industrial history and might encourage children to build small-scale reproductions of the industrial system.[18]

Immigrant education or ethnic education can be seen as a component of Jane Addams's philosophy of socialized education. In the same way that she was concerned about encouraging relationships between the individual and industrial society, so was she concerned about the relationships or connections that needed to be created between the immigrant family and the larger society. Hull House, she hoped, would be a bridge builder between the immigrants' Old World experiences and the challenges of acclimation to the New World environment.

Addams wanted the immigrants' adjustment to modern American urban and industrial society to take place through a continuum of experiences that linked the customs, traditions, and values of Europe with those of life in the United States. She feared that a sharp break or disjuncture would lead to isolation, alienation, or cultural shock. Unlike those who taught immigrant children to be Americans by first becoming ashamed of their parents and their inherited culture, Jane Addams wanted to reduce intergenerational conflict.

To demonstrate in a concrete way the importance and value of the immigrants' Old World cultural heritage, Addams created the Hull House Labor Museum. The handicraft skills and artifacts that characterized life in Europe were displayed, and in this setting, the young could experience—through demonstrations and displays—the skills, artistry, and traditions of their parents.[19] The Labor Museum was also a vehicle for interethnic and intercultural sharing and dialogue because not only did immigrants face hostility from the dominant culture, but they also encountered rivalry and antagonism from members of other ethnic and language groups. Finally, the exhibits and demonstrations in the Labor Museum illustrated the evolution and progress of industrialization in a way that linked the European handicraft past with the industrial present.

As a member of the Chicago Board of Education and as a writer and speaker on educational reform, Jane Addams urged the public schools to enter into a closer relationship with the immigrant family. She opposed the policy of Americanization into the dominant white, Anglo-Saxon, Protestant culture proposed by Cubberley and others. Addams had a more culturally pluralistic perspective of education. Anticipating contemporary programs of multicultural education, Addams wanted the schools to incorporate the history, customs, traditions, songs, crafts, and stories of the various ethnic groups into the curriculum.[20] Her multicultural perspective was congruent with her educational efforts. She wanted schools to emphasize the ecumenical values that ethnic and racial groups contributed to human civilization. Such a perspective would overcome, she believed, the narrow provincialism of a monolithic view of culture that tended to stereotype those of other languages and cultures.

As a young woman who broke through the restrictions society placed on women, Jane Addams throughout her life was an ardent advocate of women's rights and education. She was a prophet of the feminist revolution that would occur in the second half of the twentieth century. No longer were daughters and wives of the upper middle class to be social ornaments polished at finishing schools. The modern woman, Jane Addams wrote, was a person who possessed a sense of social commitment and obligation to make the world a better place.[21]

As a young woman, Jane Addams had to free herself from the constraints of family expectations and social restrictions. Daughters of middle-class families, she wrote, often found themselves in conflict situations between family claims and a sense of social responsibility. Although she did not forsake the importance of the family, Addams argued that modern women needed to participate in social life and work to solve social problems. To Addams and her associates, women needed the kind of education that equipped them to be full participants in modern life. Such an education involved not only knowledge but a sense of social obligation to those who were less fortunate.

Conclusion: An Assessment

Jane Addams' biography reveals her transformation from the reserved graduate of a small women's college into the progressive social reformer and pioneer of the settlement house movement. She shaped her own personal identity by serving others, not as a well-intentioned do-gooder but as a person who realized that she had a special mission in a country undergoing fundamental changes.

Like Theodore Roosevelt and John Dewey, Addams was a progressive thinker and doer. She was not a radical who wanted to alter the basic political, social, and educational institutions of the United States. She was, rather, a person who wanted to preserve basic institutions while creating new ones such as the settlement house and extending the social functions of existing ones such as schools. For her, the dominant need of the United States at the turn of the century was to transform its social thinking to meet the needs of a society being changed by the process of industrialization.

Addams' message was one of social service to meet the needs of a changing country. In her work at Hull House, Jane Addams took a view that knowledge should be applied in the service of persons. Like Dewey, she wanted to instrumentalize knowledge by making it apply to solving social problems. She valued research and the accumulation of information but believed that they needed to be applied to solve the problems of an industrial society.

Through her work at Hull House and her devotion to progressive causes, Jane Addams developed her philosophy of socialized education. Her conception of education was a kind of urban paedeia encompassing a wide range of educational agencies. It encompassed informal education related to the education of immigrants as well as more formal agencies such as schools and universities. It was designed to be universal in scope and to build more extensive relationships between human experience and the emergent industrial society. In particular, Addams' version of socialized education had special reference to the industrial and urban forces at work in late nineteenth and early twentieth-century America. Large cities, like Chicago, needed a renascent sense of community based on the realities of industrial society. Socialized education, both in and out of school, was to examine the history, processes, and consequences of industrialism. Above all, it was to combat the sense of isolation that industrial workers experienced when they were seen as mere appendages of machines.

At Hull House, Addams grew sensitive to the educational and social problems faced by immigrants and their children. Immigrant education was an important corollary of socialized education. In Addams's opinion, public schooling frequently separated immigrant children from their families. Addams sought to redress this tendency by urging public schools to encourage a sense of appreciation for the history, culture, traditions, and crafts of the immigrants' native countries. Contrary to such rigid Americanizers as Cubberley, Addams believed that valuing the immigrant contribution would not only reunite immigrant children with their families and their ethnic heritage but also would integrate them into American life.

In many ways, Jane Addams was as much a product of her past as she was the prophet of a new social order. The participatory democracy of the New England town meeting was to be extended to newer participants such as the immigrants who were flocking to the United States' growing cities. Although she wanted a broadened and more participatory American democracy, its outlines remained much the same but with more people involved. Through the process of a growing network of interconnections and interrelationships, the new community, the great society of an industrialized but still democratic America would arise.

Discussion Questions

1. How was Jane Addams' work at Hull House a response to the changing economic and demographic conditions of the United States?
2. Compare and contrast the assimilationist and the cultural pluralist positions on immigrant education.
3. What were the progressives' concerns about the nature of the American community?
4. How did key events in Jane Addams' life shape her social and educational philosophy?
5. What was the nature of Jane Addams' theory of socialized education?
6. Assess Jane Addams' contributions to U.S. social and educational ideas.

Research and Essay Topics

1. In an essay, examine the issues relating to the education of immigrants.
2. In an essay, compare and contrast the assimilationist and the cultural pluralist positions on immigrant education.
3. In a position paper, either defend or attack the statement: Jane Addams was a proponent of an assimilationist policy regarding the education of immigrants.
4. In an essay, examine Jane Addams' work at Hull House as an example of progressivism.
5. In an essay, analyze Jane Addams' departure from the conventional roles assigned to women at the beginning of the twentieth century.
6. In an essay, examine Hull House as both a nonformal and a formal educational institution.

Notes

1. Oscar Handlin, "The Immigrant Contribution," in Richard Leopold and Arthur Link, eds., *Problems in American History* (New York: Prentice Hall, 1952), 643–90.
2. Population Abstract of the United States (Washington, D.C.: U.S. Government Printing Office, 1980), 199.
3. Handlin.
4. *The People of Chicago* (Chicago: Department of Development and Planning, 1976), 27.
5. Salwyn E. Troen, *The Public and the Schools: Shaping the St. Louis System, 1838–1920* (Columbia: University of Missouri Press, 1975).
6. Robert M. Crunden, *Ministers of Reform: The Progressives' Achievement in American Civilization, 1889–1920* (Urbana, Ill.: University of Illinois Press, 1984).
7. Ellwood P. Cubberley, *Changing Conceptions of Education* (Boston: Houghton-Mifflin, 1907), 10–16.
8. Ibid.
9. Leonard Covello, with Guido D'Agostino, *The Teacher in the Urban Community: A Half Century in City Schools* (Totowa, NJ.: Littlefield, Adams and Co., 1970), 44–45.
10. Horace M. Kallen, *Cultural Pluralism and the American Idea: An Essay in Social Philosophy* (Philadelphia: University of Pennsylvania Press, 1956).
11. Allen F. Davis, *American Heroine: The Life and Legend of Jane Addams* (New York: Oxford University Press, 1973), 6–7.
12. Winifred E. Wise, *Jane Addams of Hull-House* (New York: Harcourt Brace and Jovanovich, 1935), 61–74, 77–80.
13. Ellen Condliffe Lagemann, ed., *Jane Addams on Education* (New York: Teachers College Press, Columbia University, 1985), 16–17.
14. Ibid., 25–26.
15. Ibid., 33–34.
16. Jane Addams, "A Function of the Social Settlement," *Annals of the American Academy of Political and Social Science* 13 (1899), 323–45.
17. Jane Addams, *Democracy and Social Ethics,* edited by Anne F. Scott (Cambridge, Mass.: Harvard University Press, 1964), 178–220.
18. Ibid.
19. Jane Addams, *Twenty Years at Hull-House* (New York: Macmillan Publishing Company, 1910).

20. Jane Addams, in Lagemann, *Jane Addams on Education,* 136–42.
21. Ibid., 64–73.

Suggestions for Further Reading

Addams, Jane. *Democracy and Social Ethics.* Edited by Anne F. Scott. Cambridge, Mass.: Harvard University Press, 1964.

———. *The Long Road of Woman's Memory.* New York: Macmillan Publishing Company, 1916.

———. *Newer Ideals of Peace.* New York: Macmillan Publishing Company, 1907.

———. *The Second Twenty Years at Hull-House.* New York: Macmillan Publishing Company, 1930.

———. *The Spirit of Youth and the City Street.* New York: Macmillan Publishing Company, 1909.

———. *Twenty Years at Hull-House.* New York: Macmillan Publishing Company, 1910.

Crunden, Robert M. *Ministers of Reform: The Progressives' Achievement in American Civilization, 1889-1920.* Urbana: University of Illinois Press, 1984.

Davis, Allen F. *American Heroine: The Life and Legend of Jane Addams.* New York: Oxford University Press, 1973.

———. *Spearheads for Reform: The Social Settlements and the Progressive Movement, 1890-1914.* New York: Oxford University Press, 1967.

Farrell, John C. *Beloved Lady: A History of Jane Addams' Ideas on Reform and Peace.* Baltimore: Johns Hopkins University Press, 1967.

Lagemann, Ellen Condliffe. *A Generation of Women: Education in the Lives of the Progressive Reformers.* Cambridge, Mass.: Harvard University Press, 1979.

Lagemann, Ellen Condliffe, ed. *Jane Addams on Education.* New York: Teachers College Press, Columbia University, 1985.

Linn, James W. *Jane Addams: A Biography.* New York: D. Appleton-Century, 1935.

John Dewey: Pragmatist Philosopher and Progressive Educator

Photograph of John Dewey; reproduction from the collections of the Library of Congress.

Chapter 19 examines the life, career, and educational contributions of John Dewey (1859–1952), one of America's most influential philosophers and educators. Dewey's ninety-three years spanned a series of momentous events that shaped the patterns of modern life. For example, Darwin published his *Origin of the Species* in the year of Dewey's birth. Two years later, the U.S. Civil War began. Dewey would later experience his nation's involvement in two World Wars. He would see the United States go through a great transformation from a predominantly rural and agricultural economy to one that was industrial and technological. He would live through the major political transformations of the progressive movement, the Great Depression, and the New Deal. Near the end of his life, the United States was one of two great world powers and humankind had entered the age of nuclear weapons and energy and space exploration. The fascinating characteristic of Dewey's work in philosophy and education was his rare ability to examine, reflect on, and incorporate the dynamics of a changing nation and world into philosophy of education.

Just as the United States and the world were changing during Dewey's life, relationships between educational institutions and society were also being altered. Dewey's pragmatic philosophy of education, experimentalism, would bridge and integrate the larger context of a changing world with the smaller setting of changing communities, neighborhoods, and schools.

In this chapter, Dewey's influence on U.S. society, philosophy, and education is examined in the historical context in which it originated and in terms of its enduring social and intellectual effect. First, the general social, political, and economic context in which Dewey lived and worked is described. Second, Dewey's biography, his education and career, is analyzed to determine the evolution of his ideas. Third, the continuing effect of Dewey's contributions to U.S. education is examined. By this analysis, we shall see how the sweep of major historical events contributed to shaping a leading thinker's educational philosophy. Dewey developed his educational philosophy as he experienced the great transformation of U.S. life that occurred as the nation moved from the nineteenth into the twentieth century. Originating in that historical context, Dewey's philosophy has left an enduring effect on pragmatism as an educational philosophy and on how we view the role of experience in education.

To help organize your thoughts as you read this chapter, you might focus on the following questions:

- What were the major trends in the historical context, the time and situation, in which Dewey lived?
- How did Dewey's life, his educational biography, shape his philosophy of education?
- How did Dewey's pragmatic philosophy influence his educational policies and practices?
- What is the enduring impact of Dewey's contributions to U.S. education?

The Historical Context of Dewey's Life

During the span of John Dewey's long life, politics, economics, society, and education experienced a great transformation in the United States and the world. Rather than attempting to follow the events that caused this change chronologically, this section of the chapter is organized around three major themes that shaped Dewey's world view and his philosophy of education:

1. The American temperament.
2. Selected U.S. political, social, and economic developments.
3. Educational developments that relate to the school and society.

To argue that a people in the course of their historical experience develop a national character is a much-discussed issue in anthropology and sociology. However, historically, groups of people over time do develop a sense of identity that creates a feeling of belonging. For the people of nations such as the United States, certain perceptions arise about what has happened and how these events help shape a national identity. At times, these group perceptions arise from concrete historical events and at other times they are based on longstanding myths. Although these myths may not be true historically, neither are they false. In fact, such myths may be powerful in creating the national ideology, those commonly held and shared ideas that vivify a feeling of identity, unity, and purpose.

In the American experience, a cluster of shared ideas has contributed to the national ideology. Among them are the effect of the westward-moving frontier, rugged individualism and entrepreneurship, and the role of the small-town community. There are many other formative ideas but, for the purpose of seeing how the American temperament influenced Dewey, these are significant. These three core ideas embrace both historical and mythic elements.

Although there were early Spanish settlements in what are now the southwestern states, the basic pattern of settlement in the United States moved from east to west. The conventional history textbook account told us that Americans first settled along the Atlantic coast in the thirteen original colonies and then moved westward in a series of settlements that occurred in the north and southwest territories east of the Mississippi River, then into the trans-Mississippi west.

Based on a demographic account of settlement, a historical interpretation of the frontier's effect on U.S. culture has developed. In *The Impact of the Frontier*, progressive historian Frederick Jackson Turner developed an interpretation that for many years was regarded as the definitive explanation of the rise of U.S. culture and character.[1] The general interpretation was that westward movement through a series of differing natural environments—coastal regions, forest lands, plains, deserts, and mountains—produced a flexible, egalitarian, and uniquely American disposition. Settlers in the western regions often found themselves in a wilderness environment. Free of the inherited mental residues of European traditionalism, Americans changed this environment, established farms and towns, and introduced their culture and institutions. As these westward-moving pioneers settled in new habitats, they too were changed by a series of interactive episodes with the environment. As a result, the American character became flexible, resourceful, and open to change. When he developed his philosophical version of pragmatism called experimentalism, Dewey captured this perceived propensity of Americans for change and incorporated it into his philosophy.

A second element in the American temperament is rugged individualism. This concept grew out of the myth that the frontier was settled by daring individuals and their families who fearlessly established homesteads in the wilderness. American individualism, often personified by the "mountain man," trapper, homesteader, and cowboy, referred to fiercely independent people who "did their own thing." The concept of frontier individualism was then blurred or merged with that of the "captain of industry," who, through entrepreneurial skills and resourcefulness, advanced U.S. industrialization while often amassing a great private fortune. The mythic conception of rugged individualism was interpreted to mean that success depended on individual initiative which was given free rein by the absence of government constraints or regulation.

Throughout his career but especially during the Depression of the 1930s, Dewey challenged what he regarded as the myth of rugged individualism. In *Individualism: Old and New*, he argued that the concept was used to block reform and a new, socially responsible version of individualism compatible with the reality of an interdependent industrial and technological society was needed.[2] The educational philosophy that Dewey developed stressed the importance of the group and shared activities and experiences in creating social intelligence.

Running through the American temperament has been a vision of community. Originating in the New England town, there emerged an idyllic Norman Rockwell-like portrait of "Our Town," a place that was a home where everyone knew each other, shared joys and sorrows, and cared about one another. Important in the daily life of the small town was the grocery store on Main Street, the church, and the school. Perhaps young John Dewey experienced such a version of small-town America in the Burlington, Vermont, of his youth. It probably seemed incongruous to him that the American temperament valued both rugged individualism and small-town togetherness.

In Dewey's thought, the theme of community, togetherness, and sharing was ever present. Like the polis of ancient Athens, the town hall was truly the cradle of U.S. democracy. Industrialization, technology, and the irresistible forces of modernization had made the older version of small-town American community obsolete. The need for community was too important to be abandoned, however. When Dewey developed his philosophical agenda for a renascent America, he incorporated a new and revitalized sense of community. It was one that retained the essence of face-to-face sharing but in the context of interdependency, industrialization, and technology. He would see the school as a miniature society that would be the catalyst for creating a new sense of community.

The principal events of the late nineteenth and early twentieth centuries that affected American and global society also shaped Dewey's world view and philosophy. Although he lived through two World Wars and a great economic depression, Dewey's emergence on the philosophical and educational scene coincided with the progressive movement in American life.[3]

A multifaceted phenomenon, the progressive movement occurred in the United States from 1890 to the U.S. entry into World War I in 1917. It was a movement that had social, political, economic, and educational consequences.[4] Because John

Dewey was positioned squarely within the framework of progressivism, especially in education, we shall examine the nature of the progressive movement and its effect on his philosophy and activities.

The longstanding historical interpretation of progressivism is that it was a movement to reform and revitalize U.S. life and institutions. By the 1880s and 1890s, reform-minded individuals realized that the United States faced a multitude of crucial issues. For example, a few large business corporations, especially in iron and steel, petroleum, and railroads, had secured virtually monopolistic control of the nation's economy and were influencing legislation at the local, state, and national levels at the expense of the public good. Progressive reformers sought to limit the power of the giant corporations by enacting and enforcing antitrust legislation.

Progressives were also concerned that certain businesses, such as the meat-packing industry and the drug and medicine industry, were selling products that were either unsanitary or dangerous to an individual's health. Upton Sinclair's expose of the meat-packing industry in Chicago is an example of progressive investigative journalism.[5] Progressive forces in the U.S. Congress, encouraged by President Theodore Roosevelt, enacted the Pure Food and Drug Act, which regulated these industries for the public health and welfare.

In U.S. political life, progressivism at the national level was associated with presidents such as Theodore Roosevelt and Woodrow Wilson. At the state level, it was often identified with leaders such as Governor Robert M. La Follette of Wisconsin. Progressives worked in local and state government to end control by political bosses. In some states, they sought to revitalize political processes by organizing campaigns to defeat or remove corrupt politicians from office. In some states, they enacted referendums by which citizens could place items on the ballot to be decided by popular vote. At the national level, progressives in both the Republican and Democratic parties sought to control trusts and monopolies, promote civil service reform, and other legislation of a reform nature.

In a broad sense, the progressive impulse in national life was educational. Progressivism meant the general populace had to be instilled with political consciousness and activism on behalf of reform and regulation. For example, President Woodrow Wilson, a former political science professor and president of Princeton University, believed that the chief executive had an educational role to perform in informing and instructing the nation's citizens.

At heart, progressivism was not a revolutionary movement that sought a radical transformation of the U.S. economic and political system. For example, it did not challenge the basic commitment to private enterprise but rather sought to ensure that the system was truly competitive. Neither did it challenge the essential framework of republican political institutions but wanted to ensure that they were genuinely representative and followed established constitutional processes.

Progressivism when applied to institutional life was highly procedural and process oriented. Its essential strategy was to:

1. Identify places where the economic, political, and educational institutions were not functioning properly and efficiently.

2. Investigate and research the problem areas with the belief that information could be used to structure solutions.
3. Develop and enact legislation designed to remedy the problem and provide the needed regulation so that the problem would not recur.
4. Enact the needed legislation so that it now became part of the general policies that governed the particular area in which the problem had initially occurred.

Progressive procedures essentially affirmed a belief that informed and enlightened citizens were capable of reforming and regulating their lives.

Those who worked on behalf of progressive reforms were basically white middle-class Protestants who came from northern European, particularly English, ethnic backgrounds. They were generally well-educated men and women who were willing to devote themselves to organizing and promoting reform causes. John Dewey, Jane Addams, and Woodrow Wilson fit this model well.[6] Those often missing from the progressive profile included immigrants from southern and eastern Europe, African Americans, and Hispanics.

Although the progressives have been conventionally seen as promoting a needed reform of U.S. life, some recent interpretations have viewed them as agents of social control. Based on their white Anglo-Saxon middle-class ideology, they are seen as trying to impose their values on the rest of the population, especially the new immigrants and first-generation ethnics. In particular, they are seen as using settlement houses and schools to impose the information, work skills, and values that would make working-class immigrants happily subordinate to the dominant, middle-class group. Critics of the group-centered education that John Dewey developed see it as a form of middle-class control by consensus. In other words, the progressives had a particular notion in mind of what the U.S. community should be, based on their own experiences. They were not willing to permit the emergence of a genuine culturally, ethnically, linguistically, and racially pluralistic society.

Although the progressive era had important formative effects on the development of Dewey's educational philosophy, the era of the Great Depression of the 1930s also shaped his outlook on life, society, and schools. During these years, Dewey was one of the "frontier thinkers" in education.[7] These individuals contributed to and were associated with an important journal, *The Social Frontier*, edited by George S. Counts. Dewey and the other frontier educators believed that U.S. political, social, economic, and educational institutions needed to be reconstructed in the light of the great technological changes that had taken place in U.S. and Western society. Essentially, they examined the basic themes of the American character identified earlier—frontier, individualism, and community—and sought to reshape them to fit the needs of a modern technological society. The frontier, they claimed, no longer meant the movement of people into geographical space. It now meant that people needed to create new frontiers in politics, society, the economy, and education. The old myth of rugged individualism also had to be reconstructed. In a modern technological society, it was wasteful, inefficient, and counterproductive to act on individual self-interests. Rather, it was important that the modern individual, although retaining the sense of personal freedom, be eager to cooperate in social, economic, and educational planning and implementation for the common good. Out of needed reconstruction would come a new sense of the American community. This new community would no longer be defined in geographical and spatial terms but would be based on an ever-expanding network of human interrelationships.

Dewey's contributions also need to be examined in terms of the major trends that had an effect on U.S. education, particularly schools, during his lifetime. In examining the educational context of Dewey's life, it is important to remember that he opposed the dichotomy that separated the school from society. He considered schools a part of society and not isolated from it. With this in mind, important movements such as progressivism and the social frontier had a significant effect on schooling.

By 1880, the public school system was institutionally and structurally in place. What Horace Mann had envisioned as a system of locally controlled and publicly supported schools, providing all the children of the community with a basic education, had been accomplished. However, many of the schools, like other institutions, had problems that reduced their effectiveness. For example, instruction had become very formal, often consisting of memorized recitations. In some cities, progressive investigative journalists found that key appointments in schools were politically rather than educationally determined.[8]

Progressive reformers sought to address these school-based problems in two ways: by curricular innovation and by educational expertise. Curricular reformers sought to improve the school's educational effectiveness by introducing innovations into the classroom. Rather than relying on teacher-directed recitations, these curricular progressives introduced a variety of innovations such as relating instruction to children's experience and needs; introducing the laboratory or experimental method as an instructional strategy; using field trips and excursions that involved visits to zoos, art galleries, parks, and museums; creating learning situations that encouraged collaborative social interaction; and relating instruction to broad social, political, and economic issues and problems. These trends were also part of Dewey's educational philosophy and practice.

Although some progressive educational reformers were working to introduce curricular reforms into the schools, others sought to make their functions more effective and efficient.[9] These administrative progressives believed that schools should be run by professional educators, not amateurs. They believed that professionally prepared administrators, superintendents and principals could use management techniques to make operating schools more efficient and businesslike. There were also educators who believed that a science of education could be devised and applied to instruction. Educators such as E. L. Thorndike believed that educational outcomes needed to be specified and measured.[10]

It was against this backdrop of social, political, economic, and educational developments that John Dewey developed his educational ideas and practices.

Dewey as a Pragmatist Philosopher and Progressive Educator

John Dewey was born in Burlington, Vermont, on October 20, 1859.[11] He was the son of Archibald Sprague Dewey and Lucina Artemisia Rich Dewey. Both of his parents were from rural farming families. They left farming to operate a family-owned grocery store in Burlington.[12] The Deweys were members of the Congregational church. Life in small-town Vermont had an important effect on Dewey who, throughout his life, cherished a vision of the face-to-face, town meeting type of community that existed in New England. This vision may have influenced his emphasis on the role of the community in shaping social intelligence and participation.

Dewey, a studious child, entered the local public elementary school in 1867. He studied the usual elementary subjects—reading, writing, spelling, arithmetic, history, and geography. In 1872, he began his secondary education in the Burlington high school, where he followed the college preparatory curriculum. Among his high school studies were Latin, Greek, French, English, mathematics, and literature.[13]

In 1875, Dewey entered the University of Vermont. The college curriculum, like the high school curriculum, was heavily oriented toward the classics. Dewey enrolled in such courses as Greek, Latin, rhetoric, and English literature. It was during his undergraduate years that Dewey developed his interest in political and social philosophy. He was especially interested in the positivism of Auguste Comte.[14]

After he was awarded his bachelor's degree in 1879, Dewey went to Oil City, Pennsylvania, as a high school teacher. Located east of Pittsburgh on the Allegheny River, Oil City was an important location for the drilling and shipping of petroleum to Pittsburgh for refining. Dewey taught Latin, algebra, and natural science in Oil City High School for two years. He then returned to Vermont where he took a teaching position at the Lake View Seminary in Charlotte. At the same time he pursued courses in philosophy at the University of Vermont and in 1881 received his master's degree.[15]

The next year, Dewey entered the new graduate institution, Johns Hopkins University, to pursue advanced study in philosophy. At the time, the university created by Daniel Coit Gilman was recognized as one of the leading research institutions in the United States. At the university, Gilman introduced the German research model in which a select group of graduate students worked in small seminars on specialized topics under the direction of a distinguished professor who was a recognized expert in the field.

At Johns Hopkins, Dewey worked under the direction of Professor George Sylvester Morris, a highly regarded interpreter of the German idealist philosopher Georg Wilhelm Hegel. Morris was the author of *A History of Philosophy from Thales to the Present*, in 1874, and *Hegel's Philosophy of the State and of History,* in 1887. Although Dewey would later reject the abstract metaphysics of Hegelianism when he fashioned his own experimentalist philosophy, his thinking did retain a propensity to reconcile apparent contradictions, or dualisms, into broad concepts such as experience, democracy, and community. Dewey's attraction to the Hegelian theme of a unifying "great community" continued. For him, the Hegelian ethical accentuation of human self-realization remained a guiding prospect but it was no longer to be reached spiritually.[16] Personal self-realization would be achieved in human experiences that were enlarged by social transactions that embraced democratic participation in the community.[17]

Dewey also studied with G. Stanley Hall, a pioneer in child and adolescent psychology. He completed a course with Charles S. Peirce, who was developing a new method of doing philosophy, called pragmaticism, which unlike abstract Hegelianism, stressed the consequences of thought when acted upon.[18]

In 1884, Dewey began his academic career on the faculty of the University of Michigan's philosophy department. At Ann Arbor, he met and wed Harriet Alice Chipman in 1886. The two shared mutual interests in intellectual and educational matters.

In 1888, Dewey went to the University of Minnesota as professor of mental and moral philosophy. Dewey, now a recognized academic philosopher, stayed at Minnesota for only one year. In 1889, he was back at the University of Michigan as head of the philosophy department. These career moves show that he was a sought-after professor who was using his prominence to rise up the academic ladder from instructor, to professor, to department head.

In 1894, Dewey was on the move again, accepting an appointment as chairman of the Department of Philosophy, Psychology, and Pedagogy at the University of Chicago. A new institution, the University of Chicago had been established only four years earlier with funds provided by the oil baron John D. Rockefeller Sr. The founding president of the University of Chicago was William Rainey Harper, who energetically recruited a faculty of distinguished professors to make his institution a leader in academic research and scholarly publication.[19]

The composition of Dewey's department at the University of Chicago was interesting in that by including professors of philosophy, psychology, and pedagogy, it brought together in one unit those disciplines with which Dewey would be involved for the rest of his career. The study of education as a university subject was still new. From the parent discipline, philosophy, would come the knowledge and insight needed for the philosophy of education. From psychology would come valuable contributions to educational psychology, child and adolescent development, and learning theory. Pedagogy—the traditional name given to principles of instruction—would become, with the foundations of philosophy and psychology, a broadened and enriched field of inquiry and application.

At the University of Chicago, Dewey established his famous Laboratory School.[20] In a school that enrolled children from age six to sixteen, Dewey developed insights into the education of children and tested them. A laboratory school to Dewey was an experimental school in which educational theories were to be tested. If validated in the actual experience of teaching and learning, those theories could be disseminated to a larger educational audience. Dewey described his Laboratory School as a "miniature society" and an "embryonic community" in which children learned by working together to solve problems. Dewey's school attracted the attention of educators during the years of its operation, 1896 to 1904, and his work continues to intrigue educational historians, philosophers, and curricular specialists. Disagreements between Dewey and Harper about the administration of the Laboratory School and other matters led to Dewey's resignation in 1904.

After a long tour of Europe, Dewey returned to the United States in 1905, where he accepted a position in the Department of Philosophy at Columbia University, a position he held until his retirement in 1930. At Columbia, Dewey formed a close association with a number of professors of education, including William Heard Kilpatrick, George S. Counts, and Harold Rugg, who were leading theorists of progressive education.

Dewey enjoyed an international reputation as a distinguished philosopher and educator. On several occasions, he lectured to audiences in foreign countries. From 1919 through 1921, when the political map of the world was being reshaped after World War I, Dewey delivered a series of lectures in major Japanese and Chinese cities. At the time of Dewey's lectures, China was struggling to become a democratic republic based on the principles of Sun Yat-sen. In 1928, Dewey visited the Soviet Union, which only eleven years earlier had overthrown its tsarist regime and established a Communist regime based on Marx's dialectical materialism. When Dewey was in the Soviet Union, its founder, Nikolai Lenin, had been dead four years and Joseph Stalin was consolidating his power in what later became a despotic tyranny. Dewey was a popular figure in the Soviet Union, which in seeking new patterns of education, had experimented with some of his ideas. When he spoke out against Stalinism a few years later, however, Dewey and his books were banned in the Soviet Union.

For twenty-two years after his retirement from Columbia University until his death in 1952, Dewey continued to speak up for social and educational reform and renewal. His reputation has remained that of a man committed to pragmatism and progressivism.

Dewey's Experimentalism

In this section, we turn to Dewey's contributions to educational philosophy by examining key ideas that emerged from his published books and articles. Because he was a prolific author, only some of his books shall be commented on.

As a philosopher, Dewey is associated with a group of U.S. philosophers including Charles S. Peirce, William James, and George H. Mead, who developed pragmatism. One of the central themes of pragmatism is that philosophy should attempt to solve human problems rather than be preoccupied with speculative metaphysics. Pragmatists assert that truth is tentative, a warranted assertion rather than universal and absolute. Further, truth is derived from human experience, which involves the testing or verification of an idea by acting upon it and determining if the consequences of such action resolve the particular problem. The pragmatist predilection to tentativeness, empiricism, and change can be contrasted with Plato's metaphysics (see Chapter 2). According to Platonic idealism, truth is based on unchanging and perfect ideas that are universally and eternally true. The goal of human cognition and behavior is conformity to these perfect ideas. As a philosophy, pragmatism fits the U.S. view, perhaps derived from the frontier experience, that sees life as interaction with changing sets of environmental conditions. For education, a goal based on pragmatism would be to create in learners an openness and willingness to accept the challenge of change.

To begin to analyze Dewey's philosophical position on human life within an ever-changing environment, we can turn to his book *The Quest for Certainty*.[21] In this book, Dewey examined Western philosophy's tendency to structure reality into two dimensions—one that was perfect and unchanging and the other that was temporary and changing. Philosophers such as Plato, arguing that reality was based on the form of the good, concentrated on a perfect world but neglected human experience.

Christian theologians emphasized a spiritual afterlife in heaven. The Western philosophical and theological tradition was the human being's way of denying his or her own death and disappearance by believing that a part of the human being, a spiritual essence or soul, would live forever. Based on this belief in two worlds, philosophy in the Western world emphasized the perfect world, which was beyond human experience, and ignored the reality of the world of everyday life. Directed to the empirical world of everyday experience, Dewey's pragmatism advised human beings to deal with the problems presented in this life.

The human quest for certainty resulted in a belief in two worlds and two dimensions of human nature—the physical, bodily nature and the spiritual or rational nature. What some philosophers called the higher and lower orders of human nature, Dewey rejected as a harmful dualism that separated mind and body and theory and practice. Dewey believed that mind and body came together to create human experience and theory and practice came together to solve the problems that arose in this experience. Rejecting dualistic philosophies, Dewey proposed a theory of knowledge based on the continuum of human experience that related rather than separated thinking and acting, fact and value, and intellect and emotion.[22]

The mind-body and theory-practice dualisms that Dewey sought to resolve had significant consequences for educational practice, especially curriculum. Traditional philosophers asserted that the mind and the pure theory derived from it were superior to solving the problems of life. According to this view, thinking was best when it stayed at the higher speculative plane. Pure theory was preferred to actually doing and making things, of discovering and inventing, and of resolving problems of politics, health, peace, and society. In such a traditional outlook, theory was superior to practice, the fine arts were better than the practical arts, liberal education was superior to vocational education, and so on. For Dewey, the challenge was to reconcile these longstanding dualisms into a unified flow of experience. The kind of education that emerged for him was unified and not segmented into separate categories. It was based on and related to human experience in the real world of the person interacting with the environment.

Instead of conjecturing a certain world, Dewey put human beings squarely within an uncertain world where they were faced with only one certainty—that everything would change. With the philosophical certainty of unchanging metaphysical categories gone, what was the human being to do in such a world? Dewey emphasized that human beings had the possibility of directing and controlling the course of change by using the scientific method. When an individual faced a personal problem or the group faced a social, political, or economic problem, the scientific method should be used to solve that problem and obtain the desired consequences.

Although informed by the bodies of scientific knowledge accumulated by experts, Dewey's concept of the scientific method was a broadly conceived procedure of scientific intelligence that was applicable to human affairs.[23] What was needed in education was to develop instructional strategies that would provide learners with a scientific method or process for controlling their destinies.

During the years of the progressive movement, Dewey developed his philosophy of education in three important books, *How We Think* (1910), *Interest and Effort in*

Education (1913), and *Democracy and Education* (1916), his most complete statement on educational philosophy.[24] From these works, we can gain further insights into Dewey's efforts to articulate a process-centered philosophy of education.

To understand how his philosophy of education evolved and to understand its implications, it is necessary to examine the effect on Dewey of certain major events. One of these crucial events was the publication of Darwinian theory.

Dewey was born in 1859, the year in which Charles Darwin's *The Origin of Species by Means of Natural Selection* was published. Darwin's theory of evolution postulated that the species of plant and animal life had evolved slowly over the course of time. This theory of adaptation to a changing environment contrasted with the literal view in the Bible's book of Genesis that the species had been created by God in their fixed and final form. Darwin's theory of evolution made an impression on Dewey, especially the emphasis of the adaptation of the species as a response to changing environmental conditions.

For Dewey, the concepts of the organism and the environment were most significant in formulating an experimentalist epistemology, or how we think, and an educational theory based on it. Somewhat similar to other simpler organisms, the human being was a living organism, physiologically composed of living tissue and possessing life-sustaining drives and impulses. The human organism, however, possessed a highly developed brain, making it a reflective creature who could hypothetically conjecture the consequences of a projected action and create plans of actions that enhanced life. Further, the human organism, with its thumb and movable forefinger, could make and use instruments. Every organism, including the human one, lived in an environment, a habitat, containing conditions that both supported and threatened life. For Dewey, life consisted of a series of connected and related interactive episodes that transpired between the human organism and its environment.

As Dewey saw it, human life was sustained through successful interactions with the environment. Instead of being pitted in an inexorable struggle with nature, Dewey advised that human beings instrumentally use nature to transform parts of the environment to increase life-sustaining possibilities. Through the use of scientific intelligence and collaborative social activity, people possess the possibility of using selected natural elements to solve problems caused by other aspects of the natural environment.[25]

Dewey called these interactive episodes "experience." Educational practice, influenced by Dewey's pragmatism, emphasizes the experience-based curriculum. In the interactive episode between the person and the environment, thinking occurs and from that education takes place. When the person encounters an obstacle or impediment to activity, a problematic situation arises. It is by resolving the problem that thinking occurs. Dewey designed a series of problem-solving steps that approximate what he considered to be the scientific method, broadly construed. Referred to as the "complete act of thought," Dewey's experimental or process-oriented method consisted of the following phases:

1. The person encounters something different, a new experience, that stops the flow of ongoing activity. It is in the context of this new element, or "deviant

particular," that the person finds himself or herself in a problematic situation. Note that the problematic situation can be used educationally when a student or group of students encounters a problem needing to be solved.

2. For the person to solve the problem, the element that is blocking activity must be located and defined. The question needs to be asked, "What is causing the problem?" Once a definition is posed, the person can begin to locate and solve the problem. In the educational situation, the ability to define the problem correctly is an important skill. The definitional phase of problem solving, if correctly done, will point the learner to the resources needed to solve the problem.

3. After the problem has been located and defined, it is then possible to gather information, do research, and consult previous experience that will shed light on the problem and point to its resolution. In the educational situation, this phase may involve researching in the library, conducting interviews, and collecting information. In this stage, the teacher functions as a resource person who facilitates students' research activities.

4. Now comes the conjectural stage in which tentative hypotheses of possible action are structured. The person or group reflects upon the possible action and mentally explores the consequences of action. Now the question becomes, "If I do this, what is likely to result?" In the educational situation, the goal is to develop reflective attitudes that contribute to planning skills. Such plans, called "ends in view," give direction to experience.

5. The last stage involves acting on the tentative hypothesis that is likely to resolve the problem by effecting the projected and desired consequences. If the problem is solved, the procedures of the complete act of thought have been followed correctly. If it is not resolved, the process needs to be reexamined to identify mistakes that may have interfered with its solution. If the problem is solved, the person resumes activity and adds the particular problem-solving episode to his or her network of experience. In the educational situation, the final step of the problem-solving sequence is of crucial importance. Unlike many conventional school situations where problem solving stays strictly academic, Dewey's process requires action, an empirical test. It is this stage that avoids the dualism of theory and practice and integrates them into complete thinking.

For Dewey, the complete act of thought, or problem solving according to the scientific method, is the proper way to think and also the most effective strategy for teaching and learning. Because of his emphasis on the scientific method, Dewey's version of pragmatism is called experimentalism. Life and learning involve a series of experiments by which human beings seek to gain control and direction of their interactions with their environment. This process is an active, ongoing, cumulative flow of human experience that unites the episodes of the past with those of the present to give direction and control over the future.

In addition to emphasizing the scientific method, Dewey's experimentalism also accentuates the person as a member of society. For Dewey, human intelligence is socially acquired as people interact with each other in solving problems in their environment. The social environment contains all of the sociocultural dimensions that the human race has created over time—political, economic, and educational infrastructures and processes as well as artistic, philosophical, and religious forms. The human group possesses the possibilities for developing and enriching shared intelligence.

As indicated earlier, Dewey and other progressives were searching to develop strategies to revitalize the American conception of the community. They wanted to preserve the face-to-face, shared experiences they believed had once characterized small-town America. However, they realized that the sense of community needed to be reconstructed to meet the requirements of an interdependent, technological, and industrial society.

For Dewey, a genuine sense of community arose through three stages: common sharing, communication, and community itself. In the first stage, the group shares common objects and pursues common activities. This is the beginning of a sense of "we feeling" or group identification. Because they use common instruments to attain common goals, the members of the group develop ways of talking about their common endeavors. When individuals communicate, they assume the perspective of the other person in developing their own understanding and behavior. Communication thus develops a commonly shared context; this context, in turn, frames the basis of community.[26] This sense of mutuality and reciprocity in making and doing, in planning and implementing, leads to a sense of full sharing in the community.

Just as he opposed metaphysically based value criteria, Dewey disputed the prevalent classical liberal orientation in U.S. society that argued that values were based on individual self-interest. He also combatted the trend in which the general community was fractured into contentious special interest groups. He saw human beings as communal participants who defined and tested collective goals.[27] In U.S. political life, Dewey was a proponent of grass-roots, face-to-face, participatory democracy.

Dewey saw U.S. society and culture as composed of smaller communities which resided within a broader encompassing community. Each of the smaller communities—racial, ethnic, gender—has its own common context, communication, and sense of membership. Each has a potentially enriching contribution to make to the greater community. While the smaller cultural communities could be expected to differ with each other on some matters, it was crucial to the welfare of the larger community, the great society, especially to its democratic processes and values that these disagreements occur within a communal framework and not degenerate into noncommunal conflict. The resolution of communal conflicts meant that they could be resolved in a procedural, nonviolent, nondestructive way. The larger community, the greater society, was one governed by commonly shared processes of conflict resolution. For Dewey, there was a communal, or communitarian, core of beliefs and values. This core, however, rested on commonly agreed to and shared democratic procedures.

In applying Dewey's general theory of community to schooling, the group should be envisioned as possessing immense educational potentialities. Collaborative group problem solving, planning, and implementation reduces the isolation of the individual from others and through mutual activities produces an enriched social intelligence. Barriers to full human association block free interaction. They impede the possibilities of individuals and groups to contribute to cultural growth by mutual sharing experience.[28] Dewey's emphasis on the group of learners is revealed in his early work at the University of Chicago Laboratory School, which he called a "miniature society . . . an embryonic community."

As a true progressive, Dewey advocated a democratic society as the environment most conducive for the application of the scientific method and for the creation of a truly sharing community. In fact, his choice of a title—*Democracy and Education*—for his most complete rendition of his philosophy of education reveals his emphasis on democratic processes. Although his view of democracy was undoubtedly shaped by his life and education in the United States, democracy for Dewey was more than political institutions. Democracy was a way of life that was free of those absolutes that blocked truly experimental inquiry. No subject, custom, or value was so sacrosanct that it was to escape inquiry. Further, the social setting was to be free of coercive and authoritarian persons who would jeopardize freedom of thought, inquiry, and experimentation.

Dewey's conception of the school curriculum integrated both the experimental qualities of the scientific method and the educative role of the group. Unlike the conventional curriculum, which was organized around tool skills such as reading, writing, and arithmetic and academic subject matter disciplines such as history, mathematics, and chemistry, Dewey structured the school's program around three broad focusing sets of activities: making and doing, history and geography, and science. It should be noted that the scientific method broadly conceived as the complete act of thought was used throughout these sets of activities.

Making and doing referred to the kinds of activities that children did in their first years of school. These activities led children from their immediate families and homes into the larger society. At school, children might sweep the floor, water plants, set the table for lunch, and go on shopping trips. These activities were similar to the kinds of things they did at home. Home experiences led easily into school experiences without isolating either from each other. The stage of making and doing was followed by history and geography. These areas of inquiry were not taught as conventional academic subjects but rather were designed to expand children's perspective into time and space. The third stage of curriculum—science—was broadly construed to mean the investigation of the various subject matter disciplines, not in insolation from each other, but in terms of what they could provide to solve problems.

By having students solve problems using the scientific method and group processes, Dewey believed they would gain a sense of reflective inquiry and practical intelligence. Dewey's experimentalism also carried the values that would underlie the new and still undefined, reconstructed U.S. community. Those who experienced an experimentalist education were to be eager to direct the course of change, flexible in their attitudes and dispositions, willing to experiment and to question inherited traditions and values, and socially involved and tolerant of others—participants in formulating a broad social consensus.

Conclusion: An Assessment

John Dewey's experimentalism has had a pervasive influence on U.S. society and education. In a general sense, his thinking was part of the progressive era that brought about a new way of viewing politics, law, art, and education. His philosophy contributed to a sense of inquiry that examined institutions and values in their response to the changing circumstances of life in the United States. For those who accepted the experimental mode, the question was, "How well does this institution or value satisfy the needs of a rapidly changing society?" No longer could institutions and values rest on traditionalism and maintenance of the status quo.

In education and in schools, Dewey's influence was broad and significant. Education was now construed as a process of intelligently solving problems using the scientific method rather than the study and mastery of bodies of knowledge organized into subjects. Especially in teacher education, Dewey and his academic disciples, many of whom were graduates of Columbia University's Teachers College, had their greatest effect. From these experimentalist educators, prospective teachers learned about the importance of the group, about the use of inquiry methods, and about the need for activities and projects.

Even though Dewey's name was gaining recognition as the leading U.S. philosopher of education at home and abroad, there was a reluctance on the part of many teachers to implement experimentalism as a working philosophy of education. Some members of the public and some professional educators who saw the curriculum as a stable body of academic subjects and values as constant rather than relative were antagonistic to Dewey's philosophy.

In some schools, teachers skimmed the surface of Dewey's philosophy and borrowed selectively certain key words and phrases such as "learning by doing," "the activity method," "problem solving," and "children's interests and needs" and designed units and lessons around them. These educators found a certain liberating appeal in these specific parts of Dewey's work without accepting his whole philosophy. Sometimes they did not accept Dewey's entire philosophy because they did not understand his difficult and often confusing prose. Others understood what Dewey was saying but accepted only parts of it. Brought up in traditional values, they did not want to sacrifice what they believed were timeless standards of academic integrity and patriotism. They did not want to examine those values that made their lives and work intellectually comfortable.

Others opposed Dewey's philosophy because of their own differing convictions. To those who saw Western civilization as derived from and resting on the universals of Judeo-Christian culture, Dewey's philosophy encouraged a dangerous relativism. Regardless of changing time and circumstances, there were certain truths that would be forever valid and certain values that would be universally applicable. For them, good and bad and right and wrong were not dependent on changing circumstances and situations but were the moral standards that schools should perennially convey to the young of each generation.

In addition to those who opposed Dewey's relativism, there were educators—especially the essentialists such as William Bagley in the 1930s, Arthur Bestor in the 1950s, and William Bennett in the 1990s—who argued that Dewey's educational philosophy was weakening the schools' primary purpose. For the essentialists and the proponents of basic education, the school's purpose was fundamentally academic. Under the direction of well-educated teachers, the school was to teach the young the basic skills of reading, writing, and arithmetic, and the fundamental intellectual disciplines of English and foreign languages, history, mathematics, and science. Anything else that was added to the school's function would dilute its primary mission, the proponents of basic education argued.

Dewey's work then was important enough to enlist dedicated disciples and equally sincere opponents. Although his philosophy differed in many fundamental ways from Plato, it can be said that Dewey shared some things with the ancient Greek philosopher. Education was so powerful and so potent a force that it could not be relegated to the school's four walls. It was, after all, the great cultural force that had the possibility of creating the new American Paideia, the great society of a renascent community.

Discussion Questions

1. What factors in the U.S. historical experience contributed to the pragmatic temperament?
2. How did the progressive movement contribute to efforts to reform U.S. society and education?
3. According to Dewey, how is the inherited concept of individualism in conflict with modern society?
4. What was Dewey's reaction to philosophical and educational dualism?
5. What is Dewey's complete act of thought?
6. How were Dewey and other progressive theorists trying to create a new concept of community?
7. Describe Dewey's work at the University of Chicago Laboratory School.
8. Apply Dewey's concepts of the common, communication, and community to the current debates over multiculturalism and bilingualism in education.

Research and Essay Topics

1. In an opinion paper, present your views on the question, Is the U.S. character still pragmatic and experimental?
2. Develop a character analysis of John Dewey.
3. In a paper, write a character sketch of a typical progressive reformer.
4. In an essay, comment on the evidences of dualism in contemporary education.
5. Prepare an extended review of Dewey's *Democracy and Education*.
6. Design a lesson plan that follows Dewey's complete act of thought of problem solving.
7. In an essay, analyze the contemporary conditions of the U.S. community.

Notes

1. Frederick Jackson Turner, "The Significance of History," *Wisconsin Journal of Education* 21 (October 1891), 230–34.
2. John Dewey, *Individualism Old and New* (New York: Capricorn Books, 1962), 74–100.
3. Lawrence A. Cremin, *The Transformation of the School: Progressivism in American Education, 1876–1975* (New York: Alfred A. Knopf, 1962).

4. Among general treatments of progressivism are J. Leonard Bates, *The United States, 1898–1928: Progressivism and a Society in Transition* (New York: McGraw-Hill Book Co., 1976); Lewis L. Gould, ed., *The Progressive Era* (New York: Syracuse University Press, 1974); and Arthur Mann, *The Progressive Era* (Hinsdale, Ill.: Dryden Press, 1975).

5. Robert M. Crunden, *Ministers of Reform: The Progressives' Achievement in American Civilization, 1889–1920* (Urbana: University of Illinois Press, 1984), 94–96.

6. Ibid., 3–15.

7. Lawrence J. Dennis, *George S. Counts and Charles A. Beard: Collaborators for Change* (Albany, N.Y.: State University of New York Press, 1989), 117–21.

8. Cremin, 3–7.

9. Raymond E. Callahan, *Cult of Efficiency* (Chicago: University of Chicago Press, 1962), 55–67, 126–29, 144–59.

10. Geraldine M. Joncich, ed., *Psychology and the Science of Education: Selected Writings of Edward L. Thorndike* (New York: Teachers College, Columbia University Press, 1962).

11. Biographical studies of Dewey are George Dykhuizen, *The Life and Mind of John Dewey* (Carbondale: Southern Illinois University Press, 1973); Neil Coughlan, *Young John Dewey: An Essay in American Intellectual History* (Chicago: University of Chicago Press, 1975); Robert B. Westbrook, *John Dewey and American Democracy* (Ithaca, N.Y.: Cornell University Press, 1991).

12. Dykhuizen, 4–9.

13. Ibid.

14. Ibid. 11–18.

15. Ibid., 19–23.

16. Westbrook, 42–43.

17. Walter Feinberg, "Dewey and Democracy at the Dawn of the Twenty-first Century," *Educational Theory*, 43, No. 2 (Spring 1993), 199.

18. Dykhuizen, 27–31.

19. Thomas W. Goodspeed, *A History of the University of Chicago: The First Quarter-Century* (Chicago: University of Chicago Press, 1972), 98–104.

20. For Dewey's laboratory school, see Arthur G. Wirth, *John Dewey As Educator: His Design for Working in Education (1894–1904)* (New York: John Wiley and Sons, 1966) and Herbert M. Kliebard, *The Struggle for the American Curriculum 1893-1958* (Boston and London: Routledge & Kegan Paul, 1986).

21. John Dewey, *The Quest for Certainty: A Study of the Relation of Knowledge and Action* (New York: G.P. Putnam's Sons, 1960).

22. Hilary Putnam and Ruth Anna Putnam, "Education for Democracy," *Educational Theory*, 43, No. 4 (Fall 1993), 364.

23. Westbrook, 141.

24. John Dewey, *Democracy and Education: An Introduction to the Philosophy of Education* (New York: Macmillan Publishing Co., 1964).

25. Fineberg, 204–5.

26. Sandra Rosenthal, "Democracy and Education: A Deweyan Approach," *Educational Theory*, 43, No. 4 (Fall 1993), 377.

27. Putnam and Putnam, 196.

28. Ibid., 364.

Suggestions for Further Reading

Cambell, James. *The Community Reconstructs: The Meaning of Pragmatic Social Thought.* Urbana, Ill.: University of Illinois Press, 1992.

Chambliss, Joseph J. *The Influence of Plato and Aristotle on John Dewey's Philosophy*. Lewiston: E. Mellen Press, 1990.

Coughlan, Neil. *Young John Dewey: An Essay in American Intellectual History*. Chicago: University of Chicago Press, 1975.

Dewey, John. *A Common Faith*. New Haven, Conn.: Yale University Press, 1934.

———. *Democracy and Education: An Introduction to the Philosophy of Education*. New York: Macmillan Publishing Company, 1964.

———. *Experience and Education*. New York: Collier Books, 1963.

———. *Individualism Old and New*. New York: Capricorn Books, 1962.

———. *Lectures on Ethics, 1900–1901*. Carbondale, Ill.: Southern Illinois University Press, 1991.

———. *Liberalism and Social Action*. New York: Capricorn Books, 1963.

———. *Philosophy & Education in Their Historic Relations*. Boulder, Colo.: Westview Press, 1993.

———. *The Political Writings*. Indianapolis: Hackett Publishing Co., 1993.

———. *The Quest for Certainty: A Study of the Relation of Knowledge and Action*. New York: G. P. Putnam's Sons, 1960.

Diggins, John P. *The Promise of Pragmatism: Modernism and the Crisis of Knowledge and Authority*. Chicago: University of Chicago Press, 1994.

Dykhuizen, George. *The Life and Mind of John Dewey*. Carbondale, Ill.: Southern Illinois University Press, 1973.

Feffer, Andrew. *The Chicago Pragmatists and American Progressivism*. Ithaca, N.Y.: Cornell University Press, 1993.

Gunn, Giles B. *Thinking Across the American Grain: Ideology, Intellect, and the New Pragmatism*. Chicago: University of Chicago Press, 1992.

Hendley, Brian P. *Dewey, Russell, Whitehead: Philosophers as Educators*. Carbondale, Ill.: Southern Illinois University Press, 1986.

Hickman, Larry A. *John Dewey's Pragmatic Technology*. Bloomington, Ind.: Indiana University Press, 1990.

Hook, Sidney. *John Dewey: An Intellectual Portrait*. Westport, Conn.: Greenwood Press, 1971.

Kliebard, Herbart M. *The Struggle for the American Curriculum 1893–1958*. Boston and London: Routledge & Kegan Paul, 1986.

Kulp, Christoper B. *The End of Epistemology: Dewey and His Current Allies on the Spectator Theory of Knowledge*. Westport, Conn.: Greenwood Press, 1992.

Kurtz, Paul. *Philosophical Essays in Pragmatic Naturalism*. Buffalo, N.Y.: Prometheus Books, 1990.

Paringer, William A. *John Dewey and the Paradox of Liberal Reform*. Albany, N.Y.: State University of New York Press, 1990.

Putnam, Hilary. *Pragmatism: An Open Question*. Cambridge, Mass.: Blackwell, 1995.

Rawls, John. *Political Liberalism*. New York: Columbia University Press, 1993.

Rice, Daniel F. *Reinhold Niebuhr and John Dewey: An American Odyssey*. Albany, N.Y.: State University of New York Press, 1992.

Rochbert-Halton, Eugene. *Meaning and Modernity: Social Theory in the Pragmatic Attitude*. Chicago: University of Chicago Press, 1986.

Rockefeller, Steven C. *John Dewey: Religious Faith and Democratic Humanism*. New York: Columbia University Press, 1991.

Ryan, Alan. *John Dewey and the High Tide of American Liberalism*. New York: W. W. Norton & Co., 1995.

Shusterman, Richard. *Pragmatic Aesthetics: Living Beauty, Rethinking Art*. Cambridge, Mass.: Blackwell, 1992.

Sleeper, R. W. *The Necessity of Pragmatism: John Dewey's Conception of Philosophy*. New Haven: Yale University Press, 1986.

Smiley, Marion. *Moral Responsibility and the Boundaries of Community: Power and Accountability from a Pragmatic Point of View*. Chicago: University of Chicago Press, 1992.

Stuhr, John J., ed. *Philosophy and the Reconstruction of Culture: Pragmatic Essays After Dewey*. Albany: State University of New York Press, 1993.

Welchman, Jennifer. *Dewey's Ethical Thought*. Ithaca, N.Y.: Cornell University Press, 1995.

West, Cornel. *The American Evasion of Philosophy: A Genealogy of Pragmatism*. Madison, Wisc.: University of Wisconsin Press, 1989.

Westbrook, Robert B. *John Dewey and American Democracy*. Ithaca, N.Y.: Cornell University Press, 1991.

Wirth, Arthur G. *John Dewey as Educator: His Design for Work in Education (1894–1904)*. New York: John Wiley and Sons, 1966.

Xu, Di. *A Comparison of the Educational Ideas and Practices of John Dewey and Mao Zedong in China: Is School Society or Society School?* San Francisco: Mellen Research University Press, 1992.

María Montessori: Proponent of Early Childhood Education

Photograph of Maria Montessori; from the National Archives.

In this chapter, we examine the life, educational philosophy, instructional methods, and contributions of Maria Montessori (1870–1952), a commanding leader in early childhood education. Montessori developed a distinctive method of early childhood education that enjoys implementation in countries around the world. She was a highly motivated person who successfully broke through many of the barriers limiting educational opportunities for women in the late nineteenth and early twentieth centuries.

Montessori's influence on early childhood education is discussed in its historical context and in terms of its enduring effect on educational philosophy, policy, and practice. First, the general social, political, economic, intellectual, and educational milieu of postrisorgimento Italy in which Montessori lived and worked is described. Many of the conditions that affected the lives of women in late nineteenth century Italy were also found in other western European nations and in the United States. Second, Montessori's biography, her background and career, is analyzed to determine the forces that contributed to shaping her educational ideas. Third, the Montessori method is considered in terms of its foundations and its implications for teaching and learning. Fourth, the continuing effect of Montessori's contributions is assessed. This analysis of the life, times, and contributions of Maria Montessori is designed to illustrate the interaction of a leading educator's biography with the development of her educational theory. For example, Montessori's educational philosophy and method emerged as she gained insights from her work in medicine, anthropology, and pedagogy. Her multidisciplinary approach to education led her to develop an educational method designed to educate the whole child—physically, mentally, and emotionally.

To organize your thoughts as you read this chapter, you might focus on the following questions:

- What were the major trends in the historical context, the culture of postrisorgimento Italy, in which Montessori lived and worked?
- How did Montessori's background, education, and career, her biography, shape her philosophy and method of education?
- How did Montessori's educational philosophy influence her educational policies and practices?
- What is Montessori's enduring influence on education in general and on early childhood education in particular?

The Historical Context of Montessori's Life

Maria Montessori was born only ten years after Italy became a united nation. Italian unification, under the royal House of Savoy, came as a result of the movement known as the "risorgimento." Spokesmen for the risorgimento, such as Camillo Cavour and Giuseppe Garibaldi, although from opposite ends of the political spectrum, were united in their desire that the various small states and principalities located on the Italian peninsula should form one country. By 1860, the political goals of the risorgimento had been accomplished. Garibaldi's volunteer army, the Carbonari, had toppled the old Bourbon kingdom of the two Sicilies and the armies of Piedmont-Sardinia had brought Victor Emmanuel to the throne of Italy, a constitutional monarchy.

Essentially, the new Italy was a product of the forces of liberalism and nationalism. Nationalists like Garibaldi wanted Italy to take its place in the political sun. Liberals such as Cavour wanted an Italy that would industrialize and modernize its economy. Although these forces enjoyed political success, there were strong conservative pockets of opinion that were uneasy about the new Italy. Serious opposition came from the pope, who opposed the annexation of the papal states to Italy, refusing to acknowledge the political reality that a united Italy presented. The pope regarded himself as the "prisoner of the Vatican." This created a dilemma for Roman Catholics in Italy such as the Montessori family who wanted to remain loyal to the pope, the head of their church, and to their king, the head of their state. Maria Montessori's uncle, Antonio Stoppani, a noted Roman Catholic priest, called for reconciliation between church and state. Maria's father, Alessandro Montessori, although remaining a committed Catholic, took a position in the new state's civil service.

Postrisorgimento Italy experienced the processes of modernization and development. Strong regional differences remained in Italy, especially the tension between the slowly industrializing north and the strongly agricultural and traditional south. Internal migration brought large numbers of former peasants to cities such as Milan and Rome to find better jobs and improve their economic conditions. In these cities, tenement districts arose to house the industrial underclass. It would be in one of these poverty-stricken districts of Rome, San Lorenzo, that Montessori would establish her first Casa dei Bambini, or Children's House. Anticipating by nearly 100 years such contemporary approaches to early childhood education as Operation Head Start in the United States, Montessori realized the crucial importance that the education of a child's early years held for later success.

The Italy in which Montessori was born was still very much the traditional, conservative Italy. In such a society, the roles that one would play were inherited across time and generations. *La famiglia,* the family, was a paramount institution that was often the Italians' primary source of identification, loyalty, and commitment. To family was added the determining factor of socioeconomic class. Although industrialization and modernization were beginning to exert peripheral modifications on Italian society, a person's education and career remained largely determined by family background and social status. The children of peasants were destined to take their parents' place on the farms and landed estates of Italy. The sons of the middle class were likely to become overseers of estates, managers of businesses, or engaged in commerce. Children of the landed aristocracy would continue to enjoy the benefits of inherited wealth that made them a leisure class.

If the positions of the males in Italian society were determined by family and class, the roles of women were even more fixed by custom and tradition. Although membership in a particular class was a conditioning factor, women were expected to become the central sustaining force in their families as wives and mothers. With their roles so determined, higher and professional education were not usually accessible to women. Indeed, social sanctions were an even more potent factor in limiting women's career choices. Society allowed and economic necessity required women of the lower socioeconomic classes to work as agricultural, domestic, or factory laborers. Daughters of the lower middle class might become elementary school teachers or nurses. Young women of the aristocracy might attend finishing schools or convent schools to learn art, music, and literature. However, Maria Montessori would challenge nineteenth century Italy's social and educational conventions. She would enter a technical secondary school to study engineering and the University of Rome's Medical School to become a doctor.

The Italian educational system in the late nineteenth century followed the continental European pattern of being heavily class determined. The Cassati Law provided for the establishment of primary or elementary schools. Compulsory education laws were not rigorously enforced, however. Italy, especially in the southern regions, had a high percentage of illiterates. At the secondary level, the schools were specialized into the highly academic college preparatory school, the *liceo,* and into a range of technical and vocational schools. Only a very small number were admitted to university studies. As a member of the middle class, Montessori had the opportunity to complete elementary school. Her determination to pursue a technical secondary education and medical school, however, were a radical departure from the educational expectations of young women at the time.

In addition to the socioeducational milieu of late nineteenth century Italy, an important aspect of the general historical context in which Montessori worked relates to the conditions and development of early childhood education. At the time that she developed her educational philosophy, conventional schooling, especially at the primary level, was dominated by the classroom teacher as the central instructional agent. Under the direction of the teacher, children followed instructional routines centered on the study and usually the memorization of textbooks, recitation, and dictation. In Italian schools, the children often used a single textbook that combined in one volume all the subjects taught—reading, writing, arithmetic, history, and geography. Like schools throughout the Western world, recitation was the favored method of instruction. Children stood when questioned by the teacher and provided accurately memorized responses from the textbook. Italian schools, in particular, featured dictation, in which students would copy word for word statements made by the teacher. Each letter of the alphabet had to be placed squarely in a small box marked on a copy book. This was the kind of elementary school Montessori attended as a child. Although it provided basic literary and mathematical skills, it stressed routine and discouraged spontaneity and creativity. When Montessori devised her unique approach to education, she developed a new pattern for schools that, although not sacrificing order and structure, did encourage the joy of spontaneous learning.

The world of educational theory that Montessori entered at the close of the nineteenth century and the early years of the twentieth century was undergoing some fundamental changes. Although school practices still were dominated by textbooks and recitations, educational theorists such as Rousseau, Pestalozzi, and Froebel had provided new insights into children's nature and education. In his theory of natural education, Rousseau had called for liberating children from oppressive social conventions (see Chapter 9). Pestalozzi had combined elements of emotional security for children and sensory training into his educational theory (see Chapter 10). Froebel stressed the inner forces of human nature that were to be developed in an educational environment that encouraged learning through self-activity (see Chapter 15). In her studies of the history of education and of pedagogy, Montessori was familiar with those important educational theories that related to early childhood education. Although they each contained something of value, she found them to be inadequate. Rousseau's wild romanticism ignored the need for educational structures although recognizing the importance of stages of development. Pestalozzi's object lesson had become too formalized and mechanical. Froebel's philosophical idealism caused his kindergarten to be steeped in a mysticism that was not grounded in modern science and psychology. Montessori would seek to remedy those deficiencies in educational theory.

Montessori was not alone in her work to develop new insights into early childhood education. In the United States, progressive educators were also working on new insights and methods. Colonel Francis Parker stressed nature studies, field trips, and activities at his school in Chicago and in approaches to teacher preparation. John Dewey, the experimentalist philosopher, was using his University of Chicago Laboratory School as a center to test new ideas about teaching and learning (see Chapter 19). William Heard Kilpatrick, who would become an early critic of Montessori, was attempting to implement Dewey's pragmatic philosophy into the project method. These progressive educators, who would become dominant figures in U.S. educational theory, were taking a different path in early childhood education from the one Montessori would follow. The progressives came to stress the school as a socially oriented embryonic society in which children learned by using the scientific method in a permissive environment. Enthusiastically calling for democracy in education, the progressives denied the role of absolute principles and urged freedom and activity. The approach to education that Montessori developed was quite different from the one the progressives were advocating in the United States.

Still another way of looking at childhood was emerging in Europe. In his development of psychoanalytic psychology, Sigmund Freud was coming to recognize the role that the irrational played in human growth and development. He was finding that childhood was more than spontaneous freedom and imitative play that Rousseau, Pestalozzi, and Froebel had suggested. It was more than the opportunity to become democratic participants in an open-ended society as the U.S. progressives were urging. For Freud, whose ideas were just beginning to reshape the conception of child nature, early childhood was also a time of sexual feelings and societal repressions that shaped the human being's psyche.

It was in this context of a new political Italy—changing but still retaining much of the binding force of custom and tradition—that Montessori was born and educated. It was in this era of changing ideas on education that she made her mark. We now turn to a biography of Montessori.

Maria Montessori: Pioneer in Early Childhood Education

Maria Montessori was born in Chiaravalle, Italy, a hill town overlooking the Adriatic Sea in the Ancona province, on August 31, 1870. She was the daughter of Alessandro Montessori, a civil servant in the Italian government, and Renilde Stoppani, a well-educated young woman. Signor Montessori, who had fought in the battles for Italian unification, was a decorated army veteran who retained his military bearing throughout his life. He exemplified the conservative temperament and values of an "old-fashioned gentleman." Maria's mother was a niece of Father Antonio Stoppani, a scholar-priest, who enjoyed an academic reputation as a naturalist and geologist. A liberal Catholic, Father Stoppani urged a policy of reconciliation between the Catholic church and the government of the new Italian state. Signor Montessori was employed as the business manager in the tobacco industry, a state monopoly.[1] Maria Montessori came from a solidly middle class Italian family whose father enjoyed a secure economic position. Like many Italians of their class, the Montessoris were committed to both the Catholic church and the new Italian state, despite the estrangement between the papacy and the government.

The Montessori family moved to Rome in 1875. Here, in one of the most important centers of Western civilization, Maria, the family's only child, was enrolled in the state elementary school located on the Via di San Nicolo da Tolentino. Her education was monitored carefully by her parents, especially her father, who encouraged her study of mathematics.

At age 12, Maria displayed what would become her characteristic independence by declaring her intention of entering a technical secondary school. For a girl to attend a technical school was a radical departure from the general Italian educational pattern in which many lower-class girls ended their formal education with completion of elementary school, whereas middle-class girls might attend a normal school or a finishing school.

In 1883, the 13-year-old Maria enrolled in the Regia Scuola Technica Michelangelo Buonarroti, a state technical school under the jurisdiction of the National Ministry of Education. Following the continental European pattern, Italian secondary schools were divided into a variety of specialized institutions such as the classical college preparatory school, the *liceo,* or technical institutes for technology, engineering, art, agriculture, and commerce. As a student in the Scuola Technica, Maria pursued a seven-year curriculum, which had been approved by the ministry and included Italian literature, French, mathematics such as algebra and geometry, sciences such as chemistry and physics, history, and geography. Instruction followed the conventional method of attending lectures, memorizing textbooks, and responding to the instructors' questions with structured recitations. The rigid structure stressed routine rather than individualized learning or self-development. Upon completing her studies at the Scuola Technica, Maria Montessori entered the Regio Instituto Technico Leonardo da Vinci to pursue engineering studies.

In 1890, Montessori made a significant career choice, which was once again a departure from Italian traditional educational practices. She left her engineering studies to enter medical school. She had the distinction of being the first woman to be admitted to the University of Rome's School of Medicine. Because medical studies were male dominated as was the medical profession, Montessori encountered regulations and practices that discriminated against women. For example, she could not enter a classroom until all the male students had taken their seats. Because dissection of the human body was regarded unseemly for a woman, she was allowed to do her laboratory work in anatomy only in the evenings when the male students were no longer present. Despite these gender-based restrictions, she proved to be an academically talented student, winning scholarships in surgery, pathology, and medicine.[2]

During her last two years of medical school, Montessori interned in the Children's Pediatric Hospital, an experience that moved her in the direction that would be her lifelong occupation. In 1896, Montessori, now 26, became the first woman in Italy to be awarded the degree of doctor of medicine. After graduating from medical school, she accepted a position at the University's San Giovanni Hospital and also began a private medical practice. Intrigued by research questions, she joined the University of Rome's Clinica Psichiatrica as a voluntary assistant and conducted special investigations of mental illness. Her research at the Clinica Psichiatrica caused her to read widely in the literature on mental illnesses and psychological disorders.

Her investigations of psychological disorders led her to the works of Jean-Marc Gaspard Itard (1774–1838) and Edouard Seguin (1812–1880), two early French psychologists who had worked with mentally deficient children. Seguin was a physician who had founded the Hospice de Dicetre, a Paris training school for children with mental disabilities. In his work with these children, Seguin used several techniques that would be used by Montessori, such as basing instruction on developmental stages, using didactic training materials, and training children to perform practical skills so that they could achieve some degree of independence.[3] Sequin's pioneering efforts in special education stimulated Montessori to delve more deeply into education. She now came to believe that mental deficiency was a problem that required a special kind of education and not only medical treatment.

At the Clinica Psichiatrica, Montessori worked with Giuseppe Montesano, a young physician with whom she developed a close personal relationship. There is academic speculation as to whether Mario Montessori—her protege—was the couple's son or if he was an adopted child. In any event, Mario Montessori was first publicly presented as her nephew and then as her adopted son.[4] Mario Montessori would be significant in continuing to publicize and implement the Montessori method after Maria's death in 1952.

Strongly motivated to examine the theoretical foundations of education, Maria Montessori decided to return to the University of Rome for further and more advanced studies. She now devoted her attention to studying psychology, anthropology, educational history and philosophy, and pedagogical principles. She began to theorize that Seguin's work with mentally disabled children, especially his concepts of developmental stages, was applicable to the education of all children.

Between 1904 and 1908, Montessori lectured at the University of Rome's School of Pedagogy. A popular lecturer, Montessori developed a following among the students because of her highly motivated and energetic presentations. Because she could draw from a variety of disciplines, ranging from medicine to anthropology and psychology, she gave her students a breadth of knowledge that was unusual at the time. She published her lectures as *Pedagogical Anthropology,* a book that combined insights from pediatric medicine, child psychology, and cultural anthropology and applied it to children's development and education.[5] What was beginning to emerge at this stage in Montessori's development as an educational theorist was a holistic conception of education that drew from a number of academic disciplines. Montessori took a transdisciplinary approach to early childhood education.

Montessori was not content with being a university lecturer and academic theoretician, however. She was convinced that her theory of the child's holistic development could be applied to schools, making them into effective centers of education. She opened her first school, the Casa dei Bambini, which enrolled children from ages 3 to 7, in a large tenement in Rome's poverty-ridden San Lorenzo district on January 6, 1907. Based upon her conception that children's freedom to learn was best accomplished in a structured and orderly environment, Montessori insisted that those attending her school and their parents should follow some explicit regulations. Despite their poverty, Montessori held that the children should come to school with clean bodies and clothing. They were also to bring with them a clean smock or apron, which remains a characteristic feature of Italian early childhood education. Believing that schools were most effective when they were closely linked to the children's homes and families, parents were expected to demonstrate interest and support in their children's education.

Within these guidelines, Montessori began her work at the Children's House. Both in terms of Montessori's theory and the actual physical location of the school, the Children's House was to be a school-home that was in close proximity to the children's family homes. Striving to connect school, society, and family, the Casa dei Bambini was designed to provide a school within a home. Parents were encouraged to visit the school and share in the educational life of their children.

Like John Dewey, Montessori exercised great care in making sure that the school's physical arrangements, the tables, chairs, and apparatus, were suited to children's needs rather than adult preferences. Even more than Dewey, Montessori stressed the educative role of the structured environment. She did not want the classroom and its furniture to limit the children's freedom of movement, as was frequently the case in the traditional school. Tables and chairs were sized according to children's heights and weights. Washstands were positioned so that they were accessible to the younger children. Further, the classrooms were lined with low cupboards where children could reach instructional materials and also take responsibility for returning them to their proper location. The Montessori school was designed to cultivate children's sensory skills and manual dexterity, to allow them a degree of choice within a structured environment, and to cultivate independence and self-assurance in performing skills.

Montessori's conception of the role of the teacher varied from that of the traditional school. Whereas teachers in conventional elementary schools occupied the center of the educational stage as the focal point for the children's attention, Montessori's teacher—or "directress"—was considered a guide for students. She was trained in the Montessori method and assisted children in their own self-development.[6]

Instruction in Montessori's school rested on the principle of encouraging children's growth at crucial times in their development, called "sensitive periods." These sensitive periods were particularly relevant to certain kinds of learning activities such as exercising motor skills, language learning, and social adaptation. In these sensitive periods, the children performed activities and used self-correcting didactic materials and apparatus. The use of these materials was based on Montessori's belief that children would acquire self-discipline and self-reliance by becoming aware of their mistakes and repeating a particular task until it was done correctly.

Montessori's success at the initial Casa dei Bambini led to the establishment of three more schools in Rome, one of which was founded in a middle-class area of the city. Her success in Rome gained the attention of the Societa Umanitaria, the Humanitarian Society of Italy, which began to popularize and provide some financial support for the Montessori method. With the society's support, a Montessori school was established in Milan, Italy's leading industrial city. It is interesting to note that several significant educational innovations such as Pestalozzi's method and the Head Start approach in the United States were initially designed to educate socially and economically disadvantaged children. As the new methods attained a reputation for getting results, they were then quickly borrowed by the middle and upper classes. The same phenomenon was now taking place with Montessori's method.

By 1910, Montessori had gained a reputation as a significant and innovative educator in her native Italy. She also was beginning to attract attention in educational circles in other European nations and in the United States. It was at this point in her career that she faced the problem of how to disseminate and perpetuate an educational innovation. This question is one that still intrigues educational innovators. Those who would reform education face two major problems. One, schools tend to be formal institutions governed by tradition and routine. When an educational innovation is introduced in a school setting, it tends to be formalized by the system and loses the unique quality that made it an innovation in the first place. However, unless the innovation finds its way into and becomes part of the institutional setting, it lies at the periphery of the educational enterprise. Two, educational innovators often attract enthusiastic but untrained or ill-disciplined disciples. When they are not in close proximity to the innovator, they often distort the innovation. Although the distortion may be unintentional, it nevertheless is an alteration that may cause the innovation to miscarry and have educational consequences other than those intended.

To reach larger audiences. Montessori used two established means of diffusing her method: lecturing and public speaking, and publication. As a university professor, Montessori was an adept lecturer and used that method to her advantage. As her reputation grew, she became a popular public speaker. Her speaking tour in 1913 in the United States is an example of her use of the public podium to introduce a wider audience to her method.[7] Again as a university professor, Montessori was familiar with and skilled in using publication to disseminate her educational ideas to audiences of both professional educators and the public. Her book, *The Montessori Method*, appeared in 1912 and was published in ten languages in addition to Italian.

Along with public speaking and publication, the Montessori method was diffused to a worldwide audience by means of educational visitation. Educational visitation is an old form of interchanging educational ideas. For example, foreign visitors came to observe Pestalozzi's schools in Switzerland in the early nineteenth century. Horace Mann and Henry Barnard, founders of the U.S. public school system, traveled to Europe to observe schools and collect educational information. In the 1970s, U.S. educators traveled to the United Kingdom to observe the innovative British primary school. Educators and other interested individuals came to Rome from other countries, including the United States, to attend Montessori's lectures, interview her, and observe her schools. Some of these visitors were intent on introducing the Montessori method to their own countries; others were educational journalists who were researching articles and books that they would publish about the Italian educator. Still others came to be trained in the method.

In terms of perpetuating an innovation, it is necessary that it have continuity across time so that it has a life that extends beyond that of its originator. To perpetuate her method and ensure that it was being introduced without distortion, Montessori turned to teacher preparation. She established a training school to prepare those who would teach in Montessori schools as directresses. A characteristic of Montessori's approach to teacher education was that the method should be learned and used without deviation from her original pattern. Although this guaranteed methodological purity of the method, it also presented obstacles to its cultural adaptation to other countries and ability to adapt to changing social and technological circumstances. To study with Dr. Montessori was a goal of many who were seeking a new way to educate children. A student from the United States who made the journey to Italy ecstatically praised Montessori as a "magical personality that makes her words seem winged messengers of light and the mighty fever of enthusiasm is amazing to the beholder."[8]

Montessori and her method aroused international interest. The United States, where more than 100 Montessori schools were functioning as of 1913, appeared to be especially receptive to the Italian educator. Enthusiasts organized a national association, called the Montessori Educational System, to promote the cause. The association, with Mrs. Alexander Graham Bell as president, included such prominent individuals on its board of directors as Margaret Wilson, the president's daughter; Philander P. Claxton, the U.S. Commissioner of Education; Samuel S. McClure, publisher of the widely regarded *McClure's* magazine; and Dorothy Canfield Fisher, a well-known writer on educational and cultural subjects.[9] Fisher, in particular, played an important role in introducing the Montessori method to its U.S. audience.

Under the auspices of the Montessori Association, Maria Montessori came to the United States in 1913 to present her educational philosophy and method in a series of lectures around the country. Her tour, which began with an inaugural presentation in Washington, D.C., was followed by appearances in New York, Philadelphia, Boston, Chicago, and San Francisco. Her lecture tour and the growing number of Montessori schools constitute what educational historians refer to as the first wave of Montessorianism in the United States. This initial enthusiasm would be short lived. Although Montessori was given a generally receptive response from her U.S. audiences and complimentary comments in newspapers and magazines, several educators began to criticize her method and its applicability to American children.

Montessori's critics generally came from two camps: Froebelian kindergarten advocates and progressive educators. At the time of Montessori's visit to the United States, the kindergarten was an established part of many public school systems. Kindergarten teachers met in annual conventions, and Froebel's writings had been translated and published in the United States. Although Montessori's school was designed to serve a wider age range, from three to seven years, than the kindergarten, the two methods, despite some theoretical and practical parallels, had some distinct conflicts.

The second category of critics included a number of university professors of education, many of whom were progressives. Walter Hallsey, a professor at the University of Omaha, labeled the Montessori method as a mere "fad promoted and advertised by a shrewd commercial spirit" that was being enthusiastically accepted by the "novelty loving American public."[10] A major attack came from William Heard Kilpatrick, a prominent professor at Columbia University's Teachers College who was associated philosophically with Dewey's pragmatism. Kilpatrick, who had developed his own group-centered project method, criticized the Montessori method as lacking sufficient initiatives for encouraging children's socialization and experimental attitudes and skills.[11]

Although a number of teachers, journalists, and lay people were receptive to Montessori, she had little effect on the educational establishment in early twentieth century America. Educational administrators were more concerned with designing facilities and schedules for large urban systems. Dewey, Kilpatrick, and other progressives were dominating the educational scene.

When Montessori made her second visit to the United States in 1917, interest was waning in her ideas and method. Nevertheless, she attracted some audiences to hear her promotion of her new book, *Dr. Montessori's Own Handbook* and to see her exhibits of didactic materials.[12] Among her instructional materials were rods of varying lengths, different-size cylinders and cubes, and stacking blocks that were designed to develop and coordinate motor skills.

The entry of the United States into World War I caused a shift in interest from European ideas about education to ways to mobilize the country to win the war. By 1917, the first wave of enthusiasm for Montessorianism was ebbing severely. It would not be until the 1950s that a second and much more substantial wave of Montessorianism would occur. This second movement would lead to the establishment of hundreds of Montessori schools throughout the country.

In the United Kingdom, the fortunes of Montessorianism paralleled what had occurred in the United States. English language translations of Montessori's books attracted a wide readership. A number of teachers from England made the journey to Rome to be trained as directresses by Montessori. An English Montessori association was formed. After the initial phase of receptivity, however, a number of critics attacked the method as being deficient culturally and aesthetically. As in the United States, the Montessori movement, after an initial burst of enthusiasm, declined in the period between the two World Wars.

On the European continent, the Montessori approach registered more permanent gains than in England and the United States. The Spanish government invited Montessori to lecture and to establish two schools in Barcelona. Except for occasional visits to lecture in Italy and in other countries, Montessori was in Spain from 1915 to 1927. While in Spain, she established a training program.

In 1922, Benito Mussolini installed a Fascist regime in Italy. The Italian dictator, bent on revitalizing nationalism in Italy, established a number of Fascist children's and youth organizations. Dressed in uniforms, young children drilled and paraded through the streets of Italy's villages and cities. In 1927, the Fascist government invited Montessori to establish schools and training centers. Although she was basically a nonpolitical person, Montessori accepted Il Duce's invitation and returned to Italy. Philosophically, Montessori's educational method had overtones of idealism, and the Italian educational system, under the leadership of the philosopher Giovanni Gentile, was moving in the direction of idealism. Mussolini's motivation in enlisting Montessori's efforts were probably more opportunistic than philosophical. Il Duce wanted to showcase prominent Italians as supporters of his Fascist government.

Cooperation between Mussolini's Fascist government and Montessori was uneasy. Although the regime was sponsoring a Montessori training college, it also wanted to use Montessori as a public personage devoted to Fascism. Montessori, however, saw her role as more international. In 1934, the Association Montessori Internationale, an organization with representatives from a number of countries, was established to coordinate Montessori schools and activities. The Italian government, seeking to capture publicity, wanted to name Montessori as Italy's children's ambassador. Montessori refused to accept the appointment unless the Italian government recognized her as the representative of Montessori Internationale. Not used to having his orders questioned, Mussolini responded quickly and ordered Montessori's schools closed. Montessori left Italy as an exile.

She went to India, where she had been invited to lecture. When World War II began, she was lecturing at the university in Madras. Although Italy and the United Kingdom were at war, the British authorities in India permitted Montessori the freedom to carry on her educational activities. In India, too, a large number of Montessori schools were established.

In 1946, Montessori went to the Netherlands, where an international headquarters was established to disseminate and coordinate activities on behalf of the method. Her lectures took her to a number of countries. She continued her writing, teaching, and lecturing until her death on May 6, 1952. Before her death, she entrusted much of the administrative responsibilities of the international society to Mario Montessori, who continued her work.

Since the 1950s, the Montessori method has experienced a significant revival in the United States. In the early 1950s, the method was rediscovered by parents seeking a more academically oriented early childhood school than was provided in many public school kindergartens or progressive private schools. Indeed, by the mid-1950s, progressive education was on the defensive and was declining. A major force in launching the U.S. revival of Montessorianism was Nancy McCormick Rambusch, the founder of the Whitby School in Greenwich, Connecticut. Although she was deeply impressed and committed to Montessori's philosophy, Rambusch believed the method needed to be modernized to incorporate some of the new developments that had taken place in education. Those who wanted a more up-to-date version of Montessorianism organized the American Montessori Society.[13] By the end of the 1950s, more than 200 Montessori schools and several large training schools were functioning. The Association Montessori Internationale, headed by Mario Montessori, was critical of the U.S. version of the method on the grounds that it departed from the founder's ideas and philosophy.

In the 1960s, the Montessori movement gained another dimension. President Lyndon Johnson's Great Society programs called for a war against poverty. Part of the anti-poverty legislation was directed toward providing compensatory education programs for children affected by poverty. Some of the Operation Head Start programs, designed to provide early learning experiences for socially and culturally disadvantaged children, adopted the Montessori approach.

The Montessori Method: Key Elements

As indicated in the previous section, Montessori based her method of education on her observations of children in her schools and on her extensive research in educational literature. In addition to her medical studies, which involved pediatrics, anatomy, and other related areas, she read widely in the fields of anthropology, psychology, and pedagogy. From research and experience, she arrived at a number of discoveries or conclusions about children's growth, development, and education.

Like Froebel, Montessori believed that children possessed an interior spiritual force that stimulated their self-activity. This self-active learning, however, was not to be wasted in chaotic activity for the sake of movement. It was a force to be used, in conjunction with the child's stages of development, to further motor, intellectual, and social growth and well-being.

Unlike conventional educators who believed that children needed to have their interests shaped for them, Montessori believed children naturally possessed a strong propensity and capacity for mental concentration. The key to exercising this self-activity came, however, from sources that were internal rather than external to the child. If they were truly interested in their activity, children would concentrate their attention and energy on it.

Rather than being disorderly creatures, children actually desired order and strongly preferred a structured environment. Rather than diminishing freedom, Montessori believed that structure enhanced the child's freedom. In a structured learning environment, expectations were clearly known by the children. Furniture and other items in their environment were made for them and their size rather than being imposed on them. If tools and didactic materials were stored in a place accessible to the children, they would make certain that this placement remained accessible by replacing them in an orderly fashion.

Further, children wanted to master new skills. On their own initiative, they would keep at the task and repeat it until they had mastered it. Children realized that the mastery of such practical skills as tying a shoelace, buttoning a jacket, and putting on gloves and overshoes without the help of an adult gave them freedom and independence. Montessori concluded that children did not have to be forced to learn, and if permitted to choose between work and play would often choose the former. In such a learning climate, artificial rewards and punishments were not only unneeded but could distort the learning experience.

Montessori also shared with Froebel a conviction that in their learning children were unfolding, or externalizing, their true personality and humanness. However, the child's early years were of such crucial importance in setting the proper course for later learning that they should not be left to chance. As Froebel created his kindergarten, Montessori devised her school, a prepared environment for children's early learning, growth, and development.

The system of education designed by Montessori is both a general philosophy of education and an instructional method that contains precise guidelines, activities, and exercises. From this blend of general philosophy and specific instructional prescription came Montessori's guiding principles:

1. Each child is to be respected as a person who has individual needs and interests.
2. All children, by their nature, have an innate drive, sensitivity, and intellectual capacity for absorbing information and for learning from the environment.
3. The first six years of a person's life are crucial for both unconscious and conscious learning.
4. Children have a need for and enjoyment of working that comes from their nature and from the task being performed.

By following these four principles, educators can assist in the holistic development of children's sensory, physical, intellectual, and sociopsychological potentialities.

Based on her observations and research, Montessori was convinced that children progressed through a series of developmental stages, each of which required an appropriate and specifically designed kind of learning.[14] She identified two major developmental stages:

1. The first stage, about which Montessori was most concerned, was the period of the absorbent mind, from birth through age 6, when children were especially sensitive to learning stimulated by their environment.
2. During the second stage, from ages 7 through 18, the child became an adolescent and was moving toward adulthood.

As a specialist in early childhood education, Montessori was primarily concerned with the sensitive periods that were part of the first stage of the "absorbent mind." The term *absorbent* reflected Montessori's belief that children absorbed sensory impressions from stimuli in the environment. The impulse for this absorption came from the child's great desire to know and to use this knowledge for self-development. The content of the knowledge so absorbed depended heavily upon the learning possibilities available in the environment. This stage she further divided into an early period, from age one to three, when the child's mind functions unconsciously and learns by interacting with and responding to the stimuli in the environment. The later period, from age three to six, was characterized by the mind becoming more aware of and directive of its mental operations.

During the period of the absorbent mind, Montessori stressed that children have a need to give order and structure to the knowledge they acquire from the environment. As they order the sensory information, they then become increasingly aware that they need still more knowledge about the larger world in which they live. Children have a great capacity for acquiring and incorporating knowledge. However, the knowledge that is presented to them must be appropriate to their particular stage of development. To make this knowledge appropriate to the stages of development, Montessori developed didactic materials and learning episodes designed to exercise the children's motor and sensory functions. It was crucial for the Montessori directress to recognize when the child had reached a sensitive period of readiness to acquire a new skill. Based on her theory of sensitive periods, Montessori fashioned a curriculum that sought to develop children in three broad areas: (1) motor and sensory training, (2) skills needed in practical life, and (3) the formal literary and computational subjects.

By using the didactic apparatus and through repeated exercises, children developed their muscular skills and physical coordination. The child's awareness of and learning about the environment comes from sensory perception. The sensory activities are designed to cultivate three kinds of skills: making comparisons, discerning color and hue, and being sensitive to smell and sound. As the child works with the didactic materials, he or she learns to recognize, group, and compare similar objects and to contrast them with dissimilar ones. By using color tablets, children learn to distinguish colors and shades. Sensory boxes are filled with spices that have distinctive odors. Tone bells cultivate the discrimination of various tones.

Practical exercises were designed to help children in developing skills needed in everyday life. Children first learned to perform what can be called "generic skills" such as tying, lacing, buckling, zipping, and buttoning that are performed daily and could be applied to related tasks. Among the range of practical activities were lacing and tying shoes, buttoning smocks and coats, setting a table with dishes and silverware, serving meals, and washing dishes.

The children then learned more formal skills and subjects including reading, writing, and arithmetic. In this area, Montessori attracted considerable attention by her claim that children of ages four and five "burst spontaneously into writing." To create readiness for writing and reading—two skills that Montessori saw being developed in close relationship—she devised letters cut out of cardboard and covered with sandpaper. As the children touch and trace these letters, the directress voices the sound of the letter. At the same time, they fix the letter in their minds and come to recognize the sound that it represents. Children discover reading when they understand that the sounds of the letters they were tracing and then writing form words. When the children know all the vowels and some of the consonants, they are ready to form simple words. Using the vowels, the directress shows the children how to compose three-letter words and to pronounce them clearly. In the next step, the children write the words dictated by the directress. After enough practice, the children are able to compose words without assistance. In teaching arithmetic, a series of colored rods of varying lengths are used.

Children learn about the natural environment by planting and cultivating gardens. There also may be some small animals in the school that introduce them to the animal kingdom. Gymnastics, group games, songs, and stories are also part of the school day.

The prepared Montessori environment also provides the milieu for using the instructional method. The method stresses the principle of choice within structure. Children are free to pursue their interests and activities at their own rate without being in competition with their peers. No one is permitted to interfere with the work of others, to disrupt the order of the school's environment, or to damage or misuse the equipment. Children are free to observe the work of other children so they can learn from it.

As indicated earlier, the primary role of the Montessori directress is helping children learn. Although not imposing tasks or activities on the children, the directress clearly establishes the ground rules, based on Montessori's principles, that will govern the school. In many ways, the directress is a diagnostician of each child's educational profile. She notes the child's previous learning, his or her readiness for new learning experiences, and is aware of special interests and needs. She exercises her influence by ensuring that the learning environment contains the materials and opportunities that excite children's desire to learn and to become independent. She then guides but does not push each child to the appropriate activity, material, or apparatus.[15]

Conclusion: An Assessment

Maria Montessori made a significant contribution to educational theory and practice in the field of early childhood education. She anticipated and led what is now the current movement to provide more and earlier educational opportunities for children. Montessori is important because of her efforts to give early childhood a more scientific base. Her work, which provided new insights into children's nature, stages of development, and the educative role of the environment, stimulated later developments in educational and child psychology.

In addition to the contribution that Montessori made to early childhood education, studying the Montessori movement provides insights into how educational theories are transported from country to country and achieve an international relevance. The two waves of Montessorianism in the United States also reveal the promises, potentialities, and pitfalls of educational innovation. These aspects of the history of the Montessori movement are especially illuminating for students of educational policy.

Maria Montessori occupies a place in educational biography that is somewhat like that of Jane Addams. Montessori, like Addams, wanted to shape her own destiny and life. Both lived at a time when women's careers were largely determined by others, either by custom and tradition or the prescriptions of a male-defined society. Montessori decided early that she would be a self-determined person rather than one whose life was directed by others. As a student of medicine and as a world-famous educator, she opened new pathways not only for herself but for other women as well.

Discussion Questions

1. How did Montessori react to the key events in her life?
2. How did Montessori overcome the gender restrictions and discrimination that were present in late nineteenth century and early twentieth century Italy?
3. What was Montessori's conception of the nature of the child?

4. Examine the Montessori school as a prepared environment.
5. Describe the preparation of a Montessori directress.
6. Examine the Montessori method as an example of the transference of educational innovations from one country to another.

Research and Essay Topics

1. Read and review a biography of Maria Montessori.
2. In a paper, define gender discrimination and analyze Montessori's reaction to the discrimination that she encountered.
3. Visit a contemporary Montessori school and prepare a paper that analyzes it as a prepared environment.
4. Interview a Montessori directress about the Montessori method. Present your findings in a paper.
5. In your opinion, why does the Montessori method enjoy such wide popularity in the United States?
6. In a paper, compare and contrast Maria Montessori and Friedrich Froebel as early childhood educators.

Notes

1. Rita Kramer, *Maria Montessori* (New York: G. P. Putnam's Sons, 1976), 22–24.
2. Lena L. Gitter, *The Montessori Way* (Seattle: Special Child Publications, 1970), 7.
3. Kathrina Myers, "Seguin's Principles of Education As Related to the Montessori Method," *Journal of Education* 77 (May 1913), 538–41.
4. Kramer, 214.
5. Maria Montessori, *Pedagogical Anthropology*. Translated by Frederick Cooper. (New York: Frederick A. Stokes, 1913).
6. Florence E. Ward, *The Montessori Method and the American School* (New York: Macmillan Publishing Company, 1913), 31. Reprinted by Arno Press and New York Times, 1971.
7. Ibid.; also see Kramer, 140.
8. Ruth M. French, "The Working of the Montessori Method," *Journal of Education* 77 (October 1913), 423.
9. E. M. Standing, *Maria Montessori* (Fresno, Calif.: Academy Library Guild, 1957), 42-44. Reprinted by New American Library, 1962.
10. Walter N. Halsey, "A Valuation of the Montessori Experiments," *Journal of Education* 77 (January 1913), 63.
11. William H. Kilpatrick, *The Montessori System Examined* (Boston: Houghton Mifflin, 1914). Reprinted by Arno Press, and New York Times, 1971.
12. Maria Montessori, *Dr. Montessori's Own Handbook* (New York: Frederick A. Stokes, Co., 1914). Reprinted by Robert Bentley, 1967.
13. Kathy Ahlfeld, "The Montessori Revival: How Far Will It Go?" *Nation's Schools* 85 (January 1970), 75–80.
14. The discussion of key elements of the Montessori method that appears in this section relies on Maria Montessori, *The Absorbent Mind* (Madras, India: Theosophical Press, 1949), translated by Claude A. Clermont, which examines the child from birth to age

six. It also relies on Montessori, *The Discovery of the Child* (Madras, India: Theosophical Press, 1948), translated by Mary A. Johnstone.

15. Ahlfeld, 75–80.

Suggestions for Further Reading

Fisher, Dorothy Canfield. *Montessori for Parents.* Cambridge, Mass.: Robert Bentley, 1965.

————. *The Montessori Manual.* Cambridge, Mass: Robert Bentley, 1964.

Gitter, Lena L. *Montessori's Legacy to Children.* Johnstown, Pa: Mafex Associates, 1970.

————. *The Montessori Way.* Seattle: Special Child Publications, 1970.

Gross, Michael J. *Montessori's Concept of Personality.* Lantham, Md.: University Press of America, 1986.

Hainstock, Elizabeth G. *The Essential Montessori.* New York: New American Library, 1978.

Kilpatrick, William H. *The Montessori System Examined.* New York: Arno Press and New York Times, 1971.

Kramer, Rita. *Maria Montessori.* New York: G. P. Putnam's Sons, 1976.

Lillard, Paula P. *Montessori: A Modern Approach.* New York: Schocken Books, 1972.

Montessori, Maria. *The Absorbent Mind.* Translated by Claude A. Clarmont. Madras, India: Theosophical Press, 1949.

————. *Childhood Education.* Translated by A. M. Joosten. Chicago: Henry Regnery Press, 1949.

————. *The Child in the Family.* Translated by Nancy Rockmore Cirillo. Chicago: Henry Regnery Press, 1970.

————. *The Discovery of the Child.* Translated by Mary A. Johnstone. Madras, India: Theosophical Press, 1948.

————. *Dr. Montessori's Own Handbook.* New York: Frederick A. Stokes, 1914. Reprinted by Robert Bentley, 1967.

————. *Education and Peace.* Translated by Helen R. Lane. Chicago: Henry Regnery Press, 1949.

————. *From Childhood to Adolescence.* New York: Schocken Books, 1948.

————. *The Montessori Method.* Translated by Anne E. George. New York: Frederick A. Stokes, 1912. Reprinted by Robert Bentley, 1967.

————. *Pedagogical Anthropology.* Translated by Frederick T. Cooper. New York: Frederick A. Stokes, 1913.

————. *The Secret of Childhood.* Translated by Barbara Barclay Carter. New York: Frederick A. Stokes, 1939.

————. *Spontaneous Activity in Education.* Translated by Florence Simmonds. New York: Frederick A. Stokes, 1917. Reprinted by Robert Bentley, 1967.

Oren, R. C. *Montessori Today.* New York: G. P. Putnam's Sons, 1971.

————, ed. *Montessori for the Disadvantaged.* New York: Capricorn Books, 1968.

————. *Montessori: Her Method and the Movement—What You Need to Know.* New York: G. P. Putnam's Sons, 1974.

Rambusch, Nancy McCormick. *Learning How to Learn.* Baltimore: Helicon Press, 1962.

Standing, E. M. *Maria Montessori: Her Life and Work.* New York: New American Library, 1962.

Ward, Florence E. *The Montessori Method and the American School.* New York: Arno Press and New York Times, 1971.

CHAPTER 21

Mohandas Gandhi:
Father of Indian Independence

Photograph of
Mohandas Gandhi;
reproduction from
the collections of
the Library of
Congress.

In this chapter, we examine the life, educational philosophy, and contributions of Mohandas Gandhi (1869–1948), the father of Indian independence. Although he sought neither economic nor political power, Gandhi was a commanding world leader. By force of his moral convictions and his philosophy of nonviolent social and political change, Gandhi was a respected and influential world figure. His broadly construed educational ideas were designed to kindle sentiments of mutual respect and cooperation. He also designed a specific educational plan of basic education to revitalize Indian village and rural life.

In this chapter, Gandhi's effect on world education is discussed in its historical context and in terms of its enduring significance on educational philosophy and policy. First, the general social, political, and economic context in which Gandhi lived and worked is described. A major characteristic of this context was the end of European imperialism and colonialism—in the case of India, British colonialism. For students of educational policy, colonialism's effect and its decline and demise are significant trends that shaped the course of human history in the twentieth century. Second, Gandhi's biography, his education and career as an independence leader, is analyzed to determine the evolution of his social and educational ideas. Third, these ideas, particularly his policy for basic education, are analyzed. Fourth, an assessment is made of Gandhi's contributions to world education. Our discussion is designed to illustrate the process of change caused by the interaction of a leading and forceful personality such as Gandhi with momentous world forces such as the decline of imperialism. Not only was he a force for change in his native India, but Gandhi's ideas of nonviolent protest and passive resistance influenced the strategy that Dr. Martin Luther King Jr. used in the Civil Rights movement in the United States in the 1950s and 1960s.

As you read the chapter, you might focus on the following questions to help organize your thoughts:

- What were the major trends in the historical context, the times and situation, in which Gandhi lived?
- How did Gandhi's life, his educational biography, shape his social and educational philosophy?
- How did Gandhi's social and educational philosophy shape his educational policies and programs?
- What is the enduring effect of Gandhi's contributions to world education?

The Historical Context of Gandhi's Life

The life of Mohandas Gandhi coincided with important worldwide trends that transformed the old order of life and brought a new social and political world into being. Gandhi was born in an India that was part of the British Empire—upon which, according to the slogan, "the sun never set." His death by an assassin's bullet came when India had gained its independence as a sovereign and independent nation. Although the struggle for Indian independence has elements that are unique to that subcontinent's history and culture, it was also part of the epic story of the decline of imperialism and the liberation of colonial peoples from foreign domination. By the end of the nineteenth century, India—divided into British India, which was ruled directly by Great Britain, and the many princely states indirectly under English rule—was regarded as the crown jewel of Britain's far-flung empire. The history of British rule in India—which began in 1639 when the Mughal rulers ceded a tract of land to the English near Madras—was part of the larger story of Western imperialism. The European nations of Great Britain, France, Spain, Portugal, the Netherlands, and Germany until its defeat in World War I had carved out colonies primarily in Africa and Asia. Great Britain controlled India, Burma, and Malaya in Asia and Nigeria, Ghana, Rhodesia, and South Africa in Africa; France controlled Morocco, Algeria, and Equatorial Africa in Africa and Indochina in Asia; and the Netherlands controlled the Dutch East Indies.

The pattern of imperialism was for a European power such as Great Britain to claim an African or Asian territory by virtue of discovery and exploration and to establish British settlements of missionaries, civil servants, soldiers, and merchants in the colony. In the case of India, the British defeated their Portuguese and French rivals and then subjugated the subcontinent either militarily or through diplomacy. Once control was established, Great Britain took over the politics and economy of the subject colony. A colonial possession such as India was the source of raw materials such as cotton, tea, and hemp, which were sent to England to be manufactured into finished products. The colony was a market for the imperial nation's manufactured products. In other words, the imperial relationship worked to the diplomatic, political, and economic benefit of Great Britain and to the disadvantage of the subject colony.

Gandhi argued that British economic policy had exploited the Indian people, especially the 75 percent of the then-500 million who inhabited thousands of small villages. In the past, the villagers had grown and spun cotton cloth as an indigenous local industry, but this was no longer done under British rule. The British commercial policy had idled village handicraft industries, and the villagers had to purchase from British merchants the cloth they once made themselves.

The policy of imperialism had important educational consequences throughout the colonial world. Europeans generally exported their educational philosophies, institutions, and policies to their colonial subjects. The educational policy practiced by the imperial nation related directly to its rule over and governance of the subject colony. In the colonies, direct rule relied on the presence of a military force. In India, the British army maintained garrisons that suppressed insurrection and revolts.

To govern a colony, especially one as vast in territory and diverse in population as India, the British brought civil servants and educators from Great Britain to staff the upper positions in the colonial government. These English administrators tended to live in enclaves that were socially isolated from the indigenous population. The role of such officials was to protect British imperial interests, which meant establishing and maintaining a British version of law and order. In India, the British constructed a great railway network that facilitated transportation and a telegraph system that facilitated communication and also served British interests. To pay the costs of the transplanted civil service, taxes were levied and collected from the indigenous population. (A similar pattern of imperial-colonial rule had been played out in North America in the eighteenth century, resulting in the American Revolution.)

To aid their rule in the colony, the European nation generally trained a small portion of the indigenous population for subordinate civil service and administrative posts. For example, a British administrator would generally have an Indian deputy and staff working under his supervision. A small group of Indians, usually from upper castes, were educated in preparatory schools, secondary schools, and universities in the English language and style. This small elite of English-speaking Indians, never more than about 2 percent of the total population, then entered the administrative ranks.

For a time, the British debated how this Indian elite should be educated. Should their education be based on the indigenous language, literature, and culture or should it be based on the English language, literature, and culture? A group of English policy makers called "orientalists" argued for the indigenous language and culture. However, a more powerful group of British policy makers called "anglicists" and headed by Lord Macaulay decided that education in India should be conducted in the British or western European mode. In India, the educational situation was complicated by the existence of seventeen major languages spoken in various regions of the subcontinent. The language issue would remain one that would complicate Indian politics and education.

The decision to impose the British language and Western attitudes on the educated elite in India had some serious educational consequences. First, the education of the vast majority of the population—the millions of children who lived in thousands of villages in India—was neglected. Village India remained a backwater of pervasive illiteracy and ignorance. For Gandhi, the illiteracy, grinding poverty, and ignorance of the underemployed and undernourished Indian villager was one of the nation's most serious problems. His policy of basic education was designed to renew village life and economy.

A second consequence of the British educational policy was that the educated elite of English-speaking Indians tended to be separated from the main problems of Indian life. Although the British intended to westernize this elite, the education they received was, in the British tradition, highly literary. According to the British civil service tradition, the best preparation for administrative duties was to study the classics, ancient history and literature, and British history and literature. This education lacked training in scientific, technological, engineering, and managerial skills and subjects. The result was that the educated elite in India were educated like the English but were regarded as inferior by their British supervisors. Further, they were culturally divorced from their heritage.

When Gandhi returned to India from South Africa, he, too, was a product of a British education. He deliberately immersed himself in Indian culture and the problems of India so that he could rediscover his roots. Many of his associates in the Congress party, the principal movement for Indian independence, were anglicized Indians who had to recapture their cultural identity before they could reach the masses and persuade them to join the independence movement.

There was still another factor operating in the educational situation in India. A unique feature of Indian society was the cultural-social-religious caste system. Although anthropologists and sociologists debate the origins of the caste system, it had a definite social and economic influence not only on Gandhi's life but on contemporary India as well. Reinforced by Hindu theology, the dominant religiocultural system of India, Indian society was rigidly segregated by membership in a particular caste. An individual was born into a caste, an ascribed status, and remained in it throughout life. The original four great castes were the following:

1. The *Brahmans,* the scholars and priests.
2. The *khasatriyas,* the warriors.
3. The *vaishyas,* the merchants.
4. The *shudras,* the farmers.

These castes were further subdivided into hundreds of *jatis,* or subcastes, which minutely and rigidly defined a person's status, role, and function. Occupation, associates, and marriage were determined by and within the confines of a given caste. In addition to the social rigidity imposed by the four major castes and their many subdivisions, there remained a large part of the Indian population known as the outcastes. The outcastes or untouchables were regarded as the dregs of Indian society. They were relegated to the most burdensome jobs—often as sweepers and scavengers—and confined to the poorest and most squalid sections of cities and villages. Indeed, if even the shadow of an untouchable fell upon a member of an upper caste, that person would have to undergo ritual purification to remove the stain of untouchability. Although Gandhi did not challenge the caste system itself, he strongly opposed untouchability. He renamed the untouchables the *harijans,* or people of God, and argued for the removal of disabilities because of caste. It should be noted that the Indian constitution, which was adopted after independence, outlaws disability because of caste and provides some compensatory assistance to untouchables. Such was not the case, however, when Gandhi assumed leadership of the Indian independence movement.

Because of ingrained Indian traditions and because of British policy, members of the upper castes tended to be those who were educated and gained entry into the administrative structure in imperial India. At that time, the concept of social mobility was nonexistent and incompatible with caste. Further, upper-caste Indians had strong inherited conceptions about the nature of work and the status of workers. The Brahman caste were intellectuals who did not do manual work. Physical labor was the task of other lower castes. Indian society had a strong dichotomy between intellectual and physical work. An educational goal was to escape physical labor. In his educational philosophy, Gandhi regarded the dichotomy to be a characteristic that had to be undone in the new India of his dreams. His educational policy was designed to emphasize the importance and dignity of physical labor.

The country that Gandhi wanted to become free and independent was a mosaic of races, languages, and ethnic groups. Although the vast majority of the population were Hindus, other religious groups were the Muslims, Sikhs, Jains, Pharsees, and Christians. Antagonism was strong between Hindus and Muslims. When the British left India, the subcontinent was divided into India, with a predominantly Hindu population, and Pakistan, with a largely Muslim population.

At the time of independence, bloody religious and communal rioting and disorders occurred that prompted Gandhi to go on a hunger strike until the religious factions laid down their arms. Still another problem was divisiveness over language. The Aryan population of the northern states of India spoke Hindi, which was derived from the ancient Sanskrit, and the people of the southern states, descended from Dravidian ethnic stock, spoke a variety of languages. In the face of such language divisions, English was the link language of government, commerce, and communication.

If India faced problems of great magnitude, it also had rich cultural resources—especially of a spiritual nature—that would nourish Gandhi's passion for freedom. Hinduism was many things to many people. Although it appeared to be a polytheistic religion of many deities and cults, there was an underlying spiritual thread. Atman or Brahma was the spiritual source of all life and to which all life sought to return. The Hindu doctrine of reincarnation held that a person experienced myriad births, deaths, and rebirths until karma, the longings of flesh were extinguished, and the person was freed from the pain of birth and death. In this cosmology what was important was eternity and not the moment. Although such a world view could carry with it a fatalism that stagnated human ambition, it brought a perspective that looked for the eternal rather than the transitory. Gandhi was willing to discipline himself, to overcome desires that diverted him from his goal, and to work patiently for his cause.

In addition to the persistence that characterized his life, Gandhi also valued nonviolence. Orthodox Hinduism, as well as Buddhism, which was originally a reform movement within Hinduism, stressed that no harm should be done to any living creature—to any other person or animal. All creatures were part of the cosmic drama and were seeking reunification in Brahma. Of all the leaders of great revolutions, Gandhi must be considered the most unusual. He proposed to free his people from British rule without taking up arms and without violence. Those who joined his movement had to be self-disciplined followers who would not take up arms, engage in terrorism, nor inflict harm on their adversaries. Gandhi forged the weapon of passive resistance and of peaceful boycotts to persuade the British their day was finished in India and that they should quit the subcontinent. As a peaceful revolutionary, Gandhi was quite a different personality than Mao Tse-tung in China.

Finally, still another aspect of Hinduism shaped the Gandhian outlook. In Hinduism, the highest state of life is free of worldly concerns and passions. This state is one of detachment from the world in which the person contemplates the meaning and the greatness of the universe. Although Gandhi was certainly an activist for Indian independence and for human rights, he did incorporate an aspect of personal detachment into his life. To free India, Gandhi determined that he had to be free from the desire for personal glory and power. He was a leader of the most unusual kind—devoid of personal egotism. It is from this general examination of the context of Indian life and society that we now turn to the life of Mohandas Gandhi, the Mahatma.

Mohandas Gandhi: Leader of Indian Independence

Mohandas Gandhi was born on October 2, 1869, at Porbandar, in Kathiawad, India. The son of Karmachand and Puthbai Gandhi, his background was upper caste. His father and grandfather had been ministers in the government of Kathiawad. His primary education was in the local school at Rajkot, where his family had moved. As was the custom, he was betrothed at age seven to marry Kasturbai, daughter of the merchant Kokuldas Makanji. He completed secondary school in Rajkot, and in 1883 he married his betrothed. He then entered undergraduate college at Sarmaldas College in Bhavnager in 1887 but left after a semester to go to England to study law. He remained in England for three years, completed his legal studies, and returned to India in 1891 to begin the practice of law in the thriving port city of Bombay.

Gandhi's career next took him to South Africa, where he served as the legal counsel of an Indian commercial firm. From 1893 to 1901, except for brief visits to India, he lived in South Africa. South Africa had a sizable Indian population consisting of many who had come as laborers and others who were small shopkeepers. Gandhi soon discovered that the South African government had enacted restrictive policies against the Indian population that severely limited their personal freedom and economic opportunities. It was at this time that Gandhi grew increasingly sensitive to violations of human rights. He organized and led the Natal Indian Congress, which sought to remove the laws that were victimizing the Indian population. During the time Gandhi lived in South Africa, he developed his strategies of nonviolent passive resistance.

In 1901, Gandhi and his family returned to India. He opened a law office in Bombay but his attention was diverted to the Indian independence movement, which was in its early stages. Because of his British education and his long absence from India, Gandhi believed he no longer knew the real India. He was determined to renew his cultural roots and for two years traveled extensively throughout India, observing local conditions and meeting local leaders of the Indian National Congress party. His reacquaintance with his native land was interrupted by an urgent call from the Indian community in South Africa, who asked him to represent their interests in the face of punitive action by the South African government.

Gandhi lived in South Africa from 1902 to 1904, representing the cause of the Indian minority and organizing them against the official repression of the government. In 1903, Gandhi began publishing the journal *Indian Opinion,* which served as a vehicle of communication for the Indian community and as a means of informing others about the plight of the Indians in South Africa.

Eventually Gandhi began to establish a theoretical base for his work on behalf of the oppressed South African Indians. He was attracted to and read the works of John Ruskin (1819–1900), the English writer, moralist, and critic, and Leo Tolstoy (1828–1910), the Russian novelist. Both Ruskin and Tolstoy had decided ideas on social justice and education that Gandhi would incorporate into his own social and educational philosophy. Gandhi was convinced that his followers needed to be morally prepared for the struggle that was ahead of them. To provide an educational environment to prepare those who were to embark on the campaign of nonviolent resistance he was planning, Gandhi established Phoenix Farm, near Durban. Phoenix Farm, Tolstoy Farm, and other centers for social and moral education that Gandhi would later establish merged the ideas of Ruskin and Tolstoy with the ancient Indian concept of the *ashram,* a school in which the disciples studied the way of life presented to them by an enlightened teacher or guru.

Gandhi's educational experiment at Tolstoy Farm, an *ashram* located in the Transvaal in South Africa, is especially illustrative of his educational philosophy and methods. The various schools Gandhi would establish when he returned to India essentially followed the pattern used at Tolstoy Farm. Located on 1,100 acres, Tolstoy Farm was an experiment in agriculturally based communal living. The residents of the farm were primarily Indians of different religions, languages, and castes. Gandhi hoped to demonstrate that a commonly practiced mutuality of interests would be stronger than the forces that traditionally had divided Indians. The school, attended by the community's children, was a focal point of the experiment. Gandhi taught in the school. Of his experiences at Tolstoy Farm, he wrote," . . . Tolstoy Farm was a family in which I occupied the place of the father, and that I should so far as possible shoulder the responsibility for the training of the young."[1]

Gandhi based his conduct of the school on his philosophy of the well-rounded intellectual, moral, and physical development of the whole person. In both the traditional Indian and the British systems of education, Gandhi believed that moral and physical development had been sacrificed to an exclusive emphasis on intellectual development. Unfortunately, in the conventional schools, intellectual education had further deteriorated, he believed, into a highly literary, verbal, and bookish method that stressed rote memorization. At Tolstoy Farm, Gandhi sought to undo the exaggerated literary bent of conventional education and emphasize total development.

Gandhi believed that all education should rest on a moral-spiritual foundation. He commented:

> I had always given the first place to the culture of the heart or the building of character, and as I felt confident that a moral training could be given to all alike, no matter how different their ages and their upbringing, I decided to live amongst them all the twenty-four hours of the day as their father.[2]

A deeply religious person, Gandhi believed moral development needed a spiritual foundation. Tending to see the expression of God's truth in the principles of the world's great religions, Gandhi's approach to spirituality was universalist rather than sectarian. However, each child was also to understand the principles of his or her particular religion. To do this, Gandhi encouraged each child to read and study the scriptures appropriate to his or her religious creed.

Within the general moral climate of the school, Gandhi believed that the subject-oriented phase of education should take place. Children were instructed in the language they spoke in their family whenever possible. They learned the primary tool skills of reading, writing, and arithmetic, in addition to studying English, history, geography, and singing.

Gandhi included vocational education both at Tolstoy Farm and in his philosophy of basic education. Vocational education was designed to emphasize the dignity of work and to teach individuals employable skills. Gandhi believed that the ancient Indian scholarly tradition, the British educational system, and the caste system all worked to diminish the importance of physical and manual labor and to relegate those who did such labor to the lower rungs of society. Further, Gandhi recognized that unemployment was a pervasive problem, especially in the Indian villages. Gandhi's emphasis on physical work and vocational education was therefore a persistent theme in his educational philosophy. At Tolstoy Farm, the teachers, including Gandhi, worked among the children. The children were engaged in gardening, performing agricultural chores, cleaning the school and its playground, and learning crafts. When he returned to India, Gandhi took up spinning cotton and making cotton cloth, which became a part of the school routine. Thus, his educational work in South Africa became the experience-tested background for his philosophy of basic education.

An unusual blending of the contemplative and activist personality, Gandhi was heavily involved in developing a political movement to redress the injuries inflicted by the restrictive laws of the South African government. Between 1905 and 1910, Gandhi was instrumental in mobilizing the Indian community against a series of repressive South African acts. His strategy involved the use of the *satyagraha,* an all-encompassing Hindi word that means awareness of the "soul force" or truth that is in each person. The person who practiced *satyagraha* was to use that spiritual force against ill-directed police, military, political, and economic pressure by engaging in nonviolent civil disobedience, passive resistance, and noncooperation against unjust laws. Although the concept of *satyagraha* was rooted in Indian philosophy, it also was expressed in Western thought by civil disobedience based on the higher law concept developed by Henry David Thoreau at Walden Pond. Similar ideas were expressed by Tolstoy in his pacifist stage. Martin Luther King Jr. drew upon similar sources of moral and political philosophy in the Civil Rights movement.

The development of the concept of *satyagraha* by Gandhi for use against South African authorities and its later use throughout the struggle for Indian independence has important educational as well as moral implications. First, Gandhi believed that all people had the moral force or power to resist social injustice within them but it needed to be raised to consciousness. Second, the use of "soul power" or moral force had to be disciplined by training that involved curbing the emotions so that the protester would not respond to violence with counterviolence. Gandhi recognized that the use of violence was a kind of terror that spawned further acts of terror, which dehumanized both the victimized person and the perpetrator of the violent action. Third, by a complete spiritual formation that led to nonviolent action the person could be prepared to participate in the movement of liberation.

Between 1906 and 1914, Gandhi organized three major *satyagraha* campaigns against the South African government. He was jailed on several occasions for inciting public unrest but always renewed his efforts upon being released. His campaign was directed against an ordinance that restricted the entry of Indians into South Africa, the registration act that compelled Indians to carry identification papers that restricted their freedom of movement, and a law that held that non-Christian marriages were invalid. Because South Africa was a member of the British Commonwealth, Gandhi's activities reached the British government and he was called to London several times as the British government attempted to mediate the impasse in South Africa. In 1914, passage of the Indian Relief Act eliminated some of the restrictions against the Indian population.

In 1915, Gandhi returned to India and began the movement to secure Indian independence, which would occupy the rest of his life. In many ways, Gandhi's nonviolent passive resistance campaigns in South Africa prepared him for the next thirty-three years. He again established an *ashram,* Satyagraha Ashram, to prepare a core of his followers for the long campaign ahead. From 1915 to 1920, he helped organize local *satyagraha* campaigns against specific injustices. As he had done in South Africa, he also turned to journalism, assuming the editorship of *Young India,* an English language weekly, and *Navajivan,* a weekly published in Gujarati, one of the Indian languages.

For the next twenty years, Gandhi was the leading voice calling for an independent India. His movement for independence involved a multidimensional strategy against British rule. First, he had to unite the various racial, ethnic, language, and religious groups that divided India into often contentious factions. His greatest difficulty in presenting a united front against the British came from the Muslim minority, who feared that they would be dominated by the Hindu majority in an independent India. His ability to keep the Muslims in his movement was always shaky and broke down when India received independence in 1947. At that time, an independent Muslim state, headed by Mohammed Ali Jinnah, was established as Pakistan. At various times, there were also outbreaks of communal disorders between the Hindus and Muslims that caused great distress for the proponent of nonviolence. When such outbreaks occurred, Gandhi would suspend his activities for independence and go on a fast, which on several occasions was life threatening, until the communal rioting and violence had ended.

A second part of Gandhi's strategy for independence was to enlist those who would become the leaders of an independent India to follow his policies of nonviolence and revitalization of village life. The major leaders of the independence movement were in the National Congress party, and Gandhi formed a close association with such promising figures as Jawaharal Nehru, Sarder Patel, and others. Although Gandhi was the undisputed moral leader of the movement, not all of the Congress party leadership believed that his nonviolent strategy would be effective. In numerous meetings Gandhi had to persuade them to accept his strategy.

Gandhi also had to deal with the British authorities. His campaign was really directed at persuading the British that they should voluntarily leave the subcontinent. It was a long process that took more than thirty years and a Britain that was worn out by World War II to accept. Gandhi would call for an all-India *satyagraha,* a campaign of massive civil disobedience, often accompanied by a cessation of work and transportation. The British would respond, often arresting Gandhi and the Congress party leaders. Gandhi would be released and the scenario would be repeated. During his lifetime, Gandhi spent a total of 2,338 days in prison. As a result of his patient but persistent strategy, India became independent in 1947 when the British voluntarily left India.

Although independence was won, the process of achieving freedom was a traumatic one. Even though Gandhi opposed the division of India, two independent nations—India and Pakistan, were created. When the two nations were created, the Hindu and Sikh religious groups that were living in the Muslim nation of Pakistan began a painful exodus to India. Many of the Muslims living in India migrated to Pakistan. In the midst of the relocation and resettlement of these millions of displaced persons, communal rioting broke out between the religious factions, resulting in massacres and pillaging. Gandhi began a fast that lasted until the rioting subsided. On January 30, 1948, Gandhi was assassinated by Vinayak Godse, a fanatical Hindu nationalist. The man who preached and practiced nonviolence was a victim of the violence he so deplored.

Gandhi's Social and Educational Theory

Gandhi's social and educational theory was a blending of spiritual, political, economic, and educational elements. Gandhi had no pretensions of being an original thinker or a systematic philosopher. He saw himself, rather, as implementing in daily life the eternal truths that governed the universe. He stated, "I do not claim to have originated any new principle or doctrine. I have simply tried in my own way to apply the eternal truths of our daily life and problems."[3]

Gandhi's religious ideas came from but were not a rigidly orthodox interpretation of Hindu theology. He shared the Hindu metaphysical view that the universe was inherently spiritual or nonmaterial. This spiritual perspective, which is also found in philosophical idealism, stresses the importance of the inner self, the spiritual essence or force, that is at the heart of human nature. In this view, the universe is the creation and the manifestation of God, a supreme spiritual presence. Following philosophical idealism, Gandhi believed that the entire universe was governed by unalterable laws. He stated that "there is an orderliness in the universe; there is an unalterable law governing everything and every being that exists or lives."[4]

In the Hindu cosmology, the purpose of human existence is to be reabsorbed into God and to end the tribulations of life. Unlike the Christian conception of salvation as an act that brings the person into the presence of God, the Hindu view was rather that of becoming part of God and being absorbed within divinity itself. The Hindu concept of reincarnation—successive births and deaths in either higher or lower orders of life depending upon one's performance in the previous existence—emphasized the sacredness of all life. Along with his acceptance of the spiritual nature of the universe, Gandhi also accepted the inherent dignity of life.

With its cosmology of absorption of all life into its spiritual source, Hinduism in India was a highly syncretistic religion. It was not creedal and dogmatic as were the various Christian denominations but was more the expression of a total way of life. Thus, Christianity in its Catholic and Protestant forms and other religions such as Buddhism and Islam could be seen as manifestations of the divine will rather than as distinctive religions. In his social and educational theory, Gandhi talked about the universal principles and truths of all the great religions. Although immersed in the Hindu religiocultural ethic, Gandhi found worth and value in all of the world's great religions. He stated, "All religions are founded on the same moral laws. My ethical religion is made up of laws which bind men all over the world."[5]

Although Gandhi was deeply impressed by the spiritual meaning of human life, he also believed that human beings—for the perfection of their own nature and for the contribution they were to make in the perfection of others—should be developed intellectually and physically as well as spiritually. According to Gandhi, the education that brought this development about involved the harmonious cultivation of the heart—or will; the mind—or intellect; and the body. For him, "man is neither mere intellect, nor the gross animal body, nor the heart or soul alone. A proper and harmonious combination of all the three is required for the making of the whole man."[6] Although each person should seek the perfection of his or her own mind, will, and body, human perfection could not be achieved in isolation but only in the cooperative mutuality of human community. The moral person, living within the moral society, lived a life of service to others. Such a moral society rested on love, the fundamental spiritual force that united individuals into a common humanity. According to Gandhi:

> Scientists tell us that without the cohesive force amongst the atoms that comprise this globe of ours, it would crumble to pieces and we would cease to exist. As even there is a cohesive force in blind matter so must there be in all things animate; and the name of that cohesive force among animate beings is love. We notice it between father and son, between brother and sister, friend and friend. But we have to learn to use that force among all that lives, and in the use of it consists our knowledge of God. Where there is love there is life; hatred leads to destruction.[7]

Gandhi then was essentially a spiritual and moral leader who became involved in politics and education to remedy what he regarded to be immoral conditions that violated the spiritual dignity of persons. His philosophy, stressing personal development through social service, had a unique spiritual base. He stated that all "social, political, and religious" activities had to be guided "by the ultimate aim of the vision of God. The immediate service of all human beings becomes a necessary part of the endeavour . . . because the only way to find God is to see Him in His creation and be one with it. This can only be done by service at all."[8]

Although based on these general philosophical considerations, several elements in Gandhi's thought rose out of the Indian context, although they had a significance that was larger than that context. Among these elements were:

- The right of people to political self-determination.
- The removal of prejudices that were either customary or statutory and that denied people opportunities for self-development.
- The emphasis of a strategy of national development located at the grass-roots level.
- The use of nonviolent passive resistance as a strategy for bringing about social and political change.

As a world figure, Gandhi's efforts to win independence for India was part of the tide of anti-imperialism and anticolonialism that swept Asia and Africa after World War II. As an advocate of human freedom, Gandhi believed that people had the right to political self-determination, which was a means to personal self-determination. If the people of Asia and Africa were forced to live in childlike submission to European overlords, their personal development would be impossible.

Gandhi's campaign for an independent India carried obvious political implications but there were educational implications as well. The kind of education the

European imperial powers imposed on colonial peoples was one that fitted them for servitude rather than for self-reliance. Education for freedom needed to awaken a sense of cultural and national identity by studying the history, language, and literature indigenous to the country. Gandhi believed that studying one's own cultural heritage, however, must not lead to a nationalist chauvinism against other nations.

In South Africa and in India, Gandhi opposed discrimination based on either custom or law. In South Africa, the government had discriminated against the Indian minority through restrictive statutes. In India, the caste system was the source of customary discrimination against members of lower castes and the untouchables. Gandhi took a stand against prejudice and discrimination by associating with the untouchables, working with them, and including them in his movement. His teachings and writings consistently opposed discrimination.

In addition to his political and social philosophies, Gandhi also had an economic theory that he hoped would revitalize the Indian economy. Gandhi believed the revival of Indian life had to begin in the villages where the great mass of the population lived. He saw small-scale industries that centered on handicraft production as the key element in such an economic revitalization. In the decade after Indian independence, government planners—although paying lip service to Gandhi's theory of small-scale local economic development—concentrated on large-scale projects designed to bring about a modern industrial economy. Since the 1980s, however, on the world scene, the trend has been to small-scale, locally initiated grass-roots development such as that which Gandhi proposed. Gandhi's strategy of civil disobedience involved strong educational components. Participants in such nonviolent activity had to be spiritually prepared for the struggle and trained in the tactics of passive resistance.

Gandhi's Theory of Basic Education

Mohandas K. Gandhi developed a theory of education designed to aid in the reconstruction of India. Gandhi's rejection of the British-imposed pattern of education as well as his desire to revitalize village life prompted his plan of basic education.[9] The ignorance, illiteracy, and poverty of the Indian masses, especially in the villages, both depressed and challenged Gandhi. He recognized that the colonial system of education, separated from the day-to-day life of the common people, had created an intellectual elite of an educated minority. The ambitions of this group had to be redirected from the security of service to the British to the uncertainty but necessary campaign of creating a revitalized and independent India. For India, the Indian people, regardless of religion or caste, had to be united, massive illiteracy combated, and popular education integrated into the mainstream of Indian life. In addition to its direct educational consequences, Gandhi believed that his projected policy of basic education had political and economic implications for an independent India. It would realize the creative and economically productive capacity of the Indian people and eventually free them from economic exploitation by a foreign power.

In expressing his educational philosophy, Gandhi defined education as the "all-round drawing out of the best in child and man—body, mind, and spirit." Concerned with the holistic and harmonious development of the human being, Gandhi in *India of My Dreams,* expressed his vision of the new India:

> I hold that the true education of the intellect can only come through a proper exercise and training of the bodily organs, e.g. hands, feet, eyes, ears, nose, etc. In other words, an intelligent use of the bodily organs in a child provides the best and quickest way of developing his intellect. But unless the development of the mind and body goes hand in hand with a corresponding awakening of the soul, the former alone would prove to be a poor lop-sided affair. By spiritual training I mean education of the heart. A proper and all-round development of the mind, therefore, can take place only when it proceeds . . . with the education of the physical and spiritual faculties of the child. They constitute an indivisible whole.[10]

For Gandhi, an education that integrated and harmonized the human faculties should be craft centered. Gandhi said he would "begin the child's education by teaching it a useful craft and enabling it to produce from the moment it begins its training."[11] Accordingly, in Gandhi's plan of basic education, primary schooling was compulsory for all children between the ages of seven and fourteen and conducted in the child's own language. The craft used in the particular school was to be one of the major occupations found in India and all instruction was to be correlated to the particular craft. Further, Gandhi believed the sale of the items produced in the schools would make education productive and self-supporting.

In 1937, an all-India conference of educators met at Wardha to consider Gandhi's educational proposals. The Wardha Conference adopted a three-point resolution in support of Gandhian basic education that was also endorsed by the Indian National Congress party. According to the party:

1. Free and compulsory education should be provided for seven years throughout India.
2. The language of instruction at the primary level should be the child's mother tongue, the vernacular spoken in his or her home.
3. The entire educational process should be craft centered and instruction should be integrally related to the central craft taught in the school.[12]

By 1939, the political and educational leaders in the independence movement strongly endorsed Gandhi's plan of basic education. However, World War II and the intensification of the independence struggle pushed educational matters into the background. It was not until 1946, on the eve of independence, that Gandhi again turned his attention to education.

He called for "education for life, through life" and once again urged the implementation of his plan for basic education. His proposals now went beyond those that had been endorsed by the Wardha Conference. The scope of basic education had been extended to cover the ages from six to fourteen. An educational agency, the Hindustani Talimi Sangh located at Wardha, was established to disseminate and prepare materials for the implementation of the plan. In particular, a comprehensive syllabus was prepared to guide and correlate instruction.[13]

Gandhi's philosophy of basic education was also an element in his design for a new India. Like other social reformers, Gandhi saw education as a method of social reconstruction that would improve both individuals and their society.[14] He saw basic education as the means to a cooperative human commonwealth. By involving the child as a participant in an interacting educational and productive group, basic education would counteract the ingrained Indian attitude that relegated physical labor to lower castes and also the modern tendency to antisocial individualism. Basic education, according to Gandhi, would inculcate a spirit of cooperation, unity, and group responsibility. It would be one of the agencies in regenerating the sense of community. Like John Dewey, Gandhi also conceived of the school as a miniature society where children as social participants had rights and responsibilities. Gandhi saw basic education as providing a common educational foundation that would reduce the gap between urban and rural India. He stated:

> Craft education will provide a healthy and moral basis of relationship between the city and the village and thus go a long way towards eradicating some of the worst evils of the present social insecurity and poisoned relationship between the classes.[15]

Believing both traditional Indian education and British education to be too verbal and passive, Gandhi advocated learning through active participation in productive occupations that had educative potentialities. For example, the craft might be cotton spinning and manufacturing. Handicraft production centering on the production of cotton cloth had a number of correlated educational possibilities. It was related to botany and to agriculture in that children could observe and participate in planting, cultivating, and harvesting cotton. It was related to small-scale industry in that children could observe and participate in ginning cotton—separating the fiber from the seeds and spinning the fiber into thread.

They could also participate in weaving the thread into cloth. Further, the cloth could be made into clothing. Thus, the participation of children in craft education—from planting the seed to manufacturing the clothing, in the case of cotton—would enable them to understand the full process of production. Further, the finished product was something they could see and appreciate as the tangible manifestation of their work. Thus, in Gandhi's mind, craft education satisfied a material need of society and served as the basis for purposeful, creative, and socially useful education.

As an educational method, Gandhi's proposed craft-centered basic education bore some resemblance to Pestalozzi's object lesson and to the efforts of such progressive educators as William H. Kilpatrick in making projects the focus of learning. There is a similarity between Gandhi's relationship of craft-centered education to economic development and to Booker T. Washington's work at Tuskegee Institute, where he saw vocational, trade, and agricultural education as the means to improving the economic status of blacks in the United States. Like these educational reformers in Europe and the United States, Gandhi had in mind a curricular and instructional reform that would make schooling an interesting and challenging experience for children.

Gandhi's proposed educational program was designed to liberate children's creative impulses by providing them with opportunities for purposeful and meaningful activity. Craft instruction was to make the school more vital and interesting to children by freeing them from routine and boredom.[16] Craft-centered education would provide children with a sense of accomplishment, dignity, and purpose. Because it was centered on making a tangible product, craft education would provide children with the opportunity to appreciate their accomplishments. Students would take pride in their work, develop self-confidence, and come to recognize the dignity of labor. By correlating instruction with meaningful work, basic education would break down old prejudices and socially integrate those of different castes.

Although resting on a vocational core, Gandhi's basic education plan also contained a cultural element. Craft instruction would break down the aesthetic separation between fine and applied art. Both dimensions of aesthetic experience would merge into an integrated flow of human activity and a correlated educational process.

Although Gandhi's life and presence on the world scene was of immense educational value to those he encountered personally and through his autobiography and writings, he should be seen as definitely contributing to educational philosophy and policy formulation. Although his general philosophy involving the affirmation of the spiritual dimension of human behavior and a strategy of nonviolent social change are large elements of the Gandhian world view, he did leave a contribution to the educational heritage in his plan of basic education.

Conclusion: An Assessment

It is not easy to assess the life of a person such as Gandhi, who was such a moral force on the global scene. His role of educational theorist, although important to him, was but one of the many dimensions of his life and personality. To assess Gandhi's contribution, we shall comment on him as a world leader, a planner for national development, and an educational theorist.

Gandhi was a moral force, a spiritual leader, rather than a political figure. He quickly learned, however, that, although moral principles can be stated in abstract documents, the ethical applications of such principles take place in political, social, and economic contexts. When Gandhi became involved in the politics of South Africa and India, struggling against unjust laws and arbitrary officials bent on enforcing such laws, he developed his strategy for social and political change. Rooted deeply in the spiritual dimension of life, Gandhi developed strategies for dealing with injustice such as nonviolent passive resistance. To use nonviolent tactics, Gandhi's followers had to be brought to a state of moral readiness for engaging in passive resistance and schooled in the appropriate behavioral response to violence when it came from those in authority. Gandhi's strategy, which was one of the factors in persuading the British to leave India, inspired the nonviolent campaign for civil rights that Martin Luther King Jr. led in the United States.

As the 1990s draw to a close, the world news is full of violence. Northern Ireland remains the scene of violence between Protestants and Catholics. The television screen carries daily accounts of terrorism and counteraction on the part of Arabs and Israelis. Student demonstrators were massacred by their own government in the People's Republic of China. Innocent people are taken hostage by terrorists, held for long periods of time, and assassinated. A moral voice and force such as Gandhi's is missing from the world scene. There is a need and place for the kind of moral persuasion that he exercised.

In his own historical period, Gandhi stands out as a leader against imperialism. The late 1940s, the 1950s, and 1960s marked the end of European imperialism in Africa and Asia, and new nations arose. Gandhi holds a place of significance in world history along with Nehru, Sukarno, Nkrumah, and other leaders of anticolonialism. As indicated in this chapter, the changes that resulted from the end of colonialism and the gaining of independence held tremendous educational implications. Education, in the form of schooling, became a force for nation building.

In terms of the implementation of Gandhi's plan for basic education in India, the results have been mixed. Less than 20 percent of Indian school children of primary age attend basic education schools. The majority attend more conventional schools. Although government authorities comment favorably on basic education, resources in India have been directed by central government planners to higher education of a scientific nature. Instead of encouraging "bottom up" development education originating in the villages as Gandhi urged, government strategy generally has been to modernize the nation from the top downward by training scientific and technological elites.

Gandhi's plan for the reconstruction of India with its basic education component was a theory of national development. From the end of World War II to the present, an important world trend has been the desire of economically underdeveloped nations in Africa, Asia, and South America to develop their economies. Such economic development is regarded as the key to improving the standard of living and providing increased social, health care, and educational opportunities.

In *India of My Dreams,* Gandhi described national development that would begin at the grass-roots level. According to such a strategy, planning would be done by the local people who would create their own small-scale industries. As indicated, basic education was the educational component of such locally directed development activities. If the local people had direct input into planning and running their economic affairs, Gandhi reasoned that they would believe themselves to be part of the process and be highly motivated to improve their economic condition.

The 1950s and 1960s, however, did not follow the pattern that Gandhi had urged. Instead of grass roots development, the strategy that was used in the newly independent third world nations was based on projects that were planned by the central government, with the assistance of developed nations such as the United States, and imposed on the local communities. These projects were generally large scale in scope, such as the construction of large dams, the change in agricultural production from subsistence farming to cash export crops, or the industrialization of the economy. Although the intention of these projects was economic growth, at times the projects actually worked against the economic interests of the lower socioeconomic classes and to the advantage of the upper classes. Further, the projects often disrupted traditional values.

In the late 1980s, there was a revitalization of interest in grass-roots development efforts such as those suggested by Gandhi. In Central and South America, Africa, and Asia, voluntary organizations and governments as well began to follow policies that encouraged projects for small-scale development planned and implemented at the grass-roots level. Gandhi's approach to small-scale development has renewed possibilities in the contemporary world.

Finally, as an educational theorist, Gandhi is significant for the relationship that he made between education and social change. His plan struck parallels with other approaches to education developed in Western educational thought. For example, Gandhi's theory of education that would develop the well-rounded person intellectually, morally, and physically was similar to Pestalozzi's method of education that emphasized training the senses through object lessons in homelike educational environments. There is a similarity between Gandhi's theory of basic education and Booker T. Washington's Tuskegee Institute in Alabama. Washington believed that the education of blacks in the United States should concentrate on vocational, trade, and agricultural education that could provide essential skills useful in establishing an economic base. Similarly, Gandhi believed that craft-centered education could provide an economic basis to revitalize India's villages. There is also a parallel between Gandhi's stress on craft-centered activities and progressive educators' emphasis on project-centered activities in the United States. Despite their metaphysical differences, Gandhi and Dewey concurred that education should be a force to build socially integrated communities.

Discussion Questions

1. Describe the educational effects of imperialism.
2. What was the context of British India and how did it affect education?
3. Identify the key events in Gandhi's life. Indicate how these events contributed to shaping his character.
4. Analyze nonviolent passive resistance as an instrument of social change.
5. How did Gandhi hope to revitalize village India?
6. What were the key elements in Gandhi's theory of basic education?

Research and Essay Topics

1. In a research paper, examine an aspect of the imposition of British educational structures on India during the colonial era.
2. Review a biography of Gandhi.
3. Prepare a research paper that compares Gandhi and Martin Luther King Jr. on the use of nonviolent passive resistance.
4. In a paper, analyze the various influences that brought Gandhi forward as leader of Indian independence.

5. In a paper, compare and contrast Gandhi and Lenin on social change.
6. In a paper, analyze the effect of untouchability on society and education.

Notes

1. Shriman Narayan, ed., *The Selected Works of Mahatma Gandhi,* vol. 2 (Ahmedabad: Navajivan Publishing House, 1968), 496.
2. Ibid., 499.
3. Narayan, vol. 6, 94.
4. Ibid., 104.
5. S. P. Chaube, *Recent Educational Philosophies in India* (Agra: Ram Pradad and Sons, 1967), 116.
6. Narayan, vol. 6, 104.
7. M. K. Gandhi, *My Philosophy of Life* (Bombay, India: Pearl Publications Private, Limited, 1961), 27–28.
8. Narayan, vol. 6, 114.
9. K. G. Saiyidain, *The Humanist Tradition in Modern Indian Educational Thought* (Madison, Wisc.: Dembar Educational Research Services, 1967), 89.
10. M. K. Gandhi, *India of My Dreams* (Ahmedabad: Navajivan Publishing House, 1947), 185.
11. Ibid., 186.
12. G. Ramanathan, *Education from Dewey to Gandhi* (London: Asia Publishing House, 1965), 4–5.
13. Ibid.
14. Humayun Kabir, *Indian Philosophy of Education* (New York: Asia Publishing House, 1961), 22.
15. Gandhi, *India of My Dreams,* 187.
16. M. Patel, *The Educational Philosophy of Mahatma Gandhi* (Ahmedabad: Navajivan Publishing House, 1953), 198.

Suggestions for Further Reading

Andrews, C. F. *Mahatma Gandhi At Work.* New York: Macmillan Publishing Company, 1931.
Ashe, Geoffrey. *Gandhi.* New York: Stein and Day, 1968.
Duncan, Ronald. *Gandhi: Selected Writings.* New York: Harper and Row, 1972.
Erikson, Eric. *Gandhi's Truth.* New York: Norton, 1972.
Fischer, Louis. *The Essential Gandhi: His Life, Work, and Ideas: An Anthology.* New York: Vintage Books, 1962.
———. *The Life of Mahatma Gandhi.* New York: Harper and Row, 1952.
Gandhi, M. K. *India of My Dreams.* Ahmedabad: Navajivan Publishing House, 1947.
———. *An Autobiography or the Story of My Experiments with Truth.* Boston: Beacon Press, 1957.
Iver, Raghavan. *The Moral and Political Writings of Mahatma Gandhi.* Oxford, England: Clarendon Press, 1986.
Kabir, Humayun. *Education in New India.* London: George Allen and Unwin, 1956.
———. *Indian Philosophy of Education.* New York: Asia Publishing House, 1961.
Moon, Penderel. *Gandhi and Modern India.* New York: Norton Press, 1969.
Mukerji, S. N. *History of Education in India.* Anand: Anand Press, 1957.
Patel, M. *The Educational Philosophy of Mahatma Gandhi.* Ahmedabad: Navajivan Publishing House, 1953.

Ramanathan, G. *Education from Dewey to Gandhi.* London; Asia Publishing House, 1965.
Saiyidain, K. G. *The Humanist Tradition in Modern Indian Educational Thought.* Madison, Wisc.: Dembar Educational Research Services, 1967.
Shirer, William. *Gandhi: A Memoir.* New York: Simon and Schuster, 1979.

CHAPTER 22

W. E. B. Du Bois: Scholar and Activist for African American Rights

Photograph of W. E. B. Du Bois; reproduction from the collections of the Library of Congress.

This chapter analyzes the life, educational philosophy, and contributions of William E. B. Du Bois (1868–1963), a distinguished sociologist and historian, who was a leader of the movement to raise black consciousness and win full equality for African Americans. Du Bois' sixteen pioneering books on sociology, history, and race relations established the scholarly foundations for the study of the African American experience.[1] He also wrote two autobiographies, several novels, and a play. Scholar and activist, Du Bois' editorship of *The Crisis*, the journal of the National Association for the Advancement of Colored People (NAACP), contributed to the momentum that led to the Civil Rights movement of the 1950s and 1960s.

Chapter 22 examines Du Bois' influence as an informal educator as well as his ideas on formal education. First, the general social, political, and economic context—especially how this context had an effect on African Americans in the United States—is discussed. Second, Du Bois' biography, his education and career, is analyzed to determine the evolution of his social and educational ideas. Third, Du Bois' major social, political, and educational ideas are identified and examined. Fourth, the continuing effect of Du Bois' contributions to U.S. education are examined. This analysis is designed to identify the forces that shaped Du Bois' life and to illustrate how his ideas and activities influenced the recent history of race relations in the United States.

To organize your thoughts as you read this chapter, you might focus on the following questions:

- What were the major trends, especially in the relationships between blacks and whites in the United States, in the historical context in which Du Bois lived?
- How did Du Bois' life, education, and career shape his social and educational philosophy?
- How did Du Bois' social philosophy determine his social and educational policy?
- What was the crux of the educational controversy between Du Bois and Booker T. Washington?
- What is the enduring effect of Du Bois' contributions on U.S. education?

The Historical Context of Du Bois' Life

The ninety-five years that W. E. B. Du Bois lived were of great significance in the history of black people in the United States. The Civil War ended three years before Du Bois was born. Sectional feelings between the victorious Union forces and the defeated eleven states of the Confederacy were still tense. From 1865 until the withdrawal of federal troops from the South in 1877 was the period of the Reconstruction of the former secessionist states into the Union.

At the time of the Reconstruction, the vast majority of African Americans lived in the southern or border states. There were small black communities in the northern cities but most African Americans still lived in the rural South. Du Bois, born in Massachusetts, was a child of parents who had been free long before the Emancipation Proclamation of President Lincoln in 1863 and the ratification of the Thirteenth Amendment to the Constitution, which ended slavery in the United States. This was not the case with

Booker T. Washington, who would eventually become Du Bois' antagonist. Washington, the son of slave parents, had been born into slavery in the rural South.

The Reconstruction and post-Reconstruction eras, from 1877 to 1910, were crucial decades in establishing the political, economic, and educational patterns that governed racial relations in the South. Despite the efforts of Lincoln's successor, Andrew Johnson, to temper Reconstruction policies, the dominant wing of the Republican party, known as "Radical Republicans," largely determined federal policies. Former Confederate leaders were disenfranchised and prevented from regaining political power. The Radical Republicans, led by former abolitionists Senator Charles Sumner and Representative Thaddeus Stevens, worked passionately to guarantee the voting and civil rights of the recently freed former slaves. In 1868, the Fourteenth Amendment to the Constitution, conferring citizenship and rights on the former slaves, was ratified. Two years later, the ratification of the Fifteenth Amendment confirmed the rights of formerly enslaved black males, the freedmen, to vote.

A coalition of Northern politicians, philanthropists, religious missionaries, and educators cooperated in advancing the civil and educational rights of blacks in the South. Although the Democratic party in the South was still regarded as the party that represented the old pattern of states' rights, the Republican party was regarded as the party of Lincoln and of freedom, particularly by blacks. Republican politicians, especially those affiliated with the party's radical wing, worked to organize blacks as a voting bloc. If they could carry the southern states in national elections for the Republican party, the party could maintain its control of the presidency and Congress. With federal troops ensuring that African Americans were permitted to vote, the Radical Republicans, supported by black voters, gained control of the legislatures throughout the South.

The interpretations of political Reconstruction have generated controversy in American historiography. The older interpretation, advanced by historians sympathetic to the "old South," was that the politics of the Reconstruction era were corrupt. According to this rendition of history, opportunistic Northern politicians, the "carpetbaggers," sojourned to the South with all of their possessions contained in a single carpetbag, determined to make their fortune in corrupt schemes. These carpetbaggers—supported by white Southern turncoats, the "scalawags"—used the politically unsophisticated black voters to win elections. They also manipulated African Americans who were elected to the state legislatures to secure power and make profits.

More recent interpretations of Reconstruction view the period as an era of substantial achievement in the development of Southern life and institutions for both whites and blacks. According to this view of history, Reconstruction legislatures embarked on internal improvement programs for the war-devastated South that involved road and railway building. These improvements laid the needed foundations for industrializing the "new South." Further, Reconstruction legislatures enacted the first levies of a fairer and a more uniform system of taxation. In education, the legislatures enacted laws that extended the common school system to the South, which hitherto had generally failed to create and support public schools. When he embarked on his career as a historian, Du Bois wrote a history of the Reconstruction that sought to challenge stereotypic fallacies about the role of African Americans.

If the South's political reconstruction left its mark on white-black racial relationships and attitudes, educational reconstruction was an equally potent factor. This educational reconstruction shaped the ideas of Booker T. Washington, the leading spokesman of African Americans throughout the rest of the nineteenth century and until his death in 1915. It also influenced Du Bois' rejection of Washington's philosophy of industrial education for African Americans and shaped his own vision of black education.

The initial efforts to educate the former slaves came from the efforts of Northern educators, many of whom had been influenced by abolitionist ideology and the New England concept of common schooling. These educators often were supported by Protestant religious denominations in the Northern states. They also received financial assistance from philanthropists who wanted to improve the condition of blacks and by the Freedmen's Bureau, a federal agency established to ease the transition from slavery to citizenship. Northern schoolmasters and school "marms," as they were called, labored with a missionary-like zeal to educate African American children. They emphasized a latter-day version of Puritanism that specified educational goals as developing diligence, orderliness, and punctuality—the old New England virtues—along with basic literacy's reading, writing, and computation.

The New England version of education made a profound impression on the South's recently emancipated blacks. The foundation of literacy and morality was further refined into what was termed "industrial education." Institutes such as the Hampton Institute, founded in 1868 and operated by Colonel Samuel Chapman Armstrong, implemented the philosophy of industrial education. Armstrong asserted that his black students needed to be "trained before they could be educated." Armstrong also postulated that for black youngsters the inculcation of moral values preceded intellectual education. Based on the "Yankee values of industriousness and thrift," Colonel Armstrong developed a thoroughly practical curriculum of vocational training.[2]

Booker T. Washington, a student at Hampton Institute, captured the attention of Colonel Armstrong, who made the industrious young man his secretary. Washington went on to endorse and implement industrial education at Tuskegee Institute in Alabama and then disseminate its doctrines throughout the South. Indeed, Washington's endorsement of industrial education extended this particular educational philosophy throughout the nation as the most suitable educational program for African Americans as well as Native Americans.

Industrial education was virtually synonymous with vocational training. Although the word *industrial* was used, the underlying philosophy was more general in content. It meant learning the various trades of brickmaking and bricklaying, shoemaking, carpentry, blacksmithing, and so on. It meant learning domestic skills of cooking, sewing, food preservation, and child care. Because blacks were often located in rural areas, industrial training also involved agricultural skills relating to maximizing the productivity of Southern farms. It was also intended to prepare black youth, especially young women, in teacher education programs to teach in black elementary schools.

Under Armstrong's tutelage, Washington became a leading proponent of industrial education. When the Alabama legislature approved and funded the establishment of an African American training school at Tuskegee, Alabama, in 1881, Washington, with Armstrong's strong endorsement, was appointed the Institute's principal or headmaster. In numerous speeches, essays, and books, Washington told the story of his successful work that made Tuskegee the leading educational institution for blacks in the United States. Washington began his work at Tuskegee on July 4, 1881. Using an old church building as a school, he taught the thirty-seven students who formed the Institute's first class. Within a decade, Washington had built the Institute into a nationally recognized institution with more than 100 buildings, a student enrollment of 1,200, and a faculty of eighty-eight instructors.[3] Just as Hampton had been the paradigm for Tuskegee, Washington's Institute became the model for other black colleges.

While Du Bois was growing up in Great Barrington, Massachusetts, and attending that community's elementary and high schools, Washington was transforming Tuskegee into an educational force. While Du Bois was pursuing advanced degrees at Harvard and the University of Berlin, Washington was gaining acknowledgment as the spokesman of black America. Although both Washington and Du Bois sought to advance the cause of African Americans in the United States, they employed very different strategies. To understand the context that shaped Du Bois' ideology, it is necessary to examine Washington's work at Tuskegee and his educational philosophy of industrial education.

Washington developed both an educational and social-political-economic philosophy. He first became known as an educator and then, because of his success in education, attracted a receptive audience to his social philosophy. At Tuskegee, Washington determined to concentrate on basic rather than higher education. Perhaps his decision was largely made for him by the conditions he faced. With minimal funding from the Alabama legislature, now in white control, Washington had to build the institution with his own labor and that of his first students.

Washington theorized that what the South's rural black population needed most was a basic education that, following the philosophy of industrial education, stressed basic health principles, literacy, and the fundamental tool skills. Washington explained his advocacy of industrial education at Tuskegee:

> First, we have found the industrial teaching useful in giving the student a chance to work out a portion of his expenses while in school. Second, the school furnishes labour that has an economic value and at the same time gives the student a chance to acquire knowledge and skill while performing the labour. Most of all, we find the industrial system valuable in teaching economy, thrift, and the dignity of labour and in giving moral backbone to students.[4]

After inculcating basic skills and the "right" moral values, these fundamentals would be followed by vocational education in the various trades, agricultural education based on the climate, topography, and crops of the southern region, domestic education, and normal training—teacher preparation—for elementary school teachers. To teach such trades as brickmaking, bricklaying, and carpentry, Washington's students constructed their own classroom buildings and dormitories. His program of agricultural education focused on raising the crops grown in Alabama—corn, cotton, and peanuts. He encouraged the research of George Washington Carver, a professor at Tuskegee, to investigate new uses for those crops that would improve the economy for rural blacks. Washington believed that a basic improvement in agricultural techniques would raise the income of black farmers, many of whom were victims of the sharecrop system. Sharecroppers were tenant farmers who cultivated land owned by someone else, usually a white landowner. In return for the use of a home and land, the tenant farmer would pay back rent by turning over a large part of the crops produced to the landowner. Washington was convinced that blacks should remain in the South and become a class of independent landowning farmers.

According to Washington:

> To . . . our aspiring youth, seeking an opening in life, to me but two alternatives present themselves, as matters now stand—to live a menial in the North, or a semi-freeman in the South. This brings us face to face with Northern competition and Southern prejudice, and between them I have no hesitancy in saying that the Negro can find his way to the front sooner through Southern prejudice than through Northern competition. The one decreases, the other increases.[5]

Washington's educational program at Tuskegee was nonthreatening to the Southern white power structure that, with the removal of federal troops in 1877, had regained political control and were now disenfranchising black voters. Further, it was providing a small but trained force of black craftsmen for what was being called the industrial "new South." Washington's educational practices, although socially conservative, had some progressive elements about them in that they involved students in learning by doing. However, unlike educational progressivism, Tuskegee's use of vocational training tended to limit further educational progress, especially into higher and professional education. When Du Bois challenged Washington's educational leadership of American blacks, his criticism was directed against restrictive characteristics of the Tuskegee educational philosophy.

As Washington's fame spread, the concept of industrial education for African Americans won endorsement from many educators in both the South and the North. For example, the Monhonk Conferences of 1890 and 1891 brought many of the nation's educators to New York to consider the issue of African American education. After being lectured by General Armstrong that blacks needed to be instilled with a sense of the dignity of work and to learn solid industrial and agricultural trades, the conference attendees voted overwhelmingly to support industrial education.

Washington's rise to prominence took place during a time when there was an intense Southern white reaction against the earlier Reconstruction period. From the end of Reconstruction through the First World War, the politics of the South created a rigid, racially segregated society. During the 1880s and 1890s, the populist movement gained political momentum in the South as disgruntled and economically hard-pressed white and black farmers challenged the rule of conservative white "bourbon" Democrats. White Farmers' Alliances and Black Farmers' Alliances were organized and some cooperation occurred between the two. Blacks had a short-lived opportunity to act as the balance of power between contending factions of white voters.

The first signs of political alliance between the economically struggling farmers were wrecked, however, on the barrier of racism. So-called poor white farmers, who tilled small farms, had in their background an intense fear of blacks as economic competitors. Using arguments of white supremacy, certain populist leaders challenged the conservative white politicians in the Democratic party primaries that nominated candidates for office. Because the South was at that time a one-party section of the country, winning the Democratic party nomination carried with it the certainty of victory in the general election. Until the 1950s, the Republican party was a negligible force in the South.

The gaining of power by the populist-inclined, agrarian Democrats over the conservative "bourbon" Democrats proved disastrous for black interests in the South. It was during this period, from 1880 to 1910, that the most severe restrictions were enacted against blacks in the South. By the 1880s, blacks had few friends in the national Republican party who were willing to take up their cause. The generation of Radical Republicans had now passed from the political scene, and party leaders were more preoccupied with maintaining the support of the "captains of industry" in the growing corporate sector. Further, the Social Darwinist ideology was in vogue both in popular and academic circles. Some Social Darwinists saw the struggle for survival as a racial combat in which the fittest race was the white race. Added to these factors was the accommodationist strategy of Booker T. Washington, who decided to go along with rather than resist the prevailing ideology.

In the late 1880s and 1890s, the southern states enacted a series of laws to limit and then virtually eliminate an African American political role. For example, Mississippi enacted a poll tax that required a fee for the privilege of voting. The poll tax eliminated many black voters from the voter registration lists. In addition, Mississippi passed a law that required voters to explain selected provisions of the state and national constitutions before they could vote. The election officials, who were white, asked complicated questions and then disqualified black voters. In Louisiana, for example, there had been 130,344 registered black voters in 1896; by 1900, only 5,320 remained on the voting lists.[6] In addition to the statutory limitations on black suffrage, the Ku Klux Klan used intimidation and terror against African Americans who challenged the system. The 1890s were a time of virulent racism. What took shape in the South was a rigid racial segregation system of separate schools and transportation facilities that, with the force of state law, relegated blacks to second-class citizenship.

While rigid segregation laws were enacted throughout the South, Booker T. Washington, continuing to hold to his philosophy of industrial education, took an accommodationist line. Speaking on September 28, 1895, to a large audience at the Atlanta Cotton Exposition, Washington made a highly significant and often quoted pronouncement on white-black racial relations in the South. The Tuskegee president told his listeners:

> No race can prosper till it learns that there is as much dignity in tilling a field as in writing a poem. It is at the bottom of life we must begin, and not at the top. . . .
>
>   The wisest among my race understand that the agitation of questions of social equality is the extremist folly, and that progress in the enjoyment of all the privileges that will come to us must be the result of severe and constant struggle rather than of artificial forcing.[7]

In 1896, the U.S. Supreme Court's landmark decision in *Plessy v. Ferguson* gave federal constitutional sanction to the segregation system that had developed in southern and border states. At issue was the constitutionality of an Alabama law that required separate railway carriages for white and "colored" passengers. The case arose when Homer A. Plessy, an African American, boarded an East Louisiana Railway train as a passenger from New Orleans to Covington. Taking a seat reserved for whites, Plessy refused to move to the black section when ordered to do so by the conductor. Plessy was arrested and brought before Judge John H. Ferguson of the Criminal District Court of New Orleans. Ferguson rejected Plessy's lawyer's argument that his arrest violated the Constitution's Fourteenth Amendment. The precedent-setting case reached the U.S. Supreme Court.

Justice Henry Brown, speaking for the majority of the justices of the Supreme Court in the Plessy case, established the precedent of "separate but equal," which would stand until overturned in the *Brown v. Board of Education of Topeka* case in 1954 that ended *de jure* racial segregation in the United States. In 1896, however, the Court, ruling that segregation was not discriminatory against blacks, stated that racially separate facilities, as long as they were equal, could be ordered legally by the states. According to the Court's decision, the object of the Fourteenth Amendment:

> . . . was undoubtedly to enforce the absolute equality of the two races before the law, but in the nature of things it could not have been intended to abolish distinction based upon color, or to enforce social, as distinguished from political equality, or a commingling of the two races upon terms unsatisfactory to either.[8]

The political and economic reality, however, was that these separate facilities, particularly schools, were not equal. By 1900, the southern states, which lagged seriously behind the other states in educational funding, were spending twice as much to educate white than black children.

This was the historical context that shaped the background of W. E. B. Du Bois' struggle for African American freedom and civil, political, and educational rights in the United States. The context involved longstanding racist attitudes in the South that were given the sanction of law. It involved a Northern attitude in which racism was real but covert. It involved an attitude on the part of politicians, including progressives, to avoid entanglement in the race question. It involved the existence of segregated institutions, especially schools, for a large part of the nation's population of children and youth.

W. E. B. Du Bois: Activist for African American Civil and Education Rights

W. E. B. Du Bois was born on February 23, 1868, in Great Barrington, Massachusetts, a New England town nestled in the Berkshire hills. His ancestry was of mixed African and European descent. Alfred Du Bois, his father, a grandson of James Du

Bois, a white plantation owner in the Bahamas, was born in Haiti. Mary Silvina Burghardt, his mother, was descended from Africans who had been brought by force to the United States by William Coenraet Burghardt, a Dutch slave trader. The Burghardt family, which dated to the prerevolutionary period, had long established roots in Great Barrington. Alfred and Mary were married in 1867 and William, their child, was born a year later. Du Bois' father left Great Barrington in search of work when William was a year old and never returned to the family. William was raised by his mother, who, although suffering from depression and the effects of a stroke, supported the household and encouraged her son's educational ambitions.[9]

William Du Bois' life as a youngster growing up in a New England town was radically different from that experienced by Booker T. Washington in the South. Unlike Washington, Du Bois' ancestors had been free since the American Revolution. He was a member of a small African American minority of twenty-five families in a town of 3,920 inhabitants which included the descendants of founding Dutch and English settlers, as well as the newly arriving Irish and Czech immigrants.[10]

Du Bois' early religious convictions were Calvinist, the bedrock theology of the Puritans which flowed into New England Congregationalism. He and his mother attended the First Congregational Church and he participated in its Sunday school. The influence of Congregationalism had been a significant force in the pre-Civil War abolitionist movement. In addition, many of the teachers who went to the South after the Civil War to teach in the Freedmen's Bureau schools had been nurtured in Congregationalism's Calvinist theological foundations. It would be a formative force in the "black Puritanism" that shaped the religious outlook of many African Americans.

In a community where blacks and whites coexisted civilly, Du Bois, though conscious that he was different, appears to have been accepted socially by his white classmates. Unlike Washington, who had to struggle against great odds to obtain an education, Du Bois attended his local elementary school, enrolling at age six. A serious student, he was a favorite pupil of his teachers. He then enrolled in Great Barrington's high school. Frank Hosmer, principal of the high school, who noticed Du Bois' academic talent, encouraged him to enroll in the college preparatory curriculum, which included algebra, geometry, Latin, and Greek.[11] After reading Macaulay's *History of England*, Du Bois, who tried to emulate the noted historian's style, developed a keen interest in history, which would become his major field at Harvard.

Du Bois also benefitted from the informal educational agencies of Great Barrington. Because his mother was the sole support of the family, Du Bois worked at a variety of jobs to supplement her income as a maid in white households. He took part-time jobs while in high school doing chores for senior citizens, working as a clerk in a local grocery store, and delivering newspapers. An avid reader, Du Bois was befriended by the owner of the local bookstore, who permitted him to read the newspapers, magazines, and books that he stocked. Showing a talent for writing, young William Du Bois also was the Great Barrington reporter for the *Springfield Republican*.[12] The fledgling reporter covered the town meetings, which in the New England tradition of local control, set the budget for the schools, roads, and other community responsibilities.

In addition to pursuing the rigorously academic college preparatory curriculum, Du Bois was active in co-curricular activities at the high school. He was co-editor of the high school newspaper, *The Howler*. He also organized a literary society, the "Sons of Freedom," which sought to advance the progress of Great Barrington's African American population.[13] Even as a high school student, Du Bois exhibited adeptness as a journalist, editor, and organizer—abilities he would employ later as one of the founders of the Niagara Movement and the National Association for the Advancement of Colored People.

In 1884, Du Bois graduated from high school. In addition to being his mother's pride, he was well regarded by both the black and white communities of Great Barrington. He received his diploma with high honors, the first black person to graduate from the high school and delivered a commencement oration on Wendell Phillips, the New England abolitionist.[14] Encouraged by his mother and the Burghardt family, he applied for admission to Harvard University. However, his mother's death in March 1885 and a lack of funds made it appear that the talented young black student would be unable to attend college. It was at this point that Frank Hosmer and several other community leaders raised enough money to send William to college. Du Bois' white benefactors decided that Du Bois should attend Fisk University, a Congregational institution for African Americans in Nashville, Tennessee, rather than Harvard.[15]

Du Bois, age seventeen, left Great Barrington in 1885 and made his first journey to the South to enroll at Fisk University, an institution of 450 students, which had been founded in 1866 by the American Missionary Society. The faculty of fifteen, fourteen whites and one black, were dedicated Congregationalists who were still motivated by the spirit of New England abolitionism. Unlike Hampton and Tuskegee's industrial training programs, Fisk's curriculum was academic in the classical sense. It included Greek, Latin, French, German, theology, natural sciences, music, moral philosophy and history, subjects Booker T. Washington would find ornamental.[16] Du Bois found his courses at Great Barrington's high school had prepared him well for college but he noted that many of his fellow students, products of segregated Southern black secondary schools, were ill-prepared for higher education. At Fisk, Du Bois excelled in Latin, Greek, French, rhetoric, botany, and calculus. Continuing his interest in history, he read Carlyle's *On Heroes, Hero-Worship, and the Heroic in History*.[17] Du Bois envisioned the great leader as a powerful change agent. Like Hosmer, Du Bois' professors at Fisk recognized that he was a person of fine academic talent, one likely to achieve distinction in the world of scholarship.

As in high school, Du Bois was attracted to journalism and editing. He worked on the staff of the *Fisk Herald*, the university newspaper, and became editor-in-chief in his senior year. He also made his first sortie into fiction, writing "Tom Brown at Fisk," which was serialized in the *Herald*.[18] Attracted to cultural activities, he was a member of the Mozart Society, a choral group that performed the classics.[19] Du Bois benefitted from his academic studies at Fisk but also came face to face with the South's racial segregation. The New England native's encounters with racism were converting him into an activist who would to do battle with prejudice.

In 1886, instead of returning to Great Barrington for summer vacation, Du Bois determined to learn firsthand about the lives and situations of rural Southern African Americans. After taking pedagogical classes at the Lebanon Teachers's Institute, he passed the elementary teachers' examination and was issued a certificate.

In the summers of 1886 and 1887, Du Bois found a job as a summer school teacher for twenty-eight dollars a month in a small rural black elementary school, near Alexandria in east Tennessee. The school, housed in an abandoned log storage barn, enrolled fifteen students, ranging in age from six to twenty.[20] Here, he not only encountered the consequences of racism and segregation but found a debilitating rural poverty. In a dilapidated school with few facilities, he taught rural black youths and gained a vivid insight into the condition of African Americans in the rural South.[21] Du Bois's attendance at Fisk University and his teaching experience made him conscious of his race and its condition in a South that was erecting rigid walls of segregation.

In June 1888, Du Bois graduated from Fisk University. In his commencement address, he gave an oration on Otto von Bismarck, the iron chancellor who had achieved German unification through a policy of diplomacy and military force. African Americans, Du Bois argued, needed to develop leaders like the German chancellor who could raise consciousness and create a mobilized and disciplined people.[22] Even at this early stage in his academic career, Du Bois was moving in the direction of the need for a highly educated black vanguard, the "talented tenth."

Du Bois had not abandoned his high school dream of earning a degree from Harvard University. He was also convinced, contrary to Booker T. Washington's doctrine of the need to create a class of black tradesmen and farmers, that the road to black equality was through higher and professional education. In 1888, Du Bois, the sixth African American to be enrolled up-to-that time at Harvard, was admitted with junior standing and awarded a scholarship to support his study.

As a Harvard student, Du Bois encountered a generation of professors who were luminaries in their academic disciplines. He studied philosophy with George Santayana. He was particularly impressed by William James, who was developing his own version of pragmatic philosophy and psychology in his books, *Principles of Psychology* and *The Will to Believe*. James became a personal friend and provided sound academic counsel to the aspiring Du Bois. His study of economics under Charles Dunbar and Frank Taussig made him a devotee of *laissez-faire* economic theory, a commitment which he later abandoned as he turned to Marxism. Once again, Du Bois impressed his professors with his academic talents. He graduated *cum laude* on June 25, 1890, earning his bachelor's degree with a concentration in philosophy .[23]

Du Bois now began his graduate study at Harvard. After some hesitation between philosophy and history as a career choice, Du Bois decided on history, a subject which he pursued under Professor Albert Bushnell Hart's direction. Hart was noted for his emphasis on basing interpretation on solid bedrock original primary sources. Du Bois's meticulously researched scholarly works followed Hart's admonitions about the proper use of the historical method. Du Bois' work with Hart was particularly useful in developing competency in historical research that Du Bois would combine with sociology. Du Bois's acumen in historical sociology was particularly useful in his research on the black community in Philadelphia, which would later earn him academic fame.[24]

From 1890 to 1892, Du Bois pursued graduate studies in history as well as doing some work in economics and political science. In 1891, he was awarded his master of arts degree in history and was admitted to the doctoral program in social science. Much of his time was devoted to researching his dissertation on the "Suppression of the African Slave Trade to the United States of America, 1638–1870."[25]

As was then the academic custom, Du Bois went to Germany to complete his higher academic studies. German universities were preeminent in the new scholarship in which a small number of carefully selected graduate students worked in seminars with distinguished professors who were specialists in their academic disciplines. Young Americans aspiring to be professors would travel to Germany, seek admission to a leading research university, and then import the new scholarship to U.S. higher education. The German universities emphasized research and publication—two activities in which Du Bois would excel as a university professor.

Supported by the Slater Fund, Du Bois traveled in 1892 to Europe with the goal of enrolling at a German university. He had long been attracted to German scholarship and leadership. In fact, he regarded Bismarck as a model statesman whose leadership skills might well be emulated by those aspiring to lead African Americans. Du Bois would compare the United States as a generally "optimistic" nation with "individual freedom" with Germany, a model of culture, efficiency and order.[26]

After some traveling through western Europe and intensive study of the German language, Du Bois enrolled at Berlin's premier Friedrich Wilhelm University, where until 1894 he studied the emerging social sciences with leading experts. He studied economics with Gustav Schmoller, political science with Rudolph von Gneist and Heinrich von Treitschke, and sociology with Max Weber. His studies at Berlin reinforced Hart's approach to historiography. Theoretical hypotheses were to be formulated only after completing very intricate and meticulous research into actual social, political, and economic phenomenon. During Du Bois' study in Berlin, German philosophy was dominated by Hegelian Idealism, which exalted the nation-state as the earthly embodiment of the Absolute. Du Bois was captivated by the Hegelian emphasis on the dialectical process in history and began to interpret race relations in terms of a clash of thesis, the former master, and the antithesis, the freed slave.

Despite his excellent academic record at the Friedrich Wilhelm University, Du Bois encountered the academic obstacles that have wounded many graduate students and often blocked their careers. The majority of the faculty voted that Du Bois was ineligible for doctoral examinations because he had not satisfied residency requirements. Unfortunately, Du Bois's scholarship support had ended and he was forced by circumstances to return to the United States to complete a Harvard doctorate rather than one at the University in Berlin. Apparently, the administrative decision at Berlin was based on academic rigidity rather than racial prejudice. Du Bois encountered little antiblack discrimination in Europe. However, he was stunned by the degree of nationalism and ethnic hostility, and the strong undercurrent of anti-Semitism.[27] Du Bois' European experience broadened his intellectual worldview to see racial relations beyond the problems that blacks faced in the United States. Du Bois's role in the movement for black freedom was informed by an international and pan-African perspective. Long before Alex Haley gained prominence as the author of *Roots*, Du Bois, who considered himself African American, saw connections between the struggle of blacks in the United States against a system of racial segregation and black Africans against an exploitive European colonialism. Black culture in the United States was a part of a larger, more international Africanism. Black people in the United States needed to become conscious and proud of their African heritage. Such heightened consciousness would be an asset in the coming struggle for civil and educational rights. Blacks in Africa, too, needed to draw on the resources of their cultural heritage in the coming struggle against colonial rule.

While in Europe, Du Bois encountered the theories of Karl Marx, which were popular in Socialist and Communist circles. His later attraction to Marxism and his international orientation brought a new dimension to his views of the black situation in the United States, to his scholarship, and to his social activism. He came to believe that blacks were victims, as were working class whites, of an exploitive capitalism. Once again, Du Bois' background departed from that of Booker T. Washington, whose life, with the exception of some European travel later in his career, was confined largely to the American South.

In 1894, his funds depleted, Du Bois returned to the United States, still lacking the doctorate that he sought so earnestly. He now completed his doctoral studies at Harvard. In 1895, Harvard University accepted his doctoral dissertation, "The Suppression of the African Slave-Trade to the United States of America, 1638–1870," which was subsequently published as a book in the Harvard Historical Studies Series.[28]

From 1894 through 1896, Du Bois was professor of classics at Wilberforce University, an institution affiliated with the African Methodist Episcopal Church, in Xenia, Ohio. Du Bois had a heavy teaching load in Latin, Greek, and German. He missed teaching history and sociology, his areas of specialization. He was a rigorous, demanding, and somewhat aloof teacher. He disliked the atmosphere of religious conformity at Wilberforce University and what he regarded as a paternalistic administration. While at Wilberforce, the young professor married Nina Gomer, an undergraduate student from Cedar Rapids, Iowa. After their marriage in Iowa, the couple returned to Wilberforce to live in a small two-room apartment in the men's dormitory.

In 1896, a research opportunity enabled Du Bois and his wife to leave Wilberforce. The University of Pennsylvania was conducting a comprehensive historical and sociological study of Philadelphia's African American population, which at 40,000 was the nation's largest Northern black community. Du Bois, appointed the project's research director, conducted a monumental and often-cited sociological study of the black community. Pioneering in sociological survey methods, Du Bois' detailed study examined family structure, neighborhoods, social organizations, educational institutions, political involvement, and economic roles. Du Bois' *The Philadelphia Negro*, published in 1899, developed significant generalizations about the development and problems of Philadelphia's African American community.[29] Although not the sole cause of black disadvantagement, Du Bois established that racial discrimination was a powerful determinant in limiting African American socioeconomic and educational opportunities. African Americans were still the historic victims of slavery which continued to affect their family structure, work ethic, and class behavior. Du Bois also discerned an evolving class structure within the Philadelphia black community: a small elite, a moderate-size middle class, a large strata of working poor, and those lowest on the socioeconomic scale, the "submerged tenth." His findings in the Philadelphia study contributed to his evolving strategy of racial change. He believed that a small well-educated elite, the talented tenth, would lead the African-American advance.[30]

Du Bois' Philadelphia study made him a visible and recognized scholar in sociology. His expertise in examining the Philadelphia blacks as a historically evolving community helped to develop the subfield of historical sociology. In addition to using archival documents, Du Bois had taken his study into the Philadelphia's streets. He surveyed several thousand members of the community and interviewed several hundred of them. He visited their institutions, homes, schools, and other agencies of community life.[31] Combining historical and sociological methods, Du Bois generated a massive data base and reached significant conclusions that could be used in later reform efforts.

In 1897, Du Bois accepted a position as a professor of economics and history at Atlanta University in Georgia. Established by Congregationalists after the Civil War, Atlanta University was an African American institution of higher learning. It offered both a traditional academic curriculum as well as some vocational programs. For thirteen years, Du Bois taught history, sociology, and economics at Atlanta University. As a teacher, Du Bois, a "no nonsense" instructor, appealed most to bright, academically inclined students. Others tended to be intimidated by his erudition and demanding course requirements.

Du Bois coordinated the annual Atlanta University Conference on Negro Problems, the proceedings of which were important in building a knowledge base on African American life and culture. The Conferences documented important changes in black communities. Migration was under way from rural to urban areas and from South to North. Using an extensive survey method, Du Bois examined the African American educational situation, documenting growing educational disparities between the schooling of black and white children.

While at Atlanta Du Bois articulated his educational concept of the talented tenth. Although all blacks should enjoy the equality of educational opportunity denied them by the institutionalized racism of a segregated society, Du Bois argued that all races, including blacks, had an intellectually gifted elite. This elite—the talented tenth— should have the advantage of higher and professional education. In the struggle for racial justice, the talented tenth would act as the vanguard of the movement.

While a professor at Atlanta University, Du Bois continued to write and publish. His *The Souls of Black Folk,* a collection of essays on African American life and culture was published in 1903.[32] *Souls of Black Folk* added a new dimension to the literature on African Americans as it examined the social and cultural psyches of people of African descent in the Americas. In 1909, *John Brown*, his biography of the radical abolitionist who led an abortive attempt to free the slaves at Harper's Ferry appeared.[33] He also served as a consultant for the U.S. Department of Labor.

Booker T. Washington, often called the "Wizard" because of his astute political sagacity, began to feel threatened by Du Bois' rising star. For a time, these two very different men had cooperated. Washington had even offered Du Bois a position at Tuskegee, which Du Bois declined. Washington had become a recognized leader of African Americans. What was called the Tuskegee Machine controlled the appointment of many African Americans to political and educational positions. Du Bois had become convinced that Washington's accommodationist policy had to be challenged and discredited so that African Americans could pursue a more militant and activist course.

Du Bois' relationship with Washington had begun as admiration for the Tuskegee educator but it had turned to apprehension that Washington was leading African Americans down a disastrous path. Finally, it deteriorated into open antagonism. Du Bois accused Washington of encouraging African Americans to renounce three necessary means of empowerment: political organization, the legal pursuit of civil rights, and participation in higher education.[34]

The two men had different origins, temperaments, and ideologies. Washington's origins and attitudes were of the rural South while Du Bois was a cosmopolitan scholar. While both were skilled speakers, Washington, the educator-politician, was expert in using crowd psychology to assess his audience and use anecdotes and humor in winning it to his point of view. The scholarly Du Bois was more of a cool intellectual who used logic and principles to put forth his agenda. For Du Bois, the higher education of able African Americans was necessary for black empowerment. For Washington, industrial education and the ownership of small businesses were the more realistic course. In his masterful biography of Du Bois, David Levering Lewis found Washington and Du Bois were addressing "two dissimilar socioeconomic orders" and "speaking past each other" rather than analyzing the same racial issues. Washington's impoverished agricultural rural South with its racism, embedded from slavery, was unready for the Du Bois' agenda. Conversely, Washington's passive accommodationism was not a viable program for racial progress in the "urban, industrial, multiethnic North." While Washington's ideology was rooted in the South's past, Du Bois spoke for a more national, indeed worldwide, future.[35]

By 1905, Du Bois joined with blacks and whites who wanted to restore civil rights to African Americans. He was part of a group of individuals dedicated to civil rights who assembled at Fort Erie, Ontario, on the Canadian side of Niagara Falls, to form an organization and develop a strategy to achieve their goals. Taking a more militant stand that ran counter to Washington's gradualism, the group, organized as the "Niagara Movement," named Du Bois its general secretary, a position he held until 1910. Many of those involved in the Niagara movement would later become members of the larger National Association for the Advancement of Colored People (NAACP).

In 1909, the National Negro Committee, which included both blacks and whites, met in New York City. The next year, this committee, which included Du Bois and others of the Niagara Movement, officially reorganized itself as the NAACP. The new organization, officially launched in 1911, elected Moorfield Storey, a past president of the American Bar Association, as its president. It united leading blacks and whites to work for the civil, social, and educational progress of African Americans. With Du Bois, the other leaders of the NAACP were Mary Ovington, a progressive organizer, Rabbi Stephen Wise, Oswald Garrison Villard, and other national figures. Two prominent black ministers, Bishop Alexander Walters and the Reverend William Brooks, were among the founders. The formation of the NAACP would have important consequences for Du Bois specifically and for blacks generally. In contrast to Washington's accommodationism, the NAACP formed a strategy to:

- Raise black consciousness and act as a unified voice for African Americans.
- Embark on a general educational program to inform both blacks and whites about the condition of African Americans in the United States.
- Begin the legal battle to end legally sanctioned racial segregation in the United States. (This battle eventually led to victory in the Brown decision that overturned *Plessy v. Ferguson.*)

In 1910, Du Bois was appointed Director of Publicity and Research, made a member of the NAACP's board of directors, and named editor of *The Crisis*, the official journal of the NAACP, which undertook the challenge of consciousness raising and education. He was ideally suited for the position of editor. Since his high school days in Great Barrington and as an undergraduate at Fisk University, he had been involved in journalism both as a writer and an editor. A first-rate scholar with proven academic credentials, Du Bois was a gifted editorialist who knew how to draft a readable argument that appealed to a wide audience. Under Du Bois's editorship, *The Crisis* addressed a wide range of issues relating to the black situation in the United States. Despite opposition from the conservative Booker T. Washington and his Tuskegee Machine, *The Crisis* was becoming a force in raising black consciousness from passive accommodation to activism.[36]

Under Du Bois' editorship, *The Crisis'* circulation steadily increased. Its subscribers who numbered 3,000 in 1911 reached 22,500 by 1912, 33,000 by 1914, and 45,000 by 1916.[37] Despite his success with *The Crisis*, Du Bois, a demanding personality, was often the center of conflict on the board of trustees.

In addition to his position in the NAACP, Du Bois continued to be the scholar, historian, sociologist, and writer. In 1911, his book *The Quest for the Silver Fleece* appeared. It was followed by *The Negro* (1915); *Darkwater: Voices from Within the Veil* (1920); and *The Gift of Black Folk* (1924).[38]

From 1910 onward, the years in which Du Bois labored to establish and give momentum to the NAACP, especially in the period between World War I and II, momentous changes were occurring among the African American population. First, blacks were no longer concentrated in the rural South. The wars generated employment needs and had expanded the job market in the United States. By the thousands, blacks migrated from the rural South to Northern cities to take jobs and improve their economic condition. Large black communities developed in the cities of New York, Philadelphia, Boston, Chicago, Detroit, and Cleveland. Blacks joined labor unions and a new spirit of activism was being born.

Second, the condition of African Americans had grown more complex and varied than it had been in the days of Booker T. Washington. An urban black community now existed along with the Southern rural and agricultural community. Further, Washington's death in 1915 left a leadership void among more conservative and accommodationist blacks. Three, a new attitude was emerging among African Americans, especially young blacks. Soldiers who had fought for democracy abroad in both World Wars were no longer willing to accept oppression in their native land. These factors gave a new momentum to the movement for civil rights and educational opportunities.

Although Du Bois never gained the prominence as the spokesman for African Americans that Washington had enjoyed for such a long time, he was nonetheless one of the leaders of the rising black movement in the United States. Along with his important role in the NAACP, Du Bois was involved in cultural, educational, and political affairs. He was especially interested in helping aspiring young black artists, writers, and poets in their careers. Achievement in the arts by blacks was both a way of contributing to U.S. and world culture generally and in raising black consciousness and self-esteem particularly. In the 1920s and early 1930s, he encouraged African American writers, artists, poets, and actors who were part of the Harlem Renaissance, such as Countee Cullen, Jean Toomer, Langston Hughes, and Claude McKay. Du Bois helped arrange conferences, performances, and concerts for them. He also arranged meetings and appointments with publishers and sponsors.

Throughout his life, Du Bois was involved in education. His articles and books were important sources for courses that dealt with African American history and culture. In addition to these formal educational activities, Du Bois was an important informal educator as editor of *The Crisis*. Along with using the law to remedy discrimination against blacks and using political organization to elect advocates of civil rights to office, Du Bois saw education as an important instrument in the struggle. His theory of the talented tenth was intended to create a leadership elite. However, he was also concerned that blacks receive the best elementary and secondary education their talents would allow. To this end, he joined forces with Jessie Redmond Fauset, a teacher in the New York City public schools, to publish *The Brownies' Book*, a children's monthly magazine. Designed to stimulate black children's early learning and to provide them with models, *The Brownies' Book* contained stories, legends, and poems.[39]

Politically, Du Bois had felt a growing attraction to Marxism. In 1911, he joined the American Socialist party then led by Eugene V. Debs. Of the political parties, Du Bois supported the Socialists, who argued that politics expressed economic class interests. He believed that blacks in the United States were victims of capitalist exploitation. During World War I, however, Du Bois supported the war effort, unlike the Socialist party. In the later part of his life, Du Bois was attracted to and participated in left-wing political organizations and movements. He saw the Republicans and Democrats as unwilling to take the necessary political risks to support full civil rights for blacks and other minority groups.

During the Great Depression, Du Bois proposed forming cooperatives to ease the economic plight of African Americans. His proposal failed to win the support of the NAACP's board of directors. Du Bois, who was a person of strong opinions, was embroiled in a series of disputes with the more conservative members of the association. In 1934, he resigned from the board of directors and as editor of *The Crisis*. He returned to Atlanta University as professor and chairman of the Department of Sociology. For the next ten years, he remained at Atlanta University, until he was reconciled with the leadership of the NAACP and returned to work for that organization. During this time, he wrote several important books. His *Black Reconstruction: An Essay Toward a History of the Part Which Black Folk Played in the Attempt to Reconstruct Democracy in America, 1860-1880*, appearing in 1935, was part of an important revisionist movement in interpreting the crucial reconstructionist period.[40] This book was followed by *Black Folk Then and Now* (1939) and *Dusk of Dawn: An Essay Toward an Autobiography of a Race Concept* (1940).[41]

In 1944, Du Bois returned to the NAACP as director of special research. When World War II ended, his activities shifted to the international scene. He was particularly interested that postwar reconstruction would end colonialism and bring political independence to the European powers' colonies in Africa and Asia. Long a proponent of pan-Africanism, he was a leader in the pan-African conferences that were held periodically. In 1945, he was a consultant to the U.S. delegation at the founding of the United Nations. Turning to international interests, he wrote *Color and Democracy: Colonies and Peace* (1945) and *The World and Africa: An Inquiry into the Part Which Africa Has Played in World History* (1947).[42]

After World War II when the general political mood in the United States was growing more anti-Communist, Du Bois moved steadily toward the left. As Cold War tensions deepened between the United States and the Soviet Union, Du Bois was accused of being a Soviet sympathizer and a member of Communist front organizations.

In the presidential election of 1948, Du Bois actively supported the Progressive party, a third party organized to support Henry A. Wallace for the presidency. Wallace, who was vice president during President Franklin D. Roosevelt's third term, from 1940 to 1944, opposed President Truman's containment policy of Soviet expansion. Wallace believed that the United States could continue to cooperate with the Soviet Union as it had done during World War II. The Progressive party also took a strong stand for civil rights.

Despite the defection of Wallace on the left and states' rights "Dixiecrafts" led by Strom Thurmond on the right from the Democratic party, President Truman defeated Governor Dewey, the Republican nominee, along with Wallace and Thurmond. It should be pointed out that Du Bois was one in a small minority of blacks in his support of Wallace's candidacy. The vast majority of the black leadership and voters supported the Democratic party and Truman in the election.

Once again, internal tensions surfaced in the NAACP. In 1949, Du Bois was dismissed from his position in the NAACP. He continued to move steadily to the left in his thinking. Du Bois believed that the Soviet Union was one of the few nations that practiced full racial equality. In 1950, he attended the All-Union Conference of Peace Proponents in Moscow. He either did not understand or misinterpreted the full effect of Stalinism in the Soviet Union and the totalitarian police state over which the Soviet dictator had presided since the 1930s. As Khrushchev revealed in the early 1960s, Stalin was a tyrant who had engineered the mass extermination of millions of Soviet citizens. Although a partisan for human freedom in many respects, Du Bois apparently had a blind spot regarding Stalinism.

In the early 1950s, the United States was experiencing a strong anti-Communist movement directed against alleged subversives in the U.S. government and in educational institutions, especially colleges and universities. The era was further characterized by the "witch hunting" activities of Senator Joseph McCarthy, who recklessly exploited the highly charged atmosphere for political advantage.

Du Bois, who did not attempt to hide his Marxist orientation or his positive attitude toward the Soviet Union, was especially suspect during this period. An official of the Peace Information Center, Du Bois was under investigation as a member of what was alleged to be a Communist "front organization." When in 1951 the U.S. Department of Justice demanded that Du Bois and the Peace Information Center register as agents of a foreign government, Du Bois refused to comply. Du Bois and other officers of the center were indicted and brought to trial. The case eventually reached the U.S. Supreme Court, where Du Bois and his associates were acquitted on the grounds that the Justice Department had not proved its allegations. In 1952, Du Bois told his version of his work for international peace, *In Battle for Peace: The Story of My 83rd Birthday*.[43]

Nina Du Bois, William Du Bois' wife of fifty-four years, died on July 1, 1950. She had been an invalid since she suffered a stroke five years earlier. In February 1951, the 83-year-old Du Bois married Shirley Graham, a close friend and co-worker from the Peace Information Center.

From 1952 to 1958, the U.S. government refused to issue a passport to Du Bois, who had received invitations to visit many of the newly independent African nations. He again turned to writing and produced a trilogy—*The Ordeal of Mansart* (1957); *Mansart Builds a School* (1959); and *The Worlds of Color* (1961).[44]

In 1958, passports were finally issued to Du Bois and his second wife, Shirley Graham-Du Bois, who embarked on a world tour. In the Soviet Union, he was awarded the Lenin Peace Prize. In 1961, dissatisfied with the slow pace of racial change and the political situation in the United States, Du Bois accepted the invitation of President Kwame Nkrumah of Ghana to direct a massive research project designed to produce an African encyclopedia. In 1963, he became a Ghanese citizen. On August 27, 1963, Du Bois died at the age of 95. The former professor, editor, and activist was accorded a state funeral on August 29, 1963, that symbolized his role as a pan-African leader.

The Social and Educational Ideas of W. E. B. Du Bois

During Du Bois' lifetime of nearly a century, the conditions of African Americans in the United States went through many changes. Through these various alterations, Du Bois was a consistent advocate for civil rights and equality of educational opportunity for blacks and other members of U.S. society who were denied these rights.

Du Bois' social and educational ideas can be examined first in terms of the strategy he developed to further African American progress. His strategy needs to be assessed in terms of its opposition to that developed by Booker T. Washington. Both Washington and Du Bois were educators who wanted to improve the social and economic conditions of African Americans in the United States. As indicated earlier, Washington's strategy was based on building an economic base for blacks in a gradual and slowly incremental way. Washington chose not to do battle with the white power structure. Du Bois challenged Washington, and the president of Tuskegee Institute responded by opposing Du Bois.

To organize and mobilize African Americans, Du Bois believed that Washington needed to be displaced as the spokesman of black America. This task, however, was formidable. Du Bois basically argued that Washington's political passivity, gradualism, and philosophy of industrial education would perpetuate a racially based caste system in the United States. Either wittingly or unwittingly, Washington was regarded by Du Bois as an accomplice in maintaining a system that relegated blacks to second-class citizenship and an inferior economic and educational position.

In *The Souls of Black Folk*, Du Bois examined the social, cultural, and educational aspects of black life in America. He appealed to African American intellectuals to take the initiative in working for voting rights, civil rights, and equal access to colleges and universities. His essay, "Booker T. Washington and Others," attacked the senior black leader for weakening black political power, for jeopardizing their civil rights, and for discouraging the entry of black youth into institutions of higher education. As a result of Washington's accommodationist strategy, blacks had been politically disenfranchised. The laws of many states, especially in the South, had legally relegated African Americans to an inferior civil and educational position.[45] In a stinging rebuke of Washington's policy of industrial education, Du Bois wrote:

1. He is striving to make Negro artisans businessmen and property-owners; but it is utterly impossible, under modern competitive methods, for workingmen and property-owners to defend their rights and exist without the right of suffrage.
2. He insists on thrift and self-respect, but at the same time counsels a silent submission to civic inferiority such as is bound to sap the manhood of any race in the long run.
3. He advocates common-school and industrial training, and depreciates institutions of higher learning; but neither the Negro common-schools, nor Tuskegee itself, could remain open a day were it not for teachers trained in Negro colleges, or trained by their graduates.[46]

In contrast to Washington's industrial education, Du Bois made higher education a key plank in his ideological platform. It was in colleges, universities, and professional schools that the African American intellectual elite, the vanguard of the movement, the talented tenth, would be educated. Again in opposition to Washington's position that the process of educational and social change for blacks should work its way upward from the bottom, Du Bois believed that it should start at the top with those blacks who had higher and professional educations. For Du Bois, social progress was "more often a pull than a push" caused by the efforts of the exceptional man to lift "his duller brethren slowly and painfully to his vantage-ground."[47] Although he saw higher education as having this special role, Du Bois strongly believed that higher education had an important cultural significance. Taking a broad and general view of higher education, Du Bois wrote:

The university is not simply to teach breadwinning, or to furnish teachers for the public schools, or to be a center of polite society: it is, above all, to be the organ of that fine adjustment between real life and the growing knowledge of life, an adjustment which forms the secret of civilization.[48]

Although Du Bois was most concerned with higher education, he also had opinions about elementary and secondary education. He took a broad view of education, defining it as all that shapes a person's outlook and behavior. In commenting on children's education, he wrote:

> Children must be trained in a knowledge of what the world is and what it knows and how it does its daily work. These things cannot be separated: we cannot teach pure knowledge apart from actual facts, or separate truth from the human mind. Above all we must not forget that the object of all education is the child itself and not what it does or makes.[49]

For Du Bois, the first years of public schooling, regardless of the child's race or class, should cultivate basic literacy and communication skills. It should also broaden children's horizons of space, time, and events by introducing them to the "extraordinary multiplicity of the world's things."[50] Like John Dewey, Du Bois recognized the educative value of a learning environment that was rich in objects that could stimulate children's interests and curiosity. The poverty-ridden neighborhood and the ramshackle school had little of the "things" that enriched a child's experience.

Unlike Washington's emphasis on vocational education, Du Bois opposed early or premature vocational education, turning children's early education into training for the trades, farming, or domestic service. Although the world of work might be introduced to students who could study the major occupations and professions that involved human beings, such an introduction should be educational and not a form of training. Too early vocational training tended to limit the child's general education and future career choice. Du Bois believed black children, like all children, should learn to read, write, calculate, and broaden their horizons by studying history, geography, and literature rather than being trained for particular jobs.

Du Bois extended this perspective to elementary, secondary, and higher education. He was especially concerned that the standard textbook treatments of world civilization and culture concentrated on the western European and North American experience and ignored African contributions. His early book, *The Negro*, in 1915, was a seminal work for Afrocentric scholarship. Taking a broad historical perspective, Du Bois explored the development of ancient African cultures in the Neolithic Age and, like the modern scholar Bernal, the Hamitic foundations of ancient civilizations. He commented on the high culture and political complexity of pre-colonial Africa.[51] *The Negro*, not only was a foray into pan-African historiography, it established the foundations for Afrocentrism. His books, *Africa—Its Place in Modern History* (1930); *Africa—Its Geography, People, and Products* (1930); and *The World and Africa: An Inquiry into the Part Which Africa Has Played in World History* (1947), provided the information base that could be used to bring the study of Africa into the historical mainstream and into the curriculum.[52] Rather than being a historical "add on," Du Bois sought to infuse African history into the general narrative of world history. Although Du Bois, as a historian, was interested in tracing African American roots to Africa, his pan-African studies were to be the basis of a worldwide black activism. According to Du Bois:

> There has been consistent effort to rationalize Negro slavery by omitting Africa from world history, so that today it is almost universally assumed that history can be truly written without reference to Negroid peoples. I believe this to be scientifically unsound and also dangerous for logical social conclusions.[53]

In addition to his pan-African orientation, Du Bois took an international perspective that stressed the reality of a multicultural world society. He emphasized the importance of life and learning in a multicultural context. In particular, African Americans needed to overcome their provincialism and isolation. They needed to be culturally and spiritually reunited with their African origins and roots. African Americans, further, needed to improve their foreign language abilities to communicate with black people in other parts of the world. Outside of the United States, many black people in Africa, South America, and the Caribbean spoke either French or Spanish. American blacks should learn to speak French, Spanish, and Portuguese. These modern languages should replace the study of the classical languages of Greek, Latin, and Hebrew. In every black community in the United States, there should be classes in the modern languages that blacks speak in other countries and there should be libraries that feature magazines and books in these languages. Through his travel and education, Du Bois had become a citizen of the world. For him, it was particularly important that African American children become multilingual. While having the self-esteem that comes from having pride in their race and their African heritage, African American children should learn they are also part of a multicultural and multiracial world.

Conclusion: An Assessment

As a leader in the movement for black civil rights and equality in the United States, W. E. B. Du Bois was of a different character, disposition, and background from others such as Roy Wilkins and Martin Luther King Jr. Whereas King had Southern roots, was immersed in black Christianity, and practiced nonviolent, Gandhi-inspired passive resistance, Du Bois combined scholarship with activism. He was the consummate researcher, historian, and sociologist who was also a political strategist. A person of commitment, he was also a man of opinions who had little tolerance for those who could not mount a clear argument. Although the NAACP, the Urban League, and later Dr. King's Southern Christian Leadership Conference arose in an American context, Du Bois took a world perspective that incorporated a devotion to pan-Africanism. Having little patience with mainstream U.S. politics, Du Bois was drawn to third parties of the political left. His perspective on the world and social change also led him to Marxism and to eventual membership in the American Communist party, which he joined near the end of his life in 1961.

Although Du Bois took a different path to reach the same goal, the prize was nonetheless reached. Painstakingly, through a long series of court cases, the strategy of the NAACP was fulfilled in 1954 in the case of *Brown v. The Board of Education of*

Topeka, Kansas. Using sociological and psychological evidence, the NAACP sought successfully to overturn the decision of the earlier *Plessy v. Ferguson* decision that had established the precedent of separate but equal. The attorneys representing the plaintiffs in the Brown case, Oliver Brown and his daughter Linda, argued that segregated schools had a negative effect on the social and psychological development of black children. Speaking for the Supreme Court, Chief Justice Earl Warren stated:

> Does segregation of children in public schools solely on the basis of race, even though the physical facilities and other "tangible" factors may be equal, deprive the children of the minority group of equal education opportunities? We believe that it does.
>
> . . . . In the field of public education the doctrine of "separate but equal" has no place. Separate educational facilities are inherently unequal. Therefore, we hold the plaintiffs and others similarly situated for whom the actions have been brought are, by reason of the segregation complained of, deprived of the equal protection of the laws guaranteed by the Fourteenth Amendment.[54]

The Supreme Court's desegregation decision in the Brown case was but one beginning of the civil rights struggle in the United States. The efforts of Martin Luther King Jr. to organize a campaign against *de facto* segregation were just starting. Racial conflicts such as those that would occur at Little Rock, Arkansas, and the University of Mississippi were still ahead. Du Bois' work, however, had moved history forward and contributed to the coming struggle for civil rights.

Although the African American struggle for civil and educational rights had enlisted Du Bois' attention for most of his life, he is also important because of his scholarly contributions in sociology and history that examined the black experience in the United States and in the world. Du Bois' books that examined black culture in both the United States and Africa were important sources that anticipated the Afro-American and black studies programs that developed at many colleges and universities. Du Bois, who was always concerned with historical accuracy and sociological validity in his research and writing, made a valuable contribution to these disciplines.

Discussion Questions

1. What was the general social, economic, and educational condition of African Americans at the end of the Reconstruction period?
2. Describe the major features of Booker T. Washington's philosophy of education.
3. How did the contexts in which Booker T. Washington and W. E. B. Du Bois lived differ?
4. How did the key events in Du Bois' life shape his social and educational perspective?
5. What were the key points in Du Bois' criticism of Washington?
6. Describe Du Bois' orientation as an African American.
7. How did Du Bois contribute to Afrocentric scholarship and curriculum?

Research and Essay Topics

1. In a paper, analyze the theoretical and practical differences between Washington and Du Bois.
2. Read and review one of Du Bois' books.
3. In a paper, analyze Du Bois' character.
4. In a research paper, examine Du Bois as a pan-Africanist.
5. In a paper, assess Du Bois' significance in U.S. social and educational thought.
6. Examine the African American Studies Program at your college or university and determine if it has been influenced by Du Bois' ideas and scholarship.

Notes

1. David Levering Lewis, *W. E. B. Du Bois: Biography of a Race, 1868–1919* (New York: Henry Holt and Co., 1993), 3.
2. Louis Harlan, *Booker T. Washington: The Making of a Black Leader, 1856–1901* (New York: Oxford University Press, 1972), 61–64.
3. Booker T. Washington, ed., *Tuskegee and Its People: Their Ideals and Achievements* (New York: D. Appleton and Co., 1905); and Washington, *The Future of the American Negro* (Boston: Small, Maynard and Co., 1900), 108–10.
4. Washington, *The Future of the American Negro*, 111–12.
5. Victoria E. Matthews, *Black-Belt Diamonds: Gems from the Speeches, Addresses, and Talks to Students of Booker T. Washington* (New York: Fortune and Scott, 1989), 8.
6. Lewis, 260.
7. E. Davidson Washington, ed., *Selected Speeches of Booker T. Washington* (New York: Doubleday, Doran, & Co., 1932), 31–36.
8. Richard Kluger, *Simple Justice* (New York: Alfred A. Knopf, 1976), 73–74.
9. Manning Marable, *W. E. B. Du Bois: Black Radical Democrat* (Boston: Twayne Publishers, 1986), 2–3.
10. Lewis, 15.
11. Virginia Hamilton, *W. E. B. Du Bois: A Biography* (New York: Thomas Y. Crowell Co., 1972), 15.
12. Marable, *W. E. B. Du Bois,* 4.
13. Ibid., 4–6.
14. Lewis, 50.
15. Marable, 7.
16. Lewis, 58–59.
17. Ibid., 75.
18. Ibid., 74.
19. Marable, 9.
20. Lewis, 68–69.
21. Marable, 9–10.
22. Lewis, 77.
23. *Ibid.,* 84–88.
24. Hamilton, *W. E. B. Du Bois,* 40.
25. Marable, 15.
26. Lewis, 117.
27. Marable, 17–20.

28. W. E. B. Du Bois, *The Suppression of the African Slave-Trade to the United States of America, 1638–1870* (New York: Longmans, Green, and Co., 1896).

29. W. E. B. Du Bois, *The Philadelphia Negro: A Social Study* (Boston: Ginn and Co., 1899).

30. Lewis, 209–10.

31. Marable, 25.

32. W. E. B. Du Bois, *The Souls of Black Folk: Essays and Sketches* (Chicago: A. C. McClurg and Co., 1903).

33. W. E. B. Du Bois, *John Brown* (Philadelphia: George W. Jacobs, 1909).

34. Lewis, 288.

35. *Ibid.*, 502.

36. Hamilton, 104.

37. Lewis, 416, 474, 514.

38. W. E. B. Du Bois, *The Quest of the Silver Fleece: A Novel* (Chicago: A. C. McClurg, 1911); Du Bois, *The Negro* (New York: Henry Holt, 1915); Du Bois, *Darkwater: Voices from Within the Veil* (New York: Harcourt Brace Jovanovich, 1920); Du Bois, *The Gift of Black Folk: Negroes in the Making of America* (Boston: Stratford Publishing Co., 1924).

39. Hamilton, 133.

40. W. E. B. Du Bois, *Black Reconstruction: An Essay Toward a History of the Part which Black Folk Played in the Attempt to Reconstruct Democracy in America, 1860–1880* (New York: Harcourt Brace Jovanovich, 1935).

41. W. E. B. Du Bois, *Black Folk Then and Now: An Essay on the History and Sociology of the Negro Race* (New York: Henry Holt and Co., 1939) and Du Bois, *Dusk of Dawn: An Essay Toward an Autobiography of a Race Concept* (New York: Harcourt Brace Jovanovich, 1940).

42. W. E. B. Du Bois, *Color and Democracy: Colonies and Peace* (New York: Harcourt Brace Jovanovich, 1945); Du Bois, *The World and Africa: An Inquiry into the Part Which Africa Has Played in World History* (New York: Viking Press, 1947).

43. W. E. B. Du Bois, *In Battle for Peace: The Story of My 83rd Birthday* (New York: Masses and Mainstream, 1952).

44. W. E. B. Du Bois, *The Ordeal of Mansart* (New York: Mainstream, 1957), *Mansart Builds a School* (New York: Mainstream, 1959), and *Worlds of Color* (New York: Mainstream, 1961).

45. W. E. B. Du Bois, *The Souls of Black Folk: Essays and Sketches* (Chicago: A.C. McClurg and Co., 1903), 15.

46. Ibid., 52.

47. Ibid., 84.

48. Du Bois, *Darkwater: Voices from Within the Veil*, 205–9.

49. Henry Lee Moon, *The Emerging Thought of W. E. B. Du Bois* (New York: Simon and Schuster, 1972), 125.

50. Ibid., 127.

51. Lewis, 462.

52. W. E. B. Du Bois, *Africa: Its Place in Modern History* (Girard, Kansas: Haldeman-Julius, 1930); Du Bois, *Africa: Its Geography, People and Products* (Girard, Kansas: Haldeman-Julius, 1930); DuBois, *The World and Africa: An Inquiry into the Part Which Africa Has Played in World History* (New York: Viking, 1947).

53. Du Bois, *The World and Africa,* vii.

54. Kluger, *Simple Justice,* 781-82.

Suggestions for Further Reading

Andrews, William L., ed. *Critical Essays on W. E. B. Du Bois*. Boston: G.K. Hall & Co., 1985.

Broderick, Francis L. *W. E. B. Du Bois: Negro Leader in a Time of Crisis*. Stanford, Calif.: Stanford University Press, 1959.

Carlisle, Rodney. *The Roots of Black Nationalism*. New York: Kennikat Press, 1975.

Du Bois, W. E. B. *Africa: Its Geography, People, and Products*. Girard, Kan.: Haldeman-Julius, 1930.

————. *Africa: Its Place in Modern History*. Girard, Kan.: Haldeman-Julius, 1930.

————. *The Autobiography of W. E. B. Du Bois: A Soliloquy on Viewing My Life from the Last Decade of its First Century*. Herbert Aptheker, ed. New York: International Publishers, 1968.

————. *Black Folk Then and Now: An Essay in the History and Sociology of the Negro Race*. New York: Henry Holt and Co., 1939.

————. *Black Reconstruction: An Essay Toward a History of the Part Which Black Folk Played in the Attempt to Reconstruct Democracy in America, 1860–1880*. New York: Harcourt Brace Jovanovich, 1935.

————. *Color and Democracy: Colonies and Peace*. New York: Harcourt Brace Jovanovich 1945.

————. *Darkwater: Voices from Within the Veil*. New York: Harcourt Brace Jovanovich, 1920.

————. *Dusk of Dawn: An Essay Toward an Autobiography of a Race Concept*. New York: Harcourt Brace Jovanovich, 1940.

————. *The Gift of Black Folk: Negroes in the Making of America*. Boston: Stratford Publishing Co., 1924.

————. *In Battle for Peace: The Story of My 83rd Birthday*. New York: Masses and Mainstream, 1952.

————. *John Brown*. Philadelphia: George W. Jacobs, 1909.

————. *The Negro*. New York: Henry Holt and Co., 1915.

————. *The Philadelphia Negro: A Social Study*. Boston: Ginn and Co., 1899.

————. *The Souls of Black Folk: Essays and Sketches*. Chicago A. C. McClurg and Co., 1903.

————. *The World and Africa: An Inquiry into the Part Which Africa Has Played in World History*. New York: Viking Press, 1947.

Foner, Philip S. *W. E. B. Du Bois Speaks: Speeches and Addresses, 1920–1963*. New York: Pathfinder Press, 1970.

Hamilton, Virginia. *W. E. B. Du Bois: A Biography*. New York: Thomas Y. Crowell Co., 1972.

Harlan, Louis. *Booker T. Washington: The Making of a Black Leader: 1856–1901*. New York: Oxford University Press, 1972.

Horne, Gerald. *Black and Red: W. E. B. Du Bois and the Afro-American Response to the Cold War*. Albany, N.Y.: State University of New York Press, 1986.

Lewis, David Levering. *W. E. B. Du Bois: Biography of a Race, 1868–1919*. New York: Henry Holt and Co., 1993.

Marable, Manning. *W. E. B. Du Bois: Black Radical Democrat*. Boston: Twayne Publishers, 1986.

Matthews, Victoria E. *Black-Belt Diamonds: Gems from the Speeches, Addresses, and Talks to Students of Booker T. Washington*. New York: Fortune and Scott, 1898.

Paschal, Andrew G., ed. *A W. E. B. Du Bois Reader*. New York: Macmillan Publishing Company, 1971.

Rampersad, Arnold. *The Art and Imagination of W. E. B. Du Bois*. New York: Schocken Books, 1990.

Washington, Booker T. *The Future of the American Negro*. Boston: Small, Maynard, and Co., 1900.

————. *Tuskegee and Its People: Their Ideals and Achievements*. New York: D. Appleton and Co., 1905.

————. *Up from Slavery*. New York: Bantam Books, 1967. Originally published in 1901.

————. *Working with the Hands*. New York: Doubleday, Page, and Co., 1904.

Mao Tse-tung: Revolutionary Educator

Poster of Mao Tse-tung; from the archives of the Hoover Institution on War, Revolution, and Peace

In this chapter, we examine the life, ideology, and educational ideas of Mao Tse-tung (1893–1976), the founding father of the People's Republic of China. An analysis of Mao's effect on China is instructive in that it allows us to consider an important educational issue—the clash of traditional knowledge and values with revolutionary thought and action. Mao led the Communist revolution that sought to create a new China based on Marxist ideology. Throughout his life, Mao viewed society and education in terms of the Marxist dialectic of opposing forces, the clash of thesis and antithesis.

An examination of Mao's life and educational ideas takes us to the context in which it occurred, a China that was tortuously leaving the ancient imperial period and heading to an uncertain future in the twentieth century. Mao's life spanned a tumultuous period in China's history—the end of the empire, the beginning of the republic, invasion by the Japanese, fratricidal civil war between Chiang Kai-shek's Nationalists and the Communists, his victory in establishing the People's Republic of China, the Great Leap Forward, and the Cultural Revolution.

To organize your thoughts as you read this chapter, you might focus on the following questions:

- What were the significant characteristics of China's historical context, the cultural situation, in which Mao Tse-tung lived?
- How did Mao's life, his career as a revolutionary, shape his political and educational ideology?
- How did Mao's ideology determine the policies of the People's Republic of China?
- What were Mao's major ideas about education and how did these ideas shape his educational policies?
- What is Mao's effect on world history and education?

The Historical Context of Mao Tse-tung's Life

In this section, we examine the historical and cultural context of China, one of the world's oldest and most enduring civilizations. The China in which Mao was born was steeped in ancient traditions and customs and was reluctantly struggling against the tides of modernity. A giant empire until the last emperor left the throne in 1912, China was tied to Confucianism, an ethical system that placed great emphasis on the need to maintain harmony and balance by observing proper relationships. Mao, the consummate revolutionary, struggled throughout his life to breach China's great wall of Confucianism. His Cultural Revolution was mounted as an ideological and educational war against the forces of tradition in Chinese society.

Mao's birth in 1893 took place in the last decade of imperial rule. It was a time when the decrepit Manchu dynasty was taking its last gasps of political control. Pursuing a half-hearted and haphazard program of defensive modernization, imperial China sought to hold off the hungry Western colonial powers and Japan which were eager to carve out zones of special economic interests.

In Mao's childhood, the traditional Chinese worldview was shaped by Confucian philosophy. The Chinese, seeing their empire as the center of the civilized world, held their language and culture to be superior to that of the barbarians, particularly the western Europeans who sought entry to China's territory and markets. The Chinese tendency to see little of value outside of China made it difficult to introduce the technological and educational innovations that might modernize the country.

In imperial China, Confucian philosophy, especially its ethics, governed political, social, economic, and educational relationships. A government official turned philosopher, Confucius (551–478 BC) devised an ethical system that emphasized tradition and custom as cultural values that would curb instability. With cultural stasis as the Confucian system's overriding goal, traditional hierarchical relationships were highly esteemed as the matrix of a properly functioning society.

The organizing principle in the Confucianist ethical code was hierarchical subordination. Politically, the subject, with a sense of filial piety, was to be compliantly subordinate to the emperor, the paternalistic ruler. In the male-dominated family, the wife was to be subordinate to her husband; the son to his father; the younger siblings to elder brothers and sisters; and young friends to older ones. The most direct and binding relationships were those of the family and kinship group. The extended family was also governed by the basic principles of subordination that held the Chinese empire together.[1] As a child, Mao rebelled against the controls that Confucianism imposed on family life. In particular, he viewed his childhood as a struggle for control rather than of his submission to his father.

Confucianism greatly influenced both formal and informal education in imperial China. It was believed that knowledge of the Confucian classics would cultivate personal virtue, morality, and loyalty and would in turn create a harmonious political state. The inherited Confucianist propensity for traditional order sharply contrasted with the chaos that Mao Tse-tung encouraged during the Cultural Revolution. A dedicated revolutionary, Mao sought throughout his career to purge the vestiges of Confucianism.

The prominence of Confucianism and the Chinese sense of cultural superiority caused the Chinese to be an inward rather than an outward looking people. Education was to preserve the culture by transmitting inherited knowledge and values from generation to generation. Traditional informal education, carried on in kinship groups, emphasized the wisdom of the elders and respect for ancestors. In contrast, Mao Tse-tung, as a dedicated revolutionary, agitated for fundamental and continuing change.

Imperial China's schools reflected Confucian ethics. The educational system reinforced a hierarchical social class structure grounded on human inequality. At the social summit were scholar-officials who ruled the empire in the emperor's name. Next in rank, came the gentry, the wealthy landowners. In descending order came the smaller landowning farmers, artisans, and merchants, At the bottom of society were the mass of landless workers.

Mao's family were small landowners. His father was bent on acquiring more land to raise his socioeconomic position. As a Marxist revolutionary, Mao sought to mobilize the bottom rungs of society, particularly the landless peasantry, into a revolutionary force that would overthrow the privileged upper classes.

An important feature of the imperial system was the power and prestige of the scholar-officials, the mandarins. Next to the emperor and the imperial court, the scholar-officials enjoyed highest social status and political authority. Embedded in the official ideology was the rationale that intellectuals, occupying the highest ranks, were to rule others. Since intellectual activity was prized over applied and manual work, the formal educational system reflected and reinforced bias for academic theory over practice. Mao despised intellectual academicians and enthusiastically encouraged their purge during the Cultural Revolution.

Potential scholar-officials had to pass crucial examinations before being assigned to the imperial civil service which in turn admitted them to the ruling circles. Students prepared for these examinations by studying ancient Chinese literature and Confucian texts with learned master teachers at imperial or temple schools. Reflecting male-dominance, women were ineligible for government service and were not admitted to schools. Deliberately separating theory and practice, the examinations stressed literary and philosophical information rather than actual administrative topics. The candidates had to run an academic gauntlet of examinations, beginning with local district ones which led to provincial examinations. Only the elite of the finalists were eligible for the empire's highest governmental positions.[2]

The highly competitive examination system perpetuated the scholar-gentry class. The scholar-officials, who largely came from the wealthy gentry class, conducted the schools that prepared candidates and used the examination system to maintain the status quo. The ingrained system perpetuated the immense social chasm between the formally educated elite and illiterate masses. The eminence accorded to scholars was an ingrained behavior in China. During the Cultural Revolution, Mao vigorously attacked any vestiges of the examination system. He believed that the tradition of the scholars' separation from society had resurfaced even in the Communist-controlled higher education where passing highly selective examinations was required for admission to universities. Mao urged the abolition of entrance examinations which he believed were perpetuating new elites of bureaucrats and discriminating against workers and peasants.

Just as its educational system was inadequate, imperial China's political and military infrastructures were unequal to the challenge they faced. As the nineteenth century began, imperial China faced internal rebellions and external pressures from western European nations and Japan. The last imperial dynasty, the Qing (Ch'ing), which had ruled China from 1644 to 1912, proved unable to react to these threats, dulled by an inertia based on its protracted reliance on tradition. The Confucian philosophy that had guided China's officials for centuries was inadequate in providing strategies to cope with the expanding crises. China's stagnating bureaucracy and its army and navy, armed with antiquated weapons, were no match for the European nations' modern military might.

Since the early nineteenth century, the European powers, challenging China's traditional isolation, had been forcing trading concessions. The Treaty of Nanking, signed on August 29, 1842, forced China to open to British economic exploitation. Other nations—Germany, Russia, France, and Japan—followed Britain in extorting concessions from China.

Imperial China's last decade, from 1901 to 1911, saw futile efforts to avert collapse. In 1901, the imperial government reluctantly began to establish a new school system, to send students to study abroad, and to adopt Western military strategies. The new school system was to replace traditional Confucian scholarship with a more functional way of training officials. The new system projected a hierarchical system, with schools at each rung of government administration: the local district, provincial, and imperial levels. The new government schools consisted of a four-year higher elementary school, a five-year middle school, a three-year higher school, and a three-year imperial university. Mao attended the primary school in his village.

The imperial dynasty was unable to stabilize a deteriorating political situation. The last emperor, Pu Yi, a young child, reigned briefly from 1909 to 1912, but the real power at court was the Empress Dowager, a crafty old woman who ruled by manipulation and intrigue. Rather than being violently overthrown by the rising forces of republicanism, old imperial China, which had lasted through the centuries, simply disintegrated.

China's republican forces were led by Dr. Sun Yat-sen (1866–1925), a physician who had been educated abroad. Heading a broad political movement, Sun's ideology rested on three principles: (1) nationalism, asserting China's rights to sovereignty; (2) democracy, the Chinese people's rights to self-government; and (3) socialism, the right to economic livelihood.[3] On January 1, 1912, Sun Yat-sen was inaugurated as the provisional president of the new Chinese republic.

The remnants of the imperial army, still the largest military force in China, were commanded by Yuan Shih-k'ai, an opportunistic general. As tensions mounted between Sun Yat-sen and Yuan Shih-k'ai, China came to the brink of civil war. To prevent conflict, a compromise was negotiated. Sun agreed to resign as president if Yuan would support the new republic. Yuan, who accepted the terms, was installed as president in 1912. However, Yuan assumed dictatorial powers, suppressed the parliament, and ruled by force until his death in 1916.

After Yuan Shih-k'ai's death, China drifted until 1928 through the war lord period, a time of personal rule by mercenary military strongmen who had little concern for the national well-being. Generals, using local armies, seized control of a region and ruled it for their personal profit. Local people were exploited and coerced into supporting the war lord. During this era, the central government actually controlled only a small part of China while real power was held in the provinces by petty military tyrants.

The Kuomintang, or Nationalist Party, led by Chiang Kai-shek, claimed to be Sun Yat-sen's ideological successor. While the Nationalists were the major force in opposition to the war lords, a new political party, the Chinese Communist Party, was being organized by Mao Tse-tung.

Under General Chiang Kai-shek, the Kuomintang, the Nationalists, sought to reunify China. Nationalist support came mainly from upper- and middle-class professionals such as government officials, industrialists and businessmen. The Communists saw the Nationalists as bourgeois capitalist exploiters of the working class. However, in Marxist terms, the Nationalists' presence on China's historical stage served to eradicate the remnants of imperial feudalism. Chiang trained an army that defeated the war lords and restored the central government's authority. By 1928, the Nationalists had secured political power.

At first, the Nationalists and Communists maintained a fragile truce, but civil war erupted between the rivals in 1927. To escape the militarily superior Nationalists, Mao Tse-tung's Communists began the desperate Long March northward to Shensi province in 1934. Thousands of Communists died, victims of Nationalist attacks or illness. When they reached Shensi, Mao's Communists proclaimed the Chinese Soviet Republic in 1935. Although Marx had written that the industrial proletariat would lead the revolution, Mao, operating in rural China, revised Marx's doctrine to proclaim the poor agricultural peasants as China's revolutionary class.

The Communists established themselves in Yenan where they successfully held off Nationalist attacks. Expropriating the land of wealthy land lords, they redistributed it to the small farmers and landless farm workers. Their land distribution policies won peasant support. Convinced that a successful revolution could be waged if Marxist ideology was adapted to the Chinese rural situation, Mao's goal was to create a strong, centralized and highly disciplined Communist Party in the coming struggle against the Nationalists. Mao's Communists organized literacy campaigns and Party schools to indoctrinate the rural masses and to win their allegiance with promises of economic improvement.

In 1931, Japan had invaded China, beginning the long war that lasted until 1945 when Japan was defeated in World War II. During the war, Nationalists and Communists had temporarily put aside their ideological differences to combat their mutual Japanese enemy.

With Japan defeated, the Nationalists and the Communists, after an unsuccessful attempt at a coalition government, resumed civil war. From 1946 through 1949, the Nationalists, supported by the United States, and the Communists, backed by the Soviet Union, were locked in combat. Chiang's Nationalists, however, had lost touch with the common people and lacked popular support. Further, the Nationalist government was plagued by internal corruption, inefficient administration, and rampant inflation. Mao's rural-based strategy worked. Nationalist armies found themselves isolated, confined to the cities, while the surrounding countryside fell to the Communists.

In 1949, Chiang's vanquished Nationalist government fled to Taiwan, still claiming to be the Republic of China's legitimate government. Chiang remained as President of the Republic until his death in 1975. Mao Tse-tung's victorious Communists proclaimed a new government, the People's Republic of China, on October 1, 1949.

Based upon this discussion of the Chinese historical context, we can now turn to an examination of Mao, the man who made the revolution.

Mao: The Making of a Revolutionary

Mao Tse-tung was born on December 26, 1893, in Hunan Province in the small isolated rural village of Shao Shan-ch'ung, in Hsiang t'an hsien County. The nearest important town, Hsiang-t'an, a commercial city and county seat, was thirty miles from Mao's home. Hunan Province, in central China, though a mountainous region, was a significant producer of agricultural products such as rice, wheat, and pork.

As customary in rural China, Shao Shan-ch'ung's villagers were organized into clans, of which the Mao clan was one of the largest. Mao's father, Mao Jen-sheng, an ambitious farmer, was bent on restoring his family's lost fortunes. Earlier, the Mao family farm had been sold for debt. Mao Jen-sheng served in the army to earn enough money to reclaim the lost family land. An efficient farmer, he acquired sufficient funds to enlarge the family's holdings. He also improved the family home and became wealthy enough to hire a tenant to work some of the land.[4]

Mao's mother, Wen Ch'i mei, was from the nearby village of Hsianghsiang. As was then common among rural Chinese women, Wen Ch'i mei was unschooled and illiterate. Known as a kindly and generous woman, Wen was a devout Buddhist who observed the local customs and religious practices.[5] As a young child, Mao Tse-tung was very close to his mother and accepted her beliefs. His father's rejection of Buddhism, however, caused family tensions.

Mao's childhood was one of conflict against his father, who in Chinese tradition as undisputed head of the household, held his wife and children in subjugation. According to Confucian ethics, the wife and children were to be properly subordinate to the father, as the nation was to the emperor. Even as a child, however, Mao challenged the old order. He disliked his father, whom he recalled as "a severe task master, a hot-tempered man who gave us no money whatsoever and the most meager food."[6] Father and son were often in conflict. While the father expected that Mao, his eldest son, would follow the Confucianist protocol and prepare himself to become head of the household and farm, the son harbored other ambitions. Mao, who showed an intellectual disposition, aspired to be a scholar. He resented the farm work his father demanded of him. Mao took great pleasure in reading and was constantly harassed by his father, who regarded reading as idleness. As an adult, Mao claimed that he learned to hate his father, who tried to deny him books. During the Cultural Revolution, in speaking to a Red Guard detachment, Mao asserted that had his father been alive, he would have been among the enemies of the people who deserved punishment. Mao seemed to personify his father with the exploiting landlord class. But while he disliked his father's materialism and authoritarianism, Mao learned to value hard physical labor. He also came to despise the academic intellectuals who avoided physical labor by escaping into the realms of theory.

In reminiscing about the family conflicts of his childhood, Mao gave them a Marxist dialectical interpretation in which two opposing factions were locked in struggle. His father, he recalled, constituted the household's "ruling power," while his mother, his brothers, and himself were the opposition "united front." Mao, the eldest son, was the child on whom the family placed its expectations and demands. However, his mother was his protector against his father. Mao even portrayed his mother as a strategist who, in the Chinese way, designed a method of indirect attack rather than overt rebellion against his father.[7] His mother's death in Mao's last year of school produced an intense period of grieving. In a poem titled "In Memory of Mother," he wrote: "Her mind was attentive and sophisticated, logical and reasonable; Never a plan miscalculated, nor a thing overlooked."[8]

Devoted to his mother and disliking his father, Mao eschewed the role that tradition would have assigned him in the Chinese extended family. According to Confucianist ethics, Mao, as the eldest son, was to be responsible for the welfare of his siblings and they in turn were to respect his status within the family. As adults, all three of his siblings, his two brothers and sister, met violent deaths because of their participation in their brother's revolutionary activities.

As a young adult Mao took another role, that of revolutionary. In the Communist ideology, the working class, united by fraternal proletarian interests, became one's sociopolitical family rather than the extended family so cherished in traditional China. Mao led his siblings into Communist Party activities. His brother, Mao Tse-min, two years younger than Mao Tse-tung, was a journalist who worked as a Party propagandist and fund-raiser. He was arrested in 1943 and executed for his Communist activities. Mao's second brother, Mao Tse-t'an, twelve years younger and also a Communist, was killed in 1934 when the Long March began. His adopted sister, Mao Tse-hung, and Mao's first wife who worked in the Communist Party, were arrested and summarily executed in 1930 when Mao was absent on Party business.

Mao, between the ages of eight and thirteen, attended the village primary school. It was here that he learned to write and read the hundreds of Chinese characters. The curriculum emphasized the study of the Confucian classics, Chinese history, and the study of the great emperors. Boys in the school learned the *Li*, the Confucian value code that stressed appropriate behavior such as obedience to one's father, respect for elders, submission to those in authority, veneration of one's ancestors, and the ceremonies and rituals of village life. Much of the teaching was done by group recitations in which students recited passages in unison.[9] It was at an early age that Mao learned to dislike Confucianism in much the same way that he learned to dislike his father.

When he was fourteen, Mao had determined that he needed a better education than that offered by the village primary school. Borrowing money from an uncle to pay tuition and to hire a replacement laborer to work in his place on the family farm, he left home. He entered the larger and more urban Tungshan Primary School, which offered a more comprehensive curriculum that included literature, writing, mathematics, history, and geography. After a year of study, he applied to and was admitted to the Fourth Normal School in Changsha. Among the professors who had the greatest effect on Mao was Yang Ch'ang-chi, who had received a degree in philosophy from the University of Edinburgh.[10]

In 1911, the republican revolution began against the decrepit Manchu dynasty. Mao, along with many other students, caught the revolutionary fire. At that time, the leader of the republican forces was Sun Yat-sen. Mao wrote his first article urging that Sun Yat-sen, then in exile, return to China to head a new government.[11]

Spurred by republican zeal, Mao joined the National Army which was in revolt against the imperial regime. Here, Mao demonstrated his penchant for revolutionary proselytizing, reading to illiterate soldiers about the republican cause. In the zigzagging course of revolutionary events, the wily, former imperial General Yuan Shih-k'ai became president. Yuan Shih-k'ai, who had effected a compromise with Sun Yat-sen averting a civil war, became a dictator.

In 1912, Mao, completing his enlistment in the army, turned again to his education. He entered the First Provincial Middle School but attended classes for only six months. He decided that he could educate himself more efficiently than the teachers at the school. He now spent days at the Hunan Provincial Library where he read voraciously on history, politics, and biography. His wide-ranging search for ideas led him to read Adam Smith's *Wealth of Nations,* Charles Darwin's *On the Origin of Species,* and Rousseau's *Social Contract.*[12]

In 1913, at age nineteen, Mao returned to formal education and was admitted to the Fourth Teachers Training School. Here, he studied for five years, from 1913 to 1918. While enrolled in the school, Mao continued to write and participate in revolutionary activities. In 1917, he published an article, "A Study in Athletics," in *The New Youth* magazine. He also helped organize the New Citizen's Society. As a member of the society, he volunteered in a literacy campaign to teach peasants and workers how to read and write.

During the Cultural Revolution, Mao criticized his own formal education. He especially was critical of its impractical academic content. He lamented the long period of time, sixteen to twenty years, to go from primary school through the university. During this time, students learned little of practical life. He argued that they could learn more from peasants and workers than from academic theoreticians.

After he finished his studies, he went to Peking where he hoped to become more directly involved in China's changing political situation. He took a menial job at the Peking National University Library which gave him access to books and people.

In Peking, Mao moved steadily in the direction of Marxism. In 1919, he joined a Marxist study group that was influenced by the Peking University librarian, Li Ta-chao. The group had only a limited access to Marx's writings, much of which had not yet been translated into Chinese. Anticipating the direction that Mao would take Marxism in the future, the group focused on developing an agenda to improve the condition of China's impoverished rural agricultural workers, many of whom were landless and exploited by rural landlords.

Mao's ideological inclination to Marxism was furthered when agents of the Comintern, the Communist International, joined the study group. In particular, the Russian agent, Grigori Voitinsky, worked with the study group, converting it to a Marxist cell. In 1921, Mao and several associates organized the first Peking Communist Party. He then went to Changsha where he had secured a teaching position at the First Normal School. He continued his political activities, founding the Hunan branch of the Socialist Youth Corps and writing revolutionary tracts.

During the 1920s, the political situation in China grew increasingly destabilized after Yuan Shi-k'ai, the dictator, died. Chiang Kai-shek sought to reunite China around the Kuomintang, or Nationalist Party. Chiang's Nationalists commenced a military campaign to defeat the war lords one-by-one. Meanwhile, the small Communist Party was beginning to organize for the long struggle that would defeat both the war lords and Chiang Kai-shek.

In May 1921, Mao, secretary of several Changsha trade unions, attended the first Chinese Communist Congress. Recognized as a leader in the fledgling Communist movement, Mao was named a delegate to the organizational meeting of the National

Chinese Communist Party. Mao saw a great potential in the new Party, arguing that "the working class of revolutionary China constitutes a powerful fighting force" that, mobilized in the Communist Party, is destined to lead the nation's revolution.[13] In 1923, he was elected to the Party's key agency, the Central Committee.

In 1925, during a period of cooperation between the Kuomintang and the Communists, Mao joined the central government as deputy director of the Peasant Movement Training Institute. The period of cooperation between the Kuomintang and the Communists was brief. In 1927, the two parties split and Chiang began a determined purge of the Communists and their leftist allies in the unions and universities. This break began a long struggle between the two leaders, Chiang and Mao, for control of China.

By 1929, Mao had organized a Communist army in Hunan province that fought against both the war lords and the Kuomintang. Facing the relentless pressure of the better-equipped Kuomintang army, Mao and his troops and their civilian supporters embarked on the famous Long March in 1934 that took them on a 6,000 mile trek. The march lasted for 368 days until they reached a safe haven at Shensi in northern China. During the journey, Mao's forces faced constant attacks from the Kuomintang army. Of the estimated 200,000 who began the march, less than 20,000 troops reached their destination on October 29, 1935. Mao regarded the Long March as having heroic dimensions in the struggle to remake China into a Marxist nation. "It is a manifesto," he said, "an agitation corps and a seeding machine" that proclaims "to the world that the Red Army is an army of heroes. . . . "[14]

It was in Yenan that Mao organized the Chinese Soviet Republic and developed his political, military, and educational strategy for creating the People's Republic of China. In this remote northern area, he ruled over three million people. He organized a Red Army that battled with the Kuomintang and the war lords. His educational program, for adults and children, included the study of Marx's doctrines and building the ideological blueprint for the new China.

Mao was married three times and was the father of ten children.[15] Following the Chinese tradition, his first marriage was arranged by his parents. Mao was fourteen and his bride was twenty. He claimed that he never lived with the woman and abandoned the arranged marriage shortly after his mother's death. He reflected that he did not consider her his wife and gave her little thought.[16]

Mao married Yang K'ai-hui, the daughter of his favorite professor, Yang Ch'ang-chi, in 1920. The couple had three sons. While Mao, now head of the Communist All-China Peasants' Union, was traveling on Party business, his wife was arrested and executed. When he was thirty-five, Mao married eighteen-year-old Ho Tzu-chen, who was active in the Communist movement. They had five daughters. Mao divorced Ho Tzu-chen in 1936.

He married Chiang Ch'ing in 1937 when he was forty-four. This was his longest and most politically significant marriage. Chiang Ch'ing was an actress. The couple had two daughters. Chiang Ch'ing was an active Communist who encouraged the Cultural Revolution. After Mao's death, she was tried as a member of the Gang of Four.

Mao came to political power in the aftermath of World War II. By 1936, the invading Japanese had occupied so much of China that the nation's survival was in doubt. The Japanese threat brought about a cessation of hostilities between the Communists and Kuomintang that allowed them to face their common enemy. After the defeat of Japan in 1945, the Communists and Kuomintang resumed the civil war. This time, the Kuomintang suffered a series of defeats that culminated in Chiang's flight to Taiwan. On October 1, 1949, Mao proclaimed the People's Republic of China in Peking.

Mao's Ideology

While China's historical context is important in understanding Mao's life and revolutionary ideology, one must also examine the effect that Karl Marx, the founder of Communism, had on his thinking. Mao relied heavily on Marx's philosophy of dialectical materialism in developing his own revolutionary ideology and strategy.

Karl Marx (1818–1883), the son of a middle-class Jewish family, was born in Germany. After studying law, philosophy, and literature at the Universities of Bonn and Berlin, he received his doctorate in philosophy from the University of Jena in 1841.[17]

While studying philosophy, Marx encountered Hegel's Idealism. Although later rejecting Hegel's nonmaterialism, Marx was intrigued by Hegel's dialectical process, which he incorporated into his own philosophy of dialectical materialism. Marx also borrowed from Ludwig Feuerbach, who emphasized the power of economic factors, or material conditions, in determining social and cultural patterns. Marx, who fused Feuerbach's materialism to Hegel's dialectic, formulated his own philosophy of dialectical materialism. When Mao gained power in China, Maoist-Marxist dialectical materialism became the official ideology.

For Marx, history—an account of class struggle—followed a dialectical process in which a thesis generated an antithesis, which in turn produced a synthesis, a new thesis. Inevitably, the dialectical struggle would culminate in a massive conflict which pitted the capitalists, the thesis, against their proletarian opponents, the antithesis. Without doubt, the working class proletariat would triumph, Marx reasoned. Embracing Marx's view that history's march was irresistible, Mao saw himself destined to lead China's coming proletarian revolution.

Mao used the Marxist dialectic to interpret both personal and political events. Recalling his childhood, he saw himself locked in dialectical conflict with his father. During the Civil War, Mao's Communists, the proletariat, were in mortal dialectical combat with Chiang's Nationalists, representing bourgeois capitalism. During the Cultural Revolution, the old patterns of Confucianist traditionalism and academic scholarship were in conflict with proletarian mass culture.

Marx became one of the commanding leaders of the international socialist movement. His study of the works of Saint Simon, the utopian socialist, reconfirmed his materialist outlook that economics predetermined the role and function of social institutions. Like Saint Simon, Marx believed an astute body of revolutionaries, the vanguard of the proletariat, would lead the coming revolution. Marx strongly opposed, however, what he called the naive and muddle-headed utopian premise

that significant political change could be accomplished without revolutionary violence. He argued that a violent but astutely guided revolution was needed to overthrow the capitalists. Mao enthusiastically accepted Marx's argument on the necessity for guided revolutionary action. Both Marx and Mao had little sympathy for
those who believed it possible to attain peaceful change through democratic political
processes. Marx and his colleague and patron, Friedrich Engels, in *The Communist
Manifesto* in 1848, began with, "a specter is haunting Europe—the specter of Communism," and concluded:

> The Communists disdain to conceal their views and aims. They openly declare
> that their ends can be attained only by the forcible overthrow of all existing social
> conditions. Let the ruling classes tremble at a Communist revolution. The prole-
> tarians have nothing to lose but their chains. They have a world to win. Working-
> men of all countries unite![18]

According to Marx's interpretation of history, just as innovations in economic
production had destroyed feudalism, capitalism, too, would be destroyed by its own
contradictions. For example, industrial capitalism created and increased the numbers of exploited, propertyless laborers—the proletariat.[19] The proletariat had supported liberal capitalists in destroying the remnants of feudalism in Europe in the
French Revolution and the Revolutions of 1848. While history's course was moving
toward capitalist ascendancy in these struggles, Marx reasoned that the alliance
between capitalists and proletariat was only temporary. The proletariat, who lived by
their labor, were denied ownership of both the means of production and the products they made. However, through their labor the workers created wealth for the
capitalists.[20] Mao used the Marxist analysis to interpret China's recent history.
Chiang's Kuomintang, representing an embryonic capitalism, had destroyed the
remnants of the feudal imperial system and the war lords who had temporarily
replaced it. The proletarian support in overthrowing the old imperial order was, for
Mao, just a temporary alliance with the Kuomintang. The Kuomintang was doomed
to follow its imperial predecessor to history's rubbish heap.

Marx prophesied that contradictions in the capitalist economic system would
cause its own destruction. These contradictions included overproduction designed
to earn greater profits, which would lead to glutted markets, unemployment, and
economic depression. To sustain their privileged position, capitalists needed to
expand production continuously and find new markets for their products.[21] Again,
Mao could interpret the West's encroachment on China as part of the capitalist
nations' insatiability for new territories to exploit. Imperialist wars, such as World
War I and II, would result as capitalist nations fought to gain control of raw materials and markets. Meanwhile, the proletariat would become more oppressed and mis-
erable as unemployment, once periodic, became chronic, creating conditions ripe
for revolt. Again, Mao's reading of Marx convinced him that China was ripe for a
Communist revolution and assumption of power.

Marx wrote that the proletariat was historically fated, through the workings of the
dialectical process, to defeat the capitalists and wrest all power from them. In the

new workers' classless society, all the instruments of production, control, and power would be lodged in the proletarian state. The dictatorship of the proletariat would root out capitalism's residues. Mao continually mobilized the proletarian peasants to destroy the remnants of the old prerevolutionary order. When the old revolution had lost its zeal and began building its own bureaucracy, Mao launched the Cultural Revolution to finish the job of purging the old ways and creating new ways.

Although primarily a political and economic philosopher rather than an educational theorist, Marx's ideology had important educational implications. He postulated that a genuine education, based on scientific socialism, required the exposure and eradication of false consciousness from the minds of the proletariat. False consciousness, the product of capitalist class ideology, was imposed upon the proletariat as a means of social control. Marx's Communist ideology was to be used to establish a revolutionary, working-class consciousness. The vanguard of the proletariat, the Communist Party, was to raise working-class consciousness to its true interests. After he secured power, Mao worked to purge schools of bourgeois ideas and bourgeois teachers.

Mao accepted Marx's conclusion that in a capitalist society, the educational system was a tool of the exploiting class. Capitalist-controlled schools indoctrinated working class children to accept their exploited station in life and trained them to become docile drones in capitalist-owned factories, mines, and mills.

Mao was determined to operationalize Marx's ideology into a revolutionary strategy for early twentieth century China. At the time, China, a vast country with massive illiteracy and industrial underdevelopment, did not meet Marx's prescribed prerevolutionary conditions. It was still very much a backward, almost feudal, nation. Whereas Marx had argued that the industrial working class was the destined revolutionary class, Mao determined that at China's state of development only the rural peasantry could make a revolution. However, Mao also realized that the Chinese peasantry were still far below the level of class consciousness needed to turn them into a genuine revolutionary class.

Mao perceived his role to be that of adapting Marxist theory into a practical revolutionary strategy. He had to raise the consciousness of China's vast proletariat and make them into a machine of revolution. Mao saw the Communist Party as having an educational mission to mobilize China's working classes into a revolutionary army that was conscious of its destined historic role. He had to translate Marx's abstract rendition of dialectical materialism into a concrete strategy for class mobilization and warfare. The true revolutionary, Mao argued, was a person who, after evaluating a political situation correctly, did not hesitate to take the needed course of action.

Before the Communists could lead the proletarian revolution, Mao reasoned that they first had to be trained as leaders who were dedicated and ruthless. Following Marx's guidelines for successful revolutionary action, these Communist leaders needed to know how to appraise a potential revolutionary situation. When the time was ripe for revolution, the spontaneous will of the proletarian masses would be at a high pitch of readiness. At this point, the Communist leadership would have to assess the proletariat's revolutionary readiness and estimate the power of the masses to make a successful revolution. As the historically destined revolutionary class, the proletariat possessed the spontaneous raw energy needed to make a revolution. However, unless this energy were organized and used efficiently, it would remain politically diffuse. For Mao, proletarian spontaneity had to be harnessed and channeled correctly by the Communist leadership.

Mao believed China's Communist Party had to exercise a program of informal education, or agitation, to raise working-class consciousness regarding its historically and dialectically determined role and to mobilize it against its capitalist adversaries. To do this, Communist leaders like Mao needed to translate Marx's abstract theory into language that ignited the consciousness of the oppressed classes. They needed to become skilled propagandists who could disseminate the Marxist message and stir the workers to revolutionary insurrection.

Along with propagandizing, the Communist leaders had to organize the masses for effective revolutionary action. This meant the leaders had to be skilled crowd psychologists who could incite the masses to action by arousing their instincts, passions, and emotions. One effective device was using slogans, simplified messages, that aroused the masses to action. Mao himself used sloganeering and revolutionary phrase-making throughout his career.

Marx's comprehensive ideology of revolutionary ideas profoundly influenced Mao in China, Lenin in the Soviet Union, Ho Chi Minh in Viet Nam, and the Communist movement internationally.

Mao's Educational Ideas

Mao employed education in many ways. In the early revolutionary period, he used it as a force to attract adherents to the Communist cause and as an instrument to oppose the old inherited educational ideas associated with the traditional Confucianist past. He used it to mobilize the masses ideologically to accomplish his plans to change the character of Chinese life and education. From the Yenan period onward, Mao, like Lenin in the Soviet Union, was committed to eradicating illiteracy. Literacy—reading and writing—was essential in molding the new Chinese Communist man and woman. When the Communists seized power in China in 1949, they faced massive illiteracy, which was most prevalent among the workers and peasants, those who were to constitute the backbone of the new social order. Mao and the Communist regime employed a variety of nonformal and formal educational programs to eradicate illiteracy and raise proletarian consciousness. Literacy classes were established on agricultural communes and spare- and part-time schools were initiated for adult learners. Mao also was concerned with schooling the young to assume their places in the new China. For him, education was a comprehensive process that was ideologically connected to the political and economic goals of the society he envisioned. According to Mao, education in the new China was "to develop morally, intellectually and physically" well-educated workers with "socialist consciousness."[22]

Prepared as a teacher, Mao had definite ideas about education and schooling. He considered education, in the broad sense a form of ideological formation, as a means to mold a world view that governed behavior. As Marx had argued, education was to rouse consciousness about class struggle and conflict. It was to build a dialectical frame of mind so that the person interpreted situations in terms of opposites to be resolved only through inevitable revolutionary conflict.

While appropriating Marx's dialectical materialism, Mao regarding it as an ideological body of doctrine that needed to be adapted to the Chinese cultural context. Although Marx had predicted that the revolution first would occur in the most highly industrialized, capitalistic countries, Mao repatterned Marxism to fit China's historical context. Even though China was a backward and industrially underdeveloped agricultural country, Mao believed he could mobilize the impoverished peasants into a revolutionary force.

For Mao, education was to purge the old ways of thinking and behaving and replace them with new ideas and actions. The purging process, epitomized in the Cultural Revolution, meant destroying the old prerevolutionary customs and traditions and replacing them with the ideological values of a collective revolutionary consciousness.

Although an intellectual, a poet, and a visionary, Mao was a highly resourceful military and political tactician and practitioner. He abhorred the traditional schooling which had deliberately separated theory and practice and thought and action.[23] He severely criticized academic subjects that were disconnected from politics and the economy. The Cultural Revolution was a dramatic conflict against academic theoreticians.

The school system that Mao helped to create in the People's Republic of China emphasized the relationship between politics and education. He was more concerned with "redness," or politically correct Marxist-Maoism, than in developing the expertise needed for China's scientific and technological modernization. Despite the victory of Communism, Mao continued to believe that China's educational system, especially secondary and higher education, still fostered an elitist attitude remote from practical politics. He considered the examinations required for university admission a sorting device that separated the intellectual elite from the masses.[24]

Despite his fame and power, Mao had opponents who envisioned China's emergence as a world power as depending on educating scientific, technological, and engineering experts. Expertise, for them, took priority over Maoist ideological political correctness.

Mao in Power

After proclaiming the People's Republic of China in 1949, Mao's Communist regime consolidated power. The new regime faced serious obstacles, however: (1) rebuilding war-devastated economic and transportation infrastructures, (2) eradicating inherited Confucianism or bourgeois values and replacing them with the new Marxist credo, and (3) resisting what it regarded as capitalist encirclement by the United States and its ally, Chiang Kai-shek. In the People's Republic's first decade, its leaders admired the Soviet Union as an ideological and economic model and looked for its economic and military aid in building Communism. The two Communist giants, the USSR and the People's Republic of China, shared the world's largest common border. Since the days of the Russian tsars and Chinese emperors, the historic relationship between the two nations had been strained and tensions would resurface. Despite their similar Marxist ideological relationship, the relationship remained tense.

Mao's new regime sought to induce ideological commitment and inaugurate economic change by purging unreliable elements, mainly from the landlord and bourgeois classes. Holding public purge trials throughout the country, Mao's government launched a concerted drive against capitalists, landlords, and those suspected of harboring bourgeois sentiments. The property, especially the landed estates, of these suspected enemies of the state and Party was confiscated and placed under state control. Farm land, which had been initially expropriated from landlords and distributed to landless peasants, was now collectivized into state-held agricultural communes. Foreign and privately owned industries were expropriated and run as state enterprises on the Soviet model. Educationally, the new government launched a massive campaign to eradicate illiteracy and to indoctrinate the people in the Communist ideology.

The period from 1953 to 1957 marked the First Five Year Plan during which government and party leaders planned to reconstruct the economy and education according to Soviet models. In agriculture, peasants were organized into collectivist cooperatives, communes, and production brigades. The produce of these collectivist units, with a subsistence allowance for the residents, went to the state. The communal structure of the agricultural collectives was designed to create a total life pattern which sought to: (1) build ideological loyalty to the Communist Party, (2) increase agricultural production for the nation's economy, (3) cultivate a shared style of life with communal social control imposed on the individual. In return for their work and loyalty, the members of the commune received educational and medical services.

In industrial development, Mao followed the Soviet model of emphasizing heavy industry rather than consumer goods. Ideologically, efforts were made to eradicate residues of traditional Confucianist ethics which esteemed intellectual effort over manual labor. As part of the Communist educational program to inculcate the collectivist work ethic, manual labor was promoted as an honorable pursuit for all people. University students were persuaded to engage in manual work to avoid falling into the traditional error of separating thinking and working. The Communists proclaimed that "all labor, whether . . . in the university, the factory, or the fields, can be directed . . . to benefit the masses."[25] Educational policy, too, followed the Soviet pattern, with textbooks and curriculum borrowed from Soviet schools.[26]

When they came to power, the Chinese Communists gave priority to reorganizing higher education. It was decided that China should emulate the Soviet example of industrialization and collectivization and that Chinese higher education, following Soviet models, should train the needed scientists and engineers.

Soviet educators advised the Chinese on creating an appropriate higher education system. Modeled after the Soviet version, Chinese higher education included general universities as well as polytechnical and technical institutes. Following the selective Soviet pattern, admission of students into higher education was based on successfully passing academically rigorous entrance examinations. Such a selective system with its accompanying examinations was compatible with the inherited Chinese tradition of higher education. The emphasis on science, engineering, and technology, however, was a new element.[27]

Although Chairman Mao acquiesced initially to the new higher education system, the old revolutionary feared that its selectivity deviated from the principle of a classless society. Mao attacked selectivity in higher education during the Great Leap Forward of 1957 when he sought to industrialize through mass popular effort rather than by relying on experts in mathematics, science, and technology. With the launching of the Cultural Revolution in 1966, Mao unleashed his most severe attack on selectivity in higher education.

By 1958, relations had soured between the Soviet Union and the People's Republic of China. Mao and the Soviet leader, Nikita Khrushchev, clashed on many issues, including the boundary between the USSR and China. Mao, growing increasingly wary of China's reliance on Soviet assistance and advice, determined that China should pursue its own path of socialist development. Arguing that China with its immense natural and human resources could stand on its own economic and military feet, Mao initiated a new economic policy, the Great Leap Forward. China's vast population, he claimed, could build the Communist state quickly through mass mobilization and grass-roots local efforts. Following Chairman Mao's directives to enlist in the campaign to transform China from a backward agricultural nation into an industrial giant, millions of peasants hastily constructed improvised backyard smelters to make iron and steel. Trees were cut down by the thousands to fuel the smelters' fires. To double crop production, farmers were told to plant two instead of one rice crop. The results were calamitous for productivity. The inefficient furnaces and smelters produced shoddy and virtually worthless steel. Drought and inept farming practices caused a steep decline in crops. Rather than a Great Leap Forward, Mao's policies, aggravated by natural calamities, precipitated a massive famine with twenty million deaths.[28]

Educationally, the Great Leap Forward also had its consequences. If the economy were capable of quick and massive expansion, Mao reasoned, there should also be rapid educational progress to eradicate illiteracy and universalize education. Educational policy makers sought to expand the number and types of schools. Spare- and part-time schools were established on agricultural communes and in factories.

After the failure of his Great Leap Forward, Mao persisted as the Communist revolution's father figure. However, his role as a key policy initiator diminished. From 1960 to 1965, the government and the Party labored to restore agricultural and industrial productivity. In agriculture, private plots were permitted and the "responsibility system" was introduced in which communes contracted with the state to set production quotas but were allowed to keep profits beyond the quota. These incentives increased agricultural productivity. Rejecting the Great Leap Forward's stress on the diffusion of many small industries, the government now emphasized large, well-run, efficient key industries, concentrated in industrial zones. In education, many of the hastily established schools on communes and in factories were closed as the emphasis shifted to restoring academic quality.

In 1965, Chairman Mao resurfaced with a vengeance, calling for a new kind of revolution, a "great proletarian cultural revolution" which would destroy old ideas, customs, and habits and replace them with a totally new culture.[29]

The Cultural Revolution

The Cultural Revolution unleashed by Mao Tse-tung in 1965 stands out as one of history's most unusual cultural and educational events. Resurfacing as an active political voice, Mao launched the Great Proletarian Cultural Revolution, an attempt to use the masses, especially youth, to reignite what he regarded as China's lagging revolutionary zeal. During the Cultural Revolution, Mao mobilized China's children and young people in a total cultural war against the government and Communist Party bureaucracy, the faculties of the secondary schools and universities, and the residues of Confucianism which still remained in Chinese culture. Thousands of Chinese youth, loosely organized as Red Guards, streamed out of the secondary schools and universities to eradicate residues of Confucianism and bourgeois capitalism. The Red Guards scoured the country, searching out those accused of harboring anti-Maoist sentiments. Their ire fell especially hard on teachers, professors, and administrators who were accused of anti-Maoist thought before mass audiences. The youthful Red Guards also sacked temples and shrines, wrecking the last vestiges of an earlier time. The Red Guards harassed Mao's opponents, conducted trials, brought the official educational system to a halt, and sought to create new educational structures and processes. In effect, the aging Chairman Mao, still a revolutionary, was leading another revolution against the revolution that he had created earlier. He wrote that the success of the Cultural Revolution depended on the "broad masses of revolutionary students and teachers in schools and on the revolutionary workers." It would be an immense process of creating a worldview of self-emancipation.[30]

The Cultural Revolution degenerated into a new reign of terror in which children and young people, the primary agents of revolutionary mob action, denounced, tried, and purged "reactionary" teachers, officials, administrators, and sometimes even their parents. Red Guard rallies were told that "destruction must come before construction."[31]

The Red Guard's destruction of the old culture degenerated into a rampage. Temples were sacked and destroyed and libraries were emptied of books regarded as counter-revolutionary. A proletarian style of dress and speech was instituted. The turmoil in the schools was so great that instruction virtually ended between 1966 and 1968 as students attacked their teachers.[32]

During the Cultural Revolution, Chairman Mao was raised to even higher pinnacles of acclaim. His photographs appeared throughout China. A Maoist cult developed in which Mao's writings became the revolutionary catechism for the Red Guards. Students, carrying the *Little Red Book of Mao Tse-Tung* and aided by the army, began a mass campaign to educate the peasants and workers in Maoist ideology.

During the Cultural Revolution, Mao presented and sought to implement his educational reforms. Early childhood preschools were to begin the process of Marxist-Maoist character formation as children acquired collectivist attitudes and values. Next came five years of primary school where students would learn reading, writing, general arithmetic and science, and basic political beliefs based on Mao's book, *Red Little Soldiers*. Secondary school was to be divided into two years of junior middle school and two years of senior middle school. The secondary curriculum would consist of political education, mathematics, chemistry, foreign languages, and labor. After completing middle school, students would serve one to three years working in rural areas with the peasants. Then the students would either remain in rural areas or be placed in industrial jobs.

Adult education took place on agricultural communes and in factories in spare-time schools. Here, full-time workers were given time for literacy studies and political indoctrination.

Mao believed that only a small percentage of students needed to proceed to higher educational institutions. He wanted to reverse the tendency for children of high party officials, government bureaucrats, and intellectuals to enter universities. In their place, he wanted children of workers and peasants to have priority in entering higher education. To equalize education, Mao wanted to eliminate university entrance examinations. He called the examinations "tickling enemies," "surprise attacks," that were full of obscure questions. They were "a method of testing official stereotyped writing."[33]

The students admitted to the universities during the Cultural Revolution were mainly older peasants and industrial workers. They no longer had to pass examinations and submit academic credentials. In *Quotations from Chairman Mao Tse-Tung*, a class of students, standing before a large portrait of Mao, is portrayed pledging: "We are determined to win honor for you and for our great socialist motherland. . . . our consciousness of continuing the revolution will not change. . . . our loyalty to you will never change."[34]

Mao and his associates in the Cultural Revolution sought to radically restructure higher education. As with secondary schools, universities were to be thoroughly politicized according to Maoist ideological doctrines. The traditional Chinese predilection to separate theory and practice was to be eliminated as higher education was combined with socially useful productive work.

Between 1966 and 1970, conditions in higher education were so chaotic that the universities were closed and the Ministry of Higher Education was abolished. With the central Ministry of Higher Education abolished and many university administrators in disgrace, the universities were taken over by University Revolutionary Committees.[35] These committees conducted a thorough purge of administrators and professors suspected of harboring bourgeois intellectual sentiments. Gangs of Red Guards occupied the universities and staged trials of suspect administrators and professors. Many of the suspect professors were sent to work in factories or on farms.

In 1970, the Cultural Revolution's higher education system appeared when ninety of the culturally purified universities were permitted to reopen. The Revolutionary Committees abolished the old admission requirements, especially entrance examinations. The new admission requirements were simply graduation from a secondary school, two years of work experience in industry, agriculture or the army, and being between the ages of twenty and twenty-five and unmarried.[36]

At all levels of schooling, especially secondary and higher education, Mao sought to change the character of teachers. Academically inclined teachers were purged as elitists during the Cultural Revolution. The new teachers were to come from the ranks of workers and peasants.[37] The most important qualification was a politically correct socioeconomic background and conformity to Chairman Mao's political ideology. Teachers were subject to self-criticism sessions in which some confessed past errors of lapsing into bourgeois sentimentality and traditional thinking.

In the schools that continued to function, a Maoist ideological line was instituted. Practical skills and work were given priority over academic subjects. Classes also were scheduled in factories with teachers working alongside students so that theory and practice could be integrated.

As the Cultural Revolution turned increasingly chaotic and violent, factions developed between units of Red Guards. Pitched battles were fought between contending groups, often on the university grounds. Even Mao, who had encouraged the Cultural Revolution, now retreated from the excesses of the Red Guard rampages. The Communist Party and the army began to reassert themselves in checking the Red Guards and ending the Cultural Revolution. The aging Mao was once again at the periphery of real power. The government and Communist Party apparatus reasserted control over the country.

The Cultural Revolution had serious negative consequences for Chinese higher education. When it ended, higher education was demoralized. Disgraced professors were working at menial jobs in remote areas as part of their "proletarian education." Libraries had been purged of suspect books and monographs and new materials had not been added for nearly a decade. Laboratories had been neglected or misused by Revolutionary Committees. Further, many students admitted under more open admission policies were unprepared for university work.

From 1966 to 1976, Mao Tse-tung and his followers vilified the administrators in the Ministry of Education. Rather than having policy drafted and implemented by educational bureaucrats, Mao wanted it made by the masses. When the Cultural Revolution ended, some professional educators returned to their positions in the Ministry of Education and in the schools and universities.

The Cultural Revolution, carried by its own mass momentum, reached excesses that even Mao began to fear. The schools and universities were either barely functioning or closed; the government and Communist Party apparatus was in disarray and the economy disrupted. The army began to intervene to restore order. Red Guards, now in disfavor, were sent to the countryside to work as agricultural laborers. By the mid-1970s, the Cultural Revolution had ended. As Mao grew increasingly ill, his wife, Chiang Ch'ing sought to influence policy. In early September 1976, Mao died. His wife and her associates, labeled the Gang of Four, were put on trial.

The Cultural Revolution left China in educational ruins. Some believed that a whole generation of young people had lost the chance for formal schooling. The reopening of schools, especially universities, was a slow process. Teachers were either missing or feared returning to their old positions. Many of the school buildings had been ransacked and damaged by the Red Guards. Previously used textbooks had been burned or discarded. No new textbooks has been published and potential authors hesitated to write new ones, not knowing what the ideological Party line would be.

China After Mao

In 1977, the Chinese government and the Communist Party launched the concerted campaign of The Four Modernizations, to modernize four key sectors—agriculture, industry, national defense, and science and technology. The drive to achieve the "four modernizations," characterized by an emphasis on science and technology, management, and planning, was a concerted effort to recover from the Cultural Revolution. Since 1977, the strongman has been Deng Xioping, (1904–) a close associate of Zhou Enlai. Under Deng's leadership, China embarked on its modernization program.

The government, seeking to modernize the country, opened it to Western technology. Part of the modernization effort involved a concerted effort to restore the academic quality of the universities. An ambitious program was begun to improve curricula and instruction in science and technology. The government initiated a program of international exchange and study in which Chinese professors of science, technology and engineering went to developed Western nations, including the United States, to learn about new developments in their fields. Professors from the developed countries were invited to China to advise, lecture and teach.

By the 1980s, a market economy had appeared, with small businesses coexisting with larger state enterprises. In agriculture, too, state control lessened as production moved toward privatization. Individuals were permitted to lease land, to pay a certain amount of their produce to the state, and to sell the surplus on the open market. Agricultural production increased as did farmers' incomes.

From the perspective of government and Party leaders, "the loss of a generation of technicians and scholars during the de-emphasis on academic quality and technical expertise produced a deep crisis in which China was essentially endangering its future as a modern socialist country." "Redness" as a paramount goal was replaced by scientific and technological expertise. In a policy linking economic productivity to education, government and party leaders, reversing their prior ideological stance, emphasized competition, and efficiency, and productivity. In education, government and party leaders called for renewed academic discipline.[38]

As part of the process of restoring the academic credibility of the universities, modernizers in the government and the Communist Party once again sought to restore selective entrance requirements, especially the examinations, to ensure that the students admitted were academically qualified. The re-established Ministry of Education prepared standardized entrance examinations which candidates for admission had to pass. The examinations were extremely rigorous so that only a small percentage of those taking the tests scored high enough to be admitted to universities.

The Chinese government believed that modernization could be selectively introduced and that the process could be centrally controlled. However, the process of change and innovation did not remain solely in science and technology but was diffused into the political and cultural areas of life. University students, motivated by values of freedom of thought and expression, organized a movement to liberalize Chinese society and politics. The students, loosely organized in the Pro-Democracy Movement, staged a sit-in at Tienanmen Square in Peking to press their demands for liberalization on the government. The response was the army's ruthless suppression of the movement with the massacre of students in Tienanmen Square in 1989.

During the Cultural Revolution, when ideological purity was emphasized, scientific and technological expertise were suspect as a form of scholarly elitism. After the Cultural Revolution, the government turned to experts to remedy the deficiencies produced by zealous amateurs. When some of the young people who had been trained abroad and influenced by foreign ideas organized the pro-Democracy movement, the government fearing change, once again turned to reliance on the Party loyalist rather than the expert.

The dramatic shifts in China's ideological postures and policies have had an effect on professors and teachers. While Chinese schools, like those in other countries, seek to instill socially and politically approved values in the young, there is uncertainty as to what these approved values will be. This is not due to the moral ambiguity found in many societies but rather to the rigidity of the regime's posture at a given period. While the schools have responded to Party dictates, Party leaders have shifted dramatically between reproducing the Communist culture and training scientific experts. The inconsistency in policy directives has produced uncertainty in curriculum, texts, and examinations. Educators who follow the official policy at one time may find themselves labeled as ideological deviants in the next period. For example, professors and teachers, accused of harboring bourgeois sentiments, were targets during the Cultural Revolution. The fear of being accused of ideological deviance and possible political persecution has caused many educators merely to read from the official syllabus and textbook without comment so they would not be accused of ideological disloyalty.[39]

China's leaders have had difficulty integrating the Maoist past with the contemporary modernization program. Policy has often taken a tortuous route, alternating in direction.[40] Crucial questions remain, such as: What elements of the traditional culture and society should be used in restructuring China? What is the relationship of Marxism and Maoism to inherited ideas? Can China become a modern nation without relying on Western science, technology, and engineering? How should science and technology be integrated into the national ideology?[41]

Conclusion: An Assessment

The heroic figure in Chinese Communist ideology is Chairman Mao Tse-tung. Mao, a consistent revolutionary, was strongly anti-Confucianism. It was more important to him to create the new Communist man and woman with correct revolutionary dedication and attitudes than to rely on scientific and technological experts to create a modern China. Mao's ideology, based on the successes of the Yenan years and the Communist revolution, called for unrelenting struggle against counter-revolutionary enemies. He believed that a new Communist China could be created out of chaos. His Great Leap Forward, from 1957 to 1960, urged the Chinese to industrialize through massive popular efforts without relying on technological expertise. The technical deficiencies of the Great Leap Forward caused economic breakdown and famine.

With the Cultural Revolution, Mao challenged the very bureaucratic and educational structures of the China that he helped to create. The Cultural Revolution was a dramatic effort to use ideology to reshape cultural and educational structures and thinking. It represented an attack on the Chinese traditional veneration of scholarly elites that were residues of Confucianism. Mao's focus on ideological purification stressed "Redness," the politically correct beliefs and behavior.

Discussion Questions

1. What events and situations in Mao's childhood shaped his revolutionary character?
2. Compare and contrast Confucianism and Maoist ideas on culture and education.
3. What key doctrines of Karl Marx were used by Mao in developing his revolutionary strategy?
4. What was the Cultural Revolution and what effect did it have on China's educational history?
5. Analyze the tension between "redness" and expertise in Chinese education.
6. What were the important contradictions in Mao's life and policies?

Research and Essay Topics

1. Read and review a biography of Mao Tse-tung.
2. Interview some international students from the People's Republic of China about Mao and the Cultural Revolution.
3. Assume you are a Red Guard, prepare a paper in which you identify and attack the major tenets of Confucianism.
4. In an interpretive essay, analyze the development of Mao as a revolutionary figure.
5. In a paper, identify and examine the relationships between Marx and Mao as ideologists.

Notes

1. John K. Fairbanks, Edwin O. Reichsauer, and Albert M. Craig, *East Asia: The Modern Transformation*, II (London: Allen and Unwin, 1965), 80–85.
2. Ibid., 87–88.
3. Ibid., 634.
4. Stuart Schram, *Mao Tse-Tung* (New York: Simon and Schuster, 1966), 15.
5. Lucian W. Pye, *Mao Tse-Tung: The Man in the Leader* (New York: Basic Books, 1976), 75.
6. Edgar Snow, *Red Star Over China* (New York: Grove Press, 1968), 132.
7. Ibid. 132–34.
8. Pye, 84.

9. George Poloczi-Horvath, *Mao Tse-Tung: Emperor of the Blue Ants* (London: Secker and Warburg, 1962), 24–25.

10. Siao-Yu, *Mao Tse-Tung and I Were Beggars* (Syracuse: Syracuse University Press, 1959), 38–41.

11. Phillippe Devillers, *Mao*, translated by Tony White (New York: Schocken Books, 1967), 23–25.

12. Jerome Ch'en, *Mao and the Chinese Revolution* (London: Oxford University Press, 1965), 32.

13. Li Jui, *The Early Revolutionary Activities of Comrade Mao Tse-Tung*, translated by Anthony W. Sariti, edited by James C. Hsiun.(New York: M. E. Sharpe 1977), 178–79.

14. Mao Tse-tung, *Selected Works*, I (London: Lawrence and Wishart, 1954), 161.

15. Edgar Snow, *The Long Revolution* (New York: Random House, 1971), 175.

16. Edgar Snow, *Red Star Over China*, 20, and George Paloczi-Horvath, *Mao Tse-Tung: Emperor of the Blue Ants*, 33.

17. David McLellan, *Karl Marx: His Life and Thought* (New York: Harper and Row, 1973), 2–6.

18. Karl Marx and Friedrich Engels, "Manifesto of he Communist Party," in Carl Cohen, ed., *Communism, Fascism and Democracy: The Theoretical Foundations* (New York: Random House, 1972), 80–98.

19. E. A. Burns, *A Handbook of Marxism* (New York: International Publishers, 1935), 30.

20. G. D. H. Coles, *What Marx Really Meant* (New York: Alfred A. Knopf, 1937), 127.

21. Sidney Hook, *Toward the Understanding of Karl Marx* (London: Victor Gallanc, 1933), p. 127.

22. Mao ZeDong, "On the Correct Handling of Contradictions Among People," in *Four Essays on Philosophy* (Peking: Foreign Language Press, 1968), 110.

23. John N. Hawkins, *Mao Tse-Tung and Education: His Thoughts and Teachings* (Hamden: Linnet Books, 1974), 71–75.

24. Theodore Hsi-en Chen, *The Maoist Educational Revolution* (New York: Praeger Publishers, 1974), 4.

25. Erica Jen, "An Experience with Peking Youth," in Terrill Ross, ed., *The China Difference* (New York: Harper Colophon Books, 1972), 147.

26. Lynn Paine, "Timeline of Chinese Policy Changes: 1945–85," *Social Education* 50 (February 1986), 110.

27. Stanley Rosen, "New Directions in Secondary Education," in Ruth Hayhoe, *Contemporary Chinese Education* (Armonk, N.Y.: M.E. Sharpe, 1984), 66–69.

28. Alasdair Clayre, *The Heart of the Dragon* (Boston: Houghton-Mifflin Co., 1985), 25–27.

29. Richard Wilson, *Mao Tse-Tung in the Scales of History: A Preliminary Assessment* (London: Cambridge University Press, 1977), 291.

30. Mao Tse-tung, *Mao Papers*, edited by Jerome Ch'en (London: Oxford University Press, 1970), 148.

31. Clare Hollingworth, *Mao and the Men Against Him* (London: J. Cape 1985), 140.

32. Ruth Hayhoe, *Contemporary Chinese Education* (Armonk, N.Y.: M. E. Sharpe, 1984), 48.

33. Theodore Hsi-en Chen, *The Maoist Educational Revolution* (New York: Praeger Publishers, 1974), 220–21.

34. Mao Tse-tung, *Quotations from Chairman Mao Tse-Tung* (Peking: Foreign Language Press, 1966), 276–77.

35. Jurgen Henze, "Higher Education:; Tension Between Quality and Equality," in Ruth Hayhoe, *Contemporary Chinese Education* (Armonk, N.Y: M. E. Sharpe, 1984), 105–7.

36. Ibid., 105–19.

37. Don-chean Chu, *Chairman Mao: Education of the Proletariat* (New York: Philosophical Library, 1980), 307–19.

38. Lynn Paine, "In Search of a Metaphor to Understand China's Changes," *Social Education*, 50 (February 1986), 107–8.
39. Suzanne Ogden, *China's Unresolved Issues: Politics, Development, and Culture* (Englewood Cliffs, N.J.: Prentice Hall, 1989), 309–10.
40. Michael G. Roskin, *Countries and Concepts: An Introduction to Comparative Politics* (Englewood Cliffs, N.J.: Prentice Hall, 1989), 282–89.
41. Ogden, 306–7.

Suggestions for Further Reading

Carter, Peter. *Mao*. New York: Viking Press, 1979.

Ch'en, Theodore H. *The Maoist Educational Revolution*. New York: Praeger, 1974.

Chu, Don-Chean. *Chairman Mao: Education of the Proletariat*. New York: Philosophical Library, 1980.

Clayre, Alasdair. *The Heart of the Dragon*. Boston: Houghton Mifflin Co., 1985.

Fitzgerald, Charles P. *Mao Tse-tung and China*. New York: Holmes and Meier Publications, 1976.

Hawkins, John N. *Mao Tse-tung and Education: His Thoughts and Teachings*. Hamden: Linnet Books, 1974.

Hayhoe, Ruth. *Contemporary Chinese Education*. Armonk, N.Y.: M. E. Sharpe, 1984.

Hollingworth, Clare. *Mao and the Men Against Him*. London: J. Cape, 1985.

Karnow, Stanley. *Mao and China: From Revolution to Revolution*. New York: Viking Press, 1972.

Mao Tse-tung. *Selected Works*. London: Lawrence and Wishart, 1954.

Paloczi-Horvath, George. *Mao Tse-tung, Emperor of the Blue Ants*. London: Secker and Warburg, 1962.

Pye, Lucian W. *Mao Tse-tung: The Man in the Leader*. New York: Basic Books, 1976.

Schram, Stuart R. *Mao Tse-tung*. New York: Simon and Schuster, 1966.

Snow, Edgar. *Red Star Over China*. New York: Grove Press, 1968.

Spence, Jonathan D. *The Search for Modern China*. New York: W. W. Norton & Co., 1990.

Wilson, Richard. *Mao Tse-tung in the Scales of History: A Preliminary Assessment*. Cambridge, U.K. and New York: Cambridge University Press, 1977.